ADOBE
FLASH CS5

Approved Certification Courseware (Adobe)

CERTIFIED ASSOCIATE — Approved Courseware (Adobe)

REVEALED

ADOBE
FLASH CS5

Adobe Approved Certification Courseware ™

CERTIFIED ASSOCIATE Approved Courseware ™

REVEALED

JIM SHUMAN

DELMAR
CENGAGE Learning™

Australia • Brazil • Japan • Korea • Mexico • Singapore • Spain • United Kingdom • United States

DELMAR
CENGAGE Learning

Adobe Flash CS5 Revealed
Jim Shuman

Vice President, Career and Professional Editorial:
Dave Garza

Director of Learning Solutions: Sandy Clark

Senior Acquisitions Editor: Jim Gish

Managing Editor: Larry Main

Product Managers: Jane Hosie-Bounar, Meaghan O'Brien

Editorial Assistant: Sarah Timm

Vice President Marketing, Career and Professional:
Jennifer Baker

Executive Marketing Manager: Deborah S. Yarnell

Marketing Manager: Erin Brennan

Marketing Coordinator: Erin Deangelo

Production Director: Wendy Troeger

Senior Content Project Manager: Kathryn B. Kucharek

Developmental Editor: Pam Conrad

Technical Editor: Sasha Vodnik

Senior Art Director: Joy Kocsis

Cover Design: Joe Villanova

Cover Art: Spitting Images

Cover Photo:

  Snow leopard: © istockphoto.com/Wrangel;

  Ski lift: © istockphoto.com/Prill Mediendesign
    & Fotografie;

  Hat/Goggles: © istockphoto.com/CyberHawk Studios;

  Snowboard: © istockphoto.com/Walik

Text Designer: Liz Kingslein

Production House: Integra Software Services Pvt. Ltd.

Proofreader: Harold Johnson

Indexer: Alexandra Nickerson

Technology Project Manager: Christopher Catalina

Printed in the United States of America
1 2 3 4 5 6 7 14 13 12 11 10

For product information and technology assistance, contact us at **Cengage Learning Customer & Sales Support, 1-800-354-9706**

For permission to use material from this text or product, submit all requests online at **www.cengage.com/permissions**

Further permissions questions can be emailed to **permissionrequest@cengage.com**

Adobe® Premiere Pro®, Adobe After Effects®, Adobe Soundbooth®, Adobe Encore®, Adobe® Photoshop®, Adobe® Illustrator®, Adobe® Illustrator®, Adobe® Flash®, Adobe® Dreamweaver®, Adobe® Fireworks®, and Adobe® Creative Suite® are trademarks or registered trademarks of Adobe Systems, Inc. in the United States and/or other countries. Third party products, services, company names, logos, design, titles, words, or phrases within these materials may be trademarks of their respective owners.

Adobe product screenshot(s) reprinted with permission from Adobe Systems Incorporated.

The Adobe Approved Certification Courseware logo is a proprietary trademark of Adobe. All rights reserved. Cengage Learning and Adobe Flash CS5–Revealed are independent from ProCert Labs, LLC and Adobe Systems Incorporated, and are not affiliated with ProCert Labs and Adobe in any manner. This publication may assist students to prepare for an Adobe Certified Expert exam, however, neither ProCert Labs nor Adobe warrant that use of this material will ensure success in connection with any exam.

Adobe Certified Associate Approved Courseware logo is a proprietary trademark of Adobe. All rights reserved. Cengage Learning and the Revealed Series are independent from ProCert Labs, LLC and Adobe Systems Incorporated, and are not affiliated with ProCert Labs and Adobe in any manner. This publication may assist students to prepare for an Adobe Certified Associate exam, however, neither ProCert Labs nor Adobe warrant that use of this material will ensure success in connection with any exam.

Library of Congress Control Number: 2010921375

Hardcover edition:
ISBN-13: 978-1-111-13054-1
ISBN-10: 1-111-13054-X

Soft cover edition:
ISBN-13: 978-1-111-13040-4
ISBN-10: 1-111-13040-X

Delmar
5 Maxwell Drive
Clifton Park, NY 12065-2919
USA

Cengage Learning is a leading provider of customized learning solutions with office locations around the globe, including Singapore, the United Kingdom, Australia, Mexico, Brazil, and Japan. Locate your local office at: **international.cengage.com/region**

Cengage Learning products are represented in Canada by Nelson Education, Ltd.

To learn more about Delmar, visit **www.cengage.com/delmar**

Purchase any of our products at your local college store or at our preferred online store **www.cengagebrain.com**

Revealed Series Vision

The Revealed Series is your guide to today's hottest multimedia applications. These comprehensive books teach the skills behind the application, showing you how to apply smart design principles to multimedia products such as dynamic graphics, animation, websites, software authoring tools, and digital video.

A team of design professionals including multimedia instructors, students, authors, and editors worked together to create this series. We recognized the unique learning environment of the multimedia classroom and created a series that:

- Gives you comprehensive step-by-step instructions
- Offers in-depth explanation of the "Why" behind a skill
- Includes creative projects for additional practice
- Explains concepts clearly using full-color visuals

It was our goal to create a book that speaks directly to the multimedia and design community—one of the most rapidly growing computer fields today. We think we've done just that, with a sophisticated and instructive book design.

—The Revealed Series

New to This Edition!

The latest edition of Adobe Flash CS5 Revealed includes many new and exciting features, some of which are listed below:

- Two chapters devoted to extensive ActionScript 3 coverage teach how to use ActionScript 3 to enhance the user experience.
- Coverage of Code Snippets, which are blocks of code that save the effort of typing ActionScript and coverage of Text Layout Framework, which provides text flowing, character coloring and column creation.
- Coverage of the improved video capabilities of Flash CS5 and coverage of features that have been enhanced in CS5, including Inverse Kinematics for character animation, and the Deco tool.
- New coverage of features including Motion Editor, and new coverage on designing for mobile devices.

Author's Vision

Writing a textbook on a web application and animation program is quite challenging. How do you take such a feature-rich program like Adobe Flash Professional CS5 and put it in a context that helps users learn? My goal is to provide a comprehensive, yet manageable, introduction to Adobe Flash Professional CS5—just enough conceptual information to provide the needed context— and then move right into working with the application. My thought is that you'll get so caught up in the hands-on activities and compelling projects that you'll be pleasantly surprised at the level of Flash skills and knowledge you've acquired at the end of each chapter.

What a joy it has been to be a part of such a creative and energetic publishing team. The Revealed Series is a great format for teaching and learning Flash, and the Revealed Series team took the ball and ran with it. I would like to thank Nicole Pinard and Jim Gish, who provided the vision for the project, and Jane Hosie-Bounar for her management expertise, and everyone at Delmar and Cengage Learning for their professional guidance. A special thanks to Pam Conrad for her hard work, editorial expertise, and constant encouragement. I also want to give a heartfelt thanks to my wife, Barbara, for her patience and support. This book is dedicated to my loving mother, Roberta Gray Shuman.

—Jim Shuman

Introduction to Adobe Flash CS5

Welcome to *Adobe Flash CS5—Revealed*. This book offers creative projects, concise instructions, and complete coverage of basic to advanced Adobe Flash CS5 skills, helping you to create and publish Flash animations, websites, and applications. Use this book both while you learn and as your own reference guide.

This text is organized into 12 chapters. In these chapters, you will learn many skills to create interesting graphics-rich applications that include animation, sound, video, and interactivity. In addition, you will learn how to publish your own Flash applications.

What You'll Do

A What You'll Do figure begins every lesson. This figure gives you an at-a-glance look at what you'll do in the chapter, either by showing you a page or pages from the current project or a tool you'll be using.

Comprehensive Conceptual Lessons

Before jumping into instructions, in-depth conceptual information tells you "why" skills are applied. This book provides the "how" and "why" through the use of professional examples. Also included in the text are tips and sidebars to help you work more efficiently and creatively, or to teach you a bit about the history or design philosophy behind the skill you are using.

Step-by-Step Instructions

This book combines in-depth conceptual information with concise steps to help you learn Flash CS5. Each set of steps guides you through a lesson where you will create, modify, or enhance a Flash CS5 file. Step references to large colorful images and quick step summaries round out the lessons. The Data Files for the steps are provided on the CD at the back of this book.

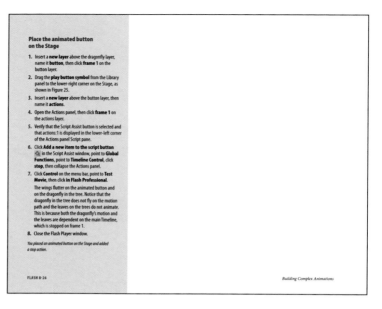

Place the animated button on the Stage

1. Insert a **new layer** above the dragonfly layer, name it **button**, then click **frame 1** on the button layer.
2. Drag the **play button symbol** from the Library panel to the lower-right corner on the Stage, as shown in Figure 25.
3. Insert a **new layer** above the button layer, then name it **actions**.
4. Open the Actions panel, then click **frame 1** on the actions layer.
5. Verify that the Script Assist button is selected and that actions:1 is displayed in the lower-left corner of the Actions panel Script pane.
6. Click **Add a new item to the script button** in the Script Assist window, point to **Global Functions**, point to **Timeline Control**, click **stop**, then collapse the Actions panel.
7. Click **Control** on the menu bar, point to **Test Movie**, then click **in Flash Professional**.

   The wings flutter on the animated button and on the dragonfly in the tree. Notice that the dragonfly in the tree does not fly on the motion path and the leaves on the trees do not animate. This is because both the dragonfly's motion and the leaves are dependent on the main Timeline, which is stopped on frame 1.
8. Close the Flash Player window.

You placed an animated button on the Stage and added a stop action.

FLASH 8-26   *Building Complex Animations*

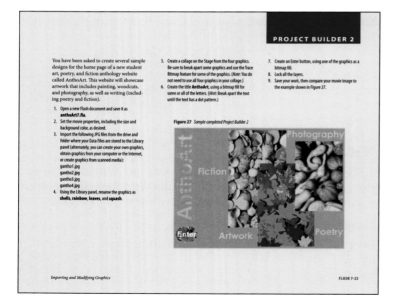

PROJECT BUILDER 2

You have been asked to create several sample designs for the home page of a new student art, poetry, and fiction anthology website called AnthoArt. This website will showcase artwork that includes painting, woodcuts, and photography, as well as writing (including poetry and fiction).

1. Open a new Flash document and save it as **anthoArt7.fla**.
2. Set the movie properties, including the size and background color, as desired.
3. Import the following JPG files from the drive and folder where your Data Files are stored to the Library panel (alternately, you can create your own graphics, obtain graphics from your computer or the Internet, or create graphics from scanned media):
   gantho1.jpg
   gantho2.jpg
   gantho3.jpg
   gantho4.jpg
4. Using the Library panel, rename the graphics as **shells**, **rainbow**, **leaves**, and **squash**.

5. Create a collage on the Stage from the four graphics. Be sure to break apart some graphics and use the Trace Bitmap feature for some of the graphics. (*Note:* You do not need to use all four graphics in your collage.)
6. Create the title **AnthoArt**, using a bitmap fill for some or all of the letters. (*Hint:* Break apart the text until the text has a dot pattern.)

7. Create an Enter button, using one of the graphics as a bitmap fill.
8. Lock all the layers.
9. Save your work, then compare your movie image to the example shown in Figure 27.

Figure 27 *Sample completed Project Builder 2*

Importing and Modifying Graphics   FLASH 7-23

Projects

This book contains a variety of end-of-chapter materials for additional practice and reinforcement. The Skills Review contains hands-on practice exercises that mirror the progressive nature of the lesson material. The chapter concludes with four projects: two Project Builders, one Design Project, and one Portfolio Project. The Project Builders and the Design Project require you to apply the skills you've learned in the chapter. Portfolio Projects encourage you to solve challenges based on the content explored in the chapter and then add the completed projects to your portfolio.

What Instructor Resources Are Available with This Book?

The Instructor Resources CD-ROM is Delmar's way of putting the resources and information needed to teach and learn effectively into your hands. All the resources are available for both Macintosh and Windows operating systems.

Instructor's Manual

Available as an electronic file, the Instructor's Manual includes chapter overviews and detailed lecture topics for each chapter, with teaching tips. The Instructor's Manual is available on the Instructor Resources CD-ROM.

Sample Syllabus

Available as an electronic file, the Sample Syllabus includes a suggested syllabus for any course that uses this book. The syllabus is available on the Instructor Resources CD-ROM.

PowerPoint Presentations

Each chapter has a corresponding PowerPoint presentation that you can use in lectures, distribute to your students, or customize to suit your course.

Data Files for Students

To complete most of the chapters in this book, your students will need Data Files. The Data Files are available on the CD at the back of this text book. Instruct students to use the Data Files List at the end of this book. This list gives instructions on organizing files.

Solutions to Exercises

Solution Files are Data Files completed with comprehensive sample answers. Use these files to evaluate your students' work. Or distribute them electronically so students can verify their work. Sample solutions to all lessons and end-of-chapter material are provided with the exception of some of the portfolio projects.

Test Bank and Test Engine

ExamView is a powerful testing software package that allows instructors to create and administer printed and computer (LAN-based) exams. ExamView includes hundreds of questions that correspond to the topics covered in this text, enabling students to generate detailed study guides that include page references for further review. The computer-based and LAN-based/online testing component allows students to take exams using the EV Player, and also saves the instructor time by grading each exam automatically.

Certification

This book, plus the material included in the Online Companion, covers the objectives necessary for Adobe Flash ACE and ACA certification. Use the Certification Grids at the back of the book to find out where an objective is covered. For information about the Online Companion, see Read This Before You Begin.

BRIEF CONTENTS

 **CHAPTER 1: GETTING STARTED WITH FLASH**

CHAPTER 5: CREATING SPECIAL EFFECTS

CHAPTER 6: PREPARING AND PUBLISHING MOVIES

CHAPTER 7: IMPORTING AND MODIFYING GRAPHICS

Intended Audience

This book is designed for the beginner or intermediate user who wants to learn how to use Adobe Flash CS5. The book is designed to provide basic and in-depth material that not only educates, but encourages you to explore the nuances of this exciting program.

Approach

The book allows you to work at your own pace through step-by-step tutorials. A concept is presented and the process is explained, followed by the actual steps. To learn the most from the use of the text, you should adopt the following habits:

- Proceed slowly: Accuracy and comprehension are more important than speed.
- Understand what is happening with each step before you continue to the next step.
- After finishing a process, ask yourself: Can I do the process on my own? If the answer is no, review the steps.

Icons, Buttons, and Pointers

Symbols for icons, buttons, and pointers are shown each time they are used.

Fonts

Data Files contain a variety of commonly used fonts, but there is no guarantee that these fonts will be available on your computer. Each font is identified in cases where fonts other than Arial or Times New Roman are used. If any of the fonts in use are not available on your computer, you can make a substitution, realizing that the results may vary from those in the book.

Windows and Macintosh

Adobe Flash CS5 works virtually the same on Windows and Macintosh operating systems. In those cases where there is a difference, the abbreviations (Win) and (Mac) are used.

Windows System Requirements

Adobe Flash CS5 requires the following:
- Intel® Pentium® 4 or AMD Athlon® 64 processor
- Microsoft® Windows® XP with Service Pack 2 (Service Pack 3 recommended); Windows Vista® Home Premium, Business, Ultimate, or Enterprise with Service Pack 1; or Windows 7
- 1GB of RAM

- 3.5GB of available hard-disk space for installation; additional free space required during installation (cannot install on removable flash-based storage devices)
- 1024x768 display (1280x800 recommended) with 16-bit video card
- DVD-ROM drive
- QuickTime 7.6.2 software required for multimedia features

Macintosh System Requirements

Adobe Flash CS5 requires the following:
- Multicore Intel processor
- Mac OS X v10.5.7 or v10.6
- 1GB of RAM
- 4GB of available hard-disk space for installation; additional free space required during installation (cannot install on a volume that uses a case-sensitive file system or on removable flash-based storage devices)
- 1024x768 display (1280x800 recommended) with 16-bit video card
- DVD-ROM drive
- QuickTime 7.6.2 software required for multimedia features

Data Files

To complete the lessons in this book, you need the Data Files on the CD located on the inside back cover. Your instructor will tell you where to store the files as you work, such as to your hard drive, a network server, or a USB storage device. When referring to the Data Files for this book, the instructions in the lessons will mention "the drive and folder where your Data Files are stored."

Projects

Several projects are presented at the end of each chapter that allow students to apply the skills they have learned in the unit. Two projects, Ultimate Tours and the Portfolio, build from chapter to chapter. You will need to contact your instructor if you plan to work on these without having completed the previous chapter's project.

Creating a Portfolio

The Portfolio Project and Project Builders allow students to use their creativity to come up with original Flash animations, screen designs and applications. Creating a portfolio is an excellent way to store and display original work.

Certification

This book covers the objectives necessary for Adobe Flash ACA certification. This book, along with material posted on the Online Companion, also covers the objectives necessary for Adobe Flash ACE certification. Use the Certification Grids at the back of the book to find out where an objective is covered. To access the Online Companion, take the following steps:

1. Open your web browser and go to: http://www.cengagebrain.com/
2. Type the author, title or ISBN of this book in the Search window. (The ISBN is listed on the back cover.)
3. Locate and click the book title in the list of search results.
4. When the book's main page is displayed, click the Access Now button.
5. Click the Student Resources link in the left navigation pane to access the PDF files you'll need.

The student resources include PDF files containing additional information about Flash features. Reading this information will help you meet the requirements for passing the Flash ACE exam. You can download and print the PDF files for your reference, or read them in Acrobat Reader.

CHAPTER **1**

GETTING STARTED WITH FLASH

1. Understand the Flash workspace

2. Open a document and play a movie

3: Create and save a movie

4. Work with the Timeline

5. Distribute an Adobe Flash movie

6. Plan an application or a website

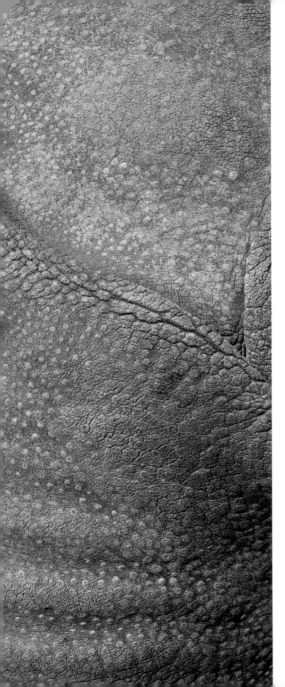

GETTING STARTED
WITH FLASH

Introduction

Adobe Flash Professional CS5 is a development tool that allows you to create compelling interactive experiences, often by using animation. You can use Flash to create entire websites, including e-commerce, entertainment, education, and personal use sites. In addition, Flash is an excellent program for developing animations that are used in websites, such as product demonstrations, banner ads, online tutorials, and electronic greeting cards. Also, Flash can be used to create applications, such as games and simulations, which can be delivered over the web and on DVDs. These applications can even be scaled to be displayed on mobile devices, such as cell phones. While it is known as a tool for creating complex animations for the web, Flash also has excellent drawing tools and tools for creating interactive controls, such as navigation buttons and menus. Furthermore, Flash provides the ability to incorporate sounds and video easily into an application.

Flash has become the standard for both professional and casual application developers, as well as for web developers. Flash is popular because the program is optimized for the web. Web developers need to provide high-impact experiences for the user, which means making sites come alive and turning them from static text and pictures to dynamic, interactive experiences. The problem has been that incorporating high-quality graphics and motion into a website can dramatically increase the download time and frustrate viewers as they wait for an image to appear or for an animation to play. Flash allows developers to use vector images, which reduce the size of graphic files. Vector images appeal to designers because they are scalable, which means they can be resized and reshaped without distortion. For example, using a vector graphic, you can easily have an object, such as an airplane, become smaller as it moves across the screen without having to create the plane in different sizes.

In addition, Flash provides for streaming content over the Internet. Instead of waiting for all the content of a web page to load, the viewer sees a continuous display of images. This chapter provides an overview of Flash and presents concepts that are covered in more detail in later chapters.

TOOLS YOU'LL USE

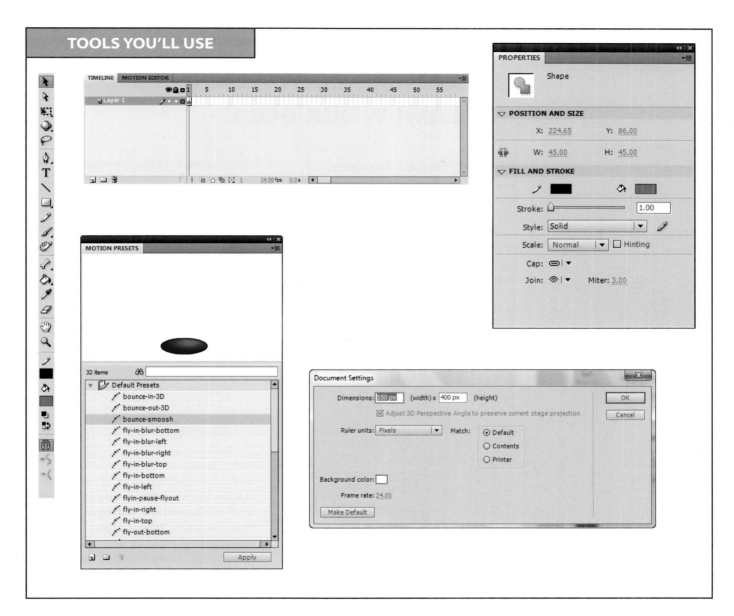

Understand the FLASH WORKSPACE

What You'll Do

In this lesson, you will learn about the development workspace in Adobe Flash and how to change Flash settings to customize your workspace.

Organizing the Flash Workspace

As a designer, one of the most important things for you to do is to organize your workspace—that is, to decide what to have displayed on the screen and how to arrange the various tools and panels. Because **Flash** is a powerful program with many tools, your workspace may become cluttered. Fortunately, it is easy to customize the workspace to display only the tools needed at any particular time.

The development process in Flash operates according to a movie metaphor: objects placed on the Stage also are incorporated in frames on a Timeline. As you work in Flash, you create a movie by arranging objects (such as graphics and text) on the Stage, and then animating the objects using the Timeline. You can play the movie on the Stage as you are working on it by using the movie controls (start, stop, rewind, and so on). Once completed, the movie can be incorporated into a website or as part of an application, such as a game.

When you start Flash, three basic parts of the workspace are displayed: a menu bar that organizes commands within menus, a Stage where objects are placed, and a Timeline used to organize and control the objects on the Stage. In addition, one or more panels may be displayed. Panels, such as the Tools panel, are used when working with objects and features of the movie. Figure 1 shows a typical Flash workspace.

Stage

The **Stage** contains all of the objects (such as drawings, photos, animations, text, and videos) that are part of the movie that will be seen by your viewers. It shows how the objects behave within the movie and how they interact with each other. You can resize the Stage and change the background color applied to it. You can draw objects directly on the Stage or drag them from the Library panel to the Stage. You can also import objects developed in another program directly to the Stage. You can specify the size of the Stage (in pixels), which will be the size of the area that displays the movie within your browser window. The gray area surrounding the Stage is the Pasteboard. You can place objects on the Pasteboard as you are creating a movie. However, neither the Pasteboard nor the objects on it will appear when the movie is played in a browser or the Flash Player.

Timeline (Frames and Layers)

The **Timeline** is used to organize and control the movie's contents by specifying when each object appears on the Stage. The Timeline is critical to the creation of movies because a movie is merely a series of still images that appear over time. The images are contained within **frames**, which are segments of the Timeline. Frames in a Flash movie are similar to frames in a motion picture. When a Flash movie is played, a playhead moves from frame to frame on the Timeline, causing the contents of each frame to appear on the Stage in a linear sequence.

The Timeline indicates where you are at any time within the movie and allows you to insert, delete, select, copy, and move frames. The Timeline contains **layers** that help to organize the objects on the Stage. You can draw and edit objects on one layer without affecting objects on other layers. Layers are a way to stack objects so they can overlap and give a 3D appearance on the Stage.

Panels

Panels are used to view, organize, and modify objects and features in a movie. The most commonly used panels are the Tools panel, the Properties panel (also called the Property inspector), and the Library panel. The **Tools panel** contains a set of tools, such as the rectangle, oval and text tools, used to draw and edit graphics and text. The **Properties panel** is used to display and change the properties of an object, such as the size and transparency of a circle. The **Library panel** is used to store and organize the various assets of your movie such as graphics, buttons, sounds, and video.

You can control which panels are displayed individually or you can choose to display panel sets. Panel sets are groups of the

Figure 1 *A typical Flash workspace*

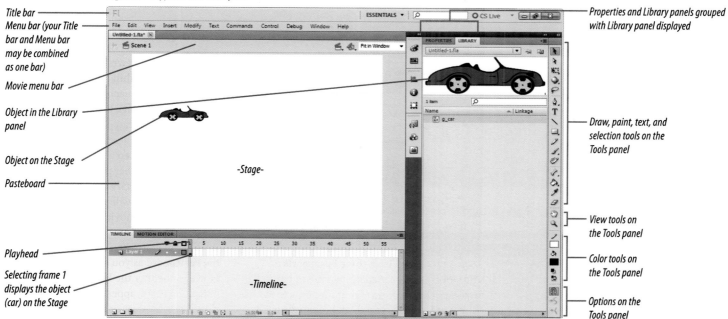

Title bar

Menu bar (your Title bar and Menu bar may be combined as one bar)

Movie menu bar

Object in the Library panel

Object on the Stage

Pasteboard

Playhead

Selecting frame 1 displays the object (car) on the Stage

-Stage-

-Timeline-

Properties and Library panels grouped with Library panel displayed

Draw, paint, text, and selection tools on the Tools panel

View tools on the Tools panel

Color tools on the Tools panel

Options on the Tools panel

most commonly used panels. For example, the Properties and the Library panels are often grouped together to make a panel set. Although several panels open automatically when you start Flash, you may choose to close them and then display them only when they are needed. This keeps your workspace from becoming too cluttered. Panels are floating windows, meaning that you can move them around the workspace. This allows you to group (dock) panels together as a way to organize them in the workspace. In addition, you can control how a panel is displayed. That is, you can expand a panel to show all of its features or collapse it to show only the title bar. Collapsing panels reduces the clutter on your workspace, provides a

larger area for the Stage, and still provides easy access to often used panels.

If you choose to rearrange panels, first decide if you want a panel to be grouped (docked) with another panel, stacked above or below another panel, placed as a floating panel, or simply positioned as a stand-alone panel. An example of each of these is shown in Figure 2. When panels are grouped and expanded, clicking on a panel's tab makes it the active panel so that the panel features are displayed.

The key to rearranging panels is the blue drop zone that appears when a panel is being moved. The drop zone is the area to which the panel can move and is indicated by either a blue line or a rectangle with a

blue border. A single blue line indicates the position for stacking a panel above or below another panel. A rectangle with a blue border indicates the position for grouping panels. If you move a panel without using a drop zone, the panel becomes a floating panel and is neither grouped nor stacked with other panels. To move a panel, you drag the panel by its tab until the desired blue drop zone appears, then you release the mouse button. Figure 3 shows the Library panel being grouped with the Properties panel. The process is to drag the Library panel tab adjacent to the Properties panel tab. Notice the rectangle with the blue border that surrounds the Properties panel. This indicates the drop

Figure 2 *Arranging panels*

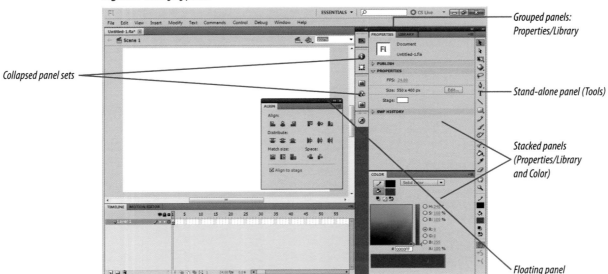

Grouped panels: Properties/Library

Collapsed panel sets

Stand-alone panel (Tools)

Stacked panels (Properties/Library and Color)

Floating panel

zone for the Library panel. (*Note*: Dragging a panel by its tab moves only that panel. To move a panel set you must drag the group by its title bar.)

Floating panels can be resized by dragging the left side, right side, or bottom of the panel. Also, you can resize a panel by dragging one of the bottom corners. In addition to resizing panels, you can collapse a panel so that only its title bar appears, and then you can expand it to display the entire panel. The Collapse to Icons button is located in the upper-right corner of each panel's title bar, as shown in Figure 3. The Collapse to Icons button is a toggle button, which means it changes or toggles between two states. When clicked,

the Collapse to Icons button changes to the Expand Panels button.

If you want to close a panel, you can click the Panel options button (shown in Figure 3) to display a drop down menu and then click the Close option. Alternately, you can right-click (Win) or [control]-click (Mac) the panel tab and choose close. If the panel is a floating panel you can click the Close button on the title bar. Finally, if the panel is expanded, you can display the Windows menu and deselect the panel (or panel group).

Arranging panels can be a bit tricky. It's easy to start moving panels around and find that the workspace is cluttered with panels arranged in unintended ways. To clean up

your workspace, you can close a panel(s) or simply display the default Essentials workspace described below.

Flash provides several preset workspace configurations that provide panels and panel sets most often used by designers, developers, and animators. The default workspace, shown in Figure 4, is named Essentials and can be displayed by clicking the ESSENTIALS button on the title bar and choosing Reset 'Essentials'. (*Note*: Your ESSENTIALS button may be on your menu bar.) Alternately, you can choose Reset 'Essentials' from the Workspace command on the Window menu. This workspace includes the Timeline panel (grouped with the Motion Editor, which is

Figure 3 *Grouping the Library panel with the Properties panel*

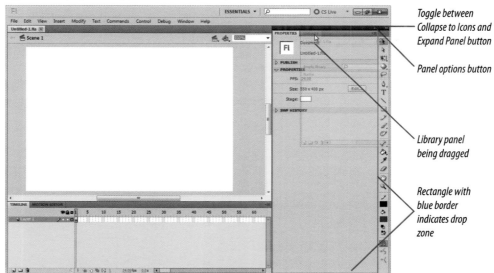

Toggle between Collapse to Icons and Expand Panel button

Panel options button

Library panel being dragged

Rectangle with blue border indicates drop zone

used to edit animations); the Tools panel which is expanded; the Properties and Library panels grouped and expanded; and several other panel sets that are stacked and collapsed. Your Essentials workspace may open with additional panel sets depending on user settings and previous use. These panels can be displayed by clicking the button icons which act as a toggle to expand and collapse the panels and panel sets. The Essentials workspace is a good development environment when learning Flash.

Regardless of how you decide to customize your development workspace, the Stage and

the menu bar are always displayed. Usually, you display the Timeline, Tools panel, Library panel, Properties panel, and one or more other panels.

Other changes that you can make to the workspace are to change the size of the Stage, move the Stage around the Pasteboard, and change the size of the Timeline panel. To increase the size of the Stage so that the objects on the Stage can be edited more easily, you can change the magnification setting using commands on the View menu or by using the View tools on the Tools panel. The Hand tool on the Tools panel and the scroll bars at the

bottom and right of the Stage can be used to reposition the Stage. The Timeline can be resized by dragging the top border. As your Flash movie gets more complex, you will use more layers on the Timeline. Increasing the size of the Timeline allows you to view more layers at one time.

QUICK TIP

When working with panels, you can collapse, move, and close them as suits your working style. Settings for an object, such as the fill color of a circle, are not lost if you close or collapse a panel. If, at any time the panels have become confusing, simply return to the Essentials workspace and open and close panels as needed.

Figure 4 *The Essentials workspace*

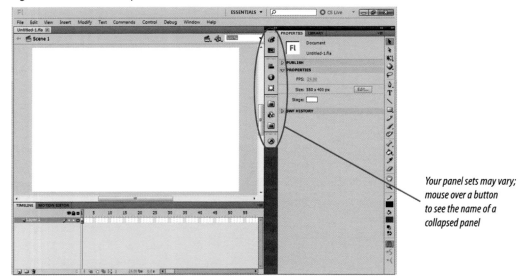

Your panel sets may vary; mouse over a button to see the name of a collapsed panel

Figure 5 *The Flash Welcome screen*

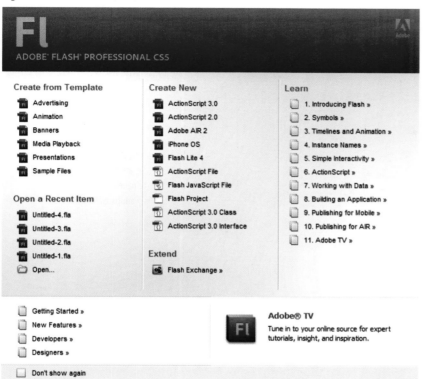

Start Adobe Flash and work with panels

1. Start the Adobe Flash Professional CS5 program **Fl**.

   The Adobe Flash CS5 Welcome screen appears, as shown in Figure 5. This screen allows you to open a recent document or create a new Flash file.

2. Click **ActionScript 3.0** under Create New.

3. Click the **ESSENTIALS button** on the title bar, then click **Reset 'Essentials'**.

   Note: The ESSENTIALS button may be on the menu bar.

   TIP When you open a new file or as you are rearranging your workspace, use the Reset 'Essentials' option to display the default workspace.

4. Click **Window** on the menu bar, then note the panels with check marks.

   The check marks identify which panels and panel sets are open.

   TIP The Properties, Library, Colors, Swatches, Align, Info, Transform, and Actions panels may be grouped, stacked, and/or collapsed, depending upon the configuration of your Essentials workspace. If so, only the panel that is active will have a check mark.

5. With the Windows menu still open, click **Hide Panels**.

6. Click **Window** on the menu bar, then click **Timeline**.

7. Click **Window** on the menu bar, then click **Tools**.

8. Click **Window** on the menu bar, then click **Library**.

   The Library and Properties panels are grouped, and the Library panel is the active panel.

   (continued)

9. Click the **Properties panel tab**.

 The Properties panel is the active tab and the panel's features are displayed.

10. Click the **Library panel tab**, then drag the **Library panel** to the left side of the Stage as a floating panel.

11. Click the **Collapse to Icons button** on the Library panel title bar.

12. Click the **Expand Panels button** on the Library panel title bar.

13. Click the **Library panel tab**, drag the **Library panel tab** to the right of the Properties panel tab, then when a rectangle with a blue border appears, as shown in Figure 6, release the mouse button to group the panels.

 Note: If the panels do not appear grouped, repeat the step making sure there is a rectangle with a blue border before releasing the mouse button.

14. Click the **Collapse to Icons button** in the upper-right corner of the grouped panels, as shown in Figure 6.

15. Click the **Expand Panels button** to display the grouped panels.

16. Click the **Color panel button** ![icon].

 The Color panel is expanded and shown grouped with the Swatches panel.

17. Click the **Collapse to Icons button** for the Color panel.

18. Click **ESSENTIALS** on the title bar, then click **Reset 'Essentials'**.

You started Flash and configured the workspace by hiding, moving, and displaying panels.

Figure 6 *Library panel grouped with the Properties panel*

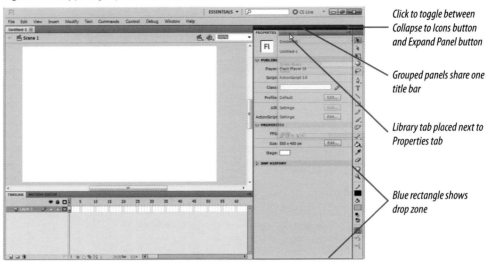

Click to toggle between Collapse to Icons button and Expand Panel button

Grouped panels share one title bar

Library tab placed next to Properties tab

Blue rectangle shows drop zone

Understanding Your Workspace

Organizing the Flash workspace is like organizing your desktop. You may work more efficiently if you have many of the most commonly used items in view and ready to use. Alternately, you may work better if your workspace is relatively uncluttered, giving you more free "desk space." Fortunately, Flash makes it easy for you to decide which items to display and how they are arranged while you work. You should become familiar with quickly opening, collapsing, expanding, and closing the various windows, toolbars, and panels in Flash, and experimenting with different layouts and screen resolutions to find the workspace that works best for you.

Figure 7 *Changing the size of the Timeline panel*

Double-headed pointer

Change the Stage view and display of the Timeline

1. Click the **Hand tool** 🖑 on the Tools panel, click the middle of the Stage, then drag the **Stage** around the Pasteboard.
2. Click **View** on the menu bar, point to **Magnification**, then click **50%**.
3. Move the pointer to the top of the Timeline title bar then, when the pointer changes to a double-headed pointer ⬍, click and drag the **title bar** up to increase the height of the Timeline, as shown in Figure 7.

   Increasing the height of the Timeline panel allows you to view more layers as you add them to the Timeline.
4. Move the pointer to the top of the Timeline title bar then, when the pointer changes to a double-headed pointer ⬍, click and drag the **title bar** down to decrease the height of the Timeline.
5. Double-click the word **TIMELINE** to collapse the Timeline.
6. Click the word **TIMELINE** again to expand the Timeline.
7. Click the **View list arrow** on the movie menu bar, then click **100%**.
8. Click **ESSENTIALS** on the title bar, then click **Reset 'Essentials'**.
9. Click **File** on the menu bar, then click **Save**.
10. Navigate to the drive and folder where your Data Files are stored, type **workspace** for the filename, then click **Save**.
11. Click **File** on the menu bar, then click **Close**.

You used a View command to change the magnification of the Stage; you used the Hand tool to move the Stage around the workspace; you resized, collapsed, and expanded the Timeline panel; then you saved the document.

Open a
DOCUMENT AND PLAY A MOVIE

What You'll Do

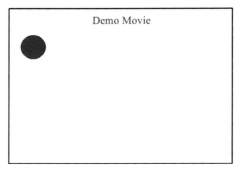

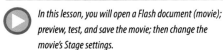

In this lesson, you will open a Flash document (movie); preview, test, and save the movie; then change the movie's Stage settings.

Opening a Movie in Flash

Flash files are called documents (or movies, interchangeably) and have an .fla file extension. If you have created a movie in Flash and saved it with the name myMovie, the filename will be myMovie.fla. Files with the .fla file extension can only be opened and edited using Flash. After they are opened, you can edit and resave them.

In order for Flash movies to be viewed on computers that do not have the Flash program installed, the movies must be changed to the Flash Player (.swf) file format. Files using the .swf file format are created from Flash movies using the Publish command. For example, when a Flash file named myMovie.fla is published using the Publish command, a new file named myMovie.swf is created. Flash .swf movies can be played in a browser without the Flash program, but the Flash Player must be installed on the computer. Flash Players are pre-installed on almost all computers. For those that do not have the player, it can be downloaded free from the Adobe website, *www.adobe.com*. Because .swf files cannot be edited in the Flash

program, you should preview the Flash .fla files on the Stage and test them before you publish them as .swf files. Be sure to keep the original .fla file so that you can make changes, if needed, at a later date.

Previewing a Movie

After creating a new Flash movie or opening a previously saved movie, you can preview it within the workspace in several ways. When you preview a movie, you play the frames by directing the playhead to move through the Timeline, and you watch the movement on the Stage.

Control Menu Commands (and Keyboard Shortcuts)

Figure 8 shows the Control menu commands and the Controller, which has buttons that resemble common DVD-type options:

- Play ([Enter] (Win) or [return] (Mac)) begins playing the movie frame by frame, from the location of the playhead to the end of the movie. For example, if the playhead is on frame 5 and the last frame is frame 40, choosing the Play command will play frames 5–40 of the movie.

- Rewind ([Shift][,]) (Win) or ([option] ⌘[R]) (Mac) moves the playhead to frame 1.
- Go To End ([Shift][.]) moves the playhead to the last frame of the movie.
- Step Forward One Frame (.) moves the playhead forward one frame at a time.
- Step Backward One Frame (,) moves the playhead backward one frame at a time.

You can turn on the Loop Playback setting to allow the movie to continue playing repeatedly. A check mark next to the Loop Playback command on the Control menu indicates that the feature is active. To turn off this feature, click the Loop Playback command.

Figure 8 *Methods to control a movie*

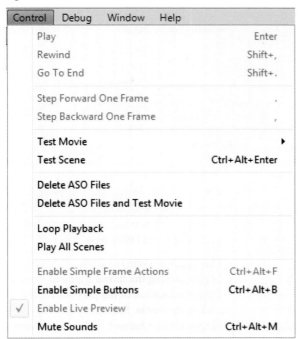

Control menu

Controller

Controller

You can also preview a movie using the Controller. To display the Controller, open the Window menu, point to Toolbars, and then click Controller.

Testing a Movie

When you play a movie within the Flash workspace, some interactive functions (such as buttons that are used to jump from one part of the movie to another) do not work. To preview the full functionality of a movie, you need to play it using a Flash Player. You can use the Test Movie command on the Control menu to test the movie using a Flash Player.

Documents, Movies, and Applications

As you work in Flash, you are creating a document. When you save your work as an .fla file, you are saving the document. This is consistent with other Adobe products, such as Photoshop, that use the word *document* to refer to work created in that program. In addition, because Flash uses a movie metaphor with a Stage, Timeline, frames, animations, and so on, the work done in Flash is often referred to as a movie. So, the phrase *Flash document* and the phrase *Flash movie* are synonymous. Movies can be as small and simple as a ball bouncing across the screen or as complex as a full-length interactive adventure game. Products such as games and educational software, as well as online advertisements and product demonstrations, are referred to as applications (see Figure 9). Applications usually contain multiple Flash documents or movies that are linked.

Using the Flash Player

To view a Flash movie on the web, your computer needs to have the Flash Player installed. An important feature of multimedia players, such as Flash Player, is the ability to decompress a file that has been compressed. Compressing a file gives it a small file size, which means it can be delivered more quickly over the Internet than its uncompressed counterpart. In addition to Adobe, companies such as Apple (QuickTime), Microsoft (Windows Media Player), and RealNetworks (RealPlayer) create players that allow applications, developed with their and other companies' products, to be viewed on the web. The multimedia players are distributed free and can be downloaded from the company's website. The Flash Player is created by Adobe and the latest version is available at *www.adobe.com*.

Figure 9 *Example of an application*

New York Philharmonic: Courtsey of http://www.nyphilkids.org/games/main.phtml?

Figure 10 *Playhead moving across Timeline*

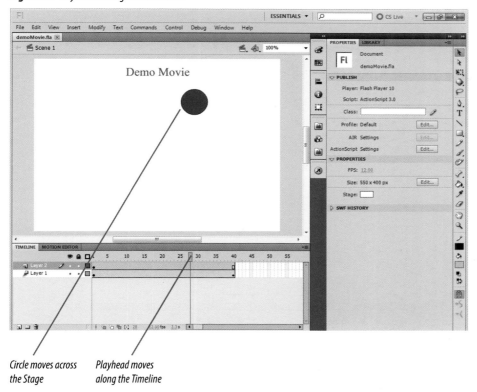

Circle moves across the Stage

Playhead moves along the Timeline

Using Options and Shortcuts

There is often more than one way to complete a particular command when using Flash. For example, if you want to rewind a movie you can use the controls on the controller panel; press [Shift] + [,]; or drag the playhead to frame 1. In addition, Flash provides context menus that are relevant to the current selection. For example, if you point to a graphic and right-click (Win) or [control]-click (Mac), a menu opens with graphic-related commands, such as cut and copy. Shortcut keys are also available for many of the most common commands, such as [Ctrl][Z] (Win) or [command][Z] (Mac) for Undo.

Open and play a movie using the Control menu and the Controller

1. Open fl1_1.fla from the drive and folder where your Data Files are stored, then save it as **demoMovie.fla**.

2. Verify the view is set to 100%.

   The view setting is displayed on the movie menu bar, which is above and to the right of the Stage.

3. Click **Control** on the menu bar, then click **Play**.

   Notice how the playhead moves across the Timeline as the blue circle moves from the left of the Stage to the right, as shown in Figure 10.

4. Click **Control** on the menu bar, then click **Rewind**.

5. Press [**Enter**] (Win) or [**return**] (Mac) to play the movie, then press [**Enter**] (Win) or [**return**] (Mac) again to stop the movie before it ends.

6. Click **Window** on the menu bar, point to **Toolbars**, then click **Controller**.

7. Use all the buttons on the Controller to preview the movie, then close the Controller.

8. Point to the **playhead** on the Timeline, then click and drag the **playhead** back and forth to view the contents of the movie frame by frame.

9. Click number **1** on the Timeline to select the frame.

10. Press the **period key** several times, then press the **comma key** several times to move the playhead one frame at a time forward and backward.

You opened a Flash movie and previewed it, using various controls.

Test a movie

1. Click **Control** on the menu bar, point to **Test Movie**, then click **in Flash Professional**.

   The Flash Player window opens, as shown in Figure 11, and the movie starts playing automatically.

2. Click **Control** on the menu bar of the Flash Player window (Win) or application menu bar (Mac), then review the available commands.

3. Click **File** on the menu bar of the Flash Player window (Win) or application menu bar (Mac), then click **Close** to close the Flash Player window.

4. Use your file management program to navigate to the drive and folder where you saved the demoMovie.fla file and notice the demoMovie.swf file.

TIP   When you test a movie, Flash automatically creates a file that has an .swf extension in the folder where your movie is stored and then plays the movie in the Flash Player.

5. Return to the Flash program.

You tested a movie in the Flash Player window and viewed the .swf file created as a result of testing the movie.

Figure 11 *Flash Player window*

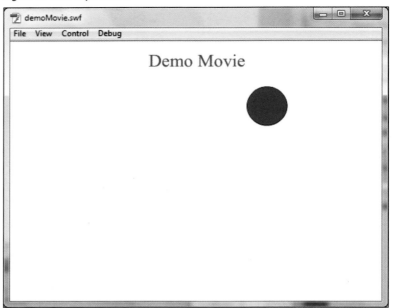

Figure 12 *Document Settings dialog box*

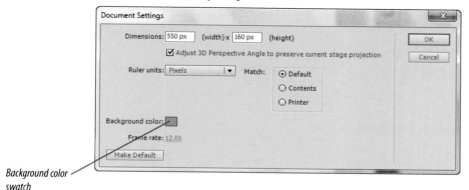

Background color
swatch

Figure 13 *Completed changes to the document properties*

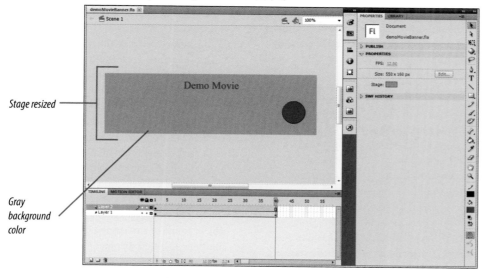

Stage resized

Gray
background
color

Change the Document Properties

1. Click **Modify** on the menu bar, then click **Document**.

   The Document Settings dialog box opens.

2. Double-click in the **height text box** to select the number, then type **160**.

3. Click the **Background color swatch**, then click a **gray (#999999) color swatch** in the far-left column of the color palette.

   Note: The color code for a color appears next to the sample color swatch above the palette as you point to a color. The Color Swatch palette allows you to click a color to choose it or to enter a number that represents the color.

4. Review the remaining default values shown in Figure 12, then click **OK**.

   The dialog box closes.

5. Click **View** on the menu bar, point to **Magnification**, then click **100%** if it is not already selected.

   Your screen should resemble Figure 13.

6. Press **[Enter]** (Win) or **[return]** (Mac) to play the movie.

7. Click **File** on the menu bar, then click **Save As**.

8. Navigate to the drive and folder where your Data Files are stored, type **demoMovieBanner** for the filename, then click **Save**.

9. Click **File** on the menu bar, then click **Close**.

You set the document properties including the size of the Stage and the background color, then you set the magnification and saved the document.

Create and SAVE A MOVIE

What You'll Do

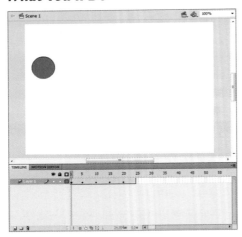

In this lesson, you will create a Flash movie that will include a simple animation, you will add animation effects, and then save the movie.

Creating a Flash Movie

Flash movies are created by placing objects (graphics, text, sounds, photos, and so on) on the Stage, editing these objects (for example, changing their brightness), animating the objects, and adding interactivity with buttons and menus. You can create graphic objects in Flash using the drawing tools, or you can create them in another program, such as Adobe Illustrator, Photoshop, or Fireworks, and then import them into a Flash movie. In addition, you can acquire clip art and stock photographs and import them into a movie. When objects are placed on the Stage, they are automatically placed on a layer and in the current frame of the Timeline.

Figure 14 shows a movie that has a circle object created in Flash. Notice that the playhead is on frame 1 of the movie. The object placed on the Stage appears in frame 1 and appears on the Stage when the playhead is on frame 1. The dot in frame 1 on the Timeline indicates that this frame is a keyframe. The concept of keyframes is critical to understanding how Flash works. A **keyframe** indicates that there is a change in the movie, such as the start of an animation, or the resizing of an object

on the Stage. A keyframe is automatically designated in frame 1 of every layer. In addition, you can designate any frame to be a keyframe.

The circle object in Figure 14 was created using the Oval tool. To create an oval or a rectangle, you select the desired tool and then drag the pointer over an area on the Stage. *Note:* Flash uses one button on the Tools panel to group the Oval and Rectangle tools, along with three other drawing tools. To display a menu of zthese tools, click and hold the rectangle (or oval) button on the Tools panel to display the menu and then click the tool you want to use. If you want to draw a perfect circle or square, press and hold [Shift] after the tool is selected, and then drag the pointer. If you make a mistake, you can click Edit on the menu bar, and then click Undo. To make changes to an object, such as resizing or changing its color, or to animate an object, you must first select it. You can use the Selection tool to select an entire object or group of objects. You drag the Selection tool pointer around the entire object to make a **marquee**. An object that has been selected displays a dot pattern or a blue border.

Getting Started with Flash

Creating an Animation

Figure 15 shows a movie that has 24 frames, as specified by the blue shading on the Timeline. The blue background color on the Timeline indicates a motion animation that starts in frame 1 and ends in frame 24. The dotted line on the Stage indicates the path the object will follow during the animation. In this case, the object will move from left to right across the Stage. The movement of the object is caused by having the object in different places on the Stage in different frames of the movie. In this case, frame 12 displays the object midway through the animation

and frame 24 displays the object at the end of the animation. A basic motion animation requires two keyframes. The first keyframe sets the starting position of the object, and the second keyframe sets the ending position of the object. The number of frames from keyframe to keyframe determines the length of the animation. If the starting keyframe is frame 1 and the ending keyframe is frame 24, the object will be animated for 24 frames. As an object is being animated, Flash automatically fills in the frames between these keyframes, with a process called **motion tweening**.

The Motion Tween Animation Process

Having an object move around the screen is one of the most common types of animations. Flash provides a process called motion tweening that makes it relatively simple to move objects. The process is to select an object on the Stage, then select the Motion Tween command from the Insert menu. If the object is not a symbol, a dialog box opens asking if you want to convert the object to a symbol. Creating a symbol allows you to reuse the object for this and other movies, as well as to apply a motion tween. Only symbols and text blocks can be motion

Figure 14 *Circle object in frame 1*

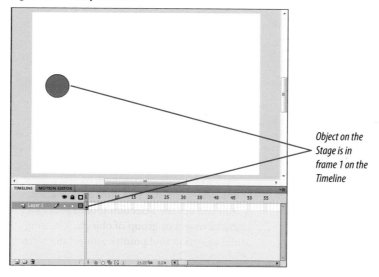

Object on the Stage is in frame 1 on the Timeline

Figure 15 *Motion animation*

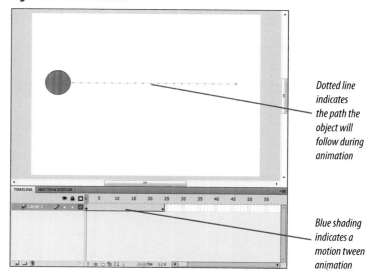

Dotted line indicates the path the object will follow during animation

Blue shading indicates a motion tween animation

tweened. The final step in the animation process is to select the ending frame for the animation and drag the object to another location on the Stage.

Two important things happen during the animation process. First, the Timeline shows the **tween span** (also called motion span), which is the number of frames in the motion tween. The tween span can be identified on the Timeline by a blue color, which, in this example, extends for 24 frames. The default tween span when starting from frame 1 of a new movie is determined by the number of frames per second setting. In this example, we used the default setting of 24 frames per second, so the initial number of frames in a tween for this movie is 24 frames. You can increase or decrease the length of the animation by pointing to either end of the span and dragging it to a new frame. The tween span will have more or fewer frames based on this action. The duration of the tween will still be based on the number of frames per second setting. For example, if we drag the tween span from frame 24 to frame 48, there are now 48 frames in the tween span. The tween span will still play at 24 frames per second because we did not change that setting. It will take two seconds to play the new tween span. If a movie has an ending frame beyond frame 1, the tween

span will extend to the end of the movie. For example, if a movie has 50 frames and you insert a motion tween starting at frame 10, the tween span will extend from frames 10 through 50. The length of the motion tween is determined automatically by the last frame in the movie or manually by you if you designate a frame other than the last frame of the movie as the end of the animation.

Second, a dotted line, called the **motion path**, represents the path the object takes from the beginning frame to the ending frame. This path can be reshaped to cause the object to travel in a non-linear way, as shown in Figure 16. Reshaping a path can be done by using the Selection tool on the Tools panel. You see the tween span on the Timeline and the motion path on the Stage.

Figure 16 *A reshaped motion path*

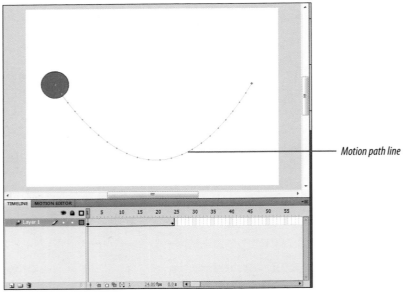

Motion path line

Getting Started with Flash

Motion Presets

Flash provides several preconfigured motion tweens that you can apply to an object on the Stage. These allow you to bounce an object across the Stage, fly-in an object from off the Stage, cause an object to pulsate and to spiral in place, as well as many other types of object animations. Figure 17 shows the Motion Presets panel where you choose a preset and apply it to an object. You can preview each preset before applying it and you can easily change to a different preset, if desired.

Adding Effects to an Object

In addition to animating the location of an object (or objects), you can also animate an object's appearance. Objects have properties such as color, brightness, and size. You can alter an object's properties as it is being animated using the motion tween process. For example, you could give the appearance of the object fading in by changing its transparency (alpha setting) or having it grow larger by altering its size over the course of the animation. Another useful effect is applying filters, such as drop shadows or bevels. All of these changes can be made using the Properties panel after selecting the object.

Figure 17 *Panel set with Motion Presets panel active*

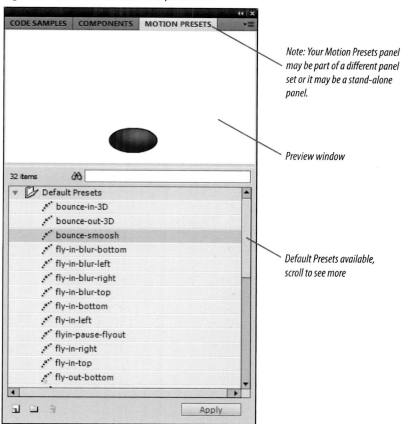

Note: Your Motion Presets panel may be part of a different panel set or it may be a stand-alone panel.

Preview window

Default Presets available, scroll to see more

Create objects using drawing tools

1. Click **ActionScript 3.0** to open a new Flash document.

2. Save the movie as **tween.fla**.

3. Verify the view is set to 100%.

4. Click and hold the **Rectangle tool** 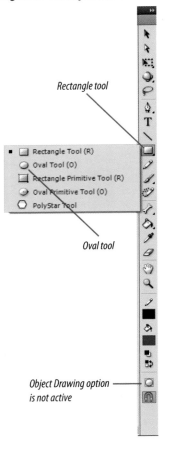 (or the Oval tool if it is displayed) on the Tools panel to display the list of tools, as shown in Figure 18, then click the **Oval tool** .

5. Verify that the Object Drawing option in the Options area of the Tools panel is not active, as shown in Figure 18.

6. Click the **Fill Color tool color swatch** on the Tools panel, then, if necessary, click the **red color swatch** in the left column of the color palette.

7. Click the **Stroke Color tool color swatch** on the Tools panel, then, if necessary, click the **black color swatch** in the left column of the color palette.

8. Press and hold **[Shift]**, drag the **pointer** on the left side of the Stage to draw the circle, as shown in Figure 19, then release the mouse button.

   Pressing and holding [Shift] creates a circle.

9. Click the **Selection tool** on the Tools panel, drag a **marquee** around the object to select it, as shown in Figure 20, then release the mouse button.

   The object appears covered with a dot pattern.

You created an object using the Oval tool, and then the object using the Selection tool.

Figure 18 *Drawing tools menu*

Rectangle tool

■ ☐ Rectangle Tool (R)
○ Oval Tool (O)
☐ Rectangle Primitive Tool (R)
◐ Oval Primitive Tool (O)
○ PolyStar Tool

Oval tool

Object Drawing option
is not active

Figure 19 *Drawing a circle*

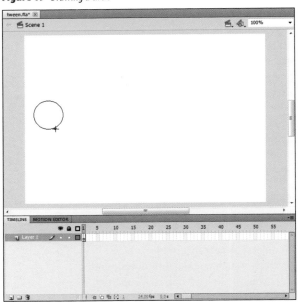

Figure 20 *Creating a marquee selection*

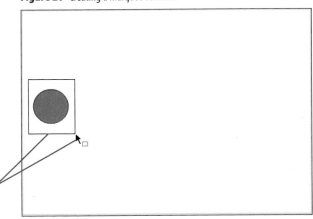

Use the Selection tool
to draw a marquee,
which selects the entire
object

Figure 21 *The circle on the right side of the Stage*

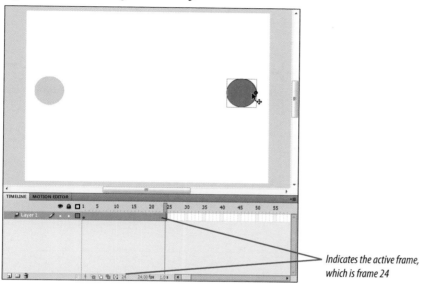

*Indicates the active frame,
which is frame 24*

Figure 22 *Pointing to the end of the tween span*

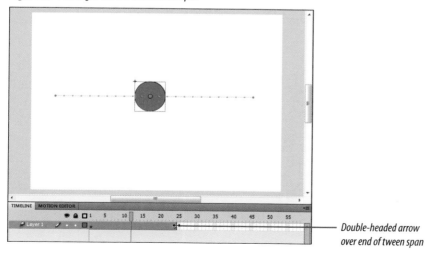

*Double-headed arrow
over end of tween span*

Create a motion tween animation

1. Click **Insert** on the menu bar, then click **Motion Tween**.

   The Convert selection to symbol for tween dialog box opens.

2. Click **OK**.

   A blue border surrounds the object indicating that the object is a symbol. Notice that, in this example, the playhead automatically moved to frame 24, the last frame in the tween span. When you move the object to a new location on the Stage, the object's new location will be reflected in frame 24.

3. Click and then drag the **circle** to the right side of the Stage, as shown in Figure 21, then release the mouse button.

4. Press **[Enter]**(Win) or **[return]**(Mac) to play the movie.

   The playhead moves through frames 1–24 on the Timeline, and the circle moves across the Stage.

5. Click **frame 12** on Layer 1 on the Timeline.

   Verify the frame number on the status bar of the Timeline is 12, and notice that the object is halfway across the screen. This is the result of the tweening process in which the frames between 1 and 24 are filled in with the object in the correct location for each frame.

6. Verify the Selection tool ![arrow] is active, then point to the end of the tween span until the pointer changes to a double-headed arrow ↔, as shown in Figure 22.

7. Click and drag the **tween span** to frame 48, then verify the frame number on the status bar is 48, or adjust as needed.

(continued)

8. Press **[Enter]**(Win) or **[return]**(Mac) to play the movie.

   Notice it now takes longer (2 seconds, not 1 second) to play the movie. Also notice that a diamond symbol appears in frame 48 indicating that it is now a Property keyframe. A Property keyframe indicates a change in the property of an object. In this case, it indicates the location of the object on the Stage has changed from frame 24 to frame 48.

9. Click **frame 24** and notice that the object is now halfway across the screen.

10. Click **File** on the menu bar, then click **Save**.

You created a motion tween animation and changed the length of the tween span.

Reshape the Motion Path

1. Click **File** on the menu bar, click **Save As**, then save the document with the filename **tweenEffects.fla**.

2. Verify the Selection tool ![cursor] is active.

3. Click **frame 1** to select it.

   Note: When you see the direction to click a frame, click the frame on the layer not the number on the Timeline.

4. Point to just below the middle of the path until the pointer changes to a pointer with an arc ![arc pointer] as shown in Figure 23.

5. Click and drag the **path** to reshape the path, as shown in Figure 24.

6. Play the movie.

   Note: When you see the direction to play the movie, press [Enter] (Win) or [return] (Mac).

(continued)

Figure 23 *Using the Selection tool to reshape a motion path*

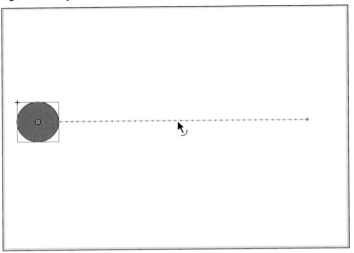

Figure 24 *Reshaping the motion path*

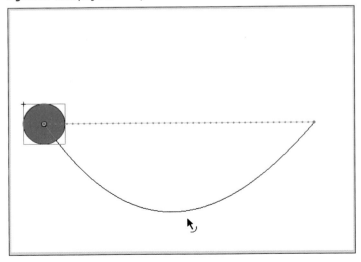

Figure 25 *The Properties panel displayed*

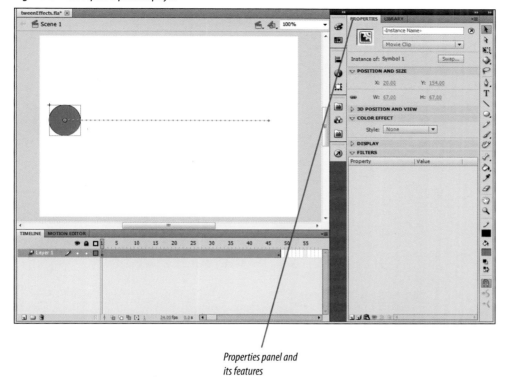

Properties panel and
its features

7. Test the movie.

   Note: When you see the direction to test the movie, click Control on the menu bar, point to Test Movie, then click in Flash Professional. Alternately, you can press [Ctrl]+[Enter] (Win) or [command]+[return](Mac).

8. View the movie, then close the Flash Player window.

9. Click **Edit** on the menu bar, then click **Undo Reshape**.

   Note: The Undo command starts with the most recent action and moves back through the actions. As a result, you may have to click Undo more than one time before you are able to click Undo Reshape.

You used the Selection tool to reshape a motion path and the Undo command to undo the reshape.

Change the transparency of an object

1. Click **frame 1** to select it, then click the **circle object** on the Stage to select it.

2. Click the **Properties panel tab** to display the Properties panel, as shown in Figure 25.

   Note: If the Properties panel is not open, click Window on the menu bar, then click Properties.

   Note: To verify the object is active, review the available settings in the Properties panel. Make sure POSITION AND SIZE is one of the options.

3. Click **COLOR EFFECT** on the Properties panel to display the Color Effect area if it is not already displayed, click the **Style list arrow**, then click **Alpha**.

(continued)

4. Drag the **Alpha slider** ⌂ to **0**.

   The object becomes transparent.

5. Click **frame 48** on the layer to select it.

6. Click a white area inside the bounding box on the Stage to select the object and check that the object's properties are displayed in the Properties panel.

   Note: To verify the object is active, review the available settings in the Properties panel. Make sure POSITION AND SIZE is one of the options.

7. Drag the **Alpha slider** ⌂ to **100**.

8. Play the movie.

9. Test the movie, then close the Flash Player window.

You used the Color Effect option on the Properties panel to change the transparency of an object.

Resize an object

1. Click **frame 1** to select it.

2. Click a white area inside the bounding box to select the **object**.

3. Click **POSITION AND SIZE** on the Properties panel if this area is not already open.

4. Review the W (width) and H (height) settings of the object.

   The width and height are the dimensions of the bounding box around the circle.

5. Click **frame 48** to select it, then click the **circle object** to select it.

6. Verify the **Lock icon** ⊖ in the Properties panel is not broken.

   Note: If the lock is broken, click the broken lock to lock it, as shown in Figure 26, to ensure the width and height change proportionally.

   (continued)

Figure 26 *Resizing the circle*

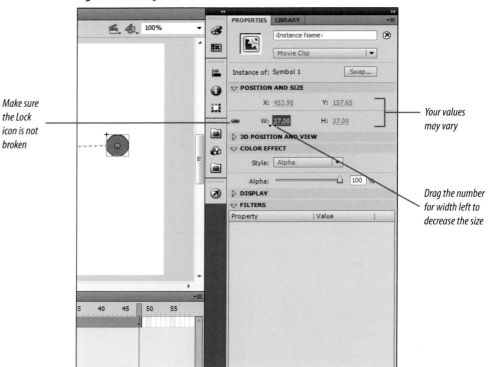

Make sure the Lock icon is not broken

Your values may vary

Drag the number for width left to decrease the size

Figure 27 *The Add filter icon*

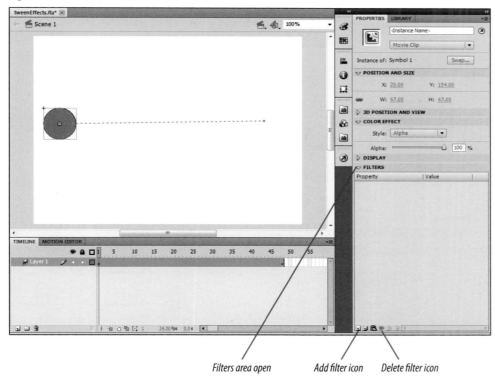

Filters area open   Add filter icon   Delete filter icon

7. Point to the number next to W: and when the pointer changes to a double-headed arrow , drag the **pointer** left to decrease the width so that the circle shrinks to about half its size, as shown in Figure 26.

   Hint: You can also double-click a value in the Properties panel and type a value.

8. Click the **circle object** on the Stage.

9. Play the movie.

10. Test the movie, then close the Flash Player window.

11. Click **frame 1** to select it, then click the **object** to select it.

12. Drag the **Alpha slider** to **100**.

You used the Position and Size option on the Properties panel to change the size of an object.

Add a filter to an object

1. Verify the object is selected by viewing the Properties panel and verifying the object's properties are displayed.

2. Click **FILTERS** on the Properties panel to display the Filters area if it is not already displayed.

3. Click the **Add filter icon** at the bottom of the Filters area, as shown in Figure 27.

4. Click **Drop Shadow**, point to the number for the angle, then when the pointer changes to a double-headed arrow, drag the pointer right to change the number of degrees to **100**.

5. Click **frame 1** to select it, then play the movie.

6. Click **frame 1** to select it, then click the **circle object** to select it.

(continued)

7. Click **Drop Shadow** in the Filters area, then click the **Delete Filter icon** 🗑 at the bottom of the Filters area.

The drop shadow filter is removed from the circle object.

8. Click the **Add filter icon** 🖵 at the bottom of the panel.

9. Click **Bevel**, test the movie, then close the Flash Player window.

You used the Filters option in the Properties panel to add and delete filters.

Add a motion preset

1. Verify the playhead is on frame 1, then click the object to select it.

2. Click **Window** on the menu bar, then click **Motion Presets**.

The Motion Presets panel opens. It may open as a stand-alone panel or it may be grouped with other panels.

3. Drag the **Motion Presets panel or the panel set** by its title bar (not one of the tabs) to the right so that it does not obscure the Stage.

4. Click the **expand icon** ▶ for the Default Presets, then click **bounce-smoosh** and watch the animation in the preview widow, as shown in Figure 28.

5. Click **Apply**.

A dialog box opens asking if you want to replace the current motion object with the new selection. You can only apply one motion tween or motion preset to an object at any one time.

(continued)

Figure 28 *The Motion Presets panel*

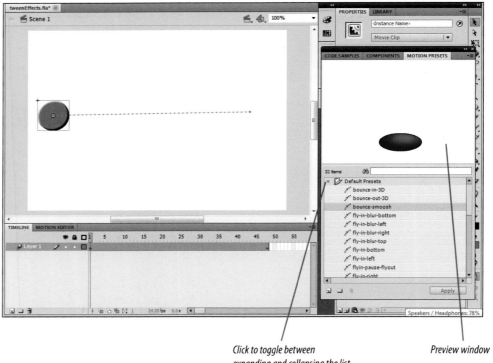

Click to toggle between expanding and collapsing the list

Preview window

Getting Started with Flash

Figure 29 *Diamond symbols indicating Property keyframes*

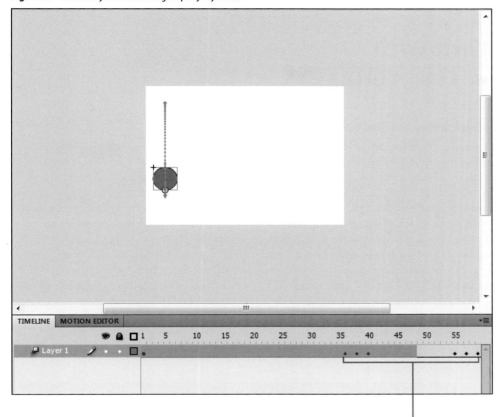

Diamond symbols
appear where the ball
is resized

6. Click **Yes**.

   The bevel filter is deleted and a new path
   is displayed.

7. Play the movie, then test the movie.

   Notice the circle object disappears from
   the Stage.

8. Close the Flash Player window.

9. Click **View** on the menu bar, point to
   Magnification, then click **50%**.

10. Click **frame 1**, click the **Selection tool**,
    draw a **marquee** around the circle object and
    the path to select both of them.

11. Press the **up arrow key [↑]** on the keyboard to
    move the circle object and the path toward the
    top of the Stage.

12. Play the movie.

    Notice the Timeline has several diamond
    symbols, as shown in Figure 29. Each one is a
    Property keyframe and indicates that there is a
    change in the object during the motion tween.
    In this case the change comes each time the
    ball is resized.

13. Click **frame 1** to select it, then drag the
    playhead from frame 1 to the last frame and
    notice the change that occurs at each keyframe.

14. Scroll the list of presets, click **pulse**, click
    Apply, then click **Yes**.

15. Play the movie.

16. Close the Motion Presets panel or panel set if
    the Motion Presets panel is part of a panel set.

17. Save and close the movie.

*You applied motion presets to an object and viewed how
keyframes identify changes in the motion tween.*

Work with
THE TIMELINE

What You'll Do

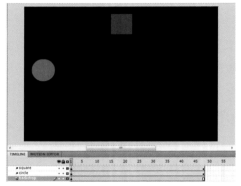

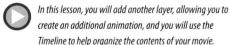

In this lesson, you will add another layer, allowing you to create an additional animation, and you will use the Timeline to help organize the contents of your movie.

Understanding the Timeline

The Timeline organizes and controls a movie's contents over time. By learning how to read the information provided on the Timeline, you can determine and change what will be happening in a movie, frame by frame. You can determine which objects are animated, what types of animations are being used, when the various objects will appear in a movie, when changes are made to the properties of an object, which objects will appear on top of others, and how fast the movie will play. Features of the Timeline are shown in Figure 30 and explained in this lesson.

Using Layers

Each new Flash movie contains one layer, named Layer 1. **Layers** are like transparent sheets of plastic that are stacked on top of each other. This is shown in Figure 31, which also shows how the stacked objects appear on the Stage. Each layer can contain one or more objects. In Figure 31, the tree is on one layer, the heading Solitude is on another layer, and the colored backdrop is on a third layer. You can add layers using the Timeline command on the Insert menu or by clicking the New Layer icon on the Timeline. Placing objects on different layers and locking the

Figure 30 *Elements of the Timeline*

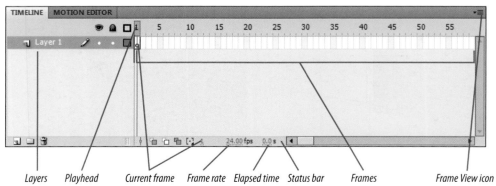

Layers   Playhead   Current frame   Frame rate   Elapsed time   Status bar   Frames   Frame View icon

Getting Started with Flash

layers helps avoid accidentally making changes to one object while editing another.

When you add a new layer, Flash stacks it on top of the other layer(s) on the Timeline. The stacking order of the layers on the Timeline is important because objects on the Stage appear in the same stacking order. For example, if you have two overlapping objects, and the top layer has a drawing of a tree and the bottom layer has a drawing of a house, the tree appears as though it is in front of the house. You can change the stacking order of layers simply by dragging them up or down in the list of layers. You can name layers, hide them so their contents do not appear on the Stage, and lock them so that they cannot be edited.

Using Frames and Keyframes

The Timeline is made up of individual segments called **frames**. The contents of each layer appear as the playhead moves over the frames, so any object in frame 1, no matter which layer it is on, appears on the Stage whenever frame 1 is played. Frames are numbered in increments of five for easy reference. The upper-right corner of the Timeline contains a Frame View icon. Clicking this icon displays a menu that provides different views of the Timeline, showing more frames or showing a preview (thumbnails) of the objects on a layer, for example. The status bar at the bottom of the Timeline indicates the current frame (the frame that the playhead is currently on), the frame rate (frames per second, also called fps), and the elapsed time from frame 1 to the current frame. Frames per second is the unit of measure for movies. If the frame rate is set to 24 frames per second and the movie has 48 frames, the movie will take 2 seconds to play.

Keyframes are locations on the Timeline where a new occurrence of an object appears or a change is made in the object. So, if you draw an object on the Stage, the current frame will need to be changed to a keyframe. In addition, if you create a motion tween, the first frame of the tween span will be a keyframe. One type of keyframe is a Property keyframe, which is used to specify locations on the Timeline where you want an animation to change. For example, you may have an animation of an object that moves across the Stage in frames 1 through 20. If you decide to resize the object in frame 5, a Property keyframe will appear on the Timeline in frame 5 when you make the change to that object. Another type of keyframe is a Blank keyframe, which is used to indicate that no content (objects) appears in that frame.

Interpreting the Timeline

The Timeline provides many clues to what is happening on the Stage. Interpreting these clues is essential to learning Flash. These clues are in the form of symbols and colors that appear on the Timeline. Figure 32 shows the most common symbols and colors. These are explained next. Others will be explained as they appear in subsequent chapters. The top layer on the Timeline in Figure 32 shows that frame 1 is a blank keyframe as indicated by the unfilled circle. No content will appear in frame 1 of this layer. In addition, the white background which extends to frame 24 indicates a span of blank frames. An unfilled rectangle appears at the end of the span and indicates the end of the blank frames.

Figure 31 *The concept of layers*

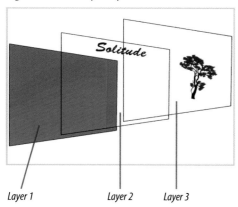

Layer 1   Layer 2   Layer 3

the Stage

The next layer shows a keyframe with content as indicated by the filled circle. The content in this frame also appears in frames 2-24 as indicated by the gray background. Again, an unfilled rectangle appears at the end of the span and indicates the end of the frames with the same content. The next layer shows a keyframe in frame 1 and a motion tween using the contents of frame 1 as indicated by the blue background in frames 2-24. No rectangle appears at the end of this span because the animation is not complete. Once frame 24 is selected and a change is made to the object being animated, such as moving it to a different location on the Stage, a keyframe will appear in frame 24. The bottom layer shows a keyframe in frame 1 and property keyframes (indicated by diamonds) in frames 5, 10, 15 and 20. Again, no symbol appears at the end of this span because no change has been made to the object in frame 24.

Figure 33 shows the Timeline of a movie created in Lesson 3 but now a second object, a square at the top of the Stage, has been added to the movie. By studying the Timeline, you can learn several things about the square object and this movie. First, the darker blue color highlighting Layer 2 indicates that this layer is active. Second, the square object is placed on its own layer, Layer 2 (indicated by the darker blue color that highlights the layer name and the motion animation). Third, the layer has a motion animation (indicated by the blue background in the frames and the motion path on the Stage). Fourth, the animation runs from frame 1 to frame 48. Fifth, if the objects intersect during the animation, the square will be on top of the circle, because the layer it is placed on (Layer 2) is above the layer that the circle is placed on (Layer 1). Sixth, the frame rate is set to 24, which means that the movie will play 24 frames per second. Seventh, the playhead is at frame 1, which causes the contents of frame 1 for both layers to appear on the Stage.

QUICK TIP

You can adjust the height of the Timeline by positioning the pointer over the top edge of the Timeline title bar until a double-headed pointer appears, and then dragging the border up or down.

Using the Playhead

The **playhead** indicates which frame is playing. You can manually move the playhead by dragging it left or right. This makes it easier to locate a frame that you may want to edit. Dragging the playhead also allows you to do a quick check of the movie without having to play it.

Figure 33 *The Timeline of a movie with a second object*

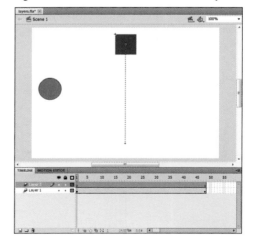

Figure 32 *Common symbols and colors on the Timeline*

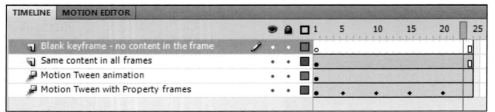

Figure 34 *Drawing a square*

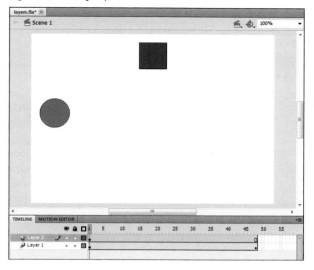

Figure 35 *Positioning the square at the bottom of the Stage*

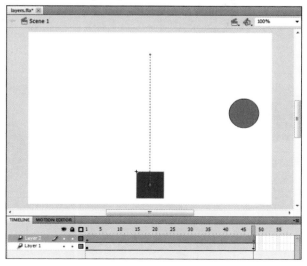

Add a layer

1. Open tween.fla, then save it as **layers.fla**.
2. Click **frame 1** on Layer 1.
3. Click **Insert** on the menu bar, point to **Timeline**, then click **Layer**.

   A new layer—Layer 2—appears at the top of the Timeline.

You added a layer to the Timeline.

Create a second animation

1. Click **frame 1** on Layer 2.
2. Click and hold the **Oval tool** ⬭ on the Tools panel, then click the **Rectangle tool** ▭ on the menu that opens.
3. Click the **Fill Color tool color swatch** 🎨 on the Tools panel, then click the **blue color swatch** in the left column of the color palette.
4. Press and hold [**Shift**], then draw a **square** resembling the dimensions and position of the square, as shown in Figure 34.
5. Click the **Selection tool** ▸ on the Tools panel, then drag a **marquee** around the square to select the object.
6. Click **Insert** on the menu bar, click **Motion Tween**, then click **OK** in the Convert selection to symbol for tween dialog box.
7. Click **frame 48** on Layer 2, then drag the **square** to the bottom of the Stage, as shown in Figure 35.

   When you click frame 48, the circle object moves to the right side of the Stage. Remember, when a frame is selected, all objects in that frame on every layer appear on the Stage.

(continued)

8. Play the movie.

The square appears on top if the two objects intersect.

You drew an object and used it to create a second animation.

Work with layers and view Timeline features

1. Click **Layer 2** on the Timeline, then drag **Layer 2** below Layer 1.

   Layer 2 is now the bottom layer, as shown in Figure 36.

2. Play the movie and notice how the square appears beneath the circle if the objects intersect.

3. Click **Layer 2** on the Timeline, then drag **Layer 2** above Layer 1.

4. Play the movie and notice how the square now appears on top of the circle if they intersect.

5. Click the **Frame View icon** 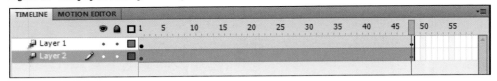 on the right corner of the Timeline title bar, as shown in Figure 37, to display the menu.

6. Click **Tiny** to display more frames.

   Notice how more frames appear on the Timeline, but each frame is smaller.

7. Click the **Frame View icon** ▾≣ , then click **Short**.

8. Click the **Frame View icon** ▾≣ , then click **Preview**.

   The object thumbnails appear on the Timeline.

9. Click the **Frame View icon** ▾≣ , then click **Normal**.

You changed the order of the layers, the display of frames, and the way the Timeline is viewed.

Figure 36 *Changing the stacking order of layers*

Figure 37 *Changing the view of the Timeline*

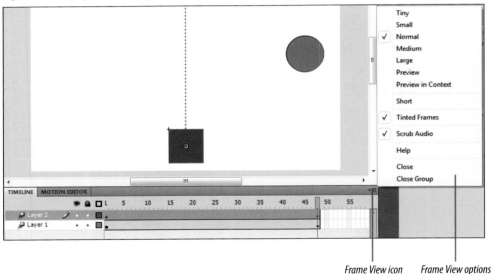

Frame View icon   Frame View options

Figure 38 *Changing the frame rate*

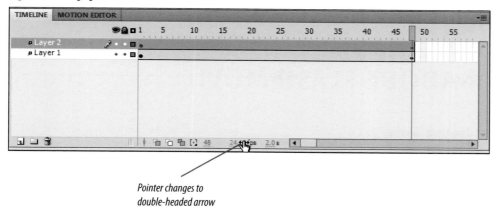

Pointer changes to
double-headed arrow

Figure 39 *Displaying the Properties option*

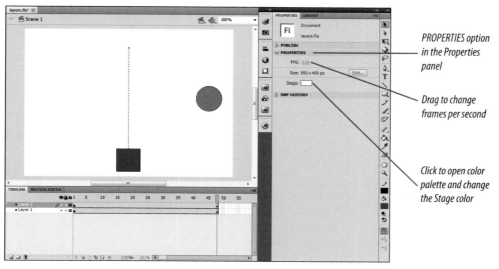

PROPERTIES option
in the Properties
panel

Drag to change
frames per second

Click to open color
palette and change
the Stage color

Modify the frame rate and change the layer names

1. Point to the **Frame Rate (fps)** on the Timeline status bar so the pointer changes to the double-headed arrow, as shown in Figure 38.

2. Drag the pointer to change the frame rate to **3**.

TIP Alternately, you can click the frame rate number, then type a new number.

3. Play the movie and notice that the speed of the movie changed.

4. Click a blank area of the Stage, then verify the Properties panel is the active panel. If not, click **Window**, then click **Properties**.

5. If the PROPERTIES options are not displayed, as shown in Figure 39, click **PROPERTIES** on the Properties panel.

   The Properties panel provides information about the Stage, including size and background color.

6. Change the frame rate (fps) to **18** and the Stage color to **black**, then play the movie.

7. Click **frame 24** on the Timeline and notice the position of the objects on the Stage.

8. Drag the **playhead** left and right to display frames one by one.

9. Double-click **Layer 1** on the Timeline, type **circle**, then press **[Enter]**(Win) or **[return]**(Mac).

10. Double-click **Layer 2** on the Timeline, type **square**, then press **[Enter]**(Win) or **[return]** (Mac).

11. Save your work.

You changed the frame rate of the movie and named layers.

Distribute an
ADOBE FLASH MOVIE

What You'll Do

 In this lesson, you will prepare a movie for distribution on the web.

Distributing Movies

When you develop Flash movies, the program saves them in a file format (.fla) that only users who have the Flash program installed on their computers can view. Usually, Flash movies are viewed on the web as part of a website or directly from a viewer's computer using the Flash Player. Flash files (.fla) cannot be viewed on the web using a web browser. They must be converted into a Flash Player file (.swf) so that the web browser knows the type of file to play (.swf) and the program needed to play the file (Flash Player). In addition, the HTML code needs to be created that instructs the web browser to play the swf file. Fortunately, Flash generates both the swf and HTML files when you use the Flash Publish command.

The process for publishing a Flash movie is to create and save a movie and then select the Publish command on the File menu. You can specify various settings, such as dimensions for the window in which the movie plays in the browser, before publishing the movie. Publishing a movie creates two files: an HTML file and a Flash Player (.swf) file. Both the HTML and swf files retain the

same name as the Flash movie file, but with different file extensions:

■ .html—the HTML document
■ .swf—the Flash Player file

For example, publishing a movie named layers.fla generates two files–layers.html and layers.swf. The HTML document contains the code that the browser interprets to display the movie on the web. The code also specifies which Flash Player movie the browser should play. Sample HTML code referencing a Flash Player movie is shown in Figure 40. If you are familiar with HTML code, you will recognize this as a complete HTML document. Even if you are not familiar with HTML code, you might recognize some of the code that the browser uses to display the Flash movie. For example, the movie source is set to layers.swf; the display dimensions (determined by the size of the Stage) are set to 550 × 400; and the background color is set to black (#000000 is the code for black).

Specifying a Background color for a Flash document will cause the HTML document that is created when using the Publish command to fill the browser window with the color.

If you want to display a background color only for the dimensions of the Stage, you can add a layer to the Flash document and draw a rectangle the same dimensions of the Stage and with the desired fill color. Be sure this backdrop layer is the bottom layer. Then, when you publish the Flash document and view it in a browser, the movie (displayed using the dimensions of the Stage) will have the rectangle color as a background color and the rest of the browser window will be a different color. A shortcut to previewing a Flash document within an HTML document is to use the Default – (HTML) option from the Publish Preview command in the File menu or simply pressing [F12].

Flash provides another way to distribute your movies that may or may not involve delivery on the web. You can create an executable file called a **projector**. When you create a projector file, you specify the type of file you want to create, such as Windows .exe files and Macintosh .app files. Projector files maintain the movie's interactivity. So, if a movie has buttons that the user clicks to play an animation, the buttons will work in a projector file.

Projector files do not need the Flash Player to play them. You can play projector files directly from a computer, or you can incorporate them into an application, such as a game, that is downloaded or delivered on a CD or DVD. In addition, Flash provides features for creating movies specifically for mobile devices, such as cell phones.

Figure 40 *Sample HTML code*

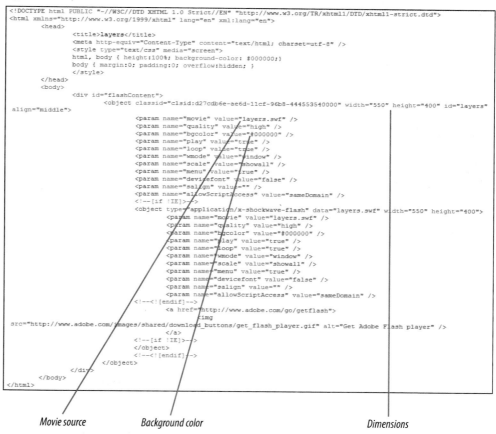

Movie source   Background color   Dimensions

Publish a movie for distribution on the web

1. Verify layers.fla is open, then save it as **layersWeb.fla**.

2. Click **File** on the menu bar, then click **Publish**.

   The files layers.html and layers.swf are automatically generated and saved in the same folder as the Flash document.

3. Use your file management program to navigate to the drive and folder where you save your work.

4. Notice the three files that begin with "layers," as shown in Figure 41.

   The three files are layersWeb.fla, the Flash movie; layersWeb.html, the HTML document; and layersWeb.swf, the Flash Player file.

5. Double-click **layersWeb.html** to play the movie in the browser.

   Note: Depending on your browser, browser settings and version, you may need to complete additional steps (such as accepting blocked content) to view the layers.html document.

TIP Click the browser button on the taskbar if the movie does not open automatically in your browser.

   Notice the animation takes up only a portion of the browser window, as shown in Figure 42. This is because the Stage size is set to 550 x 440, which is smaller than the browser window. Notice also that the entire browser window has been filled with the black background. This is because a background color was used rather than creating a backdrop layer.

6. Close the browser, and return to Flash.

You used the Publish command to create an HTML document (.html) and a Flash Player file (.swf), then you displayed the HTML document in a web browser.

Figure 41 *The three layers files after publishing the movie*

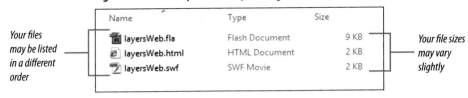

Your files may be listed in a different order

Your file sizes may vary slightly

Figure 42 *The animation played in a browser window*

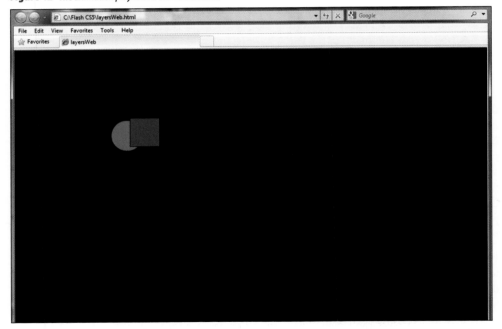

Figure 43 *Drawing a rectangle the size of the Stage*

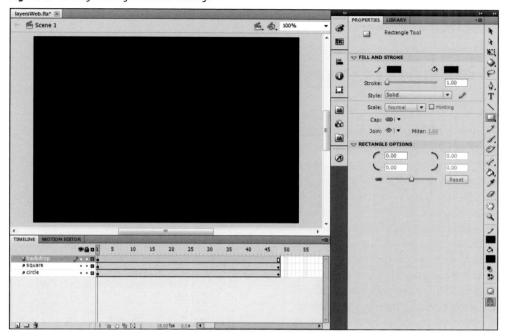

Rich Media Content and Accessibility

Flash provides the tools that allow you to create compelling applications and websites by incorporating rich media content, such as animations, sound, and video. Generally, incorporating rich media enhances the user's experience. However, accessibility becomes an issue for those persons who have visual, hearing, or mobility impairments, or have a cognitive disability. Designers need to utilize techniques that help ensure accessibility, such as providing consistency in navigation and layout, labeling graphics, captioning audio content throughout the applications and website, and providing keyboard access.

Draw a backdrop color for the Stage

1. Click **Modify** on the menu bar, then click **Document**.
2. Change the Background color to **white**, then click **OK**.
3. Click **square** on the Timeline to select the square layer.
4. Click **Insert** on the menu bar, point to **Timeline**, then click **Layer**.
5. Double-click **Layer 3** on the Timeline to select the name of the new layer, type **backdrop**, then press **[Enter]** (Win) or **[return]** (Mac).
6. Click **frame 1** of the backdrop layer.
7. Click the **Rectangle tool** ▢ on the Tools menu.
8. Use the Tools panel to set the Fill Color to **black** and the Stroke Color to **black**.
9. Draw a **rectangle** that covers the Stage, as shown in Figure 43.
10. Click **backdrop** on the Timeline, then drag the **backdrop** layer below the circle layer.
11. Click **File** on the menu bar, point to **Publish Preview**, then click **Default – (HTML)**.

    Notice how the HTML document has a white background and the Flash movie plays in an area the size of the Stage.

    Note: If a warning message opens, follow the directions to allow blocked content.
12. Close the browser and return to Flash.
13. Save and close the layersWeb.fla document.

You changed the background color of a Flash document and added a backdrop color.

Plan an APPLICATION OR A WEBSITE

What You'll Do

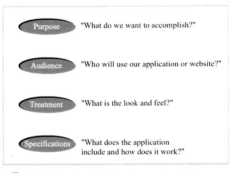

Purpose	"What do we want to accomplish?"
Audience	"Who will use our application or website?"
Treatment	"What is the look and feel?"
Specifications	"What does the application include and how does it work?"

In this lesson, you will learn how to plan a Flash application. You will also learn about the guidelines for screen design and the interactive design of web pages.

Planning an Application or a Website

Flash can be used to develop animations that are part of a product, such as a game or educational tutorial, and delivered via the internet, a CD, a DVD, or a mobile device. You can use Flash to create enhancements to web pages, such as animated logos, interactive navigation buttons, and banner ads. You can also use Flash to create entire websites. No matter what the application, the first step is planning the movie. Often, the temptation is to jump right into the program and start developing movies. The problem is that this invariably results in a more time-consuming process at best; and wasted effort, resources, and money at worst. The larger and more complex the project is, the more critical the planning process becomes. Planning an application or an entire website should involve the following steps:

Step 1: Stating the Purpose (Goals). "What, specifically, do we want to accomplish?"

Determining the goals is a critical step in planning because goals guide the development process, keep the team members on track, and provide a way to evaluate the application or website, both during and after its development.

Step 2: Identifying the Target Audience. "Who will use our application or website?"

Understanding the potential viewers helps in developing an application or a website that can address their needs. For example, children respond to exploration and surprise, so having a dog wag its tail when the mouse pointer rolls over it might appeal to this audience.

Step 3: Determining the Treatment. "What is the look and feel?"

The treatment is how the application or website will be presented to the user, including the tone, approach, and emphasis.

Tone. Will the application or website be humorous, serious, light, heavy, formal, or informal? The tone of an application or a site can often be used to make a statement—projecting a progressive, high-tech, well-funded corporate image, for instance.

Approach. How much direction will be provided to the user? An interactive game might focus on exploration such as when the user points to an object on the screen and the object becomes animated. While an informational website might provide lots of direction and include lists of options in the form of drop-down menus.

Emphasis. How much emphasis will be placed on the various multimedia elements? For example, a company may want to develop an informational application or website that shows the features of its new product line, including video demonstrations and sound narrations of how each product works. The budget might not allow for the expense of creating the videos, so the emphasis would shift to still pictures with text descriptions.

Step 4: Developing the Specifications, Flowchart, and Storyboard. "What precisely does the application or website include and how does it work?"

The **specifications** state what will be included in each screen, including the arrangement of each element and the functionality of each object (for example, what happens when you click the button labeled Skip Intro). Specifications should include the following:

Playback System. The choice of what configuration to target for playback is critical, especially Internet connection speed, browser versions, screen resolution, screen size (especially when targeting mobile devices), and plug-ins.

Elements to Include. The specifications should include details about the various elements that are to be included in the site. What are the dimensions for the animations, and what is the frame rate? What are the sizes of the various objects such as photos, buttons, and so on? What fonts, font sizes,

and font formatting will be used? Should video or sound be included?

Functionality. The specifications should include the way the program reacts to an action by the user, such as a mouse click. For example, clicking a door (object) might cause a doorbell to ring (sound), the door to open (an animation), an "exit the program" message to appear (text), or an entirely new screen to be displayed.

A **flowchart** is a visual representation of how the contents in an application or a

website are organized and how various screens are linked. It provides a guide for the developer and helps to identify problems with the navigation scheme before work begins. Figure 44 shows a simple flowchart illustrating the site organization and links.

Flowcharts vary based on the purpose of the site or application. For example, an informational website might include an extensive menu (navigation) system with lots of buttons that allow the user to easily navigate to the desired information.

Figure 44 *Sample flowchart*

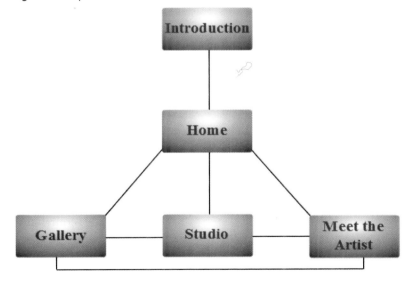

Whereas, an online sales site might have a more controlled user experience with fewer options as the user is led through product review, selection, and purchase (checkout).

A **storyboard** shows the layout of the various screens, often in the form of thumbnail sketches. It describes the contents and illustrates how text, graphics, animation, and other screen elements will be positioned. It also indicates the navigation process, such as menus and buttons. Figure 45 shows a storyboard. The exact content (such as a specific photo) does not have to be decided, but it is important to show where text, graphics, photos, buttons, and other elements, will be placed. Thus, the storyboard includes placeholders for the various elements. Storyboards can be created using the dimensions of the Flash Stage.

Flowcharts and storyboards make up the **user interface**, that is the appearance of objects (how each object is arranged on the screen) and the interactivity (how the user navigates through the site or application).

Using Screen Design Guidelines

The following screen design guidelines are used by application and web developers. The implementation of these guidelines is affected by the goals of the application or website, the intended audience, and the content.

Balance in screen design refers to the distribution of optical weight in the layout. Optical weight is the ability of an object to attract the viewer's eye, as determined by the object's size, shape, color, and so on. The storyboard in Figure 45 shows a fairly well-balanced layout, especially if the logo has as much optical weight as the text description. In general, a balanced design is more appealing to a viewer. However, for a game application or an entertainment site, a balanced layout may not be desired.

Figure 45 *Sample Storyboard*

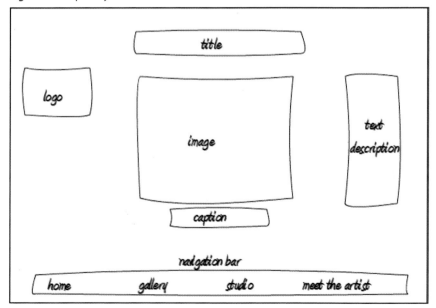

Unity helps the screen objects reinforce each other. **Intra-screen unity** has to do with how the various screen objects relate and how they all fit in. For example, a children's game might only use cartoon characterizations of animals for all the objects—including navigation buttons and sound control buttons, as well as the on-screen characters. **Inter-screen unity** refers to the design that viewers encounter as they navigate from one screen to another, and it provides consistency throughout the application or site. For example, all navigation buttons are located in the same place on each screen.

Movement refers to the way the viewer's eyes move through the objects on the screen. Different types of objects and various animation techniques can be used to draw the viewer to a location on the screen.

For example, a photo of a waterfall may cause the viewer's eyes to follow the flow of the water down, especially if the waterfall is animated. The designer could then place an object, such as a logo or a sales message, below the waterfall.

Using Interactive Design Guidelines

In addition to screen design guidelines, interactive guidelines determine the interactivity of the application. The following guidelines are not absolute rules since they are affected by the goals of the application, the intended audience, and the content:

■ Make it simple, easy to understand, and easy to use so that viewers do not have to spend time learning what the application is about and what they need to do.
■ Build in consistency in the navigation scheme. Help the users know where they are in the application and help them avoid getting lost.
■ Provide feedback. Users need to know when an action, such as clicking a button, has been completed. Changing its color or shape, or adding a sound can indicate this.
■ Give the user control. Allow the user to skip long introductions; provide controls for starting, stopping, and rewinding animations, video, and audio; and provide controls for adjusting audio.

The Flash Workflow Process

After the planning process, you are ready to start work on the Flash documents. The following steps can be used as guidelines in a general workflow process suggested by Adobe.

Step 1: Create and/or acquire the elements to be used in the application. The elements include text, photos, drawings, video, and audio. The elements become the raw material for the graphics, animations, menus, buttons, and content that populate the application and provide the interactivity. You can use the various Flash drawing and text tools to create your own images and text content; or, you can use another program, such as Adobe Photoshop, to develop the elements, and then import them into Flash. Alternately, you can acquire stock clip art and photographs. You can produce video and audio content in-house and import it into Flash or you can acquire these elements from a third party.

Step 2: Arrange the elements and create the animations. Arrange the elements (objects) on the Stage and on the Timeline to define when and how they appear in your application. Once the elements are available, you can create the various animations called for in the specifications.

Step 3: Apply special effects. Flash provides innumerable special effects that can be applied to the various media elements and animations. These include graphic and text filters, such as drop shadows, blurs, glows, and bevels. In addition, there are effects for sounds and animations such as fade-ins and fade-outs, acceleration and deceleration, morphing. and even 3D effects.

Step 4: Create the interactivity. Flash provides a scripting feature, ActionScript, which allows you to develop programming code to control how the media elements behave, including how various objects respond to user interactions, such as clicking buttons and rolling over images.

Step 5: Test and publish the application. Testing can begin before the actual development process with usability testing, which involves potential users being observed as they navigate through thumbnail sketches of the storyboard. Testing should continue throughout the development process, including using the Test Movie feature in the Control menu to test the movie using the Flash Player and to publish the movie in order to test it in a browser.

Project Management

Developing websites or any extensive application, such as a game, involves project management. A project plan needs to be developed that provides the project scope and identifies the milestones, including analyzing, designing, building, testing, and launching. Personnel and resource needs are identified, budgets built, tasks assigned, and schedules developed. Successful projects are a team effort relying on the close collaboration of designers, developers, project managers, graphic artists, programmers, testers, and others. Adobe provides various product suites, such as their Creative Suite 5 (CS5) Web Collection series, that include programs such as Flash, Dreamweaver, Photoshop, Illustrator, and Fireworks. These are the primary tools needed to develop interactive applications and websites. These programs are designed for easy integration. So, a graphic artist can use Photoshop to develop an image that can easily be imported into Flash and used by an animator. In addition, other tools in the suites, such as Adobe Bridge and Adobe Version Cue, help ensure efficient workflow when working in a team environment.

Using the Flash Help Feature

Flash provides a comprehensive Help feature that can be very useful when first learning the program. You access the Help feature from the Help menu. The Help feature is organized by categories, including Using Flash Professional CS5, which have several topics such as Workspace and Managing documents. In addition, the Help feature has a Help Search feature. You use the Help Search feature to search for topics using keywords, such as Timeline. Searching by keywords accesses the Flash Community Help feature, which displays links to content relevant to the search terms. Other resources not affiliated with Adobe are available through the web. You may find some by searching the web for Flash resources. The CS Live button on the title bar provides access to Adobe's CS Live online services, including product registration, support, and news; as well as links to Flash forums and user groups.

Figure 46 *The Flash Help categories*

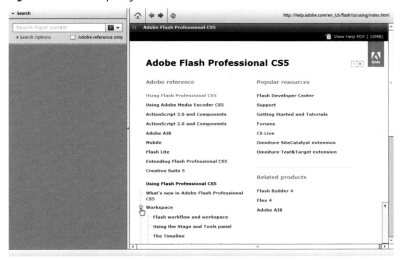

Figure 47 *The Flash Help Search feature*

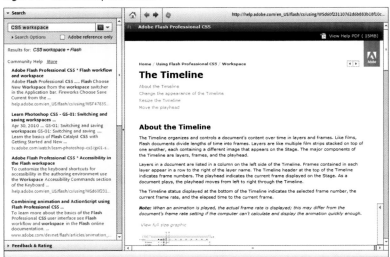

Use Flash Help

1. Start a new Flash document.

2. Click **Help** on the menu bar, then click **Flash Help**.

   Note: If you see a page not found message, be sure you are connected to the Internet.

3. Maximize the Help window, then click the **Expand button** ⊞ next to Workspace to expand the category, as shown in Figure 46.

4. Click **The Timeline**, then click **About the Timeline**.

5. Read through the text in About the Timeline.

6. Scroll to display the top of the Help window.

7. Click in the **Search text box**, type **CS5 workspace**, then verify the Flash icon is displayed to the right of the Search text box.

   Your search is refined to the Flash product when the Flash icon is displayed.

8. Press **[Enter]** (Win) or **[return]** (Mac) to access the Community Help site.

9. Study the various links provided on the site.

   Note: Figure 47 shows the results of one search using the keywords CS5 workspace. New links are added regularly because this is community-based help. Therefore, your results may differ.

10. Close the Flash Help site, then exit the Flash program.

You used the Flash Help feature to access information on the Timeline and the workspace.

Open a document and understand the Flash workspace.

1. Start Flash, open fl1_2.fla, then save it as **skillsDemo1.fla**. This movie has two layers. Layer 1 contains the heading and the line at the top of the Stage. Layer 2 contains an animation that runs for 75 frames.
2. Change the magnification to 50% using the View menu. (*Hint*: Click View, point to Magnification, then click 50%.)
3. Change the magnification to Fit in Window.
4. Change the Timeline view to Small. (*Hint*: Click the Frame View icon in the upper-right corner of the Timeline title bar.)
5. Hide all panels.
6. Display the Tools panel, Timeline panel, Properties panel, and the Library panel if it did not open with the Properties panel.
7. Group the Library and Properties panels if they are not already grouped.
8. Drag the Library panel from the Properties panel, then position it on the Stage.
9. Collapse the Library panel.
10. Close the Library panel to remove it from the screen.
11. Reset the Essentials workspace.

Play and test a movie.

1. Drag the playhead to view the contents of each frame. Use the commands on the Control menu to play and rewind the movie.
2. Press [Enter] (Win) or [return] (Mac) to play and stop the movie.

3. Use the Controller to rewind, play, and stop the movie, then close the Controller.
4. Test the movie in the Flash Player window, then close the Flash Player window.

Change the document size and background color.

1. Use the Document command on the Modify menu to display the Document Settings dialog box.
2. Change the document height to 380.
3. Change the background color to a medium gray color (#999999).
4. Click OK to close the Document Settings dialog box.
5. Play the movie.

Create and save a movie.

1. Insert a new layer above Layer 2, then select frame 1 of the new layer.
2. Draw a green ball in the middle of the left side of the Stage, approximately the same size as the red ball. (*Hint*: The green gradient color can be used to draw the ball. Several gradient colors are found in the bottom row of the color palette when you click the Fill Color tool in the Tools panel.)
3. Use the Selection tool to draw a marquee around the green ball to select it, then create a motion tween to animate the green ball so that it moves across the screen from left to right. (*Hint*: Select frame 75 on Layer 3 before repositioning the green ball.)
4. Use the Selection tool to reshape the motion path to an arc by dragging the middle of the path downward.
5. Play the movie.

6. Use the Undo command to undo the reshape. (*Note*: You may need to use the Undo feature twice.)
7. Use the Selection tool to select frame 75 of the new layer, click the green ball if it is not already selected to select it, then use the Properties panel to change the transparency (alpha) from 100% to 20%. (*Hint*: If the Properties panel COLOR EFFECT option is not displayed, make sure the Properties panel is open and click the green ball to make sure it is selected.)
8. Play the movie.
9. Click frame 75 on Layer 3 and click the green ball to select it.
10. Use the Properties panel to decrease the width of the ball to approximately half its size. (*Hint*: Make sure the lock width and height value icon in the Properties panel is unbroken. You may need to click the Stage to have the new value take effect.)
11. Play the movie.
12. Select frame 1 on Layer 3, then click the green ball to select it.
13. Use the Filters option in the Properties panel to add a drop shadow.
14. Play the movie.
15. Select frame 1 on Layer 2, then click the red ball to select it.
16. Open the Motion Presets panel, then add a bounce-smoosh preset.
17. Move Layer 3 below Layer 2.
18. Play the movie.
19. Save the movie.

Work with the Timeline.

1. Change the frame rate to 8 frames per second, play the movie, change the frame rate to 24, then play the movie again.
2. Change the view of the Timeline to display more frames.
3. Change the view of the Timeline to display a preview of the object thumbnails.
4. Change the view of the Timeline to display the Normal view.
5. Click frame 1 on Layer 1, use the playhead to display each frame, then compare your screens to Figure 48.
6. Save the movie.

Distribute an Adobe Flash movie.

1. Click File on the menu bar, then click Publish.
2. Open your browser, then open skillsDemo1.html.
3. View the movie, close your browser, then return to Flash.

Work with the Flash workspace.

1. Use the Document Settings dialog box to change the document background color to white.
2. Insert a new layer, then rename the layer **gray backdrop**.
3. Select frame 1 of the gray backdrop layer.
4. Select the rectangle tool, then set the Fill Color and the Stroke Color to the same shade of gray.
5. Draw a rectangle that covers the Stage.
6. Drag the gray backdrop layer to the bottom of the list of layers on the Timeline.

7. Rename the layers using these names: **heading**, **green ball**, and **red ball**. Use clues on the Timeline to help you know what to name each layer.

8. Play the movie in the browser, then close the browser window.
9. Save and close the Flash document.

Figure 48 *Completed Skills Review*

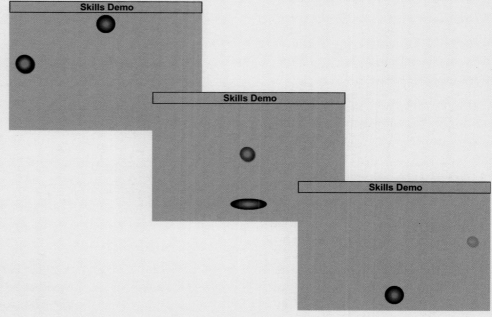

A friend cannot decide whether to sign up for a class in Flash or Dreamweaver. You help her decide by showing her what you already know about Flash. You want to show her how easy it is to create a simple animation because you think she'd enjoy a class in Flash. You decide to animate three objects. The first object is placed on the center of the Stage and pulsates throughout the movie. The second object enters the Stage from the left side and moves across the middle of the Stage and off the right side of the Stage. The third object enters the Stage from the right side and moves across the middle of the Stage and off the left side of the Stage. The motion paths for the two objects that move across the Stage are reshaped so they go above and below the pulsating object in the middle of the Stage.

1. Open a Flash document, then save it as **demonstration.fla**.
2. Verify the view is set to 100%.
3. Use the tools on the Tools panel to create a circle (or object of your choice) and color of your choice on the middle of the Stage.
4. Draw a marquee around the object to select it and apply a pulse motion preset.
5. Insert a new layer, then select frame 1 on the layer.
6. Create a simple shape or design using a color of your choice, and place it off the left side of the Stage and halfway down the Stage.
7. Select the object and insert a motion tween that moves the object directly across the screen and off the right side of the Stage. (*Hint*: Drag the object off the right side of the Stage.)
8. Reshape the motion path so that the object goes in an arc below the center pulsating object.
9. Insert a new layer, then select frame 1 on the layer.
10. Create an object using the color of your choice and place it off the right side of the Stage and halfway down the Stage.
11. Draw a marquee to select the object and insert a motion tween that moves the object directly across the screen and off the left side of the Stage.

12. Reshape the motion path so that the object goes in an arc above the center pulsating object.
13. Play the movie.
14. Add a background color.
15. Rename the layers with descriptive names.
16. Play the movie, test it , then close the Flash Player window.
17. Save the movie, then compare your movie to the sample provided in Figure 49.

Figure 49 *Sample completed Project Builder 1*

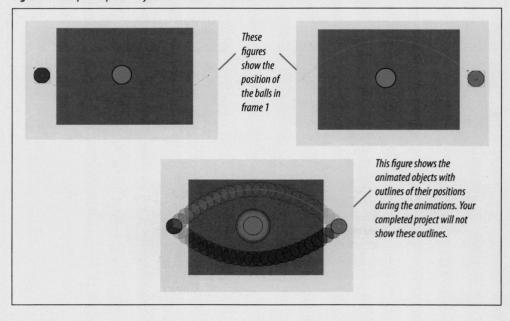

These figures show the position of the balls in frame 1

This figure shows the animated objects with outlines of their positions during the animations. Your completed project will not show these outlines.

You've been asked to develop a simple movie about recycling for a day care center. For this project, you will add two animations to an existing movie. You will show three objects that appear on the screen at different times, and then move each object to a recycle bin at different times. You can create the objects using any of the Tools on the Tools panel.

1. Open fl1_3.fla, then save it as **recycle.fla**.
2. Play the movie and study the Timeline to familiarize yourself with the movie's current settings. Currently, there are no animations.
3. Insert a new layer above Layer 2, then draw a small object in the upper-left corner of the Stage.
4. Create a motion tween that moves the object to the recycle bin. (*Hint*: Be sure to select frame 40 on the new layer before moving the object to the recycle bin.)
5. Reshape the path so that the object moves in an arc to the recycle bin. (*Note*: At this time, the object will appear outside the recycle bin when it is placed in the bin.)
6. Insert a new layer above the top layer, draw a small object in the upper-center of the Stage, then create a motion tween that moves the object to the recycle bin.
7. Insert a new layer above the top layer, draw a small object in the upper-right corner of the Stage, then create a motion tween that moves the object to the recycle bin.
8. Reshape the path so that the object moves in an arc to the recycle bin.
9. Move Layer 1 to the top of all the layers.
10. Play the movie and compare your movie to the sample provided in Figure 50.
11. Save the movie.

Figure 50 *Sample completed Project Builder 2*

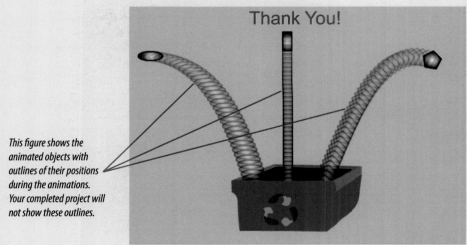

This figure shows the animated objects with outlines of their positions during the animations. Your completed project will not show these outlines.

Figure 51 shows the home page of a website. Study the figure and answer the following questions. For each question, indicate how you determined your answer.

1. Connect to the Internet, then go to *www.argosycruises.com*.
2. Open a document in a word processor or open a new Flash document, save the file as **dpc1**, then answer the following questions. (*Hint*: Use the Flash Text tool if you open a Flash document.)
   - Whose website is this?
   - What is the goal(s) of the site?
   - Who is the target audience?
   - What treatment (look and feel) is used?
   - What are the design layout guidelines being used (balance, movement, etc.)?
   - How can animation enhance this page?
   - Do you think this is an effective design for the company, its products, and its target audience? Why, or why not?
   - What suggestions would you make to improve the design, and why?

Figure 51 *Design Project*

Courtesy of www.argosy-cruises.com

There are numerous companies in the business of developing websites for others. Many of these companies use Flash as one of their primary development tools. These companies promote themselves through their own websites and usually provide online portfolios with samples of their work. Log onto the Internet, then use your favorite search engine and keywords such as Flash developers and Flash animators to locate three of these companies, and generate the following information for each one. A sample website is shown in Figure 52.

1. Company name:
2. Contact information (address, phone, and so on):
3. Website URL:
4. Company mission:
5. Services provided:
6. Sample list of clients:
7. Describe three ways the company seems to have used Flash in its website. Were these effective? Why, or why not?
8. Describe three applications of Flash that the company includes in its portfolio (or showcases or samples). Were these effective? Why, or why not?
9. Would you want to work for this company? Why, or why not?
10. Would you recommend this company to another company that was looking to enhance its website? Why, or why not?

Figure 52 *Sample website for Portfolio Project*

Courtesy of www.bluegelmedia.com

CHAPTER **2** **DRAWING OBJECTS IN ADOBE FLASH**

1. Use the Flash drawing and alignment tools
2. Select objects and apply colors
3. Work with drawn objects
4. Work with text and text objects
5. Work with layers and objects

DRAWING OBJECTS IN
ADOBE FLASH

Introduction

Computers can display graphics in either a bitmap or a vector format. The difference between these formats is in how they describe an image. A bitmap graphic represents an image as an array of dots, called **pixels**, which are arranged within a grid. Each pixel in an image has an exact position on the screen and a precise color. To make a change in a bitmap graphic, you modify the pixels. When you enlarge a bitmap graphic, the number of pixels remains the same, resulting in jagged edges that decrease the quality of the image. A vector graphic represents an image using lines and curves, which you can resize without losing image quality. Also, the file size of a vector image is generally smaller than the file size of a bitmap image, which makes vector images particularly useful for a website. However, vector graphics are not as effective as bitmap graphics for representing photo-realistic images. Even so, one of the most compelling features of Flash is the ability to create and manipulate vector graphics.

Flash images are vector graphics and they are referred to as objects. Images (objects) created using Flash drawing tools have a stroke (border line), a fill, or both. In addition, the stroke of an object can be segmented into smaller lines. You can modify the size, shape, rotation, and color of each stroke, fill, and segment.

Flash provides two drawing modes, called models. In the Merge Drawing Model, when you draw two shapes and one overlaps the other, a change in the top object may affect the object it overlaps. For example, if you draw a circle on top of a rectangle and then move the circle off the rectangle, the portion of the rectangle covered by the circle is removed. The Object Drawing Model allows you to overlap shapes which are then kept separate, so that changes in one object do not affect another object. Another way to avoid having changes in one object affect another is to place the objects on separate layers on the Timeline as you did in Chapter 1.

TOOLS YOU'LL USE

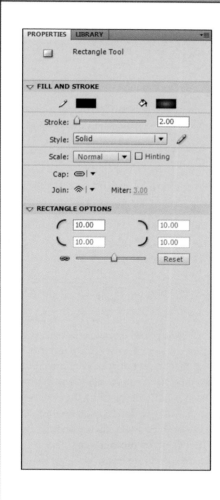

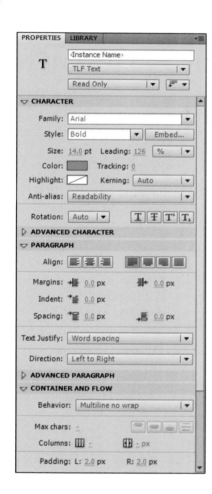

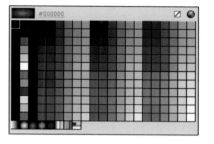

Use the Flash Drawing
AND ALIGNMENT TOOLS

What You'll Do

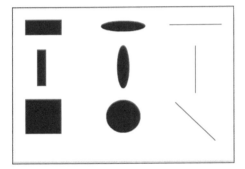

In this lesson, you will use several drawing tools to create various vector graphics.

Using Flash Drawing and Editing Tools

When you point to a tool on the Tools panel, its name appears next to the tool. Figure 1 identifies the tools described in the following paragraphs. Several of the tools have options that modify their use. These options are available in the Options area of the Tools panel when the tool is selected.

Selection—Used to select an object or parts of an object, such as the stroke or fill; and to reshape and reposition objects. The options for the Selection tool are Snap to Objects (aligns objects), Smooth (smooths lines), and Straighten (straightens lines).

Subselection—Used to select, drag, and reshape an object. Vector graphics are composed of lines and curves (each of which is a segment) connected by **anchor points**. Selecting an object with this tool displays the anchor points and allows you to use them to edit the object.

Free Transform—Used to rotate, scale, skew, and distort objects.

Gradient Transform—Used to transform a gradient fill by adjusting the size, direction, or center of the fill.

The Free and Gradient Transform tools are grouped within one icon on the Tools panel.

3D Rotation—Used to create 3D effects by rotating movie clips in 3D space on the Stage.

3D Translation—Used to create 3D effects by moving movie clips in 3D space on the Stage.

The 3D Rotation and the 3D Translation tools are grouped within one icon on the Tools panel.

Lasso—Used to select objects or parts of objects. The Polygon Mode option allows you to draw straight lines when selecting an object.

Pen—Used to draw lines and curves by creating a series of dots, known as anchor points, that are automatically connected. Other tools used to add, delete, and convert the anchor points created by the Pen tool are grouped with the Pen tool. To see the menu containing these tools, click and hold the Pen tool until the menu opens.

Text—Used to create and edit text.

Line—Used to draw straight lines. You can draw vertical, horizontal, and 45° diagonal lines by pressing and holding [Shift] while drawing the line.

Rectangle—Used to draw rectangular shapes. Press and hold [Shift] to draw a perfect square.

Oval—Used to draw oval shapes. Press and hold [Shift] to draw a perfect circle.

Primitive Rectangle and Oval—Used to draw objects with properties, such as corner radius or inner radius, that can be changed using the Properties panel.

PolyStar—Used to draw polygons and stars.

The Rectangle, Oval, Primitive, and PolyStar tools are grouped within one tool on the Tools panel.

Pencil—Used to draw freehand lines and shapes. The Pencil Mode option displays a menu with the following commands: Straighten (draws straight lines), Smooth (draws smooth curved lines), and Ink (draws freehand with no modification).

Brush—Used to draw (paint) with brush-like strokes. Options allow you to set the size and shape of the brush, and to determine the area to be painted, such as inside or behind an object.

Spray Brush—Used to spray colors and patterns onto objects. Dots are the default pattern for the spray. However, you can use a graphic symbol, such as a flag, to create a pattern.

The Brush and Spray Brush tools are grouped together.

Deco—Used to turn graphic shapes into geometric patterns or create kaleidoscopic-like effects.

Bone—Used to animate objects that have joints. For example you could use a series of linked objects, such as arms and legs to create character animations.

Bind—Used to adjust the relationships among individual bones. The Bone and Bind tools are grouped together.

Paint Bucket—Used to fill enclosed areas of a drawing with color. Options allow you to fill areas that have gaps and to make adjustments in a gradient fill.

Ink Bottle—Used to apply line colors and thickness to the stroke of an object.

The Paint Bucket and Ink Bottle are grouped together.

Eyedropper—Used to select stroke, fill, and text attributes so they can be copied from one object to another.

Eraser—Used to erase lines and fills. Options allow you to choose what part of the object to erase, as well as the size and shape of the eraser.

Hand—Used to move the Stage around the Pasteboard by dragging the Stage.

Zoom—Used to change the magnification of an area of the Stage. Clicking an area of the Stage zooms in and holding down [Alt] (Win) or [option] (Mac) and clicking zooms out.

Stroke Color—Used to set the stroke color of drawn objects.

Fill Color—Used to set the fill color of drawn objects.

Figure 1 *Flash tools*

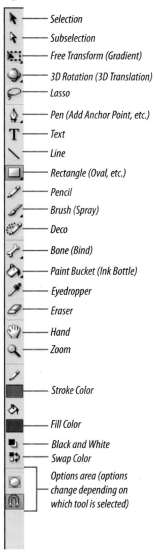

- Selection
- Subselection
- Free Transform (Gradient)
- 3D Rotation (3D Translation)
- Lasso
- Pen (Add Anchor Point, etc.)
- Text
- Line
- Rectangle (Oval, etc.)
- Pencil
- Brush (Spray)
- Deco
- Bone (Bind)
- Paint Bucket (Ink Bottle)
- Eyedropper
- Eraser
- Hand
- Zoom
- Stroke Color
- Fill Color
- Black and White
- Swap Color
- Options area (options change depending on which tool is selected)

Black and White—Used to set the stroke color to black and the fill color to white.

Swap Color—Used to swap the stroke and fill colors.

Options—Used to select an option for a tool, such as the type of rectangle (object drawing mode) or size of the brush when using the Brush tool.

Working with Grouped Tools

To display a list of grouped tools, you click the tool and hold the mouse button until the menu opens. For example, if you want to select the Oval tool and the Rectangle tool is displayed, you click and hold the Rectangle tool. Then, when the menu opens, you click the Oval tool option. You know a tool is a grouped tool if you see an arrow in the lower-right corner of the tool icon.

Working with Tool Options

Some tools have additional options that allow you to modify their use. For example, the brush tool has options to set the brush size and to set where the brush fill will be applied. If additional options for a tool are available, they appear at the bottom of the Tools panel in the Options area when the tool is selected. If the option has a menu associated with it, such as a list of brush sizes for the brush tool, then the option icon will have an arrow in the lower-right corner. Click and hold the option until the menu opens.

Tools for Creating Vector Graphics

The Oval, Rectangle, Pencil, Brush, Line, and Pen tools are used to create vector objects.

 ## Positioning Objects on the Stage

The Stage dimensions are made up of pixels (dots) matching the Stage size. So, a Stage size of 550 × 400 would be 550 pixels wide and 400 pixels high. Each pixel has a location on the Stage designated as the X (across) and Y (down) coordinates. The location of any object on the Stage is determined by its position from the upper-left corner of the Stage, which is 0,0 and the object's registration point. The registration point of an object is used to align it with the coordinates. The registration point, which is shown as a crosshair, is initially set at the upper-left corner of an object, as shown in Figure 2. So, an object having coordinates of 100,100 would be positioned at 100 pixels across and 100 pixels down the Stage, as shown in Figure 2. The Properties panel displays the X,Y values of any selected object. The most precise way to position an object on the Stage is to use the Properties panel to enter X and Y values for the object. Other ways to position objects on the Stage include using rulers, gridlines, and guides, as well as the align options. The Rulers, Grid, and Guides commands, which are found on the View menu, are used to turn on and off these features. Figure 2 shows the rulers and the ruler lines, which are used to indicate

Figure 2 *Using rulers to position an object*

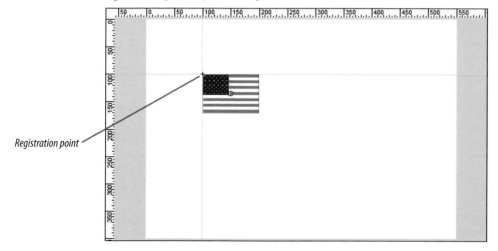

Registration point

the position of an object. (*Note:* Normally ruler lines display on top of objects on the Stage. In Figure 2, the registration point is displayed above the ruler lines to show its exact placement.)

After displaying the rulers, you can drag the lines from the top ruler or the left side ruler to the Stage. To remove a ruler line, you drag the ruler line up to the top ruler or across to the left ruler.

Figure 3 shows the Stage with gridlines displayed. The gridlines can be used to position an object. You can modify the grid size and color. In addition to using rulers and guides to help place objects, you can create a new layer as a Guide layer that you use to position objects on the Stage. When you turn gridlines and guides on, they appear on the Stage. However, they do not appear in the Flash movie when you test or publish it.

NEW Using the Align Panel

Figure 4 shows the Align panel, which allows you to position objects on the Stage either relative to the Stage or to other objects. The Align panel has four areas (Align, Distribute, Match size, Space) each with options. The Align options are used to align the edge or center of an object with the edge or center of the Stage—or, if multiple objects are selected, to align their edges and centers. The Distribute options are used to position objects across or down the Stage. The Match size options are used to resize selected objects to match the height and/or width of the largest object or to match the Stage if the Align to stage option is selected. The Space options are used to space out objects evenly across and down the Stage.

Figure 3 *Using gridlines to position an object*

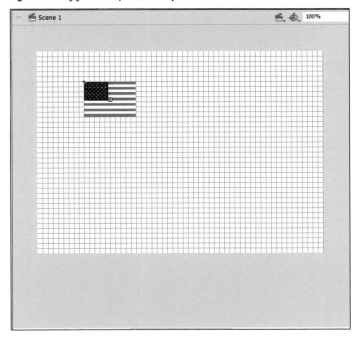

Figure 4 *The Align panel*

Show gridlines and check settings

1. Open fl2_1.fla from the drive and folder where your Data Files are stored, then save it as **tools.fla**.

2. Click **Window** on the menu bar, point to **Workspace**, then click **Reset 'Essentials'**.

3. Click **View** on the menu bar, point to **Magnification**, then click **Fit in Window**.

4. Click the **Stroke Color tool color swatch** 🖊 on the Tools panel, then click the **red color swatch** in the left column of the Color palette.

5. Click the **Fill Color tool color swatch** 🖊 on the Tools panel, then click the **blue color swatch** in the left column of the Color palette.

6. Click **View** on the menu bar, point to **Grid**, then click **Show Grid** to display the gridlines.

   A gray grid appears on the Stage.

7. Point to each tool on the Tools panel, then read its name.

8. Click the **Text tool** T , then click **CHARACTER** on the Properties panel to open the area if it is not open already.

   Notice the options in the Properties panel including the CHARACTER area, as shown in Figure 5. The Properties panel options change depending on the tool selected. For the Text tool the properties include the character family and the paragraph family.

You opened a document, saved it, set up the workspace, changed the stroke and fill colors, displayed the grid, viewed tool names on the Tools panel, then viewed the Text tool options in the Properties panel.

Figure 5 *Tool name on the Tools panel*

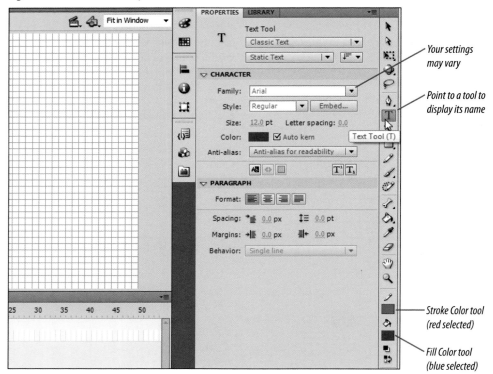

Your settings may vary

Point to a tool to display its name

Stroke Color tool (red selected)

Fill Color tool (blue selected)

Drawing Objects in Adobe Flash

Figure 6 *Objects created with drawing tools*

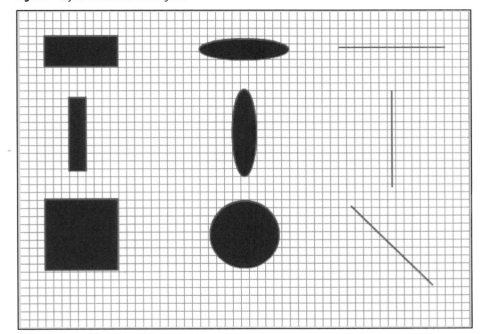

Use the Rectangle, Oval, and Line tools

1. Click the **Rectangle tool** ▢ on the Tools panel.

   Note: If the Rectangle tool is not displayed, click and hold the Oval tool to display the group of tools.

2. Verify that the Object Drawing option ◻ in the Options area of the Tools panel is not active.

   TIP When the Object Drawing option is not active, the object is drawn so that its stroke and fill can be selected separately.

3. Draw **three rectangle shapes** using Figure 6 as a guide.

   TIP Use the grid to approximate shape sizes, and press and hold [Shift] to draw a square. To undo an action, click the Undo command on the Edit menu.

   Notice the blue color for the fill and the red color for the strokes (border lines).

4. Click and hold the **Rectangle tool** ▢ on the Tools panel, then click the **Oval tool** ◯.

5. Draw **three oval shapes** using Figure 6 as a guide.

   TIP Press and hold [Shift] to draw a perfect circle.

6. Click the **Line tool** ╲ , then draw **three lines** using Figure 6 as a guide.

   TIP Press and hold [Shift] to snap the line to the nearest 45-degree increment, such as 45, 90, 180 and so on.

You used the Rectangle, Oval, and Line tools to draw objects on the Stage.

Use the Pen, Pencil, and Brush tools

1. Click **Insert** on the menu bar, point to **Timeline**, then click **Layer**.

   A new layer—Layer 2—appears above Layer 1.

2. Click **frame 5** on Layer 2.

3. Click **Insert** on the menu bar, point to **Timeline**, then click **Keyframe**.

   Since the objects were drawn in frame 1 on Layer 1, they are no longer visible when you insert a keyframe in frame 5 on Layer 2. A keyframe allows you to draw in any location on the Stage on the specified frame.

4. Click the **Zoom tool** 🔍 on the Tools panel, click near the upper-left quadrant of the Stage to zoom in, then scroll as needed to see more of the grid.

5. Click the **Pen tool** ✒ on the Tools panel, position it in the upper-left quadrant of the Stage, as shown in Figure 7, then click to set an anchor point.

6. Using Figure 8 as a guide, click the remaining anchor points to finish drawing an arrow.

TIP To close an object, be sure to re-click the first anchor point as your last action.

7. Click the **Paint Bucket tool** 🪣 , then click inside the arrow.

8. Click **View** on the menu bar, point to **Magnification**, then click **Fit in Window**.

9. Click **View** on the menu bar, point to **Grid**, then click **Show Grid** to turn off the gridlines.

10. Insert a **new layer**, Layer 3, then insert a **keyframe** in frame 10.

(continued)

Drawing Objects in Adobe Flash

Figure 7 *Positioning the Pen Tool on the Stage*

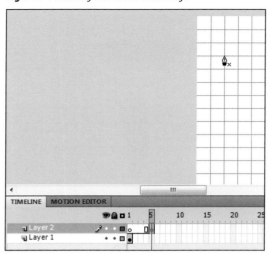

Figure 8 *Setting anchor points to draw an arrow*

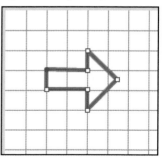

Figure 9 *Pencil Tool options*

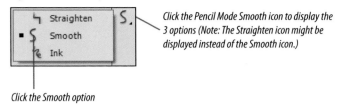

Click the Pencil Mode Smooth icon to display the
3 options (Note: The Straighten icon might be
displayed instead of the Smooth icon.)

Click the Smooth option

Figure 10 *Images drawn using drawing tools*

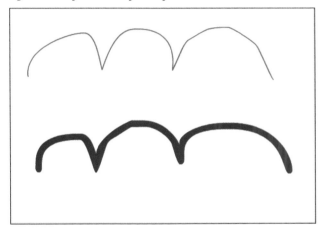

Figure 11 *The dot pattern indicating the object is selected*

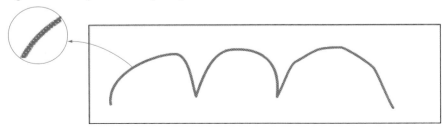

11. Click the **Pencil tool** ✐ on the Tools panel.
12. Click **Pencil Mode** ⟙ in the Options area of
    the Tools panel, then click the **Smooth** option,
    as shown in Figure 9.
13. Draw the **top image** shown in Figure 10.

    Note: The line may not appear until after you
    release the mouse button.
14. Click the **Brush tool** ✎ on the Tools panel.
15. Click the **Brush Size Icon** ▪ in the Options
    area at the bottom of the Tools panel, then click
    the fifth option from the top.
16. Draw the **bottom image** shown in Figure 10.

    Notice the Pencil tool displays the stroke color
    and the Brush tool displays the fill color.

*You added a layer, inserted a keyframe, then used the Pen tool
to draw an arrow; you selected the Smooth option for the Pencil
tool and drew an object; you selected a brush size for the Brush
tool and drew an object.*

Modify an object using tool options

1. Click the **Selection tool** ➤ on the Tools
   panel, then drag a **marquee** around the top
   object to select it.

   The line displays a dot pattern, as shown in
   Figure 11, indicating that it is selected.
2. Click the **Pencil Mode Smooth icon** ⟙ in the
   Options area of the Tools panel three times. The line
   becomes smoother as the humps tend to flatten.
3. Click and hold the **Stroke slider** △ in the FILL
   AND STROKE area of the Properties panel, then
   drag the **Stroke slider** △ to change the stroke
   size to **20.**

(continued)

4. Click the **Style list arrow** in the FILL AND STROKE area, then click **Dotted**.

5. Repeat Step 4 and change the line style to **Hairline**.

6. Save your work.

You smoothed objects using the tool options.

Use the Spray tool with a symbol

1. Click **Insert** on the menu bar, point to **Timeline**, then click **Layer**.

2. Click **frame 15** on Layer 4.

3. Click **Insert** on the menu bar, point to **Timeline**, then click **Keyframe**.

4. Click and hold the **Brush tool** 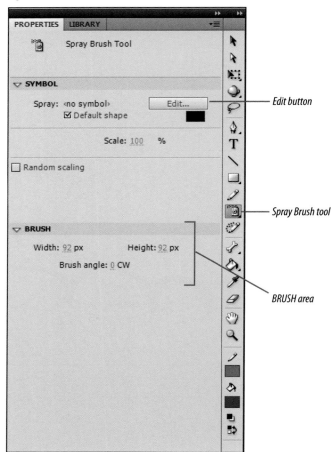 on the Tools panel, then click the **Spray Brush tool** .

5. Display the Properties panel if it is not already displayed, then click the **Edit button** in the SYMBOL area of the Properties panel, as shown in Figure 12.

   Note: If the Properties panel does not display the options for the Spray Brush tool, click the Selection tool, then click the Spray Brush tool.

   (continued)

Figure 12 *The properties for the Spray Brush tool*

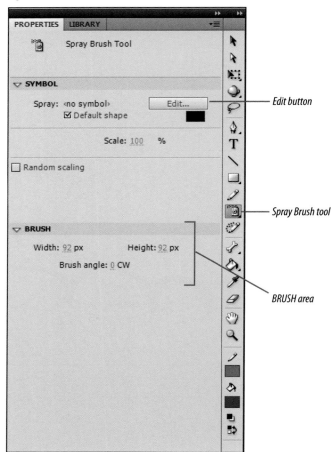

Edit button

Spray Brush tool

BRUSH area

Drawing Objects in Adobe Flash

Figure 13 *A design created using the Spray Brush tool*

6. Click **Flag** in the Select Symbol dialog box, then click **OK**.

   The flag symbol is a graphic that was imported into this Flash document.

7. Click the **Random scaling check box** to select it, then click to deselect the **Rotate symbol check box** and the **Random rotation check box** if they are checked.

8. Display the **Brush area** on the Properties panel, then set the width and height to **9 px**.

9. Click the **Spray Brush tool** in the Tools panel, then slowly draw the **U** in USA, as shown in Figure 13.

10. Continue to use the **Spray brush tool** to draw the **S** and **A**.

    Hint: If you need to redo the drawing, use the Undo command on the Edit menu or use the Selection tool to draw a marquee around the drawing, then delete the selection.

11. Save your work, then close the document.

You specified a symbol as a pattern and used the Spray Brush tool to complete a drawing.

NEW Use XY coordinates to position objects on the Stage

1. Open fl2_2.fla, then save it as **alignObjects.fla**.
2. Click the **Selection tool** ⬑ on the Tools panel, click the **flag** on the Stage, then display the Properties panel, if it is not displayed.

   Notice the X and Y coordinates are set to 100.
3. Click **View** on the menu bar, then click **Rulers**.
4. Click and hold the **horizontal ruler** at the top of the Stage, then drag a **ruler line** down to 100 on the vertical ruler, as shown in Figure 14.
5. Click and hold the **vertical ruler** at the left of the Stage, then drag a **ruler line** across to 100 on the horizontal ruler.

   The point where the two ruler lines cross identifies the X,Y coordinates 100,100. The ruler lines meet at the registration point of the object.
6. Click the **flag**, point to the **100** next to X: on the Properties panel, then, when the pointer changes to a hand with a double-headed arrow ⟨⟩, drag the ⟨⟩ pointer to the left to change the X value to **0**.

   This aligns the registration point of the object to the left edge of the Stage.
7. Repeat Step 6 to change the Y value to **0**.

   Note: You can click a value, type in a new value, and press [Enter] (Win) or [return] (Mac).
8. Type **550** for the X value and **400** for the Y value.

   Notice the flag is positioned off the Stage because the registration point is in the upper-left corner of the object.

(continued)

Figure 14 *Positioning an object on the Stage using XY coordinates*

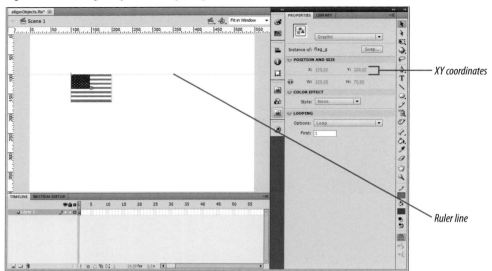

XY coordinates

Ruler line

Drawing Objects in Adobe Flash

Figure 15 *Setting the registration point*

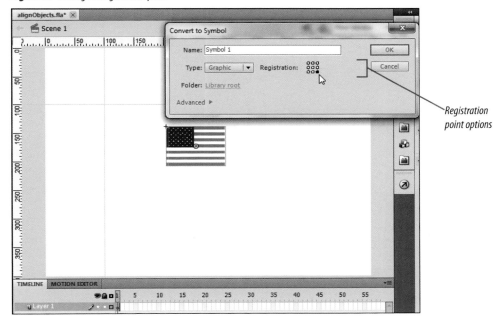

Registration
point options

9. Change the view to **50%**.

10. Point to the **flag**, then click and drag the **flag** around the Stage noticing how the values for X and Y in the Properties panel change.

11. Drag the **flag** to approximately the middle of the Stage.

12. Change the view to **Fit in Window**.

13. Use the **arrow keys** on the keyboard to move the flag one pixel at a time in all four directions, then observe the changes to the X and Y values in the Properties panel as you move the object.

14. Click the **flag** to select it, click **Modify** on the menu bar, then click **Convert to Symbol**.

    The Convert to Symbol dialog box opens allowing you to change the registration point.

15. Click the **lower-right icon** as shown in Figure 15, then click **OK**.

    Notice the registration point is now located on the lower-right corner of the flag.

16. Change the **X** and **Y** values in the Properties panel to **100** and **100**.

    Notice the flag is now positioned using the new location of the registration point.

17. Drag each **ruler line** to its respective ruler to remove it from the Stage.

18. Click **View** on the menu bar, then click **Rulers** to remove them from view.

19. Save, then close the Flash document.

You used the X and Y values of an object to position it on the Stage. You used the Convert to Symbol dialog box to change the registration point of an object.

Use the Align options

1. Open fl2_3.fla, then save it as **alignOptions.fla**.
   This document has three objects (flags) of different sizes randomly placed on the Stage.

2. Click **Window** on the menu bar, then click **Align** to open the Align panel.

TIP Alternately, you can click the Align icon that is part of a collapsed panel set on your workspace.

3. Drag the **Align panel set** by its title bar and position it adjacent to the right side of the Stage, as shown in Figure 16.

4. Verify the **Align to stage check box** in the Align panel is active, then click the Align to stage check box if it is not already active.

5. Click the **largest flag** to select it, then click the **Align left edge icon** 🖺 .

6. Point to the next **Align icon** 🖺 , read the name that appears, then click the **Align horizontal center icon** 🖺 and notice the new position of the object on the Stage.

7. Click the other **Align options** on the top row of the Align panel.

8. Click the **Align horizontal center icon** 🖺 , then click the **Align vertical center icon** 🔲 .
   When you use these two align options together, they position the center of the object with the center of the Stage.

9. Click the **Match width icon** 🖳 , then click the **Match height icon** 🔲 .

10. Click **Edit** on the menu bar, then click **Undo Match Size**.

(continued)

Figure 16 *Positioning the Align panel*

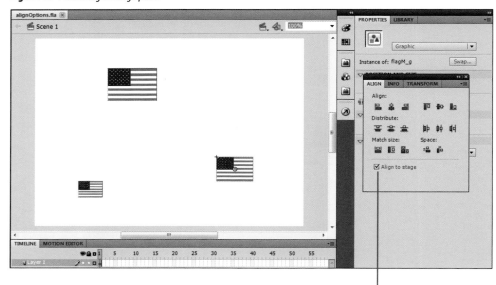

Be sure Align to stage is active (checked)

Drawing Objects in Adobe Flash

Figure 17 *All three objects selected*

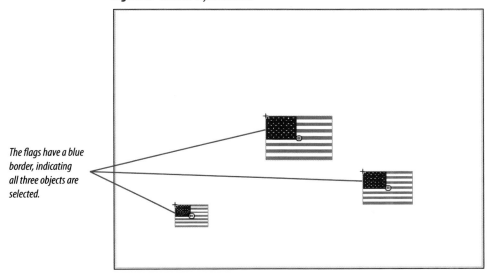

The flags have a blue border, indicating all three objects are selected.

11. Click **Edit** on the menu bar, then click **Undo Match Size**.

12. Use the **Selection tool** to draw a marquee around all three flags to select them, as shown in Figure 17.

13. Click the **Align left edge icon** , then click the **Align horizontal center icon** .

14. Click the **Space evenly vertically icon** , then click the **Align vertical center icon** .

15. Click the **Align to stage check box** to make this feature not active.

16. With all three objects selected, click each of the **Align options** on the top row of the Align panel.

    Notice that the objects align to each other instead of the Stage.

17. Click the **Match width and height icon** .

    This changes the dimension of each object to match the size of the largest object.

18. Close the Align panel, then save and close the Flash document.

You used the Align panel to position objects on the Stage relative to the Stage and to each other.

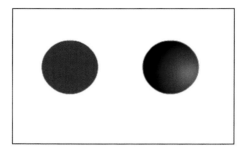

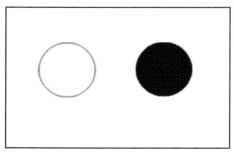

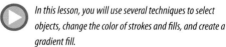

Select Objects
AND APPLY COLORS

What You'll Do

In this lesson, you will use several techniques to select objects, change the color of strokes and fills, and create a gradient fill.

Selecting Objects

Before you can edit a drawing, you must first select the object, or the part of the object, on which you want to work. Drawn objects are made up of a stroke(s) and a fill. Strokes can have several segments. For example, a rectangle has four stroke segments, one for each side of the object. These can be selected separately or as a whole. Flash highlights objects that have been selected, as shown in Figure 18. When the stroke of an object is selected, a dotted colored line appears. When the fill of an object is selected, a dot pattern appears. When the stroke and fill of an object are selected, both the stroke and the fill appear dotted. When a group of objects is selected, a bounding box appears.

Using the Selection Tool

You can use the Selection tool to select part or all of an object, and to select multiple objects. To select only the fill, click just the fill; to select only the stroke, click just the stroke. To select both the fill and the stroke, double-click the object or draw a marquee around it. To select part of an object, drag a marquee that defines the area you wish to select, as shown in Figure 18. To select

multiple objects or combinations of strokes and fills, press and hold [Shift], then click each item. To deselect an item(s), click a blank area of the Stage.

Using the Lasso Tool

The Lasso tool provides more flexibility than the Selection tool when selecting an object(s) or parts of an object on the Stage. You can use the tool in a freehand manner to draw any shape that then selects the object(s) within the shape. Alternately, you can use the Polygon Mode option to draw straight lines and connect them to form a shape that will select any object(s) within the shape.

Drawing Model Modes

Flash provides two drawing modes, called models. In the Merge Drawing Model mode, the stroke and fill of an object are separate. Thus, as you draw an object such as a circle, the stroke and fill can be selected individually as described earlier. When using the Object Drawing Model mode, the stroke and fill are combined and cannot be selected individually. However, you can use the Break Apart option from the Modify menu to separate the stroke and fill so that they can be selected individually. In addition, you can turn off either the stroke or fill when drawing an object in either mode. You can toggle between the two modes by clicking the Object Drawing option in the Options area of the Tools panel.

Working with Colors

Flash allows you to change the color of the stroke and fill of an object. Figure 19 shows the Colors area of the Tools panel. To change a color, you click the color swatch of the Stroke Color tool or the color swatch of the Fill Color tool, and then select a color swatch on the Color palette. The Color palette, as shown in Figure 20, allows you to select a color from the palette or type in a six-character code that represents the values of three colors (red, green, blue),

referred to as RGB. When these characters are combined in various ways, they can represent virtually any color. The values are in a hexadecimal format (base 16), so they include letters and digits (A–F + 0–9 = 16 options), and they are preceded by a pound sign (#). The first two characters represent the value for red, the next two for green, and the last two for blue. For example, #000000 represents black (lack of color); #FFFFFF represents white; and #FFCC33 represents a shade of gold. You do not have to memorize the codes. There are reference manuals with the codes, and many programs allow you to set the values visually by selecting a color from a palette. You can also use the Properties panel to change the stroke and fill colors.

You can set the desired colors before drawing an object, or you can change a color of a previously drawn object. You can use the Ink Bottle tool to change the stroke color, and you can use the Paint Bucket tool to change the fill color.

Working with Gradients

A gradient is a color fill that makes a gradual transition from one color to another. Gradients can be very useful for creating a 3D effect, drawing attention to an object, and generally enhancing the appearance of an object. You can apply a gradient fill by using the Paint Bucket tool. The position of the Paint Bucket tool over the object is important because it determines the direction of the gradient fill. The Color palette can be used to create and alter custom gradients.

Figure 18 *Objects or parts of objects are highlighted when selected*

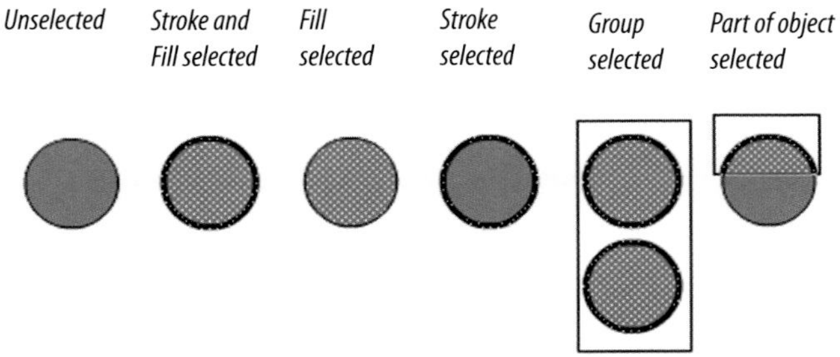

Unselected   Stroke and Fill selected   Fill selected   Stroke selected   Group selected   Part of object selected

Figure 19 *The Colors area of the Tools panel*

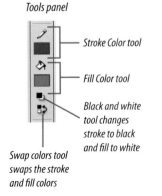

Stroke Color tool

Fill Color tool

Black and white tool changes stroke to black and fill to white

Swap colors tool swaps the stroke and fill colors

Figure 20 *Color palette showing the hexadecimal number*

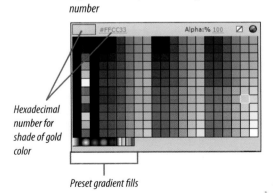

Hexadecimal number for shade of gold color

Preset gradient fills

Select a drawing using the Selection tool

1. Open tools.fla, then click **frame 1** on the Timeline.

   TIP The options available to you in the Properties panel differ depending on whether you click a frame number on the Timeline or a frame on a layer.

2. Click the **Selection tool** ![arrow] on the Tools panel if it is not already selected, then drag a **marquee** around the circle to select the entire object (both the stroke and the fill).

3. Click anywhere on the Stage to deselect the object.

4. Click **inside the circle** to select the fill only, then click outside the circle to deselect it.

5. Click the **stroke** of the circle to select it, as shown in Figure 21, then deselect it.

6. Double-click the **circle** to select it, press and hold **[Shift]**, double-click the **square** to select both objects, then click the **Stage** to deselect both objects.

7. Click the **right border** of the square to select it, as shown in Figure 22, then deselect it.

   Objects, such as rectangles, have border segments that can be selected individually.

8. Drag a **marquee** around the square, circle, and diagonal line to select all three objects.

9. Click a blank area of the Stage to deselect the objects.

10. Click **inside the oval** in row 2 to select the fill, then drag the **fill** outside the stroke, as shown in Figure 23.

11. Look at the Properties panel.

   (continued)

Figure 21 *Using the Selection tool to select the stroke of the circle*

Figure 22 *Using the Selection tool to select a segment of the stroke of the square*

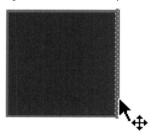

Figure 23 *Separating the stroke and fill of an object*

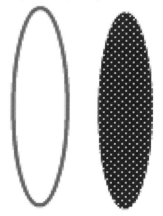

Figure 24 *Circles drawn with the Oval tool*

Figure 25 *Changing the stroke color*

Notice the stroke color is none and the fill color is blue. This is because only the object's fill is selected. You can use the Properties panel to verify what you have selected when working with the Selection tool.

12. Click **Edit** on the menu bar, then click **Undo Move**.

You used the Selection tool to select the stroke and fill of an object, and to select multiple objects.

Change fill and stroke colors

1. Click **Layer 4,** click **Insert** on the menu bar, point to **Timeline,** then click **Layer.**

2. Click **frame 20** of the new layer, click **Insert** on the menu bar, point to **Timeline,** then click **Keyframe.**

3. Select the **Oval tool**  on the Tools panel, then draw **two circles** similar to those shown in Figure 24.

4. Click the **Fill Color tool color swatch** on the Tools panel, then click the **yellow color swatch** in the left column of the Color palette.

5. Click the **Paint Bucket tool** on the Tools panel, then click the **fill** of the right circle.

6. Click the **Stroke Color tool color swatch** on the Tools panel, then click the **yellow color swatch** in the left column of the color palette.

7. Click and hold the **Paint Bucket tool** on the Tools panel, click the **Ink Bottle tool**, point to the red stroke line of the left circle, as shown in Figure 25, then click to change the stroke color to yellow.

8. Click **Edit** on the menu bar, then click **Undo Stroke.**

You used the Paint Bucket and Ink Bottle tools to change the fill and stroke colors of an object.

Apply a gradient and make changes to the gradient

1. Click the **Fill Color tool color swatch** 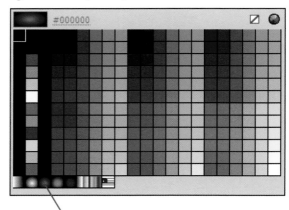 on the Tools panel, then click the **red gradient color swatch** in the bottom row of the Color palette, as shown in Figure 26.

2. Click and hold the **Ink Bottle tool** on the Tools panel, click the **Paint Bucket tool**, then click the **yellow circle**.

3. Click different parts of the right circle to view how the gradient changes.

4. Click the **right side** of the circle, as shown in Figure 27.

5. Click and hold the **Free Transform tool** on the Tools panel, then click the **Gradient Transform tool**.

6. Click the **gradient-filled circle**.

7. Drag each of the four handles shown in Figure 28 to determine the effect of each handle on the gradient, then click the **Stage** to deselect the circle.

8. Click the **Selection tool** on the Tools panel, then click inside the left circle.

9. Click the **Fill Color tool color swatch** in the FILL AND STROKE area of the Properties panel, click the **Hex Edit text box**, type **#006637** (two zeros), then press **[Enter]** (Win) or **[return]** (Mac).

   The Fill color swatch and the fill color for the circle change to a shade of green.

10. Save your work.

You applied a gradient fill, you used the Gradient Transform tool to alter the gradient, and you applied a new color using its Hexadecimal number.

Figure 26 *Selecting the red gradient*

Click red gradient color swatch to select it

Figure 27 *Clicking the right side of the circle*

Figure 28 *Gradient Transform handles*

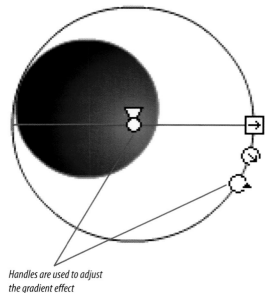

Handles are used to adjust the gradient effect

Figure 29 *Circle drawn using the Object Drawing Model mode*

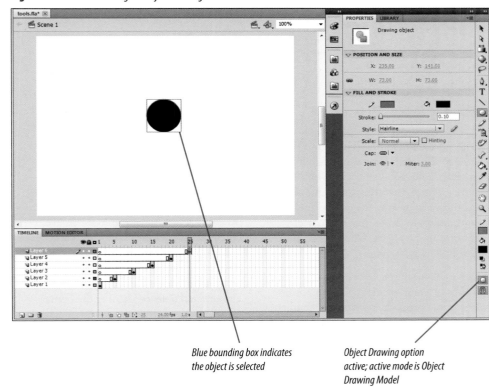

Blue bounding box indicates
the object is selected

Object Drawing option
active; active mode is Object
Drawing Model

Work with Object Drawing Model mode

1. Insert a **new layer**, then insert a **keyframe** on frame 25.
2. Select the **Oval tool** ◯, click the **Stroke Color tool color swatch** ✎, then click the **red swatch**.
3. Click the **Fill Color tool color swatch** 🪣, then click the **black swatch**.
4. Click the **Object Drawing option** ◯ in the Options area of the Tools panel to make the icon active.

   The icon is active and the mode changes to Object Drawing Model.
5. Draw a **circle** as shown in Figure 29.

   Notice that when you use Object Drawing Model mode, the object is selected automatically, which means both the stroke and fill areas of the circle are selected.
6. Click the **Selection tool** ▶ on the Tools panel, then click a blank area of the Stage to deselect the object.
7. Click the **circle** once, then drag the **circle** around the Stage.

   The entire object is selected, including the stroke and fill areas.
8. Click **Modify** on the menu bar, then click **Break Apart**.

   Breaking apart an object drawn in Object Drawing Model mode allows you to select the strokes and fills individually.
9. Click a blank area of the Stage, click the **fill** area of the circle, drag to the right, then save your work.

   Notice the fill moves but the stroke stays.

You used the Object Drawing Model mode to draw an object, deselect it, then break it apart to display and then separate the stroke and fill.

Lesson 2   Select Objects and Apply Colors

Work with Drawn OBJECTS

What You'll Do

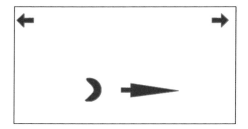

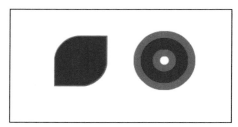

 In this lesson, you will copy, move, and transform (resize, rotate, and reshape) objects.

Copying and Moving Objects

To copy an object, select it, and then click the Copy command on the Edit menu. To paste the object, click the Paste command on the Edit menu. You can copy an object to another layer by selecting the frame on the layer prior to pasting the object. You can copy and paste more than one object by selecting all the objects before using the Copy or Paste commands.

You move an object by selecting it and dragging it to a new location. You can position an object more precisely by selecting it and then pressing the arrow keys, which move the selection up, down, left, and right in small increments. In addition, you can change the X and Y coordinates in the Properties panel to position an object exactly on the Stage.

Transforming Objects

You use the Free Transform tool and the Transform panel to resize, rotate, skew, and reshape objects. After selecting an object, you click the Free Transform tool to display eight square-shaped handles used to transform the object, and a circle-shaped transformation point located at the center

of the object. The transformation point is the point around which the object can be rotated. You can also change its location.

Resizing an Object

You enlarge or reduce the size of an object using the Scale option, which is available when the Free Transform tool is active. The process is to select the object and click the Free Transform tool, and then click the Scale option in the Options area of the Tools panel. Eight handles appear around the selected object. You drag the corner handles to resize the object without changing its proportions. That is, if the object starts out as a square, dragging a corner handle will change the size of the object, but it will still be a square. On the other hand, if you drag one of the middle handles, the object will be reshaped as taller, shorter, wider, or narrower. In addition, you can change the Width and Height settings in the Properties panel to resize an object in increments of one-tenth of one pixel.

Rotating and Skewing an Object

You use the Rotate and Skew option of the Free Transform tool to rotate an object and to skew it. The process is to select the object, click the Free Transform tool, and then click the Rotate and Skew option in the Options area of the Tools panel. Eight handles appear around the object. You drag the corner handles to rotate the object, or you drag the middle handles to skew the object, as shown in Figure 30. The Transform panel can be used to rotate and skew an object in a more precise way; select the object, display the Transform panel (available via the Window menu), enter the desired rotation or skew in degrees, and then press [Enter] (Win) or [return] (Mac).

Distorting an Object

You can use the Distort and Envelope options to reshape an object by dragging its handles. The Distort option allows you to reshape an object by dragging one corner without affecting the other corners of the object. The Envelope option provides more than eight handles to allow more precise distortions. These options are accessed through the Transform command on the Modify menu.

Flipping an Object

You use a Flip option on the Transform menu to flip an object either horizontally or vertically. You select the object, click the Transform command on the Modify menu, and then choose Flip Vertical or Flip Horizontal. Other Transform options allow you to rotate and scale the selected object. The Remove Transform command allows you to restore an object to its original state.

Reshaping a Segment of an Object

You use the Subselection tool to reshape a segment of an object. You click an edge of the object to display handles that can be dragged to reshape the object.

You use the Selection tool to reshape objects. When you point to the edge of an object, the pointer displays an arc symbol. Using the Arc pointer, you drag the edge of the object you want to reshape, as shown in Figure 31. If the Selection tool points to a corner of an object, the pointer changes to an L-shape. You drag the pointer to reshape the corner of the object.

Figure 30 *Using handles to manipulate an object*

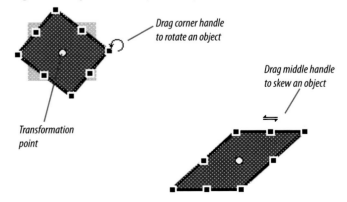

Drag corner handle
to rotate an object

Transformation
point

Drag middle handle
to skew an object

Figure 31 *Using the Selection tool to distort an object*

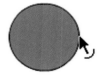

Copy and move an object

1. Click **frame 5** on the Timeline.

2. Click the **Selection tool** on the Tools panel, then draw a **marquee** around the arrow object to select it.

3. Click **Edit** on the menu bar, click **Copy**, click **Edit** on the menu bar, then click **Paste in Center**.

4. Drag the newly copied **arrow** to the upper-right corner of the Stage, as shown in Figure 32.

5. Verify the right arrow object is selected on the Stage, press the **down arrow key [↓]** on the keyboard.

   The object moves down in approximately one-pixel increments and the Y coordinate in the Properties panel changes each time the arrow key is pressed.

6. Press the **right arrow key [→]** on the keyboard.

   The object moves right in one-pixel increments and the X coordinate in the Properties panel changes each time the arrow key is pressed.

7. Select the number in the X coordinate box in the Properties panel, type **450**, as shown in Figure 33, then press **[Enter]** (Win) or **[return]** (Mac).

8. Select the **number** in the Y coordinate box in the Properties panel, type **30**, then press **[Enter]** (Win) or **[return]** (Mac).

9. Drag a **marquee** around the left arrow object, then set the X and Y coordinates to **36** and **30**, respectively.

10. Click a blank area of the Stage to deselect the object.

You used the Selection tool to select an object, then you copied and moved the object.

Figure 32 *Moving the copied object*

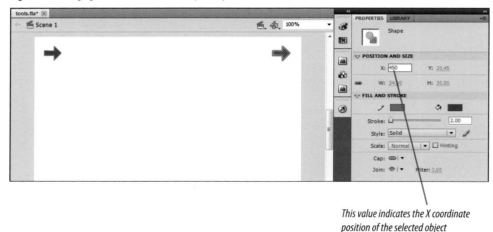

Figure 33 *Changing the X coordinate in the Properties panel*

This value indicates the X coordinate position of the selected object

Figure 34 *Resizing an object using the corner handles*

Pointer used to drag
corner handle

Figure 35 *Reshaping an object using the middle handles*

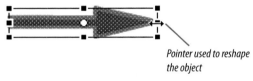

Pointer used to reshape
the object

Transform Options

Different transform options, such as rotate, skew, and scale, can be accessed through the Options area on the Tools panel when the Free Transform tool is active, the Transform command on the Modify menu, and the Transform panel via the Transform command on the Window menu.

Resize and reshape an object

1. Click the **Free Transform tool** ⊠ on the Tools panel.

   Note: You may need to click and hold the Gradient tool to display the Free Transform tool.

2. Draw a **marquee** around the arrow object on the right side of the Stage to select the object.

3. Click the **Scale option** ⊠ in the Options area on the Tools panel to make it active.

4. Drag each **corner handle** toward and then away from the center of the object, as shown in Figure 34.

   As you drag a corner handle, the object's size is changed, but its proportions remain the same.

5. Click **Edit** on the menu bar, then click **Undo Scale**.

6. Repeat Step 5 until the arrow returns to its original size.

   TIP The object is its original size when the option Undo Scale is no longer available on the Edit menu.

7. Verify the arrow is still selected and the handles are displayed, then select the **Scale option** ⊠ in the Options area on the Tools panel to make it active.

8. Drag each **middle handle** toward and then away from the center of the object, as shown in Figure 35.

   As you drag the middle handles, the object's size and proportions change.

9. Click **Edit** on the menu bar, then click **Undo Scale** as needed to return the arrow to its original size.

You used the Free Transform tool and the Scale option to display an object's handles, and you used the handles to resize and reshape the object.

Skew, rotate, and flip an object

1. Verify that the Free Transform tool and the right arrow are selected (handles displayed), then click the **Rotate and Skew option** 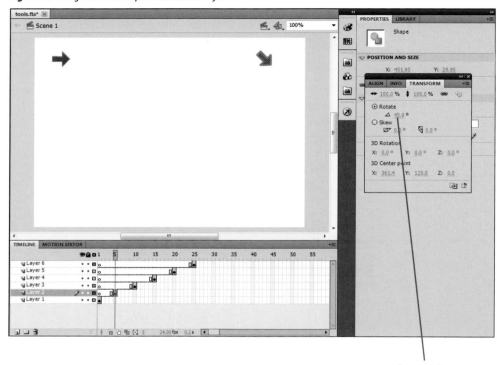 in the Options area of the Tools panel.

2. Click and drag the **upper-middle handle** to the right.

3. Click and rotate the **upper-right corner handle** of the object clockwise.

   The arrow slants down and to the right.

4. Click **Edit** on the menu bar, click the **Undo Rotate** command, then repeat, selecting the Undo Rotate and Undo Skew commands until the arrow is in its original shape and orientation.

5. Click the **Selection tool** on the Tools panel, verify that the right arrow is selected, click **Window** on the menu bar, then click **Transform**.

6. Click the **Rotate text box**, type **45**, then press **[Enter]** (Win) or **[return]** (Mac).

   The arrow rotates 45°, as shown in Figure 36.

7. Click **Edit** on the menu bar, click **Undo Transform**, then close the Transform panel if it is still open.

8. Draw a **marquee** around the arrow in the upper-left corner of the Stage to select the object.

9. Click **Modify** on the menu bar, point to **Transform**, then click **Flip Horizontal**.

10. Save your work.

You used options on the Tools panel and the Transform panel, as well as commands on the Modify menu to skew, rotate, and flip an object.

Figure 36 *Using the Transform panel to rotate an object*

Rotate text box

Drawing Objects in Adobe Flash

Figure 37 *Using the Subselection tool to select an object*

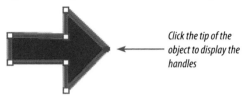

Click the tip of the
object to display the
handles

Figure 38 *Using the Subselection tool to drag a handle to reshape the object*

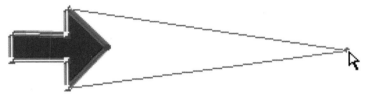

Figure 39 *Using the Selection tool to drag an edge to reshape the object*

Click here, then drag

Use the Zoom, Subselection, and Selection tools

1. Drag a **marquee** around the arrow in the upper-right corner of the Stage, click **Edit** on the menu bar, click **Copy**, click **Edit** on the menu bar, then click **Paste in Center**.

2. Click the **Zoom tool** 🔍 on the Tools panel, then click the **middle of the arrow** in the center of the Stage to enlarge the view.

3. Click the **Subselection tool** on the Tools panel, then click the **tip of the arrow** to display the handles, as shown in Figure 37.

TIP The handles allow you to change any segment of the object.

4. Click the **handle** at the tip of the arrow, then drag it, as shown in Figure 38.

5. Click the **Oval tool** on the Tools panel, then click the **Object Drawing option** in the Options area of the Tools panel so the option is not active.

6. Verify the Fill color is set to blue, then draw a **circle** to the left of the arrow you just modified.

7. Click the **Selection tool** on the Tools panel, then point to the left edge of the circle until the Arc pointer is displayed.

8. Drag the **pointer** to the position shown in Figure 39.

9. Change the **View** to **100%**.

10. Save your work.

You used the Zoom tool to change the view, and you used the Subselection and Selection tools to reshape objects.

Use the Rectangle Primitive and Oval tools

1. Insert a **new layer** above Layer 6, click **frame 30** on Layer 7, then insert a **keyframe**.

2. Click and hold the **Oval tool**  (or the Rectangle tool if it is displayed) to display the menu.

3. Click the **Rectangle Primitive tool** , then click the **Reset button** in the Properties panel RECTANGLE OPTIONS area to clear all of the settings.

4. Press and hold **[Shift]**, point to the **middle of the Stage**, then draw the **square** shown in Figure 40.

5. Click the **Selection tool** in the Tools panel, then drag **the upper-right corner handle** toward the center of the object.

   As you drag the corner, the radius of each of the four corners is changed.

6. Click the **Reset button** in the Properties panel to clear the setting.

7. Slowly drag the **slider** in the RECTANGLE OPTIONS area to the right until the radius changes to 100, then slowly drag the **slider** to the left until the radius changes to 100.

8. Click the **Reset Button** on the Properties panel to clear the radius settings.

9. Click the **Lock corner radius icon** in the Properties panel RECTANGLE OPTIONS area to unlock the individual controls.

10. Type **-60** in the upper-left corner radius text box, then type **-60** in the upper-right corner text box, as shown in Figure 41.

(continued)

Figure 40 *Drawing an object with the Rectangle Primitive tool*

The corner handles can be dragged to change the radius of the corners; in addition, the Properties panel can be used to make changes to the object

Figure 41 *Setting the corner radius of two corners*

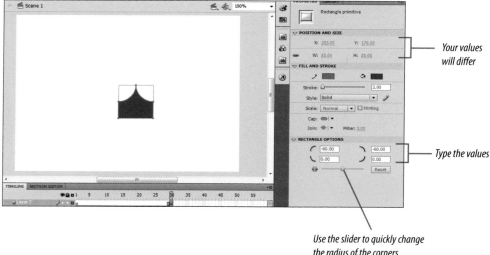

Your values will differ

Type the values

Use the slider to quickly change the radius of the corners

Figure 42 *Drawing an object with the Oval Primitive tool*

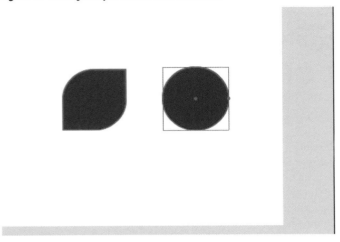

Figure 43 *Setting the stroke value to 12*

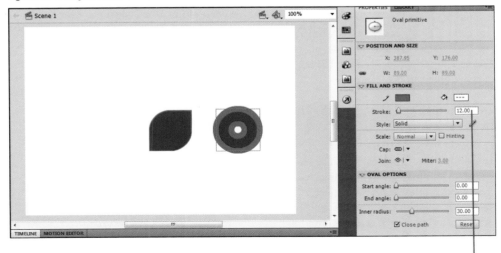

Set the stroke value to 12

11. Click the **Reset button** in the Properties panel to clear the radius settings.

12. Click the **Lock corner radius icon** to unlock the individual controls.

13. Set the upper-left corner radius to **60** and the lower-right corner to **60**.

14. Click a blank area of the Stage to deselect the object.

15. Click and hold the **Rectangle Primitive tool**, click the **Oval Primitive tool** on the Tools panel, then press and hold **[Shift]** and draw the **circle** shown in Figure 42.

TIP Remember some tools are grouped. Click and hold a grouped tool, such as the Oval tool, to see the menu of tools in the group.

16. Click the **Reset button** in the Properties panel OVAL OPTIONS area to clear any settings.

17. Drag the **Start angle slider** and the **End angle slider** to view their effect on the circle, then drag each **slider** back to 0.

18. Click the **Reset button** to clear the settings.

19. Drag the **Inner radius slider** to see the effect on the circle, then set the inner radius to **30**.

20. Display the FILL AND STROKE area of the Properties panel, then set the Stroke value to **12**, as shown in Figure 43.

21. Save your work.

You used the Primitive tools to create objects and the Properties panel to alter them.

Work with Text
AND TEXT OBJECTS

What You'll Do

 In this lesson, you will enter text using text blocks. You will also resize text blocks, change text attributes, and transform text.

Learning About Text

Flash provides a great deal of flexibility when using text. Among other settings for text, you can specify the typeface (font), size, style (bold, italic), and color (including gradients). You can transform the text by rotating, scaling, skewing, and flipping it. You can even break apart a letter and reshape its segments. There are two different text engines for working with text: Classic Text and Text Layout Framework (TLF). Classic Text mode is appropriate for many text applications and is easy to work with. Text Layout Framework mode provides advanced features and is appropriate for more text intensive applications.

Entering Text and Changing the Text Block for Classic Text

It is important to understand that text is entered into a text block, as shown in Figure 44. You use the Text tool to place a text block on the Stage and to enter and edit text. A text block expands as more text is entered and may even extend beyond the edge of the Stage. You can adjust the size of the text block so that it is a fixed width by dragging the handle in the upper-right corner of the block. Figure 45 shows the process of using the Text tool to enter text and resize the text block. Once you select the Text tool, you click the Stage where you want the text to appear. An insertion point indicates where the next character will appear in the text block when it is typed. You can resize the text block to a fixed width by dragging the circle handle. After resizing the text block, the circle handle changes to a square, indicating that the text block now has a fixed width. Then, when you enter more text, it automatically wraps within the text block. You can resize the width of a text block at any time by selecting it with the Selection tool (either clicking on the text or drawing a marquee around it) and dragging any handle.

Changing Text Attributes

You can use the Properties panel to change the font, size, and style of a single character or an entire text block. Figure 46 shows the Properties panel when a text object is selected. You select text, display the Properties panel, and make the changes. You use the Selection tool to select the entire text block by drawing a marquee around it. You use the Text tool to select a single character or string of characters by dragging the I-beam pointer over the text you want to select, as shown in Figure 47.

Working with Paragraphs

When working with large bodies of text, such as paragraphs, Flash provides many of the features found in a word processor. You can align paragraphs (left, right, center, justified) within a text block, set margins (space between the border of a text block and the paragraph text), set indents for the first line of a paragraph, and set line spacing (distance between paragraphs) using the Properties panel.

Transforming Text

It is important to understand that a text block is an object. Therefore, you can apply filters, such as drop shadows, and you can transform (reshape, rotate, skew, and so on) a text block in the same way you transform other objects. If you want to transform individual characters within a text block, you must first break apart the text block. To do this, you use the Selection tool to select the text block, then you click the Break Apart command on the Modify menu. Each character (or a group of characters) in the text block can now be selected and transformed.

NEW The Text Layout Framework (TLF)

Text Layout Framework (TLF) provides several advanced text features such as character color highlighting, underlining, strikethrough, and rotation. Text in the TLF format is displayed in a container, similar to a text block. Containers can be resized and linked using a Container icon. This allows you to flow text between them. The containers can have a border and background color, and the text in containers can be formatted into columns.

Figure 46 *The Properties panel when a text object is selected*

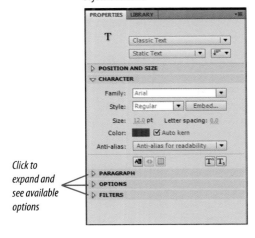

Figure 44 *A text block*

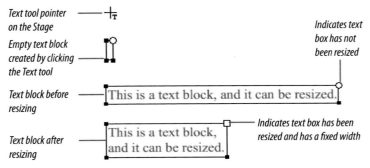

Figure 45 *Using the Text tool*

Figure 47 *Dragging the I-beam pointer to select text*

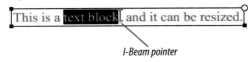

I-Beam pointer

Enter text and change text attributes

1. Click **Layer 7**, insert a **new layer**, then insert a **keyframe** in frame 35 of the new layer.

2. Click the **Text tool** T , then verify the **Text engine** is set to Classic Text mode and the Text type is set to Static Text in the T area on the Properties panel.

3. Click the left-center of the Stage, then type **We have great events each year including a Rally**!

4. Click the **I-Beam pointer** ⊺ before the word "Rally," as shown in Figure 48, then type **Car** followed by a space.

5. Drag the **I-Beam pointer** ⊺ across the text to select all the text.

6. Make the following changes in the CHARACTER area of the Properties panel: Family: **Arial**; Style: **Bold**; Size: **16**; Color: **#990000**, then click the **text box**.

   Your Properties panel should resemble Figure 49.

7. Verify the text block is selected, position the **text pointer** ⊥ᴛ over the circle handle until the pointer changes to a double arrow ←→, then drag the **handle** to just before the word each, as shown in Figure 50.

8. Select the text using the I-Beam pointer ⊺, then click the **Align center icon** ≣ in the PARAGRAPH area of the Properties panel.

9. Click the **Selection tool** ▶ on the Tools panel, click the **text object**, then drag the **object** to the lower-middle of the Stage.

TIP The Selection tool is used to select the text block, and the Text tool is used to select and edit the text within the text block.

You entered text and changed the font, type size, and text color; you also resized the text block and changed the text alignment.

Figure 48 *Using the Text tool to enter text*

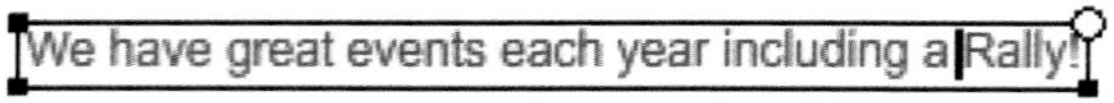

We have great events each year including a Rally!

Figure 49 *Changes to the CHARACTER area of the Properties panel*

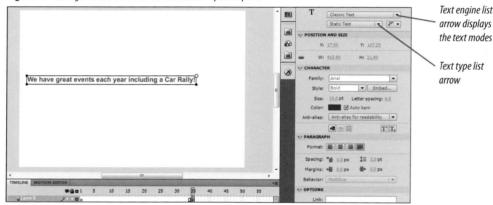

Text engine list arrow displays the text modes

Text type list arrow

Figure 50 *Resizing the text block*

Drag handle to this position

Circle handle

Figure 51 *The Filters options in the Properties panel*

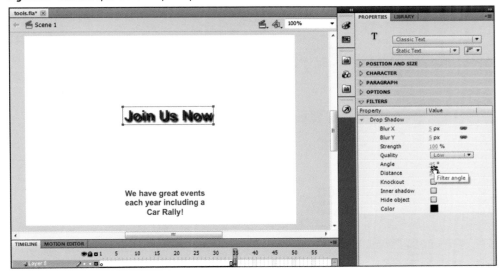

Using Filters

You can apply special effects, such as drop shadows, to text using options in the FILTERS area of the Properties panel. The process is to select the desired text, display the FILTERS area of the Properties panel, choose the desired effect, and make any adjustments, such as changing the angle of a drop shadow. You can copy and paste a filter from one object to another using the clipboard icon in the FILTERS area of the Properties panel.

Add a Filter effect to text

1. Click the **Text tool** T on the Tools panel, click the center of the Stage, then type **Join Us Now**. *Hint*: If the text box does not appear, double-click the Stage.

2. Drag the **I-Beam pointer** across the text to select it, then use the Properties panel to change the Font size to **30** and the Text (fill) color to **#003399**.

3. Click **CHARACTER** on the Properties panel to close the CHARACTER area, then close all areas in the Properties panel except for the FILTERS area.

4. Click the **Selection tool** on the Tools panel, then verify the text block is selected.

5. Click the **Add filter icon** at the bottom of the FILTERS area, then click **Drop Shadow**.

6. Point to the **Angle value** in the FILTERS area of the Properties panel, as shown in Figure 51.

7. When the pointer changes to a double-headed arrow, drag the pointer to the right to view the effect on the shadow, then set the Angle to **50**.

8. Point to the **Distance value**, when the pointer changes to a double-headed arrow, drag the pointer to the right and notice the changes in the drop shadow.

9. Set the Distance to **6**.

10. Click the **Selection tool**, click the text box to select it, drag the **text box** as needed to match the placement shown in Figure 51, then save your work.

You used the Filter panel to create a drop shadow, then made changes to it.

Skew text and align objects

1. Click the **Text tool** T to select it, click the ┼T **pointer** near the top middle of the Stage, then type **Classic Car Club**.

2. Click **CHARACTER** in the Properties panel to display the CHARACTER area.

   The attributes of the new text reflect the most recent settings entered in the Properties panel.

3. Drag the **I-Beam pointer** ⊺ to select the text, then use the CHARACTER area of the Properties panel to change the font size to **40** and the fill color to **#990000**.

4. Click the **Selection tool** ▸ on the Tools panel, click the **text box** to select it, then click the **Free Transform tool** ⬚ on the Tools panel.

5. Click the **Rotate and Skew option** ⟳ in the Options area of the Tools panel.

6. Drag the **top middle handle** to the right, as shown in Figure 52, to skew the text.

7. Click the **Selection tool** ▸ on the Tools panel.

8. Drag a **marquee** around all of the objects on the Stage to select them.

9. Click **Modify** on the menu bar, point to **Align**, click the **Align to stage check box** to make it active, then click **Horizontal Center**.

   Note: If the Modify menu closes before you select Horizontal Center, repeat Step 9.

10. Click a blank area of the Stage to deselect the objects.

You entered a heading, changed the font size and color, and skewed text using the Free Transform tool, then you aligned the objects on the Stage.

Figure 52 *Skewing the text*

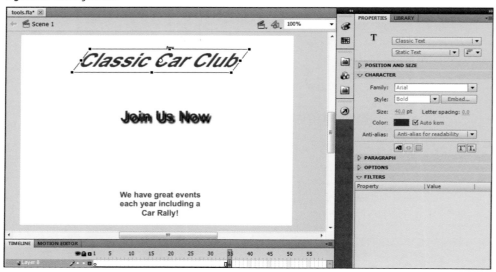

Figure 53 *Reshaping a letter*

*Drag this anchor point; notice the lines are
drawn from the anchor points on either side of
the anchor point being dragged*

Figure 54 *Applying a gradient fill to each letter*

Reshape and apply a gradient to text

1. Click the **Selection tool** ▶ , click the **Classic Car Club text block** to select it, click **Modify** on the menu bar, then click **Break Apart**.

   The letters are now individual text blocks.

2. Click **Modify** on the menu bar, then click **Break Apart**.

   The letters are filled with a dot pattern, indicating that they can now be edited.

3. Click the **Zoom tool** 🔍 on the Tools panel, then click the first **"C"** in Classic.

4. Click the **Subselection tool** ▷ on the Tools panel, then click the **edge** of the letter **"C"** to display the object's segment handles.

5. Drag a **lower anchor point** on the "C" in Classic, as shown in Figure 53.

6. Click the **Selection tool** ▶ , then click a blank area of the Stage to deselect the objects.

7. Click the **View** list arrow on the movie menu bar, then click **Fit in Window**.

8. Click the **Fill Color tool color swatch** on the Tools panel, then click the **red gradient color swatch** in the bottom row of the Color palette.

9. Click the **Paint Bucket tool** 🪣 on the Tools panel, then click the **top** of each letter to change the fill to a red gradient, as shown in Figure 54.

   Note: Click the Ink Bottle tool if you do not see the Paint Bucket tool.

10. Use the status bar to change the movie frame rate to **3**, test the movie, watch the movie, then close the Flash Player window.

11. Save your work, then close the document.

You broke apart a text block, reshaped text, and added a gradient to the text.

NEW Use the Text Layout Framework

1. Open fl2_4.fla, then save it as **TLF.fla**.
2. Click the **Text tool** T on the Tools panel, then click the **text block** on the Stage.
3. Click the **Text engine list arrow** in the T area on the Properties panel, then click **TLF Text**.

   The text block on the Stage changes to a container and displays two container icons.
4. Scroll the Properties panel as needed, then click **CONTAINER AND FLOW** to display the CONTAINER AND FLOW options.
5. Click the **Behavior list arrow**, then click **Multiline**.
6. Change the Column value to **2**, change it to **3**, then change it to **1**.
7. Point to the **middle handle** on the right side of the container, when the pointer changes to a double-headed arrow ↔, click and drag the **middle handle** left to the position shown in Figure 55, then release the mouse pointer.

(continued)

Figure 55 *Reshaping the text container*

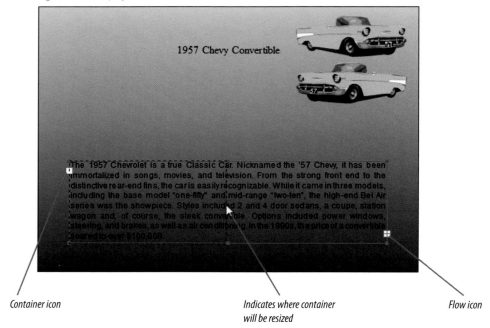

Container icon   Indicates where container will be resized   Flow icon

Figure 56 *Positioning the Flow icon pointer*

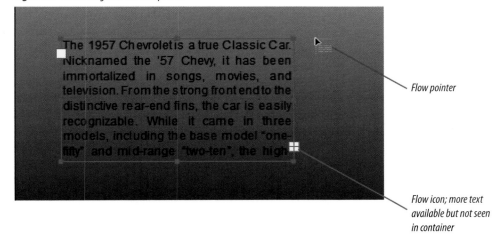

Flow pointer

Flow icon; more text
available but not seen
in container

Figure 57 *Repostioning the text container*

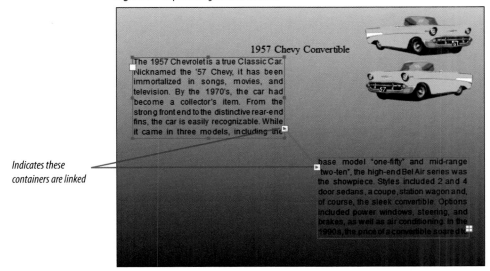

Indicates these
containers are linked

8. Click the **Container icon** on the right side of the container, position the **Flow pointer** as shown in Figure 56, then click the mouse button.

   Another container appears that is linked to the first container and with the text flowing from the first container.

9. Click before **From** in the first container, then type **By the 1970's, the car had become a collector's item**.

   Notice as you type in the first container that the text flows to the second container.

10. Click the **Selection tool** , then click and drag the **first container** to the position shown in Figure 57.

(continued)

11. Drag the **second container** to the position shown in Figure 58.

12. Click and drag the **bottom middle handle** of the second container down to display all the text if some of the text is not visible.

13. Click the **heading**, click the **Rotation list arrow** in the CHARACTER area on the Properties Panel, then click **270⁰**.

    The text rotates within the container.

14. Click **Modify** on the menu bar, point to **Transform**, then click **Rotate 90⁰ CW**.

15. Click the **heading**, then use the **arrow keys** to position the container between the two text containers.

(continued)

Figure 58 *Repositioning the second text container*

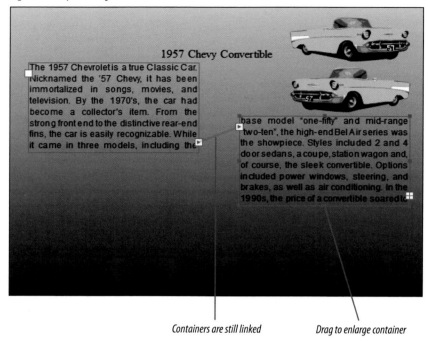

Containers are still linked   Drag to enlarge container

Drawing Objects in Adobe Flash

Figure 59 *Adding a container border*

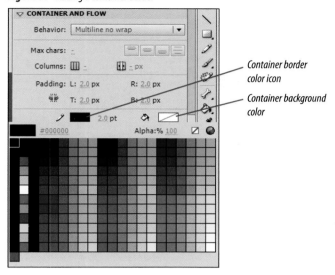

Container border color icon

Container background color

16. Click the **Container border color icon** ⟋ ▭ in the CONTAINER AND FLOW area, then click **black**.

    The border color swatch changes to black, as shown in Figure 59.

17. Change the border width to **2**.

18. Click the **Container background color icon** ✎ ▭ , then click the **car** with the Eyedropper tool ✐ to select the color.

19. Click the **Text tool** T , then click and drag the ⊥ᴛ **pointer** to select the words Nicknamed the '57 Chevy.

20. Click the **Highlight color icon** ▭ in the CHARACTER area on the Properties panel, then click the **car** to select the color.

21. Use the **Selection tool** ▸ to position the cars, as shown in Figure 60.

22. Test the movie, then save and close it.

You used the Text Layout Framework feature to display columns, create containers, add highlight color to text, add background and stroke color to a container, and rotate text.

Figure 60 *The completed document*

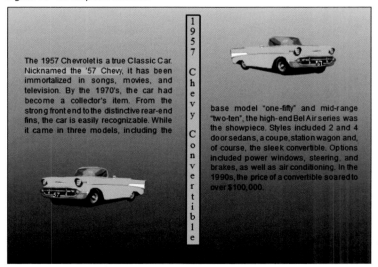

Work with Layers
AND OBJECTS

What You'll Do

 In this lesson, you will create, rename, reorder, delete, hide, and lock layers. You will also display objects as outlines on layers, use a Guide layer, distribute text to layers, and create a Folder layer.

Learning About Layers

Flash uses two types of spatial organization. First, there is the position of objects on the Stage, and then there is the stacking order of objects that overlap. An example of overlapping objects is text placed on a banner. In this case, the banner background might be placed on one layer and the banner text might be placed on a different layer. Layers are used on the Timeline as a way of organizing objects. Placing objects on their own layer makes them easier to work with, especially when reshaping them, repositioning them on the Stage, or rearranging their order in relation to other objects. In addition, layers are useful for organizing other elements such as sounds, animations, and ActionScript.

There are five types of layers, as shown in the Layer Properties dialog box displayed in Figure 61 and discussed next.

Normal—The default layer type. All objects on these layers appear in the movie.

Mask—A layer that hides and reveals portions of another layer.

Masked—A layer that contains the objects that are hidden and revealed by a Mask layer.

Folder—A layer that can contain other layers.

Guide (Standard and Motion)—You use a Standard Guide layer to set a reference point (such as a guide line) for positioning objects on the Stage. You use a Motion Guide layer to create a path for animated objects to follow.

Motion Guide, Mask, and Masked layer types are covered in a later chapter.

Working with Layers

The Layer Properties dialog box, accessed through the Timeline command on the Modify menu, allows you to specify the type of layer. It also allows you to name, show (and hide), and lock them. Naming a layer provides a clue to the objects on the layer. For example, naming a layer Logo might indicate that the object on the layer is the company's logo. Hiding a layer(s) may reduce the clutter on the Stage and make it easier to work with selected objects from the layer(s) that are not hidden. Locking a layer(s) prevents the objects from being accidentally edited. Other options in the Layer Properties dialog box allow you to view layers as outlines, change the outline color, and change layer height. Outlines can be used to help you determine which objects are on a layer. When you turn on this feature, each layer has a colored box that corresponds with the color of the objects on its layer. Icons on the Layers area of the Timeline, as shown in Figure 62, correspond to features in the Layer Properties dialog box.

Figure 61 *The Layer Properties dialog box*

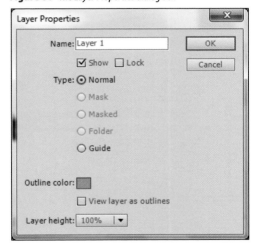

Figure 62 *The Layers area of the Timeline*

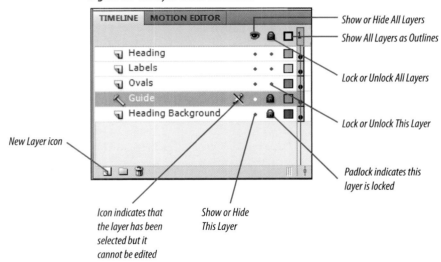

Using a Guide Layer

Guide layers are useful in aligning objects on the Stage. Figure 63 shows a Guide layer that has been used to align three buttons along a diagonal path. The buttons are on one layer and the diagonal line is on another layer, the Guide layer. To create a Guide layer, you insert a new layer above the layer containing the objects to be aligned, use the Layer Properties command from the Timeline option on the Modify menu to display the Layer Properties dialog box, select Guide as the layer type, and then draw a path (such as a guide line) that will be used as the guide to align the objects.

You then verify the Snap to Guides option from the Snapping command on the View menu is active, and drag the desired objects to the guide line. Objects have a transformation point that is used when snapping to a guide. By default, this point is at the center of the object. Figure 64 shows the process.

Figure 63 *A Guide layer used to align objects on the Stage*

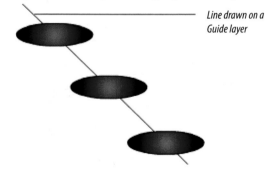

Line drawn on a Guide layer

Figure 64 *The transformation point of an object*

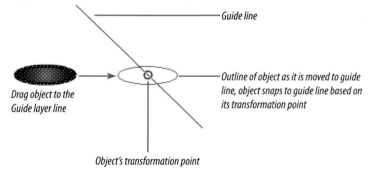

Guide line

Drag object to the Guide layer line

Outline of object as it is moved to guide line, object snaps to guide line based on its transformation point

Object's transformation point

Distributing Text to Layers

Text blocks are made up of one or more characters. When you break apart a text block, each character becomes an object that can be edited independently of the other characters. You use the Distribute to Layers command from the Timeline option on the Modify menu, which causes each character to automatically be placed on its own layer.

Figure 65 shows the seven layers created after the text block containing 57 Chevy has been broken apart and distributed to layers.

Using Folder Layers

As movies become larger and more complex, the number of layers increases. Flash allows you to organize layers by creating folders and grouping other layers in the folders. Figure 66 shows a Folder layer —carName—with seven layers in it. The process is to select the layer that is to become a Folder layer, then use the Layer Properties dialog box to specify a Folder layer. To place other layers in the Folder layer, you drag them from the Timeline to the Folder layer. The Folder layer triangle next to carName is a toggle. You click the triangle to open and close the folder.

Figure 65 *Distributing text to layers*

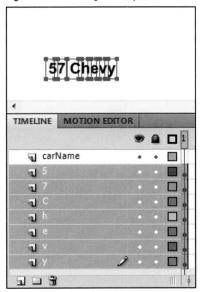

Figure 66 *A Folder layer*

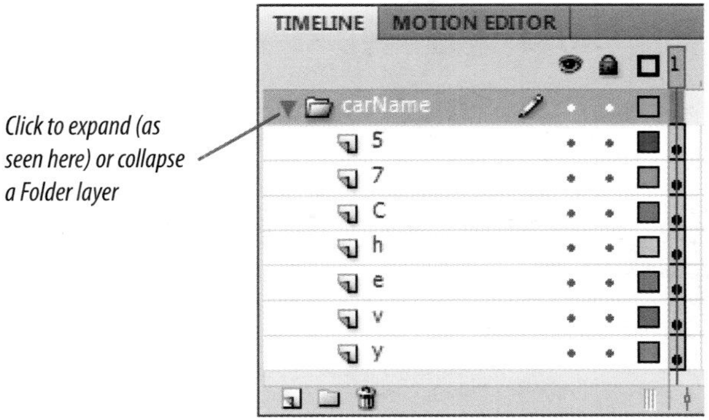

Click to expand (as seen here) or collapse a Folder layer

Create and reorder layers

1. Open fl2_5.fla from the drive and folder where your Data Files are stored, then save it as **layers2.fla**.

2. Click the **Selection tool** , click the **View list arrow** on the movie menu bar, then click **Fit in Window**.

3. Click the **New Layer icon** on the bottom of the Timeline (below the layer names) to insert a new layer, Layer 2.

4. Click **frame 1** on Layer 2.

5. Select the **Rectangle tool** on the Tools panel, then set each corner radius to **10** in the RECTANGLE OPTIONS area of the Properties panel, and set the Stroke to **2** in the FILL AND STROKE area.

6. Click the **Fill Color tool color swatch** on the Tools panel, click the **Hex Edit text box**, type **#999999**, then press **[Enter]** (Win) or **[return]** (Mac).

7. Click the **Stroke Color tool color swatch** on the Tools panel, click the **Hex Edit text box**, type **#000000**, then press **[Enter]** (Win) or **[return]** (Mac).

8. Draw the **rectangle** shown in Figure 67 so it covers the text heading.

9. Drag **Layer 1** above Layer 2 on the Timeline, as shown in Figure 68.

10. Click the **Selection tool** on the Tools panel.

11. Click a blank area of the Stage to deselect the objects.

You added a layer, drew an object on the layer, and reordered layers.

Figure 67 *Drawing a rectangle with a rounded corner*

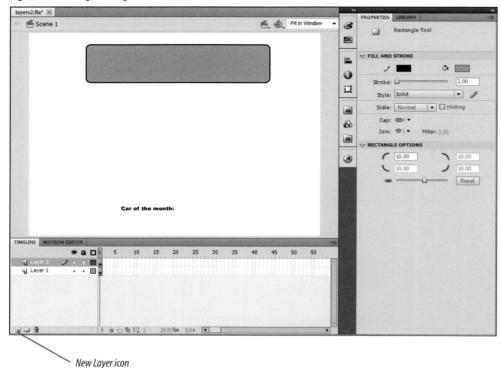

New Layer icon

Figure 68 *Dragging Layer 1 above Layer 2*

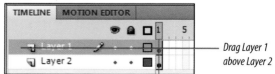

Drag Layer 1 above Layer 2

Figure 69 *Renaming layers*

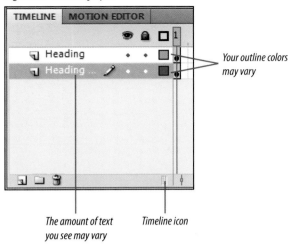

Your outline colors
may vary

The amount of text
you see may vary

Timeline icon

Figure 70 *Expanding the layer name area of the Timeline*

Drag the pointer

Rename and delete layers, and expand the Timeline

1. Double-click **Layer 1** on the Timeline, type **Heading** in the Layer Name text box, then press **[Enter]** (Win) or **[return]** (Mac).

2. Rename Layer 2 as **Heading Background**.

3. Point to the **Timeline icon** ▥, which is below the layer names and shown in Figure 69.

4. When the pointer changes to a double arrow ⬌, drag the **pointer** ⬌ to the right to display all the layer names.

   The full name of each layer is visible, as shown in Figure 70.

5. Click the **Heading layer**, then click the **Delete icon** 🗑 on the bottom of the Timeline.

6. Click **Edit** on the menu bar, then click **Undo Delete Layer**.

7. Click a blank area of the Stage to deselect all objects.

You renamed layers to associate them with objects on the layers, then deleted and restored a layer.

Hide, lock, and display layer outlines

1. Click the **Show or Hide All Layers icon** 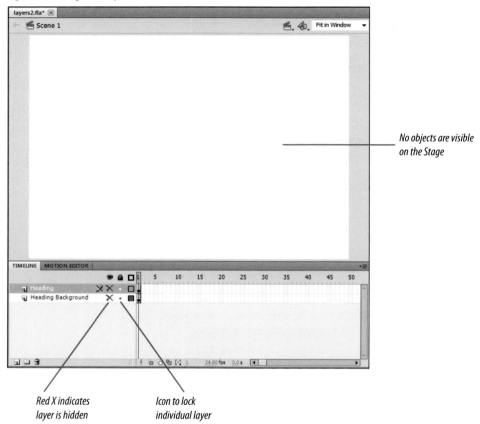 to hide all layers, then compare your image to Figure 71.

2. Click the **Show or Hide All Layers icon** to show all the layers.

3. Click the **Heading Background layer**, then click the **Show or Hide This Layer icon** next to the layer name twice to hide and then show the layer.

4. Click the **Lock or Unlock All Layers icon** to lock all layers.

5. With the layers locked, try to select and edit an object.

6. Click the **Lock or Unlock All Layers icon** again to unlock the layers.

7. Click the **Heading Background layer**, then click the **Lock or Unlock This Layer** to lock the layer.

8. Click the **Show All Layers as Outlines icon** to display the outlines of all objects.

   Notice the outlines are color-coded. For example, the two text objects are identified by their color (green) as being on the Heading layer (green).

9. Click the **Show All Layers as Outlines icon** to turn off this feature.

You hid and showed layers, you locked and unlocked layers, and you displayed the outlines of objects on a layer.

Figure 71 *Hiding all the layers*

No objects are visible on the Stage

Red X indicates layer is hidden

Icon to lock individual layer

Figure 72 *A diagonal line*

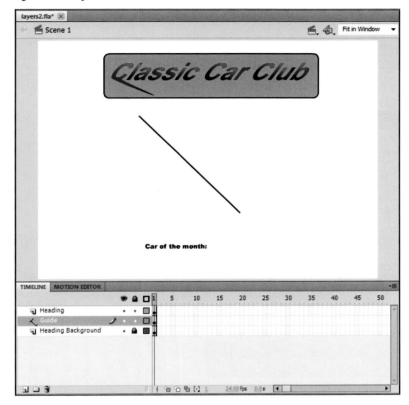

Create a guide for a Guide layer

1. Click the **Heading Background layer**, then click the **New Layer icon** on the bottom of the Timeline to add a new layer, Layer 3.

2. Rename the layer **Guide**.

3. Verify that the Guide layer is selected.

4. Click **Modify** on the menu bar, point to **Timeline**, then click **Layer Properties** to display the Layer Properties dialog box.

5. Click the **Guide option button** in the Type area, then click **OK**.

   A symbol appears next to the word Guide indicating that this is a Guide layer.

6. Click **frame 1** of the Guide layer.

7. Click the **Line tool** on the Tools panel, press and hold **[Shift]**, then draw the diagonal line, as shown in Figure 72.

8. Click the **Lock or Unlock This Layer icon** on the Guide layer to lock it.

9. Click **View** on the menu bar, point to **Snapping**, then verify Snap to Guides is selected.

You created a Guide layer and drew a guide line.

Add objects to a Guide layer

1. Add a new layer on the Timeline above the Guide layer, name it **Ovals**, then click **frame 1** on the Ovals layer.

2. Click the **Fill Color tool color swatch** on the Tools panel, then click the **red gradient color swatch** in the bottom row of the Color palette.

3. Click the **Oval tool** on the Tools panel, then verify that the **Object Drawing option** in the Options area of the Tools panel is not active.

4. Draw the **oval**, as shown in Figure 73.

5. Click the **Selection tool** on the Tools panel, then draw a **marquee** around the oval object to select it.

TIP Make sure the entire object (stroke and fill) is selected.

6. Point to the **center** of the oval, click and slowly drag the **oval** to the Guide layer line, as shown in Figure 74.

7. With the oval object selected, click **Edit** on the menu bar, then click **Copy**.

8. Click **Edit** on the menu bar, click **Paste in Center**, then drag the **copied object** to the Guide layer line beneath the first oval.

9. Click **Edit** on the menu bar, click **Paste in Center**, then drag the **copied object** to the bottom of the Guide layer line.

TIP When objects are pasted in the center of the Stage, one object may cover up another object. Move them as needed.

You created a Guide layer and used it to align objects on the Stage.

Figure 73 *An oval object*

Figure 74 *Dragging an object to the Guide layer line*

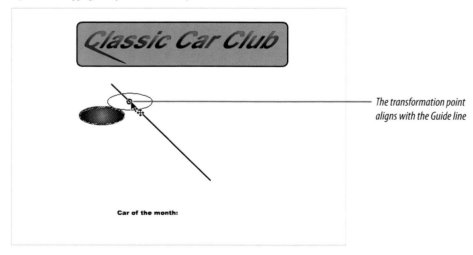

The transformation point aligns with the Guide line

Figure 75 *Adding text to the oval objects*

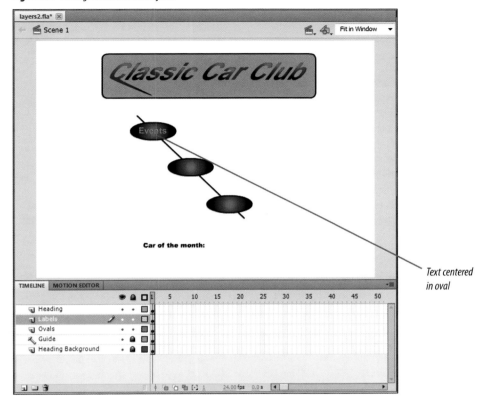

Text centered in oval

Add text on top of an object

1. Insert a **new layer** on the Timeline above the Ovals layer, then name it **Labels**.

2. Click **frame 1** of the Labels layer.

3. Click the **Text tool** T on the Tools panel, click the **top oval**, then type **Events**.

4. Drag the **I-Beam pointer** Ị across Events to select the text, then, using the Properties panel set the font family to **Arial**, the style to **Bold**, the font size to **14**, and the fill color to **#999999**.

5. Click the **Selection tool** ▶ on the Tools panel, click the **text box** to select it, then drag the **text box** to center it on the oval using the Guide layer, as shown in Figure 75.

TIP You can use the arrow keys on the keyboard to nudge the text into place.

6. Repeat Steps 3 and 5, typing **About us** and **Links** for the text blocks.

7. Lock all of the layers.

8. Test the movie, then close the Flash Player window.

   Notice the guide line does not appear in the movie.

9. Save then close the document.

10. Exit Flash.

You used the Text tool to create text blocks that were placed on objects.

Use the Flash drawing and alignment tools.

1. Start Flash, open fl2_6.fla, then save it as **skillsDemo2.fla**. Refer to Figure 76 as you complete these steps. (*Note*: Figure 76 shows the objects after changes have been made to them. For example, in Step 5 you draw a rectangle in the middle of the Stage. Then, in a later step you rotate the rectangle 45 degrees.)
2. Set the view to Fit in Window, then display the Grid.
3. Set the stroke color to black (Hex: **#000000**) and the fill color to blue (Hex: **#0000FF**).
4. Use the Oval tool to draw an oval on the left side of the Stage, then draw a circle beneath the oval. (*Hint*: Use the Undo command as needed.)
5. Use the Rectangle tool to draw a rectangle in the middle of the Stage, then draw a square beneath the rectangle. (*Hint*: Reset the RECTANGLE OPTIONS as needed.)
6. Use the Line tool to draw a horizontal line on the right side of the Stage, then draw a vertical line beneath the horizontal line and a diagonal line beneath the vertical line.
7. Use the Pen tool to draw an arrow-shaped object above the rectangle. (*Hint*: Use the Zoom tool to enlarge the area of the Stage.)
8. Use the Paint Bucket tool to fill the arrow with the blue color. (*Hint*: If the arrow does not fill, be sure you closed the arrow shape by clicking the first anchor point as your last action.)
9. Use the Pencil tool to draw a freehand line above the oval, then select the line and use the Smooth option to smooth out the line.
10. Use the Rectangle Primitive tool to draw a rectangle below the square, then use the Selection tool to drag a corner to round all the corners.
11. Save your work.

Select objects and apply colors.

1. Use the Selection tool to select the stroke of the circle, then deselect the stroke.
2. Use the Selection tool to select the fill of the circle, then deselect the fill.
3. Use the Ink Bottle tool to change the stroke color of the circle to red (Hex: **#FF0000**).
4. Use the Paint Bucket tool to change the fill color of the square to a red gradient.
5. Change the fill color of the oval to a blue gradient.
6. Save your work.

Work with drawn objects.

1. Copy and paste in center the arrow object.
2. Move the copied arrow to another location on the Stage.
3. Use the Properties panel to set the height of each arrow to 30.
4. Flip the copied arrow horizontally.
5. Rotate the rectangle to a 45° angle.
6. Skew the square to the right.
7. Copy one of the arrows and use the Subselection tool to reshape it, then delete it.
8. Use the Selection tool to reshape the circle to a crescent shape.
9. Save your work.

Work with text and text objects.

1. Select the Text tool, set the text mode to Classic Text and the type to Static, then enter the following text in a text block at the top of the Stage: **Gateway to the Pacific.**
2. Select the text, then change the text to font: Tahoma, size: 24, color: red.
3. Use the Align option on the Modify menu to horizontally center the text block.
4. Use the Selection tool and the up and down arrow keys on the keyboard to align the text block with a gridline.
5. Skew the text block to the right.
6. Save your work.

Work with layers.

1. Insert a layer into the document.
2. Change the name on the new layer to **Heading Bkgnd**, then click frame 1 on the layer.
3. Use the Rectangle Primitive tool to draw a rounded corner rectangle with a blue color that covers the words Gateway to the Pacific.
4. Switch the order of the layers.
5. Lock all layers.
6. Unlock all layers.
7. Hide the Heading Bkgnd layer.
8. Show the Heading Bkgnd layer.
9. Turn on, then turn off the view of the outlines.
10. Create a new layer as a Guide layer (be sure to change the layer type to Guide), name the layer **Guide**, draw a guideline on the new layer, lock the layer, then snap the arrows to the guideline.
11. Add a layer and use the Text tool to type **Seattle** below the heading, using Tahoma, Regular, 24 pt, and the color blue.
12. Align Seattle so it is centered horizontally across the Stage.

Use the Merge Drawing Model mode.

1. Insert a new layer and name it **MergeDraw**.
2. Select the Rectangle tool and verify that the Object Drawing option is not active.

3. Draw a square in the upper-right of the Stage, then use the Oval tool to draw a circle with a different color that covers approximately half of the square.

4. Select the stroke and fill of the circle, then using the Selection tool drag the circle off the square. (*Note*: Depending on the size of the circle and where you drew it to overlap the square, your results may vary from what is shown in Figure 76.)

Use the Object Drawing Model mode.

1. Insert a new layer and name it **ObjectDraw**.
2. Select the Rectangle tool and select the Object Drawing option to make it active.
3. Draw a square with a blue fill color, then use the Oval tool to draw a circle with a different color that covers approximately half of the square.
4. Use the Selection tool to drag the circle off the square.
5. Save your work, then compare your image to the example shown in Figure 76.

Use the Spray tool with a symbol.

1. Turn off the gridlines.
2. Add a new layer to the Timeline, then add a keyframe to frame 5 of the new layer.
3. Name the layer **Aces Wild**.
4. Select the Text tool and verify the Text option is set to TLF Text, then verify rotation is set to auto and alignment is set to Align to start.
5. Drag the pointer to create a text box that covers the lower one-fourth of the Stage.
6. Type the following using Arial, 14 pt text, black:

Ace's Wild has been providing novelty items, gifts, and toys to Seattleites since 1975. Located in Seattle's Greenlake district, we provide one stop shopping for the most unusual and unique costumes, party supplies, crafts and the strangest collection of toys ever assembled. Visit Ace's Wild to have a fun time choosing that perfect present for the hard to buy for person in your life.

7. Divide the text block into two text Containers, then use the Selection tool to position them as shown in Figure 76.
8. Use the Text tool to drag the lower middle handle of the lower text block to show a blank line if there is not a blank line.
9. Use the Text tool to select the top Container, then create a **2** pt blue border (#0066FF) and a red (#FF3300) background.
10. Select the bottom Container and create a **2 pt** red (#FF3300) border and a blue (#0066FF) background.
11. Use the Text tool to select Ace's Wild in the top Container, then create a white highlight.
12. Repeat Step 10 for the lower text Container.
13. Select the Spray Brush tool.
14. Click the Edit button in the Symbol area of the Properties panel, then select the Ace symbol.
15. Set the Scale width and height to **60**, turn on Rotate symbol (*Hint*: Be sure the check box has a check mark) and turn off the other options (*Hint*: Be sure all other check boxes do not have check marks), set the Brush width and height to 5 px, then draw the ace's as shown in Figure 76.
16. Test the movie, then save and close the document. (*Note*: If the movie displays too quickly, adjust the frame rate.)
17. Exit Flash.

Figure 76 *Completed Skills Review*

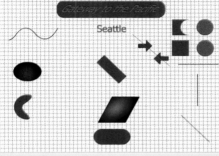

A local travel company, Ultimate Tours, has asked you to design several sample home pages for its new website. The goal of the website is to inform potential customers of its services. The company specializes in exotic treks, tours, and cruises. Thus, while its target audience spans a wide age range, they are all looking for something out of the ordinary.

1. Open a new Flash document using ActionScript 2.0 and save it as **ultimateTours2.fla**. Create the Flash movie shown in Figure 77. (*Note*: ActionScript 2.0 is used because in subsequent chapters the ultimateTours project will require this version of ActionScript.)
2. Set the document properties, including the Stage size and background color. (*Note*: You can use your choice of colors.)
3. Create the following on separate layers and name the layers:
   - A text heading; select a font size and font color. Skew the heading, break it apart, then reshape one or more of the characters.
   - A subheading with a different font size and color.
   - At least three objects that will be the background for button symbols.
   - Text that will appear on the top of the button background.

   Note: You can use different colors, shapes, and placement but your project should have all the elements shown in Figure 77.

4. Use one or more of the align features (gridlines, rulers, Align command on the Modify menu, arrow keys) to align the objects on the Stage.
5. Lock all layers.
6. Compare your image to the example shown in Figure 77.
7. Save your work.
8. Test the movie, close the Flash Player window, then close the movie.

Figure 77 *Sample completed Project Builder 1*

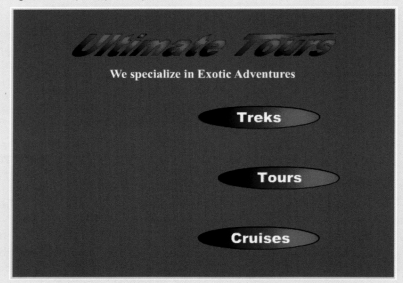

Drawing Objects in Adobe Flash

You have been asked to create several sample designs for the home page of a new organization called The Jazz Club. The club is being organized to bring together music enthusiasts for social events and charitable fundraising activities. The club members plan to sponsor weekly jam sessions and a show once a month. Because the club is just getting started, the organizers are looking to you for help in developing a website.

1. Plan the site by specifying the goal, target audience, treatment ("look and feel"), and elements you want to include (text, graphics, sound, and so on).
2. Sketch out a storyboard that shows the layout of the objects on the various screens and how they are linked together. Be creative in your design.
3. Open a new Flash document and save it as **theJazzClub2.fla**.
4. Set the document properties, including the Stage size and background color, if desired.
5. Display the gridlines and rulers and use them to help align objects on the Stage.
6. Create a heading, text objects, and drawings (such as the lines) to be used as links to the categories of information provided on the website. (*Note*: Some of the characters are individual text blocks [e.g. the S in Sessions] allowing you to move the text block without moving the other characters. *Hint*: Use the Oval, Line,

and Brush tools to create the notes. After selecting the Brush tool, experiment with the different Brush tool shapes found in the Options area at the bottom of the Tools panel.)

7. Hide the gridlines and rulers.
8. Save your work, then compare your image to the example shown in Figure 78.

Figure 78 *Sample completed Project Builder 2*

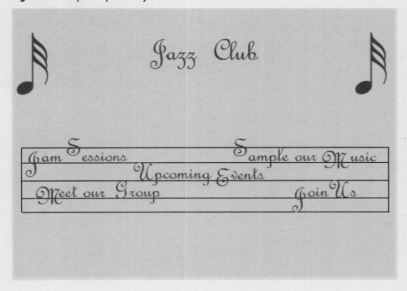

Figure 79 shows the home page of a website. Study the figure and complete the following. For each question indicate how you determined your answer.

1. Connect to the Internet, go to *www.nps.gov*, then select Explore Nature.
2. Open a document in a word processor or open a new Flash document, save the file as **dpc2**, then answer the following questions. (*Hint*: Use the Text tool in Flash.)
   - Whose website is this?
   - What is the goal(s) of the site?
   - Who is the target audience?
   - What is the treatment ("look and feel") that is used?
   - What are the design layout guidelines being used (balance, movement, and so on)?
   - What may be animated on this home page?
   - Do you think this is an effective design for the company, its products, and its target audience? Why or why not?
   - What suggestions would you make to improve the design and why?

Figure 79 *Design Project*

You have decided to create a personal portfolio of your work that you can use when you begin your job search. The portfolio will be a website done completely in Flash.

1. Research what should be included in a portfolio.
2. Plan the site by specifying the goal, target audience, treatment ("look and feel"), and elements you want to include (text, graphics, sound, and so on).
3. Sketch a storyboard that shows the layout of the objects on the various screens and how they are linked together. Be creative in your design.
4. Design the home page to include personal data (such as a Resume object that will link to your personal data), contact information (such as a Contact me link that will link to your contact information), previous employment (such as an Work History button that will link to your previous employment), education (such as an Education link that will link to information about your education), and samples of your work (such as an Animations link that will link to samples of your work).
5. Open a new Flash document using ActionScript 2.0 and save it as **portfolio2.fla**. (*Note*: ActionScript 2.0 is used because, in subsequent chapters, the portfolio project will require this version of ActionScript.)
6. Set the document properties, including the Stage size and background color, if desired.
7. Display the gridlines and rulers and use them to help align objects on the Stage.
8. Add a border the size of the Stage. (*Hint*: Use the Rectangle tool and set the fill color to none.)
9. Create a heading with its own background, then create other text objects and drawings to be used as links to the categories of information provided on the website. (*Hint*: In the example shown here, the Brush Script Std font is used. You can replace this font with Impact or any other appropriate font on your computer.)
10. Hide the gridlines and rulers.
11. Save your work, then compare your image to the example shown in Figure 80.

Figure 80 *Sample completed Portfolio Project*

CHAPTER **3** **WORKING WITH SYMBOLS AND INTERACTIVITY**

1. Create symbols and instances
2. Work with libraries
3. Create buttons
4. Assign actions to frames and buttons
5. Import graphics

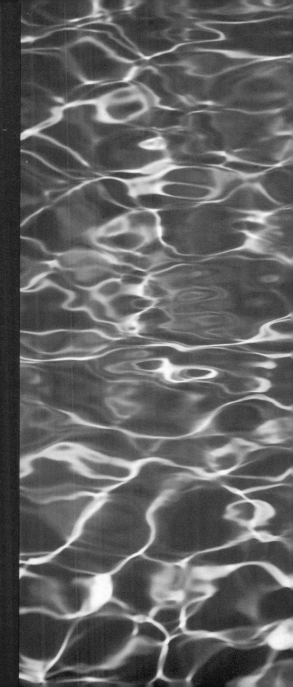

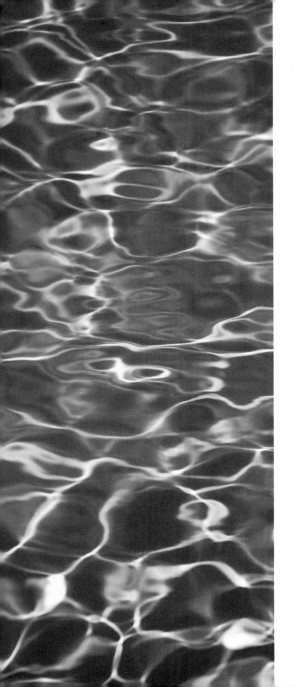

WORKING WITH SYMBOLS
AND INTERACTIVITY

Introduction

An important benefit of Flash is its ability to create movies with small file sizes. This allows the movies to be delivered from the web more quickly. One way to keep the file size small is to create reusable graphics, buttons, and movie clips. Flash allows you to create a graphic (drawing) and then make unlimited copies, which you can use throughout the current movie and in other movies. Flash calls the original drawing a **symbol** and the copied drawings **instances**. Flash stores symbols in the Library panel—each time you need a copy of the symbol, you can open the Library panel and drag the symbol to the Stage, which creates an instance (copy) of the symbol. Using instances reduces the movie file size because Flash stores only the symbol's information (size, shape, color), but Flash does not save the instance in the Flash movie. Rather, a link is established between the symbol and an instance so that the instance has the same properties (such as color and shape) as the symbol. There are two especially valuable editing features of this process. First, if you have created several instances of a symbol

and decide to change the same property for every instance, all that is needed is to edit the symbol. For example, if a logo appears in several places in a website and you need to change the color of each instance of the logo, you simply change the color of the symbol. Because the instances are linked to the symbol they are automatically updated. Second, you can change the properties of an individual instance of a symbol. For example, if your website is to contain drawings of cars that are similar but not identical, you can create just one drawing, convert it to a symbol, insert as many instances of the car as needed, and then change the properties of each individual instance, such as its size or color. When you edit a symbol, the change made to the symbol is made to all instances of the symbol. But, when you edit an instance of a symbol, you break the link between the symbol and the instance, and any changes you make to the object are not reflected in the symbol or any instances of that symbol. Likewise, if subsequently you make changes to the symbol, the changes will not be reflected in the unlinked object.

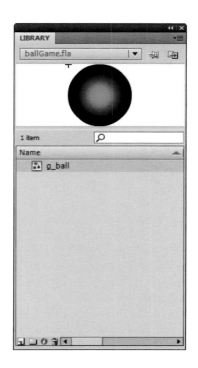

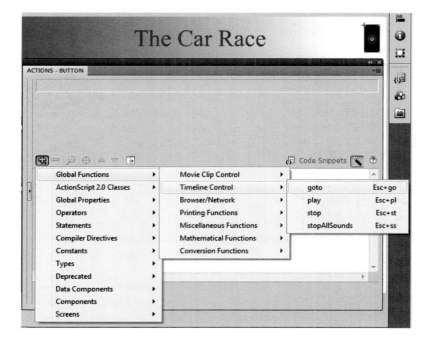

Create Symbols
AND INSTANCES

What You'll Do

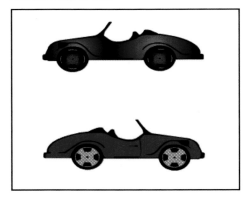

 In this lesson, you will create graphic symbols, turn them into instances, and then edit the instances.

Understanding Symbol Types

There are three categories of symbols: graphic, button, and movie clip. A graphic symbol is useful because you can reuse a single image and make changes in each instance of the image. A button symbol is useful because you can create buttons for interactivity, such as starting or stopping a movie. A movie clip symbol is useful for creating complex animations because you can create a movie within a movie. For example, you could have a movie with a car moving across the screen and its wheels rotating. The wheel animation would be created as one movie clip symbol and attached to each wheel of the animated car. Symbols can be created from objects you draw using the Flash drawing tools. In addition, you can import graphics into a Flash document that can then be converted to symbols.

Creating a Graphic Symbol

You can use the New Symbol command on the Insert menu to create and then draw a symbol. You can also draw an object and then use the Convert to Symbol command on the Modify menu to convert the object to a symbol. The Convert to Symbol dialog box, shown in Figure 1, allows you to name the symbol and specify the type of symbol you want to create (Movie Clip, Button, or Graphic). When naming a symbol, it's a good idea to use a naming convention that allows you to quickly identify the type of symbol and to group like symbols together. For example, you could identify all graphic symbols by naming them g_*name* and all buttons as b_*name*. In Figure 1, the drawing on the Stage is being converted to a graphic symbol.

After you complete the Convert to Symbol dialog box, Flash places the symbol in the Library panel, as shown in Figure 2. In Figure 2, an icon identifying the symbol as a graphic symbol and the symbol name are listed in the Library panel, along with a preview of the selected symbol. To create an instance of the symbol, you simply drag a symbol from the Library panel to the Stage. To edit a symbol, you can double-click it in the Library panel or you can use the Edit Symbols command on the Edit menu. Either way displays the symbol in an edit window, where changes can be made to it. When you edit a symbol, the changes are reflected in all instances of that symbol in your movie.

For example, you can draw a car, convert the car to a symbol, and then create several instances of the car. You can uniformly change the size of all the cars by double-clicking the car symbol in the Library panel to open the edit window, and then rescaling it to the desired size.

Working with Instances

You can have as many instances as needed in your movie, and you can edit each one to make it somewhat different from the others. You can rotate, skew (slant), and resize graphic and button instances. In addition, you can change the color, brightness, and transparency. However, there are some limitations. An instance is a single object with no segments or parts, such as a stroke and a fill. You cannot select a part of an instance. Therefore, any changes to the color of the instance are made to the entire object. Of course, you can use layers to stack other objects on top of an instance to change its appearance. In addition, you can use the Break Apart command on the Modify menu to break the link between

an instance and a symbol. Once the link is broken, you can make any changes to the object, such as changing its stroke and fill color. However, because the link is broken, the object is no longer an instance of the original symbol. So, if you make any changes to the original symbol, then the unlinked object is not affected.

The process for creating an instance is to open the Library panel and drag the desired symbol to the Stage. Once the symbol is on the Stage, you select the instance by using the Selection tool to drag a marquee around it. A blue

bounding box indicates that the object is selected. Then, you can use the Free Transform tool options (such as Rotate and Skew, or Scale) to modify the entire image, or you can use the Break Apart command to break apart the instance and edit individual strokes and fills.

Figure 2 *A graphic symbol in the Library panel*

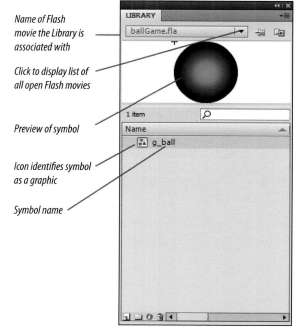

Name of Flash movie the Library is associated with

Click to display list of all open Flash movies

Preview of symbol

Icon identifies symbol as a graphic

Symbol name

Figure 1 *Using the Convert to Symbol dialog box to convert an object to a symbol*

Create a symbol

1. Open fl3_1.fla from the drive and folder where your Data Files are stored, then save it as **coolCar.fla**.

   This document has one object, a car, that was created using the Flash drawing tools.

2. Verify the Properties panel, the Library panel, and the Tools panel are displayed.

3. Set the magnification to **Fit in Window**.

4. Click the **Selection tool** on the Tools panel, then drag a **marquee** around the car to select it.

5. Click **Modify** on the menu bar, then click **Convert to Symbol**.

6. Type **g_car** in the Name text box.

7. Click the **Type list arrow** to display the symbol types, then click **Graphic**, as shown in Figure 3.

8. Set the **registration** to the upper-left corner, if necessary, as shown in Figure 3, then click **OK**.

9. Click the **Library panel tab**, then study the Library panel, as shown in Figure 4.

   The Library panel displays the symbol (red car) in the Item Preview window, an icon indicating that this is a graphic symbol, and the name of the symbol (g_car). The symbol is contained in the library, and the car on the Stage is now an instance of the symbol.

You opened a file with an object, converted the object to a symbol, and displayed the symbol in the Library panel.

Figure 3 *Options in the Convert to Symbol dialog box*

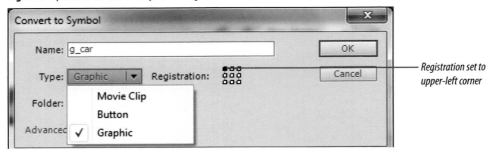

Registration set to upper-left corner

Figure 4 *Newly created symbol in the Library panel*

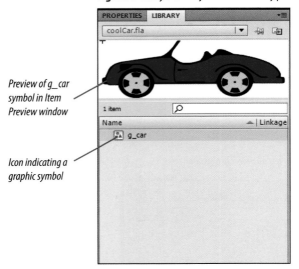

Preview of g_car symbol in Item Preview window

Icon indicating a graphic symbol

Working with Symbols and Interactivity

Figure 5 *Creating an instance*

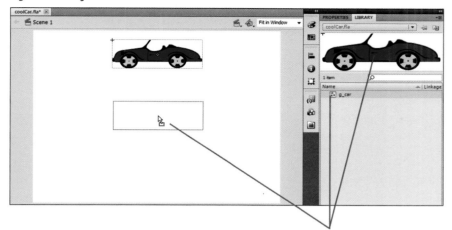

*Drag the car image, the name of the symbol,
or its icon from the Library panel to below
the original instance to create a second
instance of the symbol*

Figure 6 *The alpha set to 50%*

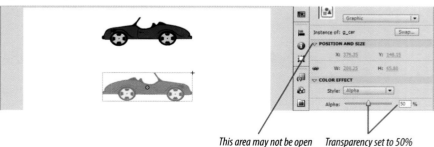

This area may not be open   *Transparency set to 50%*

Create and edit an instance

1. Point to the **car image** in the Item Preview
   window of the Library panel, then drag the
   image to the Stage beneath the first car, as
   shown in Figure 5.

   Both cars on the Stage are instances of the
   graphic symbol in the Library panel.

   TIP You can also drag the name of the symbol or its icon
   from the Library panel to the Stage.

2. Verify the bottom car is selected, click **Modify**
   on the menu bar, point to **Transform**, then click
   Flip Horizontal.

3. Display the Properties panel, then display the
   COLOR EFFECT area if it is not already showing.

4. Click the **Style list arrow**, then click **Alpha**.

5. Drag the **Alpha slider** ⬜ left then right, then set
   the transparency to **50%**.

   Notice how the transparency changes. Figure 6
   shows the transparency set to 50%.

6. Click a blank area of the Stage to deselect
   the object.

   Changing the alpha setting gives the car a more
   transparent look.

*You created an instance of a symbol and edited the instance on
the Stage.*

Edit a symbol in the edit window

1. Display the Library panel, double-click the **g_car symbol icon** 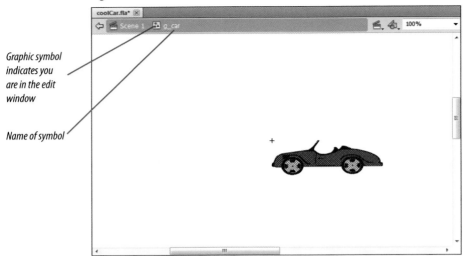 in the Library panel to display the edit window, then compare your screen to Figure 7.

   The g_car symbol appears in the edit window, indicating that you are editing the g_car symbol.

   TIP You can also edit a symbol by selecting it, clicking Edit on the menu bar, then clicking Edit Symbols.

2. Click a blank area of the window to deselect the car.

3. Verify the Selection tool is selected, then click the **light gray hubcap** inside the front wheel to select it.

4. Press and hold **[Shift]**, then click the **hubcap** inside the back wheel so both hubcap fills are selected.

5. Set the **Fill Color** to the **blue gradient color swatch** in the bottom row of the color palette, compare your image to Figure 8, then deselect the image.

6. Click **Scene 1** at the top left of the edit window to exit the edit window and return to the main Timeline and main Stage.

   Changes you make to the symbol affect every instance of the symbol on the Stage. The hubcap fill becomes a blue gradient in the Library panel and on the Stage.

   You edited a symbol in the edit window that affected all instances of the symbol.

Figure 7 *Edit window*

Graphic symbol indicates you are in the edit window

Name of symbol

Figure 8 *Edited symbol*

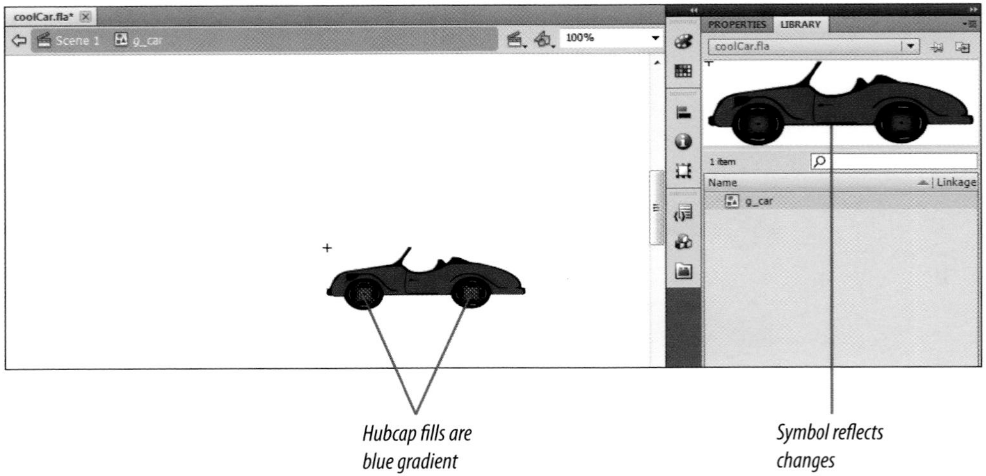

Hubcap fills are blue gradient

Symbol reflects changes

Working with Symbols and Interactivity

Figure 9 *The car with the maroon body selected*

Figure 10 *Changing the symbol affects only the one instance of the symbol*

Instance of the symbol ⎯⎯⎯

Object that is no
longer an instance
of the symbol ⎯⎯⎯

Break apart an instance

1. Drag a **marquee** around the bottom car to select it if it is not selected.

2. Click **Modify** on the menu bar, then click **Break Apart**.

   The object is no longer linked to the symbol, and its parts (strokes and fills) can now be edited.

3. Click a blank area of the Stage to deselect the object.

4. Click the blue **front hubcap**, press and hold **[Shift]**, then click the **blue back hubcap** so both hubcaps are selected.

5. Set the **Fill Color** 🎨 to the **light gray color swatch (#999999)** in the left column of the color palette.

6. Double-click the **g_car symbol icon** 🖼 in the Library panel to display the edit window.

7. Click the **maroon front body** of the car to select it, press and hold **[Shift]**, then click the **maroon back body** of the car, as shown in Figure 9.

8. Set the **Fill Color** 🎨 to the **red gradient color swatch** in the bottom row of the color palette.

9. Click **Scene 1** at the top left of the edit window, then compare your images to Figure 10.

   The body color of the car in the original instance is a different color, but the body color of the car to which you applied the Break Apart command remains unchanged.

10. Save your work.

You used the Break Apart command to break the link between one instance and its symbol, you edited the object created using the Break Apart command, and then you edited the symbol, which only affected the instance still linked to the symbol.

Work with LIBRARIES

What You'll Do

In this lesson, you will use the Library panel to organize the symbols in a movie.

Understanding the Library

The library in a Flash document contains the symbols and other items such as imported graphics, movie clips, and sounds. The Library panel provides a way to view and organize the items, and allows you to change the item name, display item properties, and add and delete items. Figure 11 shows the Library panel for a document. Refer to this figure as you read the following descriptions of the parts of the library.

Tab title—Identifies the panel title, in this case, the Library panel.

Panel options menu— Labeled in Figure 11 and shown in Figure 12, the Panel options menu provides access to several features used to edit symbols (such as renaming symbols) and organize symbols (such as creating a new folder).

Display movies list arrow—Opens a menu showing all open movies. You use this menu to select an open document (movie) and display the Library panel associated with that open document. This allows you to use the items from one movie in another movie. For example, you may have developed a drawing in one Flash movie that you converted to a symbol and now you want to use that symbol in the movie you are working on. With both documents open, you simply use the Display movies list arrow to display the library with the desired symbol, and then drag the symbol to the Stage of the current movie. This will automatically place the symbol in the library for the current movie. In addition to the movie libraries, you can create permanent libraries that are available whenever you start Flash. Flash also has sample libraries that contain buttons and other objects. The permanent and sample libraries are accessed through the Common Libraries command on the Window menu. All assets in all of these libraries are available for use in any movie.

Item Preview window—Displays the selected item. If the item is animated or a sound file, a control button appears, allowing you to preview the animation or play the sound.

Name text box—Lists the folder and item names. Each item type has a different icon associated with it. Clicking an item name or icon displays the item in the Item Preview window.

Toggle Sorting Order icon—Allows you to reorder the list of folders and items within folders.

New Symbol icon—Displays the Create New Symbol dialog box, allowing you to create a new symbol.

New Folder icon—Allows you to create a new folder.

Properties icon—Displays the Properties dialog box for the selected item.

Delete icon—Deletes the selected item or folder.

To make changes to an item, you can double-click either the item icon in the Library panel, the item in the Item Preview window, or the item on the Stage to display the edit window.

Figure 11 *The Library panel*

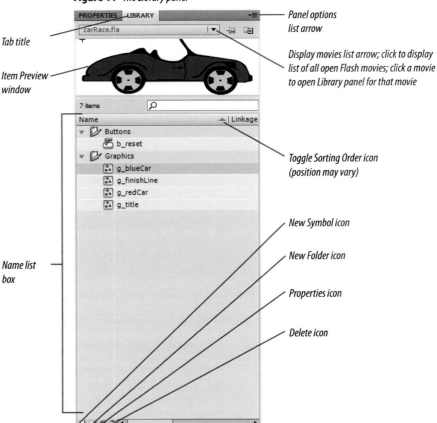

Tab title

Item Preview window

Name list box

Panel options list arrow

Display movies list arrow; click to display list of all open Flash movies; click a movie to open Library panel for that movie

Toggle Sorting Order icon (position may vary)

New Symbol icon

New Folder icon

Properties icon

Delete icon

Figure 12 *The Panel options menu*

Create folders in the Library panel

1. Open fl3_2.fla, then save it as **carRace.fla**.

2. Verify the Properties panel, the Library panel, and the Tools panel are displayed.

3. Set the magnification to **Fit in Window**.

   This movie has eight layers containing various objects such as text blocks, lines, and a backdrop. Two layers contain animations of cars.

4. Test the movie, then close the Flash Player window.

5. Click the **Show or Hide All Layers icon** 👁 on the Timeline to hide all of the layers.

6. Click each **red X** in the Show or Hide All Layers column to show the contents of each layer, click the **Show or Hide This Layer icon** ⬚ to hide the contents of that layer, then after viewing the contents of each layer, click the **Show or Hide All Layers icon** 👁 on the Timeline to show all of the layers.

   Note: The reset layer shows an empty Stage. This is because the word Reset is located in frame 65 at the end of the movie and does not appear in frame 1.

7. Click each item in the Library panel to display it in the Item Preview window.

   Notice that there is one button symbol (b_reset) and five graphic symbols.

8. Click **Name** on the Name list box title bar, as shown in Figure 13, and notice how the items are sorted.

9. Repeat Step 8 and notice how the items are sorted.

You opened a Flash movie and sorted items in the Library panel.

Figure 13 *The open Library panel*

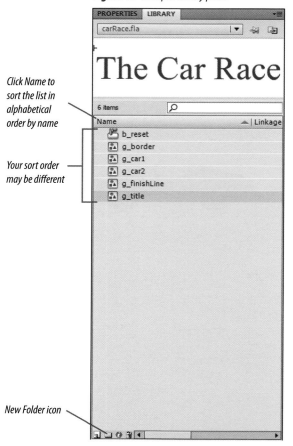

Click Name to sort the list in alphabetical order by name

Your sort order may be different

New Folder icon

Working with Symbols and Interactivity

Figure 14 *The Library panel with the folders added*

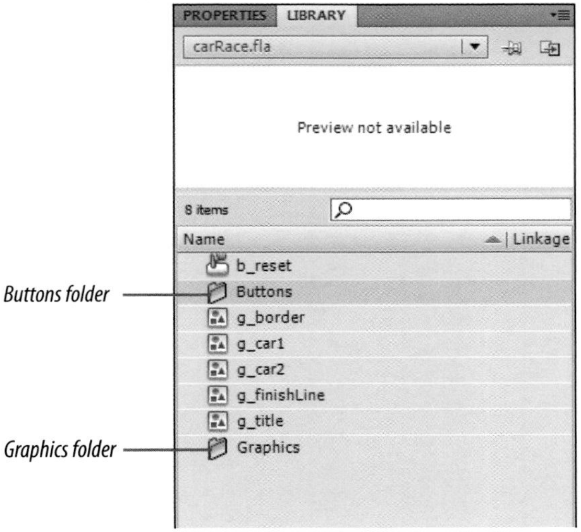

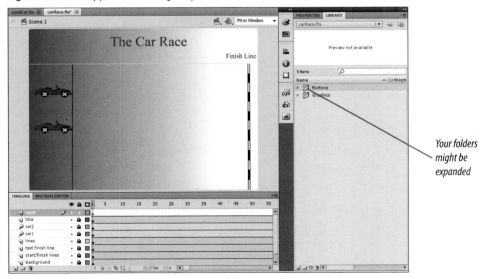

Buttons folder ———

Graphics folder ———

Figure 15 *The Library panel after moving the symbols to the folders*

Your folders
might be
expanded

Organize items within Library panel folders

1. Click the **New Folder icon** in the Library panel, as shown in Figure 13.
2. Type **Graphics** in the Name text box, then press [**Enter**] (Win) or [**return**] (Mac).
3. Click the **New Folder icon** on the Library panel.
4. Type **Buttons** in the Name text box, then press [**Enter**] (Win) or [**return**] (Mac).

   Your Library panel should resemble Figure 14.
5. Drag the **g_title symbol** in the Library panel to the Graphics folder.
6. Drag the other graphic symbols to the Graphics folder.
7. Drag the **b_reset symbol** to the Buttons folder, then compare your Library panel to Figure 15.
8. Click the **Graphics folder expand icon** to open it and display the graphic symbols.
9. Click the **Buttons folder expand icon** to open it and display the button symbol.
10. Click the **Graphics folder collapse icon** to close the folder.
11. Click the **Buttons folder collapse icon** to close the folder.

    Note: To remove an item from a folder, drag the item down to a blank area of the Library panel.

You created new folders, organized the symbols within the folders, and then opened and closed the folders.

Rename symbols and delete a symbol

1. Click the **expand icon** ▶ for the Graphics folder to display the symbols.

2. Right-click (Win) or [control]-click (Mac) the **g_car1 symbol**, then click **Rename**.

3. Type **g_redCar** in the Name text box, then press **[Enter]** (Win) or **[return]** (Mac).

4. Repeat Steps 2 and 3 to rename the g_car2 symbol as **g_blueCar**.

5. Click **g_border** in the Library panel to select it.

6. Click the **Delete icon** 🗑 at the bottom of the Library panel.

   Your Library panel should resemble Figure 16.

TIP You can also select an item and press [Delete], or you can use the Panel options menu in the Library panel to remove an item from the library. The Undo command in the Edit menu can be used to undelete an item.

You used the Library panel to rename symbols and delete a symbol.

Figure 16 *Updated Library panel*

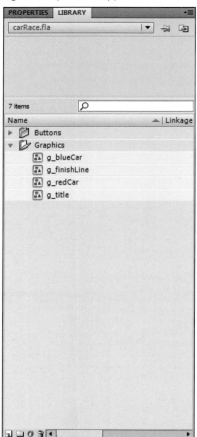

Working with Symbols and Interactivity

Figure 17 *The carRace.fla document and the coolCar.fla Library panel*

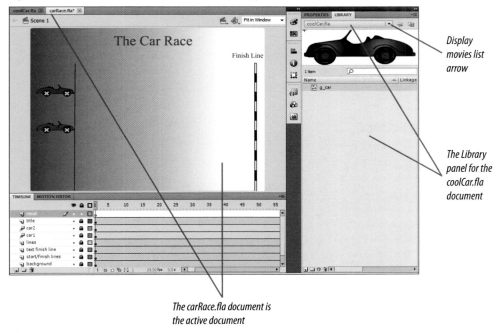

Display movies list arrow

The Library panel for the coolCar.fla document

The carRace.fla document is the active document

Use multiple Library panels

1. Click the **Display movies list arrow** near the top of the Library panel to display a list of open documents.

2. Click **coolCar.fla**, then click **g_car**.

   The Library panel for the coolCar document is displayed. However, the carRace document remains open, as shown in Figure 17.

3. Click **frame 1** on the reset layer, then drag the 📷 **g_car symbol** from the Library panel to the center of the Stage.

   The reset layer is the only unlocked layer. Objects cannot be placed on locked layers.

4. Click the **Display movies list arrow** to display the open documents.

5. Click **carRace.fla** to view the carRace document's Library panel.

   Notice the g_car symbol is added automatically to the Library panel of the carRace document.

6. Click the **g_car symbol** in the Library panel.

7. Click the **Delete icon** 🗑 at the bottom of the Library panel.

   You deleted the g_car symbol from the carRace library but it still exists in the coolCar library. The car was also deleted from the Stage.

8. Save your work.

9. Click the **coolCar.fla tab** at the top of the workspace to display the document.

10. Close the coolCar document and save the document if asked.

You used the Library panel to display the contents of another library and added an object from that library to the current document.

Create
BUTTONS

What You'll Do

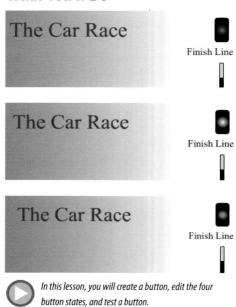

In this lesson, you will create a button, edit the four button states, and test a button.

Understanding Buttons

Button symbols are used to provide interactivity. When you click a button, an action occurs, such as starting an animation or jumping to another frame on the Timeline. Any object, including Flash drawings, text blocks, and imported graphic images, can be made into buttons. Unlike graphic symbols, buttons have four states: Up, Over, Down, and Hit. These states correspond to the use of the mouse and recognize that the user requires feedback when the mouse is pointing to a button and when the button has been clicked. This is often shown by a change in the button (such as a different color or different shape). An example of a button with different colors for the four different states is shown in Figure 18. These four states are explained in the following paragraphs.

Up—Represents how the button appears when the mouse pointer is not over it.

Over—Represents how the button appears when the mouse pointer is over it.

Down—Represents how the button appears after the user clicks the mouse.

Hit—Defines the area of the screen that will respond to the pointer. In most cases, you will want the Hit state to be the same or similar to the Up state in location and size.

When you create a button symbol, Flash automatically creates a new Timeline. The Timeline has only four frames, one for each

Figure 18 *The four button states*

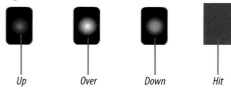

Up   Over   Down   Hit

button state. The Timeline does not play; it merely reacts to the mouse pointer by displaying the appropriate button state and performing an action, such as jumping to a specific frame on the main Timeline.

The process for creating and previewing buttons is as follows:

Create a button symbol—Draw an object or select an object that has already been created and placed on the Stage. Use the Convert to Symbol command on the Modify menu to convert the object to a button symbol and to enter a name for the button.

Edit the button symbol—Select the button and choose the Edit Symbols command on the Edit menu or double-click the button symbol in the Library panel. This displays the edit window, which includes the button Timeline, shown in Figure 19. You use the button Timeline to work with the four button states. The Up state is the original button symbol. Flash automatically places it in frame 1. You need to determine how the original object will change for the other states. To change the button for the Over state, click frame 2 and insert a keyframe. This automatically places a copy of the button that is in frame 1 into frame 2. Then, alter the button's appearance for the Over state, for instance, by changing the fill color. Use the same process for the Down state. For the Hit state, you insert a keyframe in frame 4 and then specify the area on the screen that will respond to the pointer. If you do not specify a hit area, the image for the Down state is used for the hit area. You add a keyframe to the Hit frame only if you are going to specify the hit area.

Return to the main Timeline—Once you've finished editing a button, you choose the Edit Document command on the Edit menu or click Scene 1 above the edit window to return to the main Timeline.

Preview the button—By default, Flash disables buttons so that you can manipulate them on the Stage. You can preview a button by choosing the Enable Simple Buttons command on the Control menu. You can also choose the Test Movie command on the Control menu to play the movie and test the buttons.

Figure 19 *The button Timeline*

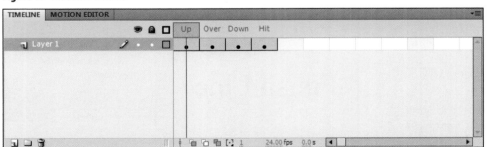

Create a button

1. Insert a **new layer** above the top layer on the Timeline, then name the layer **signal**.

2. Select the **Rectangle Primitive tool** ▭, click the **Stroke Color tool** on the Tools panel, then click the **No Stroke icon** in the upper-right corner of the color palette.

3. Set the **Fill Color** to the **red gradient color swatch** in the bottom row of the color palette.

4. Display the Properties panel, click the **Reset button** in the RECTANGLE OPTIONS area, then set the corner radius to **5**.

5. Draw the **rectangle** shown in Figure 20.

6. Click the **Zoom tool** on the Tools panel, then click the **rectangle** to enlarge it.

7. Select the **Gradient Transform tool** on the Tools panel, then click the **rectangle**.

   You may need to click and hold the Free Transform tool first.

8. Drag the **diagonal arrow** toward the center of the rectangle as shown in Figure 21 to make the red area more round.

9. Click the **Selection tool** on the Tools panel, then drag a **marquee** around the rectangle to select it.

10. Click **Modify** on the menu bar, then click **Convert to Symbol**.

11. Type **b_signal** in the Name text box, click the **Type list arrow**, click **Button**, then click **OK**.

12. Display the Library panel, then drag the **b_signal symbol** to the Buttons folder.

You created a button symbol on the Stage and dragged it to the Buttons folder in the Library panel.

Figure 20 *The rectangle object*

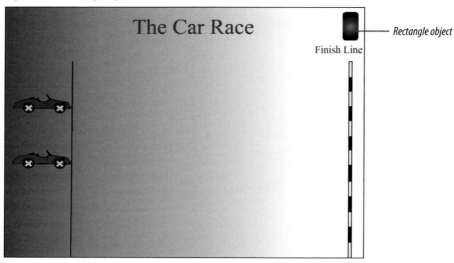

Rectangle object

Figure 21 *Adjusting the gradient*

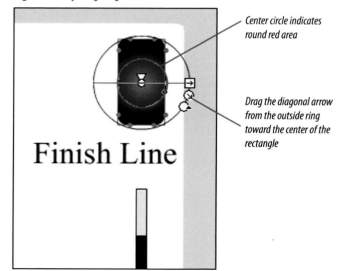

Center circle indicates round red area

Drag the diagonal arrow from the outside ring toward the center of the rectangle

Figure 22 *Specifying the hit area*

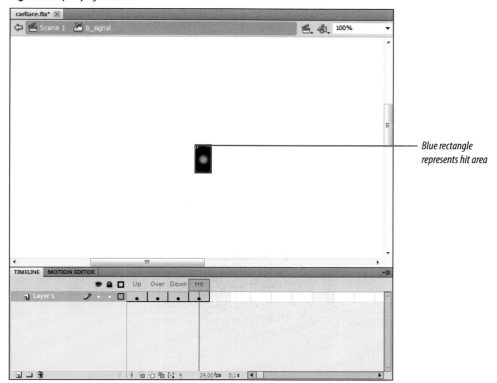

Blue rectangle represents hit area

Edit a button and specify a hit area

1. Open the Buttons folder, right-click (Win) or control-click (Mac) **b_signal** in the Library panel, then click **Edit**.

   Flash displays the edit window showing the Timeline with four button states.

2. Click the blank **Over frame** on Layer 1, then insert a **keyframe**.

TIP The [F6] key inserts a keyframe in the selected frame. The [fn] key may need to be used with some Mac keyboards.

3. Set the **Fill Color** to the **gray gradient color swatch** on the bottom of the color palette.

4. Insert a **keyframe** in the Down frame on Layer 1.

5. Set the **Fill Color** to the **green gradient color swatch** on the bottom of the color palette.

6. Insert a **keyframe** in the Hit frame on Layer 1.

7. Select the **Rectangle tool** ▢ on the Tools panel then set the **Fill Color** to the **blue color swatch** in the left column of the color palette.

8. Draw a **rectangle** slightly larger than the button, as shown in Figure 22, then release the mouse button.

TIP The Hit area will not be visible on the Stage.

9. Click **Scene 1** above the edit window to return to the main Timeline.

You edited a button by changing the color of its Over and Down states, and you specified the Hit area.

Test a button

1. Click the **Selection tool** ![selection tool icon], then click a blank area of the Stage.
2. Click **Control** on the menu bar to display the Control menu, then click **Enable Simple Buttons**.

   This command allows you to test buttons on the Stage without viewing the movie in the Flash Player window.
3. Point to the **signal button** on the Stage, then compare your image to Figure 23.

   The pointer changes to a hand ![hand icon], indicating that the object is clickable, and the button changes to a gray gradient, the color you selected for the Over state.
4. Press and hold the **mouse button**, then notice that the button changes to a green gradient, the color you selected for the Down state, as shown in Figure 24.
5. Release the mouse and notice that the button changes to a gray gradient, the color you selected for the Over state.

(continued)

Figure 23 *The button's Over state*

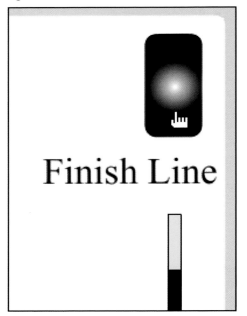

Figure 24 *The button's Down state*

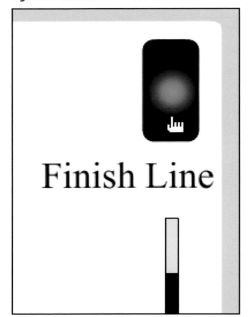

The Button Hit Area

All buttons have an area that responds to the mouse pointer, including rolling over the button and clicking it. This hit area is usually the same size and shape as the button itself. However, you can specify any area of the button to be the hit area. For example, you could have a button symbol that looks like a target with just the bulls-eye center being the hit area.

Figure 25 *The button's Up state*

Figure 26 *View options from the View list*

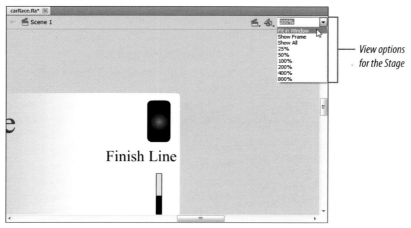

View options
for the Stage

6. Move the mouse away from the signal button, and notice that the button returns to a red gradient, the Up state color, as shown in Figure 25.

7. Click **Control** on the menu bar, then click **Enable Simple Buttons** to turn off the command.

8. Click the **View list arrow** above the Stage, then click **Fit in Window**, as shown in Figure 26.

   This shortcut allows you to change the magnification view without using the Magnification command on the View menu or the Zoom tool in the Tools panel.

9. Save your work.

You used the mouse to test a button and view the button states.

Assign Actions
TO FRAMES AND BUTTONS

What You'll Do

In this lesson, you will use ActionScript to assign actions to frames and buttons.

Understanding Actions

In a basic movie, Flash plays the frames sequentially without stopping for user input. However, you often want to provide users with the ability to interact with the movie by allowing them to perform actions, such as starting and stopping the movie or jumping to a specific frame in the movie. One way to provide user interaction is to assign an action to the Down state of a button. Then, whenever the user clicks the button, the action occurs. Flash provides a scripting language, called ActionScript, that allows you to add actions to buttons and frames within a movie. For example, you can place a stop action in a frame that pauses the movie, and then you can assign a play action to a button that starts the movie when the user clicks the button.

Analyzing ActionScript

ActionScript is a powerful scripting language that allows those with even limited programming experience to create complex actions. For example, you can create order forms that capture user input or volume controls that display when sounds are played. A basic ActionScript involves an event (such as a mouse click) that causes some action to occur by triggering the script. The following is an example of a basic ActionScript:

```
on (release) {
gotoAndPlay(10);
}
```

In this example, the event is a mouse click (indicated by the word release) that causes the movie's playback head to go to frame 10 and play the frame. This is a simple example of ActionScript code and it is easy to follow. Other ActionScript code can be quite complex and may require programming expertise to understand.

ActionScript 2.0 and 3.0

Adobe has identified two types of Flash CS5 users, designers and developers. Designers focus more on the visual features of a Flash movie, including the user interface design, drawing objects, and acquiring and editing additional assets (such as graphic images). Whereas, developers focus more on the programming aspects of a Flash movie, including creation of complex animations and writing the code that specifies how the movie responds to user interactions. In many cases, designers and developers work together to create sophisticated Flash applications. In other cases, designers work without the benefit of a developer's programming expertise. In order to accommodate the varying needs of these two types of users, Flash CS5 provides two versions of ActionScript, 2.0 and 3.0, called AS2 and AS3. ActionScript 3.0 is used by developers because it provides a programming environment that is more familiar to them and can be used to create movies that download more quickly.

However, the differences between AS2 and AS3 are transparent to designers who do not have programming expertise. AS2 allows new Flash users to create compelling applications even if they do not have a background in programming. At the same time, AS2 provides an introduction to ActionScript that can be the basis for learning ActionScript 3.0. ActionScript 2.0 will be used in this chapter. You can specify ActionScript 2.0 when creating a new document or you can use the Flash tab in the Publish Settings dialog box, which can be opened using the Publish Settings

command found on the File menu, to specify AS2.

An advantage of using AS2 is a feature called Script Assist, which provides an easy way to use ActionScript without having to learn the scripting language. The Script Assist feature within the Actions panel allows you to assign basic actions to frames and objects, such as buttons. Figure 27 shows the Actions panel displaying an ActionScript indicating that when the user clicks the selected object (a button, in this example, b_signal), the movie goes to and plays frame 2.

Figure 27 *The Actions panel displaying an ActionScript*

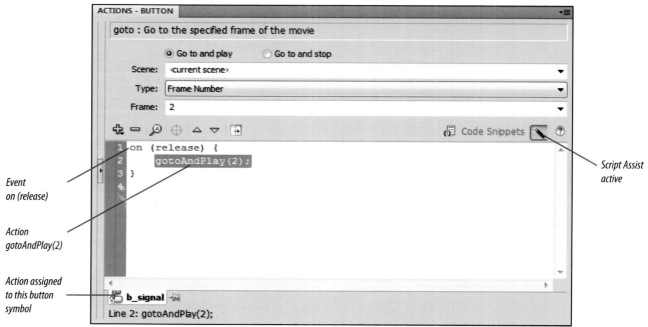

The process for assigning actions to buttons, shown in Figure 28, is as follows:

1. Select the button on the Stage that you want to assign an action to.
2. Display the Actions panel, using the Window menu.
3. Click the Script Assist button to display the Script Assist panel within the ActionScript panel.
4. Click the Add a new item to the script button to display a list of Action categories and associated menus.
5. Click the appropriate category from a menu. Flash provides several Action categories. The Timeline Control category accessed via the Global Functions menu allows you to create scripts for controlling

movies and navigating within movies. You can use the actions available via the Timeline Control menu to start and stop movies, as well as jump to specific frames. These can be in response to user mouse movements and keystrokes.

- Select the desired action, such as goto.
- Specify the event that triggers the action, such as on (release). This step in the process is not shown in Figure 28.

Button actions respond to one or more mouse events, including:

Release—With the pointer inside the button Hit area, the user presses and releases (clicks) the mouse button. This is the default event.

Key Press—With the button displayed, the user presses a predetermined key on the keyboard.

Roll Over—The user moves the pointer into the button Hit area.

Drag Over—The user holds down the mouse button, moves the pointer out of the button Hit area, and then back into the Hit area.

Using Frame Actions

In addition to assigning actions to buttons, you can assign actions to frames. Actions assigned to frames are executed when the playhead reaches the frame. A common frame action is stop, which is often assigned to the first and last frame of a layer on the Timeline.

Figure 28 *The process for assigning actions to buttons*

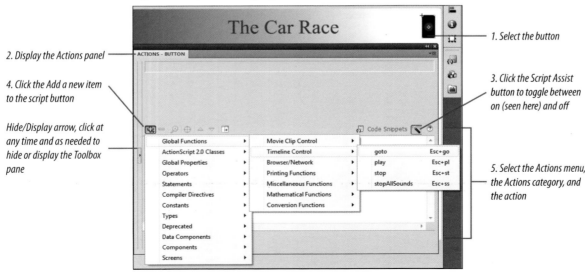

Understanding the Actions panel

The Actions panel has two panes. The left pane (also called the Toolbox pane) uses folders to display the Action categories. The right pane, called the Script pane, is used with the Script Assist feature and it displays the ActionScript code as the code is being generated. When using the Script Assist feature, it is best to close the left pane. This is done by clicking the Hide/Display arrow, which is shown in Figure 28 and Figure 29. In Figure 28, the Toolbox pane is collapsed, and in Figure 29, the Toolbox pane is expanded.

The lower-left corner of the Script pane displays the symbol name or the frame to which the action(s) will apply. Always verify that the desired symbol or frame is displayed. When the Script Assist feature is turned off (not active), you can type ActionScript code directly into the Script pane.

Using Frame Labels

Buttons are often used to move the playhead to a specific location on the Timeline. For example, clicking a Start button might cause the playhead to jump from frame 1 to frame 10 to start an animation. In addition to referencing frame numbers, like 10, you can reference frame labels in the ActionScript code. Frame labels have an advantage over frame numbers, especially in large and complex applications, because adding or deleting frames will not disrupt the navigation to a frame reference you already have in actions, since the label remains attached to the frame even if the frame moves. The process is to select a frame and use the Properties panel to specify a name. Then use the frame name in the ActionScript code instead of the frame number. Figure 30 shows the Timeline with a frame label and the Actions panel with the code that references the label.

Figure 29 *The Actions panel*

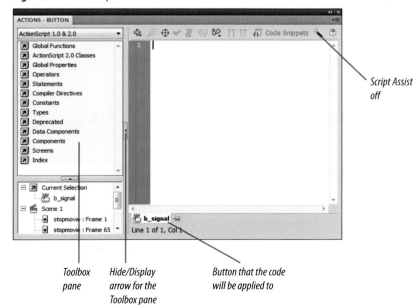

Script Assist off

Toolbox pane

Hide/Display arrow for the Toolbox pane

Button that the code will be applied to

Figure 30 *The Timeline with a frame label*

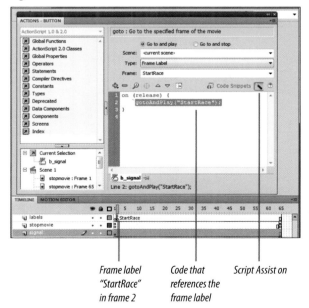

Frame label "StartRace" in frame 2

Code that references the frame label

Script Assist on

Assign a stop action to frames

1. Click **Control** on the menu bar, point to **Test Movie**, then click **in Flash Professional**.

   The movie plays and continues to loop.

2. Close the Flash Player window.

3. Insert a **new layer**, name it **stopMovie**, then click **frame 1** on the layer to select the frame.

4. Click **Window** on the menu bar, then click **Actions** to display the Actions panel.

5. Study the Actions panel. If the Toolbox pane is displayed as shown in Figure 31, then click the **Hide/Display arrow** to hide the pane.

6. Click the **Script Assist button**  to turn on the Script Assist feature if Script Assist is not active.

7. Verify stopMovie:1 (indicating the layer and frame to which the action will be applied) is displayed in the lower-left corner of the Script pane.

8. Click the **Add a new item to the script button** to display the Script categories, point to **Global Functions**, point to **Timeline Control**, then click **stop**, as shown in Figure 32.

9. Click the **Frame view icon**, click **Small**, then click **frame 65** on the stopMovie layer.

10. Insert a **keyframe** in frame 65 on the stopMovie layer, then open the Actions panel if it is no longer open.

TIP You can collapse the Actions panel to view more of the Stage, then expand the Actions panel when needed. Alternately, you can drag the bottom or sides of the Actions panel up to make the panel smaller.

(continued)

Figure 31 *The Actions panel Toolbox pane*

Hide/Display arrow for the Toolbox pane

Figure 32 *Assigning an action to frame 1 on the stopMovie layer*

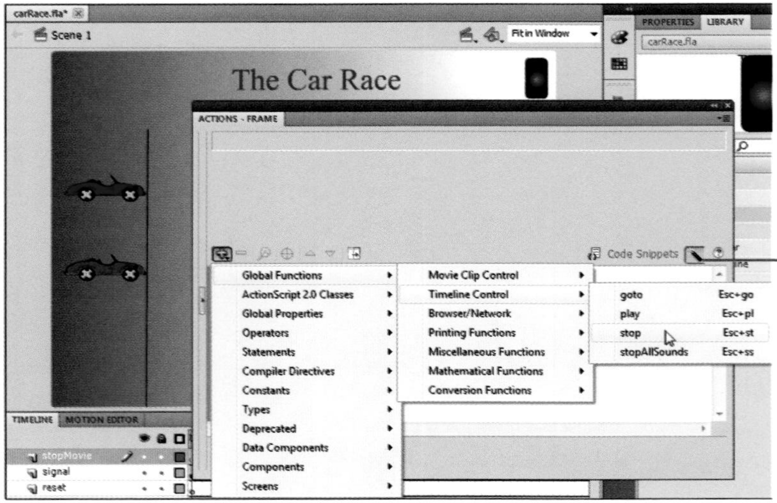

Script Assist on

Figure 33 *Script for the stopMovie layer*

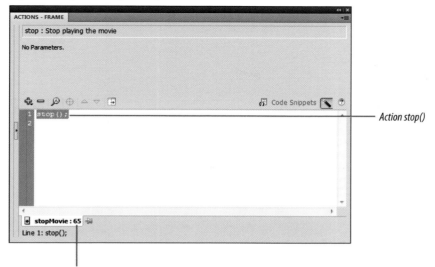

Action stop()

Action assigned to frame 65 of the stopMovie layer

Figure 34 *Assigning an event and an action to a button*

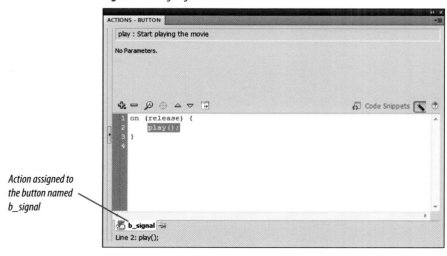

Action assigned to
the button named
b_signal

11. Verify stopMovie: 65 is displayed in the lower-left corner of the Script pane, then repeat Step 8. Compare your screen to Figure 33.

12. Test the movie.

The movie does not play because there is a stop action assigned to frame 1.

13. Close the Flash Player window.

You inserted a layer and assigned a stop action to the first and last frames on the layer.

Assign a play action to a button

1. Click **frame 1** on the signal layer.

2. Move the **Actions panel** to view the signal button on the Stage, if necessary.

3. Click the **Selection tool** ▶ on the Tools panel, then click the **button** on the Stage.

4. Verify b_signal is displayed in the lower left of the Actions panel.

This ensures that the actions specified in the Actions panel will apply to the b_signal button.

5. Click ⬧ to display the Script categories, point to **Global Functions,** point to **Timeline Control,** then click **play.**

Release is the default event for a button, as shown in Figure 34.

6. Click **Control** on the menu bar, point to **Test Movie,** then click **in Flash Professional.**

7. Click the **signal button** to play the animation.

8. Close the Flash Player window.

You used the Actions panel to assign a play action to a button.

Assign a goto frame action to a button

1. Click **Control** on the menu bar, point to **Test Movie**, then click **in Flash Professional**.

2. Click the **signal button**.

   The movie plays and stops, and the word Reset, which is actually a button, appears.

3. Click the **Reset button** and notice nothing happens because it does not have an action assigned to it.

4. Close the Flash Player window.

5. Click **frame 65** on the reset layer to display the Reset button on the Stage.

   Note: You many need to close and/or move the Actions panel to view the Reset button on the Stage.

6. Click the **Reset button** on the Stage to select it.

7. Verify b_reset is displayed in the lower left of the Actions panel.

8. Verify Script Assist in the Actions panel is active , click ⬚, point to **Global Functions**, point to **Timeline Control**, click **goto**, then verify Frame 1 is specified, as shown in Figure 35.

9. Click **Control** on the menu bar, point to **Test Movie**, then click **in Flash Professional**.

10. Click the **signal button** to start the movie, then when the movie stops, click the **Reset button**.

11. Close the Flash Player window.

You used the Actions panel to assign an action to a button.

Figure 35 *Assigning a goto action to a button*

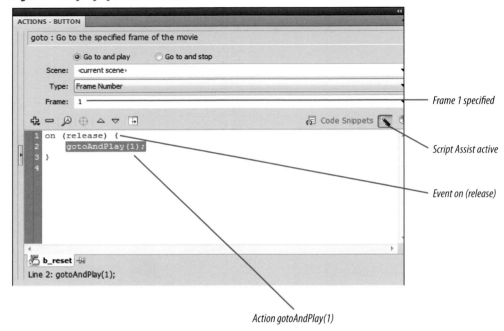

Frame 1 specified

Script Assist active

Event on (release)

Action gotoAndPlay(1)

Figure 36 *Assigning a keyPress action to a button*

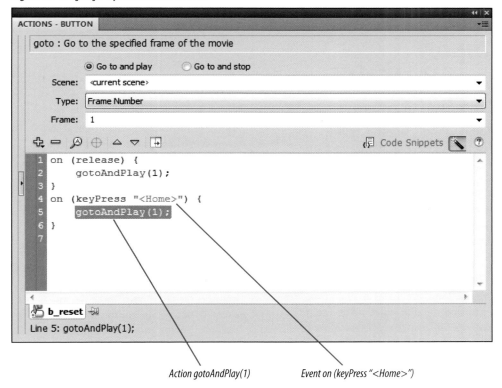

Action gotoAndPlay(1)   Event on (keyPress "<Home>")

Global Functions: Timeline Control and Movie Clip Control

The most common actions for including interactivity in a movie when using ActionScript 2.0 are added using the Global Functions categories Timeline Control and Movie Clip Control. Timeline Control actions focus on controlling the playhead (play, stop), jumping to a specific frame (goto), and stopping sounds (stopAllSounds). These actions are generally assigned to buttons. Movie Clip Control actions focus on manipulating movie clips (startDrag, stopDrag, removeMovieClip, and so on). They also provide mouse (on Release) and keyboard (Key Press) actions that can be assigned to buttons.

Assign a second event to a button

1. Click the **right curly brace** (}) in the Actions panel to highlight the brace in line 3 of the ActionScript.
2. Click 🔄, point to **Global Functions**, point to **Movie Clip Control**, then click **on**.

   The Script Assist window displays several event options. Release is selected.
3. Click the **Release check box** to deselect the option.
4. Click the **Key Press check box** to select it, then press the **[Home] key** on the keyboard.

TIP If your keyboard does not have a [Home] key, use [fn]+[←] (Mac) or one of the function keys (Win) to complete the steps.

5. Click 🔄, point to **Global Functions**, point to **Timeline Control**, then click **goto**.

   The ActionScript now indicates that pressing the [Home] key will cause the playhead to go to frame 1, as shown in Figure 36.

   The Reset button can now be activated by clicking it or by pressing the [Home] key.
6. Click **File** on the menu bar, point to **Publish Preview**, then click **Default – (HTML)**.

   The movie opens in your default browser.

   Note: If a warning message opens, follow the messages to allow blocked content.
7. Click the **signal button** to start the movie, then when the movie stops, press the **[Home] key**.
8. Close the browser window, close the Actions panel, then save and close the movie.

You added a keypress event that triggers a goto frame action.

Import GRAPHICS

What You'll Do

In this lesson, you will import and work with bitmap and vector graphics.

Understanding Graphic Types

Flash provides excellent drawing tools, which allow you to create various objects that can be changed into symbols. In addition, you can import graphics and other assets, such as photographs and sounds. There are two types of graphic files, bitmap graphics and vector graphics. They are distinguished by the way in which the image is represented.

Bitmap images are made up of a group of tiny dots of color called **pixels** (picture elements). Bitmap graphics are often used with photographic images because they can represent subtle gradients in color. However, one disadvantage of bitmap graphics is the inability to enlarge the graphic without distorting the image. This is because both the computer screen's resolution (pixels per inch) and the number of pixels making up the image are a fixed number. So, when you enlarge an image each pixel must increase in size to fill the larger image dimensions. This causes the pixels to display jagged edges, as shown in Figure 37.

Vector graphics represent an image as a geometric shape made up of lines and arcs that are combined to create various shapes, such as circles and rectangles. This is similar to Flash drawings that include strokes and fills. Flash drawing tools create vector graphics. One advantage of vector graphics is that they can be resized without distorting the image. The reason is that the geometric shapes are based on mathematical models that are recalculated when the image is resized. Figure 38 shows an example of a vector graphic before and after resizing. Vector graphics are best used for drawings rather than for images requiring photographic quality.

There are several programs that allow you to create and edit graphics including Adobe Illustrator, Fireworks, and Photoshop. There are also clip art and stock photograph collections that are available online. Filename extensions identify the file type. For example, .jpg, .tif, .bmp, and .gif are file formats for bitmap graphics; while .ai is a vector file format.

Importing and Editing Graphics

Once you have identified the graphic you would like to include in a Flash document, you can use the Import feature to bring the graphic into Flash. The process for importing is to select the Import command from the File menu and specify where to import (Stage or Library). Then you navigate to the location where the file is stored and select it. After importing a vector graphic you can work with it as you would any graphic. Because bitmap graphics are not easy to edit in Flash, you may want to use another program, like Photoshop, to obtain the desired size, color, and other enhancements before importing the graphic.

Figure 37 *Bitmap graphic enlarged*

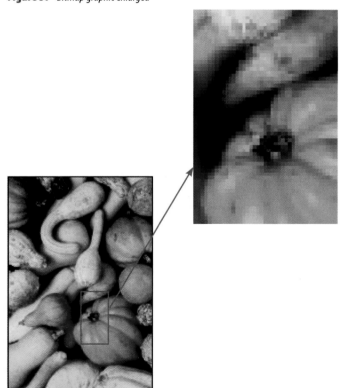

Figure 38 *Vector graphic enlarged*

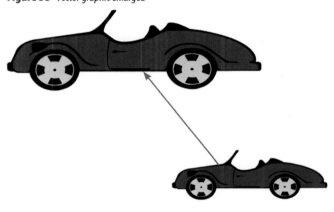

Import graphics

1. Start a new Flash document, then save it as **sailing.fla**.

2. Click **File** on the menu bar, point to **Import**, then click **Import to Library**.

3. Navigate to the folder where your Data Files are stored, click **islandview.jpg**, then click **Open**.

   Islandview.jpg is a digital photo that was edited in Photoshop and saved as a .jpg file.

4. Display the Library panel and notice the icon used for bitmap graphics.

5. Drag the **islandview icon** to the Stage, then lock the layer.

6. Click **File** on the menu bar, point to **Import**, then click **Import to Library**.

7. Navigate to the folder where your Data Files are stored, then click **sailboat.ai**.

   This graphic was created using Adobe Illustrator and is made up of several layers.

8. Click **Open**.

   A dialog box appears asking you to choose the layers to import. All layers are selected by default.

9. Click **OK**.

   The graphic is added to the Library panel as a symbol.

10. Add a new layer to the Timeline, click **frame 1** on the layer, then drag the **sailboat icon** to the Stage, as shown in Figure 39.

    (continued)

Figure 39 *Positioning the sailboat image on the Stage*

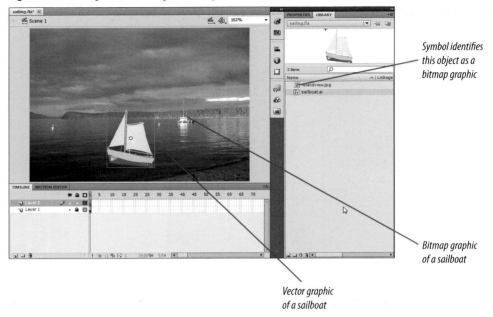

Symbol identifies this object as a bitmap graphic

Bitmap graphic of a sailboat

Vector graphic of a sailboat

Figure 40 *Changing the color of the sail*

Figure 41 *Rotating and skewing the sailboat image*

11. Click **Modify** on the menu bar, click **Break apart**, then repeat this step until the dotted pattern that indicates the image is no longer a symbol appears.

12. Click the **Selection tool** , then click a blank area of the Pasteboard.

13. Click the **left sail**, set the **Fill color icon** to the **rainbow pattern** to change the sail color, as shown in Figure 40.

    Hint: The rainbow color is found at the bottom of the palette for the Fill Color tool.

14. Use the **Selection tool** to drag a **marquee** around the entire sailboat to select it, then convert the image to a graphic symbol named **rainbowSail**.

15. Display the Properties panel, verify the Lock icon is not broken, then change the width of the boat to **60**.

16. Click the **Zoom tool** on the Tools panel, click the **sailboat** twice, then scroll as needed to view each sailboat.

    Notice how the bitmap photograph becomes distorted, while the vector sailboat does not.

17. Change the view to **Fit in Window**.

18. Click the **Free Transform tool** , click the **Rotate and Skew option** skew the sailboat slightly to the left, verify the Lock icon is not broken, change the width of the boat to **60**, then position the sailboat as shown in Figure 41.

19. Test the movie, close the Flash Player window, then save your work and exit Flash.

You imported a bitmap and a vector graphic, and edited the vector graphic.

Create a symbol.

1. Start Flash, open fl3_3.fla, then save it as **skillsDemo3.fla**. This document consists of a single object that was created using the Flash drawing tools.
2. Use the Selection tool to drag a marquee around the ball to select it.
3. Convert the ball to a graphic symbol with the name **g_beachBall**.
4. Double-click the g_beachBall symbol on the Library panel to open the edit window, change the fill color to a rainbow gradient, add a text block that sits on top of the ball with the words **BEACH BALL** (see Figure 42), formated with white, Times New Roman, 12-pt, bold, then click Scene 1 to return to the main Timeline.
5. With the ball selected, create a motion tween animation that moves the ball from the left edge of the Stage to the right edge of the Stage.
6. Use the Selection tool to drag the middle of the motion path up to near the middle of the Stage to create an arc.
7. Select the last frame of the animation on the Timeline and set Rotate to 1 time in the Rotation area of the Properties panel.
8. Play the movie.
   The ball should move across the Stage in an arc and spin at the same time.
9. Lock the beachBall spin layer.

Create and edit an instance.

1. Insert a new layer and name it **redBall**.
2. Click frame 1 on the redBall layer, then drag the g_beachBall symbol from the Library panel so it is on top of the ball on the Stage.

3. Use the arrow keys as needed to align the ball so that it covers the ball on the Stage.
4. With the ball selected, break apart the object.
5. Change the fill color of the ball to a red gradient and change the text to **RED BALL**.
6. Insert a new layer and name it **greenBall**.
7. Click frame 12 on the greenBall layer, then insert a keyframe.
8. Drag the g_beachBall symbol from the Library panel so it is on top of the ball that is near the middle of the Stage. (*Note*: Align only the balls, not the text.)
9. With the ball selected, break apart the object and change the fill color of the ball to a green gradient and the text to **GREEN BALL**.
10. Move the beachBall spin layer to above the other layers.
11. Insert a new layer and name it **title.**
12. Click frame 1 on the title layer, create a text block at the top middle of the Stage with the words **BeachBall Spin** using Arial as the font, blue as the color, and 20-pt as the font size.
13. Insert a new layer above the title layer and name it **titleBkgnd**.
14. Draw a primitive rectangle with a corner radius of 10, a medium gray fill (#999999) and no stroke that covers the BeachBall Spin title text.
15. Verify the rectangle is selected, convert it to a graphic symbol, then name it **g_Bkgnd**.
16. Move the title layer so it is above the titleBkgnd layer.
17. Play the movie, then save your work.

Create a folder in the Library panel.

1. Click the New Folder button at the bottom of the Library panel to create a new folder.
2. Name the folder **Graphics**, then move the two graphic symbols to the Graphics folder.
3. Expand the Graphics folder.
4. Rename the g_Bkgnd symbol to **g_titleBkgnd** in the Library panel.
5. Save your work.

Create a button.

1. Insert a new layer above the title layer and name it **startButton**.
2. Click frame 1 of the new layer, then drag the g_titleBkgnd symbol from the Library panel to the bottom center of the Stage.
3. Create a text block with the word **Start** formatted with white, bold, 20-pt Arial, then center the text block on top of the g_titleBkgnd object.
4. Select the rectangle and the text. (*Hint*: Drag a marquee around both objects or click the Selection tool, press and hold [Shift], then click each object.)
5. Convert the selected objects to a button symbol and name it **b_start**.
6. Create a new folder named **Buttons** in the Library panel and move the b_start button symbol to the folder.
7. Open the Buttons folder, then display the edit window for the b_start button.
8. Insert a keyframe in the Over frame.
9. Select the text and change the color to a lighter shade of gray than the background rectangle.
10. Insert a keyframe in the Down frame.

Working with Symbols and Interactivity

11. Select the text and change the color to blue.
12. Insert a keyframe in the Hit frame.
13. Draw a rectangular object that covers the button area for the Hit state.
14. Click Scene 1 to exit the edit window and return to the main Timeline.
15. Save your work.

Test a button.

1. Turn on Enable Simple Buttons.
2. Point to the button and notice the color change.
3. Click the button and notice the other color change.

Stop a movie.

1. Insert a new layer and name it **stopMovie.**
2. Insert a keyframe in frame 24 on the new layer.
3. With frame 24 selected, display the Actions panel.
4. Assign a stop action to the frame.
5. Click frame 1 on the stopMovie layer.
6. Assign a stop action to frame 1.
7. Save your work.

Assign a goto action to a button.

1. Click Control on the menu bar, then click Enable Simple Buttons to turn off this feature.
2. Use the Selection tool to select the Start button on the Stage.
3. Use Script Assist in the Actions panel to assign an event and a goto action to the button. (*Hint*: Refer to the section on assigning a goto action as needed.)
4. Test the movie.

Import a graphic.

1. Import BeachScene.jpg from the drive and folder where your Data Files are stored to the Library panel.
2. Insert a new layer and name the layer **backDrop.**
3. Select frame 1 on the backDrop layer, then drag the BeachScene image to the Stage.
4. Convert the BeachScene image to a graphic symbol with the name **g_beachScene**.

5. Move the backDrop layer to the bottom of the Timeline.
6. Move the graphic symbols to the Graphics folder in the Library panel.
7. Test the movie.
8. Save your work, then compare your image to Figure 42.
9. Exit Flash.

Figure 42 *Completed Skills Review*

The Ultimate Tours travel company has asked you to design a sample navigation scheme for its website. The company wants to see how its home page will link with one of its main categories (Treks). Figure 43 shows a sample home page and Treks screen. Using the figures or the home page you created in Chapter 2 as a guide, you will add a Treks screen and link it to the home page. (*Hint*: Assume that all of the drawings on the home page are on frame 1, unless noted.)

1. Open ultimateTours2.fla (the file you created in Chapter 2 Project Builder 1), then save it as **ultimateTours3.fla**. (*Note*: If you create a new file, you must create an ActionScript 2.0 file.)
2. Insert a layer above the Subheading layer and name it **logo**.
3. Import the UTLogo.jpg file from the drive and folder where your Data Files are stored to the Library panel.
4. Select frame 1 on the logo layer and drag the logo image to the upper-left corner of the Stage.
5. Select the logo and convert it to a graphic symbol with the name **g_UTLogo**.

6. Set the last frame of the movie by inserting a keyframe on a frame on the Logo layer at least five frames farther along the Timeline, then lock the logo layer. (*Note*: You see the logo because the keyframe you inserted on the last frame of the movie ensures everything on this layer appears on this last frame.)
7. Select the layer that the Ultimate Tours text block is on, then insert a keyframe on the last frame of the movie. (*Hint*: This should be the same frame number as the frame you set as the last frame of the movie in Step 6. *Note*: You see the logo and the heading Ultimate Tours because the keyframe you inserted on the last frame of the movie ensures everything on this layer appears on this last frame.)
8. Insert a new layer, name it **treks headings**, insert a keyframe on the last frame of the movie, then create the Treks screen shown in Figure 43, except for the home button. (*Note*: The underline was created using the Line tool.)
9. Convert the Treks graphic on the home page to a button symbol named **b_treks**, then edit the symbol so that different colors appear for the different states and be sure to set a hit area.

10. Assign a goto action to the Treks button that jumps the playhead to the Treks screen when the Treks button is clicked. (*Hint*: You need to use ActionScript 2.0 to complete the steps that follow. You can check the ActionScript version by selecting Publish Settings from the File menu and clicking the Flash tab.)
11. Insert a new layer and name it **stopMovie**. Add stop actions that cause the movie to stop after displaying the home page and after displaying the Treks page. Make sure there is a keyframe in the last frame of the stopMovie layer.
12. Insert a new layer and name it **homeButton**, insert a keyframe on the last frame of the movie, then draw the home button image with the Home text.
13. Convert the image to a button symbol named **b_home**, then edit the symbol so that different colors appear for the different states. Assign a goto action for the Home button that jumps the movie to frame 1.
14. Test the movie.
15. Save your work, then compare your web pages to the samples shown in Figure 43.

Figure 43 *Sample completed Project Builder 1*

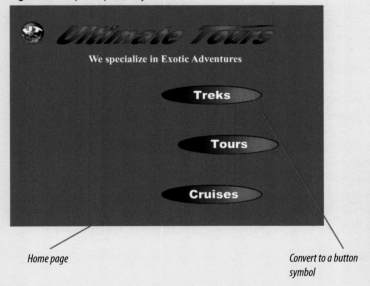

Home page

Convert to a button symbol

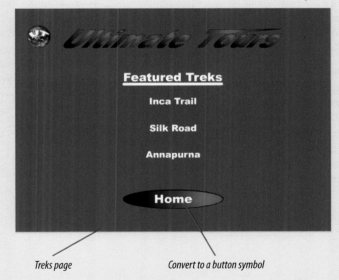

Treks page

Convert to a button symbol

You have been asked to assist the International Student Association (ISA). The association sponsors a series of monthly events, each focusing on a different culture from around the world. The events are led by a guest speaker who makes a presentation, followed by a discussion. The events are free and they are open to everyone. ISA would like you to design a Flash movie that will be used with its website. The movie starts by providing information about the series, and then provides a link to the upcoming event. Refer to Figure 44 as you create the Flash movie.

1. Open a new Flash ActionScript 2.0 document and save it as **isa3.fla**.
2. Create an initial Information screen with general information about the association's series, then insert a keyframe on the last frame of the movie so that the title and subtitle appear on all screens. The title and subtitle should appear together on one layer. Be sure to add a keyframe on this layer in the last frame of this movie so that the title and subtitle appear on every frame of the movie. (*Hint*: This movie will use a minimum of three screens so consider setting the last frame of the movie on frame 5 in case you find you need more than three frames.)
3. On a new layer, assign an action to frame 1 that stops the movie.
4. Create two more screens: a next event screen starting in frame 2 on a new layer that presents information about the next event and a series screen starting in frame 3 on a new layer that lists the series (all nine events for the school year—September through May). (*Hint*: Be sure to insert keyframes in frames 2 and 3 of the new layers when adding these screens.)
5. Create a button on the general information screen that jumps the movie to the next event screen, and create a second button on the information screen that jumps the movie to the series screen. For each button you create, specify different colors for each state of each button.
6. On the next event screen, create a Return button that jumps the movie back to the general information

screen. Be sure to specify different colors for each state when you create the Return button.
7. Copy an instance of the button you created in Step 6 to the series screen. (*Hint*: You can select the button, select Copy from the Edit menu, display the series screen and select Copy in Place from the Edit menu. Alternately, you can drag an instance of the button from the Library panel to the series screen.)
8. On the next event screen, copy an instance of the button you created in Step 5 that jumps the movie to the series screen.
9. On the series screen, copy an instance of the button you created in Step 5 that jumps the movie to the next event screen.
10. Add an action that stops the movie on the next event screen, and another action that stops the movie on the series screen. (*Hint*: Place the stop actions on the same layer as the stop action created in Step 3.)
11. Test the movie.
12. Save your work, then compare your movie to the sample shown in Figure 44.

Figure 44 *Sample completed Project Builder 2*

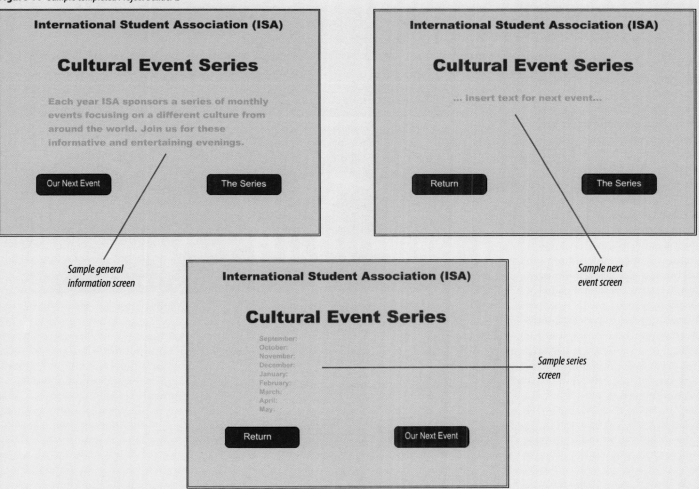

Figure 45 shows the home page of a website. Study the figure and complete the following questions. For each question, indicate how you determined your answer.

1. Connect to the Internet and go to *www.zoo.org*. Notice that this website has images that change as you visit the website.
2. Open a document in a word processor or open a new Flash document, save the file as **dpc3**, then answer the following questions. (*Hint*: Use the Text tool in Flash.)
   - Whose website is this?
   - What is the goal(s) of the site?
   - Who is the target audience?
   - What treatment ("look and feel") is used?
   - What are the design layout guidelines being used (balance, movement, and so on)?
   - What may be animated in this home page?
   - Do you think this is an effective design for the company, its products, and its target audience? Why or why not?
   - What suggestions would you make to improve the design, and why?

Figure 45 *Design Project*

Courtesy of www.zoo.org

This is a continuation of the Chapter 2 Portfolio Project, which is the development of a personal portfolio. The home page has several categories, including the following:

- Personal data
- Contact information
- Previous employment
- Education
- Samples of your work

In this project, you will create a button that will be used to link the home page of your portfolio to the animations page. Next, you will create another button to start the animation.

1. Open portfolio2.fla (the file you created in Portfolio Project, Chapter 2), then save it as **portfolio3.fla**.
2. Unlock the layers as needed.
3. Insert a new layer, name it **sampleAnimations**, then insert a keyframe in frame 2.
4. Create a Sample Animations screen that has a text block with an oval background and the words **Sample Animations** at the top of the Stage, then add another text block and oval background with the word **Tweened**. (*Note*: This screen will have several animation samples added to it later.)
5. Insert a new layer, name it **home button**, then insert a keyframe in frame 2.
6. Add a text block that says **Home** and has an oval background at the bottom of the Stage.
7. Insert a new layer, name it **tweenedAnimation**, then insert a keyframe in frame 3.

8. Create an animation(s) of your choice using objects you draw or import, or objects from the Library panel of another document. (*Note*: To create a motion tween animation when starting in a frame other than frame 1, you need to specify the beginning frame of the animation by inserting a keyframe in the starting frame and you need to specify the ending frame of the animation by inserting a keyframe before repositioning the object on the Stage. *Hint*: To create more than one animation that plays at the same time, put each animation on its own layer, such as tweenedAnimationRedCar and tweenedAnimationBlueCar.)
9. Insert a new layer, name it **animationHeading**, then insert a keyframe in frame 3.
10. Add a heading to the screen used for the animation(s) that describes the animation(s).
11. On the Sample Animations screen, convert the Tweened and Home text blocks into button symbols, then edit each symbol so that different colors appear for the different states. For the Tweened button, assign an action that jumps to the frame that plays an animation. For the Home button, assign an action to the Home button that jumps to the frame that displays My Portfolio. (*Hint*: You need to use ActionScript 2.0. You can set the ActionsScript version by selecting Publish Settings from the File menu, clicking the Flash tab and specifying ActionScript 2.0.)
12. Change the Animations graphic on the home page to a button, then edit the symbol so that different colors appear for the different states. Assign an action to the Animations button that jumps to the Sample Animations screen.
13. Insert a new layer, then name it **stopMovie**. Insert keyframes and assign stop actions to the appropriate frames.
14. Test the movie.
15. Save your work, then compare your movie to the sample shown in Figure 46.

Figure 46 *Sample completed Portfolio Project*

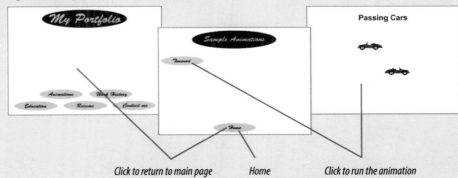

Click to return to main page   Home   Click to run the animation

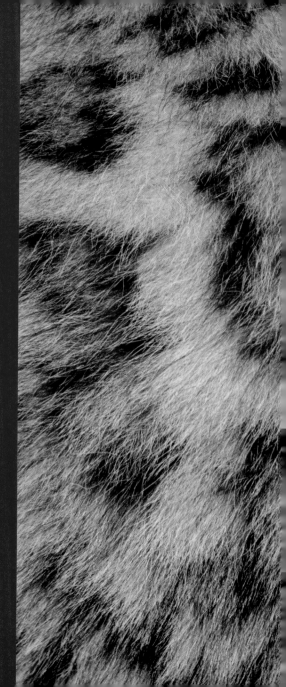

CHAPTER 4 CREATING
ANIMATIONS

1. Create motion tween animations

2. Create classic tween animations

3. Create frame-by-frame animations

4. Create shape tween animations

5. Create movie clips

6. Animate text

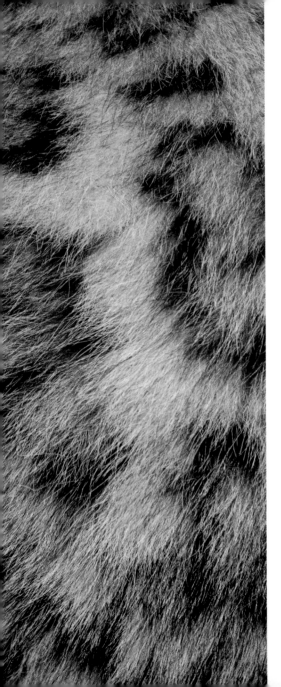

CHAPTER 4 CREATING
ANIMATIONS

Introduction

Animation can be an important part of your application or website, whether the focus is on e-commerce (attracts attention and provides product demonstrations), education (simulates complex processes such as DNA replication), or entertainment (provides interactive games).

How Does Animation Work?

The perception of motion in an animation is actually an illusion. Animation is like a motion picture in that it is made up of a series of still images. Research has found that our eye captures and holds an image for one-tenth of a second before processing another image. By retaining each impression for one-tenth of a second, we perceive a series of rapidly displayed still images as a single, moving image. This phenomenon is known as **persistence of vision** and it provides the basis for the frame rate in animations. Frame rates of 10–12 frames-per-second (fps) generally provide an acceptably smooth computer-based animation. Lower frame rates result in a jerky image, while frame

rates over 30 fps may result in a blurred image. In addition, higher frame rates may increase file size because more frames are needed for a 5 second animation running at 30 fps than at 10 fps. After creating an animation you can experiment with various frame rates to obtain the desired effect. Flash uses a default frame rate of 24 fps.

Flash Animation

Creating animation is one of the most powerful features of Flash, yet developing basic animations is a simple process. Flash allows you to create animations that can move and rotate an object around the Stage, as well as change its size, shape, or color. You can also use the animation features in Flash to create special effects, such as an object zooming or fading in and out. You can combine animation effects so that an object changes shape and color as it moves across the Stage. Animations are created by changing the content of successive frames. Flash provides two animation methods: frame-by-frame animation and tweened animation. Tweened animations can be motion, classic, or shape tweens.

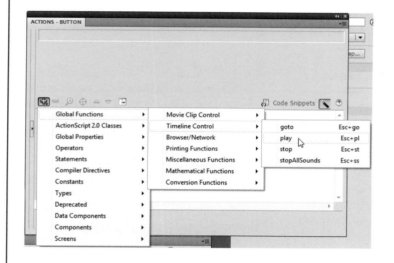

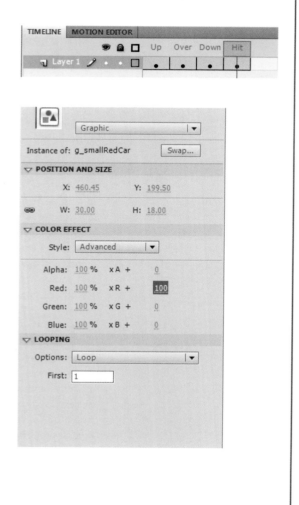

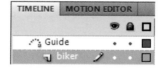

Create Motion Tween
ANIMATIONS

What You'll Do

 In this lesson, you will create and edit motion tween animations.

Understanding Motion Tween Animations

An animation implies some sort of movement in an object. However, the concept of animation is much broader. Objects have specific properties such as position, size, color, and shape. Any change in a property of an object over time (i.e., across frames on the Timeline) can be considered an animation. So, having an object start at the left of the screen in frame 1 and then having it move across the screen and end up at the right side in frame 10 would be a change in the position property of the object. Each of the in-between frames (2-9) would show the position of the object as it moves across the screen. In a motion tween animation, you specify the position of the object in the beginning and ending frames and Flash fills in the in-between frames, a process known as tweening. Fortunately, you can change several properties with one motion tween.

For example, you could have a car move across the screen and, at the same time, you could have the size of the car change to give the impression of the car moving away from the viewer. The process for creating a motion tween animation is to select the frame and layer where the animation will start. If necessary, insert a keyframe (by default, frame 1 of each layer has a keyframe). Select the object on the Stage, then select the Motion Tween command from the Insert menu. If the object is not already a symbol, you will be asked if you want to convert it to a symbol. You must convert the object to a symbol if prompted because only symbols and text fields can have a motion tween applied. Then you select the ending frame and make any changes to the object, such as moving it to another location or resizing it. After you make the change, a keyframe automatically appears in the ending frame you selected. When you create a motion tween, a tween span appears on the Timeline.

Tween Spans

Figure 1 shows a motion tween animation of a car that starts in frame 1 and ends in frame 24. The Onion Skin feature is enabled so that outlines of the car are displayed for each frame of the animation in the figure. Notice a blue highlight appears on the Timeline for the frames of the animation.

The blue highlighted area is called the tween or motion span. The length of the motion tween is determined by the last frame in the movie or by other keyframes on the layer. (*Note*: The default tween span when starting from frame 1 of a new movie is determined by the number of frames in one second of the movie. So, if the frame rate is 24 frames per second, then the span is 24 frames.) You can increase or decrease the number of frames in the span by dragging the end of the span. In addition, you can move the span to a different location on the Timeline, and you can copy the span to have it apply to another object.

Figure 1 *Sample motion tween animation*

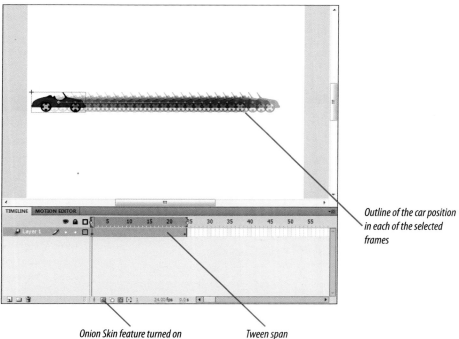

Outline of the car position in each of the selected frames

Onion Skin feature turned on   Tween span

Motion Path

The animation shown in Figure 2 includes a position change (from frame 1 to frame 24); a motion path showing the position change is displayed on the Stage. Each dot on the path corresponds to a frame on the Timeline and indicates the location of the object (in this example, the car) when the frame is played. A motion path can be altered by dragging a point on the path using the Selection tool or by using the Subselection tool to manipulate Bezier handles as shown in Figure 3. In addition, an entire path can be moved around the Stage and reshaped using the Free Transform tool.

Property Keyframes

A keyframe indicates a change in a Flash movie, such as the start or ending of an animation. Motion tween animations use property keyframes that are specific to each property such as a position keyframe, color keyframe, or rotation keyframe. In most cases these are automatically placed on the Timeline as the motion tween animation is created.

Keep in mind:

- Only one object on the Stage can be animated in each tween span.
- You can have multiple motion tween animations playing at the same time if they are on different layers.

- A motion tween is, in essence, an object animation because, while several changes can be made to an object's properties, only one object is animated for each motion tween.
- The types of objects that can be tweened include graphic, button, and movie clip symbols, as well as text fields.
- You can remove a motion tween animation by clicking the tween span on the Timeline and choosing Remove Tween from the Insert menu.

Figure 2 *The motion path*

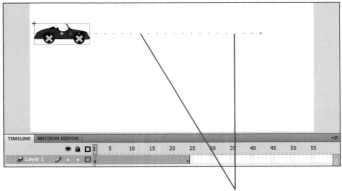

Motion path with dots; each dot corresponds to a frame on the Timeline and shows the location of the car when the frame is played

Figure 3 *Bezier handles used to alter the path*

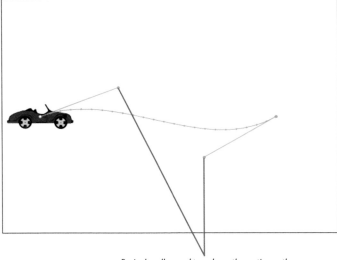

Bezier handles used to reshape the motion path

Creating Animations

Figure 4 *Positioning the car object*

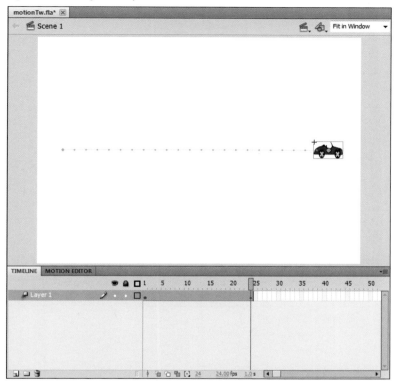

Figure 5 *Changing the end of the tween span*

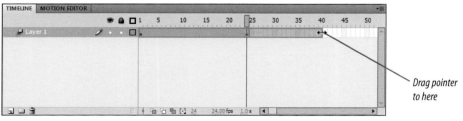

Drag pointer
to here

Create a motion tween animation

1. Open fl4_1.fla from the drive and folder where your Data Files are stored, then save it as **motionTw.fla**.

   This document has one drawn object—a car that has been converted to a symbol.

2. Click the **Selection tool** ▸ on the Tools panel, then click the **car** to select it.

3. Click **Insert** on the menu bar, then click **Motion Tween**.

   Notice the tween span appears on the Timeline. Because you started in frame 1, the number of frames in the span equals the frames per second for the movie.

4. Verify the playhead is on the last frame of the tween span, then drag the **car** to the right side of the Stage, as shown in Figure 4.

   A motion path appears on the Stage with dots indicating the position of the object for each frame. A diamond symbol appears in frame 24, which is the end of the tween span. The diamond symbol is a position keyframe and it is automatically inserted at the end of the tween path.

   Note: The end of this tween span is determined by the document frame rate, which is 24 fps. To see the diamond symbol more clearly, move the playhead.

5. Point to the end of the tween span, when the pointer changes to a double arrow ↔, drag the **tween span** to frame 40, as shown in Figure 5.

   (continued)

6. Click **frame 1** on the Timeline, then press the **period key** to move the playhead one frame at a time and notice the position of the car for each frame.

7. Play the movie, then save your work.

You created a motion tween animation, extended the length of the animation, and viewed the position of the animated object in each frame of the animation.

Edit a motion path

1. Click the **Selection tool** on the Tools panel, then click a blank area of the Stage.

2. Click **frame 1** on Layer 1.

3. Point to the middle of the motion path, as shown in Figure 6.

4. When the pointer changes to a pointer with an arc, drag the **pointer** down, as shown in Figure 7.

(continued)

Figure 6 *Pointing to the middle of the path*

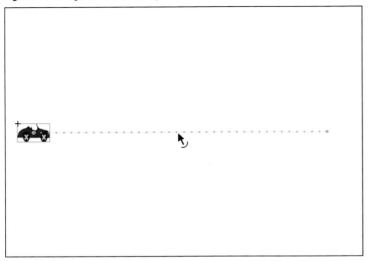

Figure 7 *Dragging the motion path down*

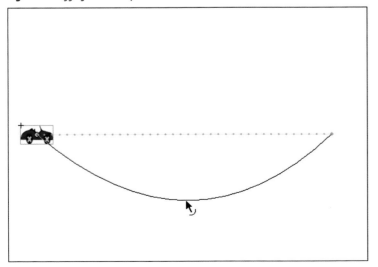

Figure 8 *Displaying the Bezier handles*

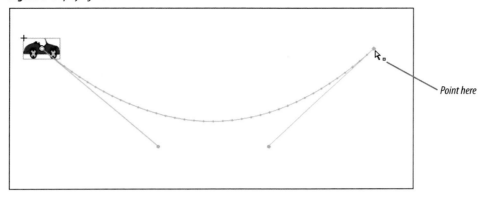

Point here

Figure 9 *Using the handles to alter the shape of the path*

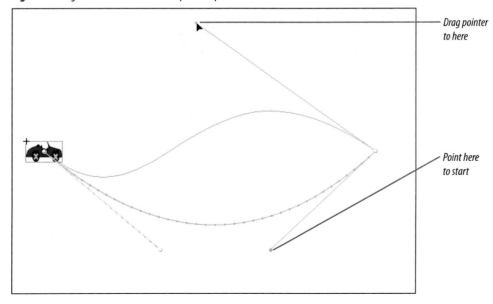

Drag pointer
to here

Point here
to start

5. Play the movie, then click **frame 1** on Layer 1.

6. Click the **Subselection tool** ▷ on the Tools panel, point to the end of the motion path, then, when the pointer changes into an arrow with a small square ▷ , click the end of path to display Bezier handles, as shown in Figure 8.

TIP Before using the Subselection tool to display the Bezier handles, you must use the Selection tool to drag the motion path, even if only slightly.

7. Point to the **lower-right handle**, then when the pointer changes to a delta symbol ▶, drag the **handle** up and toward the center of the Stage to form a horizontal S shape, as shown in Figure 9.

8. Play the movie, then save your work.

You edited a motion path by using the Selection tool to drag the path and by using the Subselection tool to display and reposition Bezier handles.

Change the ease value of an animation

1. Play the movie and notice that the car moves at a constant speed.

2. Display the **Properties panel**, then click **frame 1** on Layer 1.

3. Point to the **Ease value**, when the pointer changes to a hand with a double arrow 🖑, drag the 🖑 **pointer** to the right to set the value at **100**, as shown in Figure 10.

4. Click **frame 1** on Layer 1, then play the movie.

   The car starts moving fast and slows down near the end of the animation. Notice the word "out" is displayed next to the ease value on the Properties panel indicating that the object will ease out, slow down, at the end of the animation.

5. Click **frame 1** on Layer 1.

6. Point to the Ease value on the Properties panel, then drag the 🖑 **pointer** to the left to set the value to **−100**.

7. Click **frame 1** on Layer 1, then play the movie.

   The car starts moving slowly and speeds up near the end of the animation. Notice the word "in" is displayed next to the ease value on the Properties panel. Also, notice the dots are grouped closer together at the beginning of the motion path indicating that the object does not move very far in that section of the path.

8. Click **frame 1** on Layer 1, then set the ease value to **0**.

9. Save your work.

You changed the ease out and ease in values of the animation.

Figure 10 *Changing the ease value*

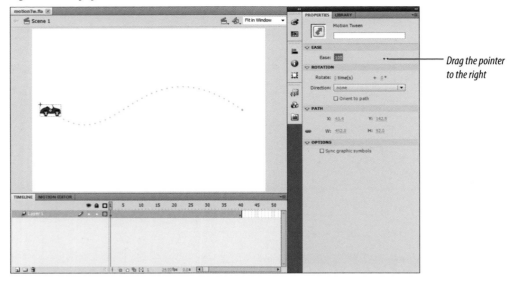

Drag the pointer to the right

Figure 11 *Changing the width of the object*

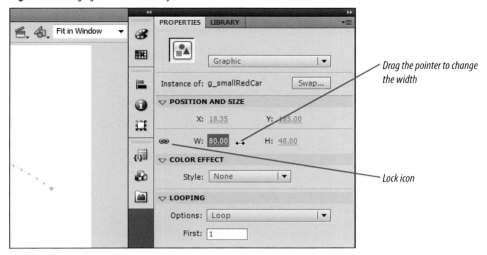

Drag the pointer to change the width

Lock icon

Figure 12 *Using the Free Transform tool to skew the object*

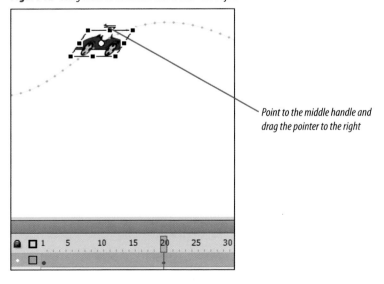

Point to the middle handle and drag the pointer to the right

Resize and reshape an object

1. Verify frame 1 is selected, click the **Selection tool** , then click the **car**.

2. Display the Properties panel, verify the lock icon is unbroken, point to the **W: value**, then, when the pointer changes to a hand with a double arrow , drag the **pointer** to the right to set the value to **80**, as shown in Figure 11.

3. Click the **car**, then play the movie.

4. Click **frame 40** on Layer 1, then click the **car**.

5. Point to the **W: value** on the Properties panel, then, when the pointer changes to a hand with a double arrow , drag the **pointer** to the left to set the value to **30**.

6. Click the **car**, then play the movie.

   The car starts out large and ends up small.

7. Click **frame 20** on Layer 1.

8. Click the **Free Transform tool** on the Tools panel, then click the **Rotate and Skew option** if it is not active.

9. Point to the **top middle handle**, then, when the pointer changes to a double line , drag the **pointer** to the right to skew the object, as shown in Figure 12.

   A keyframe indicating a change in the property (skew) of the object appears in frame 20.

10. Play the movie, use the Undo command on the Edit menu to undo the skew, then save the movie.

    The skew keyframe is removed from frame 20.

    Note: You may have to click the Undo command more than one time to undo the skew.

You resized and skewed a motion tween object.

Create a color effect

1. Click the **Selection tool** on the Tools panel.

2. Click **frame 40** on Layer 1.

3. Click the **car** to select it.

4. Click **COLOR EFFECT** to display that area if it is not open, then click **Style list arrow** in the COLOR EFFECT area of the Properties panel.

5. Click **Alpha**, then drag the **slider** to set the value to **0%**, as shown in Figure 13.

6. Play the movie.

   Notice the car slowly becomes transparent.

7. Reset the Alpha to **100%**.

8. Click **frame 40** on Layer 1.

9. Click the **car** to select it.

10. Click the **Style list arrow** in the COLOR EFFECT area of the Properties panel.

11. Click **Advanced**, then set the x R + value for Red to **100**, as shown in Figure 14.

12. Click the **car**, then play the movie.

    Notice the car slowly changes to a new shade of red. Because the car is a symbol, it is one part (not a composite of pieces). As a result, changes made to the color value affect the entire car.

13. Set the x R + value back to **0**, then save your work.

You changed the alpha and advanced color option for an object.

Figure 13 *Setting the Alpha (transparency) value*

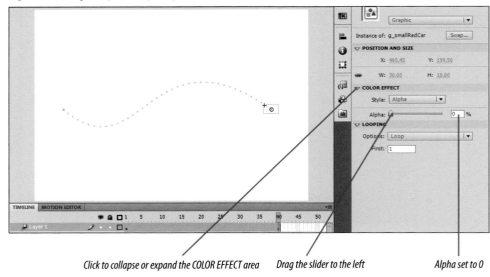

Click to collapse or expand the COLOR EFFECT area   Drag the slider to the left   Alpha set to 0

Figure 14 *Changing a color value for the object*

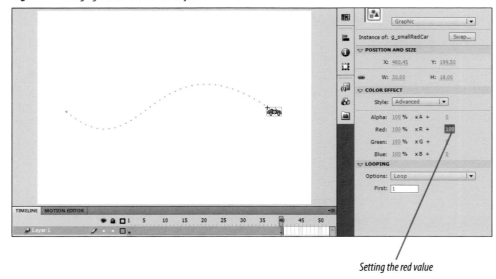

Setting the red value

Figure 15 *Aligning the car to the path*

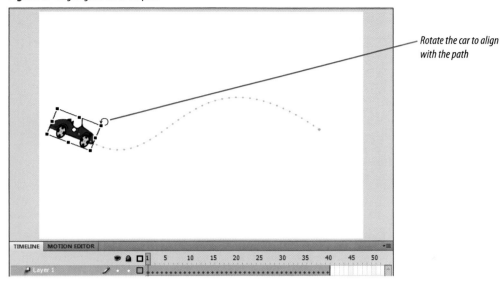

Rotate the car to align with the path

Figure 16 *Aligning the car to the end of the motion path*

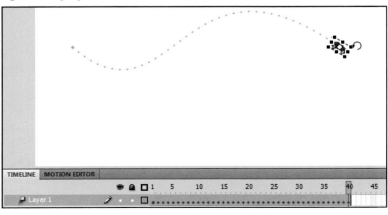

Orient an object to a path

1. Play the movie.

   Notice the car follows the path but it is not oriented to the path.

2. Click **frame 1** on Layer 1.

3. Click the **Orient to path check box** in the ROTATION area of the Properties panel.

4. Click the **Free Transform tool** on the Tools panel, then click the **Rotate and Skew option** near the bottom of the Tools panel if it is not active.

5. Point to the upper-right corner of the car, then, when the pointer changes into a circular arrow, rotate the front of the car so that it aligns with the path, as shown in Figure 15.

6. Click **frame 40** on Layer 1, then rotate the car so that its back end aligns with the path, as shown in Figure 16.

7. Play the movie.

   The car is oriented to the path.

   Notice the diamond symbols in the frames on Layer 1. These are rotation keyframes that indicate the object will change in each frame as it rotates to stay oriented to the path.

8. Test the movie, then close the Flash Player window.

9. Save your work, then close the document.

You oriented an object to a motion path and aligned the object with the path in the first and last frames of the motion tween.

Copy a motion path

1. Open fl4_2.fla, save it as **tweenEdits.fla**, then play the movie.

2. Insert a **new layer** and name it **biker2**, then click **frame 1** on the biker2 layer.

3. Click the Selection tool ![selection tool icon] on the Tools panel, then drag the **g_biker symbol** from the Library panel to the Stage, as shown in Figure 17.

4. Click any frame on the tween span on the biker layer.

5. Click **Edit** on the menu bar, point to **Timeline**, then click **Copy Motion**.

6. Click the new instance of the biker, click **Edit** on the menu bar, point to **Timeline**, then click **Paste Motion**.

7. Play the movie, then hide the biker layer.

8. Click **frame 1** on the biker2 layer, click the **Free Transform tool** ![free transform icon] on the Tools panel, then click the **path** to select it, as shown in Figure 18.

9. Click **Modify** on the menu bar, point to **Transform**, then click **Flip Horizontal**.

(continued)

Figure 17 *Dragging the biker symbol to the Stage*

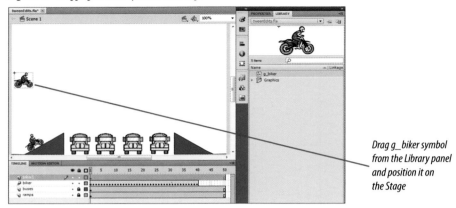

Drag g_biker symbol from the Library panel and position it on the Stage

Figure 18 *Selecting the path to display the handles*

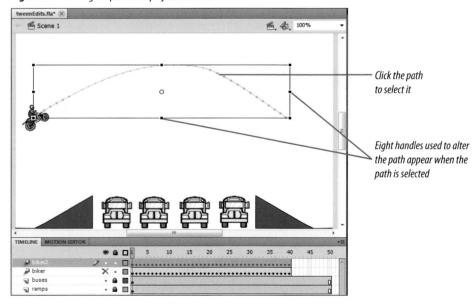

Click the path to select it

Eight handles used to alter the path appear when the path is selected

Creating Animations

Figure 19 *Positioning the path*

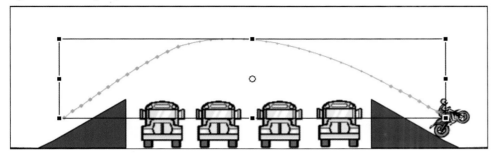

Figure 20 *Aligning the biker to the path*

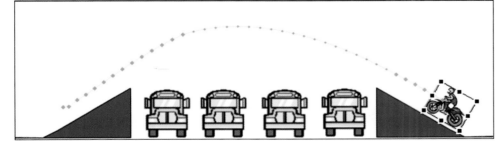

10. Use the arrow keys on the keyboard to position the path, as shown in Figure 19.
11. Click the **biker object**, click **Modify** on the menu bar, point to **Transform**, then click **Flip Horizontal**.
12. Use the Free Transform tool 🔲 and the arrow keys to align the biker, as shown in Figure 20.
13. Play the movie, then save your work.

You copied a motion path to another object.

Rotate an object

1. Click **frame 1** on the biker2 layer, then display the Properties panel.

2. Point to the **Rotate times value** in the ROTATION area of the Properties panel, then, when the pointer changes to a hand with a double arrow 🖑, drag the 🖑 **pointer** to the right to set the count to **1**, as shown in Figure 21.

3. Click the **Direction list arrow**, click **CW** (Clockwise), click **frame 1** on the biker2 layer, then play the movie.

   The biker object rotates one time in a clockwise direction. Look at the Timeline. Notice some of the keyframes have been removed from the motion tween span. This is because, as the biker rotates, he is no longer oriented to the path. Motion tweens do not allow an object to be rotated and oriented to a path simultaneously because orienting an object to a path rotates the object in each frame along the path. You can use a classic tween to rotate and orient an object to a path at the same time. The remaining keyframes at the beginning and ending of the tween span are used to align the biker to the ramp.

4. Click **frame 1** on the biker2 layer, set the rotation count to **2**, set the Direction to **CCW** (Counter Clockwise), then play the movie.

5. Click **Orient to path** to select it.

   The rotate value is automatically set to no times (indicated by a 0), as shown in Figure 22.

6. Play the movie, then save your work.

You caused an object to rotate by setting the rotate value and specifying a rotation direction.

Figure 21 *Changing the rotate value*

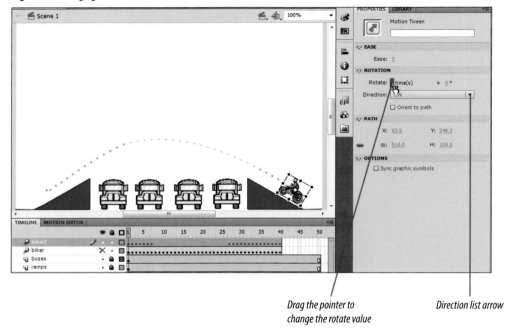

Drag the pointer to change the rotate value

Direction list arrow

Figure 22 *The Properties panel showing that the rotate value is set to 0 times*

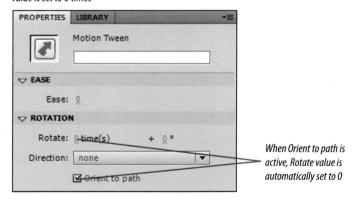

When Orient to path is active, Rotate value is automatically set to 0

Figure 23 *Timeline showing the motion tween removed*

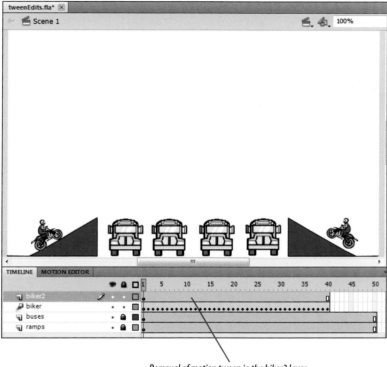

Removal of motion tween in the biker2 layer removes the blue highlight on the Timeline

Remove a motion tween

1. Unhide the **biker layer**, then play the movie.

2. Click **frame 1** on the biker2 layer to select the tween span on the Timeline.

   Note: You can click any frame on the tween span to select it.

3. Click **Insert** on the menu bar, then click **Remove Tween**.

4. Click **frame 1** on the buses layer, then notice that the blue highlight on the biker2 layer is gone, as shown in Figure 23.

5. Play the movie and notice that the biker on the biker2 layer is visible but it does not move.

6. Use the Undo command in the Edit menu to undo the Remove Tween process.

   Note: You may need to select the Undo command more than one time.

7. Click **biker2** on the Timeline to select the layer.

8. Click the **Delete icon** 🗑 at the bottom of the Timeline to delete the biker2 layer that includes the motion tween.

9. Test the movie, then close the Flash Player window.

10. Save your work.

You removed an object's motion tween, undid the action, then deleted a layer containing a motion tween.

Work with multiple motion tweens

1. Click frame **40** on the biker layer, then click the **biker** on the Stage.

2. Lock the **biker layer**, then insert a **new layer** above the biker layer and name it **bikeOffStage**.

3. Click frame **40** on the bikeOffStage layer.

4. Click **Insert** on the menu bar, point to **Timeline**, then click **Keyframe**.

5. Drag an instance of the **g_biker symbol** from the Library panel so it is on top of the biker on the Stage, as shown in Figure 24.

6. Use the Free Transform tool 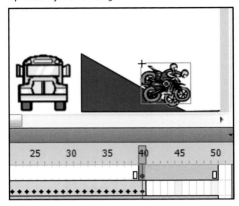 and the arrow keys on the keyboard to align the two biker objects.

7. Click frame **41** on the **bikeOffStage** layer, then insert a **keyframe**.

8. Use the **arrow keys** on the keyboard and the **Free Transform tool** to align the biker with the bottom of the ramp, as shown in Figure 25.

9. Click the **Selection tool** , then click the **biker**.

(continued)

Figure 24 *Placing an instance of the g_biker symbol on top of the object on the Stage*

Figure 25 *Aligning the biker with the ramp*

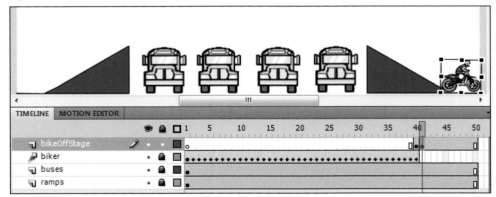

Creating Animations

Figure 26 *Dragging the biker object off the Stage*

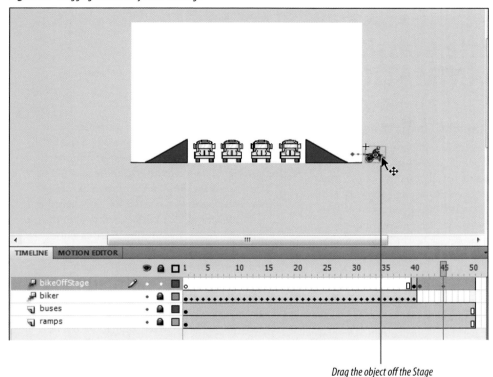

Drag the object off the Stage

10. Click the **View list arrow**, then click **50%**.

11. Click **Insert** on the menu bar, then click **Motion Tween**.

12. Click **frame 45** on the bikeOffStage layer, then drag the **biker** off the Stage, as shown in Figure 26.

13. Test the movie, close the Flash Player window, save your work, then close the document.

You created a second motion tween for the movie.

Create Classic Tween
ANIMATIONS

What You'll Do

 In this lesson, you will create a motion guide and attach an animation to it.

Understanding Classic Tweens

Classic tweens are similar to motion tweens in that you can create animations that change the properties of an object over time. Motion tweens are easier to use and allow the greatest degree of control over tweened animations. Classic tweens are a bit more complex to create, however, they provide certain capabilities that some developers desire. For example, with a motion tween (which consists of one object over the tween span), you can alter the ease value so that an object starts out fast and ends slow. But, with a classic tween, you can alter the ease value so that an object starts out fast, slows down, and then speeds up again. The process for creating a classic tween animation that moves an object is to select the starting frame and, if necessary, insert a keyframe. Next, insert a keyframe at the ending frame, and click anywhere on the layer between the keyframes. Then select classic tween from the Insert menu, select the ending frame, and move the object to the position you want it to be in the ending frame.

Understanding Motion Guides

When you use motion tweening to generate an animation that moves an object, a motion path that shows the movement is automatically created on the Stage. When you use classic tweening, the object moves in a straight line from the beginning location to the ending location on the Stage. There is no path displayed. You can draw a path, called a **motion guide**, that can be used to alter the path of a classic tween animation, as shown in Figure 27. A motion guide is drawn on the motion guide layer with the classic tween animation placed on its own layer beneath a motion guide layer, as shown in Figure 28. The process for creating a motion guide and attaching a classic tween animation to it is:

- Create a classic tween animation.
- Insert a new layer above the classic tween animation layer and change the layer properties to a Guide layer. Drag the classic tween animation layer to the guide layer so that it indents, as shown in Figure 28. This indicates that the classic tween animation layer is associated with the motion guide layer.
- Click the Guide layer and draw a path using the Pen, Pencil, Line, Circle, Rectangle, or Brush tools.
- Attach the object to the path by clicking the first keyframe of the layer that

contains the animation, and then dragging the object by its transformation point to the beginning of the path. Click the end keyframe and then repeat the steps to attach the object to the end of the path.

Depending on the type of object you are animating and the path, you may need to orient the object to the path.

The advantages of using a motion guide are that you can have an object move along any path, including a path that intersects itself, and you can easily change the shape of the path, allowing you to experiment with different motions. A consideration when using a motion guide is that, in some instances,

orienting the object along the path may result in an unnatural-looking animation. You can fix this by stepping through the animation one frame at a time until you reach the frame where the object is positioned poorly. You can then insert a keyframe and adjust the object as desired.

Transformation Point and Registration Point

Each symbol has a transformation point in the form of a circle (O) that is used to orient the object when it is being animated. For example, when you rotate a symbol, the transformation point is the pivot point around which the object rotates.

The transformation point is also the point that snaps to a motion guide, as shown in Figure 27. When attaching an object to a path, you can drag the transformation point to the path. The default position for a transformation point is the center of the object. You can reposition the transformation point while in the symbol edit mode by dragging the transformation point to a different location on the object. Objects also have a registration point (+) that determines the X and Y coordinates of an object on the Stage. The transformation and registration points can overlap—this is displayed as a plus sign within a circle ⊕.

Figure 27 *A motion guide with an object (motorbike) attached*

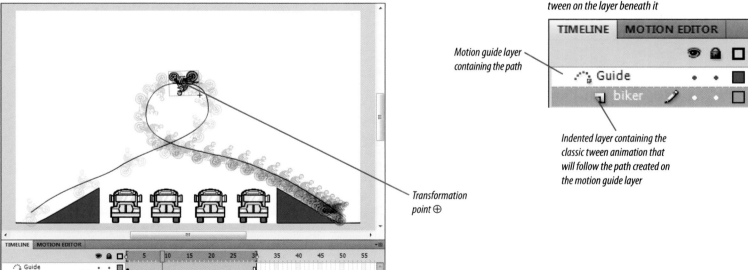

Motion guide layer containing the path

Transformation point ⊕

Figure 28 *A motion guide layer with a classic tween on the layer beneath it*

Indented layer containing the classic tween animation that will follow the path created on the motion guide layer

Create a classic tween animation

1. Open fl4_3.fla, then save it as **cTween.fla**.
2. Insert a **new layer**, then name it **biker**.
3. Click **frame 1** on the biker layer, then drag the **biker symbol** from the Library panel to the Stage, as shown in Figure 29.
4. Click **frame 30** on the biker layer, click **Insert** on the menu bar, point to **Timeline**, then click **Keyframe**.
5. Drag the **biker** to the position shown in Figure 30.
6. Click **frame 2** on the biker layer, click **Insert** on the menu bar, then click **Classic Tween**.

    An arrow appears on the Timeline indicating that this is a classic tween.

7. Play the movie.

You created an animation using a classic tween.

Add a motion guide and orient the object to the guide

1. Insert a **new layer**, then name it **Guide**.
2. Click **Modify** on the menu bar, point to **Timeline**, then click **Layer Properties**.
3. Click the **Guide option button**, click **OK**, then drag the **biker layer** up to the Guide layer, as shown in Figure 31.

    The biker layer indents below the Guide layer.

4. Click **frame 1** on the Guide layer, click the **Pencil tool** on the Tools panel, select **Smooth** in the Options area at the bottom of the Tools panel, then set the stroke color to **black**.
5. Point to the middle of the biker, then draw a **line** with a loop similar to the one shown in Figure 32.

(continued)

Figure 29 *Positioning the biker symbol on the Stage*

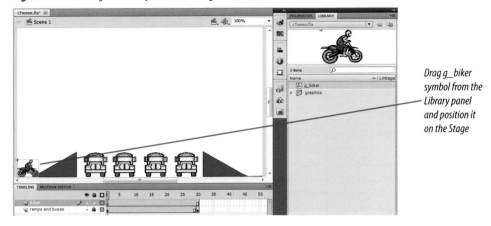

Drag g_biker symbol from the Library panel and position it on the Stage

Figure 30 *Repositioning the biker*

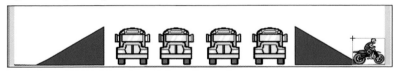

Figure 31 *Dragging the biker layer up to the Guide layer*

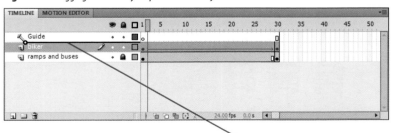

Drag biker layer up to but not above the Guide layer

Figure 32 *Drawing a guide path on a Guide layer*

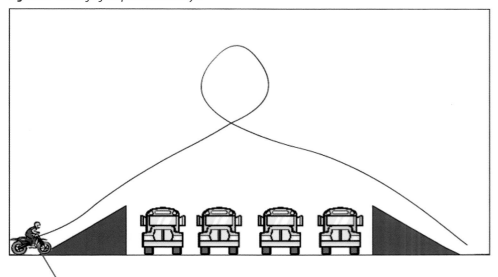

Point to the middle of the biker object

Figure 33 *Aligning the object with the guide path*

Figure 34 *Aligning the object with the end of the guide path*

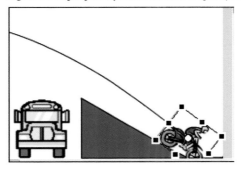

Lesson 2   Create Classic Tween Animations

Note: You may not see the line you are drawing until you are done drawing it.

6. Click **frame 30** on the biker layer, click the **Selection tool** , then drag the **biker** so that it snaps to the end of the line.

   Hint: Use the Zoom tool to zoom in on the biker to make it easier to see you have placed the transformation point on the path.

7. Play the movie.

   The biker should follow the path. If not, make sure the biker is attached to the beginning and end of the path.

8. Click **frame 1** on the biker layer, then click the **biker** to select the object.

9. Click the **Free Transform tool** on the Tools panel, then rotate the **biker,** as shown in Figure 33.

10. Click **frame 30** on the biker layer, then rotate the **biker**, as shown in Figure 34.

11. Click the **Selection tool** , then click **frame 1** on the biker layer.

12. Display the Properties panel, then click the **Orient to path check box**.

13. Play the movie.

14. Click **frame 1** on the biker layer, set the Ease value on the Properties panel to **100**, then click **frame 1** on the biker layer to accept the value.

15. Insert a **keyframe** on the frame on the biker layer that displays the highest point in the animation, set the ease value to **100**, then click **frame 1** on the biker layer to accept the value.

16. Test the movie, save your work, then close the document.

You added a motion guide, oriented the animated object to the guide, and set ease values.

Create Frame-by-Frame
ANIMATIONS

What You'll Do

In this lesson, you will create frame-by-frame animations.

Understanding Frame-by-Frame Animations

A frame-by-frame animation (also called a frame animation) is created by specifying the object that is to appear in each frame of a sequence of frames. Figure 35 shows three images that are variations of a cartoon character. In this example, the head and body remain the same, but the arms and legs change to represent a walking motion. If these individual images are placed into succeeding frames (with keyframes), an animation is created.

Frame-by-frame animations are useful when you want to change individual parts of an image. The images in Figure 35 are simple—only three images are needed for the animation. However, depending on the complexity of the image and the desired movements, the time needed to display each change can be substantial. When creating a frame-by-frame animation, you need to consider the following points:

- The number of different images. The more images there are, the more effort is needed to create them. However, the greater the number of images, the less

change you need to make in each image and the more realistic the movement in the animation may seem.
- The number of frames in which each image will appear. Changing the number of frames in which the object appears may change the effect of the animation. If each image appears in only one frame, the animation may appear rather jerky, since the frames change very rapidly. However, in some cases, you may want to give the impression of a rapid change in an object, such as rapidly blinking colors. If so, you could make changes in the color of an object from one frame to another.
- The movie frame rate. Frame rates below 10 may appear jerky, while those above 30 may appear blurred. The frame rate is easy to change, and you should experiment with different rates until you get the desired effect.

Keyframes are critical to the development of frame animations because they signify a change in the object. Because frame animations are created by changing the object, each frame in a frame animation may need to be a keyframe. The exception is when you want an object displayed in several frames before it changes.

Creating a Frame-by-Frame Animation

To create a frame animation, select the frame on the layer where you want the animation to begin, insert a keyframe, and then place the object on the Stage. Next, select the frame where you want the change to occur, insert a keyframe, and then change the object. You can also add a new object in place of the original one. Figure 36 shows the first three frames of an animation in which three different objects are placed one on top of the other in succeeding frames. In the figure, the movement is shown as shadows. These shadows are visible because the Onion Skin feature is turned on. In this movie, the objects stay in place during the animation. However, a frame animation can also involve movement of the object around the Stage.

Using the Onion Skin Feature

Normally, Flash displays one frame of an animation sequence at a time on the Stage. Turning on the Onion Skin feature allows you to view an outline of the object(s) in any number of frames. This can help in positioning animated objects on the Stage.

Figure 35 *Three images used in an animation*

Figure 36 *A frame-by-frame animation of three figures appearing to walk in place*

Onion Skin feature is turned on so that all of the objects in frames 1-3 are viewable even though the playhead is on frame 1

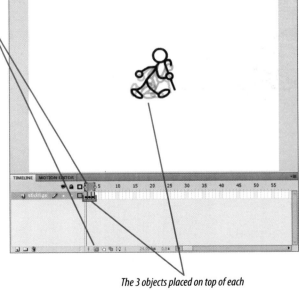

The 3 objects placed on top of each other on the Stage, each in its own frame on the Timeline

Create an in-place frame-by-frame animation

1. Open fl4_4.fla, then save it as **frameAn.fla**.
2. Set the view to **Fit in Window**.
3. Insert a **new layer**, name it **stickfigs**, click **frame 1** of the stickfigs layer, then drag **stickfig1** from the Library panel to the center of the Stage so it touches the white walkway.

   Note: You can use the Align panel to center the object horizontally across the Stage.

4. Click **frame 2** of the stickfigs layer to select it, click **Insert** on the menu bar, point to **Timeline**, then click **Keyframe**.
5. Drag **stickfig2** so it is on top of stickfig1, as shown in Figure 37, use the arrow keys on the keyboard to align the heads, then click a blank area of the Stage to deselect stickfig2.
6. Select **stickfig1** by clicking the foot that points up, as shown in Figure 38, then press **[Delete]**.
7. Click **frame 3** on the stickfigs layer to select it, insert a **keyframe,** drag **stickfig3** so it is on top of stickfig2, then use the **arrow keys** on the keyboard to align the heads.
8. Click a blank area of the Stage to deselect stickfig3.
9. Select stickfig2 by clicking the foot that points down, as shown in Figure 39, then press **[Delete]**.
10. Change the frame rate to **12**.
11. Play the movie.

You created a frame-by-frame animation.

Figure 37 *Dragging stickfig2 on top of stickfig1*

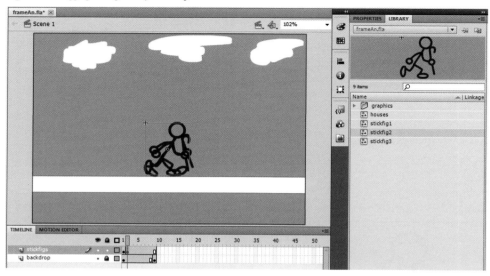

Figure 38 *Selecting stickfig1*

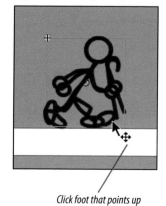

Click foot that points up

Figure 39 *Selecting stickfig2*

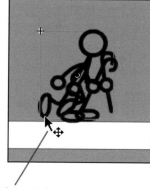

Click foot that points down

Figure 40 *Moving the houses layer below the stickfigs layer*

Figure 41 *Positioning the houses symbol on the Stage*

Figure 42 *Repositioning the houses object*

Copy frames and add a moving background

1. Click **frame 1** of the stickfigs layer, press and hold **[Shift]**, then click **frame 3**.

2. Click **Edit** on the menu bar, point to **Timeline**, click **Copy Frames**, then click **frame 4** of the stickfigs layer.

3. Click **Edit** on the menu bar, point to **Timeline**, then click **Paste Frames**.

4. Click **frame 7**, then repeat step 3.

5. Click **frame 10** of the stickfigs layer, press and hold **[Shift]**, then click **frame 13**.

6. Click **Edit** on the menu bar, point to **Timeline**, then click **Remove Frames**.

7. Insert a **new layer**, name the layer **houses**, then drag the **houses layer** below the stickfigs layer, as shown in Figure 40.

8. Click **frame 1** of the houses layer, drag the **houses symbol** from the Library panel to the Stage, then position the houses, as shown in Figure 41.

9. Play the movie.

10. Click **frame 1** of the houses layer, click **Insert** on the menu bar, then click **Motion Tween**.

11. Click **frame 9** on the houses layer, then drag the **houses object** to the left, as shown in Figure 42.

12. Test the movie, close the Flash Player window, save your work, then close the document.

You copied frames and added a motion tween to a movie with an in-place frame-by-frame animation.

Create a frame-by-frame animation of a moving object

1. Open fl4_5.fla, then save it as **frameM.fla**.

   This document has a backdrop layer that contains a row of houses and clouds.

2. Insert a **new layer**, then name it **stickFigs**.

3. Click **View** on the menu bar, point to **Magnification**, then click **50%**.

4. Click **frame 5** on the stickFigs layer, then insert a **keyframe**.

5. Drag **stickfig1** from the Library panel to the left edge of the Stage, as shown in Figure 43.

6. Click **frame 6** on the stickFigs layer, click **Insert** on the menu bar, point to **Timeline**, then click **Blank Keyframe**.

   A blank keyframe keeps the object in the previous frame from appearing in the current frame.

7. Click the **Edit Multiple Frames button** 🔲 on the Timeline status bar to turn it on.

   This allows you to view the contents of more than one frame at a time.

8. Drag **stickfig2** to the right of stickfig1, as shown in Figure 44.

9. Click **frame 7** on the stickFigs layer, then insert a **Blank Keyframe**.

10. Drag **stickfig3** to the right of stickfig2, as shown in Figure 45.

(continued)

Figure 43 *Positioning stickfig1 on the Stage*

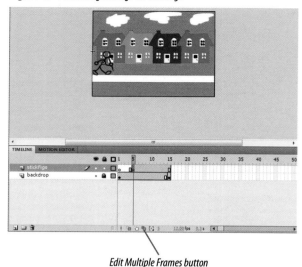

Edit Multiple Frames button

Figure 44 *Positioning stickfig2 on the Stage*

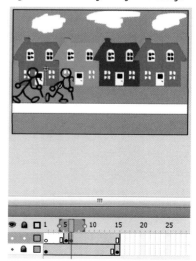

Figure 45 *Positioning stickfig3 on the Stage*

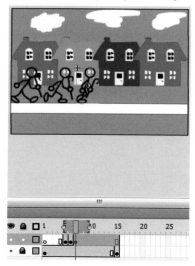

Figure 46 *Adding stickfig3 as the final object*

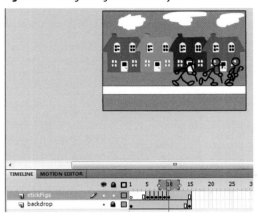

Working with Frames

Selecting frames
To select one frame: click the frame.
To select a range of contiguous frames: Shift-click additional frames.
To select non-contiguous frames: Control-click (Win) or ⌘-click (Mac).
To select a span of frames: double-click between keyframes.
To select all frames on the Timeline: choose Select All Frames from the Timeline option on the Edit menu.

Removing frames
Select the frame(s), then choose Remove Frames from the Timeline option on the Edit menu.
This removes frames from the timeline and moves the contents of succeeding frames left based on the number of frames removed.

Copy and paste
Select the frame(s), choose Copy Frames from the Timeline option on the Edit menu, select the frame(s) to copy to, then choose Paste Frames from the Timeline option on the Edit menu.
(*Note*: Use Cut Frames instead of Copy Frames to move frames).

Clear contents
Select the frame(s), then choose Clear Frames from the Timeline option on the Edit menu.
This leaves the frame(s) on the Timeline but the content is cleared and not available for pasting.

11. Click **frame 8** on the stickFigs layer, insert a **Blank Keyframe**, then drag **stickfig1** from the Library panel to the right of stickfig3.

12. Click **frame 9** on the stickFigs layer, insert a **Blank Keyframe**, then drag **stickfig2** to the right of stickfig1.

13. Click **frame 10** on the stickFigs layer, insert a **Blank Keyframe**, then drag **stickfig3** to the right of stickfig2.

    Your screen should resemble Figure 46.

14. Click **frame 11** on the stickFigs layer, then insert a **Blank Keyframe**.

15. Click the **Edit Multiple Frames button** on the Timeline status bar to turn it off.

16. Test the movie, then close the Flash Player window.

17. Change the frame rate to **6 fps**.

18. Test the movie, then close the Flash Player window.

19. Save the movie, then close the document.

You created a frame-by-frame animation that causes objects to appear to move across the screen.

Create Shape Tween
ANIMATIONS

What You'll Do

In this lesson, you will create a shape tween animation and specify shape hints.

Understanding Shape Tweening

In previous lessons, you learned that you can use motion tweening to change the shape of an object. You accomplish this by selecting the Free Transform tool and then dragging the handles to resize and skew the object. While this is easy and allows you to include motion along with the change in shape, there are two drawbacks. First, you are limited in the type of changes (resizing and skewing) that can be made to the shape of an object. Second, you must work with the same object throughout the animation. When you use **shape tweening**, however, you can have an animation change the shape of an object to any form you desire, and you can include two objects in the animation with two different shapes. As with motion tweening, you can use shape tweening to change other properties of an object, such as its color, location, and size.

Using Shape Tweening to Create a Morphing Effect

Morphing involves changing one object into another, sometimes unrelated, object. For example, you could turn a robot into a man, or turn a football into a basketball. The viewer sees the transformation as a series of incremental changes. In Flash, the first object appears on the Stage and changes into the second object as the movie plays. The number of frames included from the beginning to the end of this shape tween animation determines how quickly the morphing effect takes place. The first frame in the animation displays the first object and the last frame displays the second object. The in-between frames display the different shapes that are created as the first object changes into the second object.

When working with shape tweening, you need to keep the following points in mind:

- Shape tweening can be applied only to editable graphics. To apply shape tweening to instances, groups, symbols, text blocks, or bitmaps, you must break apart the object to make it editable. To do this, you use the Break Apart command on the Modify menu. When you break apart an instance of a symbol, it is no longer linked to the original symbol.
- You can shape tween more than one object at a time as long as all the objects

Creating Animations

are on the same layer. However, if the shapes are complex and/or if they involve movement in which the objects cross paths, the results may be unpredictable.

- You can use shape tweening to move an object in a straight line, but other options, such as rotating an object, are not available.
- You can use the settings in the Properties panel to set options (such as the ease value, which causes acceleration or deceleration) for a shape tween.
- Shape hints can be used to control more complex shape changes.

Properties Panel Options

Figure 47 shows the Properties panel options for a shape tween. The options allow you to adjust several aspects of the animation, as described in the following:

- Adjust the rate of change between frames to create a more natural appearance during the transition by setting an ease value. Setting the value between −1 and −100 will begin the shape tween gradually and accelerate it toward the end of the animation. Setting the value between 1 and 100 will begin the shape tween rapidly and decelerate it toward the end of the animation. By default, the rate of change is set to 0, which causes a constant rate of change between frames.
- Choose a blend option. The Distributive option creates animation in which the in-between shapes are smoother and more irregular. The Angular option preserves the corners and straight lines and works only with objects that have these features. If the objects do not have corners, Flash defaults to the Distributive option.

Shape Hints

You can use shape hints to control the shape's transition appearance during animation. Shape hints allow you to specify a location on the beginning object that corresponds to a location on the ending object. Figure 48 shows two shape animations of the same objects, one using shape hints and the other not using shape hints. The figure also shows how the object being reshaped appears in one of the in-between frames. Notice that with the shape hints, the object in the in-between frame is more recognizable.

Figure 47 *The Properties panel options for a shape tween*

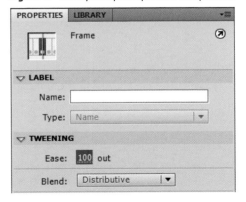

Figure 48 *Two shape animations (A morphing into B) with and without shape hints*

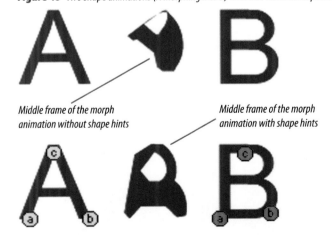

Middle frame of the morph animation without shape hints

Middle frame of the morph animation with shape hints

Create a shape tween animation

1. Open fl4_6.fla, then save it as **antiqueCar.fla**.

2. Set the view to **Fit in Window**.

3. Click **frame 30** on the shape layer, then insert a **keyframe**.

4. Click the **Selection tool** on the Tools panel, then click a blank area of the pasteboard to deselect the car.

5. Move the pointer over the top of the car near the right side until it changes to an arc pointer, then use the arc pointer to drag the **car top** to create the shape shown in Figure 49.

6. Click anywhere on the shape layer between frames 1 and 30.

7. Click **Insert** on the menu bar, then click **Shape Tween**.

8. Click **frame 1** on the shape layer, then play the movie.

9. Click **frame 30** on the shape layer.

10. Click the **Selection tool** on the Tools panel, then drag a **marquee** around the car to select it if it is not already selected.

11. Drag the **car** to the right side of the Stage.

12. Play the movie, then save and close it.

You created a shape tween animation, causing an object to change shape as it moves over several frames.

Figure 49 *The reshaped object*

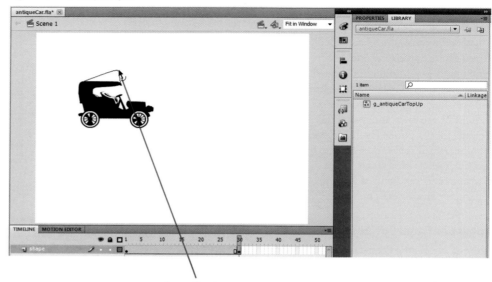

Drag up from here

Figure 50 *Positioning the car instance on the Stage*

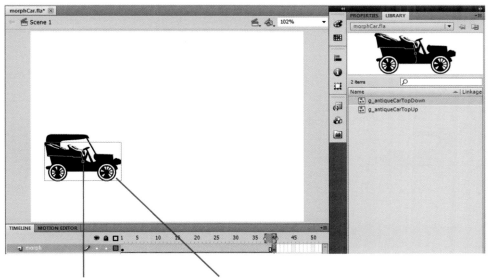

Transformation point appears when the mouse is released

Line up both cars so it appears that there is only one car; use the spokes on the wheels to help you know when the two objects are aligned

Create a morphing effect

1. Open fl4_7.fla, then save it as **morphCar.fla**.
2. Click **frame 40** on the morph layer.
3. Click **Insert** on the menu bar, point to **Timeline**, then click **Blank Keyframe**.

TIP Inserting a blank keyframe prevents the object in the preceding keyframe from automatically being inserted into the frame with the blank keyframe.

4. Click the **Edit Multiple Frames button** on the Timeline.

   Turning on the Edit Multiple Frames feature allows you to align the two objects to be morphed.

5. Display the Library panel.
6. Drag the **g_antiqueCarTopDown graphic** symbol from the Library panel directly on top of the car on the Stage, as shown in Figure 50.

TIP Use the arrow keys to move the object in small increments as needed.

7. Make sure the g_antiqueCarTopDown object is selected, click **Modify** on the menu bar, then click **Break Apart**.
8. Click the **Edit Multiple Frames button** to turn off the feature.
9. Click anywhere between frames 1 and 40 on the morph layer, click **Insert** on the menu bar, then click **Shape Tween**.
10. Click **frame 1** on the Timeline, then play the movie.

    The first car morphs into the second car.
11. Save the movie.

You created a morphing effect, causing one object to change into another.

Adjust the rate of change in a shape tween animation

1. Click **frame 40** on the morph layer.

2. Click the **Selection tool** ➤ on the Tools panel, then drag a **marquee** around the car to select it, if it is not already selected.

3. Drag the **car** to the right side of the Stage.

4. Click **frame 1** on the morph layer.

5. Set the ease value on the Properties panel to **−100**, as shown in Figure 51.

6. Click the **Stage**, then play the movie.

   The car starts out slow and speeds up as the morphing process is completed.

7. Repeat Steps 4 and 5, but change the ease value to **100**.

8. Click **frame 1** on the Timeline, then play the movie.

   The car starts out fast and slows down as the morphing process is completed.

9. Save your work, then close the movie.

You added motion to a shape tween animation and changed the ease value.

Figure 51 *Setting the ease value of the morph*

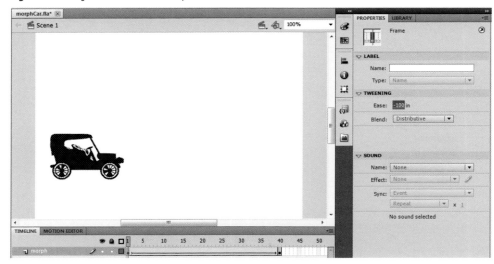

Figure 52 *Positioning a shape hint*

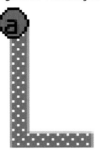

Figure 53 *Adding shape hints*

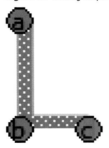

Figure 54 *Matching shape hints*

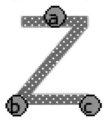

Use shape hints

1. Open fl4_8.fla, then save it as **shapeHints.fla**.
2. Play the movie and notice how the L morphs into a Z.
3. Click **frame 15** on the Timeline, the midpoint of the animation, then notice the shape.
4. Click **frame 1** on the hints layer to display the first object.
5. Make sure the object is selected, click **Modify** on the menu bar, point to **Shape**, then click **Add Shape Hint**.
6. Drag the **Shape Hint icon** to the location shown in Figure 52.
7. Repeat Steps 5 and 6 to set a second and third Shape Hint icon, as shown in Figure 53.
8. Click **frame 30** on the hints layer.

   The shape hints are stacked on top of each other.
9. Drag the **Shape Hint icons** to match Figure 54.
10. Click **frame 15** on the hints layer, then notice how the object is more recognizable now that the shape hints have been added.
11. Click **frame 1** on the Timeline, then play the movie.
12. Save your work, then close the movie.

You added shape hints to a morph animation.

Create Movie
CLIPS

What You'll Do

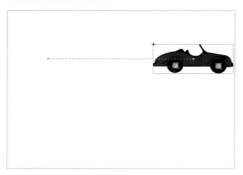

 In this lesson, you will create, edit, and animate a movie clip.

Understanding Movie Clip Symbols

Until now you have been working with two kinds of symbols, graphic and button. A third type is a **movie clip symbol**, which provides a way to create more complex types of animations. A movie clip is essentially a movie within a movie. Each movie clip has its own Timeline, which is independent of the main Timeline. This allows you to nest a movie clip that is running one animation within another animation or in a scene on the main Timeline. Because a movie clip retains its own Timeline, when you insert an instance of the movie clip symbol into a Flash document, the movie clip continues in an endless loop even if the main Timeline stops.

The wheels on a car rotating while the car is moving across the screen is an example of a movie (the moving car) with a nested animation (the rotating wheels). The nested animation is a movie clip. To create the animated movie clip, a drawing of a wheel separate from the car is converted into a movie clip symbol. Then the movie clip symbol is opened in the edit window, which includes a Timeline that is unique to the movie clip. In the edit window, an animation is created that causes the wheel to rotate. After exiting the edit window and returning to the main Timeline, an instance of the movie clip symbol is placed on each wheel of the car. Finally, the car, including the wheels, is animated on the main Timeline. As the car is moving across the screen, each wheel is rotating according to the movie clip Timeline. This process is shown in Figure 55.

In addition to allowing you to create more complex animations, movie clips help to organize the different reusable pieces of a movie and provide for smaller movie file sizes. This is because only one movie clip symbol needs to be stored in the Library panel while an unlimited number of instances of the symbol can be used in the Flash document.

An animated movie clip can be viewed in the edit window that is displayed when you double-click the movie clip symbol in the Library panel; and it can be viewed when you test or publish the movie that contains the movie clip. It is important to note that an animated movie clip cannot be viewed simply by playing the movie on the main Timeline.

In this lesson, you will learn how to create a movie clip symbol from a drawn object, edit the movie clip to create an animation, and nest the movie clip in another animation.

Figure 55 *The process of nesting a movie clip within an animation*

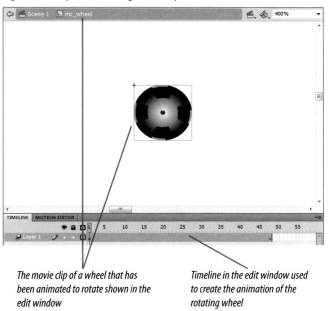

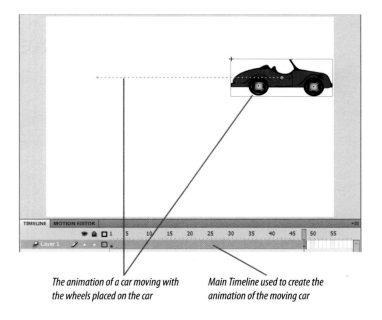

The movie clip of a wheel that has been animated to rotate shown in the edit window

Timeline in the edit window used to create the animation of the rotating wheel

The animation of a car moving with the wheels placed on the car

Main Timeline used to create the animation of the moving car

Break apart a graphic symbol and select parts of the object to separate from the graphic

1. Open fl4_9.fla, then save it as **mClip.fla**.

   This document has one graphic symbol—a car that has been placed on the Stage.

2. Click the **Selection tool** on the Tools panel, then click the **car** to select it.

3. Click **Modify** on the menu bar, then click **Break Apart**.

4. Click a blank area of the Stage to deselect the object.

5. Click the **Zoom tool** on the Tools panel, then click the **front wheel** two times to zoom in on the wheel.

6. Click the **Selection tool** on the Tools panel.

7. Click the **gray hubcap**, press and hold **[Shift]**, then click the rest of the wheel, as shown in Figure 56.

   Hint: There are several small parts to the wheel, so click until a dot pattern covers the entire wheel, but do not select the tire. Use the Undo command if you select the tire.

8. Drag the **selected area** down below the car, as shown in Figure 57.

9. Compare your selected wheel to Figure 57, if your wheel does not match the figure, use the Undo command to move the wheel back to its original position, and repeat step 7.

You broke apart a graphic symbol and selected parts of the object to separate from the graphic.

Figure 56 *Selecting the wheel*

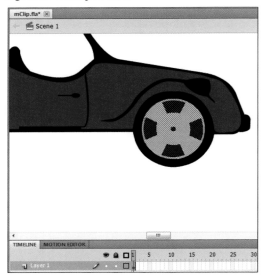

Figure 57 *Separating the wheel from the car*

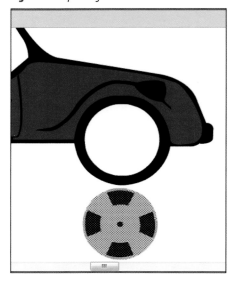

Figure 58 *Selecting the gray area of the wheel*

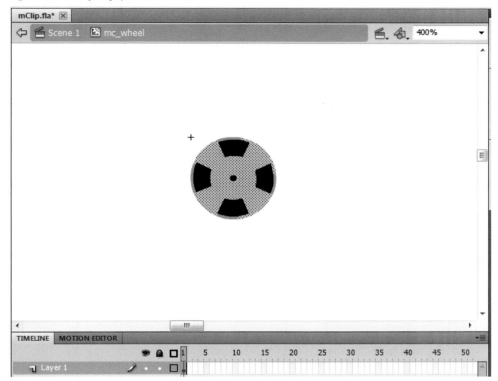

Create and edit a movie clip

1. Verify the wheel is selected, click **Modify** on the menu bar, then click **Convert to Symbol**.

2. Type **mc_wheel** for the name, select **Movie Clip** for the Type, then click **OK**.

   The mc_wheel movie clip appears in the Library panel.

3. Double-click the **mc_wheel icon** on the Library panel to display the edit window.

4. Click the **Zoom tool** 🔍 on the Tools panel, then click the **wheel** twice to zoom in on the wheel.

   The movie clip has been broken apart as indicated by the dot pattern.

5. Click the **Selection tool** �, click a blank area of the Stage to deselect the object, then click the **gray area** of the wheel to select it, as shown in Figure 58.

6. Click the **Fill color tool color swatch** on the Tools panel, then click the **gray gradient color swatch** in the bottom row of the palette.

You created a movie clip symbol and edited it to change the color of the object.

Animate a movie clip

1. Click the **Selection tool** , then drag a **marquee** around the entire wheel to select it.

2. Click **Insert** on the menu bar, click **Motion Tween**, then click **OK** for the Convert selection to symbol for tween dialog box.

3. Point to the end of the tween span on Layer 1 of the Timeline, then, when the pointer changes to a double-headed arrow ↔, drag the **span** to frame 48, as shown in Figure 59.

4. Click **frame 1** on Layer 1.

5. Display the Properties panel.

6. Change the rotate value to **4** times and verify the Direction is CW (Clockwise), as shown in Figure 60.

   Hint: If you don't see the Rotate option, click the Selection tool, then drag a marquee around the object.

7. Set the frame rate on the Timeline status bar to **12**, test the movie, then close the Flash Player window.

8. Click **Scene 1** near the top left side of the edit widow to exit the edit window.

9. Drag the **wheel** on the Stage up and position it so it is back inside the front tire of the car.

   (continued)

Figure 59 *Increasing the motion span on the Timeline*

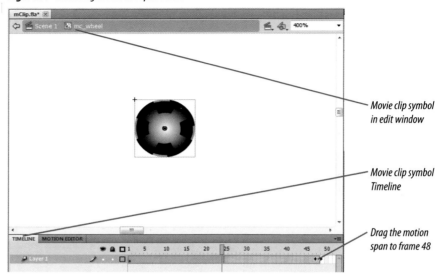

Movie clip symbol in edit window

Movie clip symbol Timeline

Drag the motion span to frame 48

Figure 60 *Changing the rotate value*

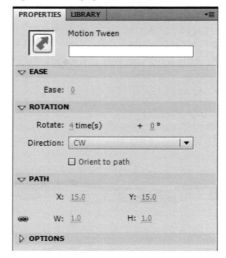

Creating Animations

Figure 61 *Repositioning the car*

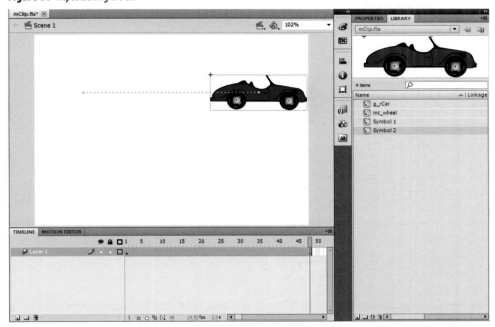

10. Drag the **mc_wheel movie clip** from the Library panel and position it using the arrow keys as needed so it is on the back wheel.

11. Click **View** on the menu bar, point to **Magnification**, then click **Fit in Window**.

12. Test the movie and notice how the wheels turn, then close the Flash Player window.

13. Click the **Selection tool** , then drag a **marquee** around the car to select it and the wheels.

14. Click **Insert** on the menu bar, click **Motion Tween**, then click **OK**.

15. Drag the **tween span** on Layer 1 to frame 48.

16. Click **frame 48** on Layer 1, then drag the **car** to the right side of the Stage, as shown in Figure 61.

17. Test the movie, then close the Flash Player window.

18. Save your work, then close the document.

You edited a movie clip to create an animation, then nested the movie clip in an animation on the main Timeline.

Animate TEXT

What You'll Do

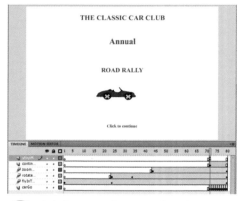

 In this lesson, you will animate text by scrolling, rotating, zooming, and resizing it.

Animating Text

You can motion tween text block objects just as you do graphic objects. You can resize, rotate, reposition, and change the colors of text blocks. Figure 62 shows three examples of animated text with the Onion Skin feature turned on. When the movie starts, each of the following occurs one after the other:

■ The Classic Car Club text block scrolls in from the left side to the top center of the Stage. This is done by creating the text block, positioning it off the Stage, and creating a motion-tweened animation that moves it to the Stage.

■ The Annual text block appears and rotates five times. This occurs after you create the Annual text block, position it in the middle of the Stage under the heading, and use the Properties panel to specify a clockwise rotation that repeats five times.

■ The ROAD RALLY text block slowly zooms out and appears in the middle of the Stage. This occurs after you create the text block and use the Free Transform tool handles to resize it to a small block at the beginning of the animation. Then, you resize the text block to a larger size at the end of the animation.

Once you create a motion animation using a text block, the text block becomes a symbol and you are unable to edit individual characters within the text block. You can, however, edit the symbol as a whole.

Figure 62 *Three examples of animated text*

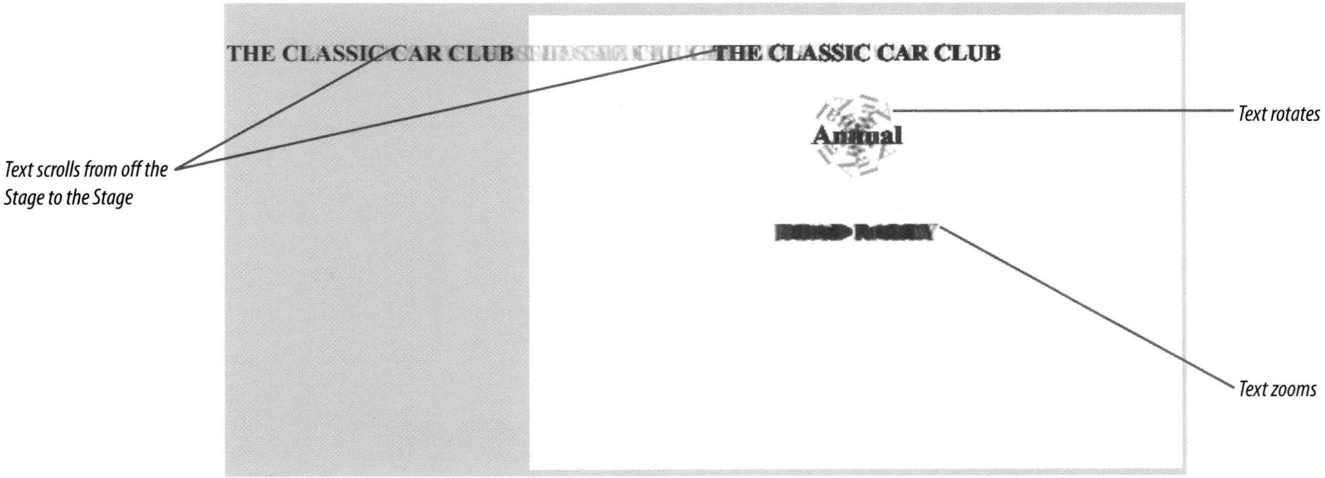

THE CLASSIC CAR CLUB

THE CLASSIC CAR CLUB

Annual

ROAD RALLY

Text scrolls from off the
Stage to the Stage

Text rotates

Text zooms

Select, copy, and paste frames

1. Open fl4_10.fla, then save the movie as **textAn.fla**.

   This document has a heading and a frame-by-frame animation of a car where the front end rotates up and down, and then the car moves off the screen.

2. Play the movie, then click **frame 1** on the Timeline.

3. Press the **period key** to move through the animation one frame at a time and notice the changes to the object in each frame.

4. Change the view to **Fit in Window**.

5. Click the **Frame View icon** ▾≡ near the upper right of the Timeline, then click **Small**.

6. Point to the **vertical line** on the Timeline until the ◂┼▸ pointer appears, then drag the ◂┼▸ **pointer** to the left until frame 80 appears on the Timeline, as shown in Figure 63, if you do not see frame 80.

7. Click **frame 1** on the carGo layer, press and hold **[Shift]**, then click **frame 9** to select all the frames, as shown in Figure 64.

8. Click **Edit** on the menu bar, point to **Timeline**, then click **Cut Frames**.

9. Click **frame 72** on the carGo layer.

10. Click **Edit** on the menu bar, point to **Timeline**, then click **Paste Frames**.

11. Click **frame 1** on the carGo layer.

12. Play the movie, then save your work.

You selected frames and moved them from one location on the Timeline to another location on the Timeline.

Figure 63 *Expanding the view of the Timeline*

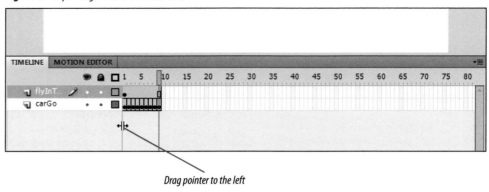

Drag pointer to the left

Figure 64 *Selecting a range of frames*

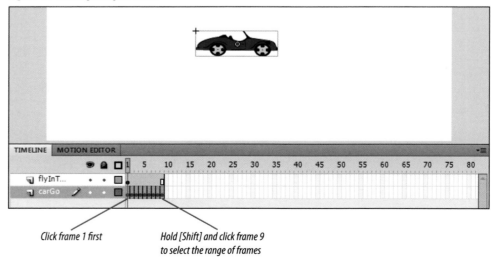

Click frame 1 first

Hold [Shift] and click frame 9 to select the range of frames

Figure 65 *Positioning the text block outside the Stage*

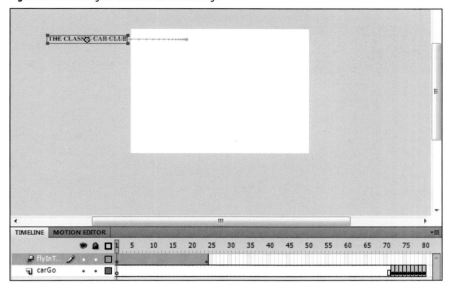

Figure 66 *Centering the text block*

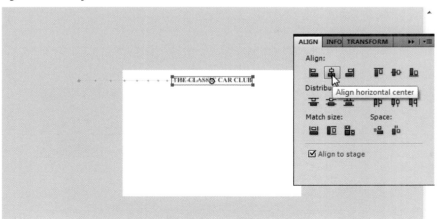

Animate text using a motion preset

1. Change the view to **50%**.
2. Click **frame 1** on the flyInText layer.
3. Open the Motion Presets panel, display the **Default Presets**, then click **fly-in-left**.
4. Click **Apply**, read the information box, then click **OK**.

   A motion tween is applied to the text block and a motion path appears.

5. Click the **Selection tool** , then draw a **marquee** around the text and the path.
6. Use the **left arrow key** to position the object and path, as shown in Figure 65.

   Alternately, you can drag the object and path to reposition it. Using the arrow key prevents any vertical movement when repositioning the object and path.

7. Click **frame 24** on the flyInText layer.
8. Click a **blank area** of the Stage to deselect the object and the path.
9. Click the **text object** to select it, then use the align panel to **center** the text horizontally across the Stage, as shown in Figure 66.
10. Click **frame 80** on the flyInText layer, then insert a **keyframe**.
11. Change the view to **Fit in Window**.
12. Test the movie, then close the Flash Player window.

You used a motion preset to animate an object by having it fly in from the left side of the Stage.

Create rotating text

1. Insert a **new layer**, then name it **rotateText**.

2. Insert a **keyframe** in frame 24 on the rotateText layer.

3. Click the **Text tool** **T** on the Tools panel, position the pointer beneath the "A" in "CLASSIC," then click to display a blank text block.

4. Change the Character properties in the Properties panel to **Times New Roman**, size **24**, style **bold** and color **blue** (#0000FF).

5. Type **Annual**, then compare your image to Figure 67.

6. Click the **Selection tool** **↖** on the Tools panel, then use the Align panel to center the text block horizontally across the Stage.

7. Verify Annual is selected, click **Insert** on the menu bar, then click **Motion Tween**.

8. Click **frame 24** on the rotateText layer, then set the Rotate value on the Properties panel to **2** times with a **CW** (clockwise) direction.

9. Point to the end of the tween span (frame 80) until the pointer changes to ↔, then drag the ↔ **pointer** to frame 34, as shown in Figure 68.

10. Click **frame 80** on the rotateText layer, then insert a **keyframe**.

11. Click **frame 1** on the Timeline, then play the movie.

    The Annual text rotates clockwise two times.

You inserted a new layer, created a rotating text block, applied a motion tween to text, and used the Properties panel to rotate the text block.

Figure 67 *Adding the Annual text block*

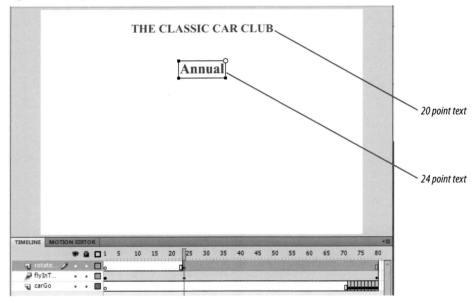

THE CLASSIC CAR CLUB

Annual

20 point text

24 point text

Figure 68 *Resizing the motion span from frame 80 to frame 34*

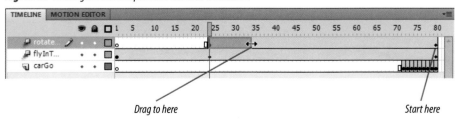

Drag to here

Start here

Figure 69 *Using the Text tool to type ROAD RALLY*

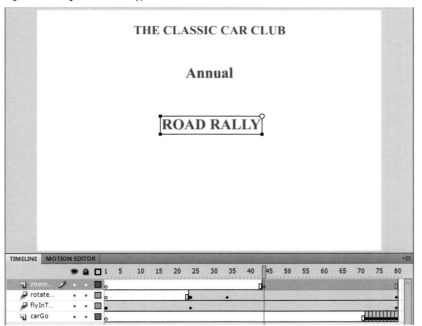

Figure 70 *Resizing the Text block*

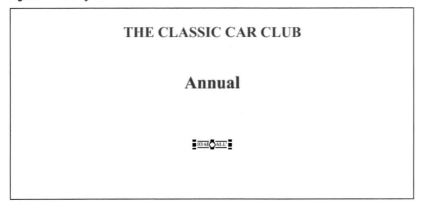

Resize and fade in text

1. Insert a **new layer**, name it **zoomText**, then insert a **keyframe** in frame 44 on the layer.

2. Click the **Text tool** T , position the pointer beneath the Annual text block, then type **ROAD RALLY**, as shown in Figure 69.

3. Click the **Selection tool** ▶ , then use the Align panel to center the text block horizontally across the Stage.

4. Click **frame 44** on the zoomText layer, click **Insert** on the menu bar, then click **Motion Tween**.

5. Click **frame 44** on the zoomText layer, click the **Free Transform tool** , then click the **Scale button** in the Options area of the Tools panel.

6. Drag the **upper-left corner handle** inward to resize the text block, as shown in Figure 70.

7. Click **frame 80** on the zoomText layer, verify the Scale option in the Options area of the Tools panel is selected, then drag the **upper-left corner handle** outward to resize the text block to approximately its original size.

8. Test the movie, then close the Flash Player window.

You created a motion animation that caused a text block to zoom out.

Make a text block into a button

1. Insert a **new layer**, then name it **continueBTN**.

2. Insert a **keyframe** in frame 72 on the continueBTN layer.

3. Click the **Text** tool **T** on the Tools panel, position the **Text tool pointer** beneath the car, then type **Click to continue**.

4. Drag the **pointer** over the text to select it, then change the character size on the Properties panel to **12**.

5. Click the **Selection tool** on the Tools panel, center the text block horizontally across the Stage, then compare your image to Figure 71.

6. Verify that the text block is selected, click **Modify** on the menu bar, click **Convert to Symbol**, type **b_continue** in the Name text block, set the Type to **Button**, then click **OK**.

7. Double-click the **text block** to edit the button.

8. Insert a **keyframe** in the Over frame, then set the fill color to the **black color swatch** in the left column of the color palette.

9. Insert a **keyframe** in the Down frame, set the fill color to the **bright green color swatch** in the left column of the color palette.

10. Insert a **keyframe** in the Hit frame, click the **Rectangle tool** on the Tools panel, then draw a **rectangle** that covers the text block, as shown in Figure 72.

11. Click **Scene 1** at the top left of the edit window to return to the main Timeline.

You made the text block into a button.

Figure 71 *Adding a button*

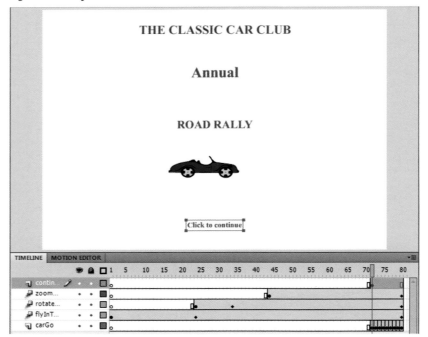

Figure 72 *The rectangle that defines the hit area*

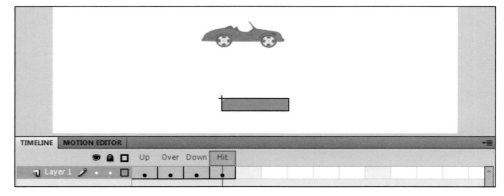

Figure 73 *Adding a play action*

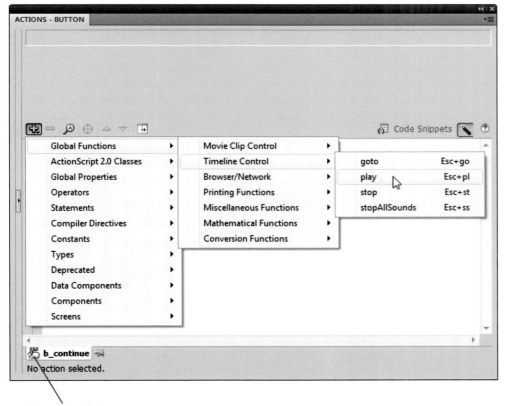

Action will be applied to this button

Add an action to the button

1. Display the Actions panel.
2. Click the **Selection tool** ![selection tool icon] on the Tools panel, then click the **Click to continue button** on the Stage.
3. Verify the Script Assist button is turned on, then verify the button symbol and b_continue are displayed in the lower-left corner of the Actions panel.

   Note: You need to have ActionScript 2.0 active. You can check your ActionScript version by choosing Publish Settings on the File menu, then selecting the Flash tab.
4. Click the **Add a new item to the script button** ![icon] in the Script Assist window, point to **Global Functions**, point to **Timeline Control**, then click **play**, as shown in Figure 73.
5. Insert a **new layer**, name it **stopMovie**, then insert a **keyframe** in frame 72 on that layer.
6. Verify that stopmovie:72 is displayed in the lower-left corner of the Actions panel.
7. Click the **Add a new item to the script button** ![icon] in the Script Assist window, point to **Global Functions**, point to **Timeline Control**, then click **stop**.
8. Click **Control** on the menu bar, point to **Test Movie**, click **in Flash Professional**, then click the **Click to continue button** when it appears.

   The movie begins by playing the animated text blocks. When you click the Click to continue button the movie plays the animated car and then the movie loops back to frame 1.
9. Close the Flash Player movie window, save and close the movie, then exit Flash.

You inserted a play button and added a play action to it, then inserted a stop action on another layer.

Create a motion tween animation.

1. Start Flash, open fl4_11.fla, then save it as **skillsDemo4.fla**.
2. Insert a keyframe in frame 20 on the ballAn layer.
3. Display the Library panel, then drag the g_vball graphic symbol to the lower-left corner of the Stage.
4. Click frame 20 on the ballAn layer, then insert a motion tween.
5. Point to the end of frame 20, when the pointer changes to a double-headed arrow, drag the pointer to frame 40 to set the tween span from frames 20 to 40.
6. With frame 40 selected, drag the object to the lower-right corner of the Stage.
7. Change the view of the Timeline to Small so more frames are in view.
8. Insert a blank keyframe in frame 41.
9. Play the movie, then save your work.

Edit a motion tween.

1. Click frame 20 on the ballAn layer, then use the Selection tool to alter the motion path to form an arc.
2. Use the Subsection tool to display the Bezier handles, use them to form a curved path, then play the movie.
3. Select frame 20, use the Properties panel to change the ease value to **100**, then play the movie.
4. Select frame 20, change the ease value to **–100**, then play the movie.
5. Select frame 40, select the object, use the Properties panel to change the width of the object to **30**, then play the movie. (*Hint*: Verify the Lock width and height values together chain is not broken. This will

ensure that when one value is changed, the other value changes proportionally.)
6. Select frame 35, select the object, use the Free transform tool to skew the object, then play the movie.
7. Select frame 40, select the object, use the Properties panel to change the alpha setting to **0**, then play the movie.
8. Change the alpha setting back to **100**.
9. Select frame 40, select the object, then use the Advanced Style option in the COLOR EFFECT area of the Properties panel to create a red color.
10. Lock the ballAn layer.
11. Play the movie, then save your work.

Create a classic tween.

1. Insert a new layer and name it **v-ball**.
2. Insert a keyframe in frame 76 on the v-ball layer.
3. Insert a keyframe in frame 41 on the v-ball layer.
4. Drag an instance of the g_vball symbol from the Library panel to the lower-left corner of the Stage.
5. Insert a keyframe in frame 50 on the v-ball layer and drag the ball to the lower-right corner of the Stage.
6. Click any frame between 41 and 50 on the v-ball layer and insert a Classic tween.
7. Insert a blank keyframe at frame 51 on the v-ball layer.
8. Play the movie, then save your work.

Create a motion guide.

1. Insert a new layer above the v-ball layer and name it **path**.
2. Insert a keyframe in frame 76 on the path layer.
3. Change the path layer to a Guide layer.
4. Insert a keyframe at frame 41 on the path layer.

5. Select the pencil tool, point to the middle of the ball and draw a path with a loop.
6. Insert a keyframe in frame 50 on the path layer.
7. Drag the v-ball layer up to the path layer so that it indents below the path layer.
8. Click frame 41 on the v-ball layer and attach the ball to the path.
9. Click frame 50 on the v-ball layer and attach the ball to the path.
10. Click frame 41 on the v-ball layer and use the Properties panel to orient the ball to the path.
11. Lock the v-ball and path layers.
12. Hide the path layer.
13. Play the movie, then save the movie.

Create a frame-by-frame animation.

1. Insert a new layer above the path layer and name it **corner-ball**.
2. Insert a keyframe in frame 76 on the corner-ball layer.
3. Insert a keyframe in frame 51 on the corner-ball layer, then drag the g_vball graphic from the Library panel to the lower-left corner of the Stage.
4. Insert a blank keyframe in frame 55 on the corner-ball layer, then drag g_vball graphic from the Library panel to the upper-left corner of the Stage.
5. Insert a blank keyframe in frame 59 on the corner-ball layer, then drag the g_vball graphic from the Library panel to the upper-right corner of the Stage.
6. Insert a blank keyframe in the frame 63 on the corner-ball layer, then drag the g_vball graphic from the Library panel to the lower-right corner of the Stage.

7. Insert a blank keyframe in frame 67 on the corner-ball layer.
8. Lock the corner-ball layer.
9. Change the movie frame rate to 3 frames per second, then play the movie.
10. Change the movie frame rate to 12 frames per second, play the movie, then save your work.

Create a movie clip.

1. Insert a new layer and name it **spin-ball**.
2. Insert a keyframe at frame 76 on the spin-ball layer.
3. Insert a keyframe at frame 51 on the spin-ball layer.
4. Drag an instance of the g_vball symbol from the Library panel to the center of the Stage.
5. Select the ball and convert it to a movie clip with the name **mc_ball**.
6. Display the edit window for the mc_ball movie clip.
7. Create a motion tween that rotates the ball 6 times counterclockwise in 12 frames.
8. Exit the edit window.
9. Insert a blank keyframe in frame 67 of the spin-ball layer.
10. Lock the spin-ball layer.
11. Test the movie, close the Flash Player window, then save your work.

Animate text.

1. Insert a new layer above the spin-ball layer and name it **heading**.
2. Click frame 1 on the heading layer.
3. Use the Text tool to click at the top-center of the Stage, then type **Having fun with a**.
4. Change the text to Arial, 20 point, light gray (#CCCCCC), and bold.
5. Select frame 1 on the heading layer and create a pulse motion using the Motion Presets panel.
6. Drag the motion span to frame 76.
7. Play the movie and save your work.
8. Lock the heading layer.
9. Insert a new layer and name it **zoom**.
10. Insert a keyframe in frame 76 on the zoom layer.
11. Insert a keyframe in frame 11 on the zoom layer.
12. Use the Text tool to type **Volleyball** below the heading, then center it as needed.
13. Select frame 11 on the zoom layer and create a motion tween.
14. Insert a keyframe in frame 20 on the zoom layer.
15. Click frame 11 on the zoom layer and select the text block.
16. Use the Free Transform tool to resize the text block to approximately one-fourth its original size.
17. Select frame 20 on the zoom layer, and resize the text block to approximately the size shown in Figure 74.
18. Lock the zoom layer.
19. Test the movie, close the Flash Player window, save your work.

Create a Shape Tween Animation.

1. Insert a new layer above the zoom layer and name it **morph**.
2. Insert a keyframe in frame 66 on the morph layer.
3. Drag the g_vball symbol to the center of the Stage so it covers the other ball (mc_ball movie clip) in the center of the Stage. Because the mc_ball movie clip (spinning ball) ends in frame 66 and the morph begins in frame 66, this will give the impression of the spinning ball morphing.
4. Use the Properties panel to resize the width to **60 px**. (*Hint*: Verify the Lock width and height values together chain is unbroken. This will ensure that when one value is changed, the other value changes proportionally.)
5. Reposition the smaller ball so it is over the center of the larger ball, then break apart the object.
6. Insert a blank keyframe in frame 76 on the morph layer.

7. Turn on the Edit Multiple Frames feature.
8. Drag the g_fball symbol to the Stage and use the Properties panel to resize the width to 60 px. (*Hint*: Verify the Lock width and height values together chain is not broken. This will ensure that when one value is changed, the other value changes proportionally.)
9. Center the football on top of the volleyball.
10. Break apart the football object.
11. Turn off the Edit Multiple Frames feature.
12. Click frame 66 on the morph layer and insert a shape tween.
13. Test the movie, then close the Flash Player window.
14. Add shape hints to the volleyball and the football.
15. Lock the morph layer.
16. Test the movie, close the Flash Player window, then save your work.
17. Exit Flash.

Figure 74 *Completed Skills Review*

The Ultimate Tours travel company has asked you to design several sample animations for its website. Figure 75 shows a sample home page and the Cruises screen. Using these (or one of the home pages you created in Chapter 3) as a guide, complete the following:

(*Hints*: If you need to insert frames, select the frame where the inserted frame is to go and press [F5] or use the Frame command via the Timeline option on the Insert menu. To insert several frames, select a range of frames and press [F5] or use the Frame command via the Timeline option from the Insert menu. To move the contents of a frame(s), you can select the frame(s) you want to move, then use the Cut and Paste commands via the Timeline option on the Edit menu.)

1. Open ultimateTours3.fla (the file you created in Chapter 3 Project Builder 1) and save it as **ultimateTours4.fla**. (*Hint*: Read through all of the steps and determine how many frames you will need to create the animation before taking any action.)
2. Animate the heading Ultimate Tours on the home page so that it zooms out from a transparent text block.
3. Have the logo appear next.
4. After the heading and logo appear, make the subheading We Specialize in Exotic Adventures appear.
5. Create motion tweens that cause each of the button shapes (Treks, Tours, Cruises) to scroll from the bottom of the Stage to its position on the Stage. Stagger the buttons on the Timeline so they scroll onto the Stage one after the other.
6. Assign a stop action after the home page appears.
7. Add a new layer, name it **cruises headings**, then add the text blocks shown in Figure 75 (Featured Cruises, Panama Canal, Caribbean, Galapagos).
8. Insert keyframes in the ending frames for the Ultimate Tours title, logo, and home button so that they appear on the cruises screen.
9. Import the graphic file ship.gif from the drive and folder where your Data Files are stored to the Library panel. (*Hint*: To import a graphic to the Library panel, click File on the menu bar, point to Import, then click Import to Library. Navigate to the drive and folder where your Data Files are stored, then select the desired file and click Open.)
10. Add a new layer and drag the ship.gif from the Library panel to the stage.
11. Convert the ship graphic to a graphic symbol named **g_ship**, create a motion tween animation that moves the ship across the screen, then alter the motion path to cause a dip in it, similar to the path shown in Figure 75. (*Hint*: Use the Selection tool to create an arc in the path. Then use the Subselection tool to display the Bezier handles and further alter the path.)
12. Orient the boat to the motion path.
13. Assign a goto action to the Cruises button so it jumps to the frame that has the Cruises screen.
14. Test the movie, then compare your movie to the example shown in Figure 75.

Figure 75 *Sample completed Project Builder 1*

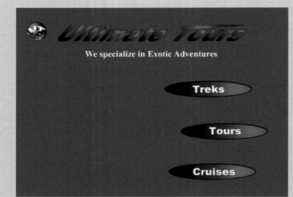

Home page

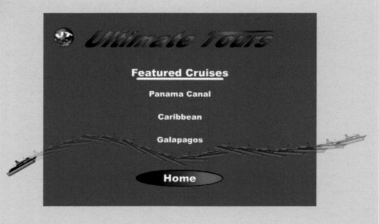

Featured Cruises Page

You have been asked to demonstrate some of the animation features of Flash. You have decided to create a movie clip that includes a frame-by-frame animation and then use the movie clip in a motion tween animation. Figure 76 shows the stick figure that will walk across the screen and jump up at each line on the sidewalk. The movement across the screen is created using a motion tween. The jumping up is created using a movie clip, as shown in Figure 76.

To complete this project, do the following:

1. Start a new Flash document and name it **jumper4.fla**.

2. Add a background color, sidewalk with lines, and houses or other graphics of your choice, adding layers as needed and naming them appropriately. (*Note*: You can open a previous movie that used the stick figures, such as frameAn, then with your movie open, click the Display movies list arrow under the Library panel tab. This displays a list of all open documents. Click the name of the file that has the stick figures to display its Library panel, then drag the symbols you need to the Pasteboard of your movie. Verify the objects are in the jumper4 Library panel, then delete them from the Pasteboard.)

3. Create a new movie clip. (*Note*: You can create a new movie clip by selecting New Symbol from the Insert menu, then you can drag objects from the Library panel to the movie clip edit window.)

4. Edit the clip to create a frame-by-frame animation of the stick figures walking in place. In the movie clip, place the stick figures one after the other but have one of the stick figures in the sequence placed above the others to create a jumping effect. You will use each stick figure two times in the sequence.

5. Exit the edit window and place the movie clip on the Stage, then create a motion tween that moves the movie clip from the left side to the right side of the Stage.

6. Test the movie. Change the fps setting as needed to create a more realistic effect, then retest the movie. (*Note*: Movie clips do not play from the Stage, you must use the Test Movie command.)

7. Close the Flash Player movie, then save the movie.

Figure 76 *Sample completed Project Builder 2*

Jumper4 movie

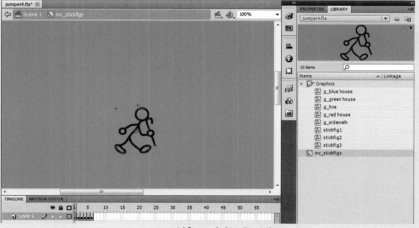

mc_stickfigs symbol in edit window

Creating Animations

Figure 77 shows a website for kids. Study the figure and complete the following. For each question, indicate how you determined your answer.

1. Connect to the Internet, then go to *www.smokeybear.com/kids*.

2. Open a document in a word processor or open a new Flash document, save the file as **dpc4**, then answer the following questions. (*Hint*: Use the Text tool in Flash.)
   - What seems to be the purpose of this site?
   - Who would be the target audience?
   - How might a frame animation be used in this site?
   - How might a motion tween animation be used?
   - How might a motion guide be used?
   - How might motion animation effects be used?
   - How might the text be animated?

Figure 77 *Design Project*

Smokey Bear image used with the permission of the USDA Forest Service.

This is a continuation of the Portfolio Project in Chapter 3, which is the development of a personal portfolio. The home page has several categories, including the following:

- Personal data
- Contact information
- Previous employment
- Education
- Samples of your work

In this project, you will create several buttons for the sample animations screen and link them to the animations.

1. Open portfolio3.fla (the file you created in Portfolio Project, Chapter 3) and save it as **portfolio4.fla**.
2. Display the Sample Animation screen and change the heading to Sample Animations.
3. Add layers and create buttons with labels, as shown in Figure 78, for the tweened animation, frame-by-frame animation, motion path animation, and animated text.
4. Create a tween animation or use the passing cars animation from Chapter 3, and link it to the appropriate button on the Sample Animations screen by assigning a goto action to the button.
5. Create a frame-by-frame animation, and link it to the appropriate button on the Sample Animations screen.
6. Create a motion path animation, and link it to the appropriate button on the Sample Animations screen.
7. Create several text animations, using scrolling, rotating, and zooming; then link them to the appropriate button on the Sample Animations screen.
8. Create a shape tween animation, and link it to the appropriate button on the Sample Animations screen.
9. Create a shape tween animation that produces a morphing effect, and link it to the appropriate button on the Sample Animations screen.
10. Create a shape tween animation that produces a morphing effect using shape hints, and link it to the appropriate button on the Sample Animations screen.
11. Add a layer and create a Home button that links the Sample Animations screen to the Home screen.
12. Create frame actions that cause the movie to return to the Sample Animations screen after each animation has been played.
13. Test the movie.
14. Save your work, then compare sample pages from your movie to the example shown for two of the screens in Figure 78.

Figure 78 *Sample completed Portfolio Project*

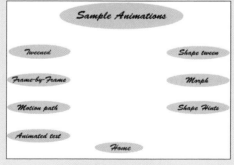

Sample Animations page

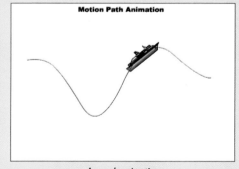

A sample animation

CHAPTER 5 CREATING SPECIAL EFFECTS

1. Create a mask effect
2. Add sound
3. Add video
4. Create an animated navigation bar
5. Create character animations using inverse kinematics
6. Create 3D effects
7. Use the Deco tool

5

CREATING SPECIAL
EFFECTS

Introduction

Now that you are familiar with the basics of Flash, you can begin to apply some of the special features, such as special effects and sound effects, that can enhance a movie. Special effects can provide variety and add interest to a movie, as well as draw the viewer's attention to a location or event in the movie. One type of special effect is a spotlight that highlights an area(s) of the movie or reveals selected content on the Stage. You can use sound effects to enhance a movie by creating moods and dramatizing events. In addition, you can add sound to a button to provide feedback to the viewer when the button is clicked. Video can be incorporated into a Flash movie and effects, such as fading in and out, can be applied to the display of the video.

Another type of special effect is an animated navigation bar, for example, one that causes a drop-down menu to open when the user rolls over a button. This effect can be created using masks and invisible buttons.

Additional features of Adobe Flash CS5 are Inverse Kinematics, 3D Effects, and the Deco tool. Inverse Kinematics allows you to easily create character animations and even allows users to interact with the character when viewing the Flash movie. The 3D tools allow you to create 3D effects such as objects moving and rotating through 3D space. The Deco tool provides a variety of drawing effects that can be used to create environments and decorative patterns.

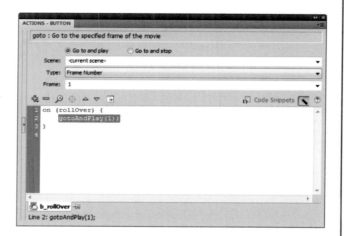

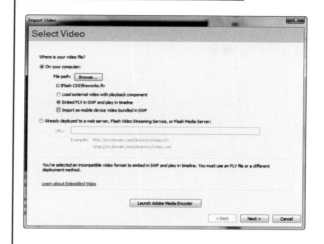

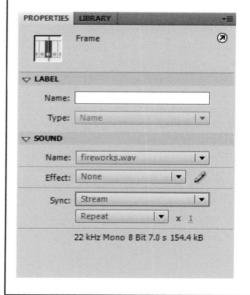

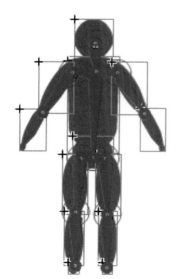

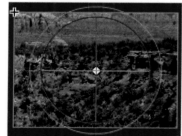

Create A
MASK EFFECT

What You'll Do

Classic Car lub

 In this lesson, you will apply a mask effect.

Understanding Mask Layers

A **mask layer** allows you to cover up the objects on one or more layers and, at the same time, create a window through which you can view objects on those layer(s). You can determine the size and shape of the window and specify whether it moves around the Stage. Moving the window around the Stage can create effects such as a spotlight that highlights certain content on the Stage, drawing the viewer's attention to a specific location. Because the window can move around the Stage, you can use a mask layer to reveal only the area of the Stage and the objects you want the viewer to see.

You need at least two layers on the Timeline when you are working with a mask layer. One layer, called the mask layer, contains the window object through which you view the objects, which are on a second layer below the mask layer. The second layer, called the masked layer, contains the object(s) that are viewed through the window. Figure 1 shows how a mask layer works: The top part of the figure shows the mask layer with the window in the shape of a circle. The next part of the

figure shows the layer to be masked. The last part of the figure shows the result of applying the mask. Figure 1 illustrates the simplest use of a mask layer. In most cases, you want to have other objects appear on the Stage and have the mask layer affect only a certain portion of the Stage.

The process for using a mask layer follows:

- Select an original layer that will become the masked layer—it contains the objects that you want to display through the mask layer window.
- Insert a new layer above the masked layer that will become the mask layer. A mask layer always masks the layer(s) immediately below it.
- Draw a filled shape, such as a circle, or create an instance of a symbol that will become the window on the mask layer. Flash ignores bitmaps, gradients, transparency colors, and line styles on a mask layer. On a mask layer, filled areas become transparent and non-filled areas become opaque when viewed over a masked layer.

Creating Special Effects

- Select the new layer and open the Layer Properties dialog box. To open the Layer Properties dialog box, click Modify on the menu bar, point to the Timeline, then click Layer Properties. In the Layer Properties dialog box, select Mask as the layer type. Flash converts the layer to the mask layer.

- Select the original layer and open the Layer Properties dialog box, then select Masked as the layer type. Flash converts the layer to the masked layer.
- Lock both the mask and masked layers.
- To mask additional layers: Drag an existing layer beneath the mask layer, or create a new layer beneath the mask layer

and use the Layer Properties dialog box to convert it to a masked layer.
- To unlink a masked layer: Drag it above the mask layer, or select it and select Normal from the Layer Properties dialog box.

Figure 1 *A mask layer with a window*

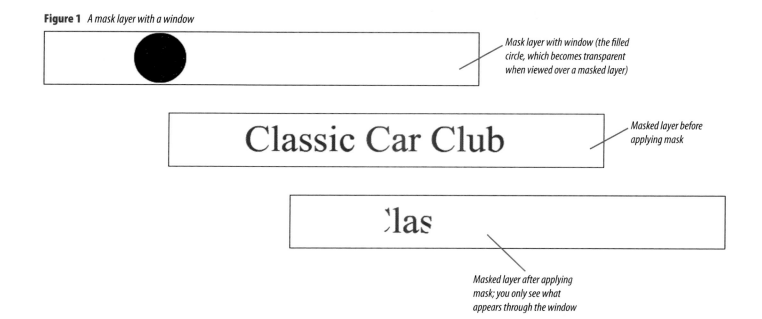

Mask layer with window (the filled circle, which becomes transparent when viewed over a masked layer)

Classic Car Club

Masked layer before applying mask

ʾlas

Masked layer after applying mask; you only see what appears through the window

Create a mask layer

1. Open fl5_1.fla, then save it as **classicCC.fla**.

2. Insert a **new layer**, name it **mask**, then click **frame 1** on the mask layer.

3. Select the **Oval tool** ⊙ on the Tools panel, set the **Stroke Color** to **No Stroke** on the top row of the color palette.

4. Set the Fill Color to the **black color swatch** in the left column of the color palette.

5. Draw the circle shown in Figure 2, click the **Selection tool** ↖ on the Tools panel, then drag a **marquee** around the circle to select it.

6. Click **Insert** on the menu bar, click **Motion Tween**, then click **OK** to convert the drawing into a symbol so that it can be tweened.

   Note: Flash converts the object to a movie symbol as the default symbol type. To convert the object to a different symbol type, you must convert the symbol manually.

7. Click **frame 40** on the mask layer, then drag the **circle** to the position shown in Figure 3.

8. Click **mask** on the Timeline to select the mask layer, click **Modify** on the menu bar, point to **Timeline**, then click **Layer Properties**.

9. Verify that the Show check box is selected in the Name area, click the **Lock check box** to select it, click the **Mask option button** in the Type area, then click **OK**.

   The mask layer has a shaded mask icon next to it on the Timeline.

   Hint: Alternately, you can lock the layer using the Lock This Layer icon on the Timeline.

   (continued)

Figure 2 *Object to be used as the window on a mask layer*

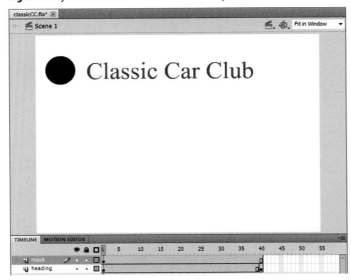

Figure 3 *Repositioning the circle*

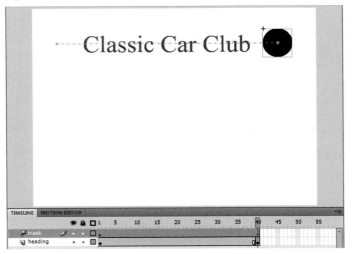

Creating Special Effects

Figure 4 *The completed Layer Properties dialog box*

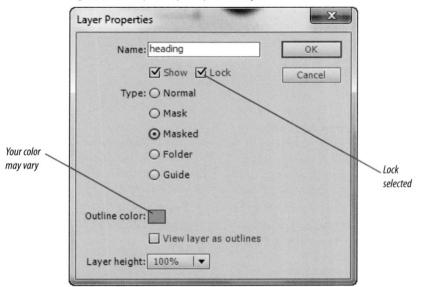

Your color may vary

Lock selected

10. Play the movie from frame 1 and notice how the circle object covers the text on the heading layer as it moves across the Stage.

    Note: The circle object will not become transparent until a masked layer is created beneath it.

You created a mask layer containing a circle object that moves across the Stage.

Create a masked layer

1. Click **heading** on the Timeline to select the heading layer, click **Modify** on the menu bar, point to **Timeline,** then click **Layer Properties** to open the Layer Properties dialog box.

2. Verify that the Show check box is selected in the Name area, click the **Lock check box** to select it, click the **Masked option button** in the Type area, compare your dialog box to Figure 4, then click **OK.**

    The text on the Stage seems to disappear. The heading layer is indented and has a shaded masked icon next to it on the Timeline.

3. Play the movie and notice how the circle object acts as a window to display the text on the heading layer.

4. Click **Control** on the menu bar, point to **Test Movie,** then click **in Flash Professional.**

5. View the movie, then close the Flash Player window.

6. Save your work, then close the movie.

You used the Layer Properties dialog box to create a masked layer.

Add SOUND

What You'll Do

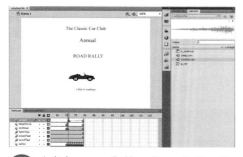

 In this lesson, you will add sound to an animation and to a button click event.

Incorporating Animation and Sound

Sound can be extremely useful in a Flash movie. Sounds are often the only effective way to convey an idea, elicit an emotion, dramatize a point, and provide feedback to a user's action, such as clicking a button. How would you describe in words or show in an animation the sound a whale makes? Think about how chilling it is to hear the footsteps on the stairway of a haunted house. Consider how useful it is to hear the pronunciation of "buenos dias" as you are studying Spanish. All types of sounds can be incorporated into a Flash movie: for example, CD-quality music that might be used as background for a movie; narrations that help explain what the user is seeing; various sound effects, such as a car horn beeping; and recordings of special events, such as a presidential speech or a rock concert.

The process for adding a sound to a movie follows:

- Import a sound file into a Flash movie; Flash places the sound file in the movie's library.
- Create a new layer.
- Select the desired frame on the new layer where you want the sound to play and drag the sound symbol to the Stage.

You can place more than one sound file on a layer, and you can place sounds on layers that have other objects. However, it is recommended that you place each sound on a separate layer so that it is easier to identify and edit. In Figure 5, the sound layer shows a wave pattern that extends from frame 1 to frame 24. The wave pattern gives some indication of the volume of the sound at any particular frame. The higher spikes in the pattern indicate a louder sound. The wave pattern also gives some indication of the pitch. The denser the wave pattern, the lower the pitch. You can alter the sound by adding or removing frames. However, removing frames may create undesired effects. It is best to make changes to a sound file using a sound-editing program.

You can use options in the Properties panel, as shown in Figure 6, to specify special effects (such as fade in and fade out) and to synchronize a sound to an event (such as clicking a button). You can import the following sound file formats into Flash:

- ASND (Windows or Macintosh)
- WAV (Windows only)
- AIFF (Macintosh only)
- MP3 (Windows or Macintosh)

If you have QuickTime 4 or later installed on your computer, you can import these additional sound file formats:

- AIFF (Windows or Macintosh)
- Sound Designer II (Macintosh only)
- Sound Only QuickTime Movies (Windows or Macintosh)
- Sun AU (Windows or Macintosh)
- System 7 Sounds (Macintosh only)
- WAV (Windows or Macintosh)

Figure 5 *A wave pattern displayed on a sound layer*

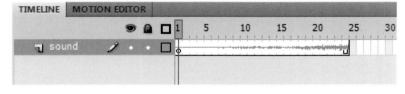

Figure 6 *Sound Effect options in the Properties panel*

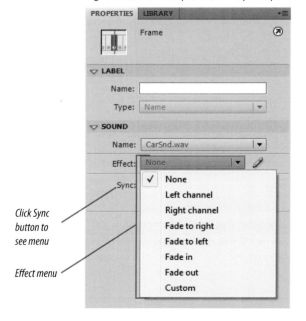

Click Sync button to see menu

Effect menu

Add sound to a movie

1. Open fl5_2.fla, then save it as **rallySnd.fla**.

2. Play the movie and notice that there is no sound.

3. Click the **stopMovie layer**, insert a **new layer**, then name it **carSnd**.

4. Insert a **keyframe** in frame 72 on the carSnd layer.

5. Click **File** on the menu bar, point to **Import**, then click **Import to Library**.

6. Use the Import to Library dialog box to navigate to the drive and folder where your Data Files are stored, click the **CarSnd.wav file**, then click **Open**.

7. Display the Library panel, click **CarSnd.wav**, then click the **Play button** ▶ in the Preview window.

8. Click **frame 72** on the carSnd layer.

9. Drag the **CarSnd sound symbol** 🔊 to the Stage, as shown in Figure 7.

   After releasing the mouse button, notice the wave pattern that has been placed on the carSnd layer starting in frame 72.

TIP The wave pattern may not appear on the layer until the movie is played one time.

10. Change the frame rate to **12 fps**.

11. Click **Control** on the menu bar, point to **Test Movie**, then click **in Flash Professional**.

12. Click the **Click to continue button** to test the sound.

13. Close the Flash Player window.

You imported a sound and added it to a movie.

Figure 7 *Dragging the CarSnd symbol to the Stage*

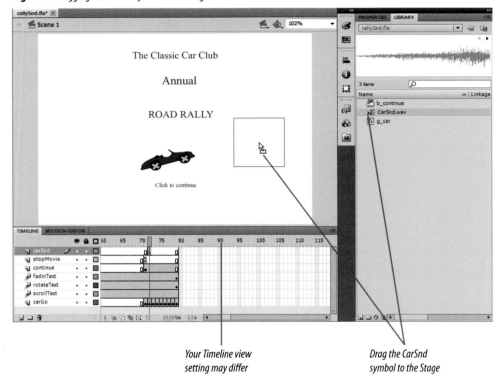

Your Timeline view setting may differ

Drag the CarSnd symbol to the Stage

Creating Special Effects

Figure 8 *The Timeline for the button with the sound layer*

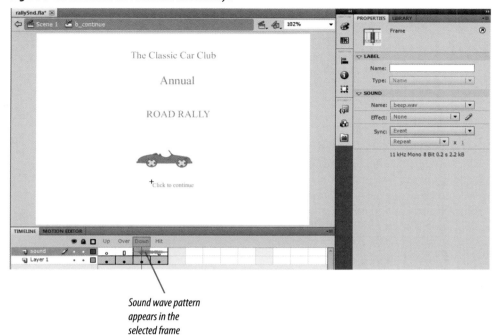

Sound wave pattern
appears in the
selected frame

1. Click **frame 71** on the carSnd layer.

2. Click the **Selection tool** ▶ on the Tools panel, drag a **marquee** around "Click to continue" to select the button, then double-click the **button** to display the button's Timeline.

3. Insert a **new layer** above Layer 1, then name it **sound**.

4. Click the **Down frame** on the sound layer, click **Insert** on the menu bar, point to **Timeline**, then click **Blank Keyframe**.

5. Click **File** on the menu bar, point to **Import**, then click **Import to Library**.

6. Use the Import to Library dialog box to navigate to the drive and folder where your Data Files are stored, click the **beep.wav file**, then click **Open**.

7. Display the Properties panel, click the **Name list arrow** in the SOUND area, then click **beep.wav**.

8. Click the **Sync list arrow** in the Properties panel, click **Event**, then compare your screen to Figure 8.

9. Click **Scene 1** on the upper left of the edit window title bar to display the main Timeline.

10. Test the movie.

11. Click the **Click to continue button** and listen to the sounds, then close the Flash Player window.

12. Save your work, then close the movie.

You added a sound layer to a button, imported a sound, then attached the sound to the button.

Add VIDEO

What You'll Do

In this lesson, you will import a video, add actions to video control buttons, and then synchronize sound to a video clip.

Incorporating Video

Adobe Flash allows you to import FLV (Flash video) files that then can be used in a Flash document. Flash provides several ways to add video to a movie, depending on the application and, especially, the file size. Video content can be embedded directly into a Flash document, progressively downloaded, or streamed.

Embedded video becomes part of the SWF file similar to other objects, such as sound and graphics. A placeholder appears on the Stage and is used to display the video during playback. If the video is imported as a movie clip symbol, then the placeholder can be edited, including rotating, resizing, and even animating it. Because embedded video becomes part of the SWF file, the technique of embedding video is best used for small video clips in order to keep the document file size small. The process for embedding video is to import a video file using the Import Video Wizard. Then, you place the video on the Stage and add controls as desired. Figure 9 shows a video placeholder

for an embedded video. The video file (fireworks.flv) is in the Library panel and the video layer on the Timeline contains the video object. The embedded video plays when the Play button is clicked.

Progressive downloading allows you to use ActionScript to load an external FLV file into a SWF file; the video then plays when the SWF file is played. With progressive downloading, the FLV file resides outside the SWF file. As a result, the SWF file size can be kept smaller than when the video is embedded in the Flash document. The video begins playing soon after the first part of the file has been downloaded.

Streaming video provides a constant connection between the user and the video delivery. Streaming has several advantages over the other methods of delivering video, including starting the video more quickly and allowing for live video delivery. However, streaming video requires the Flash Media Server, an Adobe software product designed specifically for streaming video content.

Using the Import Video Wizard

The Import Video Wizard is used to import FLV files into Flash documents. The wizard, in a step-by-step process, leads you through a series of windows that allow you to select the file to be imported and the deployment method (embedded, progressive, streaming). In addition, you can specify whether or not to have the video converted to a movie clip symbol which allows you to animate the placeholder. The wizard appears when you choose the Import Video command from the Import option on the File menu.

Using the Adobe Media Encoder

The Adobe Media Encoder is an application used by Flash to convert various video file formats, such as .mov, .avi, and .mpeg, to the FLV (Flash Video) format so the videos can be used with Flash. The Encoder allows you to, among other things, choose the size of the placeholder the video will play in, edit the video, and insert cue points that can be used to synchronize the video with animations and sound. Figure 10 shows the Encoder ready to convert the fireworks.mov video (Source Name) to fireworks.flv (Output File). The Start Queue button is used to start the process. When the conversion is complete, a green check mark is displayed in the Status column. The Adobe Media Encoder can be accessed through the Import Video Wizard.

Figure 9 *An embedded video*

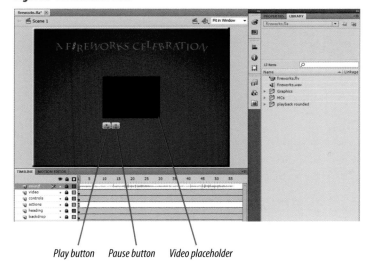

Play button   Pause button   Video placeholder

Figure 10 *The Adobe Media Encoder*

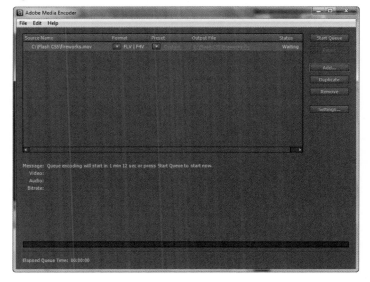

Import a video

1. Open fl5_3.fla, then save it as **fireworks.fla**.

   Note: If the Missing Font Warning message appears, click Use Default.

   The movie has four layers and 85 frames. The actions layer has a stop action in frame 1. The heading layer contains the text object. The controls layer contains start and pause buttons that will be used to control the video. The backdrop layer contains a blue gradient backdrop object. The Library panel contains the two button symbols and a sound file as well as graphics and movie clip files.

2. Set the view to **Fit in Window**.

3. Insert a **new layer** above the controls layer, name it **video**, then click **frame 1** on the video layer.

4. Click **File** on the menu bar, point to **Import**, then click **Import Video**.

   The Import Video Wizard begins by asking for the path to the video file and the desired method for importing the file, as shown in Figure 11.

5. Click the **Embed FLV in SWF and play in timeline option button**.

6. Click **Browse**, navigate to the drive and folder where your Data Files are stored, click **fireworks.mov**, then click **Open**.

   A message appears indicating that the video format is not valid for embedding video. You must convert the file to the FLV format.

7. Click **OK**, then click the **Launch Adobe Media Encoder button**.

   (continued)

Figure 11 *The Import Video Wizard*

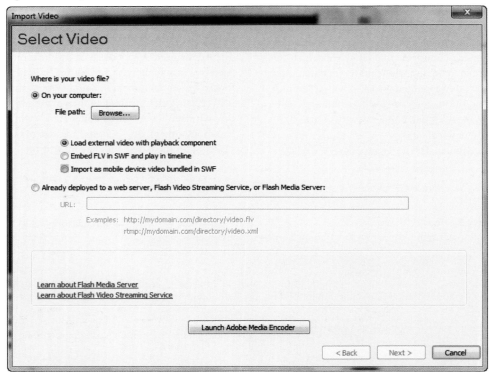

Figure 12 *The completed Select Video window*

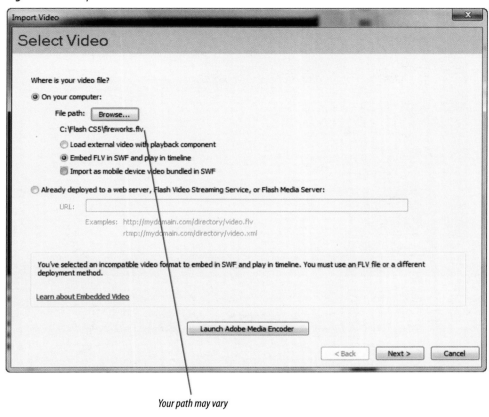

Your path may vary

Note: If a message about browsing to the file after it is converted opens, click OK.

After several moments the encoder opens.

Note: Click the Adobe Media Encoder button on the taskbar if the encoder does not open automatically in its own window.

8. Click **Start Queue**, then, when the process is done as indicated by a green check mark, close the encoder window.

9. Click **OK** to close the message window if one opens, then click the **Browse button**.

10. Click **fireworks.flv**, then click **Open**.

Note: If you do not see fireworks.flv, navigate to the drive and folder where you saved your solution file.

The Select Video screen now displays the path to the fireworks.flv file, as shown in Figure 12.

11. Click **Next** (Win) or **Continue** (Mac) in the wizard.

The Embedding window opens, which allows you to specify how you would like to embed the video.

12. Read the screen and verify all the options have a check mark.

13. Click **Next** (Win) or **Continue** (Mac).

14. Read the Finish Video Import screen, then click **Finish**.

The video is encoded and placed on the Stage and in the Library panel.

You imported a video then specified the encoding and embed type.

Lesson 3 Add Video

FLASH 5-15

Attach actions to video control buttons

1. Test the movie, then click the **control buttons**.

   Nothing happens because there is a stop action in frame 1 and no actions have been assigned to the buttons.

2. Close the Flash Player window.

3. Open the Actions panel.

4. Click the **play button** on the Stage, then verify the btn_play button symbol appears in the lower-left corner of the Script pane.

5. Turn on Script Assist if it is off.

6. Click the **Add a new item to the script button** , point to **Global Functions**, point to **Timeline Control**, then click **play** as shown in Figure 13.

7. Click the **Pause button** on the Stage, then verify the btn_pause button symbol appears in the lower-left corner of the Script pane.

8. Click the **Add a new item to the script button** , point to **Global Functions**, point to **Timeline Control**, then click **stop**.

9. Close the Actions panel.

10. Test the movie, click the **play button**, then click the **pause button**.

    The video plays, however there is no sound.

11. Close the Flash Player window.

You assigned play and stop actions to video control buttons.

Figure 13 *Using Script Assist to assign a play action to a button*

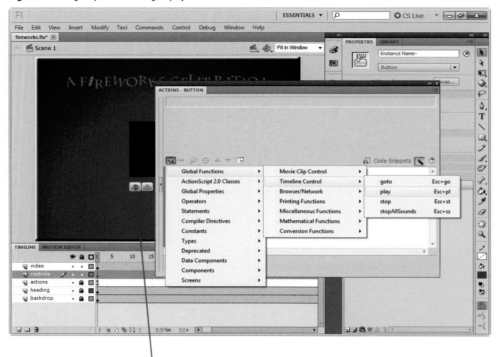

Play button selected

Figure 14 *The completed Properties panel*

Synchronize sound to a video clip

1. Insert a **new layer** above the video layer, then name it **sound**.

2. Click **frame 1** on the sound layer.

3. Display the Properties panel, then display the SOUND area options.

4. Click the **Name list arrow** in the SOUND area, then click **fireworks.wav**.

5. Click the **Sync sound list arrow** in the SOUND area, then click **Stream**.

6. Click the **Repeat list arrow**, click **Loop**, then compare your Properties panel to Figure 14.

7. Test the movie, click the **play button**, then click the **pause button**.

8. Close the Flash Player window.

9. Lock all layers.

10. Save your work, then close the file.

You inserted a layer, then you synchronized a sound to the video clip.

Create an Animated NAVIGATION BAR

What You'll Do

 In this lesson, you will work through the process to create one drop-down menu. A navigation bar has been provided, as well as the necessary buttons.

Understanding Animated Navigation Bars

A common navigation scheme for a website is a navigation bar with drop-down menus, such as the one shown in Figure 15. Using a navigation bar has several advantages. First, it allows the developer to provide several menu options to the user without cluttering the screen, thereby providing more screen space for the website content. Second, it allows the user to go quickly to a location on the site without having to navigate several screens to find the desired content. Third, it provides consistency in function and appearance, making it easy for users to learn and work with the navigation scheme.

There are various ways to create drop-down menus using the animation capabilities of Flash and ActionScript. One common technique allows you to give the illusion of a drop-down menu by using masks that

Figure 15 *Navigation bar with drop-down menus*

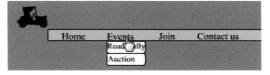

reveal the menu. When the user points to (rolls over) a menu item on the navigation bar, a list or "menu" of buttons is displayed ("drops down"). Then the user can click a button, which might go to another location in the website or trigger some other action, depending on the action assigned to the button. The dropping down of the list is actually an illusion created by using a mask to "uncover" the menu options.

The process for creating a drop-down menu follows:

- **Create a navigation bar.** This could be as basic as a background graphic in the shape of a rectangle with buttons that represent the navigation bar menu items.
- **Position the drop-down buttons.** Add a drop-down buttons layer beneath the navigation bar layer. Next, select an empty frame adjacent to the first frame containing the navigation bar. Place the buttons that will be used to create the drop down list on the Stage below their respective menu items on the navigation bar. For example, if the navigation bar has an Events button with two choices, Road Rally and Auction, that you want

to appear as buttons on a drop-down menu, position these two buttons below the Events button on the drop-down buttons layer.

- **Create an animated mask.** Add a mask layer above the drop-down buttons layer and create an animation of an object that starts above the drop-down buttons and moves down to reveal them. Then change the layer to a mask layer and the drop-down buttons layer to a masked layer.
- **Assign actions to the drop-down buttons.** Select each drop-down button and assign an action, such as "on (release) gotoAndPlay."
- **Assign a roll over action to the navigation bar menu item button.** The desired effect is to have the drop-down buttons appear when the user points to a navigation bar button. Therefore, you need to assign an "on rollOver" action to the navigation bar button that causes the playhead to go to the frame that plays the animation on the mask layer. This can be done using the Script Assist feature.
- **Create an invisible button.** When the user points to a navigation bar button, the drop-down menu appears showing the drop-down buttons. There needs to be a way to have the menu disappear when the user points away from the navigation bar button. This can be done by creating a button on a layer below the masked layer. This button is slightly larger than the drop-down buttons and their navigation bar button, as shown in Figure 16. A rollOver action is assigned to this

button so that when the user rolls off the drop-down or navigation bar buttons, he or she rolls onto this button and the action is carried out. This button should be made transparent so the user does not see it.

Using Frame Labels

Until now, you have worked with frame numbers in ActionScript code when creating a goto action. Frame labels can also be used in the code. You can assign a label to a frame as an identifier. For example, you could assign the label home to frame 10 and then create a goto home action that will cause the playhead to jump to frame 10. One advantage of using frame labels is that if you insert frames on the Timeline, the label adjusts for the added frames. So, you do not have to change the ActionScript that uses the frame label. Another advantage is that the descriptive labels help you identify parts

of the movie as you work with the Timeline. You assign a frame label by selecting the desired frame and typing a label in the Frame text box in the Properties panel.

Understanding Scenes

When you create a movie, the phrase Scene 1 appears above the Stage. You can add scenes to a movie at any time. Scenes are one way to organize long movies. For example, a movie created for a website could be divided into several scenes: an introduction, a home page, and content pages. Each scene has its own Timeline. You can insert new scenes by using the Insert menu and view them using the Other Panels option on the Windows menu. Scenes can be given descriptive names, which will help you find them easily if you need to edit a particular scene. One drawback to using scenes is potentially larger file sizes.

Figure 16 *A button that will be assigned a rollOver action*

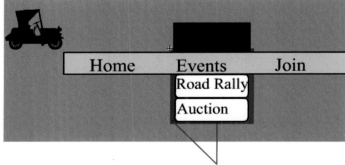

When the user rolls over any part of the blue button with the pointer, a script is executed that causes the drop-down menu to disappear

Position the drop-down buttons

1. Open fl5_4.fla, then save it as **navBar.fla**.

2. Click the **homeBkgrnd layer**, insert a **new layer**, then name it **roadRally**.

3. Click **frame 2** on the roadRally layer, then insert a **keyframe**.

4. Display the Library panel, open the Buttons folder, then drag the **b_roadRally button** to the position just below the Events button on the Navigation bar, as shown in Figure 17.

5. Insert a **new layer** above the homeBkgrnd layer, then name it **auction**.

6. Click **frame 2** on the auction layer, then insert a **keyframe**.

7. Drag the **b_auction button** from the Library panel and position it below the b_roadRally button.

8. Click the **Zoom tool** 🔍 on the Tools panel, then click the **Events button** on the navigation bar to enlarge the view.

9. Click the **Selection tool** ▶ on the Tools panel, then click each button and use the arrow keys to position each button, as shown in Figure 18.

   The bottom border of the navigation bar must overlap the top line of the Road Rally button, and the bottom border of the Road Rally button must overlap the top border of the Auction button.

You placed the drop-down buttons on the Stage and repositioned them.

Figure 17 *Positioning the b_roadRally button*

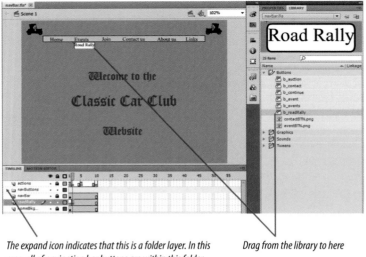

The expand icon indicates that this is a folder layer. In this case, all of navigation bar buttons are within this folder. Clicking the arrow reveals the contents of the folder.

Drag from the library to here

Figure 18 *Positioning the buttons*

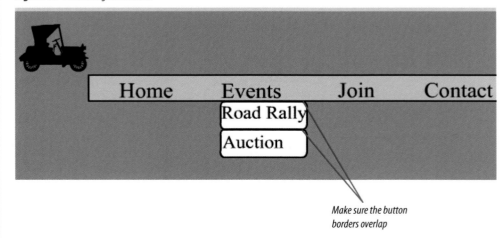

Make sure the button borders overlap

Creating Special Effects

Figure 19 *The drawn rectangle that covers the buttons*

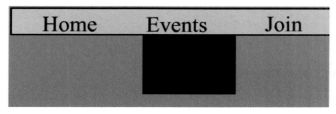

Home   Events   Join

Figure 20 *Dragging the rectangle above the buttons*

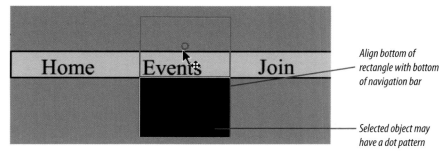

Home   Events   Join

Align bottom of rectangle with bottom of navigation bar

Selected object may have a dot pattern

Figure 21 *Positioning the rectangle over the buttons*

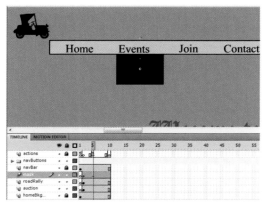

Add a mask layer

1. Click the **roadRally layer**, insert a **new layer** above the roadRally layer, then name it **mask**.

2. Click **frame 2** on the mask layer, then insert a **keyframe**.

3. Select the **Rectangle tool** ▭ on the Tools panel, set the Stroke Color to **none** ⬜ , then set the Fill Color to **black**.

4. Draw a **rectangle** that covers the buttons, as shown in Figure 19.

5. Click the **Selection tool** ▸ on the Tools panel, then drag the **rectangle** to above the buttons, as shown in Figure 20.

6. Verify the rectangle is selected, click **Insert** on the menu bar, click **Motion Tween**, then click **OK**.

   Note: Flash automatically converts the object to a movie symbol, which can have a motion tween applied to it. If you want the object to be a different type of symbol, you need to convert the object to the symbol type of your choice before inserting the motion tween.

7. Click **frame 5** on the mask layer, then insert a **keyframe**.

8. Use the **Selection tool** ▸ to move the **rectangle**, as shown in Figure 21.

9. Click **mask** on the Timeline, click **Modify** on the menu bar, point to **Timeline**, click **Layer Properties**, click the **Mask option button**, then click **OK**.

10. Click **roadRally** on the Timeline.

(continued)

11. Click **Modify** on the menu bar, point to **Timeline**, click **Layer Properties**, click the **Masked option button**, then click **OK**.

12. Click **auction** on the Timeline, then repeat step 11.

13. Drag the **playhead** along the Timeline, noticing how the mask hides and reveals the buttons.

You added a mask that animates to hide and reveal the menu buttons.

Assign an action to a drop-down button

1. Change the view to **Fit in Window**.

2. Click **frame 2** on the roadRally layer, then click the **Road Rally button** to select it.

3. Open the **Actions panel** and verify the Script Assist button is active and b_roadRally is displayed in the lower-left corner of the Script pane, as shown in Figure 22.

   b_roadRally in the lower-left corner of the Script pane tells you that the b_roadRally button symbol is selected on the Stage and that the ActionScript you create will apply to this object.

4. Click the **Add a new item to the script icon** ⊞ , point to **Global Functions,** point to **Timeline Control,** then click **goto.**

5. Click the **Scene list arrow,** point to **Scene 2** as shown in Figure 23, then click.

6. Verify the Type is set to Frame Number and the Frame is set to 1.

7. Collapse the Actions panel.

You used the Script Assist window to assign a goto action to a menu button.

Figure 22 *The Actions panel with the b_roadRally button selected*

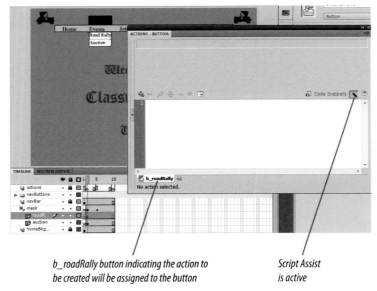

b_roadRally button indicating the action to be created will be assigned to the button

Script Assist is active

Figure 23 *Selecting the scene to go to*

Scenes, which have their own Timeline, are a way to organize large movies. In this case, Scene 2 contains the Road Rally screen for the website.

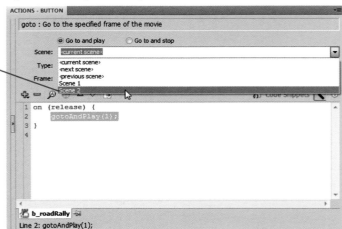

Figure 24 *Specifying a frame label*

Figure 25 *The completed Actions panel*

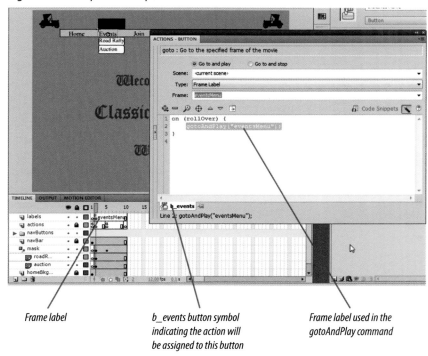

Frame label

b_events button symbol indicating the action will be assigned to this button

Frame label used in the gotoAndPlay command

Add a frame label and assign a rollOver action

1. Insert a **new layer** at the top of the Timeline, name it **labels**, then insert a **keyframe** in frame 2 on the labels layer.

2. Display the Properties panel, click inside the **Name text box** in the LABEL area, then type **eventsMenu**, as shown in Figure 24.

3. Click the **Events button** on the Stage to select it.

4. Expand the Actions panel, then verify b_events is displayed in the lower-left corner of the Script pane.

5. Click the **Add a new item to the script icon**, point to **Global Functions**, point to **Movie Clip Control**, then click **on**.

6. Click the **Release check box** to deselect it, then click the **Roll Over check box** to select it.

7. Click the **Add a new item to the script icon**, point to **Global Functions**, point to **Timeline Control**, then click **goto**.

8. Click the **Type list arrow**, then click **Frame Label**.

9. Click the **Frame list arrow**, then click **eventsMenu**.

   Your screen should resemble Figure 25.

10. Click **Control** on the menu bar, point to **Test Movie**, then click **in Flash Professional**.

11. Point to **Events**, then click **Road Rally**.

12. Close the Flash Player window, collapse the Actions panel, then save your work.

You added a frame label and assigned a rollOver action using the frame label.

Add an invisible button

1. Click **Control** on the menu bar, point to **Test Movie**, then click **in Flash Professional**.

2. Move the pointer over Events on the navigation bar, then move the pointer away from Events.

   Notice that when you point to Events, the drop-down menu appears. However, when you move the pointer away from the menu, it does not disappear.

3. Close the Flash Player window.

4. Insert a **new layer** above the homeBkgrnd layer, then name it **rollOver**.

5. Insert a **keyframe** in frame 2 on the rollOver layer.

6. Click the **Zoom tool** 🔍 on the Tools panel, then click the **Events button** on the navigation bar to enlarge the view.

7. Select the **Rectangle tool** ▭ on the Tools panel, verify that the Stroke Color is set to **none**, then set the Fill Color to **blue**.

8. Draw a **rectangle**, as shown in Figure 26.

9. Click the **Selection tool** ▶ on the Tools panel, then click the **blue rectangle** to select it.

10. Click **Modify** on the menu bar, then click **Convert to Symbol**.

11. Type **b_rollOver** for the name, click the **Type list arrow**, click **Button**, then click **OK**.

12. Expand the Actions panel.

(continued)

Figure 26 *Drawing the rectangle*

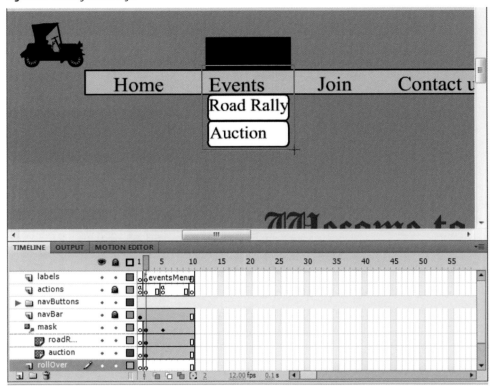

Figure 27 *The Actions panel displaying ActionScript assigned to the b_rollOver button symbol*

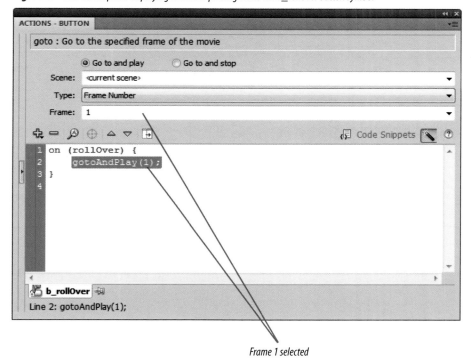

Frame 1 selected

13. Verify the rollOver button is selected and b_rollOver is displayed in the lower-left corner of the Script pane.

14. Click the **Add a new item to the script icon**, point to **Global Functions**, point to **Movie Clip Control**, then click **on**.

15. Click the **Release check box** to deselect it, then click the **Roll Over check box** to select it.

16. Click the **Add a new item to the script icon**, point to **Global Functions**, point to **Timeline Control**, then click **goto**.

17. Verify Frame 1 is specified, as shown in Figure 27.

18. Close the Actions panel.

19. Click the **Style list arrow** in the COLOR EFFECT area of the Properties panel, click **Alpha**, then set the percentage to **0**.

20. Click **Control** on the menu bar, point to **Test Movie**, then click **in Flash Professional**.

21. Point to **Events** to display the drop-down menu, then slowly move the pointer away from Events.

    The drop-down menu disappears.

22. Close the Flash Player window, then save and close the movie.

You added a button and assigned a rollOver action to it, then made the button transparent.

Create Character Animations
USING INVERSE KINEMATICS

What You'll Do

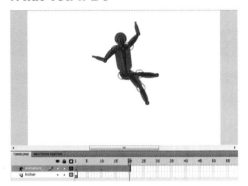

In this lesson, you will use the bone tool to create a character animation and create a movie clip that can be manipulated by the viewer.

Understanding Inverse Kinematics

One way to create character animations is to use the frame-by-frame process in which you place individually drawn objects into a series of successive frames. You did this with the stick figure graphics in an earlier chapter. Those graphics were simple to draw. However, if you have more complex drawings, such as fill shapes that are more realistic, and if you want to create animations that show an unlimited number of poses, the time required to develop all of the necessary drawings would be considerable.

Flash provides a process that allows you to create a single image and add a structure to the image that can be used to animate the various parts of the image. The process is called **Inverse Kinematics (IK)** and involves creating an articulated structure of bones that allow you to link the parts of an image. Once the bone structure is created, you can animate the image by changing the position of any of its parts. The bone structure causes the related parts to animate in a natural way. For example, if you draw an image of a person, create the bone structure, and then move the person's right foot, then all parts of

the leg (lower leg, knee, upper leg) respond. This makes it easy to animate various movements.

Figure 28 shows a drawing of a character before and after the bone structure is added. Figure 29 shows how moving the right foot moves the entire leg. The image is made up of several small drawings, each one converted to a graphic symbol. These include a head, torso, upper and lower arms, upper and lower legs, hips, and feet. Together these form the IK object.

Creating the Bone Structure

The bone structure can be applied to a single drawn shape, such as an oval created with the Flash drawing tools. More often it is applied to an image, such as a character, made up of several drawings. When this is the case, each drawing is converted to a graphic symbol or a movie clip symbol and then assembled to form the desired image. If you import a graphic, it needs to be broken apart using the Modify menu and the individual parts of the imported graphic converted to graphic symbols or movie clip symbols. However, if the imported graphic has only one part (such as a bitmap), it needs to be broken apart and treated as a single drawn shape.

Once the image is ready, you use the Bone tool to create the bone structure, called the armature, by clicking and dragging the Bone tool pointer to link one part of the image to another. You continue adding bones to the structure until all parts of the image are linked. For a human form you would link the head to the torso and the torso to the upper left arm and the upper left arm to the lower left arm, and so on. The bones in an armature are connected to each other in a parent-child hierarchy, so that adjusting the child adjusts the parent.

Animating the IK Object

As you are creating the bone structure, a layer named Armature is added to the Timeline, and the image with the bone structure is placed in frame 1 on that layer. This new layer is called a **pose layer**. Each pose layer can contain only one armature and its associated image. Animating the image is done on this layer by inserting a keyframe in any frame after frame 1 on the Armature layer and then changing the position of one or more of the bones. This is referred to as creating a pose. Once you specify the start and end positions of the image, Flash interpolates the position of the parts of the image for the in-between frames. So, when one bone moves, the other connected bones move in relation to it. Additional poses can be set along the Timeline by inserting keyframes and adjusting the bone structure. Animations of IK objects, other than those within movie clips, only allow you to change the shape, position, and ease in the animation.

Figure 28 *Drawings showing before and after the bone structure is added*

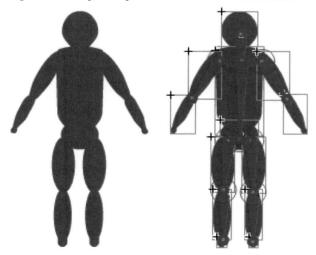

Figure 29 *Moving the foot moves the other parts of the leg*

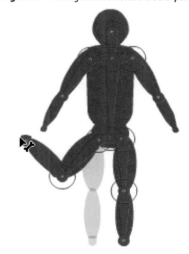

Creating a Movie Clip with an IK Object

Movie clips provide a great deal of flexibility when animating IK objects. You can change properties such as the color effect and you can nest one movie clip within another. So, you could have a movie clip of a character walking and nest another movie clip within it to have its mouth move. In addition, you can apply a motion tween to a movie clip.

So, you could have a movie clip of a character walking and have it play within a motion tween which causes the character (movie clip) to jump over an obstacle.

Runtime Feature

Flash provides a runtime feature for manipulation of an IK object. That is, you can allow the user to click the object and adjust the image. This is useful if you are creating a game or just wanting to provide some interaction on a website. The process is to click a frame on the Armature layer, then use the Properties panel to set the Type to Runtime. The runtime feature only works with IK structures connected to drawn shapes or movie clip symbols, not graphic or button symbols. In addition, only one pose can used.

IK Objects

As you are working with IK objects, keep in mind the following:

- The Undo feature can be used to undo a series of actions such as undoing a mistake made when creating the bone structure.
- The bone structure may disappear as you are working on it. This could be caused by going outside the image as you are connecting the parts of the image. If the bone structure disappears, use the Undo feature to Undo your last action.
- To delete an individual bone and all of its children, click the bone and press [Delete]. You can select multiple bones to delete by holding down [Shift] and clicking each bone.
- To delete all bones, select the image and choose the Break Apart command from the Modify menu.
- To create IK animations, ActionScript 3.0 and Flash Player 10 need to be specified in the Publish Settings dialog box, which is displayed by choosing Publish Settings from the File menu.

Figure 30 *Connecting the head and torso*

Figure 31 *Connecting the torso and the upper arm*

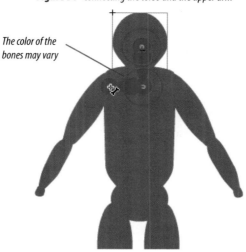

The color of the bones may vary

Figure 32 *Connecting the upper and lower arms*

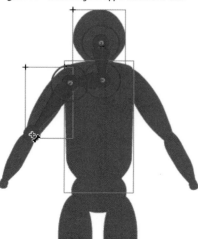

Figure 33 *The completed bone structure*

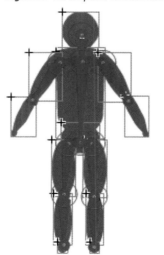

Create the bone structure

1. Open fl5_5.fla, then save it as **kicker.fla**.

   This document has a graphic symbol made up of 13 individual drawings to form a character shape.

2. Click the **Selection tool** ↖ , then drag a **marquee** around the image to select it.

   Notice the separate objects.

3. Click a blank area of the Stage to deselect the image.

4. Click the **Zoom tool** 🔍 , then click the **image** to zoom in on it.

5. Scroll the Stage to view the head, then click the **Bone tool** 🦴 on the Tools panel.

6. Point to the middle of the head, when the pointer changes to a bone with a cross ⚑ , drag the ⚑ **pointer** down to the torso as shown in Figure 30, then release the mouse button.

7. Point to the bottom of the bone, then drag the ⚑ **pointer** to the left as shown in Figure 31.

8. Point to the left end of the bone, then drag the ⚑ **pointer** down as shown in Figure 32.

   Notice that a bone connects two overlapping objects, such as the bone used to connect the upper arm and lower arm.

9. Using Figure 33 as a guide, complete the drawing of the other bones.

   Hint: Use the Undo command as needed if your connections do not match Figure 33.

10. Save your work.

You created a bone structure by connecting objects on the Stage with the Bone tool.

Animate the character

1. Change the view to **Fit in Window**.
2. Click **frame 10** on the Armature layer, then insert a **keyframe**.

   Note: The name of your Armature layer will include a number.
3. Click the **Selection tool** ![selection icon], then click a blank area of the Stage to deselect the object if it is selected.
4. Point to the **right foot**, then, when the pointer changes to a bone with a delta symbol ![bone icon], drag the ![bone icon] **pointer** to position the foot as shown in Figure 34.
5. Point to the **right arm**, then use the ![bone icon] pointer to position it as shown in Figure 35.
6. Use the ![bone icon] pointer to position the left arm and left foot as shown in Figure 36.

   Hint: To position the left foot, move the left knee first, then move the left foot.
7. Click **frame 20** on the Armature layer, then insert a **keyframe**.
8. Adjust the arms and legs as shown in Figure 37.

   Hint: Move the right leg to the position shown to create a kicking motion.
9. Click the **Free Transform tool** ![tool icon] on the Tools panel, then drag a **marquee** around the image to select it if it is not already selected.
10. Point to the **upper-right handle**, then, when the pointer changes to an arc ![arc icon], drag the ![arc icon] **pointer** to the left as shown in Figure 38.
11. Test the movie, close the Flash Player window, then save the movie.

You animated the character by adjusting the armatures of the various bones.

Figure 34 *Positioning the right foot*

Figure 35 *Positioning the right arm*

Figure 36 *Positioning the left arm and left foot*

right leg

Figure 37 *Positioning the arms and legs*

right leg

Figure 38 *Rotating the object*

Figure 39 *Increasing the length of the motion span*

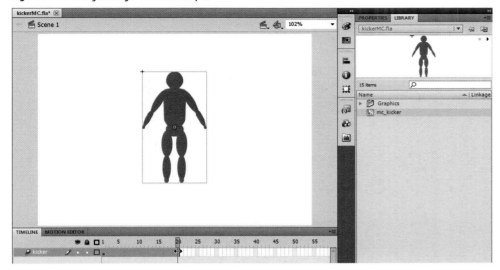

Create a movie clip of the IK object and animate the movie clip

1. Click **File** on the menu bar, click **Save as**, type **kickerMC**, then click **Save**.

2. Click **frame 1** on the Armature layer.

3. Click the **Selection tool** ![selection tool], then drag a **marquee** around the entire image to select it.

4. Click **Modify** on the menu bar, then click **Convert to Symbol**.

5. Type **mc_kicker** for the name, select **Movie Clip** for the Type, then click **OK**.

6. Click **Armature** on the Timeline, then click the **Delete icon** ![delete icon] to delete the layer.

7. Click **frame 1** on the kicker layer, display the Library panel, then drag the **mc_kicker symbol** to the Stage.

8. Insert a **motion tween**.

9. Drag the **tween span** on the Timeline to **frame 20**, as shown in Figure 39.

10. Click **frame 10** on the kicker layer.

11. Verify the object is selected, then press the **up arrow** [↑] on the keyboard 10 times.

12. Click **frame 20**, then press the **down arrow** [↓] on the keyboard 10 times.

    Steps 11 and 12 will give the impression of the character jumping up then coming down during the kicking motion.

13. Test the movie, close the Flash Player window, then save your work.

You created a movie clip and applied a motion tween to it.

Apply an ease value

1. Double-click the **mc_kicker symbol** in the Library panel to display the edit window, then scroll as needed to see the entire object.

2. Display the Properties panel.

3. Click **frame 10** on the Armature layer.

4. Set the Ease Strength to **-100**.

5. Click the **Type list arrow** in the EASE area, then click **Simple (Fastest)**

   The EASE type is set to Simple (Fastest), as shown in Figure 40. Frame 10 is the start of the motion tween where the right leg begins to kick downward. Setting the ease value to -100 will cause the leg motion to start out slow and accelerate as the leg follows through to the end of the kicking motion. This is a more natural way to represent the kick than to have the leg speed constant throughout the downward motion and follow through.

6. Click **Scene 1** on the edit window title bar to return to the main Timeline.

7. Test the movie, close the Flash Player window, save your work, then close the file.

You added an ease value to the movie clip.

Figure 40 *Setting the ease value*

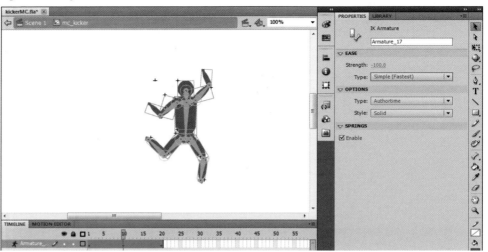

Creating Special Effects

Figure 41 *The completed armature structure*

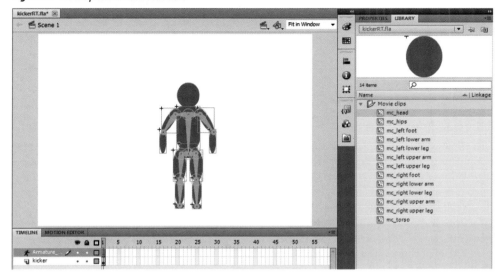

Set the play to runtime

1. Open fl5_6.fla, then save it as **kickerRT.fla**.

   This character is similar to the one used in the kicker movie, however it has been created using movie clips instead of graphic symbols. Also, only one pose is used.

2. Use the **Bone tool** to create the armature structure as shown in Figure 41.

   Hint: Each bone should connect two body parts.

3. Click **frame 1** on the Armature layer.

   Hint: If you have trouble clicking a frame, select a larger frame view setting and try again.

4. Display the Properties panel, click the **Type list arrow** in the OPTIONS area of the Properties panel, then click **Runtime**.

5. Click **File**, point to **Publish Preview**, then click **Default - (HTML)** to display the movie in a browser.

   Hint: Press [F12] (Win) or [command][F12] (Mac) to display the movie in a browser.

6. Drag each part of the character, such as an arm or a leg.

7. Close your browser.

8. Save your work, then close the document.

You created an animated character, set the play to runtime and manipulated the character in a browser.

Create 3D
EFFECTS

What You'll Do

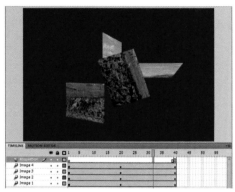

In this lesson, you will create a movie with 3D effects.

Understanding 3D Effects

Flash allows you to create 3D effects by manipulating objects in 3D space on the Stage. Until now you have been working in two dimensions, width and height. The default settings for the Stage are 550 pixels wide and 400 pixels high. These are represented by an x axis (across) and a y axis (down). Any position on the Stage can be specified by x and y coordinates. The upper-left corner of the Stage has an x value of 0 and a y value of 0, and the lower-right corner has an x value of 550 and a y value of 400, as shown in Figure 42. In 3D space there is also a z axis that represents depth. Flash provides two tools, 3D Translation and 3D Rotation that can be used to move and rotate objects using all three axes. In addition, Flash provides two other properties that can be adjusted to control the view of an object. The Perspective Angle property controls the angle of the object and can be used to create a zooming in and out effect. The Vanishing Point property more precisely controls the direction of an object as it moves away from the viewer. The Perspective Angle and the Vanishing Point settings are found in the Properties panel.

The 3D Tools

The 3D tools are available on the Tools panel. By default the 3D Rotation tool is displayed on the Tools panel. To access the 3D Translation tool, click and hold the 3D Rotation tool to open the menu. Toggle between these two 3D tools as needed.

The process for creating 3D effects is to create a movie clip (only movie clips can have 3D effects applied to them), place the movie clip on the Stage, create a motion tween and then click the object with either of the 3D tools. When you click an object with the 3D Translation tool, the three axes X, Y, and Z appear on top of the object, as shown in Figure 43. Each has its own color: red (X), green (Y), and blue (Z), which you see only when the 3D Rotation tool is active. The X and Y axes have arrows and the Z axis is represented by a black dot when the 3D Translation tool is active. You point to an arrow or the black dot and drag it to reposition the object. Dragging the X axis arrow moves the object horizontally. Dragging the Y axis arrow moves the object vertically. Dragging the Z axis dot zooms the object in and out.

When you click the object with the 3D Rotation tool, the three axes X, Y, and Z appear on top of the object, as shown in Figure 44. Dragging the X axis (red) will flip the object horizontally. Dragging the Y axis (green) will flip the object vertically. Dragging the Z axis (blue) will spin the object. A fourth option, the orange circle, rotates the object around the X and Y axes at the same time.

Using a Motion Tween with a 3D Effect

Creating 3D effects requires a change in the position of an object. A motion tween is used to specify where on the Timeline the effect will take place. This allows you to create more than one effect by selecting various frames in the tween span and making adjustments as desired. If you are animating more than one object, each object should be on its own layer.

Figure 42 *The x and y coordinates on the Stage*

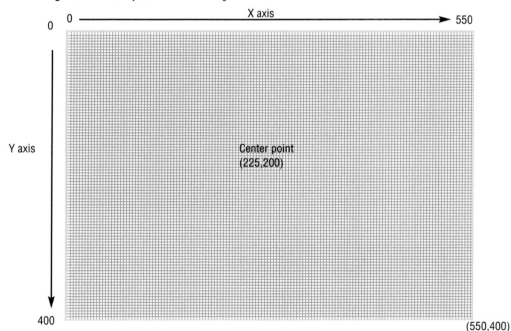

Figure 43 *The 3D Translation tool*

Figure 44 *The 3D Rotation tool*

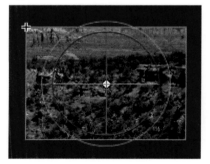

Create a 3D animation

1. Open fl5_7.fla, then save it as **puzzle.fla**.

   Note: The document opens with the ruler feature turned on and showing the vertical and horizontal lines that intersect at the center of the Stage.

2. Change the view to **Fit in Window**.

3. Click **frame 1** on the Image 1 layer, insert a **motion tween**, then drag the **tween span** to frame 40.

4. Click **frame 20** on the Image 1 layer, then select the **3D Translation tool** ⟁ from the Tools panel.

   Note: You may need to click the 3D Rotation tool on the Tools panel to display the 3D Translation tool.

5. Click the **image** in the upper-right corner of the Stage, point to the **green arrow tip**, then use the ▶Y pointer to drag the image down to the horizontal ruler line, as shown in Figure 45.

6. Click the **red arrow tip**, then use the ▶X pointer to drag the image to the left, as shown in Figure 46.

7. Select the **3D Rotation tool** ⦿ from the Tools panel, point to the **green line Y axis** on the right side of the object, then, when the pointer changes to a delta symbol with a Y, drag the ▶Y **pointer** down and to the left, as shown in Figure 47, to flip the image horizontally.

8. Click **frame 40** on the Image 1 layer, then select the **3D Translation tool** ⟁ from the Tools panel.

   (continued)

Figure 45 *Using the 3D Translation tool to position the image vertically*

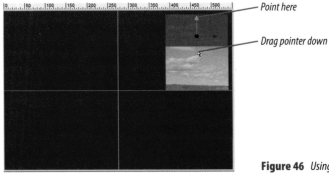

Point here

Drag pointer down

Figure 46 *Using the 3D Translation tool to position the image horizontally*

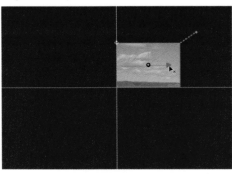

Figure 47 *Using the 3D Rotation tool to flip the image horizontally*

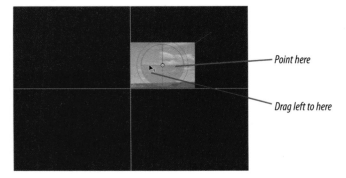

Point here

Drag left to here

Figure 48 *Using the 3D Translation tool to position the image again*

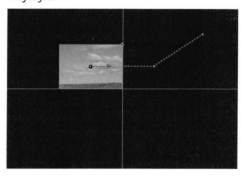

Figure 49 *Using the 3D Translation tool to position a second image*

Figure 50 *Using the 3D Rotation tool to flip the image vertically*

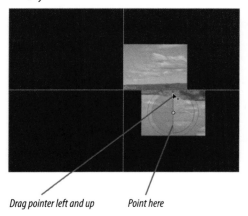

Drag pointer left and up   Point here

Figure 51 *Using the 3D Translation tool to reposition the second image*

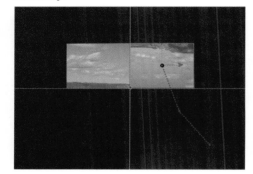

9. Click the **red arrow tip**, then use the ▶︎ₓ pointer to move the image to the position shown in Figure 48.

10. Select the **3D Rotation tool** 🔮, point to the **green line Y axis** on the left side of the object, then drag the ▶︎ᵧ **pointer** down and to the right to flip the image horizontally again.

11. Click **frame 1** on the Image 2 layer, insert a **motion tween**, then drag the **tween span** to frame 40.

12. Click **frame 20** on the Image 2 layer, then select the **3D Translation tool** 🔧.

13. Point to the **red and green arrow tips** and use the ▶︎ₓ pointer and the ▶︎ᵧ pointer respectively to drag the image to the position shown in Figure 49.

14. Select the **3D Rotation tool** 🔮, then point to the **bottom red line X axis**.

15. When the pointer changes to a delta symbol with an X, use the ▶︎ₓ pointer to drag the line to the left and up to flip the image vertically, as shown in Figure 50.

16. Click **frame 40** on the Image 2 layer, then select the **3D Translation tool** 🔧.

17. Point to the **red and green arrow tips** and use the ▶︎ₓ pointer and the ▶︎ᵧ pointer respectively to position the image as shown in Figure 51.

18. Select the **3D Rotation tool** 🔮, then point to the bottom red line X axis.

19. When the pointer changes to a ▶︎ₓ, drag the **line** to the left and up to flip the image vertically again.

(continued)

20. Click **frame 1** on the Image 3 layer, insert a **motion tween**, then drag the **tween span** to frame 40.

21. Click **frame 20** on the Image 3 layer, then select the **3D Translation tool** ⬩.

22. Point to the **red and green arrow tips** and use the ▶ₓ pointer and the ▶ᵧ pointer respectively to drag the image to the position shown in Figure 52.

23. Select the **3D Rotation tool** ◐, then point to the **blue circle Z axis**, as shown in Figure 53.

24. When the pointer changes to ▶_z, drag the circle to rotate the image clockwise 180 degrees, as shown in Figure 54.

25. Click **frame 40** on the Image 3 layer, then select the **3D Translation tool** ⬩.

26. Point to the **red and green arrow tips** and use the ▶ₓ pointer and the ▶ᵧ pointer respectively to position the image as shown in Figure 55.

27. Select the **3D Rotation tool** ◐, point to the **blue circle Z axis**, then use the ▶_z pointer to drag the circle and to rotate the image clockwise 180 degrees again.

28. Click **frame 1** on the Image 4 layer, insert a motion tween, then drag the **tween span** to frame 40.

29. Click **frame 20** on the Image 4 layer, then select the **3D Translation tool** ⬩.

(continued)

Figure 52 *Using the 3D Translation tool to position the third image*

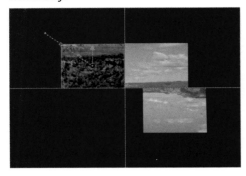

Figure 53 *Pointing to the blue circle Z axis on the 3D Rotation tool*

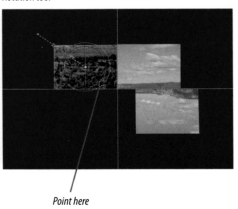

Point here

Figure 54 *Using the 3D Rotation tool to rotate the image*

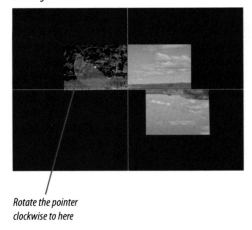

Rotate the pointer clockwise to here

Figure 55 *Using the 3D Translation tool to reposition the third image*

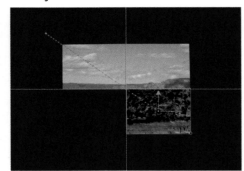

Creating Special Effects

Figure 56 *Using the 3D Translation tool to position the fourth image*

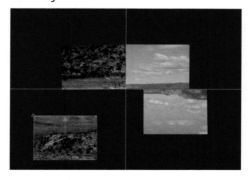

Figure 57 *Using the 3D Rotation tool to rotate the image*

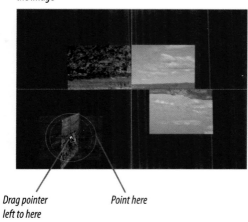

Drag pointer
left to here

Point here

Figure 58 *Using the 3D Translation tool to reposition the fourth image*

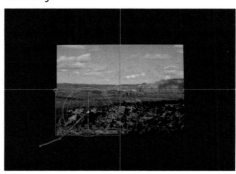

Figure 59 *The completed 3D effects movie*

30. Point to the **red and green arrow tips** and use the ►ₓ pointer and the ►ᵧ pointer respectively to position the image as shown in Figure 56.

31. Select the **3D Rotation tool** , then point to the right side of the **orange circle**.

32. When the pointer changes to a Delta symbol, drag the **► pointer** to the middle of the image as shown in Figure 57.

33. Click **frame 40** on the Image 4 layer, point to the left side of the orange circle, then drag the **► pointer** to the center of the image.

34. Use the **3D Translation tool** to position the image as shown in Figure 58.

35. Click the **Selection tool** , drag the **ruler lines** to remove them, then use the 3D tools and the red and green arrow tips to make adjustments as needed so your screen resembles Figure 59.

Hint: Use the arrow keys on the keyboard to make minor adjustments to the position of an object.

36. Test the movie, then close the Flash Player window.

37. Save your work, then close the document.

You created a movie with 3D effects.

Use the
DECO TOOL

What You'll Do

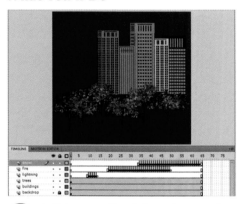

In this lesson, you will use the Deco tool to create and animate a cityscape.

Understanding the Deco Tool

The Deco tool provides a variety of drawing effects that can be used to quickly create environments, such as city landscapes, and to create various animations. In addition, the Deco tool can be used to create decorative patterns that incorporate imported graphics and those drawn in Flash. These patterns can be animated and added to a movie to create special effects. Flash has a number of Deco tool brushes and effects. In addition, Adobe has designed the Deco tool so that other brushes and effects can be added by developers. This allows users to develop tools for their specific needs. Because the Deco tool is easy to use and can be used to quickly create a design and add animation, it is a valuable tool for creating prototypes in the early stages of developing an application. One drawback of using the Deco tool is that animations created with the Deco tool often result in movie file sizes that are large. This is because the images created with the brush tools are made up of small segments and the animations are frame-by-frame animations.

Basic Types of Deco Effects

There are 13 drawing effects available with the Deco tool, as shown in Figure 60.

Figure 60 *The Deco drawing tools*

Creating Special Effects

These drawing effects are available in the Properties panel when the Deco tool is selected from the Tools panel. They are grouped into three basic types, although there is some overlap in the groups.

- Fills—the Vine Fill, Grid Fill, and Symmetry Brush create patterns that can be used as fill for graphics or a backdrop for a movie. Figure 61 shows a vine and a grid fill. Flash allows you to create your own fill using an image of your choice, such as a logo. In addition, you can set various properties such as the pattern scale.
- **NEW** Brushes—several brushes including the building, lightning, tree, and flower brushes can be used to create drawings that can be combined to construct environments, like the one shown in Figure 62. The Decorated Brush has 20 variations, including those shown in Figure 63.
- **NEW** Animations—a few brushes, such as the Lightning Brush, Fire Animation, Smoke Animation, and Particle System, create animations as they are used. However, any effect created using the Deco tool can be selected, converted to a graphic or movie clip symbol, and animated by inserting a motion tween or using another animation process in Flash.

Hint: Select a keyframe before selecting the Deco tool and use different layers for each Deco tool effect.

Figure 61 *A vine fill and a grid fill*

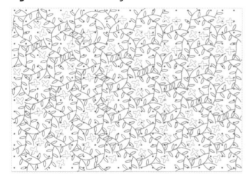

Figure 62 *Cityscape created using Deco tools*

Figure 63 *Patterns created using selected Decorative Brushes*

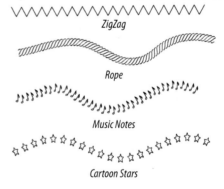

ZigZag

Rope

Music Notes

Cartoon Stars

Create screen design and animations with the Deco tool

1. Open fl5_8 .fla, then save it as **decoLand.fla**.

   This movie has six layers, dimensions of 400 x 400 pxs, a length of 65 frames, and a dark blue backdrop.

2. Change the view for the Timeline to **Small** if necessary to see all 65 frames, then set the view to **Fit in Window**.

3. Click **frame 1** on the buildings layer, click the **Deco tool** on the Tools panel, then display the Properties panel.

4. **NEW** Click the **DRAWING EFFECT list arrow**, then click **Building Brush**.

5. Verify your Properties panel displays DRAWING EFFECT: Building Brush; ADVANCED OPTIONS: Random Building and Building Size **1**.

6. Point to the Stage, then click and drag the **pointer** to the position shown in Figure 64.

   Note: The Random Building option may cause your building to display differently.

   Hint: You can use the undo command in the Edit menu to undo an action(s).

7. Continue to create four more buildings similar to Figure 65.

8. Click **frame 1** on the trees layer.

9. Click the **Deco tool** on the Tools panel, then use the Properties panel to change the DRAWING EFFECT to **Tree Brush** and the type to **Gingko Tree**.

10. Use the **pointer** to draw trees similar to the ones shown in Figure 66.

    (continued)

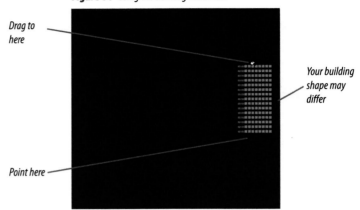

Figure 64 *Using the Building Brush tool*

Drag to here

Your building shape may differ

Point here

Figure 65 *The completed buildings*

Figure 66 *The completed trees*

Creating Special Effects

Figure 67 *Using the Lightning Brush*

Point here

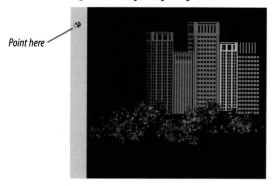

Figure 68 *Inserting a blank keyframe*

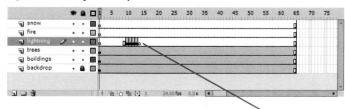

Blank keyframe inserted after the keyframes of the animation.
Note: There may be a different number of keyframes in your animation.

Figure 69 *Positioning the pointer*

Point here

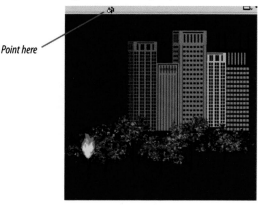

11. Insert a **keyframe** in frame 10 on the lightning layer.
12. Click the **Deco tool** 🖉 on the Tools panel, change the DRAWING EFFECT to **Lightning Brush** and the color to **white**, then verify animation is checked.
13. Point off the Stage as shown in Figure 67, then drag the 🔧 **pointer** toward the trees and release the mouse button.
14. Insert a **blank keyframe** in the frame following the last keyframe in the lightning animation, as shown in Figure 68.
15. Click **frame 20** on the fire layer, then insert a **keyframe**.
16. Click the **Deco tool** 🖉 on the Tools panel, then change the DRAWING EFFECT to **Fire Animation** and the Fire duration to **30 frames**.
17. Click the **tree top** on the far left of the Stage, click **frame 50** on the fire layer, then insert a **blank keyframe**.
18. Click **frame 35** on the snow layer, then insert a **keyframe**.
19. Click the **Deco tool** 🖉 on the Tools panel, change the DRAWING EFFECT to **Particle System**, verify Particle 1 and Particle 2 have a check mark, and set the particle color to **white** for each particle.
20. Point to the sky, as shown in Figure 69, then click the 🔧 **pointer**.
21. Click **frame 35**, repeat Steps 19 and 20 **three times** placing the 🔧 **pointer** in different areas across the sky.
22. Test the movie, close the Flash Player window, save your work, then close the document.

You created a cityscape environment, including animations, with the Deco tool.

Create a mask effect.

1. Start Flash, open fl5_9.fla, then save it as **skillsDemo5.fla**. (*Hint*: When you open the file, you may receive a missing font message, meaning a font used in this document is not available on your computer. You can choose a substitute font or use a default font.)
2. Verify the frame rate is set to 12 and the Flash Publish Settings (accessed from the File menu) are set to Flash Player 10 and ActionScript 3.0.
3. Insert a new layer above the table layer, then name it **heading**.
4. Select frame 1 on the heading layer, then use the Text tool to create the Aces Wild heading with the following characteristics: size 48, color #006633 (a dark green), and Byington (or similar) font. (*Hint*: Look at Figure 70 and find a font that matches the heading text. Use the samples provided to find a similar font, such as Constania.)
5. Use the Selection tool to select the heading, then use the Align command in the Modify menu to center the heading across the Stage.
6. With the heading still selected, convert it to a graphic symbol with the name **g_heading**.
7. Insert a keyframe in frame 40 on the heading layer.
8. Insert a new layer above the heading layer, then name it **ending-heading**.
9. Insert a keyframe in frame 40 on the ending-heading layer.
10. Drag the g_heading symbol from the Library panel and position it on top of the heading on the Stage, then use the keyboard arrow keys as needed to position the g_heading symbol.
11. Lock the ending-heading layer.
12. Insert a new layer above the heading layer, then name it **circle**.
13. Select frame 1 on the circle layer, then use the Oval tool to create a black-filled circle that is slightly larger in height than the heading text.
14. Place the circle to the left of the heading.
15. Convert the circle to a graphic symbol with the name **g_mask**.
16. Create a motion tween that moves the circle across and to the right side of the heading.
17. Verify the tween span on the Timeline extends to frame 40.
18. Change the circle layer to a mask layer and lock the layer.
19. Change the heading layer to a masked layer and lock the layer.
20. Insert keyframes in frame 40 on the table, arms, and the head and body layers.
21. Insert a new layer above the table layer, name it **stopMovie**, move the stopmovie layer below the table layer, then insert a keyframe in frame 40.
22. Open the Actions panel, verify Script Assist is turned off and stopMovie: 40 is displayed in the lower-left corner of the Script pane, then type **stop( );** for the code. (*Note*: Because ActionScript 3.0 is needed when working with Inverse Kinematics and with the 3D feature, both of which you will do shortly, you cannot use the Script Assist feature of Flash, which is why you typed the code directly into the Actions pane.)
23. Close the Actions panel.
24. Test the movie, then save your work.

Create a character animation using inverse kinematics.

1. Select frame 1 on the Timeline, then use the Zoom tool to enlarge the view of the character.
2. Use the Bone tool to join the head to the body, then to join the body with the upper and lower left arm, and with the upper and lower right arm. (*Note*: The bone structure stops at the elbow on each arm.)
3. Click the Selection tool on the Tools panel, click frame 40 on the Armature layer, then insert a keyframe.
4. Select frame 6 on the Armature layer.
5. Use the Selection tool to move the ends of the arms so that the lower left and lower right arms are horizontal and touch at the chest. This will cause the elbows to point out away from the body.
6. Select frame 12 on the Armature layer.
7. Use the Selection tool to move the end of the right arm so that it is straight and pointing to the upper-left corner of the Stage.
8. Change the view to Fit in Window.
9. Test the movie, then save your work.

Create a frame-by-frame animation.

1. Select frame 4 on the card layer, then insert a keyframe.
2. Use the Zoom tool and the keyboard arrow keys as needed to reposition the card so that it is at the end of the right arm.
3. Select frame 5 on the card layer, then insert a keyframe.
4. Use the arrow keys on the keyboard to reposition the card so that it is at the end of the right arm.

5. Repeat steps 3 and 4 in frame 6 through frame 12 on the card layer. (*Note*: The hand moves a small increment in each frame, which is why you must reposition the card so it stays connected to the hand.)

6. Select frame 13 on the card layer, then insert a blank keyframe.

7. Test the movie, close the Flash Player window, then save your work.

Create a 3D effect.

1. Insert a new layer above the card layer, then name it **ace3D**.

2. Select frame 12 on the ace3D layer, then insert a keyframe.

3. Drag the mc_aceD movie clip from the Library panel to the Stage, display the Properties panel, verify the Lock width and height values together icon is not a broken link, then resize the width to 10.6.

4. Reposition the ace to on top of the card held by the character.

5. Verify frame 12 on the ace3D layer is selected, then create a motion tween.

6. Verify the tween span on the Timeline extends from frame 12 through frame 40.

7. Select frame 40 on the ace3D layer.

8. Use the 3D Translation tool to reposition the card to the upper-left corner of the Stage in a diagonal line that extends from the character's right shoulder. (*Hint*: Use both the red and green arrow tips to move the card to create a diagonal line.)

9. Use the Free Transform tool and the Scale option at the bottom of the Tools panel to resize the card to a width of between 80 and 90.

10. Select frame 26 on the ace3D layer.

11. Use the 3D Rotation tool to add a 3D effect.

12. Select frame 40 on the ace3D layer.

13. Use the 3D Rotation tool to add a 3D effect that causes the card to display right side up, as seen in Figure 70.

14. Test the movie, close the Flash Player window, then save your work.

Add sound to a movie.

1. Insert a new layer at the top of the Timeline, then name it **sound**.

2. Insert a keyframe in frame 5 on the sound layer.

3. Drag introSound.wav from the Library panel to the Stage.

4. Insert a keyframe in frame 40 on the sound layer.

5. Test the movie, if a warning box opens, read the message then click OK, compare your movie to the images in Figure 70, close the Flash Player window, save your work, then close the file.

Add video.

1. Open fl5_10.fla, then save it as **skillsDemo5-video.fla**.

Figure 70 *Completed Skills Review-IK 3D Animation*

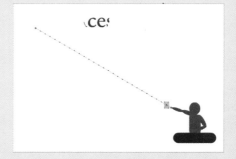

2. Add a new layer above the headings layer, then name it **video**.

3. Import the file tour-video.mov as an embedded video from the drive and folder where you store your Data Files to the Library using the Import Video command. (*Note*: You will need to use the Adobe Media Encoder to convert the file to the flv format, then you will need to browse to the drive and folder where you save your Solution Files to open the converted file.)

4. Verify that the video is in the Library panel and on the center of the Stage, note the number of frames needed to display the entire video. (*Note*: You may need to drag the video from the Library panel to the Stage. If a message appears asking if you want frames inserted into the Timeline, click Yes. *Hint*: Be sure to position the video placeholder, if necessary, to prevent overlapping the text subheading.)

5. Add a new layer, name it **controls**, then select frame 1 on the layer.

6. Use the Text tool to create a text box with the word **Play** beneath and to the left side of the video. Set the text

characteristics to the following: family Arial, style Narrow (Win) or Regular (Mac), size 20 pt, and color White.

7. Convert the text to a button symbol with the name **b_play**.

8. Edit the over and down states of the button symbol, for example, make the color of the letters change when the mouse pointer is over the word Play and when the user clicks the button.

9. Use the Actions panel and Script Assist to assign a play action to the button that plays the movie when the mouse is released.

10. Use the Text tool to create a text box with the word **Pause** beneath and to the right side of the video. Use the same text characteristics used for the Play button.

11. Convert the text to a button symbol with the name **b_pause**.

12. Edit the button symbol to match what you did in step 8.

13. Use the Actions panel to assign a stop action to the button when it is released.

14. Add a new layer, then name it **stopMovie**.

15. Add a stop action to frame 1 on the stopMovie layer.

16. Add a keyframe at the end of the movie on the headings layer. (*Note*: If a message appears asking if you want frames inserted into the timeline, click No because the frames are already inserted.)

17. Test the movie, compare your screen to Figure 71, close the Flash Player window, then save your work.

18. Close the Flash document.

Work with TLF text and create an animated navigation bar.

1. Open fl5_11.fla, then save it as **skillsDemo5-TLF.fla**.

2. Add a new layer and name it **photo**.

3. Select frame 1 of the photo layer and drag the g_birchBay graphic symbol from the Library panel to the center of the Stage.

4. Use the Align panel to center the graphic on the Stage.

5. Lock the heading and photo layers.

6. Add a new layer at the top of the Timeline and name it **text**.

7. Select frame 1 of the text layer and drag the g_text graphic from the Library panel to the middle of the Stage.

8. Verify the text image is selected, then click Modify on the menu bar and select Break Apart. (*Note*: The original text block was changed to a graphic symbol and placed in the Library panel. In order to edit the text, the symbol must be broken apart.)

9. Display the Properties panel and change the text from Classic Text to TLF Text.

10. Change the Size in the CHARACTER area to 13 pt.

11. Change the Behavior in the CONTAINER AND FLOW area of the Properties panel to Multiline.

12. Using Figure 72 as a guide complete the following:
    - Use the Selection tool to resize the Container and create a second linked Container.
    - Use the Text tool to type in the words "in the majestic Pacific Northwest" at the end of the first sentence.
    - Use the Selection tool to select the containers.
    - Justify the text using the "Justify with last line aligned to start" button in the PARAGRAPH area of the Properties panel, and adjust the text box widths as needed to closely match the line wrap shown in Figure 72.

13. Lock the text layer.

14. Test the movie, then close the Flash Player window.

15. Save your work.

Figure 71 *Completed Skills Review - video*

Creating Special Effects

Create the drop-down buttons

1. Save the Flash document as **skillsDemo5-navBar.fla**.
2. Insert a new layer, name it **navBar Background**, create the white horizontal bar shown in Figure 72, then lock the layer.
3. Insert a new layer, name it navBar Buttons, then create the three text headings using Classic text and a black color.
4. Convert the Take a Tour heading to a button, then edit the button symbol to add a hit area around it. (*Note*: Be sure to make the hit area long enough so that it will fall below the navBar Background rectangle when the Take a Tour button is positioned on the navBar.)
5. Position the Take a Tour button so that its hit area falls below the navBar Background rectangle.
6. Insert keyframes in frame 10 of all the layers.
7. Insert a layer above the navBar Buttons layer, name it **videoBtn**, then insert a keyframe in frame 2 of the layer.
8. Create the video button, edit the button symbol to add a hit area to the button, then position it below Take a Tour.
9. Insert a layer, name it **slidesBtn**, then insert a keyframe in frame 2 of the layer.
10. Create the slides button, then position it below the video button.

Add a mask layer

1. Insert a layer, name it **cover**, then insert a keyframe in frame 2 of the layer.
2. Draw a rectangle that covers the video and slide buttons and move it above Take a Tour.
3. Verify the rectangle is selected and Insert a motion tween.

4. Insert a keyframe in frame 5 of the cover layer, then move the rectangle down to cover the buttons.
5. Change the layer properties for the cover layer to mask.
6. Select the slidesBtn layer and change it to a masked layer, if it has not changed to a masked layer.
7. Select the videoBtn layer and change it to a masked layer.

Assign actions to buttons and frames

1. Click File on the menu bar, click Publish Settings, click the Flash tab, then change the Script to ActionScript 2.0. (*Note*: ActionScript 2.0 is needed when assigning actions to buttons.)
2. When the warning message appears, click OK, then click OK to close the Publish Settings dialog box.
3. Select frame 2 on the videoBtn layer, click to select the Video button, then use ScriptAssist to add the on(release) code that causes the playhead to go to the next scene. (*Note*: The next scene will contain the video, although the scene has not been created yet.)
4. Insert a layer above the cover layer, name it **labels**, then insert a keyframe in frame 2 of the layer.
5. Add a frame label named **tourMenu**.
6. Select the Take a Tour button, then use ScriptAssist to add the code so the playhead goes to and plays the frame labeled tourMenu when the mouse pointer rolls over the button.
7. Insert a layer above the labels layer, name it **actions**, then, in frames 1 and 5 (be sure to add a keyframe) on the actions layer, use the Script pane (ScriptAssist turned off) to type **stop();**.
8. Insert a layer above the heading layer, name it **rollOver**, then insert a keyframe in frame 2 of the layer.

Figure 72 *Completed Skills Review - TLF and Animated Navigation Bar*

Add an invisible button

1. Draw a rectangle that covers the Take a Tour, Video and Slides buttons, then convert the rectangle to a button with the name **rollOverBtn**.
2. Use ScriptAssist to add ActionScript code that causes the playhead to go to frame 1 when the mouse pointer rolls over the button.
3. Select the rollOverBtn button and use the Properties panel to change the alpha setting to 0.
4. Test the movie, then save and close it.
   Note: If your text columns do not display as justified, unlock the text layer if it is locked, select a text block and set the Anti-alias option in the CHARACTER area of the Properties panel to Anti-alias for readability.

Work with the Deco tool.

This is a continuation of the Deco tool exercise you completed in this chapter. Figure 73 shows the changes you will make to the decoLand.fla document as you complete the following steps.

(*Hint*: Use the Undo command in the Edit menu to undo drawings as necessary.)

1. Open decoLand.fla and save it as **skillsDemo5-deco.fla**.
2. Change the view to Fit in Window.
3. Lock all the layers.
4. Insert a new layer above the backdrop layer, name it **road**, then select frame 1 on the road layer.
5. Select the Deco tool and display the Properties panel.
6. Change the DRAWING EFFECT to Decorated Brush, the ADVANCED OPTIONS to 18: Bumps, and the color to white.

7. Use the Deco pointer to draw the road below the buildings.
8. Lock the road layer.
9. Insert a new layer above the snow layer and name it **stars**.
10. Select frame 1 of the stars layer.
11. Select the Deco tool and display the Properties panel.
12. Change the ADVANCED OPTIONS to 16: Shiny Stars, then set the color to white, the pattern size to 30, and the pattern width to 20.
13. Use the Deco pointer to create the stars at the top of the Stage. (*Hint*: You can click and drag the pointer, and you can move the pointer to a new location then click and drag again to create a more scattered effect.)

14. Lock the stars layer.
15. Insert a new layer above the stars layer and name it **flowers**.
16. Select frame 1 of the flowers layer.
17. Select the Deco tool and display the Properties panel.
18. Change the DRAWING EFFECT to Flower Brush, then change the ADVANCED OPTIONS to Rose, and the flower and leaf size to 50%.
19. Click and drag to create the row of flowers at the bottom of the Stage.
20. Lock the flowers layer.
21. Save the movie.
22. Test the movie, then close the Flash Player window.
23. Exit Flash.

Figure 73 *Completed Skills Review - deco*

The Ultimate Tours travel company has asked you to design several sample animations for its website. Figure 74 shows a sample Cruises screen with a mask effect, as the spotlight rotates across the screen and highlights different ships. Complete the following for the Cruises screen of the Ultimate Tours website:

1. Open fl5_12.fla, then save it as **assets.fla**.
2. Open ultimateTours4.fla (the file you created in Chapter 4 Project Builder 1), and save it as **ultimateTours5.fla**.
3. Insert a new layer at the top of the Timeline and select frame 1 on the layer.
4. Display the Library panel, then click the Display movies list arrow below the Library tab to display the list of open documents.

5. Select assets.fla and drag each of the symbols in the Library panel to the Stage, delete the layer from the Timeline, click the assets.fla tab above the Stage, then close the assets file. (*Note:* You added the objects from the assets file to the ultimateTours5 Library panel, and then closed the assets.fla file.)
6. Display the Library panel for ultimateTours5.
7. Insert a new layer at the top of the Timeline, then name it **backdrop**.
8. Insert a keyframe in a frame that is higher than the last frame in the current movie (such as frame 100) on the backdrop layer, then draw a dark gray rectangle (#333333) that covers the Stage.
9. Insert a keyframe that is at least 30 frames higher on the backdrop layer (such as frame 130), then lock the layer. (*Note:* All of the subsequent layers you add will use the same starting frame, such as 100.)

10. Insert a new layer, name it **heading**, insert a keyframe in frame 100 (or the frame specified in Step 8), and create the Mystery Ships heading.
11. Insert a new layer, name it **lighthouse**, insert a keyframe in frame 100 (or the frame specified in Step 8), and place the g_lighthouse symbol on the Stage.
12. Insert a new layer, name it **searchlight**, insert a keyframe in frame 100 (or the frame specified in Step 8), and place the g_searchlight symbol to the left of the lighthouse.
13. Use the Free Transform tool to create a motion tween that causes the searchlight to rotate from the left to the right of the lighthouse.
    (*Hint:* The searchlight will rotate (pivot) around the transformation point (small circle) of the graphic.)

Figure 74 *Sample completed Project Builder 1*

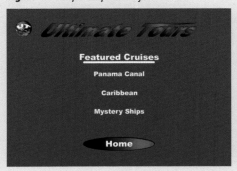

14. Create a new layer for each of the three ships, name each layer appropriately (**ship1**, **ship2**, and **ship3**), and insert keyframes in frame 100 (or the frame specified in Step 8) of each layer.

15. Using frame 100 (or the frame specified in Step 8), place the ships on the Stage so that the searchlight highlights them as it moves from left to right across the Stage.

16. Insert a new layer above the ship layers, name it **searchlight mask**, insert a keyframe in frame 100 (or the frame specified in Step 8), add an instance of the g_searchlight symbol from the Library panel to on top of the searchlight on the stage, then add a motion tween that duplicates the one created in Step 13.

17. Create a mask effect that has a searchlight as the mask and reveals the ships when the searchlight is over them. (*Note*: The two searchlight motion tweens are needed on different layers because one will become a mask and will not be visible in the movie.)

18. Insert a new layer, name it **sound**, insert a keyframe in frame 100 (or the appropriate frame) on the layer, then drag the foghorn.wav sound file to the Stage.

19. Insert a new layer, name it **homeBTN**, insert a keyframe in the last frame of the movie, then add the b_home button to the bottom center of the Stage. (*Note*: This button does not appear on the MYSTERY SHIPS screen in Figure 74 because the last frame of the movie has not been reached.)

20. Add an action to the home button to have the playhead go to frame 1 of the movie when the button is clicked.

21. Insert a new layer, name it **stopAction**, then add a keyframe and a stop action at the end of the movie.

22. Add a new layer, name it **labels**, insert a keyframe in frame 100 (or the appropriate frame), then create a frame label named **mystery**.

23. Click frame 1 on the Timeline, drag (scrub) the playhead on the Timeline to locate the first frame that shows the Galapagos text (cruises headings layer for example), then unlock the cruise heading layer (or layer that has the Galapagos text).

24. Change the Galapagos text to **Mystery Ships**, then create a button that changes the text color for the different button states.

25. Add an action to the mystery ship button to have the playhead go to the frame labeled mystery.

26. Test the movie, then compare your image to the example shown in Figure 74.

27. Close the Flash Player window.

28. Lock all layers, save your work, then close the document.

You have been asked to develop a website illustrating the signs of the zodiac. The introductory screen should have a heading with a mask effect and 12 zodiac signs, each of which could become a button. Clicking a zodiac sign button displays an information screen with a different graphic to represent the sign and information about the sign, as well as special effects such as sound, mask effect, and character animation (inverse kinematics). Each information screen would be linked to the introductory screen. (*Note*: Using the inverse kinematics feature requires ActionScript 3.0, therefore, you will start with a movie that has the ActionScript for the buttons and stop actions already developed.)

1. Open fl5_13.fla, save it as **zodiac5.fla**, then change the frame rate to **12 fps**. (*Hint*: When you open the file, you may receive a missing font message, meaning a font used in this document is not available on your computer. You can choose a substitute font or use a default font.)
2. Test the movie, then study the Timeline to understand how the movie works.
3. Refer to Figure 75 as you complete the introductory screen with the following:
   - A new layer above the signs layer named **heading** with the heading, **Signs of the** that appears from frame 1 through frame 31
   - A new layer named **masked** that contains the word **Zodiac** and that appears from frame 1 through frame 31
   - A mask layer that passes across the heading Zodiac (*Notes*: Use a fill color that can be seen on the black background. After creating the motion tween, drag the end of the tween span on the Timeline to frame 31. Be sure to set the Layer Properties for the mask and masked layers.)
   - A new layer that displays the word **Zodiac** in frame 31 only (*Note*: Remove frames 32–80 from the layer by using the Remove Frames option from the Timeline command of the Edit menu.)
   - A new layer with a sound that plays from frame 1 through frame 31 as the mask is revealing the contents of the masked layer
4. Refer to Figure 75 as you complete the scorpio screen with the following: (*Notes*: The scorpio screen starts in frame 51. Remove frames in other layers containing content that you do not want displayed after frame 31, such as the Zodiac heading.)
   - A new layer with the three-line heading
   - An inverse kinematics animation that moves the tail (*Note*: Be sure to connect the head to the tail.)
5. Test the movie.
6. Save the movie as **zodiac5-mc.fla**.
7. Select frame 51 on the Armature layer and convert the IK animation to a movie clip.
8. Edit the movie clip and add a stop action on a separate layer at the end of the movie clip, then return to the main Timeline.
9. Delete the Armature layer, then select frame 51 on the scorpio layer and drag the movie clip to the Stage.
10. Create a motion tween to animate the movie clip so the scorpion moves across the screen.
11. Test the movie, compare your screens to Figure 75, close the Flash Player window, then save the movie.

Figure 75 *Sample completed Project Builder 2*

Tail moves while scorpion moves across the screen

Figure 76 shows the home page of a website. Study the figure and complete the following questions. For each question, indicate how you determined your answer.

1. Connect to the Internet, then go to *www.nikeid.com*, and display the women's basketball shoes. Go to the site and explore several links to get a feeling for how the site is constructed. Use Figure 76 to answer the questions.

2. Open a document in a word processor or open a new Flash document, save the file as **dpc5**, then answer the following questions. (*Hint*: Use the Text tool in Flash.)

   - Whose site is this and what seems to be the purpose of this site?
   - Who would be the target audience?
   - How might a character animation using inverse kinematics be used?
   - How might video be used?
   - How might a mask effect be used?
   - How might sound be used?
   - How might 3D be used?
   - What suggestions would you make to improve the design and why?

Figure 76 *Design Project*

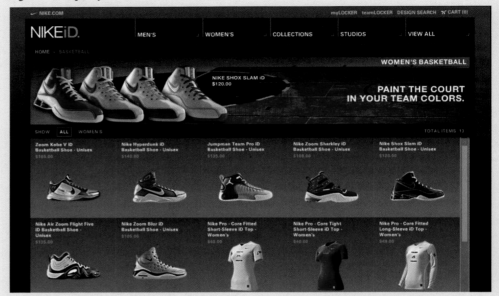

Creating Special Effects

This is a continuation of the Portfolio Project in Chapter 4, which is the development of a personal portfolio. The home page has several categories, including the following:

- Personal data
- Contact information
- Previous employment
- Education
- Samples of your work

In this project, you will create several buttons for the Sample Animations screen and link them to their respective animations.

1. Open portfolio4.fla (the file you created in Portfolio Project, Chapter 4) and save it as **portfolio5.fla**.
2. Display the Sample Animations screen. You will be adding buttons to this screen. Each of these new buttons links to a screen that plays its corresponding animation. In each case, have the animation return to the Sample Animations screen at the end of the animation.
3. Add a button for a character animation so it appears on the Sample Animations screen, add a new layer and create a character animation (inverse kinematics) on that layer, then link the character animation button to the character animation.
4. Add a button for a mask effect so it appears on the Sample Animations screen, add new layers to create a mask effect (such as to the words My Portfolio) on that layer, add a sound that plays as the mask is revealing the contents of the masked layer, then link the mask effect button to the mask effect animation.

5. Add a button for an animated navigation bar so it appears on the Sample Animations screen, add a new layer and create an animated navigation bar on that layer, then link the navigation bar button to the animated navigation bar.

6. Test the movie, then compare your Sample Animation screen to the example shown in Figure 77.
7. Close the Flash Player window, then save your work.

Figure 77 *Sample completed Portfolio Project*

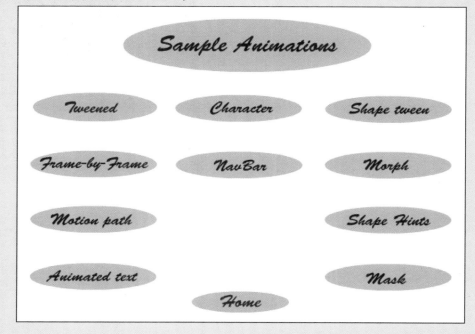

CHAPTER 6 PREPARING AND PUBLISHING MOVIES

1. Publish movies

2. Reduce file size to optimize a movie

3. Create a preloader

4. Use HTML publish settings

NEW 5. Create and test applications for mobile devices

PREPARING AND PUBLISHING MOVIES

Introduction

The most common use of Flash is to develop movies that provide web content and applications. During the planning process for an Adobe Flash movie, you are concerned with, among other things, how the target audience will view the movie. Flash provides several features that help you generate the files that are necessary for delivering movies successfully to the target audience over the Internet.

When you deliver content over the Internet, you want to provide compelling movies. However, it is important that you keep the file size down so that the movies play smoothly regardless of the user's connection speed. Flash allows you to test movies to determine where problems might arise during download and to make changes to optimize the movies.

Adobe provides a program, Device Central, that allows you to preview and test mobile content on an assortment of mobile devices. This is especially useful when designing Flash movies because of the reduced viewing size for mobile devices, such as cell phones, and the limited download speeds available for mobile devices. Using Device Central, you can specify the model of a cell phone and simulate the display of Flash movies for that phone. Then you can make adjustments in your movie to optimize the design and lighting, and even choose from an array of languages. Adobe provides a version of its Flash Player, called Flash Lite, that is specifically developed to optimize the playing of Flash movies using mobile devices.

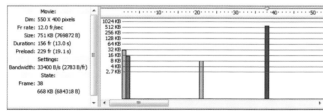

Publish MOVIES

What You'll Do

In this lesson, you will use the Flash Publish Settings feature to publish a movie, create a GIF animation, and create a JPEG image from a movie.

Using Publish Settings

The Flash Publish feature generates the files necessary to deliver the movies on the web. When you publish a movie using the default settings, a Flash (.swf) file is created that can be viewed using the Flash Player. In addition, an HTML file is created with the necessary code to instruct the browser to play the Flash file using the Flash Player. If you are not distributing the movie over the Internet or if you know the Flash Player will not be available, you can use the Publish Settings feature to create alternate images and stand-alone projector files.

Figure 1 shows the Publish Settings dialog box with a list of the available formats for publishing a Flash movie. By default, the Flash and HTML formats are selected and their related tabs are available. You can choose a combination of formats, and you can specify a different name (but not file extension) for each format. The GIF, JPEG, and PNG formats create still images that can be delivered on the web. The projector formats in the Publish Settings dialog box are executable files (which were discussed in Chapter 1). When you select a format (such as GIF image), its related tab (in this example, GIF) appears. When you click a tab, the tab opens with settings specifically for the selected format. Figure 2 shows the Flash tab in the Publish Settings dialog box. On the Flash tab, you can choose settings for several options, including:

- A profile, which is a set of selected settings that have been saved for later use; the Default profile is selected in Figure 2
- The version of the Flash Player
- The version of ActionScript
- The quality for JPEG images and audio

- Other options, such as compressing the movie

QUICK TIP

Not all features of Flash CS5 work when using Flash Player versions earlier than version 10

Figure 1 *The Publish Settings dialog box*

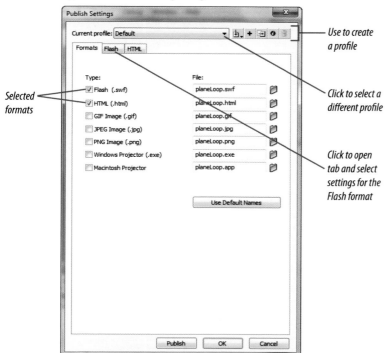

Selected formats

Use to create a profile

Click to select a different profile

Click to open tab and select settings for the Flash format

Figure 2 *The Flash tab and settings available for Flash*

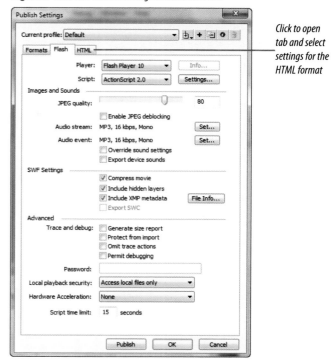

Click to open tab and select settings for the HTML format

Figure 3 shows the GIF tab in the Publish Settings dialog box. This tab appears after selecting GIF Image on the Formats tab. GIF files, which are compressed bitmaps, provide an easy way to create images and simple animations for delivery on the web. GIF animations are frame-by-frame animations created from Flash movie frames. Using this tab, you can change several settings, including the following:

- The dimensions in pixels (or you can match the movie dimensions)
- Playback as a static image or an animated GIF
- Whether an animation plays (loops) continuously or repeats a certain number of times
- A range of appearance settings, such as optimizing colors and removing gradients

Using Publish Preview

You can use the Publish Preview command on the File menu to publish a movie and display the movie in either your default browser or the Flash Player. In addition, you can use this command to view HTML, GIF, JPEG, PNG, and Projector files.

Figure 3 *The GIF tab and settings available for Gif files*

Preparing and Publishing Movies

Figure 4 *The three planeLoop files*

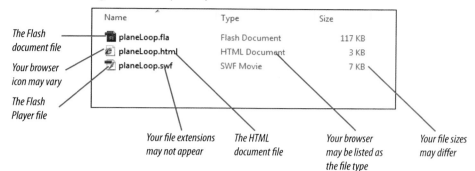

The Flash document file

Your browser icon may vary

The Flash Player file

Name	Type	Size
planeLoop.fla	Flash Document	117 KB
planeLoop.html	HTML Document	3 KB
planeLoop.swf	SWF Movie	7 KB

Your file extensions may not appear

The HTML document file

Your browser may be listed as the file type

Your file sizes may differ

Publish using the default settings

1. Open fl6_1.fla from the drive and folder where your Data Files are stored, save it as **planeLoop.fla**, then play the movie.

2. Click **File** on the menu bar, click **Publish Settings**, then verify the Formats tab is active.

3. Verify that the Flash and HTML check boxes are the only ones selected, then click the **Flash tab**.

4. Verify that the version is set to Flash Player 10 and that the Compress movie check box under SWF Settings is selected.

5. Accept the remaining default settings, click **Publish**, then click **OK**.

6. Use your file management program to navigate to the drive and folder where you save your Data Files, then notice the three files with filenames that start with "planeLoop", as shown in Figure 4.

7. Display the Flash program, click **File** on the menu bar, point to **Publish Preview**, then click **Default - (HTML)**.

   The movie plays in a browser. When the movie plays in the browser, it plays in the Flash movie window but not in the Flash Player. You will learn more about the Flash movie window in a later lesson.

   Note: If a warning message opens, follow the messages to allow blocked content.

8. Close the browser, then display the Flash program.

You published a movie using the default publish settings and viewed it in a browser.

Create a GIF animation from a movie

1. Click **File** on the menu bar, click **Publish Settings**, then click the **Formats tab**.

2. Click the **GIF Image (.gif) check box**, then click the **GIF tab**.

3. Click the **Match movie check box** to turn off this setting, double-click the **Width text box**, type **275**, double-click the **Height text box**, then type **200**.

4. Click the **Animated option button**, then verify the remaining default settings match those shown in Figure 5.

5. Click **Publish**, then click **OK**.

6. Open your browser, then use the browser to open planeLoop.gif from the drive and folder where you save your work.

TIP Many browsers have an Open command on the File menu. Use this command to navigate and open files for display within the browser. If you do not see the GIF file, change the file type to All Files.

7. Notice the GIF animation plays in the browser with the modified settings.

   Because the GIF file is not an SWF file, it does not require the Flash Player to play—it can be displayed directly in a web browser.

8. Close the browser.

You changed the publish settings for a GIF image, then created a GIF animation and viewed it in your web browser.

Figure 5 *The completed GIF format dialog box*

Figure 6 *The JPEG image displayed in the browser*

Your browser
may vary

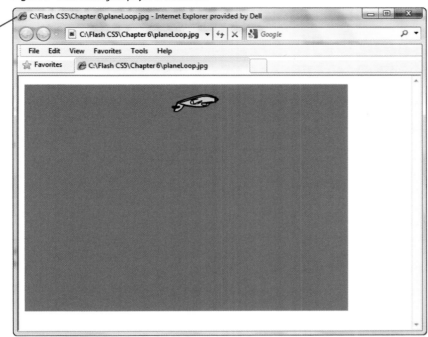

Create a JPEG image from a frame of a movie

1. Display the Flash program, then click **frame 10** on the plane layer.

2. Click **File** on the menu bar, then click **Publish Settings**.

3. Click the **Formats tab**, click the **GIF Image check box** to deselect it, then click the **JPEG Image check box** to select it.

   Deselecting the GIF format will prevent the GIF file from being created again.

4. Click the **JPEG tab**, review the default settings, click **Publish**, then click **OK**.

5. Open your browser, then use the browser to open the planeLoop.jpg file from the drive and folder where you save your work.

   TIP If you do not see the JPG file, change the file type to All Files.

6. Notice that the static JPEG image appears in the browser, as shown in Figure 6.

7. Close your browser, then display the Flash program.

8. Save your work, then close the movie.

You reviewed the default publish settings for a JPEG image, then created a JPEG image and viewed it in your web browser.

Reduce File Size
TO OPTIMIZE A MOVIE

What You'll Do

In this lesson, you will test a movie and reduce its file size.

Testing a Movie

The goal in publishing a movie is to provide the most effective playback for the intended audience. This requires that you pay special attention to the download time and playback speed. Users are turned off by long waits to view content, jerky animations, and audio that skips. These events can occur as the file size increases in relation to the user's Internet connection speed.

Before you publish a movie, be sure you have maximized its optimization in order to improve its delivery. As you develop Flash movies, keep in mind and practice these guidelines for optimizing movies:

- Use symbols and instances for every element that appears in a movie more than once.
- Use tween animations rather than frame-by-frame animations when possible.
- Use movie clips rather than graphic symbols for animation sequences.
- Confine the area of change to a keyframe so that the action takes place in as small an area as possible.
- Use bitmap graphics as static elements rather than in animations.

- Group elements, such as related images.
- Limit the number of fonts and font styles.
- Use gradients and alpha transparencies sparingly.

When you publish a movie, Flash optimizes it using default features, including compressing the entire movie, which is later decompressed by the Flash Player. However, Flash provides various ways to test a movie before you publish it to determine where changes/optimizations can improve its delivery. Two features for testing are discussed next.

Using the Bandwidth Profiler

When a movie is delivered over the Internet, the contents of each frame are sent to the user's computer. Depending on the amount of data in the frame and the user's connection speed, the movie may pause while the frame's contents download. The first step in optimizing a movie is to test the movie and determine which frames may create a pause during playback. The test should be done using a simulated Internet connection speed that is representative of the speed of your target audience. You can set a simulated speed using the **Bandwidth Profiler**, shown in Figure 7. The Bandwidth Profiler allows you to view a graphical representation of the size of each frame. Each bar represents one frame of the movie, and the height of the bar corresponds to the frame's size. If a bar extends above the red baseline, the movie may need to pause to allow the frame's contents to be downloaded. Figure 7 shows the following:

- Movie information: dimensions, frame rate, file size, duration, and preload
- Settings: simulated bandwidth (specified in the View menu option)
- State: number of the selected frame and size of the contents in that frame

The Bandwidth Profiler shown in Figure 7 indicates that downloading frame 38 may result in a pause because of the large size of the contents in this frame in relationship to the connection speed and the frame rate. If the specified connection speed is correct for your target audience and the frame rate is needed to ensure acceptable animation quality, then the only change that can be made is in the contents of the frame.

Using the Simulate Download Feature

When testing a movie, you can simulate downloading Flash movies using different connection speeds. The most common connections are Dial-up, broadband (both DSL and cable), and T1. Dial-up is a phone connection that provides a relatively slow download speed. Broadband is a type of data transmission in which a wide band of frequencies is available to transmit more information at the same time. DSL provides a broadband Internet connection speed that is available through phone lines. DSL and cable are widely used by homes and businesses. T1 provides an extremely fast connection speed and is widely used in businesses, especially for intranet (a computer network within a company) applications. You can test the movie that you are developing at the different speeds to evaluate the download experience for potential users.

QUICK TIP

NEW A quick way to track the changes in the .swf file size when a change is made to a Flash document is to view the SWF HISTORY area of the Properties panel.

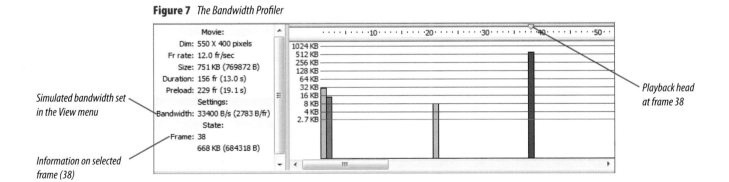

Figure 7 *The Bandwidth Profiler*

Simulated bandwidth set in the View menu

Information on selected frame (38)

Playback head at frame 38

Movie:
Dim: 550 X 400 pixels
Fr rate: 12.0 fr/sec
Size: 751 KB (769872 B)
Duration: 156 fr (13.0 s)
Preload: 229 fr (19.1 s)
Settings:
Bandwidth: 33400 B/s (2783 B/fr)
State:
Frame: 38
668 KB (684318 B)

Test the download time for a movie

1. Open fl6_2.fla, then save it as **planeFun.fla**.

2. Turn on your computer speakers or plug in headphones if you would like to hear the audio that is part of this movie.

3. Change the view to **Fit in Window**.

4. Click **Control** on the menu bar, point to **Test Movie**, then click **in Flash Professional**.

5. Maximize the Flash Player window.

6. Click **View** on the menu bar, point to **Download Settings**, then click **DSL (32.6 KB/s)**, as shown in Figure 8.

   The connection speeds (especially DSL) are affected by several factors including your Internet service provider capabilities, distance to telecom equipment, your computer and Internet connectivity equipment and the amount of Internet traffic. The Download Simulator provides relative connection speeds and is used to help determine where in a movie a download problem might exist.

7. Click **View** on the menu bar, then click **Simulate Download**.

   The movie is loaded and ready to play in the Flash Player using the simulated speed of 32.6 KB/s.

   (continued)

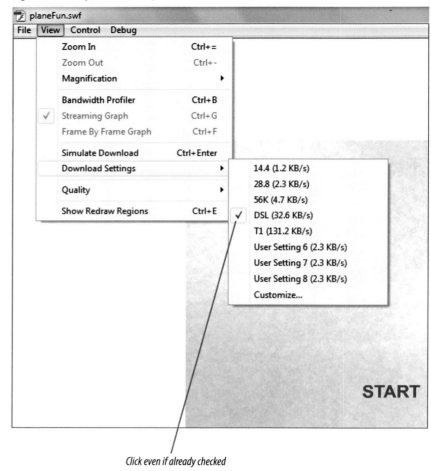

Figure 8 *Selecting the connection speed for a simulated download*

Click even if already checked

Figure 9 *A pause in the movie*

Movie pauses at this point

8. Click **Start**, then notice the pause in the movie when the plane begins to morph into the hot air balloon, as shown in Figure 9.

   You may have to wait several moments for the movie to continue. The pause is caused by the simulated browser waiting for the remaining contents of the movie to be downloaded.

9. Click **View** on the menu bar, point to **Download Settings**, then click **T1 (131.2 KB/s)**.

10. Click **View** on the menu bar, verify the Simulate Download feature is off (no check mark next to it), then click **Simulate Download** to turn on the feature.

    When you change a download setting, you need to be sure the Simulate Download feature is off, and then turn it on again to start the simulation with the new setting. The movie is loaded and ready to play in the Flash Player at the simulated download speed of 131.2 KB/s.

11. Click **Start**, then notice the pause in the movie is shorter with the simulated T1 line speed.

TIP If you don't notice a difference, turn the Simulate Download feature off and then on again.

Note: To see a dramatic difference, select one of the simulated dial-up speeds (14.4, 28.8, or 56 K). If you do this, be prepared to wait up to several minutes for the plane to morph into a hot air balloon. If you have users that connect via a dial-up connection, be sure to simulate a dial-up connection and make adjustments as needed so the movie displays as smoothly as possible.

You used the Flash Player window to simulate the download time for a movie using different connection speeds.

Use the Bandwidth Profiler

1. Verify that the Flash Player window is still open.
2. Click **View** on the menu bar, point to **Download Settings**, then click **DSL (32.6 KB/s)** to select it.
3. Click **View** on the menu bar, then click **Bandwidth Profiler**.
4. Click **View** on the menu bar, then verify Frame By Frame Graph is selected.
5. Click **View** on the menu bar, then click **Simulate Download**.

   Notice the green bar as it scrolls at the top of the Bandwidth Profiler to indicate the frames being downloaded. The bar pauses at frame 37, as shown in Figure 10.

6. Click **frame 37** on the Timeline, then notice that the only object in the frame is the morphing balloon, and its size is less than 1 KB.
7. Click **frame 38** on the Timeline, then notice the large color photograph.

   The frame setting in the State area indicates that the file size is over 600 KB. It takes several moments to download this large image, which causes the pause in the movie. One way to optimize the movie is to replace the image with the large file size in frame 38 with an image that is a smaller file size.

8. Close the Flash Player window.

You used the Bandwidth Profiler to determine which frame causes a pause in the movie.

Figure 10 *The Bandwidth Profiler indicating the pause at frame 37*

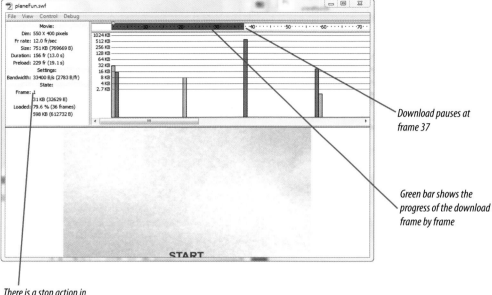

Download pauses at frame 37

Green bar shows the progress of the download frame by frame

There is a stop action in frame 1 causing the movie to stay at frame 1 while the rest of the movie is downloading

Figure 11 *Positioning the cloud image*

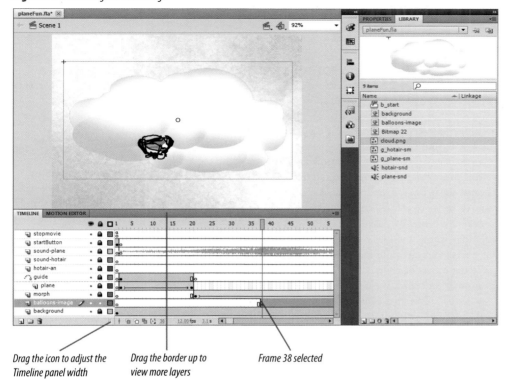

Drag the icon to adjust the Timeline panel width

Drag the border up to view more layers

Frame 38 selected

Optimize a movie by reducing file size

1. Point to the **top border** of the Timeline, then, when the pointer changes to a double-arrow ⭫, drag the **top border** up to view the balloons-image layer.

   TIP If the layer name appears cut off, then drag the Adjust Timeline panel width icon to the right until the layer name is fully visible.

2. Click **frame 38** on the balloons-image layer to view the image on the Stage.

3. Click the **balloon photographic image** on the Stage, click **Edit** on the menu bar, then click **Cut**.

   The balloon photograph is no longer visible on the Stage.

4. Display the Library panel.

5. Verify frame 38 is selected, then drag the **cloud.png** graphic from the Library panel to the center of the Stage, as shown in Figure 11.

6. Click **Control** on the menu bar, point to **Test Movie**, click **in Flash Professional**, then maximize the Flash Player window if it is not already maximized.

7. Click **View** on the Flash Player window menu bar, click **Simulate Download**, wait for the download to finish, then click **Start**.

   Notice the movie no longer pauses.

8. Click **frame 38** on the Timeline in the Flash Player window and notice that the file size is now just above the 8 KB line.

9. Click **View**, click **Bandwidth Profiler** to close the Bandwidth Profiler, close the Flash Player window, save your work, then close the movie.

You replaced an image that had a large file size with one having a small file size to help optimize a movie.

Create a
PRELOADER

What You'll Do

> Loading . . .

In this lesson, you will create a preloader for the planeFun movie. Ten frames have been added to the beginning of the movie and labels have been added to the start and ending frames of the movie.

Preloading a Movie

One way to improve the playback performance of large or complex movies is to preload the movie frames. Preloading frames prevents the browser from playing a specified frame or series of frames until all of the frames have been downloaded. Commonly, a **preloader** frame includes a simple animation that starts in frame 1 and loops until the rest of the movie has been downloaded. The animation could consist of the words "Please wait" flashing on the screen, the word "Loading" with a series of scrolling dots, or the hand of a clock sweeping around in a circle. The purpose of the animation is to indicate to the viewer that the movie is being loaded. The animation is placed on its own layer. A second layer contains the ActionScript code that checks to see if the movie has been loaded and, if not, causes a loop that continues until the last frame of the movie has been loaded.

For example, assume a movie has 155 frames. An additional 10 frames could be added to the beginning of the movie for the preloader, and the preloader animation would run from frames 1 to 10. A label, such as **startofMovie**, would be added to frame 11 (the first frame of the actual movie). Another label, such as **endofMovie**, would be added to frame 165, the last frame of the entire movie. Then the following ActionScript code would be placed in frame 1 of the movie on the preLoaderScript layer:

ifFrameLoaded ("endofMovie") {
**   gotoAndPlay ("startofMovie");**
}

This ActionScript code is a conditional statement that checks to see if the frame labeled endofMovie is loaded. If the statement is true, then the next line of the script is executed and the playhead goes to the frame labeled startofMovie. This

ActionScript code is placed in frame 1 on the preLoaderScript layer. So each time the playhead is on frame 1, there is a check to see if the entire movie has been downloaded. If the condition is false, the playhead moves on to frames 2, 3, 4, and so on. Then the following ActionScript code would be placed in frame 10.

gotoAndPlay (1);

This creates a loop. When the movie first starts, the playhead is on frame 1 and there is a check to see if the movie has been loaded. If not, the playhead continues to frame 10 (playing the preloader animation) where this script (gotoAndPlay (1);) causes it to

loop back to frame 1 for another check. The looping process continues until all movie frames have been loaded.

Figure 12 shows the Timeline that displays the two preloader layers after the preloader has been created.

Figure 12 *The completed preloader with the animation and ActionScript*

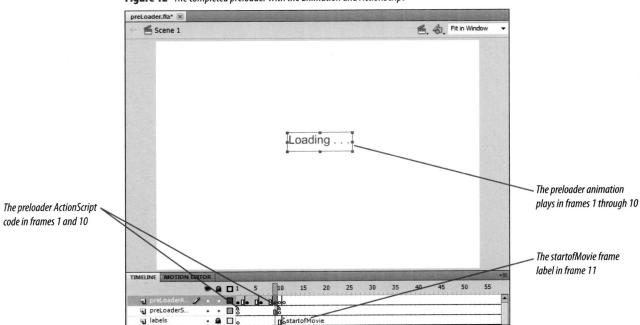

The preloader ActionScript code in frames 1 and 10

The preloader animation plays in frames 1 through 10

The startofMovie frame label in frame 11

Add layers for a preloader

1. Open fl6_3.fla, then save it as **preLoader.fla**.

   This movie is similar to the planeFun.fla movie except that the first 10 frames contain no content, and the movie again contains the larger graphic file photo of the hot air balloons.

2. Change the view to **Fit in Window**.

3. Click the **labels layer** at the top of the Timeline, then click the **New Layer icon** 🖫 to insert a **new layer**.

4. Name the new layer **preLoaderScript**.

5. Insert a **new layer** above the preLoaderScript layer, then name it **preLoaderAnimation**.

6. Click **frame 10** on the preLoaderAnimation layer, then insert a **keyframe**.

7. Insert a **keyframe** in frame 10 on the preLoader-Script layer.

   Your screen should resemble Figure 13.

You added two layers that will be used to create a preloader. One layer will contain the ActionScript and the other layer will contain the animation for the preloader.

Figure 13 *The preloader layers added to the Timeline*

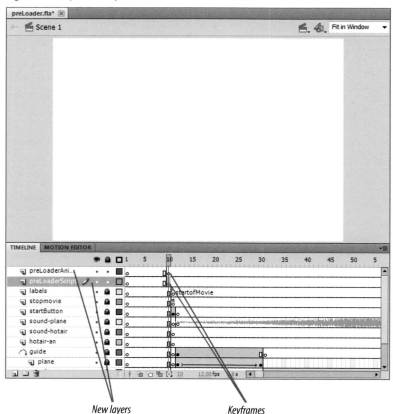

New layers   Keyframes

Figure 14 *The Actions panel showing frame to which action will be applied*

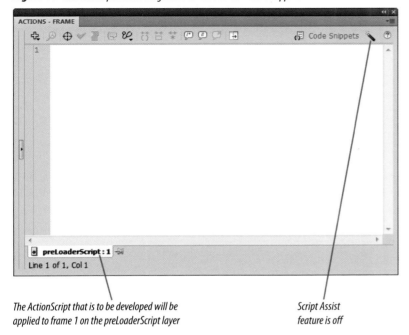

The ActionScript that is to be developed will be applied to frame 1 on the preLoaderScript layer

Script Assist feature is off

Figure 15 *The ActionScript code used to check if the last frame in the movie has been downloaded*

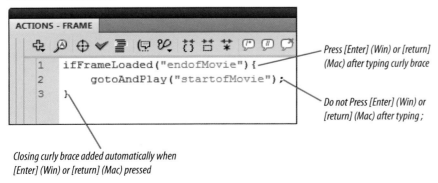

Press [Enter] (Win) or [return] (Mac) after typing curly brace

Do not Press [Enter] (Win) or [return] (Mac) after typing ;

Closing curly brace added automatically when [Enter] (Win) or [return] (Mac) pressed

Add actions to the preloader

1. Open the Actions panel, then turn off the Script Assist feature if it is on.

2. Click **frame 1** on the preLoaderScript layer.

3. Verify that preLoaderScript:1 is displayed in the lower-left corner of the Actions panel Script pane, as shown in Figure 14.

4. Click the **Actions panel Script pane**, then type the following code, matching use of capital letters, spacing, and punctuation exactly.

   ifFrameLoaded ("endofMovie") {

       gotoAndPlay ("startofMovie");

   Your screen should match Figure 15.

   Note: Be sure there is only one closing curly brace.

5. Click **frame 10** on the preLoaderScript layer, then verify preLoaderScript:10 is displayed in the lower-left corner of the Actions panel Script pane.

6. Click the **Actions panel Script pane**, then type the following code.

   gotoAndPlay (1);

7. Close the Actions panel.

You added actions to frames on the preLoaderScript layer that create a loop. The loop includes a check to see if the entire movie has been loaded and, if so, jumps to a starting place in the movie.

Create the preloader animation

1. Click **frame 1** on the preLoaderAnimation layer.
2. Click the **Text tool** T on the Tools menu, verify the text type is set to Classic Text, click the middle of the Stage, then type **Loading**.
3. Double-click to select **Loading**, then use the Properties panel to set the font to **Arial**, the size to **20**, and the color to **blue**.
4. Insert a **keyframe** in frame 3 on the preLoader-Animation layer.
5. Using the **Text ⊥̵ₜ pointer**, point to the right of the g in Loading, click, press the **spacebar**, then type a **period [.]**.
6. Insert a **keyframe** in frame 6 on the preLoaderAnimation layer.
7. Point to the right of the period, click, press the **spacebar**, then type a **period [.]**.
8. Insert a **keyframe** in frame 9 on the preLoader-Animation layer, point to the right of the period, click, press the **spacebar**, then type a **period [.]**.

   Your screen should resemble Figure 16.
9. Click **frame 10** on the preLoaderAnimation layer, click **Insert** on the menu bar, point to **Timeline**, then click **Blank Keyframe**.

   Inserting a blank keyframe prevents the contents of the previous frame from being inserted into the frame.
10. Drag the **playhead** back and forth across frames 1 through 10 and view the animation.

You created an animation that causes the word Loading to appear, followed by three dots, as the playhead loops waiting for the movie to load. You can create any animation for the preloader and use as many frames as desired.

Figure 16 *The text used in the preloader animation*

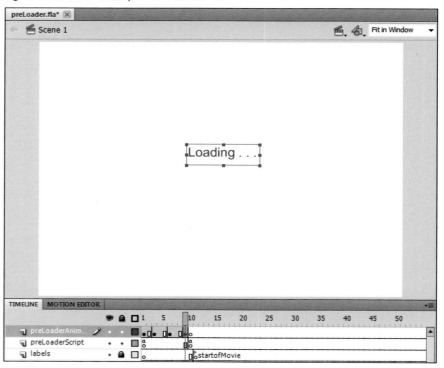

Figure 17 *The Bandwidth Profiler showing the delay in downloading frame 48*

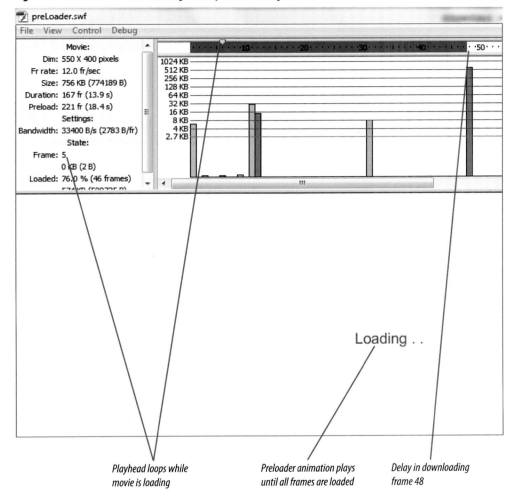

Playhead loops while
movie is loading

Preloader animation plays
until all frames are loaded

Delay in downloading
frame 48

Testing the preloader

1. Click **Control** on the menu bar, point to **Test Movie**, then click **in Flash Professional**.

2. Maximize the Flash Player window if it is not already maximized.

3. Click **View** on the menu bar, then click **Bandwidth Profiler** to display it if it is not already displayed.

4. Click **View** on the menu bar, point to **Download Settings**, then verify that DSL (32.6 KB/s) is selected.

5. Click **View** on the menu bar, then click **Simulate Download**.

   Notice the playhead loops, causing the preloader animation Loading . . . to play over and over in the Flash Player window as the frames are loaded. There is a delay in down-loading frame 48, as shown in Figure 17, as the large JPG file is loaded. Once all frames are loaded, the screen with the Start button appears in the Flash Player window.

6. Repeat Step 5 twice (to turn off and then turn on the Simulated Download feature) to run the simulation again, then drag the **scroll bar** on the Bandwidth Profiler to the right as needed to view the last frames of the movie (through frame 165).

7. Close the Bandwidth Profiler, then close the Flash Player window.

8. Save and close the movie.

You tested the preloader by simulating a download and you viewed the information on the Bandwidth Profiler during the simulation.

Use HTML
PUBLISH SETTINGS

What You'll Do

Having PlaneFun!!!

In this lesson, you will use the HTML Publish Settings to align the Flash movie window in a browser window and change the code of an HTML document.

Understanding HTML Publishing Options

During the publishing process, Flash automatically creates an HTML document that allows a Flash movie to be displayed on the web. When you test a Flash movie, you see it in the Flash Player window. When you see a Flash movie on the web, you view it in a **Flash movie window** in your browser. The Flash movie window is a container for displaying a Flash movie. Unlike the Flash Player, which a user can see, the Flash movie window is transparent to the user. Information about where the Flash movie should be placed in the browser window and information on how the Flash movie should look are in the HTML code for the web page.

The HTML code specifies, among other things, the movie's background color, its size, and its placement in the browser window. In addition, the attributes for the OBJECT (Internet Explorer for Win) and EMBED (all other browsers for Win and Mac) tags are specified in the HTML document. These tags are used to direct the browser to display the Flash movie using the specified dimensions and alignment settings. You can specify the settings using options available on the HTML tab in the Publish Settings dialog box.

A description of options available on the HTML tab in the Publish Settings dialog box follows:

Template—Flash provides several templates that create different HTML coding. For example, selecting Flash HTTPS creates HTML coding suitable for a secure HTTP connection.

Dimensions—This option sets the values for the Width and Height attributes in the OBJECT and EMBED HTML tags and it is used to set the size of the Flash movie window in the browser. You can set the size of the Flash movie window to match the size of the movie, you can resize the Flash movie window by entering its size in pixels, or you can set the Flash movie window dimensions as a percentage of the browser window.

Playback—These options control the movie's playback and features, including:

- Paused at start—pauses the movie until the user takes some action.
- Loop—repeats the movie.
- Display menu—displays a shortcut menu (with options such as zoom in and out, step forward and back, rewind, and play) when the user right-clicks (Win) or [control]-clicks (Mac) the movie in the browser.

- Device font (Win)—allows you to substitute system fonts for fonts not installed on the user's computer.

Quality—This option allows you to specify the quality of the appearance of objects within the frames. Selecting low quality increases playback speed but reduces image quality, while selecting high quality results in the opposite effect.

Window Mode—This option allows you to specify settings for transparency and opaqueness.

HTML alignment—This option allows you to position the Flash movie window in the browser window. Center alignment is the default setting.

Scale—If you have changed the movie's original width and height, you can use this option to place the movie within specified boundaries.

Flash alignment—This option allows you to align the Flash movie (when it is a smaller size than the Flash movie window) within the Flash movie window.

Determining Movie Placement in a Browser Window

When you publish a movie for delivery on the Internet, you need to be concerned with where the movie will appear in a browser window. This is especially important when you have a Flash movie, such as an animation displayed as a banner, that you want to place in a specific location on a web page. The placement is controlled by settings in the HTML document. You can specify the settings when you publish the movie. A Flash movie is displayed within a Flash movie window in your browser window. You can have the Flash movie window match the size of the Flash movie or you can use the HTML tab in the Publish Settings dialog box to specify a different size. Figure 18 shows the relationships among the Flash movie dimensions, the Flash movie window, the browser window, and the HTML settings. In this example, the dimensions for the Flash

movie window are set to Percent (Width: 50%, Height: 25%). This means that the Flash movie window will span only one half the width of the browser window and the height of the Flash movie window will be one quarter the height of the Flash movie. The height of the Flash movie is 400 px, so 25 percent of that height is 100 px, which sets the height of the Flash movie window at 100 px. The HTML alignment, that is where the Flash movie window appears in the browser, is set to right. The Flash alignment, that is where the Flash movie appears in the Flash movie window, is also set to right.

When you reduce the percent of one Flash movie window dimension to below 100, then the other Flash movie dimension is reduced to keep the same aspect ratio. In this example, the Flash movie window height of 25 percent causes the Flash movie height to be resized to 100. Then, the Flash movie width is resized to 100 to maintain the same 1:1 aspect ratio (as the original dimensions, which were 400 x 400).

Figure 18 *Relationships among the movie dimensions, movie and browser windows, and the HTML settings*

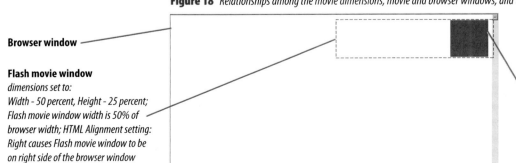

Browser window

Flash movie window
dimensions set to:
Width - 50 percent, Height - 25 percent;
Flash movie window width is 50% of
browser width; HTML Alignment setting:
Right causes Flash movie window to be
on right side of the browser window

Flash Movie
dimensions set to:
Width - 400 px, Height - 400 px
Actual display size is 100 x 100
caused by Flash movie window
dimensions;
Flash Alignment Horizontal
setting: Right causes Flash
movie to be on right side of the
Flash movie window

Change HTML publish settings

1. Open planeFun.fla, then save it as **planeFunRev.fla**.

2. Click **File** on the menu bar, click **Publish Settings**, then click the **HTML tab**.

3. Click the **Dimensions list arrow**, then click **Percent**.

4. Double-click the **Height text box**, type **50**, then compare your settings on the HTML tab to Figure 19.

   Specifying 100 percent for the width and 50 percent for the height causes the Flash movie window to be as wide as the browser window and approximately one-half the height of the browser window.

5. Click **Publish**, then click **OK**.

6. Click **File** on the menu bar, point to **Publish Preview**, then click **Default - (HTML)**.

7. Click the **Start button**, then view the movie.

   The Flash movie window, which is transparent to the visitor, is the full width of the browser because the width setting of the Flash movie window was specified as 100% in the HTML settings. But, the height of the window is 50% of the browser window because the height setting of the Flash movie window was specified as 50%. The Flash movie is centered within the Flash movie window in the browser because the horizontal alignment for the Flash movie was specified as centered.

8. Close the browser.

You resized the Flash movie window by changing the HTML publish settings, which in turn resized the Flash movie.

Figure 19 *Changing the HTML publish settings*

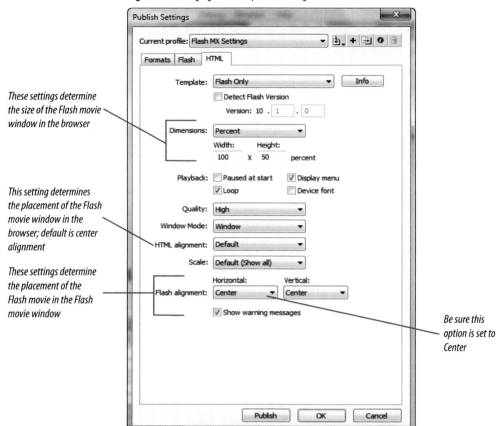

These settings determine the size of the Flash movie window in the browser

This setting determines the placement of the Flash movie window in the browser; default is center alignment

These settings determine the placement of the Flash movie in the Flash movie window

Be sure this option is set to Center

Preparing and Publishing Movies

Figure 20 *Changing the HTML code*

Code to insert a heading
below the Flash movie
window

Edit an HTML document

1. Open a text editor such as Notepad (Win) or TextEdit (Mac).

2. Click **File** on the text editor menu bar, click **Open**, change the Files of type to **All Files** if All Files is not displayed, navigate to planeFunRev.html, verify the Ignore rich text commands check box is checked (Mac), click **planeFunRev.html**, click **Open** in the text editor window, then maximize the editor window.

3. Scroll to the bottom of the window, click to the left of </div>, then press **[Enter]** to insert a blank line above </div>.

4. Click the **blank line**, type **
, then press **[Enter] (Win) or **[return]** (Mac).

5. Type **<h3> <font color="red"> Having PlaneFun!!!</font> </ h3>**, then compare the text you typed with the boxed text in Figure 20.

6. Save the file with the file name **planeFunRev-caption.html**, then close the text editor.

7. Use your file management program to navigate to the folder where you save your Data Files, then double-click **planeFunRev-caption.html** to open the movie in your browser.

   The text you added appears centered on the screen in red.

8. Close your browser.

9. Save the movie, then close the movie.

You edited an HTML document to display formatted text below the Flash movie.

Create and Test Applications
FOR MOBILE DEVICES

What You'll Do

In this lesson, you will use Flash to develop an application for a mobile device and test the application using Adobe Device Central.

NEW Understanding Flash Lite

You have been using the Flash Player to view .swf files when testing and publishing Flash movies. Adobe makes available another player, **Flash Lite**, that is a subset of the Flash Player. Flash Lite is optimized for mobile devices such as cell phones. In addition, Adobe provides a program, **Device Central**, that allows you to test Flash movies on various models of mobile devices. This is important because mobile devices vary in screen size and capabilities (e.g. navigation controls) that may cause unexpected user problems if not detected through testing. Figure 21 shows the Device Central Emulation screen. The TEST DEVICES panel at the left of the screen displays a list of mobile device profiles. Many of these are generic profiles developed by Adobe. Others are available from vendors and can be added to the TEST DEVICES list using the BROWSE command on the Device Central menu bar. Figure 21 also shows the selected device, Nokia 6600 slide, which is displaying a Flash movie. In addition, the INFO panel at the upper-right side of the screen shows information about the Flash movie and player as explained below.

Content Type—There are several content types including Screensaver, Wallpaper, and Embedded in HTML. In this case the type is set to Standalone Player, which is appropriate for .swf files.

Player Version—Adobe began with version 1.0 and has created new versions that take advantage of emerging technologies, such as touch screens. The figure shows Flash Lite 3.0 will be used.

File—Displays the Flash .swf file that is being tested.

Dimensions—Displays the Stage dimensions for the .swf file being tested.

Due to screen and memory limitations, as well as processor speeds of mobile devices, there are several considerations to take into account when developing applications for mobile devices. Keep in mind the following guidelines as you are developing Flash movies for deployment on mobile devices:

- Specify Fit to Fullscreen to help ensure that the content will cover the entire screen.
- Keep vector shapes as simple as possible.
- Convert smaller graphics to bitmaps.

- Keep animations simple, especially reduce the amount of screen redrawing during the animation.
- Avoid alpha transparencies.
- Avoid overlapping motion tweens.

While testing a Flash application using Device Central is an essential part of the development process, testing directly on the device should also be done. This can be accomplished in several ways including connecting the device to a computer and uploading the .swf file to the device; transferring the application via a memory card; placing the application on a web server and transferring via a browser; or sending the application as an e-mail attachment.

Figure 21 *The Device Central Emulation screen*

List of mobile device profiles

INFO panel provides information specific to the selected device

Nokia 6600 slide phone in preview area

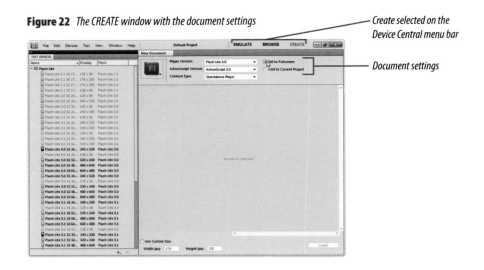 Set up Adobe Device Central

1. Open a new Flash ActionScript 2.0 document, click **File** on the menu bar, click **New**, click **Adobe Device Central**, then click **OK**.

   Device Central opens.

2. Verify CREATE is selected on the menu bar.

3. Click the **Player Version list arrow**, click **Flash Lite 3.0**, then verify the ActionScript Version is 2.0.

4. Click the **Content Type list arrow**, click **Standalone Player**, then click **Set to Fullscreen** as shown in Figure 22.

5. Click **BROWSE** on the menu bar.

6. Scroll the device list in the Device Library panel to display Nokia 6600 slide, then double-click the **Nokia 6600 slide device icon**.

   A picture of the cell phone appears with general information, such as its display size (240 x 320 px) and its Flash Lite version (3.0).

7. Click **FLASH** above the general information to view the acceptable graphic (and video file formats).

8. Click the **cell phone image**, then drag the **cell phone image** to the TEST DEVICES Name list if it is not already included in the list.

9. Click **CREATE** on the menu bar.

10. Double-click **Nokia 6600 slide** in the Name list on the Test Devices panel.

    The device appears in the New Document window, as shown in Figure 23.

11. Click the **Create button** at the bottom right of the screen, then if a message appears asking if you want to queue this command, click **Yes**.

    The Flash workspace appears.

You opened Device Central, specified a Flash Lite version, and selected a device to use for testing.

Figure 22 *The CREATE window with the document settings*

Create selected on the Device Central menu bar

Document settings

Figure 23 *The Nokia 6600 slide phone displayed in the CREATE window*

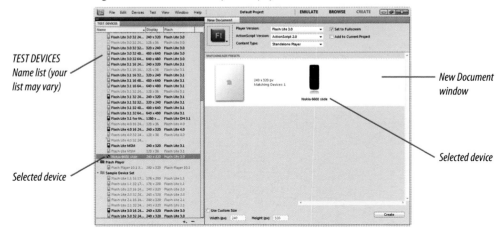

TEST DEVICES Name list (your list may vary)

Selected device

New Document window

Selected device

Figure 24 *Creating the text block centered above the graphic*

Figure 25 *Creating the motion tween that causes the text block to move*

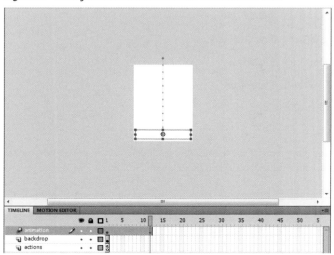

NEW Create a Flash application for a mobile device

1. Save the document with the name **palms.fla**.

2. Change the view to **50%**, then verify the frame rate is 12 fps.

3. Name Layer 1 **actions**, insert a **new layer**, then name it **backdrop**.

4. Click **File** on the menu bar, point to **Import**, then click **Import to Library**.

5. Navigate to the drive and folder where your Data Files are stored, click **palmTrees.jpg**, then click **Open**.

6. Click **frame 1** on the backdrop layer.

7. Drag the **palmTrees graphic** from the Library panel, then align the palmTrees graphic on the Stage by setting the X and Y values in the POSITION AND SIZE area of the Properties panel to 0.

8. Insert a **new layer**, then name it **animation**.

9. Click **frame 1** on the animation layer.

10. Click the **Text tool** T on the Tools panel, then use the Properties panel to set the font to **Lithos Pro** or another font, such as Bodoni MT, the style to **Black**, and the size to **26** and the color to **white**.

11. Position the text tool above the graphic, type **The Big Island**, then center the text block as shown in Figure 24.

12. Insert a **motion tween** that causes the text block to move from above the graphic to the bottom of the graphic as shown in Figure 25.

(continued)

13. Click **frame 12** on the backdrop layer, then insert a **keyframe**.

14. Click **frame 1** on the actions layer, then display the Actions panel.

    The code on line 1 was generated when you selected Set to Fullscreen in the Device Central New Document window.

15. Click at the **end of line 1**, then press **[Enter]** (Win) or **[return]** (Mac).

16. Type the code exactly as shown in Figure 26 and explained in the sidebar.

17. Click **frame 12** on the actions layer, then insert a **keyframe**.

18. Click **line 1** in the Actions panel, then type **stop();**

19. Save the movie.

20. Click **Control** on the menu bar, point to **Test Movie**, then click **in Flash Professional**.

21. When the movie appears in the Flash Player window, press the **spacebar**.

    The movie starts and the animation plays.

22. Close the Flash Player window.

You created an animation, including a press key event, for a mobile device.

Figure 26 *The code to create a key press action*

```
ACTIONS - FRAME

1  fscommand2("FullScreen", "true");
2  stop();
3
4  var pressKey:Object = new Object();
5  pressKey.onKeyDown = function() {
6      gotoAndPlay("2");
7  };
8  Key.addListener(pressKey);
```

NEW Explanation of the ActionScript code shown in Figure 26.

fscommand2("FullScreen", "true");

Sets the display area to full screen; this code was generated when you selected the Set to Fullscreen option.

stop();

Stops the playhead so the animation does not play.

var pressKey:Object = new Object();

Declares a variable called pressKey.

pressKey.onKeyDown = function() {

        gotoAndPlay("2");

};

Assigns a function (line of code) to the pressKey variable when a key is pressed (onKeyDown). The function is to move the playhead to frame 2.

Key.addListener(pressKey);

Listens for the pressKey action. That is, this allows Flash to recognize when there is an onKeyDown action and then to execute the line of code within the function.

Figure 27 *Playing a Flash movie in a mobile device*

Click the center button to
play the Flash movie

Test a movie using Device Central

1. Click **Control** on the menu bar, point to **Test Movie**, then click **in Device Central**.

   Device Central opens. *Note:* If the Flash workspace reappears minimize the window.

2. Verify that EMULATE FLASH is active on the menu bar, Standalone Player is specified for the Content Type, and that the Nokia cell phone is displayed.

3. Point to the button shown in Figure 27, then click the **button** to play the movie.

   The movie plays because the ActionScript code uses the onKeyPress command, which is not key specific. Additional code would be needed to specify a specific key.

4. View the information in the INFO panel at the upper-right side of the screen.

5. Click the **Display tab** on the right side panel, change the Backlight to **50%**, then repeat step 3 to test the movie.

   Note: You will have to click the button two times. The first time resets the movie and the second time plays the movie.

6. Change the Backlight to **100%**, then test the movie. *Note:* The output panel grouped with the Timeline panel may display a "FSCommand2 FullScreen command found" message. This verifies that the SWF file is communicating with the Flash Lite player.

7. Click **File** on the Device Central menu bar, then click **Quit** (Win), or click **Device Central** on the menu bar, then click **Quit Device Central** (Mac).

8. Close the Flash document.

9. Exit Flash.

You tested a Flash movie using Device Central and changed a property of the display.

Publish using default settings.

1. Start Flash, open fl6_4.fla, then save it as **skillsDemo6.fla.** (*Notes*: When you open the file, you may receive a warning message that a font is missing. You can replace this font with the default, or with any other appropriate font on your computer. If a message appears indicating that you need QuickTime, you will need to install the program to continue.)
2. Open the Publish Settings dialog box.
3. Verify that the Formats tab is selected and the Flash and HTML options are the only Format types checked.
4. Click Publish, then click OK to close the dialog box.
5. Use your file management program to navigate to the drive and folder where you store your work to view the skillsDemo6.html and skillsDemo6.swf files.
6. Return to the Flash program.
7. Use the Publish Preview feature to display the movie in a browser.
8. Close your browser, return to the Flash program, then save your work.

Create a JPEG image.

1. Select frame 60 on the Timeline.
2. Open the Publish Settings dialog box.
3. Click the JPEG Image check box, then click the JPEG tab.
4. Click Publish, then click OK to close the dialog box.
5. Open your browser, and then open the skillsDemo6.jpg file.
6. Close the browser, return to the Flash program, then save your work.

Test a movie.

1. Test the movie in the Flash Player window, then maximize the Flash Player window if it is not already maximized.
2. Turn off the loop feature. (*Hint*: Click Control on the Flash Player menu bar, then deselect the Loop check box.)
3. Set the Download Setting to DSL (32.6 KB/s) if it is not already set to that setting.
4. Display the Bandwidth Profiler if it is not already displayed, click View on the menu bar, then click Frame By Frame Graph if it is not already selected.
5. Use controls on the Control menu to rewind the movie. (Notice the bar on the Timeline for frame 1 is just under 256 KB, which is way above the red base line. The large photo is in frame 1, which could cause the movie to have a slow start.)
6. Close the Flash Player window.

Reduce file size to optimize a movie.

1. Select frame 1 on the sedona-photo layer, verify the image is selected on the Stage, then delete the image.
2. Replace the image with the sedona-sm graphic from the Library panel.
3. Position the sedona-sm image approximately two-thirds of the way down the Stage and centered across the Stage.
4. Save the movie.
5. Test the movie within the Flash Player window by simulating a DSL download. (Notice the bar on the Timeline for frame 1 is near 32 KB. This allows the movie to start more quickly.)
6. Close the Flash Player window.

Use HTML Publish Settings.

1. Display the Publish Settings dialog box, and then click the HTML tab.
2. Change the Dimensions to Percent, then change the width to **100%** and the height to **40%**.
3. Click Publish, then click OK to close the dialog box.
4. Use the Publish Preview feature to view the movie in a browser.
5. Close the browser.
6. Save your work.

Edit an HTML document.

1. Open a text editor.
2. Open the skillsDemo6.html file, then save it as **skillsDemo6-caption.html**.
3. Scroll to the end of the window, insert a blank line before the </div> tag.
4. Type </br> on the blank line above </div>, then press [Enter] (WIN) or [return] (Mac) to insert a new line in the Flash document.
5. Type **<h3> <font color="green"> Beautiful Northern Arizona</font> </h3>**.
6. Save your work.
7. Display skillsDemo6-caption.html in your browser.
8. Close the browser, then close the text editor.

Add a background.

1. Verify skillsDemo6.fla is the active file, then insert a new layer and move it below the sedona-photo layer.
2. Name the new layer **background**.
3. Select frame 1 on the background layer.
4. Display the Library panel (if necessary).

Preparing and Publishing Movies

5. Drag the g_background graphic symbol to the center of the Stage.
6. Click the last frame on the Timeline associated with content so your screen looks like Figure 28. (*Note*: Your heading font may differ.)
7. Use the Publish Preview feature to view the movie in a browser, close the browser, then save your work.

Create a preloader.

1. Click frame 1 on the Timeline.
2. Click Edit on the menu bar, point to Timeline, then click Select All Frames.
3. Point to any frame on the Timeline and drag the frames to the right so they start in frame 11.
4. Insert a new layer and name it **labels**.
5. Click frame 11 on the labels layer to select it, insert a keyframe, then display the Properties panel and type **startofMovie** in the Name text box in the LABEL area.
6. Insert a keyframe in frame 70 on the labels layer and type **endofMovie** in the Name text box in the LABEL area.
7. Add a new layer and name it **preLoaderScript**.
8. Insert an ifFrameLoaded action in frame 1 to check if all the frames have been loaded and, if so, go to and play the startofMovie frame. Also, insert a keyframe in frame 10 on the preLoaderScript layer, then insert a gotoAndPlay(1) action in frame 10 to cause a loop in the preloader frames.
9. Add a new layer and name it **preloader Animation**, then have the words "**Please wait**" appear in the first four frames and not appear in the last six frames of the ten frames used for the preloader. This will cause the words Please wait to flash until all the frames are loaded.

10. Test the movie, and use the Simulate Download feature to view the preloader.
11. Save your work.

Create and test a Flash application for a mobile device

1. Save the document as **skillsDemo6-mobile.fla**.
2. Change the view to 50%, then change the document size to 240 width and 320 height.
3. Select the Please Wait text and center it on the Stage, then lock the preloader Animation layer.
4. Select frame 11 on the background layer, click the background graphic, resize it to the same dimensions as the Stage, then lock the background layer.
5. Select the Sedona photo, change the width to 236, center the photo on the Stage, then lock the Sedona-photo layer.

Figure 28 *Completed Skills Review*

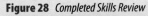

6. Click frame 11 on the heading-An layer, draw a marquee around the heading, then drag it above the photo.
7. Click frame 70 on the heading-An layer, use the Free Transform tool (with the Scale option at the bottom of the Tools panel selected) to resize the heading to fit the Stage and center the heading above the photo.
8. Display the Publish Settings dialog box, select the Flash tab, then change the Player to Flash Lite 3.0.
9. Save the movie.
10. Select Control on the menu bar, point to Test Movie, then click in Device Central. (*Note*: The movie plays in the device as Device Central opens because no press key event was specified. If Nokia 6600 slide is not in the preview window, browse to select the Nokia 6600 slide device and test the movie using it).
11. Change the display to Fullscreen.
12. Close Device Central and exit Flash.

The Ultimate Tours travel company has asked you to create a website and a JPEG image using movies you created in previous chapters.

1. Open ultimateTours5.fla (the file you created in Chapter 5 Project Builder 1) and save it as **ultimateTours6.fla**.
2. Use the Publish Settings dialog box to publish the movie using the following settings for the Flash and HTML formats:
   Flash Player: 10
   Flash Script: ActionScript 2.0
   HTML Dimensions: Match Movie
3. Use the Publish Preview feature to display the movie in the browser.
4. Create a JPEG image of the Mystery Ships screen, as shown in Figure 29.
5. Display the JPEG image in your browser.
6. Use the HTML publish settings panel to change the HTML Dimensions: Percent, then set Width to 100 and Height to 40.
7. Display the movie in your browser, then save the document to the drive and folder where you save your work.
8. Edit the HTML document using a text editor to add a caption.
9. Save the edited HTML file as **ultimatetours6-caption.html**, then display the movie in your browser.
10. Save the ultimateTours6.fla file.

Figure 29 *Sample completed Project Builder 1*

In this project you will choose a Flash movie you developed for this book or one you developed on your own. You will make changes to the publish settings, create a JPEG image, create and edit the HTML document, and create an application for a mobile device. Figure 30 shows a JPEG image with a caption for a sample movie and the movie in a mobile device.

1. Open a movie you developed from this book or one you developed on your own, then save it as **publish6.fla**.
2. Use the Publish Settings dialog box to publish the movie using the following settings for the Flash and HTML formats.
   Flash Player: 10
   Flash Script: ActionScript 2.0
   HTML Dimensions: Match Movie
3. Use the Publish Preview feature to display the movie in the browser.
4. Create a JPEG image of an interesting frame of your movie.
5. Display the JPEG image in your browser.
6. Change the HTML publish settings to HTML Dimensions: Percent, with Width set to 100 and Height set to 50
7. Display the movie in your browser, then save the document to the drive and folder where you save your work.
8. Edit the HTML document using a text editor to add a caption.
9. Save the edited HTML file as **publish6-caption. html**, then display the movie in your browser.
10. Save the publish6.fla file.

11. Save the document with the name **publish6-mobile.fla**.
12. Change the Publish Settings by removing the check-mark for the JPEG format and setting the Flash player to Flash Lite 3.0.
13. Click Control on the menu bar, point to Test Movie, then click in Device Central.
14. Click BROWSE on the menu bar and scroll the list or use the Search box to display Nokia 3600 slide. (*Note*: You can type a device name in the Search text box, and press [Enter] (Win) or [return] (Mac) to quickly find a device.)

15. Drag the phone icon to the TEST DEVICES panel, then scroll the panel to view the name.
16. Click the name in the TEST DEVICES panel to view the phone information in the Device Library.
17. Click EMULATE FLASH on the menu bar and view the movie playing in the phone display window.
18. Click the DISPLAY panel tab, then click Set to Fullscreen to select it.
19. Close Device Central and return to Flash.
20. Close the Flash document.

Figure 30 *Sample completed Project Builder 2*

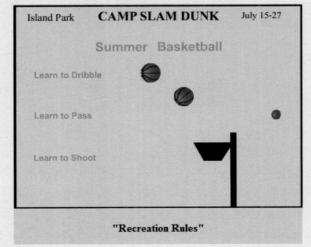

Figure 31 shows the home page of a website. Study the figure and complete the following questions. For each question, indicate how you determined your answer.

1. Connect to the Internet, go to *www.yha.com.au/itinerary/index.cfm*, then click the link Find a Hostel in the quick links area of the web page.

2. Open a document in a word processor or open a new Flash movie, save the file as **dpc6**, then answer the following questions. (*Hint*: Use the Text tool in Flash.)
   - What seems to be the purpose of this site?
   - Who would be the target audience?
   - How might the Bandwidth Profiler be used when developing this site?
   - Assuming there is a pause in the playing of a Flash movie on the site, what suggestions would you make to eliminate the pause?
   - What would be the value of creating a GIF animation from one of the animations on the site?
   - What would be the value of creating a JPEG image from one of the animations on the site?
   - What suggestions would you make to improve the design, and why?

Figure 31 *Design Project*

This is a continuation of the Portfolio Project in Chapter 5, which is the development of a personal portfolio. In this project, you will create a website and a JPEG image with the movies you have created.

1. Open portfolio5.fla (the file you created in Portfolio Project, Chapter 5) and save it as **portfolio6.fla**.
2. Use the Publish Settings dialog box to publish the movie.
3. Use the Publish Preview feature to display the movie in the browser.
4. Create a JPEG image of the first frame of the movie.
5. Display the JPEG image in your browser, and compare it to the example shown in Figure 32.
6. Use the Bandwidth Profiler to display a frame-by-frame graph of the movie and to determine which frame may cause a pause in the movie at a 28.8 (2.3 KB/s) connection speed. (*Note*: Specifying 28.8 (2.3 KB/s) as the connection speed enables you to identify any pauses and practice using the Bandwidth Profiler. This option can take a very long time to load.)
7. Make a change in the movie to help optimize it.
8. Make a change in the HTML publish settings, display the movie in your browser, then save the document to the drive and folder where you save your work.
9. Edit the HTML document using a text editor to add a caption, then save the edited HTML file as **portfolio6-caption**.html, then display the movie in your browser.
10. Save portfolio6.fla.

Figure 32 *Sample completed Portfolio Project*

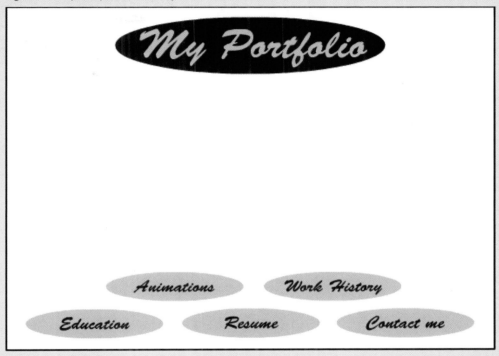

CHAPTER

7

IMPORTING AND
MODIFYING GRAPHICS

1. Understand and import graphics
2. Break apart bitmaps and use bitmap fills
3. Trace bitmap graphics

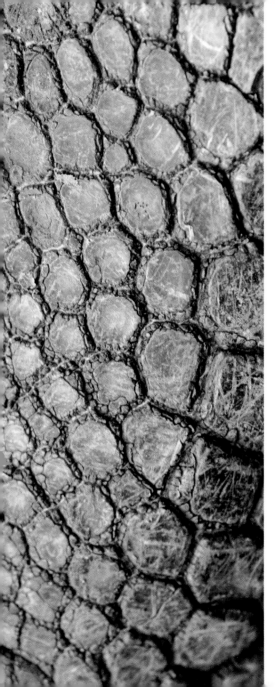

CHAPTER 7

IMPORTING AND MODIFYING GRAPHICS

Introduction

Graphics are vital to websites and applications. A single drawing, chart, or photograph can illustrate what might take many pages of narrative text to communicate. In the end, the image may do a better job of creating a lasting impression or establishing a mood. As you create movies, you may often find yourself wanting to use a logo or image that originated in another application. In previous chapters, you learned to create graphics using the drawing tools on the Tools panel. And, as you have seen in previous chapters, you are not limited to just what you can draw within your movie. You can also import and even animate vector and bitmap graphics that have been created or modified in other applications.

Importing vector graphics from an application, such as Adobe Fireworks or Adobe Illustrator, is easy—the vector graphics are treated almost the same as if

you created them in Adobe Flash. Importing bitmap graphics is easy, too, but working with them can be more difficult. Also, remember that using bitmap graphics can increase the file size of your movies dramatically, resulting in slower download times. When considering images for your movies, it is most efficient to use vector graphics or to create graphics directly within Flash.

In this chapter, you will practice importing graphics that have been created outside the Flash environment. For those who are "artistically challenged," importing graphics from other applications can often help to make up for less-than-perfect drawing skills. You can import a wide variety of vector and bitmap graphics, including drawings and photographs. Once the graphics are in your library, you can place them on the Stage, where you can trace them, break them apart, use them to fill an object, optimize them, and animate them.

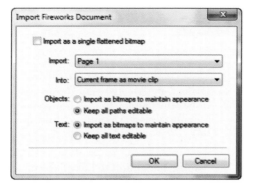

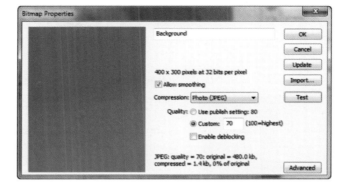

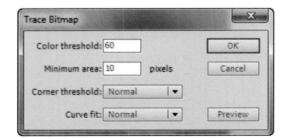

Understand and
IMPORT GRAPHICS

What You'll Do

In this lesson, you will import graphics that were created using different drawing and image-editing programs.

Understanding the Formats

Because Flash is a vector-based application, all graphics and motion within the application are calculated according to mathematical formulas. This vector-based format results in a smaller file size, as well as a robust ability to resize movies without a notable loss in quality.

When you import bitmapped graphics, you usually lose some of the vector-based benefits or these benefits change dramatically. A bitmap graphic, also called a **raster graphic**, is based on pixels, not on mathematical formulas. As discussed previously, importing multiple bitmap graphics increases the file size of your movie and decreases flexibility in terms of resizing the movie.

Flash makes it possible to import both vector and bitmap graphics from applications such as Adobe Fireworks, Illustrator, and Photoshop. In many cases, you can retain features, such as layers, transparency, and animation, when you import graphics.

Importing Different Graphic Formats: An Overview

There are several ways of bringing external graphics into your movie, including import

or cut and paste. Generally, the best way to bring a graphic into your movie is to **import** it by selecting the Import option on the File menu. Then, you can choose the Import to Stage command to have the graphic placed on the Stage and in the library, or you can choose the Import to Library command to have the graphic placed only in the library. Next, in the Import dialog box, you navigate to the graphic of your choice. Figure 1 displays the Import to Library dialog box with the All Files option selected. In most cases, you would import graphics to the Library before developing a movie. At times during the development process, you may want to add a new graphic directly to the Stage. In these cases, you could use the import to Stage feature to save the step of dragging the graphic from the Library panel to the Stage.

If the original graphic has layers, Flash can create new layers associated with that graphic in your document, depending on the file type and the settings you specify when you import the graphic. Flash automatically places the additional layers on the Timeline or inside a movie clip symbol, when applicable.

If you are importing large numbers of graphics, you can import a group of graphics (of the same file type and from a single folder), all of which will automatically use the same settings, enabling you to choose your import preferences just once.

You can also copy and paste graphics from an application, such as a graphics-editing program, directly into a Flash movie. Some graphics applications, such as Adobe Illustrator and Adobe Fireworks, create vector graphics which are maintained during the copy and paste process. However, when you copy and paste using other applications, the graphic may become a flattened bitmap, which means the advantages of using vector graphics in Flash, such as smaller file sizes, editing strokes and fills, and resizing without distortion, are lost.

Using Fireworks PNG Files

Graphics created in Fireworks are PNG files. You can import Fireworks PNG files as either flattened bitmap graphics or as editable objects. Fireworks uses Pages to contain selected layers, which in turn contain the paths. Paths are the segments, such as lines, of a graphic that can be individually edited. In addition to paths, pages also contain the settings such as size, color, and image resolution that are applied to different parts of a graphic. For example, in a picture of a child on a bike, one page might contain the settings for the bike and the other page might contain the settings for the child. If a PNG file has more than one page, you can specify which pages to import.

Figure 1 *Import to Library dialog box*

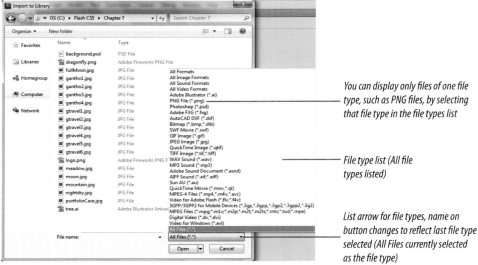

You can display only files of one file type, such as PNG files, by selecting that file type in the file types list

File type list (All file types listed)

List arrow for file types, name on button changes to reflect last file type selected (All Files currently selected as the file type)

Figure 2 shows the Import dialog box for a Fireworks file, which you use to specify the import settings for a PNG file. If, in the Import dialog box for a Fireworks file, you choose to import a PNG file as a flattened graphic, Flash will automatically convert the graphic to a flattened bitmap image. If, in the Import dialog box for a Fireworks file, you choose to import a PNG file as an editable object, the graphic retains its vector format as well as its layers, transparency features, and filters (such as bevels). If you click the Keep all paths editable option, Flash imports the PNG file as a movie clip symbol. All the features of the PNG file will be intact inside the movie clip symbol that is stored in the library. To edit features of an imported file, open the movie clip in the edit window and make the changes.

QUICK TIP

The Import dialog box is specific to the type of document being imported. The Name in the title bar changes to reflect the type of document being imported, and the options available in the dialog box are specific to the type of document being imported. For example, compare Figure 2 and Figure 3 to see how the Import dialog box changes.

Importing Adobe Illustrator Files

Adobe Illustrator is an excellent program for creating artwork that is to be imported into Flash. Graphics created in Illustrator are AI files. Illustrator AI files are vector-based. So, when imported as a movie clip, AI files preserve most of their attributes including filters (such as drop shadows) and blends (such as transparency settings). In addition, in the Import dialog box for an Illustrator file, you can choose to convert Illustrator graphic layers to Flash layers. This allows quite a bit of flexibility when editing and animating an Illustrator file in Flash.

Importing Adobe Photoshop Files

Flash also allows you to import Photoshop files into a Flash document. One advantage of using Photoshop to create graphics and enhance photographs is that the drawing and selection tools, as well as the photo-retouching features, allow you to produce more creative and complex images. The Photoshop tools allow you to create high-quality artwork before you import the graphic into Flash. Graphics created in Photoshop are PSD files. In the Import dialog box for a Photoshop file, you can choose to have the Photoshop layers imported as Flash layers. This allows you to edit individual parts of an image, such as animating text, or to use the entire graphic, such as creating a button using a photograph, once the graphic is in your Flash document.

The process for importing Photoshop files into Flash follows. First, open a Flash document and select the Import option from the File menu. Then, choose to import to the Stage or to the library, and then navigate to and select the PSD file you want to import. The Import dialog box for a Photoshop file opens, as shown in Figure 3. You select options in this dialog box that determine whether or not you want to be able to edit the contents (text, image, background, etc.) of each PSD layer. If you choose not to make a layer editable, the contents of that layer are flattened as a bitmap image. If you choose to make a layer editable,

Figure 2 *Import dialog box for Fireworks file*

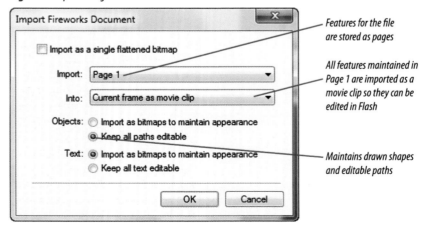

Features for the file are stored as pages

All features maintained in Page 1 are imported as a movie clip so they can be edited in Flash

Maintains drawn shapes and editable paths

a movie clip symbol that contains the graphic information is created using the layer contents. Therefore, depending on the choices you make in the Import dialog box, you could end up with several items (graphic symbols and movie clip symbols as well as bitmaps) in the Library. All of the information (flattened bitmap images and editable images) for the PSD file is imported into one folder in your Flash movie.

When importing to the Stage, other options allow you to specify that the contents of the imported file retain the same relative position they had in Photoshop and that the Flash Stage resizes so it is the same size as the Photoshop document.

Importing Bitmaps

Flash allows you to use and modify imported bitmaps in a variety of ways. You can control the size, compression, and **anti-aliasing** of an imported bitmap. Anti-aliasing is the process of smoothing the edges of a graphic so they appear less jagged. This is done by blending colors. For example, if there is a black graphic on a white background, the pixels on the edges of the graphic would be turned to shades of gray. You can also use a bitmap as a fill, or you can convert a bitmap to a vector by tracing it or breaking it apart.

Once you import a bitmap, it becomes a graphic object in the library. To edit the

graphic from the Library panel, double-click the object to open the Bitmap Properties dialog box. Using the dialog box, you can compress the graphic and allow for smoothing (anti-aliasing) on the graphic.

When an instance of a bitmap symbol is on the Stage, you can use the Properties panel to:

- numerically change the dimensions of the graphic
- swap the bitmap for another bitmap within the Library (this is useful if you want to quickly view how another graphic will look in the same location in your movie)
- edit the bitmap in another application (for example, Photoshop if that program is available)

NEW Copyrights

Copyright laws apply to digital images, including those obtained from companies that provide stock photographic images and clipart. These laws are intended to protect the intellectual property rights of the creator of the work, as well as to ensure compensation for the creativity and work involved by the artist. Some works, such as those created by government agencies, *may* be in the public domain; while others, such as those used for education, *may* fall under fair use and not be subject to copyright restrictions. However, unless you produce the graphics yourself, you should assume that any other graphics you want to use in your Flash movies are protected under copyright laws. Be sure to read the terms of use associated with any graphic you obtain for use in your movies and to follow the stated permissions requirements regarding that graphic.

Figure 3 *Import dialog box for Photoshop "background.psd" file*

background.psd consists of two layers: Sun and Background

Sun layer is selected; it is converted to a movie clip so its features will be editable

Once imported, each layer in background.psd will exist on its own layer in Flash

Import a layered Fireworks PNG file as a movie clip symbol

1. Start Flash, create a new **Flash (ActionScript 2.0) document**, save it as **gsamples.fla**, then verify the Stage size is 550 × 400 pixels.

2. Display the Library panel.

3. Click **File** on the menu bar, point to **Import**, click **Import to Stage**, then navigate to the drive and folder where your Data Files are stored.

4. Click the **list arrow** for the file types, click **PNG File (*.png)**, click **dragonfly.png**, then click **Open**.

TIP If you have difficulty finding the file types list arrow, refer to Figure 1.

5. In the Import dialog box, verify the Import as a single flattened bitmap check box is not checked and the Into: option is set to Current frame as movie clip.

6. Click the **Keep all paths editable option button** in the Objects area to select it, then click **OK**.

7. Set the view to **Fit in Window**, then click the **Pasteboard**.

8. Click the **expand icon** ▶ next to the Fireworks Objects folder in the Library panel, then continue to expand folders until there are no more to expand, as shown in Figure 4.

9. Click the **collapse icon** ▼ next to the Fireworks Objects folder in the Library panel.

10. Name Layer 1 **dragonfly**.

You imported a Fireworks PNG file as a movie clip to the Stage, which automatically generated a folder containing the movie clip and supporting files in the Library panel.

Figure 4 *Imported Fireworks PNG graphic file*

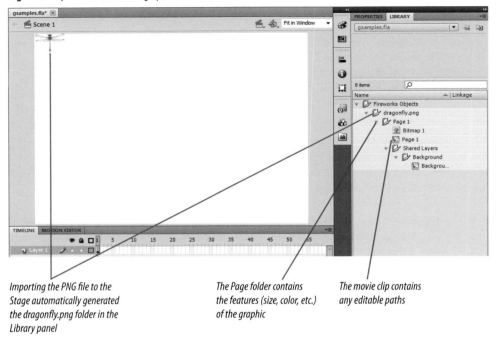

Importing the PNG file to the Stage automatically generated the dragonfly.png folder in the Library panel

The Page folder contains the features (size, color, etc.) of the graphic

The movie clip contains any editable paths

Figure 5 *Tree on the Stage after importing*

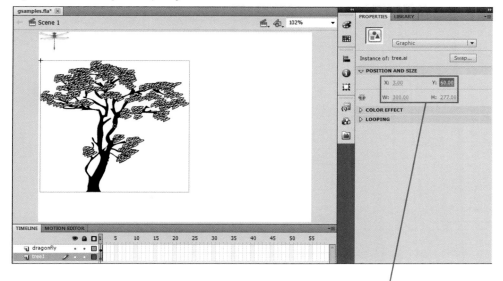

Position coordinates
and size

1. Click **File** on the menu bar, point to **Import**, then click **Import to Library**.

2. Click the **list arrow** for the file types, click **Adobe Illustrator (*.ai)**, click **tree.ai**, then click **Open**.

   The Import to Library dialog box for an Illustrator file appears. A check mark next to a layer means that layer will be imported.

3. Verify the Convert layers to option is set to Flash Layers, then verify both Import unused symbols and Import as a single bitmap image check boxes do not have check marks.

4. Click **OK**.

   A new graphic symbol, tree.ai, appears in the Library panel.

5. Insert a **new layer**, name it **tree1**, then drag the **tree1 layer** beneath the dragonfly layer.

6. Verify that frame 1 of the tree1 layer is selected, then drag the **tree.ai graphic symbol** from the Library panel to the left side of the Stage beneath the dragonfly.

7. Display the Properties panel, click the tree on the Stage, then verify the Lock width and height values together symbol ⊕ is broken.

8. Change the width to **300** and the height to **277**.

9. Set the X: coordinate to **3.0** and the Y: coordinate to **60.0**.

10. Compare your screen to Figure 5.

You imported an Illustrator file to the library, dragged the graphic symbol to the Stage, and then resized and repositioned it.

Import an Adobe Photoshop PSD file

1. Click **File** on the menu bar, point to **Import**, then click **Import to Stage**.

2. Click the **list arrow** for the file types, click **Photoshop (*.psd)**, click **background.psd**, then click **Open**.

   The Import to Stage dialog box for a Photoshop file opens. A check mark next to a layer means the layer will be imported.

3. Click the **Background layer** (not its check box), then verify the Flattened bitmap image option button is selected.

4. Click the **Sun layer** (not its check box), then click the **Editable paths and layer styles option button**.

5. Verify the Convert layers to option is set to Flash Layers, then verify the Set stage size to . . . option does not have a check mark, as shown in Figure 6.

6. Click **OK**, notice the two layers that are added to the Timeline, then press **[Esc]** to deselect the newly inserted graphics.

7. Click the **Sun layer**, then click the **Delete icon** 🗑.

8. Drag the **Background layer** below the tree1 layer.

9. Click the **background graphic** to select it, then use the Properties panel to change the width to **550** and the height to **400**.

10. Verify the X: coordinate is set to 0.00 and the Y: coordinate is set to 0.00.

    Your screen should resemble Figure 7.

11. Lock the Background layer.

You imported a PSD file to the library, resized it, set its position on the Stage, and then locked its layer.

Figure 6 *Completed Import dialog box for Photoshop "background.psd" file*

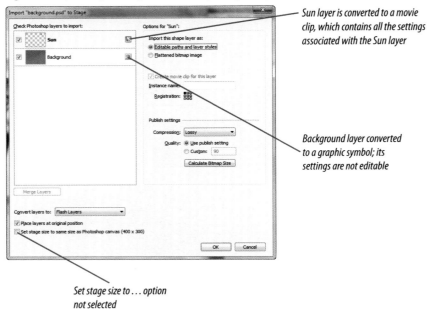

Sun layer is converted to a movie clip, which contains all the settings associated with the Sun layer

Background layer converted to a graphic symbol; its settings are not editable

Set stage size to . . . option not selected

Figure 7 *The imported graphics placed on the Stage*

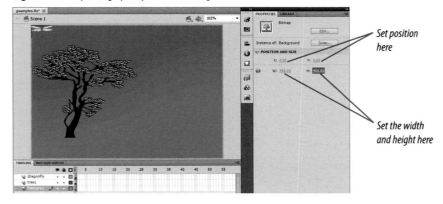

Set position here

Set the width and height here

Figure 8 *Bitmap Properties dialog box*

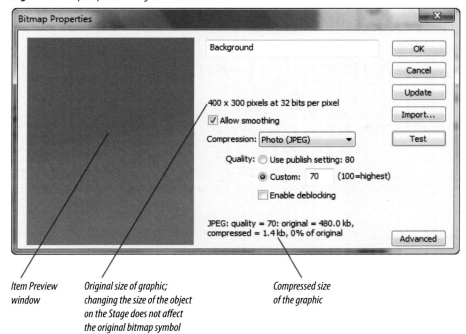

Item Preview window

Original size of graphic; changing the size of the object on the Stage does not affect the original bitmap symbol

Compressed size of the graphic

Change the compression settings of a bitmap

1. Display the Library panel, then double-click the **background.psd Assets** folder to display the Assets folder and the symbols for the two objects: the Background bitmap symbol and the Sun movie clip symbol.

   Note: When you specified in the Import dialog box that the Sun layer would be imported as "Editable paths and layer styles", the movie clip that contains the graphic information was created.

2. Right-click (Win) or [control]-click (Mac) the **Background bitmap symbol** in the Library panel, then click **Properties** to open the Bitmap Properties dialog box.

3. Click the **Allow smoothing check box** to select it.

4. Verify that Photo (JPEG) is selected for Compression, then click the **Custom option button** in the Quality area.

5. Type **100** in the Custom text box, then click **Test**.

   Study the quality of the graphic in the Preview window and notice the compressed size of the graphic is approximately 25 kb.

6. Change the Custom setting to **20**, then click **Test**.

   Notice the quality of the graphic has diminished as the compressed size has dropped.

7. Change the Custom setting to **70**, then click **Test**.

   Your screen should resemble Figure 8. The compressed size of the graphic has been reduced to less than 2 kb, with no significant reduction in the appearance of the image.

8. Click **OK**.

9. Save your work.

You compared the file sizes of different compressions and then compressed a bitmap file.

Break Apart Bitmaps
AND USE BITMAP FILLS

What You'll Do

In this lesson, you will break apart bitmap graphics and manipulate bitmap fill graphics to create new effects.

Breaking Apart Bitmaps

Bitmap graphics, unlike vector graphics, are made up of groups of pixels. You can break apart a bitmap graphic and edit individual pixels. Breaking apart a bitmap graphic allows increased flexibility in how you can use it within a movie. If you do break apart a bitmap graphic, you can select different areas of the graphic (with the Selection tool and the Lasso and Magic Wand tools) to manipulate them separately from the graphic as a whole, including deleting an area or changing its color. In addition, you can use the Eraser tool to delete parts of a bitmap graphic that has been broken apart.

> **QUICK TIP**
>
> There is no need to break apart a bitmap graphic that you do not plan to manipulate.

Using the Lasso Tool and the Magic Wand Tool

The Lasso tool lets you select an irregularly shaped part of a graphic, which you can then move, scale, rotate, reshape, or delete. You can use the Magic Wand tool, which is available in the Options area of the Tools panel when the Lasso tool is selected, to select areas of similar color in a bitmap graphic you have broken apart. For example, if you have a graphic of a girl with a blue background and you decide to delete the blue background, you can use the magic wand to select the blue background and then delete the selection. If there are other shades of blue adjacent to the background, you can use the magic wand settings to specify a color similarity threshold number between 0 and 200. A higher number means more matching colors will be selected.

> **QUICK TIP**
>
> Introducing bitmaps will always increase the file size of your movie, resulting in increased download times for the users.

Using Bitmap Fills

Until now, you have been applying solid colors and gradient fills to objects. Flash allows you to apply a bitmap fill to any drawn shape or text that has been broken apart. A **bitmap fill** is created by breaking apart a bitmap graphic and using it to fill another graphic.

To do this, you break apart a bitmap graphic, use the Eyedropper tool to select the graphic, and then use the Paint Bucket tool to apply the bitmap fill to a different graphic.

Figure 9 shows different bitmap fill effects. You can apply a bitmap fill to any drawn shape. If necessary, Flash will tile (repeat) the bitmap to fill the shape. You can use the Gradient Transform tool to change the size, shape, rotation, and skew of your fill, which allows you to position the original graphic exactly as you want it in the new shape.

In addition to filling shapes with a bitmap, you can also apply your bitmaps as a fill by using the Brush tool. This process involves breaking apart the bitmap graphic, selecting it with the Eyedropper tool, and then choosing a Brush tool and brush size. When you begin painting, you will see your bitmap graphic as a fill.

Selecting a Bitmap Fill Using the Color Panel

If the bitmap graphic you want to use for a fill is not on the Stage, you can use the Color panel to select it. The process is to open the Color panel, choose Bitmap as the Type of fill, and then select the bitmap of your choice from the library area. If you select bitmap fill using the Color panel and there are no bitmaps available in the library area, a dialog box opens so you can navigate to the file you want to use as the bitmap fill. In this situation, you do not have to break apart the bitmap. Figure 10 shows the Color panel with a bitmap fill selected.

Figure 9 *Different bitmap fill effects*

Bitmap fill applied with the Brush tool

Bitmap fill in a circle applied with the Paint Bucket tool

Bitmap fill in text applied with the Paint Bucket tool

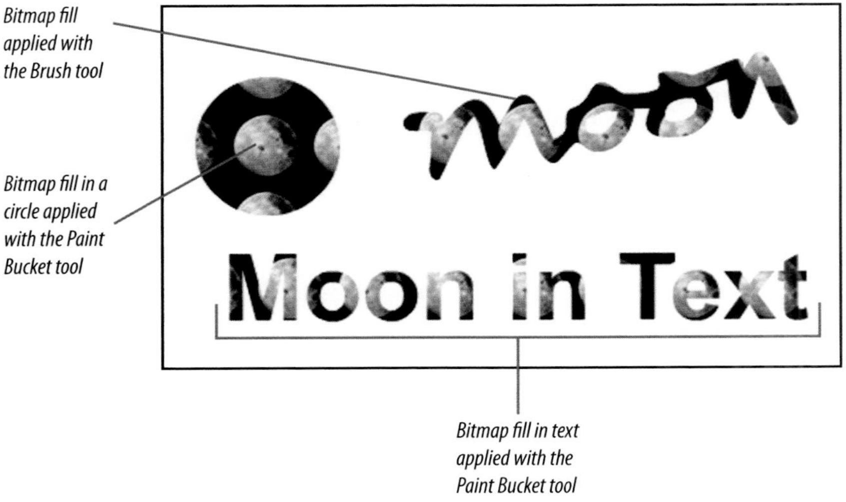

Figure 10 *Bitmap fill selected in Color panel*

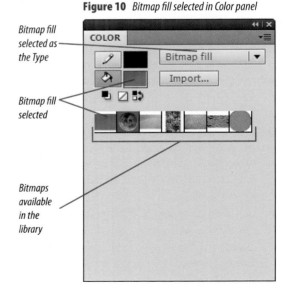

Bitmap fill selected as the Type

Bitmap fill selected

Bitmaps available in the library

Break apart a bitmap

1. Verify the gsamples.fla document is open, click **File** on the menu bar, point to **Import**, then click **Import to Library**.

2. Click the **list arrow** for the file types, click **JPEG Image (*.jpg)**, click **moon.jpg**, then click **Open**.

3. Insert a **new layer**, move it to just above the background layer, then name it **moon**.

4. Click **frame 1** on the moon layer, then drag the **moon graphic symbol** to the Stage, as shown in Figure 11.

5. Verify the moon is selected, click **Modify** on the menu bar, then click **Break Apart**.

6. Click the **Selection tool** , then click the **Pasteboard** to deselect the moon graphic.

7. Click the **Lasso tool** on the Tools panel, then click the **Magic Wand Settings tool** in the Options area of the Tools panel.

8. Click the **Smoothing list arrow** in the Magic Wand Settings dialog box, click **Pixels**, set the Threshold to **20**, then click **OK**.

9. Click the **Magic Wand tool** in the Options area of the Tools panel, point to the **blue background** of the moon graphic as shown in Figure 12, then click to select the blue background.

10. Click **Edit** on the menu bar, then click **Cut**.

11. Click the **Selection tool** , drag the **moon graphic** to the upper-right corner of the Stage, click the **Pasteboard**, then compare your Stage to Figure 13.

You broke apart and edited a bitmap graphic.

Figure 11 *Moon on Stage after importing*

Figure 12 *Using the Magic Wand to select the background color*

Figure 13 *Positioning the moon image*

Figure 14 *Selecting a bitmap fill*

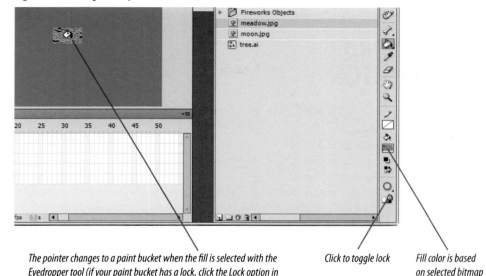

The pointer changes to a paint bucket when the fill is selected with the Eyedropper tool (if your paint bucket has a lock, click the Lock option in the Options area of the Tools panel to turn off the Lock)

Click to toggle lock

Fill color is based on selected bitmap

Figure 15 *Filling a shape with a bitmap*

Meadow bitmap tiles to fill the rectangle

1. Click **File** on the menu bar, point to **Import**, click **Import to Library**, then open **meadow.jpg**.

2. Insert a **new layer**, move it to just below the tree1 layer on the Timeline, then name it **meadow**.

3. Click **frame 1** of the meadow layer, then drag the **meadow graphic symbol** from the Library panel to an empty area of the Stage.

4. Click **Modify** on the menu bar, then click **Break Apart**.

5. Click the **Eyedropper tool** 🖊 on the Tools panel, click the **meadow graphic** on the Stage, then compare your screen to Figure 14.

   The Eyedropper tool lets you select a fill from an existing object so you can apply it to another object. Notice the color swatch for the Fill color tool in the Tools panel displays the meadow pattern and the pointer changes to a paint bucket.

6. Click the **Selection tool** ▶ on the Tools panel, then verify the meadow graphic on the Stage is selected.

7. Click **Edit** on the menu bar, then click **Cut** to remove the graphic from the Stage.

8. Select the **Rectangle tool** ☐ on the Tools panel, then set the Stroke color to **No color** ☑.

9. Using Figure 15 as a guide, draw a **rectangle** covering a small part of the tree trunk across the bottom of the Stage.

   The rectangle fills with a tiling bitmap of the meadow.

10. Save your work.

You used the Eyedropper tool to select a fill from an object, then applied the fill to another object.

Trace Bitmap
GRAPHICS

What You'll Do

In this lesson, you will trace a bitmap graphic to create vectors and special effects.

Understanding Tracing

Tracing is an outstanding feature if you are illustration-challenged or if you need to convert a bitmap graphic into a vector graphic for animation purposes. When you apply the trace function, you change a bitmap graphic into vector paths and fills with varying degrees of detail. If you keep all the detail in a graphic, you end up with very detailed, intricate vector paths, which tend to increase file size. If you remove some of the detail, you can turn a photograph into a more abstract-looking drawing, which usually requires less file size.

Once traced, you can remove the original graphic from the library and work with only the traced paths and shapes, thereby reducing the movie's file size. The traced shapes act just like shapes you have drawn, with fills, lines, and strokes that you can manipulate and change. Tracing allows a graphic to act as a graphic drawn directly in Flash, which is why you are able to select vector fills based on color and change the color. You can also select vector paths (lines) and manipulate the paths to alter the shape of a graphic.

QUICK **TIP**

Tracing bitmaps can often take a long time, especially if it is a detailed trace or a large graphic.

Figure 16 shows the before and after effects of tracing a graphic. In this example, you can see how tracing makes the original photograph appear more abstract.

Using the Trace Settings

It is possible to trace a graphic using very detailed or less detailed settings. Your traced graphic will look more like the original graphic if you retain more detail. If you want the traced graphic to look more abstract, use less detail. Remember, the greater the detail, the greater the file size. In Figure 17, three different trace effects are created by adjusting the trace values.

There are four options that affect how detailed the trace will appear: Color threshold, Minimum area, Corner threshold, and Curve fit. Color threshold compares two side-by-side pixels; if the difference is less than the color threshold, the two are considered the same color. Color threshold options include integers between 1 and 500. Minimum area sets the number of surrounding pixels to consider, with options between 1 and 1000. Corner threshold works with sharp edges to retain them or smooth them out. Curve fit determines how smoothly outlines are drawn. Figure 18 shows the Trace Bitmap dialog box. You can use the Preview button to display how various settings will affect the graphic.

One of the challenges with using the trace feature comes when you try to animate a traced graphic. Tracing creates paths and shapes, but every piece of the original graphic remains on one layer. To animate or tween between pieces of the shape, you often have to isolate parts of the object onto their own layers. Figure 19 shows the sections of the moon that have been isolated. The sections are selected by color according to

the settings in the Trace Bitmap dialog box. The Selection tool is used to click a color and drag the color section. Once isolated, a selection can be converted to a graphic symbol and animated.

QUICK TIP

You can no longer trace a bitmap graphic once you break it apart. The magic wand tool does not work on traced bitmaps.

Figure 16 *Before and after tracing a bitmap*

Figure 17 *Three different effects with different trace settings*

Figure 18 *Trace Bitmap dialog box*

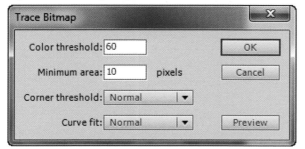

Figure 19 *Dividing a traced graphic by color*

Sections of the moon selected by color and moved

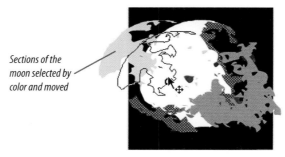

Trace a bitmap graphic

1. Click the **Selection tool** on the Tools panel, click the **moon graphic** on the Stage to select it, then press **[Delete]**.

2. Click **frame 1** on the moon layer to select the frame, then drag the **moon.jpg graphic** from the Library panel to the upper-right corner of the Stage.

3. Verify the moon is selected, click **Modify** on the menu bar, point to **Bitmap**, then click **Trace Bitmap**.

4. Type **60** in the Color threshold text box.

5. Double-click the **value** in the Minimum area text box, then type **10**.

6. Click the **Corner threshold list arrow** to view the options, then click **Normal**.

7. Click the **Curve fit list arrow** to view the options, then click **Normal**,

8. Click **OK**, click the **Pasteboard** to deselect the moon, then compare your graphic to Figure 20.

9. Click the **Zoom tool** on the Tools panel, then click the **moon** to enlarge it, as shown in Figure 21.

You traced a bitmap graphic and zoomed in on it.

Figure 20 *The traced bitmap image*

Bitmap graphic traced

Figure 21 *Zooming in on the moon*

Importing and Modifying Graphics

Figure 22 *Specifying a fill color*

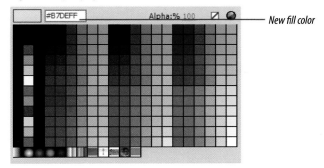

New fill color

Figure 23 *Changing the fill color*

Figure 24 *The completed screen*

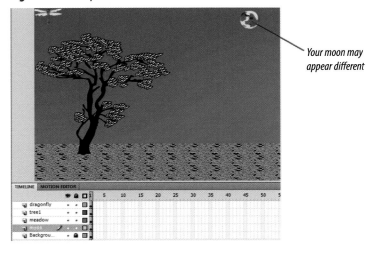

Your moon may appear different

Edit a traced bitmap graphic

1. Click the **Selection tool** ▶ on the Tools panel.
2. Click the **Paint Bucket tool** 🪣 on the Tools panel, then verify the Lock Fill option 🔒 option in the Options area of the Tools panel is not selected.
3. Set the Fill color to **#B7DEFF**, as shown in Figure 22, then press **[Enter]**.
4. Click various parts of the moon graphic with the Paint Bucket tool 🪣 to change the color to resemble Figure 23.

   Note: Click Edit on the menu bar, then click Undo to use the undo command, as needed.
5. Click the **Selection tool** ▶ on the Tools panel.
6. Set the view to **Fit in Window**.

   Your screen should resemble Figure 24.
7. Save your work, then close the document.

You edited a traced bitmap graphic by changing the color of parts of the bitmap.

Import graphics.

1. Create a new Flash document with a size of **550 × 400** pixels and a white background color, the view set to Fit in Window, and the frame rate to **9** fps, then save it as **skillsDemo7.fla**.
2. Click the Library tab to display the Library panel.
3. Import the logo.png file from the drive and folder where your Data Files are stored to the library with the following settings:
   Import: Page 1
   Into: Current frame as movie clip
   Objects: Keep all paths editable
   Text: Keep all text editable
4. Import fullMoon.jpg to the library.
5. Import mountain.jpg to the library.
6. Import nightsky.jpg to the library.
   (*Note*: You can import more than one graphic at a time by selecting multiple graphics. Click a graphic, then press and hold [Ctrl] (Win) or [command] (Mac) and click another graphic.)
7. Save your work.

Break apart bitmaps and use bitmap fills.

1. Rename Layer 1 **nightsky**.
2. Click frame 1 on the nightsky layer, then drag the nightsky graphic to the Stage and break it apart.
3. Click the nightsky graphic with the Eyedropper tool, then delete the nightsky graphic from the Stage.
4. Use the Rectangle tool to create a rectangle (with nightsky for the fill and no stroke color) that spans the width of the Stage and covers the top half of the Stage.
5. Insert a new layer, name it **logo**, click frame 1 on the logo layer, and drag the logo graphic symbol to the upper-left corner of the Stage.
6. Create a new layer named **mountain**, click frame 1 on the mountain layer, and drag the mountain symbol to the bottom-center of the Stage.
7. Use the Properties panel to change the width of the mountain so that it is as wide as the Stage, 550 pixels, then move the mountain graphic so it is flush with the bottom and sides of the Stage.
8. Lock the nightsky and logo layers.
9. Save your work.

Trace bitmap graphics.

1. Trace the mountain graphic, using settings of **100** for Color threshold, **10** for Minimum area, and Normal for Corner threshold and Curve fit.
2. Deselect the graphic.
3. Verify the Fill color on the Tools panel displays the nightsky and the Stroke color is set to none.
4. Use the Paint Bucket tool to change the blue sky, in the background of the mountain, to stars.
5. Lock the mountain layer.
6. Save your work.

Create an animation.

1. Add a keyframe to frame 30 of each layer.
2. Insert a new layer at the top of the Timeline and name it **moon**. Do not add a keyframe to frame 30 on this layer.
3. Click frame 1 of the moon layer.
4. Drag the fullMoon graphic to the Stage and break it apart.
5. Click a bank area of the Pasteboard to deselect the graphic.

6. Click the Lasso tool on the Tools panel, click the Magic Wand Settings button in the Options area of the Tools panel, then set the Threshold to **10** and the Smoothing to Pixels.

7. Use the Magic Wand to select the blue background, then delete the background.

8. Use the Selection tool to select the moon and convert it to a graphic symbol with the name g_Moon.

9. Change the view to 50%.

10. Move the moon off the left side of the Stage and above the mountains.

11. Insert a motion tween that moves the moon across the Stage and off the right side of the Stage.

12. Verify the motion span on the Timeline extends to frame 30.

13. Using the Selection tool, point to just below the motion path on the Stage, then click and drag the path to create an arc shaped path.

14. Click frame 1 on the moon layer, then use the Properties panel to set the rotation to **2** times.

15. Test the movie, then close the Flash Player window.

16. Click frame 23 on the moon layer, then compare your movie to Figure 25.

17. Save your work, then exit Flash.

Figure 25 *Completed Skills Review*

Ultimate Tours is rolling out a new "summer in December" promotion in the coming months and wants a Flash website to showcase a series of tours to Florida, Bermuda, and the Caribbean. The website should use bright, "tropical" colors and have a family appeal. Though you will eventually animate this site, Ultimate Tours would first like to see still pictures of what you are planning to do.

1. Open a new Flash document, then save it as **ultimateTours7.fla**.
2. Set the movie properties, including the size and background color as desired.
3. Create the following text objects using Classic Text on separate layers, then lock the layers:
   - A primary headline **Ultimate Tours Presents...** with an appropriate font and color.
   - A subheading **Our new "Summer in December" Tour Packages!** in a smaller font size.
4. Import the following JPG files from the drive and folder where your Data Files are stored to the Library panel (alternately, you can create your own graphics, obtain graphics from your computer or the Internet, or create graphics from scanned media):
   gtravel1.jpg   gtravel4.jpg
   gtravel2.jpg   gtravel5.jpg
   gtravel3.jpg   gtravel6.jpg
5. Using the Library panel, rename the graphics **sand**, **umbrella**, **boat**, **castle**, **starfish**, and **boy**.
6. Drag the sand graphic to the Stage, break it apart, create a bitmap fill, then delete the sand graphic from the Stage.

7. Add a layer and create a rectangle using the sand bitmap fill that appears as a background for the other graphics.
8. Add the castle, boat, boy, and starfish to the Stage to create an appealing vacation collage, as follows:
   - Use separate layers.
   - Trace each graphic to give it an artistic look. (*Hint*: Some of the sample files have a white background. To delete the background or any part of the graphic after tracing the graphic, use the Selection tool to select the desired part(s) and delete them or use the Eraser tool. *Note*: The magic wand will only work on bitmap graphics that have been broken apart. It will not work on traced bitmaps.)
   - Resize and arrange the graphics as desired.
   - Lock each layer when not in use.
9. Add a layer and create the two buttons, Home and Buy Now. Use the Paint Brush tool with the sand bitmap fill.
10. Add the umbrella to a new layer, then lock all the layers.
11. Save your work, then compare your image to the example shown in Figure 26.

Figure 26 *Sample completed Project Builder 1*

You have been asked to create several sample designs for the home page of a new student art, poetry, and fiction anthology website called AnthoArt. This website will showcase artwork that includes painting, woodcuts, and photography, as well as writing (including poetry and fiction).

1. Open a new Flash document and save it as **anthoArt7.fla**.
2. Set the movie properties, including the size and background color, as desired.
3. Import the following JPG files from the drive and folder where your Data Files are stored to the Library panel (alternately, you can create your own graphics, obtain graphics from your computer or the Internet, or create graphics from scanned media):
   gantho1.jpg
   gantho2.jpg
   gantho3.jpg
   gantho4.jpg
4. Using the Library panel, rename the graphics as **shells**, **rainbow**, **leaves**, and **squash**.

5. Create a collage on the Stage from the four graphics. Be sure to break apart some graphics and use the Trace Bitmap feature for some of the graphics. (*Note*: You do not need to use all four graphics in your collage.)
6. Create the title **AnthoArt**, using a bitmap fill for some or all of the letters. (*Hint*: Break apart the text until the text has a dot pattern.)

7. Create an Enter button, using one of the graphics as a bitmap fill.
8. Lock all the layers.
9. Save your work, then compare your movie image to the example shown in Figure 27.

Figure 27 *Sample completed Project Builder 2*

DESIGN PROJECT

Figure 28 shows the home page of the NASA website. Study the figure and complete the following. For each question, indicate how you determined your answer.

1. Connect to the Internet, type the URL *www.nasa.gov/missions/highlights/index.html*, then click Current Missions in the left navigation pane.

2. Open a document in a word processor or open a new Flash document, save the file as **dpc7**, then answer the following questions. (*Hint*: Use the Text tool in Flash.)

   ■ Are photographs used well in this website? Why or why not?
   ■ Could the goals and intent of the website be accomplished without the use of photographs?
   ■ Do the graphics contribute to the design of the site? If so, how?
   ■ Which file format do you think was used for the images?
   ■ Can you guess what file format the logo was before it was brought into Flash? Or, do you think it was recreated in the application?
   ■ Do you think the graphics in this site should be changed in any way? How?
   ■ Who do you think is the target audience for this website?

Figure 28 *Design Project*

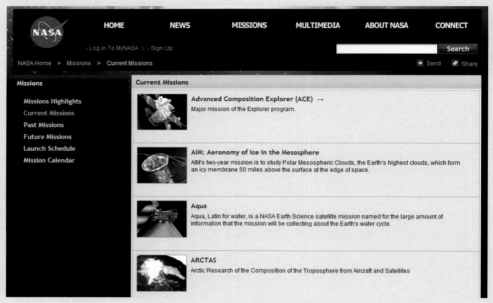

Importing and Modifying Graphics

To showcase your broad range of skills, you want to add some web-related work to your portfolio. This will allow you to improve upon and continue to use websites and artwork you created previously. Try to create at least four samples of your work.

1. Open portfolio6.fla (the project you created in Portfolio Project, Chapter 6), then save it as **portfolio7.fla**.
2. Change the Education button label to **Web Sites**. (The education information will eventually be created as part of the Resume page.)
3. Lock all layers, then add a new layer and name it **webSites**.
4. Insert a keyframe on the websites layer one frame past the last frame in the movie.
5. Create a heading with the text **Sample Web Sites**.
6. Import the graphics that will be used on this page to the Library panel.
   (*Note*: You can use the Publish Settings option in Flash to create PNG and JPG images of the websites you have created for this course. Alternately, you can use other images for the graphics that you place on this page.)
7. Place the graphics on the Stage so that their placement is visually pleasing.
8. Copy the Home button from another part of the movie to this frame.
9. Lock the webSites layer.
10. Insert a new layer and name it **portfolioCase**.
11. Import the portfolioCase.jpg file to the Library panel.

(*Note*: You can use another image, such as a photo of yourself, for the graphic that appears in the center of the home page.)

12. Place the graphic on the Stage, break it apart, and delete the blue background.
13. Import the ganthro2.jpg file to the Library panel, then rename it **rainbow**.
14. Use the rainbow graphic to create a bitmap fill, and apply the fill to the portfolio case. (*Hints*: Turn off the Lock option for the Paint Bucket tool in the Options area of the Tools panel. Click in the middle of the rainbow graphic with the Eyedropper tool and click in the middle of the portfolio case.)
15. Create a text block that uses the settings of your choice to place your name on the portfolio case.
16. Insert a blank keyframe in frame 2 on the portfolioCase layer, then lock all layers.
17. Add ActionScript code to the Web Sites button on the home page that jumps the playhead to the frame that displays the website graphics.
18. Save your work, then compare your movie to the example shown in Figure 29.

Figure 29 *Sample completed Portfolio Project*

8 BUILDING COMPLEX ANIMATIONS

CHAPTER

1. Plan for complex movies and animations

2. Create an animated graphic symbol

3. Create a movie clip symbol

4. Animate buttons using movie clip symbols

5. Edit an animation using the Motion Editor

CHAPTER **8** BUILDING COMPLEX
ANIMATIONS

Introduction

As your movies become more complex and you begin utilizing more advanced features of Flash, planning your work is critical. Part of the planning process is determining how to develop a clean Timeline, that is, with objects that are easy to recognize and manipulate, and how to optimize file size by reusing symbols as much as possible.

Creating animated graphic symbols and movie clip symbols can help meet both goals. A well-built movie consists of many small pieces of animation put together and often, of movies nested within movies. For example, in an earlier chapter, you used movie clip symbols of rotating wheels on a moving car. While the concept of movies within movies might sound confusing, it is actually very logical from a file management, media management, and animation perspective. Building movies with 40 layers and lengthy tween spans can be unwieldy. The alternative is to split the many animations on the Stage into smaller, reusable pieces, and then insert these smaller pieces as needed. Creating Flash movies using reusable pieces such as movie clip symbols allows you to have fewer motion tweens and layers in the movie. Creating animated graphic symbols and movie clip symbols also allows you greater flexibility in adding ActionScript to elements, as well as in placing elements on and off the Stage.

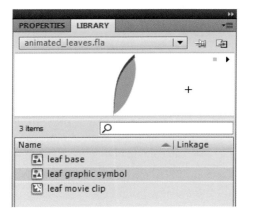

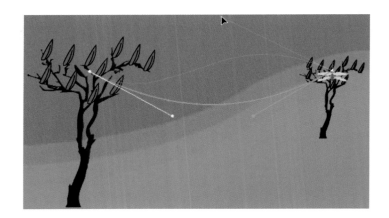

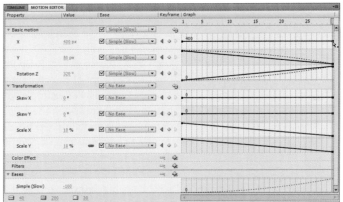

Plan for Complex Movies
AND ANIMATIONS

What You'll Do

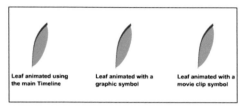

Leaf animated using the main Timeline

Leaf animated with a graphic symbol

Leaf animated with a movie clip symbol

In this lesson, you will work with and compare animated graphic and movie clip symbols.

Making Effective Use of Symbols and the Library Panel

It is important to plan out in advance what you are trying to accomplish in a movie. In addition to making development work easier, planning ahead also allows you to organize your Library panel with more accuracy. Consider the following questions as you plan your project:

- Are there any repeated elements on the Stage? If yes, you should make them into graphic symbols. Graphic symbols should include any still element that is used on the Stage more than once. Graphic symbols might also be elements that you want to be able to tween. Keep in mind one graphic symbol can contain other graphic symbols. For example, you could have a sailboat in which the sails are graphic symbols within the boat symbol.
- Are there any repeating or complex animations, or elements on the Stage that animate while the rest of the movie is still? If so, make these animated graphic symbols or movie clip symbols.
- What kind of interactivity will your Flash movie have? You can assign ActionScript

to button symbols and to movie clip symbols, but not to graphic symbols. You should use button symbols for elements used for navigation or elements that you want to be clickable. Button symbols can contain both graphic and movie clip symbols inside them.

Remember, your Library panel should house all of the building blocks for your movies. To build a logical Library panel, you should have a solid plan in place for the different elements you expect to use.

Understanding Animated Graphic Symbols

Just as you can create a graphic symbol from multiple objects on the Stage, you can convert an entire multiple-frame, multiple-layer animation into a single **animated graphic symbol** that you can store in the Library panel. Creating a single animated graphic symbol removes all of the associated keyframes, layers, and tweening of the animation from your Timeline, which results in a much cleaner Timeline. Animated graphic symbols can also reduce file size if you expect to use the animation in more than one place in a movie.

Compare the two Timelines in Figure 1. On the left is a tree animated through the main Timeline; each individual leaf on the tree has its own layer. On the right is a Timeline for a movie with the same animation but with the leaves grouped into an animated graphic symbol and appearing on a single layer.

An animated graphic symbol is tied to the Timeline of the movie in which you place the symbol. This means that there must be enough frames on the Timeline for the animation to run, and that if the movie stops, the animation stops too.

Understanding Movie Clip Symbols

A **movie clip symbol**, which is essentially a movie within a movie, is a more robust way to store complex animations in the Library panel. The biggest difference between a movie clip symbol and an animated graphic symbol is that the movie clip symbol retains its own independent Timeline when you insert an instance of the symbol into a movie. This creates a nested effect, which means the movie clip instance Timeline plays within the main Timeline. Because the movie clip instance Timeline is independent of the main Timeline, it will repeat if its Timeline is shorter than the main Timeline. For example, if the main Timeline is 40 frames in length and the movie clip instance's Timeline is 10 frames in length, when the movie clip instance is inserted in frame 1 of the main Timeline it will repeat 4 times. This would be useful if you have an animation, such as a flashing logo, that you want to repeat as the main Timeline is playing. One technique for stopping an animated movie clip is to insert a blank keyframe at the end of the layer on the main Timeline that displays the movie clip.

Figure 1 *Comparing Timelines*

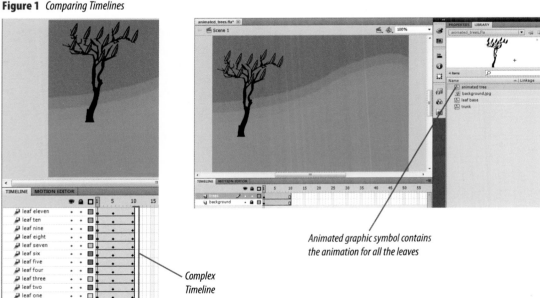

Complex Timeline

Animated graphic symbol contains the animation for all the leaves

In addition, you can use ActionScript to control the playing of a movie clip. For instance, you could have buttons that start and stop a movie clip.

Consider Figure 2, which looks like a drawing of a still living room. However, if it were animated, the fire could be crackling and the candles flickering. To create the animation for these elements (the fire and the candle flame), each one of these animated elements might reside in its own movie clip symbol (one containing the fire animation and a different one containing the candle flame). That way, when placed on the Stage in a movie, each of the movie clip symbols would move according to its own independent Timeline, as well as only taking up one layer and, potentially, only one keyframe on the Timeline. Not only does this help to organize the different pieces of a movie, it also allows you to isolate animated elements and have animations repeat. For example, the animation of the candle flame could be done by using a few frames in which the flame is moved back and forth one time. The animation could be converted to a movie clip with its own Timeline. This allows the movie clip to be repeated (independent of the main Timeline) giving the flame a fluttering effect.

In this lesson, you will view the same animation (animated leaf) created in three different ways: using the main Timeline, a graphic symbol, and a movie clip.

Figure 2 *Using movie clip symbols*

You could create one movie clip symbol of a flickering flame, and use it to animate all three candles

You could create one movie clip symbol of the fire, which would continuously crackle and move as fires do

Figure 3 *Adding an animated graphic symbol to the Stage*

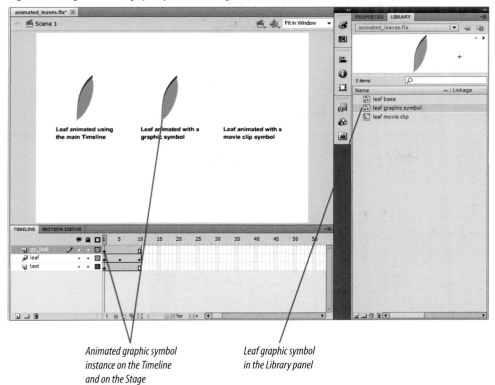

Animated graphic symbol instance on the Timeline and on the Stage

Leaf graphic symbol in the Library panel

Work with an animated graphic symbol

1. Open fl8_1.fla, then save it as **animated_leaves.fla**.
2. Display the Library panel.
3. Press [**Enter**] (Win) or [**return**] (Mac) to play the animation.

   The motion tween in the leaf layer on the Timeline causes the leaf to move.
4. Double-click the **leaf graphic symbol** in the Library panel to display it in the edit window.
5. Press [**Enter**] (Win) or [**return**] (Mac) to play the animation.

   This is the same animation as the one on the main Timeline. It was developed by creating a new graphic symbol (named leaf graphic symbol) of the leaf, copying the motion tween on the main Timeline, and pasting it into the Timeline of this leaf graphic symbol.
6. Click **Scene 1** at the top left of the workspace to return to the main Timeline.
7. Insert a **new layer** above the leaf layer, then name it **gs_leaf**.
8. Click **frame 1** on the gs_leaf layer, then drag the **leaf graphic symbol** from the Library panel to the Stage above the text, as shown in Figure 3.

   The animated graphic symbol version of the leaf still takes up 10 frames on the Timeline, but the symbol's motion tween (blue shading and keyframe on the Timeline) does not display because it is saved as part of the symbol.
9. Press [**Enter**] (Win) or [**return**] (Mac) to view the animations.

You opened a graphic symbol animation in the edit window and you moved an instance of an animated graphic symbol to the Stage.

Work with a movie clip symbol

1. Insert a **new layer** above the gs_leaf layer, then name it **mc_leaf**.
2. Drag the **leaf movie clip symbol** from the Library panel to the Stage above the text, as shown in Figure 4.
3. Click **frame 1** on the mc_leaf layer, then press **[Enter]** (Win) or **[return]** (Mac) to view the animations.

   The movie clip symbol version of the leaf does not move because movie clips on the Stage play only when you export, publish, or test the movie in the Flash Player. Although this movie clip has been provided for you to use in this lesson, you will learn how to create this movie clip symbol in a later lesson.

4. Click **Control** on the menu bar, point to **Test Movie**, then click **in Flash Professional** to test the movie.

   All three leaves animate in place continually.

5. Close the Flash Player window.
6. Save your work.

You placed an instance of a movie clip symbol on the Stage, then tested the movie.

Assign a stop action to the Timeline

1. Insert a **new layer** above the mc_leaf layer, then name it **stopAction**.
2. Insert a **keyframe** in frame 8 of the stopAction layer.
3. Open the Actions panel, then verify the Script Assist button is active.

(continued)

Figure 4 *Adding a movie clip symbol to the Stage*

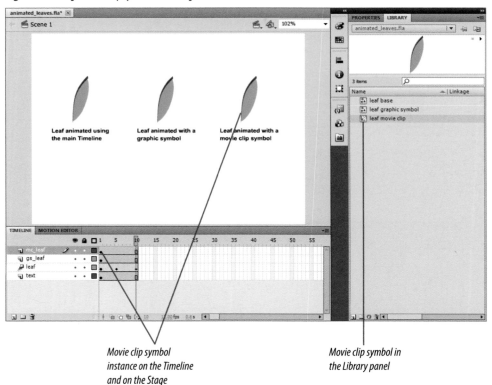

Movie clip symbol instance on the Timeline and on the Stage

Movie clip symbol in the Library panel

Figure 5 *Inserting a* **stop** *action using the Actions panel*

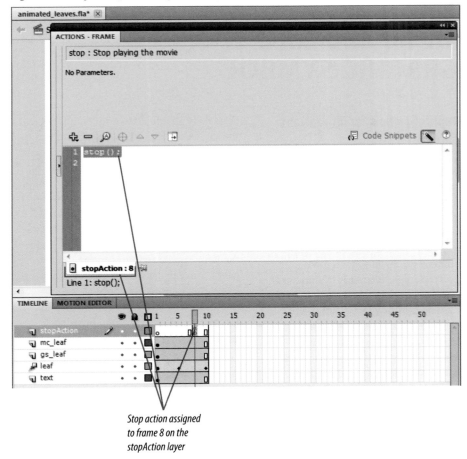

Stop action assigned
to frame 8 on the
stopAction layer

4. Verify that stopAction:8 is displayed in the lower-left corner of the Actions panel Script pane.

   This indicates that the ActionScript code will be assigned to frame 8 on the stopAction layer.

5. Click the **Add a new item to the script button** ⊕ in the Script Assist window, point to **Global Functions**, point to **Timeline Control**, then click **stop**.

   Your screen should resemble Figure 5.

6. Test the movie.

   The first two instances move briefly and then stop because of the stop action in frame 8 on the main Timeline. The movement of the first two instances of the leaf are dependent on the main Timeline. Only the movie clip symbol continues to move because it has an independent Timeline.

7. Close the Flash Player window.

8. Click **frame 8** on the stopAction layer, click **Modify** on the menu bar, point to **Timeline**, then click **Clear Keyframe**.

9. Click **frame 1** on the stopAction layer.

10. Open the Actions panel, verify stopAction:1 is displayed in the lower-left corner of the Script pane, Click the **Add a new item to the script button** ⊕ in the Script Assist window, point to **Global Functions**, point to **Timeline Control**, then click **stop**.

11. Close the Actions panel.

12. Test the movie.

    The first two instances do not move at all because of the stop action in frame 1 on the main Timeline. Only the movie clip symbol moves because it has an independent Timeline.

13. Save your work, then close the movie.

You assigned a stop action to the Timeline and tested the movie.

Create an Animated **GRAPHIC SYMBOL**

What You'll Do

 In this lesson, you will convert an animation on the Timeline into an animated graphic symbol.

Using Graphic Symbols for Animations

Most of the time, you will want to use movie clip symbols instead of animated graphic symbols to store animations. However, there are some situations where creating an animated graphic symbol is useful, such as a sequential animation you want to play only one time, rather than repeat continuously like a movie clip. Or, you might want an animation to synchronize with other elements on the Stage, and because animated graphic symbols use the main Timeline, it can be easier to achieve this effect. Also, you can preview animated graphic symbols you place on the Stage right from the Flash editing environment by dragging the playhead back and forth across the Timeline (also called scrubbing). This makes animated graphic symbols easy to test within a Flash movie.

You create an animated graphic symbol in the same way you create a static graphic symbol, by choosing the Graphic option in the Create New Symbol dialog box. In the Library panel, an animated graphic symbol looks the same as a static graphic symbol. However, when you select the animated graphic symbol or a movie clip symbol, it is displayed with Stop and Play buttons in the Item Preview window in the Library panel. You can click these buttons, shown in Figure 6, for testing purposes.

Copying Motion Tweens, Frames, and Layers from the Timeline

Despite good preliminary planning, you may end up drawing and animating objects in a movie, and decide later that the animation would be better placed inside an animated graphic or movie clip symbol. Fortunately, it is easy to copy motion tweens, frames, and layers from the main Timeline and paste them into a new symbol.

To copy multiple layers and frames from within a movie to a symbol, first select the layers and keyframes that you want to copy. To select multiple frames in one or more layers, click the first frame you want to select, and then drag to the last frame. Also, you can click the first frame, press and hold [Shift], and then click the last frame in order to select those frames and all the frames in between.

To select noncontiguous layers, click the name of the first layer you want to select, press and hold [Ctrl] (Win) or [command] (Mac), and then click each layer name. To select contiguous layers, click the first layer name, press and hold [Shift], and then click the last layer name in order to select those layers and all the layers in between. Figure 7 shows a selection across multiple frames and layers. Once you select the frames, click Edit on the menu bar, point to Timeline, and then click Cut or Copy Frames. Create or open the symbol, place the insertion

point in a keyframe, click Edit on the menu bar, point to Timeline, and then click Paste Frames. Flash pastes each individual layer from the original movie into the Timeline for the symbol, and even maintains the layer names.

Note that you cannot copy sound or interactivity in an animation from the main Timeline to an animated graphic symbol. If you want to include sound or interactivity in an animation, you should create a movie clip symbol instead of a graphic symbol.

Figure 6 *Stop and Play buttons in the Library panel Item Preview window*

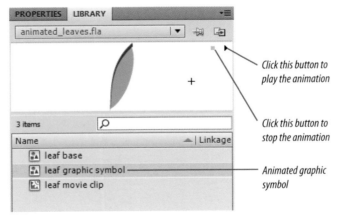

Click this button to play the animation

Click this button to stop the animation

Animated graphic symbol

Figure 7 *Multiple frames and layers selected*

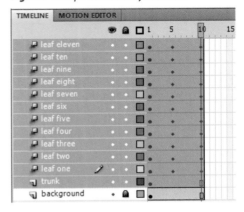

Delete objects from the Timeline

1. Open fl8_2.fla, then save it as **animated_trees.fla**.

2. Verify the Library panel is open, drag the **border** at the top of the Timeline up to display the trunk layer and all 11 leaf layers, then set the view to **Fit in Window**.

3. Play the movie.

   The leaves animate on 11 separate layers.

4. Click the **trunk layer** to select it, press **[Shift]**, click the **leaf eleven layer**, then release **[Shift]**.

   The trunk layer, all numbered leaf layers, and all frames in each layer on the Timeline are selected, as shown in Figure 8.

   TIP You can press and hold [Ctrl] (Win) or [command] (Mac), then click one or more layer names to select all frames in each layer you click.

5. Click **Edit** on the menu bar, point to **Timeline**, then click **Cut Frames**.

   The tree is no longer visible on the Stage. Notice that you cut the frames but not the layers from the main Timeline.

   You selected and then cut the frames on the layers on the Timeline that made up the tree.

Figure 8 *Layers and frames pasted on graphic symbol Timeline*

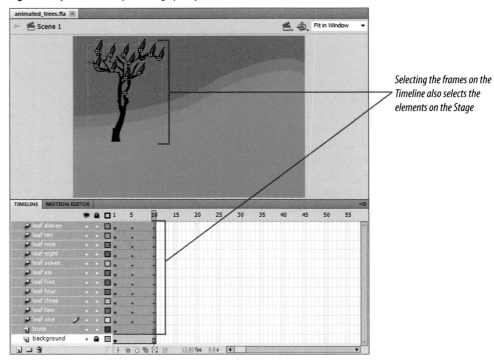

Selecting the frames on the Timeline also selects the elements on the Stage

Figure 9 *Layers and frames pasted on graphic symbol Timeline*

Move frames to create an animated graphic symbol

1. Click **Insert** on the menu bar, then click **New Symbol**.

2. Type **animated tree** in the Name text box, select **Graphic** as the type, then click **OK**.

   You are now in the edit window for the animated tree graphic symbol.

3. Click **frame 1** on Layer 1, click **Edit** on the menu bar, point to **Timeline**, then click **Paste Frames**.

   The tree trunk and leaves appear on the Stage, as shown in Figure 9.

4. Play the movie, then click **Scene 1** at the top left of the workspace to return to the main Timeline.

5. Select all the layers, except the background layer, then click the **Delete icon** 🗑 to delete them.

6. Click **ESSENTIALS** on the title bar, then click **Reset 'Essentials'**.

You pasted frames from the main Timeline into a graphic symbol to create an animated graphic symbol. You then deleted the layers from the main Timeline.

Move an animated graphic symbol to the Stage

1. Insert a **new layer** above the background layer, then name it **trees**.

2. Click **frame 1** on the trees layer, then drag the **animated tree graphic symbol** from the Library panel to the left side of the Stage, as shown in Figure 10.

3. Play the movie.

4. Click **frame 1** on the trees layer, then drag the **animated tree graphic symbol** from the Library panel to the right side of the Stage to create another instance of the tree.

(continued)

Figure 10 *Moving an instance of the tree symbol to the Stage*

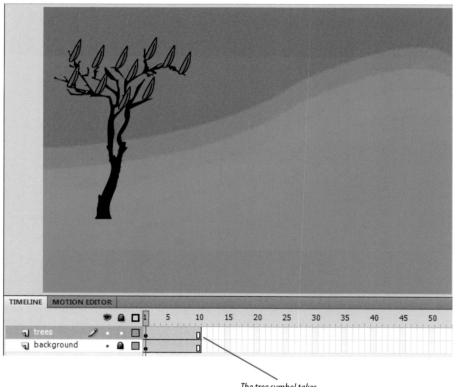

The tree symbol takes up only one layer on the Timeline

Figure 11 *Resizing the second instance of the tree symbol*

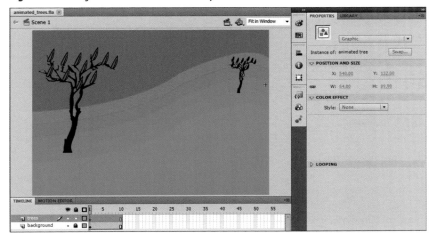

5. Click the **Properties panel**, then in the POSITION AND SIZE area, verify the Lock icon is not broken, and set the width to **64** and the X and Y values to **540** and **132**, respectively.

6. Compare your screen to Figure 11.

7. Play the movie and watch the leaves animate on the Stage.

8. Save your work, then close the movie.

You created two instances of an animated graphic symbol on the Stage.

Create a Movie
CLIP SYMBOL

What You'll Do

 In this lesson, you will create a movie clip symbol and nest movie clip symbols within one another.

Using Movie Clip Symbols for Animations

Movie clip symbols are usually the most efficient choice for creating and storing complex animations. The main advantage of movie clip symbols is that they maintain their own independent Timeline, which is especially useful for animating continuous or looping actions. Movie clip symbols require only one frame in the main movie, regardless of the complexity of the animation, which can make it easier to work with the Timeline.

Movie clip symbols offer many other sophisticated features not available with animated graphic symbols. For instance, you can add sound and associate ActionScript statements to movie clip symbols, or you can create an animation for a movie clip in the main Timeline (such as a motion tween) while another movie clip continues to play its own animation on its independent Timeline. For example, you could have an animation of a plane flying across the screen developed as a motion tween on the main Timeline. At the same time, you could have an animation of a spinning windmill developed as another movie clip that plays continuously. In addition, you can use movie clip symbols to animate a button.

To start building a movie clip symbol, create a new symbol and then choose Movie Clip in the Create New Symbol dialog box. You can create the movie clip animation from scratch, or cut and copy frames and layers from the main Timeline, as you did with the animated graphic symbol in the previous lesson. You can also copy a motion tween from another animated object and paste it to a movie clip symbol.

QUICK TIP

While you're working with the main Timeline, you see only a static image of the first frame of a movie clip symbol on the Stage. To view the full animation, you must export, publish, or test the movie.

Nesting Movie Clips

As you learned in Chapter 4, a movie clip symbol is often made up of many other movie clips, a process called **nesting**. You can nest as many movie clip symbols inside another movie clip as you like. You can also place a

Building Complex Animations

symbol, graphic, or button inside a movie clip symbol. Figure 12 shows a diagram of nesting.

Nesting movie clips creates a **parent-child relationship** that will become increasingly important as you enhance the interactivity of your movies and begin to deploy more sophisticated ActionScript statements. When you insert a movie clip inside another movie clip, the inserted clip is considered the child and the original clip the parent. These relationships are hierarchical, as indicated in Figure 12. Notice that both the movie clips and the graphic symbol are children of the parent clip. Also, keep in mind that if you place an instance of a parent clip into a movie and then change it, you will also affect all its nested child clips. Any time you change the instance of a parent clip, the associated child clips update automatically. For example, if you have a car that is the parent clip and it has wheels that are child clips and you resize the car, the wheels resize proportionally.

Understanding the Movie Explorer Panel

The Movie Explorer panel, shown in Figure 13, allows you to inspect the nesting structure of your entire movie. This is a useful reference to print, so as you work on a movie, you can easily view the movie's structure and see which elements are nested inside each other. You can also apply a filter to view just the elements you want. To access the Movie Explorer, click Window on the menu bar, then click Movie Explorer.

The Panel options button opens the Options menu, which you can use to select a variety of actions to perform on the elements listed in the Movie Explorer. For example, you can go to the element on the Stage and Timeline, find the element in the Library panel, or open all panels relevant to the element so you can edit the object using the panels.

Figure 12 *Diagram of a nested movie clip animation*

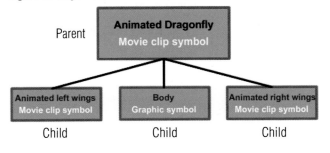

Figure 13 *Movie Explorer panel*

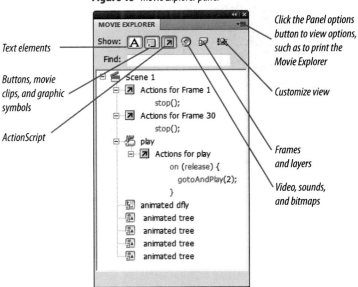

Create a movie clip symbol

1. Open fl8_3.fla, save it as **dragonfly.fla**, then change the frame rate to **10** fps.
2. Display the Library panel, then notice the symbols.

   The Library panel contains the dfly body, left wings, and right wings graphic symbols, as well as the animated left wings movie clip symbol. These symbols will form the basis of your movie clip.
3. Click the **animated left wings movie clip symbol** in the Library panel, then click the **Play button** ▶ in the Item Preview window.

   Note: Be sure you click the movie clip symbol and not the name next to the movie clip symbol.

   The wings appear to flutter. Next, you will create another movie clip symbol to animate a set of right wings for the dragonfly.
4. Click **Insert** on the menu bar, then click **New Symbol**.
5. Type **animated right wings** in the Name text box, select **Movie Clip** for the type, then click **OK** to display the edit window.
6. Click **frame 1** on Layer 1 on the Timeline, then drag the **right wings graphic symbol** from the Library panel to the center of the Stage so that the circle is over the centering cross-hair, as shown in Figure 14.
7. Display the Properties panel, click **frame 1** on the Timeline, then click the **wings**.
8. Change the X and Y coordinates to X: **0**, Y: **0**.

   Setting the coordinates to 0,0 provides an anchor point that will remain the same as you resize the wings, which provides the appearance of fluttering.

   (continued)

Figure 14 *Positioning the wings in the edit window*

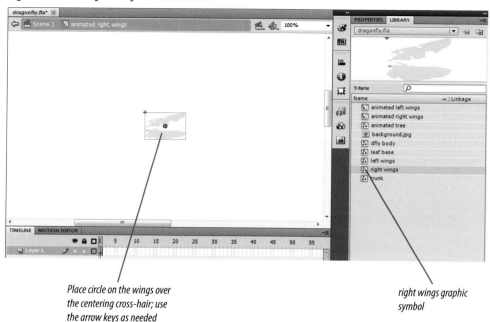

Place circle on the wings over the centering cross-hair; use the arrow keys as needed

right wings graphic symbol

Figure 15 *Setting values for frame 5 of the motion tween*

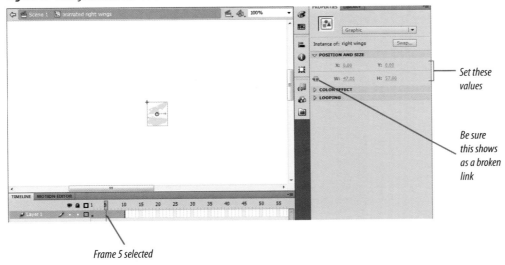

Set these values

Be sure this shows as a broken link

Frame 5 selected

Figure 16 *Assembled animated dragonfly*

Animated left wings movie clip symbol attached here

Animated right wings movie clip symbol attached here

9. Click **Insert** on the menu bar, then click **Motion Tween**.

10. Click **frame 5** on the Timeline, click the **wings**, then use the Properties panel to set the following values: W: **47**, H: **57**, as shown in Figure 15.

    Note: Make sure the Link icon for the width and height is broken.

11. Click **frame 10** on the Timeline, click the **wings**, then use the Properties panel to set the following values: W: **84**, H: **57**.

12. Play the animation.

13. Click **Scene 1** at the top left of the workspace to return to the main Timeline.

You created a movie clip symbol containing a motion tween animation.

Nest movie clip symbols

1. Click **Insert** on the menu bar, then click **New Symbol**.

2. Type **animated dfly** in the Name text box, verify Movie Clip is selected for the type, then click **OK**.

3. Drag the **dfly body graphic symbol** from the Library panel to the center of the Stage.

4. Drag the **animated left wings movie clip symbol** from the Library panel to the Stage, then attach it to the upper-left side of the dragonfly's body.

5. Drag the **animated right wings movie clip symbol** to the upper-right side of the body.

    Compare your image to Figure 16.

6. Click **Scene 1** at the top left of the workspace to return to the main Timeline.

You nested two movie clips inside a new movie clip symbol.

Move the movie clip symbol to the Stage, rotate, and resize it

1. Insert a **new layer** above the trees layer, then name it **dragonfly**.

2. Click **frame 1** on the dragonfly layer, then drag the **animated dfly movie clip symbol** from the Library panel so it is on top of the left tree on the Stage, as shown in Figure 17.

3. Play the movie.

   Because the dragonfly is an animated movie clip, the animation does not play on the Stage.

4. Test the movie to view the animation, then close the Flash Player window.

5. Verify the dragonfly graphic on the Stage is selected.

6. Click **Modify** on the menu bar, point to **Transform**, then click **Scale and Rotate**.

7. Type **180** for the Rotate value, then click **OK**.

8. Display the Properties panel, click **frame 1** on the dragonfly layer, then click the **dragonfly**.

9. Verify the Lock icon is unbroken, change the width to **49** in the Properties panel, then use the Selection pointer ▸₊ to place the dragonfly so it is centered on the branches.

You added an instance of a movie clip symbol to the Stage, rotated it 180 degrees, and resized it.

Animate an instance of a movie clip and resize an object

1. Click **frame 1** on the dragonfly layer, click **Insert** on the menu bar, then click **Motion Tween**.

(continued)

Figure 17 *Animated dragonfly instance placed on the Stage*

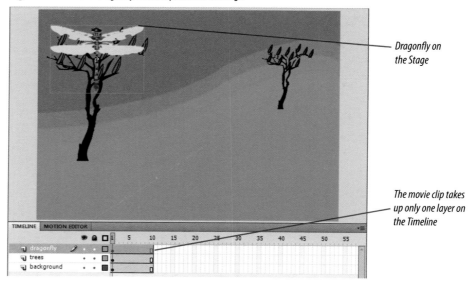

Dragonfly on the Stage

The movie clip takes up only one layer on the Timeline

Figure 18 *Reshaping the path with the Selection tool*

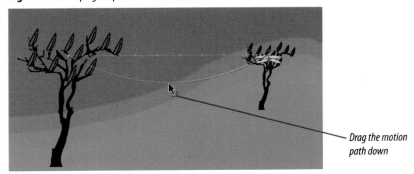

Drag the motion
path down

Figure 19 *Dragging the Bezier handle up to complete the curve*

Drag the
handle up

Figure 20 *Completed path*

Your path may vary

2. Click **frame 10** on the dragonfly layer, then drag the **dragonfly** to the leaves on the small tree.

3. Using the **Selection pointer** ↖⊕, point to the middle of the motion path, then, when the pointer changes to ↖, drag the **path** down, as shown in Figure 18.

4. Click the **Subselection tool** ↘, point to the left end of the motion path, then, when the pointer changes to an arrow with an unfilled square ↘□, click to display the Bezier handles.

5. Point to the right-side handle, then, when the pointer changes to a delta symbol ▲ drag the **handle** up to the position shown in Figure 19.

6. Drag the **solid path** down slightly with the Subselection pointer with a filled square ↘■.

   Notice the dots from the original path are now on the reshaped path, as shown in Figure 20.

7. Click **frame 1** on the dragonfly layer, then click **Orient to path** in the Properties panel.

8. Click the **Free Transform tool** ▦, then rotate a corner handle to align the front of the dragonfly to the path.

9. Click **frame 10** on the dragonfly layer, click the **dragonfly**, then resize the dragonfly to width **22**.

10. Drag the **tween span** on the dragonfly layer to **frame 30**, then insert **keyframes** in frame 30 on the other layers.

11. Test the movie, close the Flash Player window, then save your work.

You animated and resized an instance of a movie clip.

Animate Buttons Using
MOVIE CLIP SYMBOLS

What You'll Do

 In this lesson, you will create an animated button and put together a short interactive movie using ActionScript.

Understanding Animated Buttons

As you learned in a previous chapter, a button symbol does not have the standard Timeline, but instead has four states associated with it. You can animate a button by nesting a movie clip symbol inside any one of the three visible states of the button: Up, Over, or Down—although Up and Over are the most common placements.

Depending on the state in which you nest the symbol, you will have different results. If you nest the animation inside the Up state, the movie/button will continue to animate as long as the button is visible on the Stage in the main Timeline. If you nest the movie inside the Over state, the animation will be visible only when the user's mouse is over the button. If the animation is nested inside

the Down state, the users will see only a brief flicker of animation when they click the mouse. The first two are the most common and both have obvious interface benefits as well—if your users see something animated, they are more inclined to interact with it and discover it is actually a button.

Building an Animated Button Symbol

To build an animated button symbol, you need at least two symbols in the Library panel. First, you need to create a movie clip symbol with the animation. In building this animation, make sure you design it to repeat cleanly, especially if you plan to use it in the Up state of a button. Once you have built the movie clip symbol, you need to create a button symbol in which to nest the animation. Remember, because movie clips have independent Timelines, the clip will run continually while the button symbol is on the Stage, even if the main movie pauses or stops. Figure 21 shows the Information bar for the edit window of a movie clip symbol nested inside a button.

As with a movie clip, you must publish the movie or test it using the Flash Player to see the animation of a button. The Enable Simple Buttons option will not play the movie clip—you will see only a static view of the first frame of the clip.

Creating an Interactive Movie

Adding interactivity to a movie simply means you are asking your user to be involved in the movie in some way other than watching it. It can be as simple as adding a button for a user to click or giving the user a choice to make. Interactivity can also be complex, for example, the game shown in Figure 22 in which a user must assemble a puzzle. Because adding interactivity means you are forcing users to become involved in your movie, you are more likely to hold your users' interest.

You can also create complex interactions by using ActionScript in combination with movie clip symbols. With ActionScript, you can set up movie clips to play, pause, or perform other actions based on user input such as clicking the mouse or pressing a key on the keyboard, similar to the interactions you can create with a button. You can also use ActionScript to instruct movie clips to perform actions without waiting for user input and to jump to specific frames on the Timeline of a movie clip symbol.

Figure 21 *Movie clip symbol nested inside a button*

Button symbol   Animated movie clip

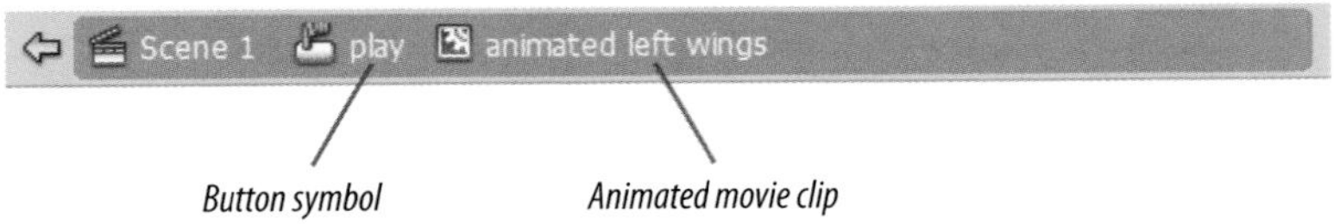

Figure 22 *Interactive game created with symbols, buttons, and ActionScript*

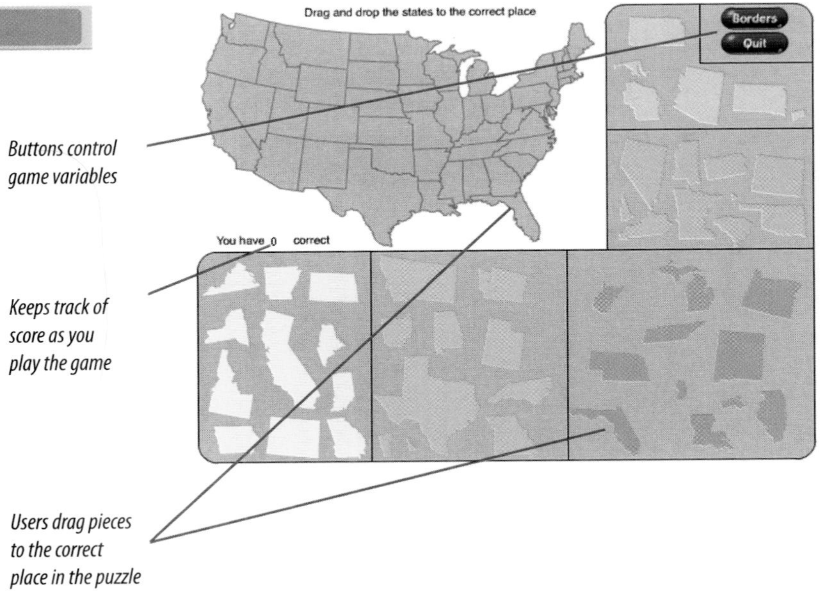

Buttons control game variables

Keeps track of score as you play the game

Users drag pieces to the correct place in the puzzle

Create an animated button by nesting an animation in the button's Up state

1. Verify that the dragonfly document is open, click **Insert** on the menu bar, then click **New Symbol**.

2. Type **play** in the Name text box, change the Type to **Button**, then click **OK**.

3. Click the **Up frame** on Layer 1, click the **Text tool** T on the Tools panel, then click the **Text tool pointer** $+\frac{}{I}$ in the center of the Stage.

4. Use the Properties panel to change the Character family to **Verdana**, the style to **bold**, the size to **24**, and the color to **black**.

   Note: If you see TFL Text at the top of the Properties panel, click the list arrow and then select Classic Text. If you see Dynamic Text or Input Text below Classic Text, click the list arrow and then select Static Text.

5. Type **PLAY**.

6. Click the **Selection tool** ▶ on the Tools panel, drag the **animated left wings movie clip symbol** from the Library panel to the left of the word "PLAY," then drag the **animated right wings movie clip symbol** from the Library panel to the right side of the word "PLAY", as shown in Figure 23.

7. Click the **Selection tool** ▶ on the Tools panel, click the word **PLAY** on the Stage, click the **Text (fill) color box** on the Properties panel, position the Eyedropper pointer ✐ over a wing, then click.

(continued)

Figure 23 *Adding the animated wings to the text*

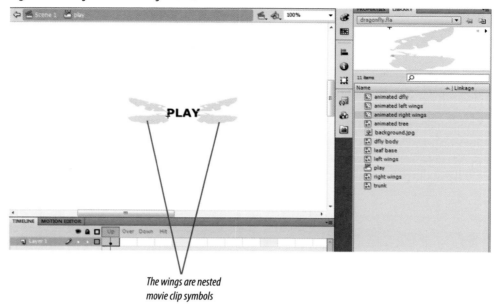

The wings are nested movie clip symbols

Figure 24 *Setting the Hit area*

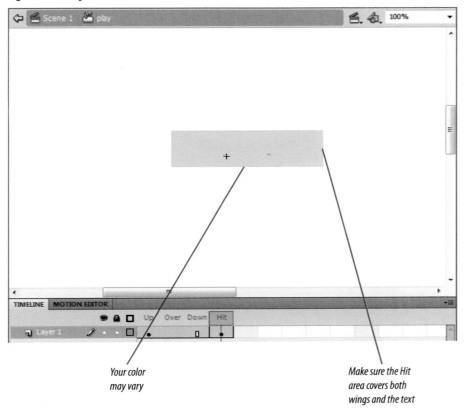

Your color
may vary

Make sure the Hit
area covers both
wings and the text

TIP When you move the Eyedropper pointer to the Stage, do not pass over any other clickable element in the Properties panel. If, as you move the Eyedropper pointer, the pointer changes to a shape other than the Eyedropper, go back and click the Text (fill) color box and try again.

The text and the wings are now the same color.

8. Insert a **keyframe** in the Hit frame of the button Timeline, select the **Rectangle tool** on the Tools panel, then draw a **box** around both sets of wings and the text, as shown in Figure 24.

TIP Remember that the Hit state is invisible on the Stage, but it defines the clickable area of a button.

9. Click the **Selection tool** ▶ on the Tools panel.

10. Click **Scene 1** at the top left of the workspace to return to the main Timeline.

You created a button symbol and placed an animation inside the Up state of the button symbol.

Place the animated button on the Stage

1. Insert a **new layer** above the dragonfly layer, name it **button**, then click **frame 1** on the button layer.

2. Drag the **play button symbol** from the Library panel to the lower-right corner on the Stage, as shown in Figure 25.

3. Insert a **new layer** above the button layer, then name it **actions**.

4. Open the Actions panel, then click **frame 1** on the actions layer.

5. Verify that the Script Assist button is selected and that actions:1 is displayed in the lower-left corner of the Actions panel Script pane.

6. Click **Add a new item to the script button** ⊕ in the Script Assist window, point to **Global Functions**, point to **Timeline Control**, click **stop**, then collapse the Actions panel.

7. Click **Control** on the menu bar, point to **Test Movie**, then click **in Flash Professional**.

   The wings flutter on the animated button and on the dragonfly in the tree. Notice that the dragonfly in the tree does not fly on the motion path and the leaves on the trees do not animate. This is because both the dragonfly's motion and the leaves are dependent on the main Timeline, which is stopped on frame 1.

8. Close the Flash Player window.

You placed an animated button on the Stage and added a stop action.

Figure 25 *Placing the button on the Stage*

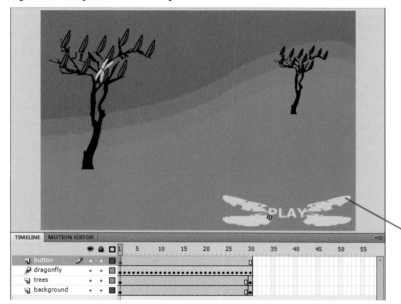

The animated button is made up of text and two movie clip symbols

Figure 26 *Adding the button action in the Actions panel*

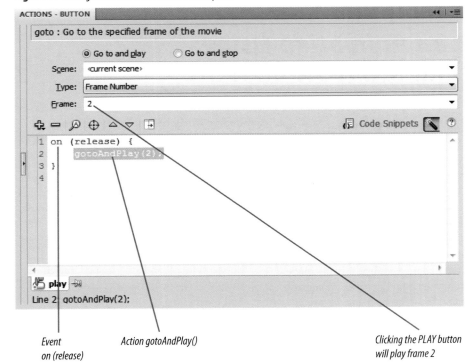

Event
on (release)

Action gotoAndPlay()

Clicking the PLAY button
will play frame 2

1. Click the **Selection tool** ▶, then click the **PLAY button** on the Stage to select it.

2. Display the Actions panel, then verify that the play button symbol is displayed in the lower-left corner of the Actions panel Script pane.

3. Click **Add a new item to the script button** ⊹, point to **Global Functions**, point to **Movie Clip Control**, then click **on**.

4. Click **Add a new item to the script button** ⊹, point to **Global Functions**, point to **Timeline Control**, then click **goto**.

5. Change the Frame number to **2**, as shown in Figure 26.

6. Click **frame 30** on the actions layer, click **Insert** on the menu bar, point to **Timeline**, then click **Blank Keyframe**.

7. Click **Add a new item to the script button** ⊹, point to **Global Functions**, point to **Timeline Control**, click **stop**, then close the Actions panel.

8. Click **Control** on the menu bar, point to **Test Movie**, then click **in Flash Professional**.

    The dragonfly in the tree and the PLAY button are animated because they use their movie clip Timelines, which are independent of the main Timeline.

9. Click the **PLAY button**.

    The leaves on the trees animate and the dragonfly flies on the motion path, which are actions associated with the main Timeline.

10. Close the Flash Player window, save your work, then close the movie.

You added actions to the movie, creating interactivity.

Edit an Animation Using
THE MOTION EDITOR

What You'll Do

 In this lesson, you will use the Motion Editor to make changes in the properties of an animation.

NEW Understanding the Motion Editor

Flash provides a feature called Motion Editor that allows you to edit motion tween animations by changing the property values such as the position, rotation, color effects, and ease value. The advantages of using the Motion Editor are that you can quickly make changes to an animation without having to use the Properties panel and you can view the effect of a change while it is being made. In addition, you can more precisely control the changes that are to be made. Figure 27 shows the Motion Editor panel displayed below the Stage. The Essentials workspace groups the Timeline and Motion Editor panels. When MOTION EDITOR is clicked the Motion Editor panel opens in place of the Timeline panel at the bottom of the Flash workspace. In Figure 27, the Stage view has been set to 25% so that the entire Motion Editor panel can been seen. The PLAY button, which has been given a motion tween, is selected and all changes made in the Motion Editor will affect this button symbol.

The Motion Editor includes several columns with the headings across the top of the panel: Property, Value, Ease, Keyframe, and Graph. The Property, Value, and Ease columns are used together. They represent the properties of the selected object (in this case the button symbol) and are grouped into three categories: Basic motion, Transformation, and Eases.

■ Basic motion includes the position of the button symbol (X and Y values) on the Stage, the Rotation Z value, and the type of ease, if any, for each property. Currently, the button symbol has X and Y coordinates of 400 px and 375 px, respectively. No ease and no rotation has been specified.

- Transformation includes skew and scale (used to resize the symbol) values; color effects such as transparency and brightness; and filters such as drop shadow, blur, and glow. None of these properties has been changed.
- Eases has several types including slow, medium, and fast, as well as values from −100 to 100. Setting the type of ease and ease value for a specific property is a two-step process. If you want to specify an ease (for example, when moving an object), first you select the type of ease and the value within this category. Then, you click the list arrow for a property, such as the X coordinate, and select the ease type.

The Keyframe column is used to add and remove keyframes. When you need to change a property you must select a keyframe or insert one. Keyframes are displayed on the graph as black rectangles. Currently there are keyframes in frames 1 and 30 because the motion tween begins and ends on these frames. The Graph column provides a frame-by-frame visual representation of the values specified for the various properties. You can drag keyframes along a graph line to change a value. For example, if you want to change the position of the object on the Stage, you could enter a value for the X or Y coordinates or you could drag the keyframe in frame 1 for the X or Y coordinates up or down.

QUICK TIP

Use the Undo command from the Edit menu to undo your actions as necessary.

Figure 27 *The Motion Editor panel*

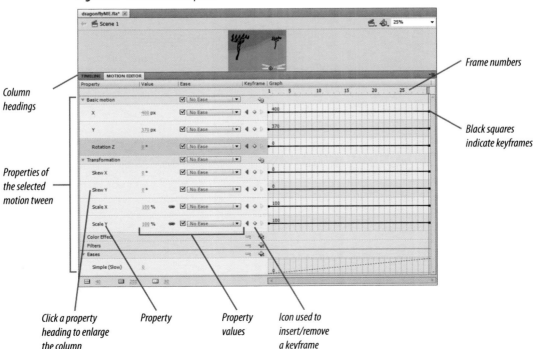

Column headings

Properties of the selected motion tween

Frame numbers

Black squares indicate keyframes

Click a property heading to enlarge the column

Property

Property values

Icon used to insert/remove a keyframe

Use the Motion Editor to change properties of a motion tween animation

NEW

1. Open dragonfly.fla, then save it as **dragonflyME.fla**.

2. Click **frame 1** on the button layer, insert a **motion tween**, click **frame 30**, then insert a **keyframe**.

3. Change the View to Fit in Window, then collapse the Properties panel.

4. Click **MOTION EDITOR** on the Timeline.

5. Drag the **top** of the MOTION EDITOR panel up to display the Motion Editor panel.

6. Click the **Viewable Frames value** at the bottom of the Motion Editor and change the value to **30**, as shown in Figure 28.

7. Click **frame 30** on the MOTION EDITOR Graph Timeline.

8. In the Basic motion area, click the **Y value**, type **80**, then press **[Enter]** (Win) or **[return]** (Mac).

   Notice the button symbol on the Stage moves and the graph line on the Motion Editor changes.

9. Change the rotation Z value to **320**.

(continued)

Figure 28 *Displaying the entire Motion Editor panel*

Drag top line of the Motion Editor panel up to display the entire panel

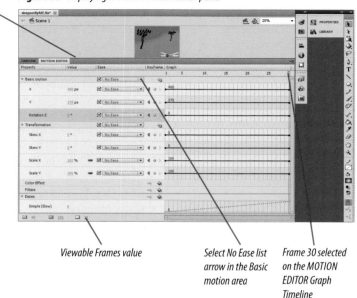

Viewable Frames value

Select No Ease list arrow in the Basic motion area

Frame 30 selected on the MOTION EDITOR Graph Timeline

Figure 29 *Selecting a keyframe to drag*

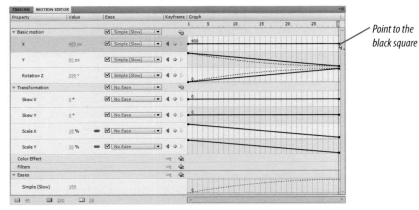

Point to the
black square

Figure 30 *The completed Motion Editor panel*

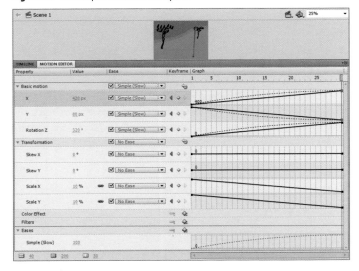

10. In the Transformation area, verify the link for the X and Y scales is not broken, then change the Scale X to **10%**.

    Notice the Scale Y is set to 10% automatically because the lock is not broken.

11. In the Eases area, change the Simple (Slow) value to **100**.

12. On the Basic motion bar, click the **No Ease list arrow**, then click **Simple (Slow)**.

    All the ease settings in the Basic Motion area change to Simple (Slow).

13. Click **Control** on the menu bar, point to **Test Movie**, then click **in Flash Professional**.

14. Click the **PLAY button**.

15. Close the Flash Player window.

16. Point to the **keyframe** in **frame 30** on the X coordinate graph line, as shown in Figure 29.

17. Drag the **line** up to change the value to **420** and notice how the top of the motion path on the Stage moves toward the tree.

    Your screen should resemble Figure 30.

18. Test the movie, then close the Flash Player window.

19. Save your work, close the document, then exit Flash.

You used the Motion Editor to change the properties of a motion tween animation.

Plan for complex movies and animations, and create an animated graphic symbol.

1. Start Flash, open fl8_4.fla from the drive and folder where your Data Files are stored, then save it as **skillsDemo8.fla**.
2. Set the view to Fit in Window.

In this Flash document, you will create a movie that will display a clock (a movie clip) with a minute hand (a movie clip) and an hour hand (a movie clip) that are rapidly spinning. The clock will be a button so that when the user clicks the clock it displays wings (two movie clips) and flies around the screen. All of the necessary graphic objects are available in the Library panel. The movie currently has a background graphic (water and clouds) and a text title (Time Flies).

Create a movie clip symbol.

1. Create a new movie clip symbol named **mc_minuteHand**.
2. Verify you are in the edit window for the mc_minuteHand movie clip, then drag the g_minute hand graphic symbol to the Stage.
3. Use the Properties panel to set the X and Y position values to 0 and 0.
4. Click the Free Transform tool and verify the object is selected.
5. Change the view to 800%, then drag the transformation point (the white circle) of the minute hand object to the middle of the colored circle at the bottom of the object. This will set the pivot point for the object as it spins around.

6. Click frame 1, then create a motion tween.
7. Drag the end of the tween span on the Timeline back to frame 5.
8. Verify frame 5 is selected, then use the Properties panel to set the rotate value to 1 and the direction to clockwise.
9. Play the movie clip, then return to the main Timeline.
10. Change the view to Fit in window, then create a new movie clip symbol named **mc_hourHand**.
11. Verify you are in the edit window for the mc_hourHand movie clip, then drag the g_hour hand graphic symbol to the Stage.
12. Use the Properties panel to set the X and Y position values to 0 and 0.
13. Change the view to 800%, then drag the transformation point (white circle) to the middle of the bottom of the object, which is actually to the left.
14. Click frame 5, then insert a keyframe.
15. Click Modify on the menu bar, click Transform, click Scale and Rotate, set the rotate value to 30 degrees, then click OK.
16. Click frame 10, insert a keyframe, then repeat Step 15 to set the rotate value to 30 degrees.
17. Repeat Step 15 for frames 15, 20, 25, 30, 35, 40, 45, 50, 55, and 60. (*Hint*: Do not just copy and paste frames because the action of rotating the hand will not be copied and pasted to the new frames. You can use shortcut keys. The [F6] key will insert a keyframe. The [Ctrl]+[Alt]+S keys (Win) [option]+[command]+S display the Scale and Rotate

dialog box. Then pressing [Enter] Win or [return] [Mac] will accept the values in the dialog box.)
18. Play the movie clip, then return to the main Timeline.
19. Create a new movie clip symbol named **mc_clock**.
20. Verify you are in the edit window for the mc_clock movie clip, rename Layer 1 **clockFace**, then drag the g_clock face graphic symbol to the Stage.
21. Use the Properties panel to set the X and Y position values to 0 and 0.
22. Add a new layer, name it **hourHand**, zoom to 400, scroll to see the clock, drag the mc_hourHand movie clip so the colored circle at the bottom of the hand aligns with the clock's registration symbol.
23. Add a new layer, name it **minuteHand**, drag the mc_minuteHand movie clip to the middle of the clock so that the bottoms of the objects overlap, use the arrow keys to align the two hands, then change to Fit in Window.
24. Add a new layer named **wings**, move it below the clockFace layer, then drag the mc_left wings to the upper-left side of the clock.
25. Drag the mc_right wings to the upper-right side of the clock.
26. Use the Free Transform tool and the arrow keys to rotate the wings as needed to place the wings so they appear to be connected to the clock.
27. Insert keyframes in frame 60 on all the layers, then return to the main Timeline.
28. Add a layer, name it **clock**, insert a keyframe in frame 2 on the layer.
29. Drag the mc_clock movie clip symbol to the lower middle of the Stage.

Animate the movie clip symbol.

1. Verify frame 2 on the clock layer is selected, then create a motion tween.
2. Select frame 60 on the clock layer, then drag the clock to the upper-left corner of the Stage.
3. Use the Properties panel to resize the clock to approximately one-fourth of its original size, then adjust the position of the clock so it is in the upper-left corner of the Stage, as shown in Figure 31.
4. Use the Selection tool to reshape the motion path to an arc.
5. Use the Subselection tool to display the Bezier handles and reshape the motion path to an S curve, then compare your screen to Figure 31.

Animate buttons using movie clip symbols.

1. Display the mc_clock symbol in the edit window.
2. Select the clockface and both hands layers (not the wings layer).
3. Click Edit on the menu bar, point to Timeline, click Copy Frames, then return to the main Timeline.
4. Create a new movie clip symbol with the name **mc_clockButton**.
5. Verify you are in the edit window for the mc_clockButton symbol, click frame 1, click Edit on the menu bar, point to Timeline, click Paste Frames, then return to the main Timeline.
6. Create a new button symbol with the name **b_clockButton**, then insert the mc_clockButton symbol into the Up state of the button.
7. Insert a keyframe in the Hit state of the button, return to the main Timeline, insert a new layer above the clock layer, then name it **button**.

8. Click frame 1 on the button layer, then click the Edit Multiple Frames icon at the bottom of the Timeline.
9. Drag the button symbol to the Stage and place it directly on top of the clock. (*Hint*: Use the arrow keys to align the two clocks.)
10. Turn off the Edit Multiple Frames feature, then remove frames 2–60 on the button layer.
11. Insert a new layer above the button layer, name it **stopAction**, then insert stop actions in frame 1 and 60. (*Hint*: Be sure to add a keyframe to frame 60.)
12. Add a goto action to the button on the Stage, and specify 2 as the frame to go to. (*Hint*: Be sure the button symbol is displayed in the lower-left corner of the Actions panel Script pane.)
13. Test your movie, be sure to click the clock button, then save your work.

Edit an animation using the Motion Editor.

1. Save the document as **skillsDemo8-ME.fla**.

2. Click frame 1 on the gtext layer. The text block has been converted to a graphic symbol, a motion tween has been inserted and a keyframe placed in frame 60.
3. Change the view to Fit in Window, display the Motion Editor panel and adjust the panel height to view the entire panel.
4. Change the viewable frames to 60.
5. Verify the text symbol is selected, click frame 60 on the Graph Timeline and make the following changes:
   - X value: **450**
   - Y value: **350**
   - Z value: **360**
   - Scale X value: **50**
   - Color Effect: Tint, black, **50%** (*Hint*: Click the Add Color, Filter, or Ease button on the Color Effect bar, then change the settings.)
6. Test the movie, then compare your screen with Figure 32.
7. Save your work, then exit Flash.

Figure 31 *Motion path for clock movie clip symbol*

Figure 32 *Completed Skills Review*

Ultimate Tours has decided it wants to add animation to the opening page of its "Summer in December" website, which is promoting a series of tours to Florida, Bermuda, and the Caribbean. The management would like the animation to draw attention to the company name and to the navigation button (which in this case is the sun graphic), so visitors will click to find out more information about specific tours. Though the site is still at an early stage, they would like to see some prototypes of potential animations. The company would like a

new look that differs from the prototype developed in Chapter 7 (ultimateTours7.fla).

1. Start a new Flash document and save it as **ultimateTours8.fla**.
2. On paper, plan how you might add animations to this page that will fulfill the criteria Ultimate Tours has established.
3. Build the animation you have planned for emphasizing the company name or the promotion subtitle text. For example, you might convert the text of the promotion ("Our new Summer . . .") to a graphic symbol, then create a movie clip symbol

in which the text dissolves and reappears, changes color, rotates, or moves across the screen.
4. Build the animation you have planned that will encourage visitors to click the continue button. For example, you might create an animation of a yellow ball representing the sun rolling out from the heading. Then, you could create a direction line telling visitors to click the sun to continue. (*Note:* For this project, the button does not have to be active.)
5. Save your work, then compare your image to the example shown in Figure 33.

Figure 33 *Sample completed Project Builder 1*

You have been asked to create a short interactive movie on ocean life for the local elementary school, which is planning a visit to an oceanographic institute. This project should be colorful, interactive, and full of images that appeal to 7- to 12-year-old students.

The opening page of the site should show some images of sea creatures which, when clicked, lead to more information. You must include at least three clickable objects on this opening page.

1. Obtain some images of fish, coral, and other ocean creatures from resources on your computer or the Internet, or from scanned media. (*Note*: Be sure to use only images you have permission to use.)

2. Create a new Flash document, then save it as **ocean_life8.fla**.

3. Set the document properties, including the size and background color, if desired.

4. Create animated movie clips for at least three ocean creatures. Use different types of animation for these movie clips. For example, you might use motion tweening to move, resize, or rotate objects, or fade them in or out.

5. Use the Motion Editor to make adjustments to one of the tweens.

6. Create buttons for the ocean creature images using your animated movies in the Up state and also designating a Hit state. (*Hint*: Be creative about the appearance of the buttons—use different shapes and sizes, or try cropping and making the images themselves clickable.)

7. Place the three buttons on the Stage.

8. Add some explanatory text.

9. Save your work and compare your image to the example shown in Figure 34.

Figure 34 *Sample completed Project Builder 2*

The starfish movie clip contains the graphic image of the starfish and a motion tween that causes the starfish to rotate and get larger as it rotates

Click an image to learn about these ocean creatures...

Figure 35 shows a birthday card created in Flash. Study the figure and complete the following. For each question, indicate how you determined your answer.

1. Connect to the Internet, then go to *www.rubberchickencards.com/site/search.htm?id = 197*.
2. Open a document in a word processor or create a new Flash document, save the file as **dpc8**, then answer the following questions. (*Hint*: Use the Text tool in Flash.)

- Without seeing the source file in this movie, make a list of objects you believe to be in the Library panel and why you think they should be stored there.
- Do you think all the images in this work were drawn in Flash? Explain.
- What in this movie could be animated?
- Would you use animated graphic symbols or movie clip symbols to create the animations? Explain.
- Are there any animated graphic symbols or movie clip symbols you could create once and use in multiple places?

- What other buttons would you add and why?
- Suppose you want to create an animation in which one jester strums his lute, some text appears and then dissolves, the other jester bangs his tambourine, more text appears and dissolves, then both jesters play simultaneously while the words "Happy Birthday" float across the screen. Plan a strategy for creating this animation that will streamline the Timeline, reuse symbols to conserve file size, and allow you to easily set up the timing of the sequence so the text appears at the appropriate time.

Figure 35 *Design Project*

To add some pizzazz to your existing portfolio, you want to change the navigation on your home page. Your goal is to have visitors mouse over the navigation buttons and see an animation that you hope will better entice employers and potential clients with your skills. The animation should be fairly subtle and elegant, and showcase your animation skills.

1. Start a new Flash document and save it as **portfolio8.fla**.
2. Create a movie clip symbol named **animated button**.
3. Inside the movie clip symbol create an animation that would be appropriate for the mouse-over of your primary navigation buttons in the portfolio.
4. Open each of your button symbols and place the animation in the Over state. (*Hint*: Insert a keyframe in the Over state, then drag the animated button movie clip to the Stage. It will be a nested movie clip within the button symbol.)
5. Save your work, then compare your movie to the example shown in Figure 36. (*Note*: Each of the balls rotate and flip when the pointer rolls over it.)

Figure 36 *Sample completed Portfolio Project*

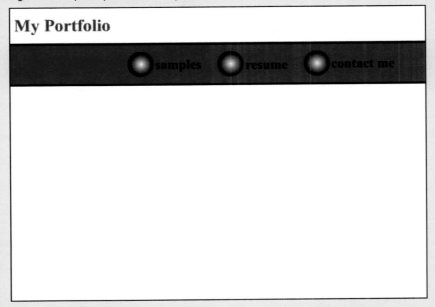

CHAPTER **9** **INTRODUCTION TO ACTIONSCRIPT 3.0**

1. Understand ActionScript 3.0

2. Work with instances of movie clip symbols

3. Use code snippets

4. Work with variables

 Introduction

Until now, you have generally used ActionScript 2.0 (AS2) to code various actions, such as stop events within frames and goto events within buttons. Using AS2 allows you to use Script Assist to enter code that controls the Timeline and creates user interactivity. ActionScript 3.0 (AS3) allows you to do everything you did using AS2 and more. In addition, using AS3 significantly improves the performance of Flash movies by delivering large and complex applications, such as games and websites, more rapidly. Increased performance greatly enhances the user experience by not having to wait for movies to download, as well as making complex animations work more smoothly.

AS2 and AS3 are scripting languages with intuitive code (instructions) such as *gotoAndPlay*. However, AS3 is based on Object Oriented Programming (OOP) standards. OOP is a way to organize code (a set of instructions). You use AS3 code to define objects and send messages between objects. Conceptually, you have been working in an object oriented environment in the previous chapters. That is, you have been working with items (objects) on the

Stage and assigning them actions or having them react to actions.

You can build on this conceptual knowledge formed while using AS2 to learn AS3 and to apply the basic concepts of Object Oriented Programming, including understanding its terminology and understanding the rules (the syntax) regarding how AS3 code is written. Having a basic understanding of AS2 gives you a frame of reference as you begin learning AS3.

The goal of this chapter is for you to understand how you can use AS3 to create applications. The examples used in this chapter are simple but give you a basic understanding of AS3 and how AS3 can be used to create complex applications that would be more difficult, time consuming, less flexible or even impossible to create using AS2. Indeed, many new features of recent editions of Flash (especially CS4 and CS5) require that the movie be created with AS3. These features include inverse kinematics (using the Bone tool), and 3D effects. Adobe requires a basic knowledge of ActionScript 3.0 for its Associate's certification. Thus, having fundamental skills in AS3 makes a person more employable.

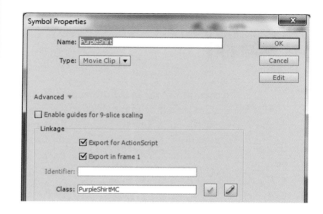

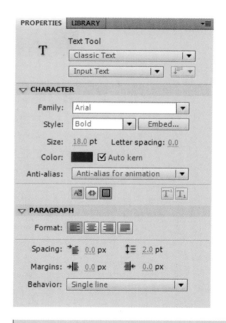

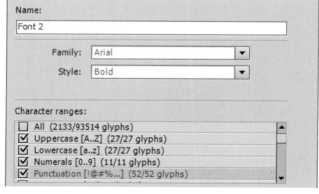

Understand
ACTIONSCRIPT 3.0

What You'll Do

In this lesson, you will use ActionScript to create an object, animate the object, and create interactivity.

NEW Understanding How ActionScript 3.0 Works

In the previous chapters, the process for creating movies has focused on the Timeline and on using Flash tools (such as the Tools panel, the Properties panel, and the Library panel). You selected a frame on a layer, used tools to create and place objects on the Stage, and used menu items to animate the objects. For example, in previous chapters, you used Flash tools to draw an oval on the Stage with a specific color and size. Then you used the menu options to change the drawing into a symbol, such as a button, and the edit window to change the colors of the button states and to specify the hit area. Finally, you selected the button instance on the Stage and used the Actions panel and AS2 code to specify an *on release mouse* event and *goto* action that jumps the playhead to another frame that has a motion tween.

Depending on the complexity and length of a movie, the Timeline for a movie created in this manner could get very long and have many layers. With AS3, the emphasis shifts from the Timeline to objects, both on and off the Stage. So, for example, with AS3, all of the AS2 examples cited above can be

done without using the drawing tools, menu system, or edit window. That is, you can write the code directly in the Actions panel that defines the button and specifies the event (*mouse click*) that triggers the action (*goto*) or simply plays the motion tween without moving the playhead. This provides a great deal more flexibility because the code can be reused or executed from other places in the movie.

When you start a new Flash Movie, you choose AS2 or AS3. Specifying AS3 means that when writing code in the Actions panel you must adhere to the AS3 rules. However, it does not prevent you from using the features (drawing tools to create and place objects on the Stage, to create Timeline animations, and so on) that you have already learned. In fact, most Flash movies are a combination of these activities and ActionScript code. However, you can only develop using one ActionScript version. You can switch versions (using the Publish Settings option), but, if you do, then all of the code that you have developed already will need to be rewritten. In order to understand AS3, you must understand the concept of objects. In AS3, an object is an instance similar to the instances you created from movie clip, graphic, and button symbols. In previous chapters, the instances you placed on the Stage were defined (form, color, size, and so on) by the symbols used to create the instances. With AS3, instances are defined by **classes** instead of by symbols. This is useful because a class has certain attributes (properties) and functionality (methods) that are passed on to its objects. The **properties** of an object describe the object, such as the size and color; the **methods** explain what the object can do, such as rotate or accept a mouse click, or what can be done to an object, such as fill it with color. (*Note*: The properties of a class are similar to those of an instance of a symbol, which are also passed on.) Figure 1 summaries the concepts and terminology related to Classes, Objects, Properties and Methods.

The Flash program has many predefined classes, such as the Shape class, which are available for use as soon as you start an AS3 document. If a class is not predefined in Flash, you can import a class, such as Tween, or you can create your own class. For example, you could create a cell phone class. After creating the cell phone class, when you place an instance of the cell phone class on the Stage, it has all of the properties of the class and can perform all of the methods associated with the class. The class contains the AS3 code that defines the object. Based on the AS3 code, Flash knows what the object is and what it can do. As you work with AS3,

you will be working with objects that are defined by their class. For example, you will use the Shape class to create instances of objects such as circles and rectangles.

![NEW] Understanding Display Lists and the addChild() Method

Flash files have a **display list**. The display list is transparent to the user but Flash uses it to manage every object on the screen when the movie is published. In order for an object to be on the display list, it must be part of the **DisplayObjects** class. Objects

that can be part of the display list include movie clips, buttons, text, shapes, bitmaps, and video. Objects created with AS3 are not automatically visible on the screen when a movie is published. They must be added to the display list with the **addChild()** method. The syntax for using the addChild method is addChild(my_Object), where my_Object is the name of the object to be added to the display list. Each time you create an object that you want to be visible on the screen in the Flash Player when the movie is published, you must use the addChild() method.

Figure 1 *Summary of specific AS3 concepts and terms*

Term	Definition	Example	Notes
Class	AS3 code that defines the attributes (properties) and functionality (methods) of an object	CellPhone	A class can have a subclass such as webEnabledCellPhones
Object	One instance of a class that inherits the attributes (properties) and functionality (methods) of that class	myCellPhone	
Property	Each attribute of an object, such as its size or color (i.e. "What does it look like?")	Height, width, color, weight, screen, buttons, and so on.	
Method	The functionality of an object (i.e. "What can it do?" or "What can be done to it?")	makeCall, receiveCall, textMessage, playVideo, takePicture, and so on.	

Understanding Variables and Data Types

A **variable** is a container that holds data. You assign each variable a **Data Type**, which indicates the class used to populate the variable. There are scores of data types including Number, String (text), MovieClip, and Shape. The syntax for creating a variable is *var variableName:DataType*, where you specify the variable name and the data type. So, using this syntax, you could create a variable to hold a user's age by typing **var age:Number**. In this example, the variable name is age and Data Type is Number. It is useful to create a variable name that says something about the information that is held in the variable. And, it is imperative to use the correct Data Type, which can be found in the Help section of Flash CS5. An important use of variables is to hold instances of objects that can be referred to throughout the AS3 code. For example, you could create a variable named myAnimatedLogo_mc and assign it an animated movie clip. Then anytime you wanted to display the movie clip you would refer to the variable in your code.

Getting Started with AS3

The process for working with AS3 is to plan your application including how you will be developing objects (such as by importing them to the Library, drawing them on the Stage, or creating them using AS3), and how you will be using the Timeline (such as by developing motion tweens using the Timeline or by developing the motion tweens using AS3). The planning also involves how to construct the user interactivity (such as using buttons, goto actions, and so on). Figure 2 shows a simple movie that has a border and a circle. Figure 2 also shows the Actions panel with the code used to develop the circle. The movie uses two layers and only one frame on the Timeline. The Flash drawing tools were used to create the border, which was placed on its own layer. AS3 was used to create the circle. The process for creating a circle using AS3 is to add a layer with an appropriate name, such as actions, then open the Actions panel and type in the code. The Shape class is used to create a vector object (lines, arcs, circle, and rectangles) and the Graphics subclass is used to create the circle named my_circle. The Graphics subclass has several methods (such as drawCircle) that make it easy to create various shapes. An explanation of the code follows.

var my_circle:Shape = new Shape();

This line of code does three things. First, it creates a variable called my_circle. (Remember, you must determine the variable name.) Next, it specifies Shape as the Data Type for the variable. Finally, it creates an instance of the class by specifying new Shape (), which means it will create an instance of the circle. (*Note:* Many data types, such as Shape and MovieClip, describe the class used to fill the variable. So, they are both data types and classes.)

my_circle.graphics.beginFill(0x00FF00);

This line of code uses the beginFill method to specify the fill color property for the object. The first two characters (0x) indicate that a hexadecimal value will follow. You have used hexadecimal numbers with the Fill Color tool on the Tools panel. 00FF00 is a shade of green. Notice you do not type the # sign before the numbers when you are specifying a color code in AS3.

my_circle.graphics.drawCircle (250, 100, 20);

This line of code uses the drawCircle method to set the location and size of the object. The first two values are the X and Y Stage coordinates and the last value is the radius of the circle. So, this circle will be located in the top middle of the Stage and have a diameter of 40 px.

Figure 2 *A movie with a circle and the AS3 code used to create the circle*

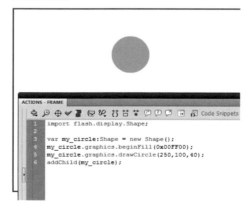

```
addChild(my_circle);
```

This line of code adds the object (my_circle) to the display list so that the object will be visible on the screen when the movie is played in the Flash Player.

With just four lines of code you can create a circle and specify a fill color, size, and Stage location. Other properties that are easy to add would be a stroke (line size and color) and a transparency (alpha) value. You might also add a line of code to indicate the fill process is complete (`my_circle.graphics.endFill();`). This line was omitted in order to simplify the example.

When this movie is published, frame 1 plays displaying the area with the blue border and the green circle. Now the question is "Why not just draw the circle on the Stage, convert it to a symbol, and give it an instance name?" The answer is once you have created this object and placed it in a variable container it becomes easily accessible for inclusion in other AS3 code. In addition, using Display Objects rather than drawn objects reduces the Flash file size significantly because code generated that creates an object by drawing on the Stage is less efficient than code written in the Actions panel to create an object.

Importing Classes

Many, but not all, classes are built into a Flash document. By including only commonly used classes, such as Shape, the Flash file size can be kept smaller. Depending on the configuration of the Flash program on the computer you are using, these built-in classes may be added automatically to the Actions panel as you type AS3 code that references the class. For example, when you type: `var my_circle:Shape = new Shape();` which references the Shape class, the code `import flash.display.Shape;` may appear in the Actions panel. If the import code does not appear, the code you typed will still work. For those classes not built-in, you need to import them as shown in the following section on adding Tweens.

Adding Tweens Using ActionScript 3

To make the example we have been discussing more interesting, we can use AS3 to add a motion tween to the circle. AS3 provides a Tween class that can be used to create motion tweens. Before you can use the Tween class, you must import it. Tweens involve a change in an object's size, transparency, or position, and these changes could also involve easing. Therefore, in addition to importing the Tween class, you need to import the Easing class too. The code for these two imports is:

```
import fl.transitions.Tween;
import fl.transitions.easing.*;
```

After importing these two classes, the following code can be added to create a tween that causes the circle to move down the screen.

```
var moveCircle:Tween = new Tween
    (my_circle,"y",None.easeOut,0,220, 5, true)
```

This line of code does several things:

```
var moveCircle:Tween
```

Creates a variable named moveCircle and specifies Tween as the Data Type.

```
new Tween
```

Creates an instance of the object (the circle created using AS3).

```
(my_circle
```

Identifies the object to be animated.

```
y
```

Identifies the property of the object that is to be controlled, i.e., the y location on the Stage.

```
None.easeOut
```

Specifies the type of ease (in, out) for the tween. In this case there is no ease.

```
0
```

Names the object's starting x or y position.

```
220
```

Names the object's ending x or y position.

```
5, true)
```

These two values work together. The first value indicates the duration of the tween in either the number of seconds or the number of frames. The second value indicates if the duration is to be specified in seconds or frames. A true value specifies seconds. A false value specifies frames.

The entire line of code causes the circle to move from its current location 220 pixels down the Stage in 5 seconds.

NEW Adding Interactivity Using AS3

Now that an object and a motion tween have been developed using AS3, a button could be used to provide interactivity, such as playing an animation when the user clicks the button.

A common type of interactivity is to have the user click a button, which causes some action (such as the playhead jumping to a frame on the Timeline that plays a motion tween). With AS2, you used Script Assist to assign a button action, such as "on release," and then you specified the desired results, such as gotoAndPlay. With AS3, you do not assign code to a button or any other objects on the Stage; instead, you reference the object within the code. Figure 3 shows a button added to the Stage in frame 1 of a layer named button. This button was created using the Flash drawing tools. The drawing was converted to a button symbol named b_play, and the Properties panel was used to give the button an instance name of playBtn. The instance name can be used in AS3 code to reference the button. There are three steps involved in a basic button interaction.

1. An event, such as a mouse click, occurs.
2. Flash recognizes that the event has occurred by using an **Event Listener**. Flash is constantly "listening" to "hear" when an event occurs.
3. Flash executes a block of code in response to the event. The block of code is called a **function**. The important thing about functions is that they are reusable blocks of code. They can be written one time and executed as often as desired, which helps keep the file size of a Flash movie small.

An example of the AS3 code that carries out these three steps follows.

```
playBtn.addEventListener(MouseEvent.
    CLICK, animateCircle);
```

This line of code does three things:

```
playBtn.addEventListener
```

Adds an event listener method to the instance (playBtn) of the button on the Stage.

```
MouseEvent.CLICK
```

Identifies the event as a mouse click (there are several other mouse events such as MOUSE_ OVER, MOUSE_UP, and MOUSE_DOWN).

```
animateCircle
```

Creates a function with the name animateCircle. In the same way that you must give a variable a name, you also must create the name for the function. It is helpful to give functions meaningful names.

The function has been named and now it needs to be defined. This involves using the function (animateCircle), specifying the event type (MouseEvent), and typing the lines of code that are to be executed inside curly braces {}. The following code defines the animateCircle function in response to a mouse event.

```
function animateCircle(event:MouseEvent)
{
var moveCircle:Tween = new Tween(my_
    circle,"y",None.easeOut,0,220, 5, true);
}
```

Figure 3 *A button added to the Stage in frame 1*

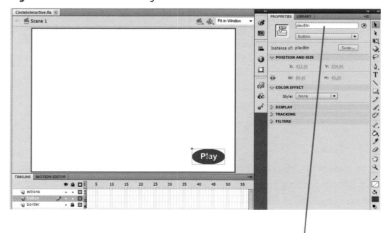

Instance name for object on the Stage

Notice that the code for the moveCircle tween is within the curly braces. As a result, the code for the moveCircle tween will be executed when the user clicks the Play button on the Stage because, when the Event Listener for the playBtn "hears" the click event, it "calls" the animateCircle function.

A variation of this function would be to include the code that creates the circle within the curly braces, followed by the code shown above to animate the circle. Then, when the user clicks the Play button, the circle appears and is animated.

NEW Understanding ActionScript 3.0 Syntax and Format

AS3 is a strict code environment. This means when you write AS3 code, you must adhere to specific syntax rules including spelling, punctuation, capitalization, and use of special characters. For example, you must use exact case for action names, such as when typing the gotoAndPlay action, you must be sure to capitalize the "A" and "P." Also, remember the structure, that is the how the lines of code are organized and formatted, is critical. For example, a semicolon(;) terminates an ActionScript statement. Text strings appear between quotation marks. To group actions, you enclose them in curly braces—{}—as shown in Figure 4. In addition, there are certain conventions that while not required are considered good coding practices. These will be pointed out as you work through the chapter. A seemingly minor error, such as typing a colon instead of a semicolon will cause an error when the ActionScript code is executed. If you need help, you can display code hints. Code hints give the syntax or possible parameters for an action in a pop-up window as you are entering the action. To see a code hint, type the action statement, and then type an opening parenthesis. To dismiss the code hint, type a closing parenthesis or press [Esc]. To disable the code hints, click Edit on the menu bar, click Preferences, and then click to deselect the Code Hints check box in the ActionScript category.

Flash provides two features that are useful when working with the Actions panel, **Check syntax** and **Auto format**. Clicking the Check syntax button checks for any errors in the syntax of the coding and, if found, displays a message in the Compiler Errors panel. This helps you determine what changes need to be done. When an error occurs the Compiler Errors panel appears grouped with the Timeline panel. In many cases the mistakes are in spelling or use of special characters. Clicking the Auto format button formats the code in accordance with ActionScript formatting conventions. This may add spaces, lines, and indents to make the code more readable.

Figure 4 *Syntax for AS3 code*

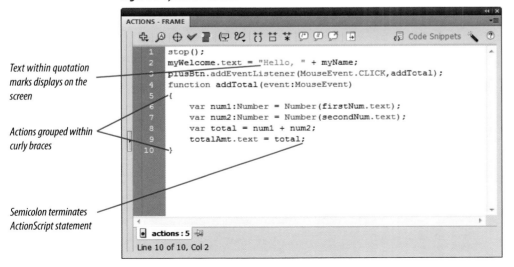

Text within quotation marks displays on the screen

Actions grouped within curly braces

Semicolon terminates ActionScript statement

Using the Actions Panel

The specific steps used when working with AS3 vary depending on what you would like done within your movie. The process can be as simple as starting a new AS3 Flash document, opening the Actions panel and typing the desired code. Or, the process can be as complex as utilizing the Timeline, adding content and functionality spread throughout multiple layers (in the same way you added content in an AS2 document), and then using AS3 code to enhance the movie. Either approach involves the Actions panel. (*Note*: When you work with ActionScript you are creating a text file. It is possible to create the file outside of Flash using programs designed for writing and debugging AS3 code.)

The Actions panel has two windows and three panes, as shown in Figure 5:

- **Actions toolbox pane**—provides the categories of actions that can be selected to build ActionScript code. This provides an alternative to typing code in the Script pane.
- **Script navigator pane**—provides a list of frames that contain scripts used in the movie. This pane can be used to quickly locate a frame and display its code in the Script pane.
- **Script pane**—used to type in the code and a toolbar for editing the code.

Configuring the Actions Panel

In previous chapters, you have used the Actions Panel mainly to insert code using Script Assist. As just discussed, there are two windows, left and right, in the Actions panel. The left window displays the Actions toolbox pane and the Script navigator pane. The right window displays the Script pane where the ActionScript code is displayed and edited. You will need to display the right window at all times. Before writing any code, be sure to check the layer name and frame number/name displayed in the lower-left corner of the Script pane to verify it is the frame you want to apply the code to. You can collapse and expand the left window by clicking the Expand/Collapse arrow between the windows. You can resize the windows by dragging the border between the two windows left or right. You can resize the panes in the left window by dragging the border between the two panes up or down. You can press [F9] to open and close the Actions panel.

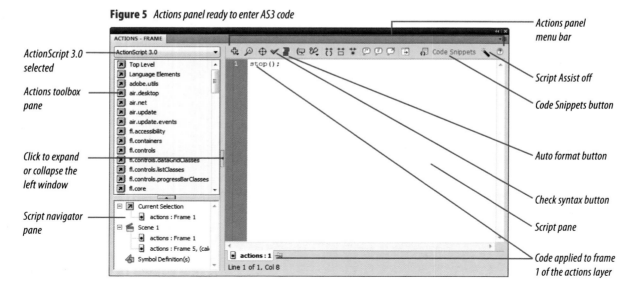

Figure 5 *Actions panel ready to enter AS3 code*

Figure 6 *The code to create a circle*

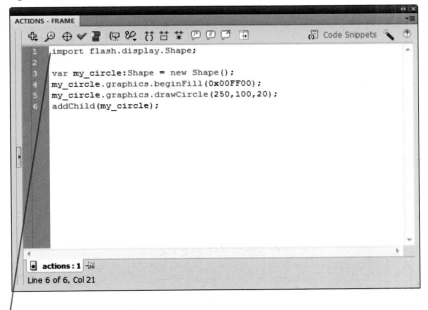

```
ACTIONS - FRAME

import flash.display.Shape;

var my_circle:Shape = new Shape();
my_circle.graphics.beginFill(0x00FF00);
my_circle.graphics.drawCircle(250,100,20);
addChild(my_circle);
```

actions : 1
Line 6 of 6, Col 21

This statement may be added automatically as you type the code to create a shape. Note: ignore code hints throughout this chapter if they appear as you type.

Using the Check syntax and Auto format buttons

It is good practice to always check syntax after typing code. Click the Check syntax button throughout this chapter after typing code even if you are not directed to do so in the steps. If there is an error in the code the Compiler Errors panel will appear next to the Timeline and display a message. Some errors may not be recognized until the movie is tested in the Flash Player.

It is also good practice to use the Auto format button to ensure your code is formatted according to AS3 structure. This will make your code easier to read and easier to find errors, if any.

NEW Use ActionScript to create an object

1. Open fl9_1.fla, then save it as **CircleObject.fla**.
2. Change the view to Fit in Window.

   This movie has one layer named border with a blue border in frame 1.
3. Insert a **new layer**, name it **actions**, then click **frame 1** on the actions layer.
4. Open the Actions panel, then collapse the Actions panel left window if it is open.
5. Verify actions:1 is displayed in the lower-left corner of the Script pane and that Script Assist is not active.
6. Click at the top of the Script pane, then type the following as shown in Figure 6.

   var my_circle:Shape = new Shape();

   my_circle.graphics.beginFill(0x00FF00);

   my_circle.graphics.drawCircle(250, 100, 20);

   addChild(my_circle);
7. Click the **Check syntax button** ✔ on the Actions panel menu bar and correct any errors.
8. Collapse the Actions panel, then press **[Enter]** (Win) or **[return]** (Mac) to play the movie.

   Nothing appears on the Stage. The object only appears when the movie is published.
9. Click **Control** on the menu bar, point to **Test Movie**, then click **in Flash Professional**.

   The green circle appears in the Flash Player window.
10. Close the Flash Player window, then save your work.

You used ActionScript 3.0 to create and display an object.

NEW Use ActionScript to change the properties of an object

1. Save the document as **CircleObject2.fla**.

2. Open the Actions panel, then change the fill color of the object to **0xFF0000**.

3. Test the movie and notice the color of the circle is now red.

4. Close the Flash Player window.

5. Change the position of the object to **50**, **50** and the radius to **40**.

6. Test the movie, notice the red circle is larger and in the upper-left corner of the Flash Player window, then close the Flash Player window.

7. Drag the **mouse pointer** to highlight the four lines of code starting with var.

8. **Right-click** (Win) or **[control]-click** (Mac) the code, then click **Copy**.

9. Click the end of addChild line, then press **[Enter]** (Win) or **[return]** (Mac) to move down a line.

10. **Right-click** (Win) or **[control]-click** (Mac) the new blank line, then click **Paste**.

11. For the newly copied lines change the four occurrences of my_circle to **my_circle2**, then change the position to **250**, **250**, as shown in Figure 7.

12. Test the movie.

    Notice another object (my_circle2) is displayed.

13. Close the Flash Player window, save your work, close the Actions panel, then close the movie.

You used ActionScript 3.0 to change the properties of an object and create a second object.

Figure 7 *The code to create a second circle*

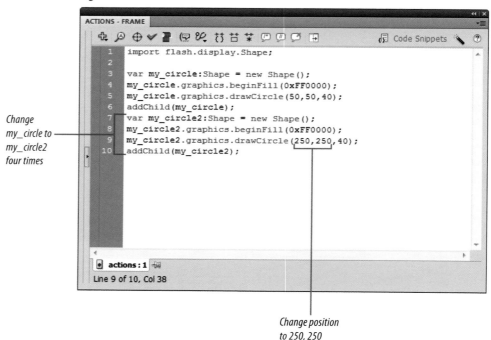

Change my_circle to my_circle2 four times

Change position to 250, 250

Figure 8 *The code to allow the Tween class to be used*

Your Actions panel may not display this line of code

Type these 2 lines

Insertion point initially placed before var

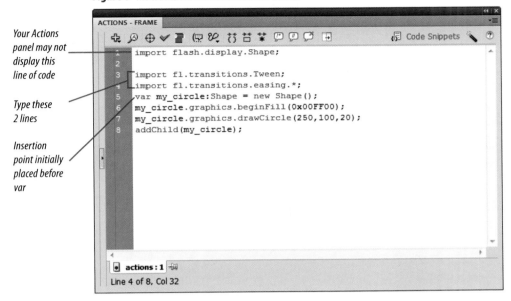

```
1    import flash.display.Shape;
2
3    import fl.transitions.Tween;
4    import fl.transitions.easing.*;
5    var my_circle:Shape = new Shape();
6    my_circle.graphics.beginFill(0x00FF00);
7    my_circle.graphics.drawCircle(250,100,20);
8    addChild(my_circle);
```

actions : 1
Line 4 of 8, Col 32

Figure 9 *The code to create the motion tween*

This line creates the motion tween

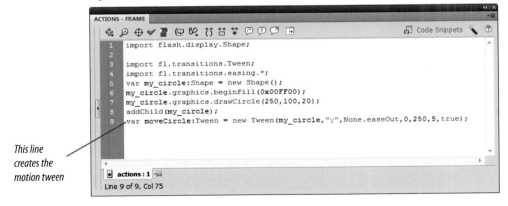

```
1    import flash.display.Shape;
2
3    import fl.transitions.Tween;
4    import fl.transitions.easing.*;
5    var my_circle:Shape = new Shape();
6    my_circle.graphics.beginFill(0x00FF00);
7    my_circle.graphics.drawCircle(250,100,20);
8    addChild(my_circle);
9    var moveCircle:Tween = new Tween(my_circle,"y",None.easeOut,0,250,5,true);
```

actions : 1
Line 9 of 9, Col 75

NEW **Use ActionScript 3.0 to create a motion tween**

1. Open CircleObject.fla, then save it as **CircleTween.fla**.
2. Change the view to Fit in Window.
3. Click **frame 1** on the actions layer, then display the Actions panel.

   Note: Pressing F9 (Win) or [option]+F9 (Mac) opens and closes the Actions panel.
4. Click before **var** on line 3 to position the insertion line at the beginning of that line.

   Note: if code is not automatically added to your Actions panel, then your line numbers will differ from those referenced in the text and shown in the figure. Your code needs to match the figure exactly but your line numbers do not.
5. Press **[Enter]** (Win) or **[return]** (Mac) to create a blank line.
6. Click the blank **line 3**, then type the following two lines as shown in Figure 8.

   import fl.transitions.Tween;
   import fl.transitions.easing.*;

   This code allows the Tween class to be used.
7. Click the end of the last line of code, then press **[Enter]** (Win) or **[return]** (Mac) to move to a blank line.
8. Type the following code on one line.

   var moveCircle:Tween = new Tween (my_circle,"y",None.easeOut,0,250, 5, true);

   Your Actions panel should match Figure 9.
9. Test the movie, then close the Flash Player window.
10. Change the seconds (5) to **2**.

(continued)

11. Test the movie, then close the Flash Player window.

12. Save your work, close the Actions panel, then close the document.

You used ActionScript to create a motion tween and changed the speed of the tween.

Use ActionScript to create user interactivity

1. Open fl9_2.fla, then save it as **CircleInteractive.fla**.

2. Change the view to Fit in Window.

This movie has three layers: border, button, and actions. The button was created with the Flash tools. The actions layer has code that animates a circle.

3. Test the movie, let the animation play, then click the **Play button**.

Notice there is no effect when the Play button is clicked.

4. Close the Flash Player window.

5. Click the **Play button** on the Stage, display the Properties panel, then notice the instance name is playBtn.

This instance name will be used in the code you develop.

6. Click **frame 1** on the actions layer, then display the Actions panel.

7. Click **line 5** in the Script pane, press **[Enter]** (Win) or **[return]** (Mac), then type the code shown in Figure 10.

This creates an event listener for a mouse click on the playBtn instance and names a function (in this case animateCircle) to be executed.

(continued)

Figure 10 *The code to create an event listener for a mouse click on the playBtn instance*

```
1   import flash.display.Shape;
2
3   import fl.transitions.Tween;
4   import fl.transitions.easing.*;
5
6   playBtn.addEventListener(MouseEvent.CLICK, animateCircle);
7   var my_circleNew:Shape = new Shape();
8   my_circleNew.graphics.beginFill(0xFF0000);
9   my_circleNew.graphics.drawCircle(50, 50, 40);
10  addChild(my_circleNew);
11  var moveCircle:Tween = new Tween(my_circleNew,"y",None.easeOut,0,300,2,true);
12
```

actions : 1

Line 6 of 12, Col 59

This line creates the event listener

Introduction to ActionScript 3.0

Figure 11 *The completed code*

```
ACTIONS - FRAME

1   import flash.display.Shape;
2
3   import fl.transitions.Tween;
4   import fl.transitions.easing.*;
5   import flash.events.MouseEvent;
6
7   playBtn.addEventListener(MouseEvent.CLICK, animateCircle);
8   function animateCircle(event:MouseEvent)
9   {
10  var my_circleNew:Shape = new Shape();
11  my_circleNew.graphics.beginFill(0xFF0000);
12  my_circleNew.graphics.drawCircle(50, 50, 40);
13  addChild(my_circleNew);
14  var moveCircle:Tween = new Tween(my_circleNew,"y",None.easeOut,0,300,2,true);
15  }

actions : 1
Line 15 of 15, Col 2
```

This statement may be added automatically as you type the code for a MouseEvent

8. Press **[Enter]** (Win) or **[return]** (Mac), then type the following.

   function animateCircle(event:MouseEvent)

   {

   These two lines of code begin the process of identifying the block of code included in the function, named animateCircle.

9. Click the blank line at the bottom of the code, then type **}**.

   This curly brace indicates the end of the function's block of code. Your screen should match Figure 11.

10. Test the movie, click the **Play button**, then notice the object appears and animates.

11. Click the **Play button** again, then notice another instance of the object appears and is animated.

   Each time the Play button is clicked the function is called and the code is executed.

12. Close the Flash Player window, save your work, close the Actions panel, then close the document.

You used ActionScript to add user interactivity to a button.

Work with Instances
OF MOVIE CLIP SYMBOLS

What You'll Do

In this lesson, you will use ActionScript to control instances of movie clip symbols.

Working with Movie Clips

Most large Flash documents include many movie clips. Using movie clips helps you manage your document by breaking complex tasks into smaller components, and using movie clips also lets you reuse content and reduce file size. Another advantage to movie clips is you can use actions with them, allowing you greater control over the objects on the Stage.

You can set the actions you associate with movie clips to run when a user performs an action, to run automatically when the movie plays, or to run when a condition is met, such as if the movie clip has been dropped on top of another movie clip. Some common uses of AS3 with movie clips include creating actions that run a specific frame within the movie clip's Timeline and making a movie clip draggable, so users can move it in games, to shopping carts, or in simulations.

> **QUICK TIP**
>
> The AS3 that you associate with movie clips will run only when you test, export, or publish your movie.

NEW Exporting a Movie Clip for Use in ActionScript

When a movie clip has been created and added to the Library panel it is not yet ready to be used with ActionScript. To keep the file size down, objects in the Library are not by default included in the swf file when the movie is published. Objects placed on the Stage are automatically included in a swf file. However, objects that are added at runtime, such as those created using ActionScript, need to be identified. This is done by turning on the Export for ActionScript feature found in the Symbol Properties dialog box. Figure 12 shows the process for exporting a movie clip, named PurpleShirt, for use in ActionScript. First, you open the Symbol Properties dialog box and check the Export for ActionScript check box in the Linkage area of the dialog box. A class is created that references the movie clip. You can specify a class name or accept the default name. This name appears in the Linkage column of the Library panel. The linkage name can be used to reference the movie clip in ActionScript.

For example, as shown below, a variable can be used to create an instance of a movie clip, then the addChild method can be used to have the instance appear on the screen when the movie is published.

var PurpleShirtInstance:PurpleShirtMC=
    new PurpleShirtMC();

var PurpleShirt:PurpleShirtMC

This creates a variable with the name PurpleShirtInstance and uses PurpleShirtMC as the data type, which in this case would be the movie clip data type. (*Note*: It is important to understand that PurpleShirtMC is a name you specify. Flash knows that it is a Movie Clip because it is linked with PurpleShirt which is a Movie Clip in the Library. So, Flash knows that PurpleShirtMC is a Movie Clip data type.)

= new PurpleShirtMC();

This creates a new instance of the PurpleShirt movie clip using the PurpleShirtMC linkage name.

QUICKTIP

To ensure that your ActionScript will run correctly, do not include spaces in movie clip symbol instance names.

Figure 12 *The process for exporting a movie clip for use in AS3*

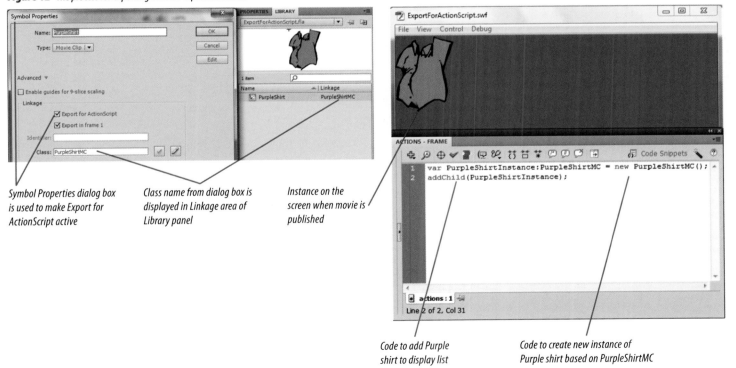

Symbol Properties dialog box is used to make Export for ActionScript active

Class name from dialog box is displayed in Linkage area of Library panel

Instance on the screen when movie is published

Code to add Purple shirt to display list

Code to create new instance of Purple shirt based on PurpleShirtMC

NEW Make movie clip instances so they can be referenced in ActionScript

1. Open fl9_3.fla, then save it as **shirts.fla**.

   This movie has five layers and one frame.

2. Test the movie, then click each of the buttons.

   None of the buttons are functional.

3. Close the Flash Player window.

4. Display the Library panel, then open the **shirt folder**.

5. Click each of the movie clips and view them in the Item Preview window.

   In the completed movie, when the user clicks a button, the appropriate movie clip (displaying a color or pattern) will appear on the shirt.

6. **Right-click** (Win) or **[control]-click** (Mac) **PurpleShirt** in the Library panel, then click **Properties**.

7. Click **Advanced** in the Symbol Properties dialog box to expand the box if it is not already expanded.

8. Click the **Export for ActionScript check box** if it is not already checked.

   Flash automatically inserts PurpleShirt for the Class name.

9. Change PurpleShirt to **PurpleShirtMC**, as shown in Figure 13, then click **OK**.

   A message appears indicating that Flash will create a definition for this class.

   (continued)

Figure 13 *Changing the class name*

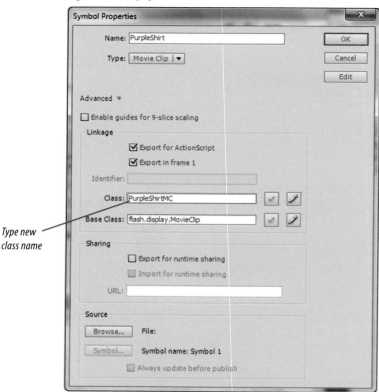

Type new class name

Figure 14 *Viewing the linkage name in the Library panel*

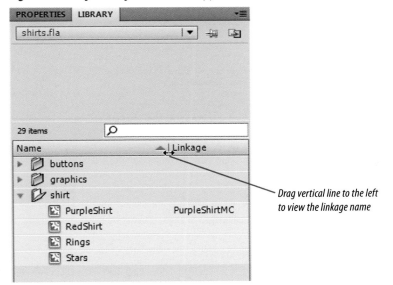

Drag vertical line to the left to view the linkage name

Figure 15 *The code for creating the four variables*

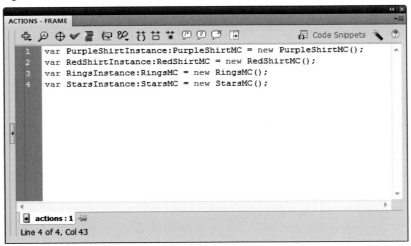

10. Click **OK**.

11. Drag the **vertical line** next to Linkage in the Library panel to the left to view the Linkage name, as shown in Figure 14.

12. Repeat steps 6-10 for the remaining three movie clips giving them class names of **RedShirtMC**, **RingsMC**, and **StarsMC**.

13. Insert a **new layer** at the top of the Timeline, then name it **actions**.

14. Click **frame 1** on the actions layer.

15. Open the **Actions panel**, then type the following code on one line.

    var PurpleShirtInstance:PurpleShirtMC = new PurpleShirtMC();

    This creates a variable named PurpleShirtInstance, sets the data type to PurpleShirtMC, and creates an instance of the object.

16. Type the code for the other three objects as shown in Figure 15.

17. Close the Actions panel.

18. Save your work.

You specified Export for ActionScript for movie clip symbols in the Symbols Properties dialog box, gave class names to each one, then created a variable and instance for each movie clip so the movie clips can be referenced in AS3 code.

NEW Add an event listener and function to a button instance

1. Click the **purple button** on the Stage to select it.

2. Display the Properties panel, then note the instance name of the button.

3. Click **frame 1** on the actions layer, open the Actions panel, verify the insertion point is at the end of the last line of code, press **[Enter]** (Win) or **[return]**(Mac) one time, then type the following on one line.

   purpleBtn.addEventListener(MouseEvent. CLICK, displayPurple);

   This adds an event listener to the button instance named purpleBtn. It also specifies the event as a mouse click event and defines a function, displayPurple, that will execute when the event occurs.

4. Press **[Enter](Win)** or **[return]**(Mac) to move the insertion point to the next blank line, then type the following on two lines.

   function displayPurple(event:MouseEvent) {

   These two lines of code begin the block of code for the function, displayPurple. Any code placed after the brace { will be part of the block of code that is executed when the purple button is clicked.

5. Press **[Enter]** (Win) or **[return]** (Mac) to move the insertion point to the next blank line, then type the following on one line.

   addChild(PurpleShirtInstance).x=125, (PurpleShirtInstance).y=93;

   (continued)

Figure 16 *The code for creating an event listener and function for a button*

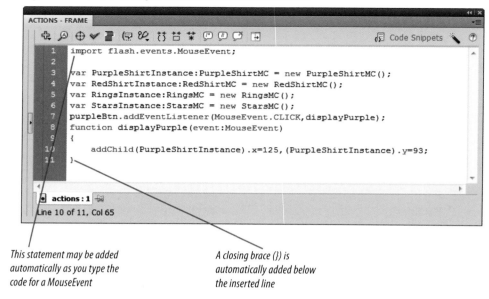

This statement may be added automatically as you type the code for a MouseEvent

A closing brace (}) is automatically added below the inserted line

Figure 17 *The completed code for all the buttons*

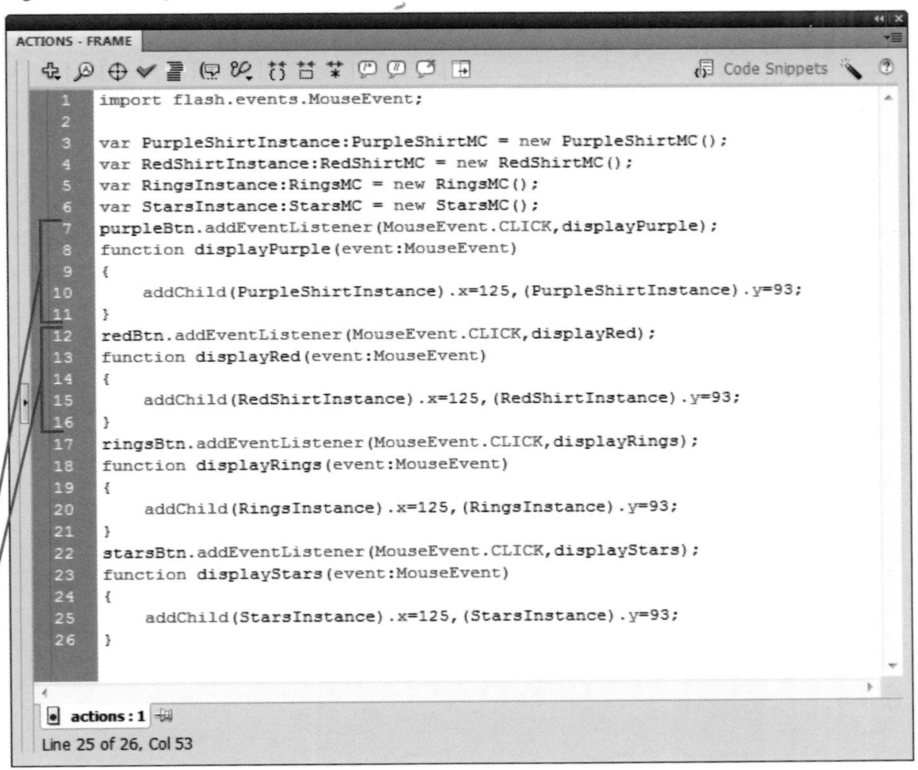

```
ACTIONS - FRAME

                                                          Code Snippets
 1   import flash.events.MouseEvent;
 2
 3   var PurpleShirtInstance:PurpleShirtMC = new PurpleShirtMC();
 4   var RedShirtInstance:RedShirtMC = new RedShirtMC();
 5   var RingsInstance:RingsMC = new RingsMC();
 6   var StarsInstance:StarsMC = new StarsMC();
 7   purpleBtn.addEventListener(MouseEvent.CLICK,displayPurple);
 8   function displayPurple(event:MouseEvent)
 9   {
10       addChild(PurpleShirtInstance).x=125,(PurpleShirtInstance).y=93;
11   }
12   redBtn.addEventListener(MouseEvent.CLICK,displayRed);
13   function displayRed(event:MouseEvent)
14   {
15       addChild(RedShirtInstance).x=125,(RedShirtInstance).y=93;
16   }
17   ringsBtn.addEventListener(MouseEvent.CLICK,displayRings);
18   function displayRings(event:MouseEvent)
19   {
20       addChild(RingsInstance).x=125,(RingsInstance).y=93;
21   }
22   starsBtn.addEventListener(MouseEvent.CLICK,displayStars);
23   function displayStars(event:MouseEvent)
24   {
25       addChild(StarsInstance).x=125,(StarsInstance).y=93;
26   }

  actions : 1
Line 25 of 26, Col 53
```

You can copy the AS3 code for the purpleBtn, paste it in the Script pane, and then replace information specific to the purpleBtn object with information specific to the another object, such as redBtn

This adds the PurpleShirtInstance to the display list and places an instance of the purple shirt at x and y coordinates 125 and 93, respectively.

6. Click the **Check syntax button** in the Script pane, then correct any errors.

7. Click the **Auto format button**, then compare your Script pane to Figure 16 on the previous page.

8. Test the movie, click the purple button, then close the Flash Player window.

9. Complete the code for the other buttons as shown in Figure 17.

10. Save your work.

You added event listeners and functions that display objects on the Stage.

NEW Change the visibility of objects

1. Test the movie, click the **Purple button**, then click the **Red button**.

   The red shirt covers the purple shirt.

2. Click the **Stars button**, then click the **Rings button**.

   The rings are placed on top of the stars. To have only one pattern appear at a time, you can change the visibility values for the instances.

3. Close the Flash Player window, then add the following below the addChild(RingsInstance) line and before the closing }, as shown in Figure 18.

   RingsInstance.visible = true;

   This code sets the visible property of the RingsInstance (rings pattern on the Stage) to true when the Rings button is clicked.

4. Add the following below the RingsInstance.visible=true; line and before the closing }.

   StarsInstance.visible = false;

   This code sets the visible property of the StarsInstance (star pattern on the Stage) to false when the Rings button is clicked.

5. Add the following below the addChild(StarsInstance) line.

   StarsInstance.visible = true;

   RingsInstance.visible = false;

   This code causes the stars to display and the rings to disappear when the Stars button is clicked.

   (continued)

Figure 18 *Setting the visibility for the RingsInstance to true*

```
17   ringsBtn.addEventListener(MouseEvent.CLICK,displayRings);
18   function displayRings(event:MouseEvent)
19   {
20       addChild(RingsInstance).x=125,(RingsInstance).y=93;
21       RingsInstance.visible = true;
22   }
23   starsBtn.addEventListener(MouseEvent.CLICK,displayStars);
24   function displayStars(event:MouseEvent)
25   {
26       addChild(StarsInstance).x=125,(StarsInstance).y=93;
27   }
```

Note: your line numbers may vary

Type this line to set the visibility for the object to true

Figure 19 *The complete code to set all the visibility values*

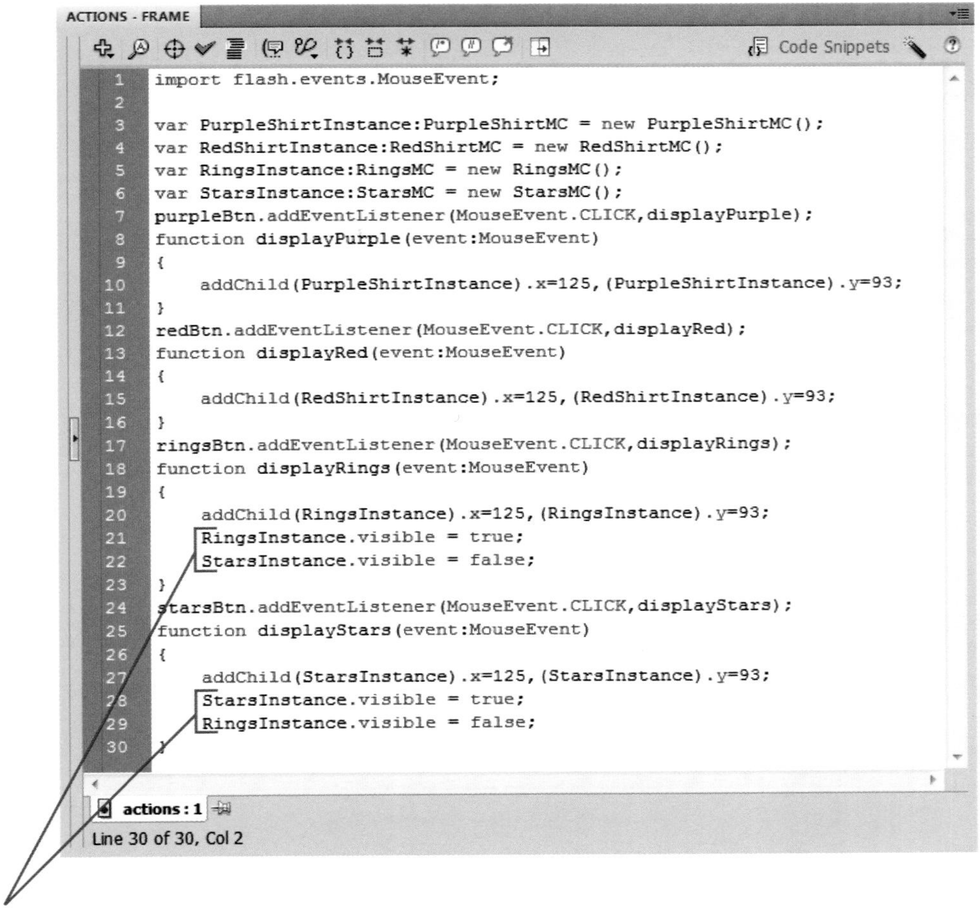

```
ACTIONS - FRAME

    ⊕ 🔎 ⊕ ✓ 彐 ⊡ ⅔ ⅃⅄ ⅄ ✱ ⊡ ⊡ ⊡ ⊡              🗐 Code Snippets  ✎ ⑦

1    import flash.events.MouseEvent;
2
3    var PurpleShirtInstance:PurpleShirtMC = new PurpleShirtMC();
4    var RedShirtInstance:RedShirtMC = new RedShirtMC();
5    var RingsInstance:RingsMC = new RingsMC();
6    var StarsInstance:StarsMC = new StarsMC();
7    purpleBtn.addEventListener(MouseEvent.CLICK,displayPurple);
8    function displayPurple(event:MouseEvent)
9    {
10        addChild(PurpleShirtInstance).x=125,(PurpleShirtInstance).y=93;
11   }
12   redBtn.addEventListener(MouseEvent.CLICK,displayRed);
13   function displayRed(event:MouseEvent)
14   {
15        addChild(RedShirtInstance).x=125,(RedShirtInstance).y=93;
16   }
17   ringsBtn.addEventListener(MouseEvent.CLICK,displayRings);
18   function displayRings(event:MouseEvent)
19   {
20        addChild(RingsInstance).x=125,(RingsInstance).y=93;
21        RingsInstance.visible = true;
22        StarsInstance.visible = false;
23   }
24   starsBtn.addEventListener(MouseEvent.CLICK,displayStars);
25   function displayStars(event:MouseEvent)
26   {
27        addChild(StarsInstance).x=125,(StarsInstance).y=93;
28        StarsInstance.visible = true;
29        RingsInstance.visible = false;
30   }

  ◀ actions : 1 ⊞
  Line 30 of 30, Col 2
```

Code to set
visibility values

6. Click the **Check syntax button** ✓ in the Script pane, then correct any errors.

7. Click the **Auto format button** 彐 , then compare your Script pane to Figure 19.

8. Test the movie, then click each button several times.

9. Close the Flash Player window, then close the Actions panel.

10. Save your work, then close the document.

You used ActionScript to set the visibility values of objects.

Use
CODE SNIPPETS

What You'll Do

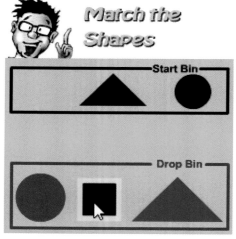

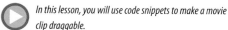

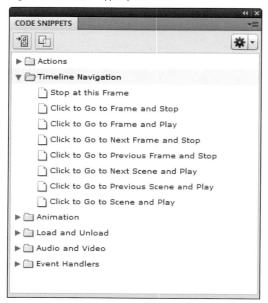

In this lesson, you will use code snippets to make a movie clip draggable.

NEW Working with Code Snippets

In previous chapters, you used AS2 and Script Assist to enter predefined code in the Scripts pane. AS3 allows you to enter predefined blocks of AS3 code called code snippets, which provide a quick way to insert AS3 code into the Script pane.

Figure 20 shows the Code Snippets panel with the list of categories and the Timeline Navigation category expanded to show the code snippets available in that category. Figure 21 shows the "Click to Go to Frame and Play" code snippet in the Script pane. The code begins with several comment lines

Figure 20 *The Code Snippets panel*

that are grayed out. These are instructions that guide you through the use of the code. The code starts in line 11 with an add mouse click event listener for a button instance named startBtn followed by a function named, fl_ClickToGoToAndPlayFromFrame. This is a generic function name that you can change to be more descriptive of what is happening in the function. Line 13 identifies the start of the function and line 15 has the code that is executed when the user clicks the startBtn. The instructions indicate that you replace the number 5 with the frame number you would like the playhead to move to when the symbol instance (startBtn) is clicked. The process for using this code snippet follows.

- Create a button symbol and give it an instance name.
- Select the button instance on the Stage. (*Note*: Even though you select the button on the Stage, the AS3 code will be placed in a frame on a layer named actions (or Actions), not in a frame containing the button. If there is no layer named actions or Actions, Flash will create one and name it Actions.)

- Open the Code Snippets panel and click the desired snippet to enter that code in the Script pane.
- Edit the code as needed, such as changing the function name and editing the actions you want executed. For instance, you can change the frame number that the function should go to and play when the code is executed.

Think of code snippets as templates that allow you to make changes to customize the code. These could be changes in function names, frame numbers, or properties such as ease values.

Figure 21 *The Script pane after adding a code snippet*

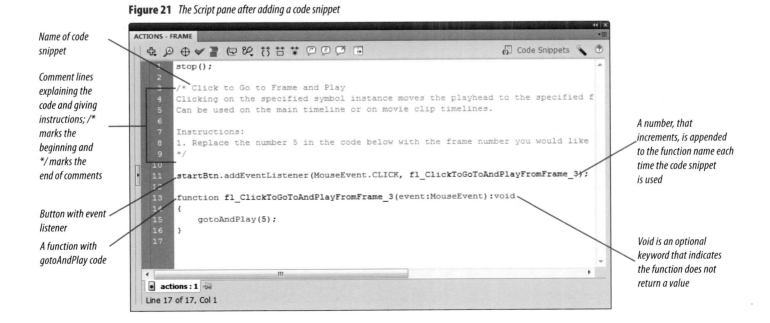

Name of code snippet

Comment lines explaining the code and giving instructions; /* marks the beginning and */ marks the end of comments

Button with event listener

A function with gotoAndPlay code

A number, that increments, is appended to the function name each time the code snippet is used

Void is an optional keyword that indicates the function does not return a value

NEW Adding Comments to Your AS3 Code

As you write more and more code, it becomes useful to provide comments, like those shown in Figure 21, to help clarify what is happening in a particular section of code. Comments can be inserted easily using the Apply block comment button or Apply line comment button on the Actions menu bar. You can also add a comment to your ActionScript code by typing a slash and an asterisk (/*) at the beginning and an asterisk and a slash (*/) at the end of one or more lines of text. Any code between this set of symbols is treated as a comment and it is ignored when the ActionScript code runs. Alternately, if your comment is only a single line, you can place two slashes (//) at the beginning of the line, and that line will be ignored when the ActionScript runs. Comments appear in the Script pane as gray text, and they are not part of the executable code.

Understanding Interactive Movie Clips

Using AS3 with movie clip symbols offers many opportunities for creating a richer user experience. With the startDrag and stopDrag actions, you can make a movie clip draggable while a movie is playing; that is, you can allow a user to click the movie clip and then move it to another location on the screen. You have probably seen draggable movie clips in games created with Flash, as shown in Figure 22, or in user interface features such as scroll bars and sliders in web applications created with Flash.

AS3 code can also change the properties of movie clip symbols as a movie is playing. You can control such properties as position, rotation, color, size, and whether the movie clip is visible or hidden. Actions that change movie clip properties are often used in combination with actions that test for user input or interactions. For example, you can create ActionScript that makes a movie clip disappear when it is dragged onto another movie clip.

QUICK TIP

As you work through this lesson, you will be opening the Actions and Code Snippets panels and viewing objects on the Stage. If your workspace gets cluttered, you can move, collapse, and resize panels as needed to work more efficiently. If the workspace becomes confusing you can click the ESSENTIALS button above the menu bar and choose Reset 'Essentials'.

Figure 22 *Draggable movie clips in a Flash game*

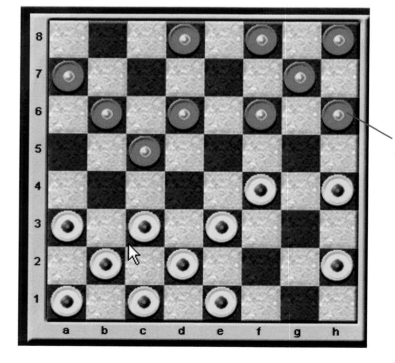

Each checker is a movie clip symbol, which you can drag to a square

Introduction to ActionScript 3.0

Figure 23 *Changing the goto frame number in a code snippet*

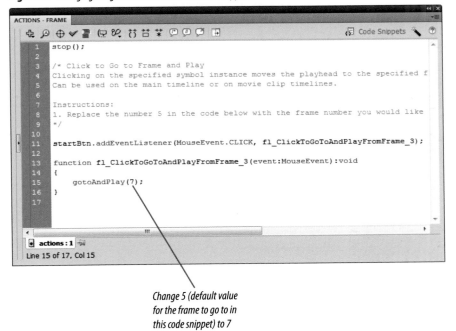

```
ACTIONS - FRAME

 1   stop();
 2
 3   /* Click to Go to Frame and Play
 4   Clicking on the specified symbol instance moves the playhead to the specified f
 5   Can be used on the main timeline or on movie clip timelines.
 6
 7   Instructions:
 8   1. Replace the number 5 in the code below with the frame number you would like
 9   */
10
11   startBtn.addEventListener(MouseEvent.CLICK, fl_ClickToGoToAndPlayFromFrame_3);
12
13   function fl_ClickToGoToAndPlayFromFrame_3(event:MouseEvent):void
14   {
15       gotoAndPlay(7);
16   }
17

  actions : 1
Line 15 of 17, Col 15
```

Change 5 (default value for the frame to go to in this code snippet) to 7

NEW Use code snippets to make a button interactive

1. Open fl9_4.fla, then save it as **shapes.fla**.

2. Drag the **playhead** through the Timeline.

   This movie contains two screens. The first screen has a button that when clicked will jump the playhead to the second screen.

3. Click **frame 1** on the actions layer, then open the Actions panel.

4. Click **Code Snippets** on the Actions panel menu bar.

5. Click the **Timeline Navigation expand arrow** ▶ to display the options.

6. Arrange the Actions and Code Snippets panels so that the Start button is visible on the Stage.

7. Click the **Start button** to select it.

   Note: You select the Start button so that Flash knows what object to apply the code snippet code to.

8. Display the Properties panel, then type **startBtn** for the instance name.

9. Verify the Start button is selected on the Stage, then double-click **Click to Go to Frame and Play** in the Code Snippets panel.

10. Drag the **Actions panel** to the center of the screen and resize it to display the code.

11. Click inside the Script pane to remove the highlighting, select **5** in the code, then type **7** for the frame to go to, as shown in Figure 23.

12. Test the movie, click the **Start button**, close the Flash Player window, then save your work.

You used code snippets to add interactivity to a button.

NEW Use code snippets to enter code into the Script pane

1. Collapse the Code Snippets and the Actions panels.

2. Click **frame 7** on the Timeline to display the next screen, then click the **black square** in the Start Bin.

3. Display the Properties panel, then type **square** for the instance name.

4. Click **frame 7** on the actions layer.

5. Expand the Code Snippets panel, then click the **Actions list arrow** ▶ .

   The Actions area of the Code Snippets panel is expanded, as shown in Figure 24.

6. Click the **black square** on the Stage.

7. Double-click **Drag and Drop** in the Code Snippets panel.

(continued)

Figure 24 *Actions area in the Code Snippet panel expanded*

Figure 25 *The code snippet displayed in the Actions panel*

```
ACTIONS - FRAME                                              Code Snippets

1  stop();
2
3  /* Drag and Drop
4  Makes the specified symbol instance moveable with drag and drop.
5  */
6
7  square.addEventListener(MouseEvent.MOUSE_DOWN, fl_ClickToDrag_2);
8
9  function fl_ClickToDrag_2(event:MouseEvent):void
10 {
11     square.startDrag();
12 }
13
14 stage.addEventListener(MouseEvent.MOUSE_UP, fl_ReleaseToDrop_2);
15
16 function fl_ReleaseToDrop_2(event:MouseEvent):void
17 {
18     square.stopDrag();
19 }
20

  actions : 7
Line 20 of 20, Col 1
```

8. Click inside the Script pane to remove the highlight, then read the comments and code, as shown in Figure 25.

Line 7 of the code adds a mouse down event listener for the square instance and defines a function named fl_ClickToDrag_2 (*Note*: The 2 may vary).

Lines 9–12 of the code identify the function so that when the mouse pointer is over the square and the mouse button is pressed, the square will be moveable.

Line 14 of the code adds a mouse up event listener to the Stage. That is, when the mouse pointer is on the Stage and the mouse button is released, Flash will recognize it as a mouse up event.

Lines 16–19 of the code identify the function so that when the mouse button is released, the square will not be moveable.

9. Test the movie, then click the **Start button**.

10. Drag the **black square** in the Start Bin to on top of the yellow square in the Drop Bin, then release the mouse button.

11. Close the Flash Player Window, then close the Actions and Code Snippets panels.

12. Save your work, then close the document.

You used code snippets to add interactivity to a movie and to enable an object to be draggable.

Work WITH VARIABLES

What You'll Do

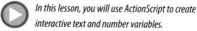
In this lesson, you will use ActionScript to create interactive text and number variables.

Understanding Variables

A **variable** is a container that holds information. Variables are dynamic; that is, the information they contain changes depending on an action a user takes or another aspect of how the movie plays. For example, a variable would be used in a Flash game that keeps track of scores or in a form in which a user enters credit card information while making an online purchase.

You create variables in ActionScript with the **var** keyword. You have to specify a name and a data type for the variable when you create it. It is good practice to give the variable an initial value so you can keep track of how it changes as you use it in expressions. To create a **string variable**, which is a sequence of characters including letters, numbers, and punctuation, place quotation marks around the string. For example, the ActionScript statement var myExam:String = "Pop Quiz"; creates a variable named myExam, with a data type called String, and assigns the string Pop Quiz to it. To create a **number variable**, just write the number. For example,

var myScore:Number = 93;
creates a number variable named myScore

and assigns the number 93 to it. No quotation marks are needed around a value assigned to a number variable.

Flash includes the following data types for variables including: String, Number, Boolean, Object, and MovieClip. See the Flash Help system for a full explanation of each type.

> **QUICK TIP**
>
> To ensure your ActionScript will run correctly, do not include spaces in variable names.

Using Text Fields to Collect User Information

One of the most powerful uses of variables is to collect and work with information from users. To do this, you create input text fields to collect the data and dynamic text fields to display the data. You can manipulate variables using ActionScript before displaying them in the dynamic text field (for example, adding a greeting with a person's name), using the instance name.

An **input text field** takes information entered by a user and stores it as a variable. To create an input box, you select the Text tool, open the Properties panel, and change the text type to Input, as shown in Figure 26. You can also set properties, such as font family and style, whether the input text box appears with a border, and the maximum number of characters allotted for user input. Then, you use the Text tool to draw the box on the Stage and assign an instance name to it.

A **dynamic text field** displays information derived from variables. A dynamic text field can be used together with an input text box. For example, you could have a user enter his/her name into an input text field in one part of a movie and have the name displayed in a dynamic text box in another part of the movie. You create a dynamic text box the same way you create an input text box by using the Text tool and Properties panel, where you select Dynamic Text as the text type.

Text input fields work with string data. If you want the user to input numbers so calculations can be performed, you must convert the string data type to a number data type. For example, you could have an input text box with an instance name of inputAge where the user types in her age. The following code could be used to change the data that the user types from text to a number.

```
var age:Number = Number(inputAge.text);
```

In the code, a variable named age is created with the Number data type. Then, the data

from the inputAge text box is converted to a number and assigned to the variable age. This process of changing one data type to another is called **casting**.

NEW Embedding Fonts

When you include input text fields in your Flash movie you need to embed the font so that it is available to the users no matter what fonts they have on their computer.

Embedding the font ensures the text maintains the appearance you desire. The process for embedding fonts is to click the Embed button in the Character area of the Properties panel. This displays the Font Embedding dialog box that you use to specify which font(s) and characters to embed. A font file is created that accompanies the swf file when the Flash document is published.

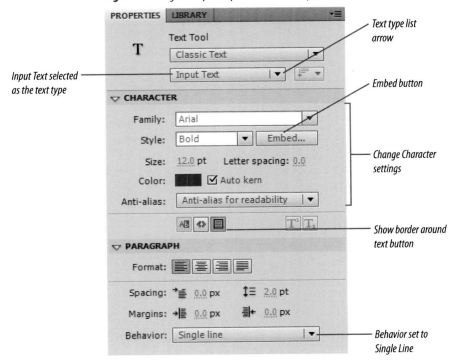

Figure 26 *Using the Properties panel to create an input text field*

NEW Understanding Expressions

Expressions are formulas for manipulating or evaluating the information in variables. This can range from string expressions that concatenate (join together) user and system-derived text (as in a paragraph that inserts a user's name right in the text) to numeric expressions that perform mathematical calculations like addition, subtraction, or incrementing a value. Flash also lets you enter logical expressions that perform true/false comparisons on numbers and strings, with which you can create conditional statements and branching.

Note that some expressions have different results depending on whether they are performed on string or number variables. For example, the comparison operators >, >=, <, and <= determine alphabetical order when used with string variables, and the mathematical operator + concatenates strings. In addition, the equal sign is used to test whether or not two values are identical.

Figure 27 shows an expression in which the value of one variable (num1) is added to the value of another variable (num2) and the result is assigned to a third variable (total). The code defines the addTotal function that is executed when the plusBtn object is clicked.

Figure 27 *Example of an expression used for a calculation*

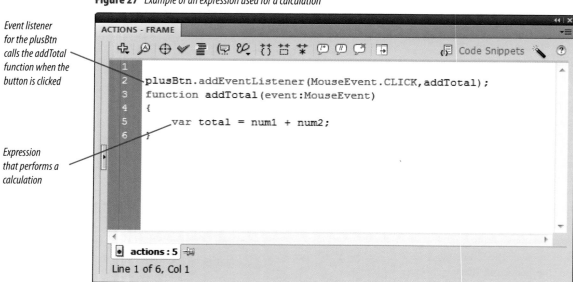

Event listener for the plusBtn calls the addTotal function when the button is clicked

Expression that performs a calculation

```
plusBtn.addEventListener(MouseEvent.CLICK,addTotal);
function addTotal(event:MouseEvent)
{
    var total = num1 + num2;
}
```

Figure 28 *Drawing the text box for the input text field*

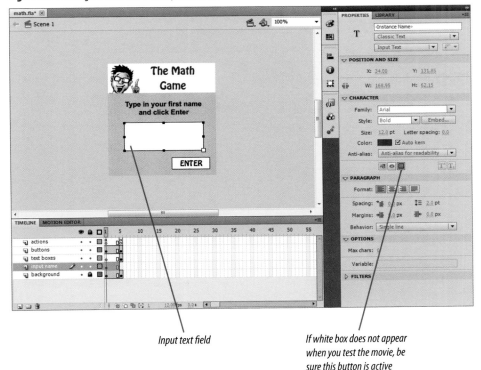

Input text field

If white box does not appear
when you test the movie, be
sure this button is active

Create an input text box

1. Open fl9_5.fla, then save it as **math.fla**.
2. Drag the **playhead** through the Timeline.

   This movie has two screens, an introduction that allows you to type in a name, and a calculations screen to enter numbers and perform calculations.
3. Click **frame 1** on the input name layer, then click the **Text tool** T on the Tools panel.
4. Verify the Properties panel is displayed, verify Classic Text is displayed, click the **Text type list arrow**, then click **Input Text**.
5. Make the following changes: Family: **Arial**; Style: **Bold**; Size: **18**; Color: #990000, click the **Show border around text button** to turn it on, set the alignment to Align Left , then verify the Behavior is set to Single line.

   Note: If the Properties panel does not display the CHARACTER area, click the pasteboard, make the changes above, then delete the text box on the pasteboard.
6. Draw a **text box** as shown in Figure 28.

   TIP Use the pointer to move the box. Use the handles to resize the box.

7. Verify the text box is selected on the Stage, then use the Properties panel to enter **inputNameBox** as the instance name.
8. Test the movie.

   A white input text box appears on the screen. In addition, a message appears in the Output panel indicating that fonts should be embedded.
9. Try to type **Jesse** into the input name box.

   (continued)

The letters do not appear because the font is not available at runtime.

10. Close the Flash Player window.

You created an input text box in which users can type their name. You also specified the formatting for the input text.

NEW Embed fonts for use with input text fields

1. Click the **Selection tool** on the Tools panel, then click the **input text box** on the Stage to select it.

   Note: If you cannot select the input text box, click the Pasteboard, and then click the input text box.

2. Verify the Properties panel is displayed, then note the **font** that appears in the Character area.

3. Click the **Embed button** in the Character area.

   The Font Embedding dialog box appears with the name of font that was specified for the input text box.

4. Click **Uppercase**, **Lowercase**, **Numerals**, and **Punctuation** in the Character ranges area to select them.

5. Click the **Add new font button** ➕.

   A font name that represents the selected font character ranges is created and added to the Font list automatically, as shown in Figure 29.

6. Click **OK** to close the dialog box.

7. Test the movie, type **Jesse** in the input box, then click the **Enter button**.

8. Close the Flash Player window.

9. Save your work.

You embedded fonts for an input text box.

Figure 29 *Selecting the font character ranges in the Font Embedding dialog box*

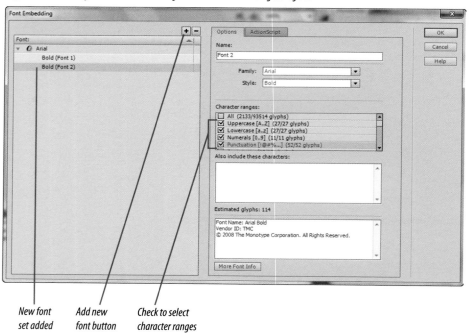

New font set added   Add new font button   Check to select character ranges

Figure 30 *Drawing the text box for the dynamic text field*

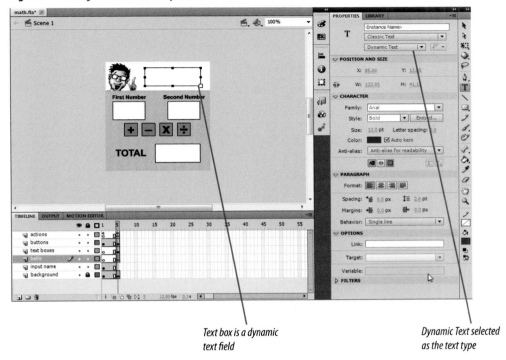

Text box is a dynamic
text field

Dynamic Text selected
as the text type

Create a dynamic text box

1. Click the **Selection tool** ⬆ on the Tools panel, then click the **TIMELINE tab** to display the Timeline.

2. Insert a **new layer** above the input name layer, then name it **hello**.

3. Insert a **keyframe** in frame 5 of the hello layer.

4. Click the **Text tool** T on the Tools panel, then use the Properties panel to change the text type to **Dynamic Text**.

5. Click the white area next to the character's head, and then use the Selection tool ⬆ to move or resize the box as necessary so it matches Figure 30.

6. Verify the text box is selected.

7. Use the Properties panel to enter **myWelcome** as the instance name.

8. Save your work.

You created a dynamic text box to hold the name the user enters.

Use ActionScript to collect and modify string variables

1. Click **frame 1** on the actions layer, then display the Actions panel.

2. Click after the **;** in stop();, press **[Enter]**(Win) or **[return]**(Mac) to insert a blank line, then type:

   var myName:String = "";

   This defines a variable named myName with a String (text) Data Type. This variable will be used to hold the name typed into the inputText box. The "" gives the variable an initial value of null (that is, an empty container).

3. Click before the **g** in the goto line within the function, press **[Enter]**(Win) or **[return]**(Mac) to insert a blank line, press **[↑]**, then type:

   myName = inputNameBox.text;

   This takes the text that is typed in the input text box and assigns it to the myName variable.

4. Verify your Script pane matches Figure 31.

5. Click **frame 5** on the actions layer.

6. Expand the Actions panel, type the following below the stop(); line.

   myWelcome.text = "Hello, " + myName;

   This statement takes the value in the myName variable and concatenates it with Hello, . So, when the user clicks the Enter button, this ActionScript takes the name the user has entered in the myName input field, prefaces it with the word "Hello, " then displays the text string in the myWelcome dynamic text box.

7. Click the **Check syntax button** ✔ in the Script pane.

   (continued)

Figure 31 *The script pane showing the code that collects the data from the input field*

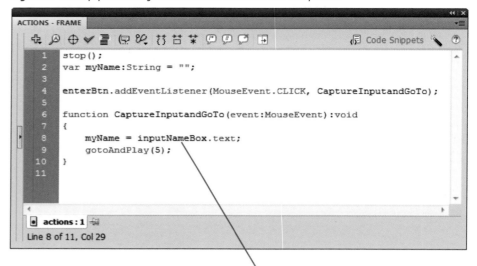

Data typed into the inputNameBox (which is an input text field) is assigned to the myName variable (which is a string variable)

Figure 32 *The completed code to have the input text appear in the dynamic text box*

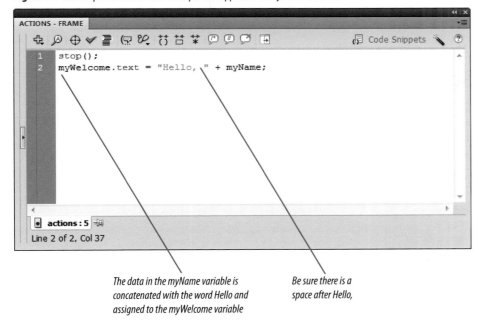

```
ACTIONS - FRAME

1   stop();
2   myWelcome.text = "Hello, " + myName;
```

Code Snippets

actions : 5
Line 2 of 2, Col 37

The data in the myName variable is concatenated with the word Hello and assigned to the myWelcome variable

Be sure there is a space after Hello,

If there are errors in the code, check your code and be sure it matches the code in Figure 32.

8. Click the **Auto format button** ≡ in the Script pane.

9. Test the movie, click the **name input field**, type **Jesse**, then click the **Enter button**.

   The name "Jesse" appears in the dynamic text field, prefaced by "Hello, ".

10. Close the Flash Player window, close the Actions panel, then save your work.

You used ActionScript to modify a text variable and place it in a dynamic text box.

Use ActionScript to perform a mathematical operation on a numeric variable

1. Verify the calculation screen is displayed.

   This screen already contains two input text boxes (First Number and Second Number) and a dynamic text box (Total).

2. Click the **Selection tool** ▸ , click the **Input text box** below First Number, then give it an instance name of **firstNum**.

3. Click the **Input text box** below Second Number, then give it an instance name of **secondNum**.

4. Click the **Dynamic text box** next to Total, then give it an instance name of **totalAmt**.

5. Click the **plus button**, then give it an instance name of **plusBtn**.

6. Click **frame 5** of the actions layer, open the Actions panel, then type the code that follows on one line below the myWelcome line.

(continued)

plusBtn.addEventListener(MouseEvent. CLICK, addTotal);

This adds a mouse click event listener to the plusBtn instance and creates a function named addTotal.

7. Type the remaining lines of code shown Figure 33 below the plusBtn line.

This code defines the block of code for the addTotal function that is called when the user clicks the plusBtn button. The first two lines of code inside the curly braces take the input typed by the user in the First Number and Second Number input text boxes and assigns them to number variables. The third line adds the two numeric variables and assigns the result to a variable named total. The last line assigns the value in the total variable to the totalAmt text field (the instance name for the dynamic text field) and displays it in the Total text box.

8. Test the movie, type a **name**, then click the **Enter button**.

9. Type a **number** into the First Number box, type a **number** into the Second Number box, then click the **plus button**.

10. Close the Flash Player window, then save your work.

You used ActionScript to create a mathematical operation that works with variables.

Copy ActionScript code

1. Click the **Selection tool** on the Tools panel, click the **minus button** on the Stage to select it, verify the Properties panel is displayed, then type **minusBtn** for the instance name.

(continued)

Figure 33 *The completed code to perform a calculation on input data*

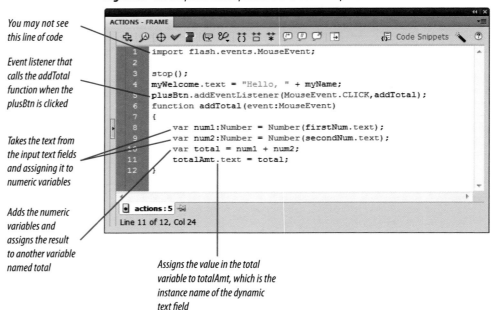

You may not see this line of code

Event listener that calls the addTotal function when the plusBtn is clicked

Takes the text from the input text fields and assigning it to numeric variables

Adds the numeric variables and assigns the result to another variable named total

Assigns the value in the total variable to totalAmt, which is the instance name of the dynamic text field

```
import flash.events.MouseEvent;

stop();
myWelcome.text = "Hello, " + myName;
plusBtn.addEventListener(MouseEvent.CLICK,addTotal);
function addTotal(event:MouseEvent)
{
    var num1:Number = Number(firstNum.text);
    var num2:Number = Number(secondNum.text);
    var total = num1 + num2;
    totalAmt.text = total;
}
```

actions : 5
Line 11 of 12, Col 24

Figure 34 *Highlighting the code*

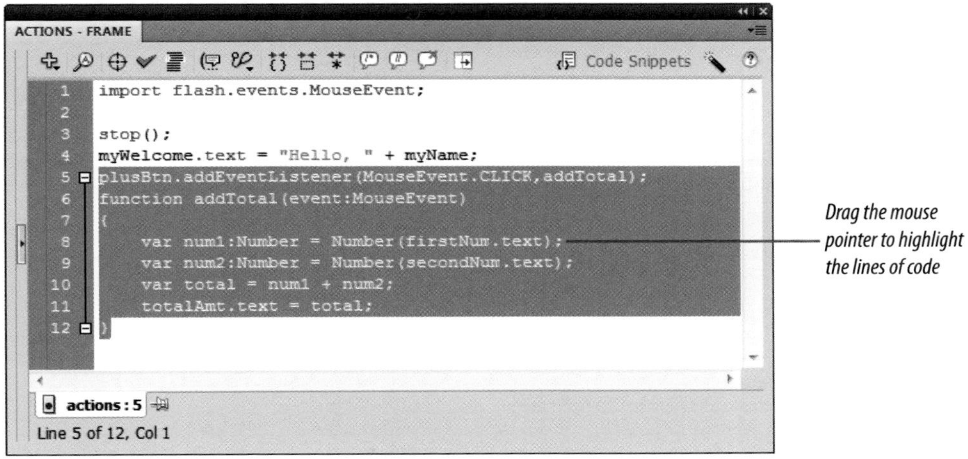

```
ACTIONS - FRAME

                                                            Code Snippets

   1    import flash.events.MouseEvent;
   2
   3    stop();
   4    myWelcome.text = "Hello, " + myName;
   5    plusBtn.addEventListener(MouseEvent.CLICK,addTotal);
   6    function addTotal(event:MouseEvent)
   7    {
   8        var num1:Number = Number(firstNum.text);
   9        var num2:Number = Number(secondNum.text);
  10        var total = num1 + num2;
  11        totalAmt.text = total;
  12    }

  actions : 5
  Line 5 of 12, Col 1
```

Drag the mouse pointer to highlight the lines of code

Figure 35 *The completed ActionScript to perform the mathematical calculations*

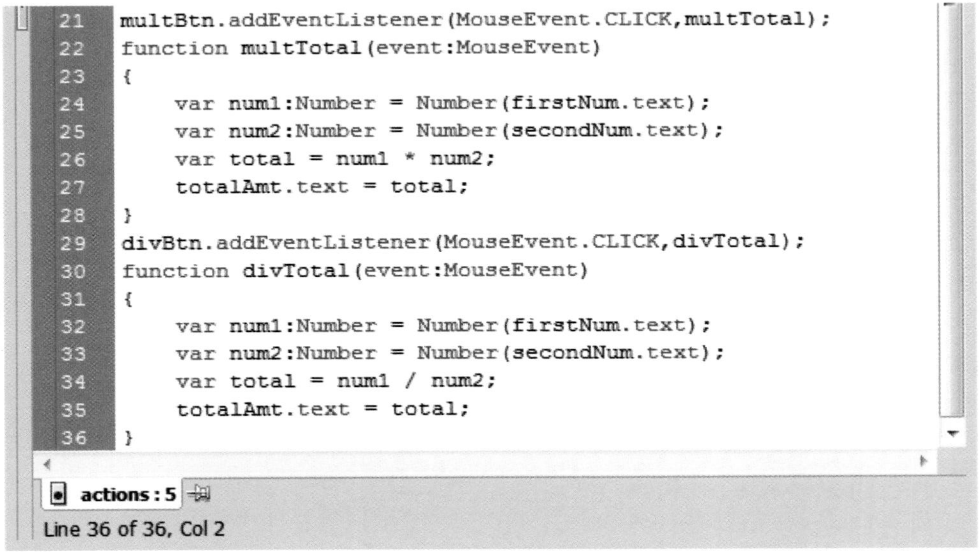

```
  21    multBtn.addEventListener(MouseEvent.CLICK,multTotal);
  22    function multTotal(event:MouseEvent)
  23    {
  24        var num1:Number = Number(firstNum.text);
  25        var num2:Number = Number(secondNum.text);
  26        var total = num1 * num2;
  27        totalAmt.text = total;
  28    }
  29    divBtn.addEventListener(MouseEvent.CLICK,divTotal);
  30    function divTotal(event:MouseEvent)
  31    {
  32        var num1:Number = Number(firstNum.text);
  33        var num2:Number = Number(secondNum.text);
  34        var total = num1 / num2;
  35        totalAmt.text = total;
  36    }

  actions : 5
  Line 36 of 36, Col 2
```

2. Click **frame 5** on the actions layer, then display the Actions panel.

3. Drag the **mouse pointer** to highlight the plusBtn line and the function lines as shown in Figure 34.

4. **Right-click** (Win) or **[control]-click** (Mac) the highlighted text, then click **Copy**.

5. Click at the end of the code, press **[Enter]** (Win) or **[return]**(Mac) to insert a blank line below the code, then **right-click** (Win) or **[control]-click** (Mac) and click **Paste**.

6. Change **plusBtn** to **minusBtn**, change **addTotal** to **subtTotal** for both instances of addTotal, then change + to −.

   This creates a new mouse click event listener for the minus button and changes the function to subtract the numbers typed into the input boxes.

7. Test the movie, enter **two numbers**, then click the **minus button**.

8. Close the Flash Player window.

9. Repeat Steps 1 – 6 for the multiplication and division buttons using **multBtn** and **divBtn** for the instance names; **multTotal** and **divTotal** for the function names; an asterisk (*) for the multiplication operator; and a slash (/) for the division operator.

10. Compare your screen to Figure 35.

11. Test the movie, type in various numbers and test all of the buttons, then close the Flash Player window.

12. Close the Actions panel, save your work, then close the document.

Your copied ActionScript code from one object to another and made changes to the code.

Use ActionScript to create an object and change its properties.

(*Hint*: Use the Check syntax and Auto format features when typing ActionScript code.)

1. Start Flash, open a new ActionScript 3.0 document, then save it as **skillsDemo9-object.fla**.
2. Rename Layer1 **actions**.
3. Display the Actions panel.
4. Type the code to create a rectangle using the variable name **myRectangle** with a **Shape** data type, a **000099** fill, positioned at **100** pixels for the x and y coordinates, and with a width of **50** pixels and a height of **80** pixels (*Note*: The code for drawing a rectangle is drawRect (x-coordinate, y-coordinate, width, height). Then type the code to add the object to the display list.
5. Check the syntax and format the code.
6. Test the movie, then close the Flash Player window.
7. Change the rectangle color to **660000** and the x position to **50**.
8. Test the movie, close the Flash Player window, then change the x position to **100**.
9. Test the movie to verify your change, close the Flash Player window, then save your work.

Use ActionScript to create a motion tween and user interactivity.

1. Add the code to import the tween and easing classes.
2. Add the code to create a variable named **animateRectangle** with a **Tween** data type, create an instance of the myRectangle object, then specify an x movement, with no ease, of **300** pixels in **3** seconds.
3. Test the movie, then close the Flash Player.

4. Click frame 1 of the actions layer, then type a stop action at the top of the Actions panel.
5. Insert a new layer, then name it **button**.
6. Click frame 1 of the button layer, then create a button on the Stage and give it an instance name of **playBtn**.
7. Click frame 1 of the actions layer, display the Actions panel, then type the code above the existing line of code that begins var myRectangle . . . and that will add a mouse click event listener to the button and define a function.
8. Type the code to create the function that will animate the object. (*Hint*: Move the code that defines the variable and the tween code to within the curly braces of the function.)
9. Check the syntax and format the code.
10. Close the Actions panel.
11. Test the movie, then click the button.
12. Close the Flash Player window, save your work then close the document.

Add an event listener and function to a button instance.

1. Open fl9_6.fla, then save it as **skillsDemo9-seasons.fla**.
2. Scrub the playhead to look at all the frames in the movie. This movie has two screens, which are displayed in frames 1 and 6. There are stop actions in frames 1 and 6.
3. Click the Start button on the Stage and give it an instance name of **startBtn**.
4. Click frame 1 on the actions layer, then open the Actions panel.
5. Type the code for an event listener to the startBtn object that will execute a function (you specify

the function name, such as playSeason) when the startBtn object is clicked.
6. Type the code for the function that will cause the playhead to go to and play frame 6.
7. Check the syntax and format the code.
8. Test the movie and click the Start button.
9. Close the Flash Player window, then save your work.

Add Code to make a button interactive.

1. Click frame 6 on the Timeline.
2. Click the Restart button on the Stage and give it an instance name of **restartBtn**.
3. Click frame 6 on the actions layer.
4. Add code for an event listener to the restartBtn object that will execute a function (you specify the function name) when the restartBtn object is clicked.
5. Add code for the function that will cause the playhead to go to and play frame 1.
6. Check the syntax and format the code.
7. Test the movie, click the Start button, then click the Restart button.
8. Close the Flash Player window, then save your work.

Use code snippets to enter code into the script pane.

1. Click the scarf on the Stage to select it, then give it an instance name of **scarfDrag**.
2. Open the Code Snippets panel, then expand the Actions folder.
3. Verify the scarf is selected on the Stage, then double-click the Drag and Drop code snippet in the Actions folder.
4. Close the Code Snippets panel.
5. View the code in the Actions panel.

6. Change stage to **scarfDrag** for the mouse up event listener. (*Hint*: This will prevent a click anywhere on the Stage from executing the function.)
7. Test the movie, click the Start button, then drag and drop the scarf under one of the pictures. (*Note*: For this test of the movie, you are simply testing the drag and drop functionality of the scarf.)
8. Close the Flash Player window, then close the Actions panel.
9. Save your work.

Make movie clip instances able to be referenced with ActionScript.

1. Open the Library panel, then open the movieclips folder.
2. Right-click (Win) or [control]-click (Mac) winterScene, then click Properties.
3. Display the Advanced area of the Symbol Properties dialog box, check Export for ActionScript, change the class name to **winterSceneMC**, then click OK twice.
4. Click frame 6 on the actions layer, then open the Actions panel.
5. Add code on a blank line after the closing brace for the gotoAndPlay function to create a variable named **winterSceneInstance**, set the Data Type to **winterSceneMC**, and create an instance of the object.
6. Add code to add the Instance to the Display List so that it appears on the screen when the movie is viewed in the Flash Player. (*Hint*: Use the addChild method and set the x value to **310** and the y value to **2**.)
7. Check the syntax and format the code.
8. Test the movie, then click the Start button to view the winter scene that has been added.

9. Close the Flash Player window.
10. Add code within the fl_ReleaseToDrop function for the mouse up event to set the visible property of the winterSceneInstance to **false**.
11. Add the same code (setting the visible property to false for the winterSceneInstance) above the gotoAndPlay(1); line in the function for restartBtn. This will prevent the winterInstance object from appearing on the first screen when the Restart button is clicked.
12. Test the movie, click the Start button, then drag and drop the scarf below the winter scene, which causes the winter image to disappear.
13. Close the Flash Player window.
14. Close the Actions panel, then save your work.

Create an input text field box.

1. Insert a new layer above the background layer, then name it **input text**.
2. Click frame 6 on the input text layer, then insert a blank keyframe.
3. Click frame 1 of the input text layer.
4. Click the Text tool, display the Properties panel, then make the following changes: Family: Arial; Style: Bold; Size: **14**; Color: **#000099**.
5. Click the Text type list arrow in the Properties panel, click Input Text, click the Show border around text button to turn it on, then verify the Behavior is set to Single line.
6. Draw a text box below "What is your favorite season?".
7. Verify the text box is selected on the Stage, then type **inputSeason** for the instance name.
8. Save your work.

Embedding fonts for use with input text fields.

1. Click the Selection tool, then click the input text box on the Stage to select it.
2. Display the Properties panel, then note the font that appears in the CHARACTER area.
3. Click the Embed button in the CHARACTER area.
4. Click Uppercase, Lowercase, Numerals, and Punctuation in the Character ranges area to select them.
5. Click the Add new font button.
6. Click OK to close the dialog box.
7. Test the movie, type **Winter** in the input box, then click the Start button.
8. Close the Flash Player window.
9. Save your work.

Create a dynamic text box.

1. Insert a new layer above the input text layer, then name it **display text**.
2. Insert a keyframe in frame 6 of the display text layer.
3. Click the Text tool, use the Properties panel to change the text type to Dynamic Text with the same font settings as the Input text, except change the font color to white.
4. Click the Show border around text button to deselect the button, then select the Multiline option as the Behavior in the PARAGRAPH area on the Properties panel.
5. Draw a text box above the scarf approximately the same height as the images.
6. Add myFavorite as the instance name for the dynamic text box.
7. Save your work.

Use ActionScript to collect and modify string variables.

1. Click frame 1 on the actions layer, then display the Actions panel.
2. Insert a blank line below the stop(); line, then type the code to create a variable named **mySeason** with the **String** data type and an initial null value.
3. Insert a blank line above the goto line within the function, then type the code to assign the text entered into the inputSeason text box to the mySeason variable.
4. Click frame 6 on the actions layer, open the Actions panel, insert a line below the stop(); line, then type the code to assign the data in the mySeason variable to the myFavorite dynamic text box after the words "I like ".
5. Check the syntax, then auto format the code.
6. Test the movie, type **Winter** in the input text box, then click the Start button and view the text displayed above the scarf.
7. Drag and drop the scarf below the winter scene.
8. Close the Flash Player window, close the Actions panel, then save your work.

Use ActionScript to perform a math calculation.

1. Insert a new layer above the scarf game layer, then name it **temperature**.
2. Insert a keyframe in frame 6 of the temperature layer.
3. Select the Text tool, change the font size to 10, the color to black, and the text type to Static. (*Hint*: If the Properties panel does not display the CHARACTER area, click the pasteboard, make the changes above, then delete the text box on the pasteboard. Also, change the Anti-alias setting to Anti-alias for Readability to make the text more readable.)
4. Use the Text tool to type **Enter Fahrenheit Click for Celsius**, as shown in Figure 36.
5. Add an input text field box below "Click" with Arial, bold, 12 pt, black with a border and single line Behavior.
6. Add an instance name of **tempIn** for the input text box.
7. Create a dynamic text box to the right of the input text box, then give it an instance name of **celTemp**.
8. Create a button with a **Convert** label, place it below the text boxes, then give it an instance name of **convertBtn**.

9. Click frame 6 on the actions layer, then open the Actions panel.
10. Type the code to add a click event listener to the convertBtn object that creates a function named **convert**.
11. Type the code to associate the function with a mouse event, then type the three lines of code that are executed when the convertBtn object is clicked causing the convert function to execute.
    - A variable named **fahrenheit** with a Number data type that is assigned tempIn text as a number
    - A variable named **celsius** that is assigned a formula for converting the value in the fahrenheit variable to a Celsius value: $((fahrenheit-32)/9*5)$
    - The celsius variable assigned to the celTemp dynamic text box.
12. Test the movie, enter a season, click the Start button, drag the scarf to beneath the winter scene, type **70** for the Fahrenheit value, then click the Convert button.
13. Continue adding Fahrenheit values, then click the Restart button and repeat the process.
14. Close the Flash Player window.
15. Save your work, then close the document.
16. Exit Flash.

Figure 36 *Completed Skills Review*

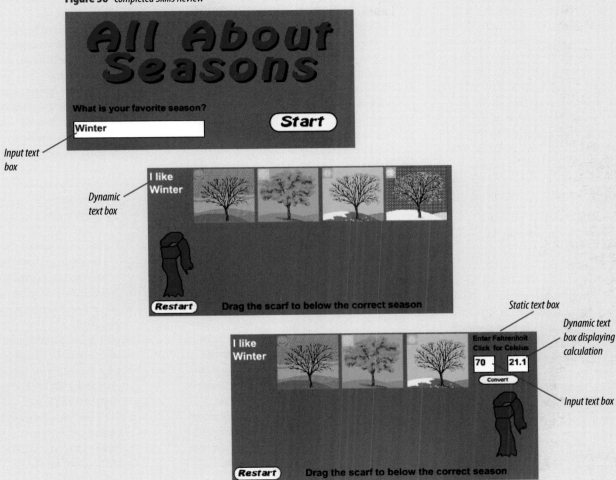

Input text box

Dynamic text box

Static text box

Dynamic text box displaying calculation

Input text box

Ultimate Tours wants to add pages to their website that will provide information for the Package Tour of the month. The information will include the destination, features for various types of accommodations, and cost per week. Ultimate Tours would like the pages to be interactive and allow the visitor to enter a name (which is displayed later), enter the number of adults (used to calculate the cost) going on the trip, and select the type of accommodations (used to calculate the cost). It would also like the pages to have some visual interest beyond just a series of text and numbers so that it engages to the visitor.

1. Open ultimateTours8.fla (the file you created in Chapter 8 Project Builder 1) and save it as **ultimateTours8-reference.fla**.
   This movie was done using ActionScript 2.0 so you will need to start a new Flash ActionScript 3.0 document. Use the ultimateTours8-reference.fla as a guide and use the assets from the document. (*Hint*: You can move the assets from one document to another using the Library panel. Open both documents. With the new document active, open the Library panel and click the Display movies list arrow to display the list of all open documents. Click the ultimateTours8-reference.fla document to display its Library panel. Drag the desired items (including folders) to the Stage. Then delete them from the Stage.)

2. Start a new ActionScript 3.0 document, name it **ultimateTours9.fla**, then use the assets from the ultimateTours8-reference.fla file to create page 1.

3. Create a second page that is displayed when the visitor clicks the sun navigation button on the home page. The second page is a movie clip that contains the destination information. (*Hint*: To create a movie clip page, create a new movie clip symbol and use the edit window to design the page. Then return to the main Timeline, insert a keyframe where the new page will appear, drag the movie clip from the Library panel and align it on the Stage.)

4. Refer to Figure 37 as you include the following on the second page. Be sure to include all elements and to check spelling and punctuation.
   - A background that is the same as the home page but that has been dimmed (e.g. set the brightness to 55)
   - A heading with the destination **Cozumel**
   - A static text box with the text: **Enter your name:**; followed by an input text box that allows the visitor to enter a name
   - Two buttons: one that, when clicked, displays the features associated with Deluxe accommodations in a box, and another button, that when clicked, displays the features associated with Standard accommodations in a box (*Hint*: Use a movie clip with the Export for ActionScript feature turned on)
   - Two additional buttons: one that that, when clicked, displays a third page with the price package for Deluxe accommodations; a different one that, when clicked, displays a fourth page with the price package for the Standard accommodations

5. Buttons on page 2 and their functions include:
   - A Deluxe button
     - Displays the features associated with Deluxe accommodations; create as a movie clip within the destination movie clip
   - A Standard button
     - Displays the features associated with Standard accommodations; create as a movie clip with the destination movie
   - Two "Click to see your Package Price" buttons— one for Deluxe accommodations (page 3) and one for Standard accommodations (page 4)
     - Displays the Welcome text and name entered into the input field
     - Displays an input box for entering the number of adults
     - Calculates the package cost by multiplying the accommodation amount times the number of adults from the input text box
     - Displays the package cost in a dynamic text field
   - The sun graphic included as part of each of the buttons

6. Include the following on the third and fourth pages:
   - Same background and heading as on the second page
   - A dynamic text box that displays a message (such as Welcome,) followed by the name from the input text box on page 2
   - A static text box with the text: **Enter number of adults:**; followed by an input text box that allows the visitor to enter a number (the number of adults going on the trip)

- A button that, when clicked, calculates the cost
- A static text block that displays the words
  Total cost: $
- A dynamic text field that follows the words Total cost: $ and displays a number that is calculated based on the number of adults times the rate

for the type of accommodation selected (2000 for Deluxe and 1000 for Standard) (*Hint*: Put these numbers in the ActionScript code when calculating the total cost)

- The selected accommodation type and its list of features

- A back button that when clicked displays page 2 (Cozumel)

7. Save your work, then compare your image to the example shown in Figure 37.

Figure 37 *Sample completed Project Builder 1*

Page 1

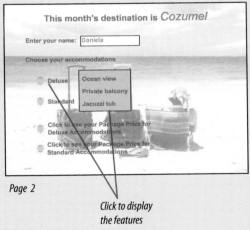

Page 2

Click to display the features

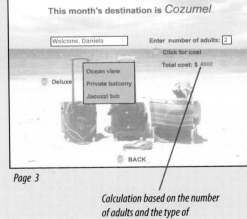

Page 3

Calculation based on the number of adults and the type of accommodation

PROJECT BUILDER 2

You work in the multimedia department of a school. An instructor asks you to build an interactive study guide in Flash that includes a series of practice test questions. The instructor would like to see a prototype of a matching style test question. The prototype should include feedback showing students the correct answer.

1. Create a new Flash ActionScript 3.0 document, then save it as **dragToMatch.fla**.
2. Set the movie properties, including the size, background color, graphics, and text headings as desired.
3. Use the Text tool to create a drag and drop matching-style exercise of your own, or use the example shown in this Project Builder. The exercise should have at least four choices.
4. Create an input text box in which students can type their names.

5. Create a dynamic text box to display the student's name and a message.
6. Create a feedback screen to indicate the correct answers. The feedback screen shows where the answers should have been dropped.
7. Create navigation buttons to jump to the various screens in the movie.
8. Save your work, then compare your movie to the example shown in Figure 38.

Figure 38 *Sample completed Project Builder 2*

Home page

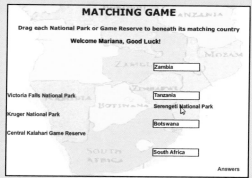

Matching page

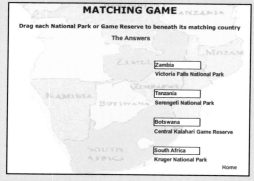

Answers page

Figure 39 shows a page from a website created using Flash. Study the figure and complete the following. For each question, indicate how you determined your answer.

1. Connect to the Internet, type the URL *www.nyphilkids.org/games/main.phtml?*, click instrument Frenzy, then read and follow the directions on the screen to play the game.

2. Open a document in a word processor or create a new Flash document, save the file as **dpc9**, then answer the following questions. (*Hint*: Use the Text tool in Flash.)

In this game, the visitor uses the arrow keys on the keyboard to move the maestro back and forth. The maestro has to catch the instrument as it drops. The visitor then moves the maestro to the correct bin for the captured instrument and presses the down arrow to drop it in the bin by category (woodwind, brass, percussion, strings). If the instrument is dropped into the correct bin, the visitor is awarded points. Missed catches are also tabulated.

- What are some of the actions that might be used to enable the user to drag and drop an instrument to the correct bin rather than using the arrow keys?

- Which elements of the movie must be movie clip symbols? Would all the movie clips need instance names?
- What actions might be used to allow the visitor to enter a name at the beginning of the game and have the name displayed at the end of the game?

- When the question mark (?) button near the lower right of the screen is clicked, instructions for playing the game appear. How would you create this navigation?
- Suppose you wanted the Maestro's eyes to animate when the mouse pointer moved over them. How would you do this?

Figure 39 *Design Project*

PORTFOLIO PROJECT

In a previous chapter, you created a page for your portfolio website that contained thumbnail pictures of work samples. Another way to highlight your work might be to create a slide show that runs continuously, to display different samples. Such a strategy could motivate the visitor to look at more samples, and would allow you to display a larger area for the samples without forcing the visitor to follow a link.

1. Open portfolio8.fla, then save it as **portfolio8-reference.fla**.
   This movie was done using ActionScript 2.0 so you will need to start a new Flash ActionScript 3.0 document. You can use portfolio8-reference.fla as a guide and you can use the assets from the document. (*Hint*: You can move the assets from one document to another using the Library panel. Open both documents. With the new document active, open the Library panel and click the Display movies list arrow to display the list of all open documents. Click the portfolio8-reference.fla document to display its Library panel. Drag the desired items (including folders) to the Stage. Then delete them from the Stage.)

2. Start a new ActionScript 3.0 document, name it **portfolio9.fla**, then use the assets from the portfolio8-reference.fla file to create page 1.

3. Create a series of screen shots with at least four samples of your work, or use the screen shots you created for the Portfolio Project at the end of Chapter 7.

4. Create a new screen with the title **Samples of My Web Work**.

5. Create a movie clip symbol that includes a series of screens each with a sample of your work and some explanatory text. Each sample and associated text should appear in a separate frame. The samples should be spaced out on the movie clip Timeline to allow for a few seconds between when one appears and the next one appears.

6. Return to the main Timeline and use the first frame for the My Portfolio screen. Use the Samples button to jump to frame 2, which is the Samples of My Web Work screen.

7. Add a button with the text **Slide Show** on the Samples of My Web Work page, then program the Over and Down states for the button in any way you'd like.

8. Turn on the Export for ActionScript feature for the movie clip and use the linkage name in the code when creating a variable that will become an instance of the object.

9. Type the code that displays the movie clip when the user clicks the Slide Show button. Use the addChild method, and the x and y values to position the movie clip on the Stage.

10. Use a home button to create navigation from the samples page to the main portfolio page. Add a line of code in the function to turn off the visibility of the movie clip when the home button is clicked. This will prevent the movie clip from appearing on the home page.

11. Save your work, then compare your movie to the example shown in Figure 40.

Figure 40 *Sample completed Portfolio Project*

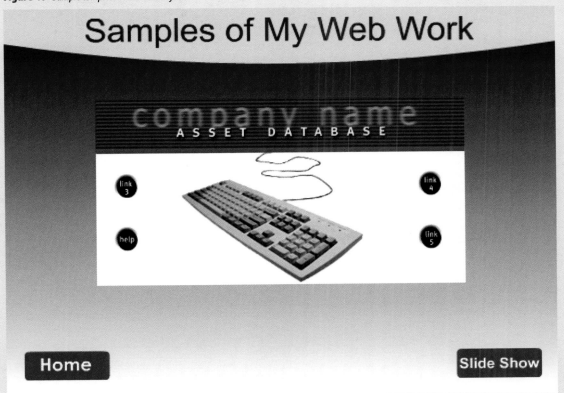

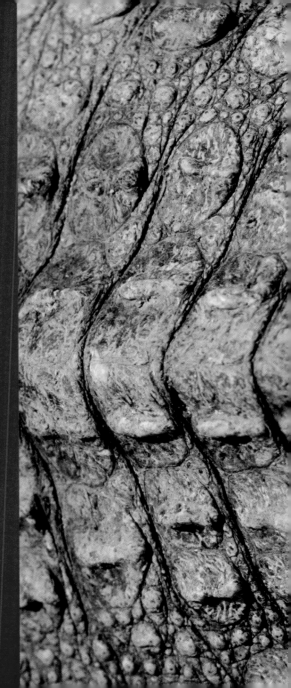

CHAPTER

10 USING ACTIONSCRIPT TO ENHANCE
USER EXPERIENCE

1. Create complex interactivity

2. Load movies at runtime

3. Work with conditional actions

4. Use ActionScript to create external links

USING ACTIONSCRIPT TO ENHANCE
USER EXPERIENCE

NEW Introduction

In this chapter, you will continue to build on your knowledge of ActionScript, with an emphasis on adding actions that encourage user interaction and enhance the user experience. Some examples of how you can use ActionScript to accomplish these goals follow. You can replace the mouse cursor with a custom cursor. You can track user interactions and offer feedback based on the data you gather. You can break your movies into multiple, smaller movies and then use ActionScript to load these movies when appropriate, which will help you organize a large website and provide users relief from lengthy downloads. You can create conditional actions to implement complex branching in your movies. You can create looping actions to help streamline your ActionScript and to provide a way to repeat a set of actions based on a value provided by the user or on a task you want the user to perform.

With all the new actions and cool techniques you will see in this chapter, remember that you're still just scratching the surface of ActionScript. The more you research and experiment, the more surprised you will be by all you can accomplish with ActionScript, and the more your users will appreciate your efforts.

```
ACTIONS - FRAME
                                            Code Snippets
1    import flash.events.MouseEvent;
2    stop();
3    Mouse.hide();
4    stage.addEventListener(MouseEvent.MOUSE_MOVE,follow);
5    {
6        myCursor.x = mouseX;
7        myCursor.y = mouseY;
8    }
9    startBtn.addEventListener(MouseEvent.CLICK, goto2);
10   function goto2(Event:MouseEvent)
11   {
12       gotoAndPlay(2);
13   }

actions : 1
Line 8 of 13, Col 2
```

```
ACTIONS - FRAME
                                            Code Snippets
1    import flash.events.MouseEvent;
2
3    stop();
4    var n:Number = 0;
5    loginBtn.addEventListener(MouseEvent.CLICK,checkPW);
6    function checkPW(Event:MouseEvent)
7    {
8        if (pwEntered.text == "letmein")
9        {
10           gotoAndStop(2);
11       }
12       else
13       {
14           n++;
15           tries.text = "Sorry,"+(3-n)+" triesleft";
16           pwEntered.text = "";
17           if (n == 3)
18           {
19               gotoAndStop(3);
20           }
21       }
22   }

actions : 1
Line 22 of 22, Col 2
```

```
ACTIONS - FRAME
                                            Code Snippets
6
7
8    fishBtn.addEventListener(MouseEvent.CLICK,loadMovie1);
9    function loadMovie1(event:MouseEvent)
10   {
11       myLoader.load(new URLRequest("fish.swf"));
12       addChild(myLoader);
13   }
14
15
16
17

actions : 1
Line 19 of 30, Col 1
```

```
ACTIONS - FRAME
                                            Code Snippets
3
4    websiteBtn.addEventListener(MouseEvent.CLICK,goWeb);
5    function goWeb(Event:MouseEvent)
6    {
7        var targetURL:URLRequest = new URLRequest("http://www.adobe.com/");
8        navigateToURL(targetURL,"_blank");
9    }
10
11
12
13
14

actions : 1
Line 16 of 21, Col 53
```

Create Complex
INTERACTIVITY

What You'll Do

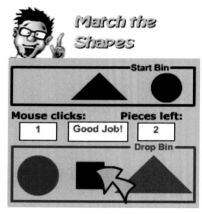

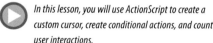

In this lesson, you will use ActionScript to create a custom cursor, create conditional actions, and count user interactions.

Creating a Custom Cursor

Creating a custom cursor is a fun way to make a Flash site distinctive. You might create a cursor with your face on it for a personal site, or you can tie the cursor into the theme of the site, such as using a picture of a yo-yo for an e-business site selling toys. You can also integrate a custom cursor with the purpose of the site; for example, in a game site, the custom cursor might be a cartoon figure the user leads through a maze with the mouse. The custom cursor can be a graphic, photograph, or even an animation. The only requirement is that it be a movie clip symbol.

The first step toward implementing a custom cursor is to hide the regular cursor. You do this with the Mouse.hide method. There is a corresponding Mouse.show method you can use to redisplay the cursor at any point. After hiding the regular cursor you display the custom cursor. This means you will have two cursors on the Stage, but only the custom cursor is visible.

The next step is to set up an event listener that "listens" for when the mouse moves. When the mouse moves, a function is called which causes the custom cursor to follow the hidden cursor. Flash tracks the x and y Stage position of the hidden cursor. By setting the custom cursor to the same x and y coordinates, it follows the hidden cursor.

Mouse movement is tracked by mouseX and mouseY properties, which return the coordinates of the mouse pointer. As the user moves the mouse, the mouseX and mouseY values are updated constantly to reflect the current position of the mouse pointer. Because the custom cursor is following the hidden cursor, these values are assigned to the coordinates of the custom cursor (which is an instance of a movie clip).

Figure 1 shows the ActionScript for a custom cursor implemented using this method.

 ## Using Multiple Objects to Call a Function

One of the values of ActionScript 3.0 is the ability to reuse lines of code. This is especially applicable to functions (which are made up of blocks of code). For example, you could have one event listener (such as mouse down) that **calls** (executes) the same function (such as startToDrag) for more than one object (such as for a circle, square, and triangle). Figure 2 shows three objects (with instance names of mySquare, myTriangle, and myCircle) that, when they receive a mouse down event, will call the clickToDrag function. The function has one line of code that makes the object receiving the mouse down event draggable. Notice that the instance names of the objects are not used in the function. Rather, event.target is specified as the draggable object. Event.target refers to the instance that is assigned to the listener. So, if the mySquare object receives the mouse down event it becomes the event.target, which means the mySquare object becomes draggable. Without event.target, you would need to type the same function three times, once for each object.

Creating Conditional Actions

If-then statements are familiar to anyone who has had minimal programming exposure. ActionScript includes an if action that can test whether certain conditions have been met and, if so, can perform other actions. (You used an If statement when you created the preloader in a previous chapter.) Conditional statements offer many possibilities for building more interactive movies. You should enclose all the actions you want Flash to carry out in braces following the if action. If the conditions are not met, the actions in the braces are ignored, and Flash jumps to the next action.

When creating conditions in ActionScript, you must use two equal signs (= =). A single equal sign (=) assigns a specific value to a variable. For example, n=9 in ActionScript assigns the value 9 to a variable named n,

Figure 1 *ActionScript to create a custom cursor by setting X and Y coordinates*

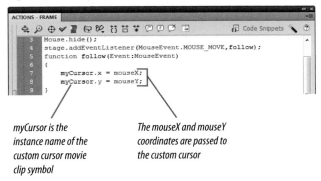

myCursor is the instance name of the custom cursor movie clip symbol

The mouseX and mouseY coordinates are passed to the custom cursor

Figure 2 *Three objects that call the same function*

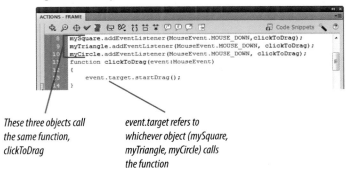

These three objects call the same function, clickToDrag

event.target refers to whichever object (mySquare, myTriangle, myCircle) calls the function but n = = 9 is a conditional statement that checks if the variable n has a value of 9, and if so, performs another action. Figure 3 shows an example of a conditional statement.

NEW Working with Parent Movie Clips

In Chapter 9, you learned about the Display List which is a list of all of the items that will be visible on the screen in a Flash document. It includes movie clips, drawn shapes, text fields, videos, and bitmaps. These items are Display Object types. Some of these display objects can have children. For example, a movie clip could be made up of one drawn shape, such as a square. The square would be a child of the movie clip and the movie clip would be a parent of the square. This is important because when you want to refer to the square in your ActionScript code you may need to specify that the square is a child of the movie clip. You do this using this format: parent= =child. In this example, parent refers to the movie clip, and child is substituted with the instance name of the object you want to reference. For example, let's say you have written the code to make a black square (an object with an instance name of mySquare) a draggable object. You want the black square to be dragged to and dropped on the yellow square (which is the child of a movie clip). In order to determine if the black square was dropped on the yellow square (which has an instance name of targetSquare), you would use

Figure 3 *Example of a conditional statement*

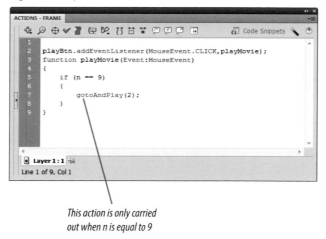

This action is only carried out when n is equal to 9

the dropTarget property. This concept is illustrated in Figure 4 and discussed next:

```
if (mySquare.dropTarget.parent ==
    targetSquare)
```

This line of code checks to see if the drop target of the mySquare object being dragged is targetSquare (the yellow square contained in the movie clip).

if makes this a conditional statement; it lets you know that something will happen if the condition (the dropTarget) is correct.

mySquare is the instance name of the object being dragged, in this example the black square.

dropTarget is the property that specifies on which object the mySquare object is dropped.

parent == targetSquare identifies the yellow square (targetSquare) as the child of the parent.

The entire line of code checks to see that the dropTarget is the parent (the movie clip in this example) of the dropTarget object (the yellow square child in this example).

Tracking User Interactions

One aspect of interactivity involves responding to user actions, such as jumping to a different point in a movie when a user clicks a button. Another aspect involves providing users with individual feedback based on the actions they take or information they supply. This can be as simple as creating a dynamic text box

to display the user's name in a greeting, as you did in Chapter 9. Or, this can be as complex as using ActionScript to gather and display more complex information, such as the number of times a user clicks the mouse or a user's progress in a game or quiz. Collecting such information presents many opportunities to offer users custom feedback. Tracking interactions can also provide you with insight on the way people work with your site or application.

The increment and decrement actions are useful when tracking user interactions. The **increment action**, ++ (two plus signs), adds 1 unit to a variable or expression;

the **decrement action**, – – (two minus signs), subtracts 1 unit. For example, the ActionScript statement x++ is the equivalent of the expression $x = x+1$. Both add 1 to the variable. You might use the increment operator to keep track of and display the number of correct answers a user has given during an online test.

QUICK TIP

The increment and decrement operators are also useful when setting up the number of times to run a conditional loop. For example, you might want to allow a user to attempt to answer a question a specified number of times before providing the correct answer to the user.

Figure 4 *Using parent to target a shape within a movie clip instance*

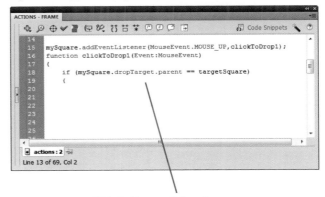

This is checking to see if the mySquare object has been dropped on top of the parent (a movie clip) of the targetSquare object

Hide the cursor

1. Open fl10_1.fla from the drive and folder where your Data Files are stored, then save it as **interactive.fla**.

2. Drag the **playhead** to view the contents of the frames.

   This movie has two screens, a welcome screen in frame 1 and a drag and drop screen in frame 2.

3. Click **frame 1** on the actions layer, then open the Actions panel.

   Frame 1 of the actions layer has an import flash.events.MouseEvent statement; a stop action and a goto action for the Start button. Frame 2 of the actions layer has an import flash.events.MouseEvent statement and a stop action.

4. Type the following line of code below the stop(); line in the Script pane for frame 1 of the actions layer, as shown in Figure 5: **Mouse.hide();**

5. Test the movie.

   The mouse cursor is not visible.

   TIP The cursor reverts to the shape for your operating system when you position the mouse pointer on the title bar or menu bar of the Flash Player window.

6. Close the Flash Player window.

7. Collapse the Actions panel.

8. Save your work.

You used ActionScript to hide the mouse cursor.

Figure 5 *ActionScript to hide the mouse cursor*

Code to type

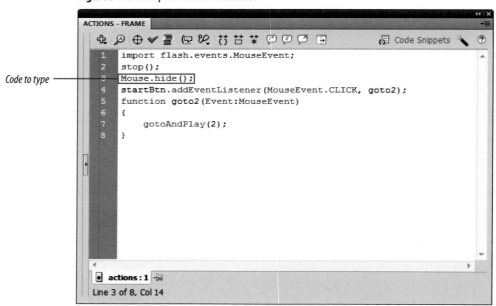

Figure 6 *Instance of the custom cursor movie clip symbol on the Stage*

Create a custom cursor using X and Y coordinates

1. Insert a **new layer** above the shapes layer, name it **cursor**, then click **frame 1**.

2. Display the Library panel, open the movieClips folder, then drag the **cursor movie clip symbol** to the center of the Stage, as shown in Figure 6.

3. Verify the cursor movie clip symbol is selected on the Stage, display the Properties panel, type **myCursor** for the instance name, then press **[Enter]** (Win) or **[return]** (Mac).

4. Click **frame 1** of the actions layer, display the Actions panel, then type the following as a single line of code below the Mouse.hide(); line:

   stage.addEventListener(MouseEvent. MOUSE_MOVE, follow);

   This creates an event listener that "listens" for the mouse to move. Also, it names a function (follow) that is called when the mouse moves.

   (continued)

5. Press **[Enter]** (Win) or **[return]** (Mac), then type the following lines of code, as shown in Figure 7 (*Note: A closing right brace (}) is added automatically when you press [Enter] (Win) or [return] (Mac) after typing the opening left brace ({)):

function follow(Event:MouseEvent)
{
myCursor.x = mouseX;
myCursor.y = mouseY;

This defines the function (named follow) to set the x and y positions of the custom cursor, myCursor, to the x and y positions of the regular cursor, which is hidden.

6. Test the movie, use the custom cursor to click the **Start button** on the first screen, then try to drag and drop the shapes on the second screen.

7. Close the Flash Player window.

8. Save your work.

You used ActionScript to designate an instance of a movie clip symbol to act as the mouse cursor using X and Y coordinates.

NEW Use multiple objects to call a function

1. Click **frame 2** on the actions layer, then display the Actions panel.

2. Type the following line of code below the stop(); line:
   mySquare.addEventListener(MouseEvent.MOUSE_DOWN, clickToDrag);

   This creates an event listener and names a function, clickToDrag, that is called when there is a mouse down action on the mySquare object.

(continued)

Figure 7 *ActionScript that sets the position of the custom cursor to the position of the regular cursor*

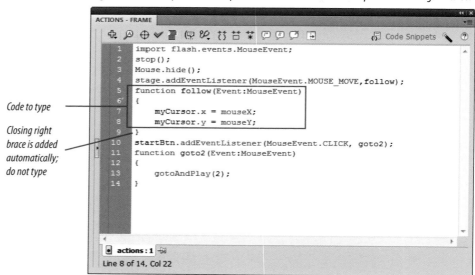

Code to type

Closing right
brace is added
automatically;
do not type

```
1   import flash.events.MouseEvent;
2   stop();
3   Mouse.hide();
4   stage.addEventListener(MouseEvent.MOUSE_MOVE,follow);
5   function follow(Event:MouseEvent)
6   {
7       myCursor.x = mouseX;
8       myCursor.y = mouseY;
9   }
10  startBtn.addEventListener(MouseEvent.CLICK, goto2);
11  function goto2(Event:MouseEvent)
12  {
13      gotoAndPlay(2);
14  }
```

actions : 1

Line 8 of 14, Col 22

Figure 8 *ActionScript to define the clickToDrag function using event.target*

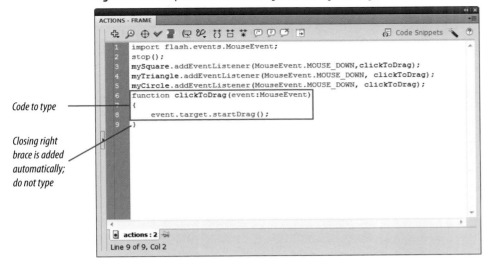

Code to type —

Closing right
brace is added
automatically;
do not type

```
1  import flash.events.MouseEvent;
2  stop();
3  mySquare.addEventListener(MouseEvent.MOUSE_DOWN,clickToDrag);
4  myTriangle.addEventListener(MouseEvent.MOUSE_DOWN, clickToDrag);
5  myCircle.addEventListener(MouseEvent.MOUSE_DOWN, clickToDrag);
6  function clickToDrag(event:MouseEvent)
7  {
8      event.target.startDrag();
9  }
```

actions : 2

Line 9 of 9, Col 2

3. Press **[Enter]** (Win) or **[return]** (Mac), then type
   the following two lines of code:

   **myTriangle.addEventListener(MouseEvent.
   MOUSE_DOWN, clickToDrag);**

   **myCircle.addEventListener(MouseEvent.
   MOUSE_DOWN, clickToDrag);**

   This code creates mouse down event listeners for
   the myTriangle and myCircle objects and calls the
   same function, clickToDrag.

4. Press **[Enter]** (Win) or **[return]** (Mac), then type
   the following lines of code, as shown in Figure 8:

   function clickToDrag(event:MouseEvent)

   {

   event.target.startDrag();

   This defines the clickToDrag function as a
   mouse event and allows the event.target
   object to be draggable.

5. Test the movie, click the **Start button**, drag the
   black square around the screen, then release
   the mouse button.

   Notice the object is draggable. You are not able to
   drop the object at this time.

6. Close the Flash Player window, close the Action
   panel, then save your work.

*You used event.target to allow multiple objects to call the
same function.*

Create dynamic text boxes

1. Insert a **new layer** above the shapes layer, then name it **text boxes**.

2. Click **frame 2** on the text boxes layer, then insert a **keyframe**.

3. Click the **Text tool** T on the Tools panel, display the Properties panel, click the **Text type list arrow**, click **Dynamic Text**, click the **Show border around text button** 📧 to select it, click the **Align center** button ☰ in the PARAGRAPH area.

4. Use the Properties panel to set the text properties to: Family: **Arial**; Style: **Bold**; Size: **12**; Text fill color: **#990000**.

5. Using Figure 9 as a guide, draw a **text box** below the words Mouse clicks.

6. With the text box selected, type **mouseClicks** for the instance name.

7. Using Figure 10 as a guide, create **two more dynamic text boxes**.

8. Give the middle text box an instance name of **reply** and the right side text box an instance name of **piecesLeft**.

9. Click the **Embed button** in the CHARACTER area of the Properties panel, then click the check boxes for **Uppercase**, **Lowercase**, **Numerals**, and **Punctuation** to select them.

10. Click the **Add new font icon** ➕, then click **OK**.

11. Save your work.

You created three dynamic text boxes, gave them instance names, and embedded fonts.

Figure 9 *Drawing the dynamic text box*

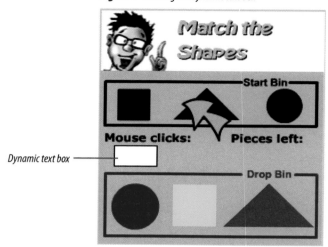

Dynamic text box

Figure 10 *Drawing the other dynamic text boxes*

If one of the text boxes overlaps other elements on the screen, click the Selection tool on the Tools panel after drawing the text box, then use the mouse or arrows keys to move the box.

Figure 11 *Creating a conditional statement*

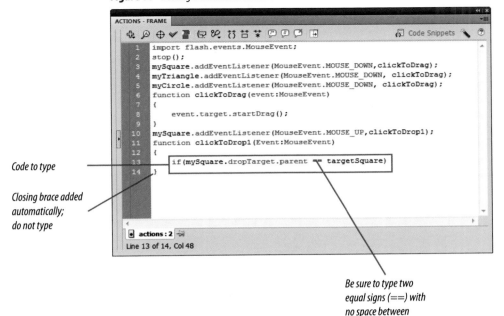

Code to type

Closing brace added automatically;
do not type

Be sure to type two
equal signs (==) with
no space between

Create a conditional statement

1. Click **frame 2** on the actions layer, then open the Actions panel.

2. Insert a **blank line** below the last line of code, then type the following as a single line of code:

   mySquare.addEventListener(MouseEvent. MOUSE_UP, clickToDrop1);

   This adds a mouse up event listener to the mySquare object on the Stage and names a function clickToDrop1.

3. Press **[Enter]** Win or **[return]** (Mac) to add a new line, then type the following lines of code:

   function clickToDrop1(Event:MouseEvent)

   {

   This begins the process of defining the clickToDrop1 function.

4. Press **[Enter]** Win or **[return]** (Mac) to add a new line, then type the following as a single line of code, as shown in Figure 11:

   if (mySquare.dropTarget.parent == targetSquare)

   This creates a conditional statement that says if mySquare is dropped on targetSquare then complete the following lines of code. (*Note*: targetSquare is the instance name of the yellow square, and the yellow square is the child of the parent movie clip.)

   (continued)

5. Press **[Enter]** Win or **[return]** (Mac) to add a new line before the closing brace (}), then type the following lines of code:

{

reply.text = "Good Job!";

targetSquare.visible = false;

The two lines within the curly braces identify the code to be executed if the conditional statement is true. The first line assigns Good Job! to reply.text, which is the middle text box on the screen. The second line causes the targetSquare object to disappear from view.

6. Insert a **blank line** between the last two curly braces (}) at the end of the code, then type **mySquare.stopDrag();** as shown in Figure 12.

Notice the stopDrag line is placed outside the conditional statement so that it is executed whether or not the statement is true. The } completes the block of code for the clickToDrop1 function.

7. Test the movie, click the **Start button**, then drag the **black square** to the yellow square.

Notice Good Job! is displayed in the reply text box and the yellow square (targetSquare instance) disappears from the screen.

Note: If errors occur, compare your code to Figure 12.

8. Close the Flash Player window.

9. Save your work.

You created a conditional statement within a function.

Figure 12 *Placing the stopDrag line outside the conditional statement*

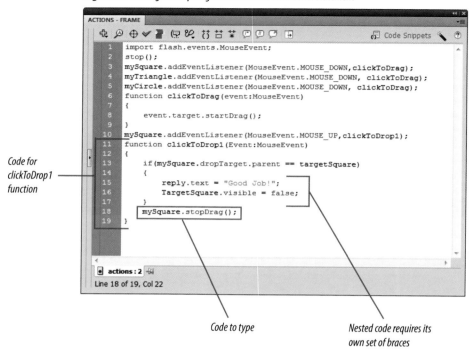

Code for clickToDrop1 function

Code to type

Nested code requires its own set of braces

Using ActionScript to Enhance User Experience

Figure 13 *ActionScript to increment the variable value and assign it to a text box*

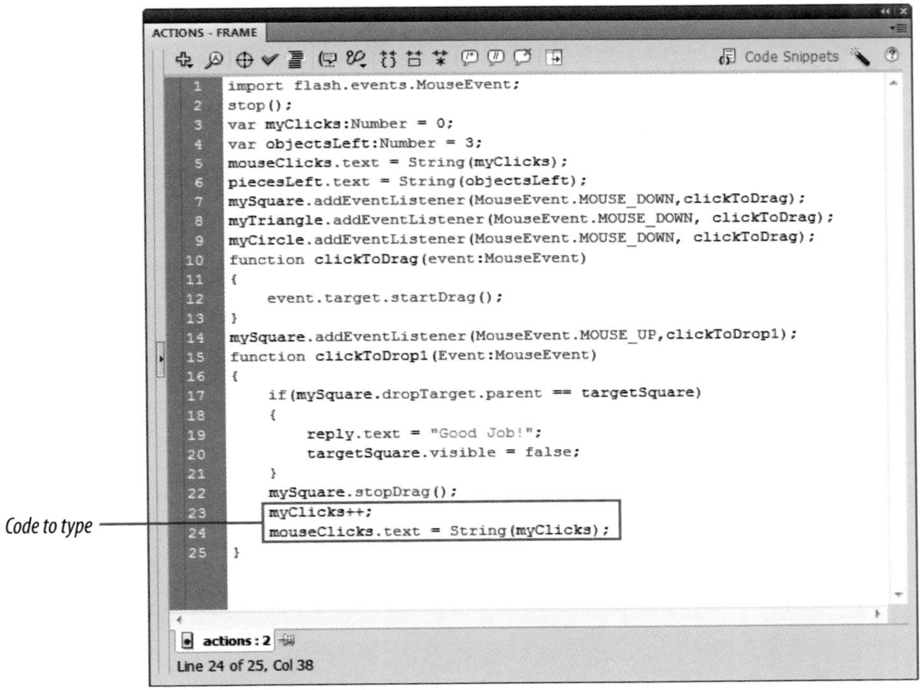

Code to type

```
1   import flash.events.MouseEvent;
2   stop();
3   var myClicks:Number = 0;
4   var objectsLeft:Number = 3;
5   mouseClicks.text = String(myClicks);
6   piecesLeft.text = String(objectsLeft);
7   mySquare.addEventListener(MouseEvent.MOUSE_DOWN,clickToDrag);
8   myTriangle.addEventListener(MouseEvent.MOUSE_DOWN, clickToDrag);
9   myCircle.addEventListener(MouseEvent.MOUSE_DOWN, clickToDrag);
10  function clickToDrag(event:MouseEvent)
11  {
12      event.target.startDrag();
13  }
14  mySquare.addEventListener(MouseEvent.MOUSE_UP,clickToDrop1);
15  function clickToDrop1(Event:MouseEvent)
16  {
17      if(mySquare.dropTarget.parent == targetSquare)
18      {
19          reply.text = "Good Job!";
20          targetSquare.visible = false;
21      }
22      mySquare.stopDrag();
23      myClicks++;
24      mouseClicks.text = String(myClicks);
25  }
```

actions : 2

Line 24 of 25, Col 38

Changing the data type to display data in dynamic text boxes

Dynamic text boxes display characters (including numbers) as string data. Therefore, if you have a number that is to be displayed in a dynamic text box it must be changed to a string data type. The process is to append *.text* to the instance name of the dynamic text box using the format: *instanceName.text*. Then, take the numeric variable and preface it with String using the format: *String(variable Name)*. Finally, the text box (using the instance name) is assigned the value in the variable using the format: *instanceName.text = String(variableName)*. If the variable name is **myClicks** and the dynamic text box instance name is **mouseClicks** the code would be **mouseClicks.text = String(myClicks)**.

Track user interactions

1. Insert a **blank line** after the stop(); line in the Actions panel.

2. Type the following lines of code:

   var myClicks:Number = 0;

   var objectsLeft:Number = 3;

   The first line creates a numeric variable named myClicks and assigns it an initial value of 0. This variable will keep track of the number of times the mouse button is clicked. The second line creates a numeric variable named objectsLeft and assigns it an initial value of 3. The number for this variable will be reduced each time an objected is dragged.

3. Press **[Enter]** Win or **[return]** (Mac) to add a new line, then type the following lines:

   mouseClicks.text = String(myClicks);

   piecesLeft.text = String(objectsLeft);

   The first line takes the numeric value in the myClicks variable, changes it into a string value and assigns it to the mouseClicks text box. The second line takes the numeric value in the objectsLeft variable, changes it into a string value, and assigns it to the piecesLeft text box. This allows the numeric values to be displayed in the dynamic text field boxes.

4. Type the following lines of code after the mySquare.stopDrag line and before the closing brace (}), as shown in Figure 13:

   myClicks++;

   mouseClicks.text = String(myClicks);

   The first line increments the value for myClicks by 1. The second line updates the value in the mouseClicks text box.

   (continued)

5. Press **[Enter]** Win or **[return]** (Mac) to add a new line, then type the following lines of code, as shown in Figure 14:

objectsLeft--;

piecesLeft.text = String(objectsLeft);

The first line decrements the value for objectsLeft by 1. The second line updates the value in the piecesLeft text box.

Note: Be sure to type two minus signs (--) after objectsLeft.

6. Test the movie, then click the **Start button**.

Notice the Mouse clicks and Pieces left text boxes display the initial values.

Note: If errors occur, compare your code to Figure 14.

7. Drag the **black square** to on top of the yellow square.

Notice the Mouse clicks and Pieces left text boxes display the updated values.

8. Close the Flash Player window.

9. Save your work.

You tracked user interactions with the increment and decrement operators.

Figure 14 *ActionScript to decrement the variable value and assign it to a text box*

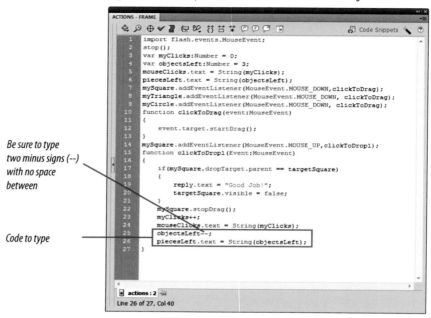

Be sure to type
two minus signs (--)
with no space
between

Code to type

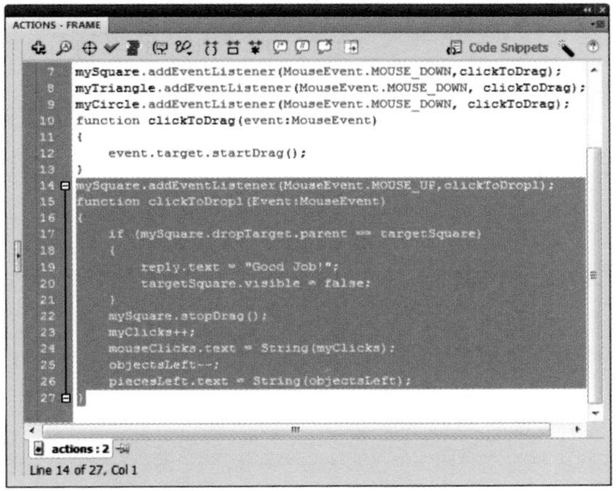

Figure 15 *Highlighting the lines of code*

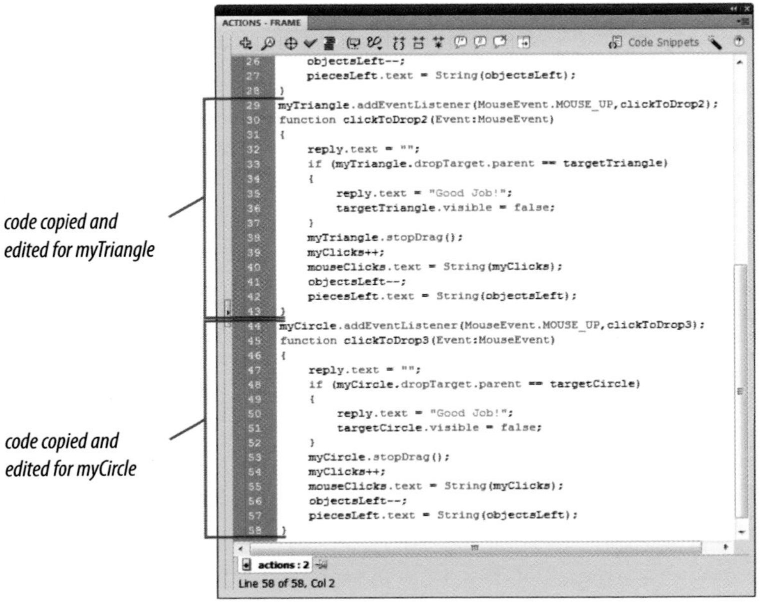

Figure 16 *The copied and edited lines of code*

code copied and
edited for myTriangle

code copied and
edited for myCircle

Copy ActionScript code

1. **Drag the pointer** to highlight the lines shown in Figure 15.

2. **Right-click** (Win) or **[control]-click** (Mac) on the highlighted area, then click **Copy**.

3. Insert a **blank line** at the bottom of the ActionScript code, **right-click** (Win) or **[control]-click** (Mac), then click **Paste**.

4. Change **mySquare** to **myTriangle** (3 occurrences) to the code you just pasted.

5. Change **clickToDrop1** to **clickToDrop2** (2 occurrences).

6. Change **targetSquare** to **targetTriangle** (2 occurrences).

7. Repeat Steps 1 through 6 using **myCircle**, **clickToDrop3**, and **targetCircle**.

8. Insert a **blank line** above the first if statement, then type:

    reply.text = "";

    This code will clear the text in the reply.text text box of the words "Good Job!".

9. Repeat Step 8 for the other two if statements.

10. Click the **Check syntax button** ✔ on the Actions panel menu bar, click the **Auto format button** ▤ , then compare your screen to Figure 16.

11. Test the movie, click the **Start button**, then drag **each of the objects** in the Start Bin to the corresponding objects in the Drop Bin.

12. Close the Flash Player window, then close the Actions panel.

13. Save your work, then close the document.

You copied ActionScript code and changed object names.

Load Movies
AT RUNTIME

What You'll Do

In this lesson, you will load and unload movies into the Flash Player so that they play along with the content of the original movie.

Understanding Multiple Movies

In previous chapters, you have seen how you can use scenes and movie clip symbols to break large movies into smaller, more manageable components. Another strategy is to split a single movie into a number of different movies, and then use ActionScript to load the movies as needed. For example, you might have a site with a number of discrete areas, not all of which are of interest to every user. By splitting each area into its own movie, you can save download time for the user because, instead of having to download a large movie for the entire site, the movie for each area will be downloaded only when the user visits that area or specifically requests it, such as by clicking a link. Multiple movies can create smoother transitions between pages because the new movies load into the current HTML page. Using multiple movies can also help you keep organized during development of a movie, especially if different people are working on different parts of the movie. Figure 17 shows an example of one way to use multiple movies.

Loading Movies

The Loader class along with the addChild method can be used to load an external movie (or other object such as a graphic, text block, or sound). You must know the name of the Flash Player movie file you want to load (Flash Player files have an .swf extension) and also its location. The location can be on your computer or on a network. The location is specified using the URLRequest class. When you are creating a link to a file, you can include an **absolute path**, which specifies the exact location of the file, or a **relative path**, which indicates the location based on the current location of your movie file. For example, if the SWF file you are referencing is in a folder named myMovie and your Flash document is in the same folder, you can include just the filename, without any path, in your code. Figure 18 shows the ActionScript for loading an SWF file located in the same folder as the Flash document.

You can load a new movie with the original document or into a movie clip symbol. If you load a new movie with the original document, the new movie inherits the frame rate, dimensions, and background color of the original document. The new movie appears starting in the upper-left corner of the original document, which may cause design issues if your movies are not the same size; make sure to test how the additional movies will load before publishing a site. You can specify the x and y Stage coordinates for the SWF file when loading it. Loading a new movie into a movie clip gives you more control over the size and placement of the movie. One useful technique is to create a blank movie clip symbol that you name, position on Stage where you want the new movie to appear, and then load the new movie into the blank movie clip symbol.

Unloading Movies

The removeChild method can be used to unload movies. Including this action when you no longer need a movie loaded can create smoother transitions between movies, ensure there's no visual residue between movies of different sizes, and reduce the memory required by the Flash Player. When a movie is unloaded, it is removed from the player but it is still available to be replayed without having to download it again.

Figure 17 *A Flash site that takes advantage of using multiple movies*

Each tab could open a different SWF file, saving the user download time.

Figure 18 *ActionScript for loading an SWF file in the same location as the Flash document*

Code to load fish.swf file

Load a movie

1. Open fl10_2.fla, then save it as **letterF.fla**.

   This movie has three buttons and the letter F displayed on the Stage. The instance names for the buttons are fishBtn, unloadBtn, and frogBtn.

TIP The steps use relative paths to load new movies. Be sure to copy the two movies you will load, fish.swf and frog.swf, to the same drive and folder where you save the letterF.fla file.

2. Click **frame 1** on the actions layer, then open the Actions panel.

3. Type the following line of code below the stop(); line:

   var myLoader:Loader = new Loader();

   This creates a variable named myLoader with a Loader data type and creates an instance of the Loader.

4. Press **[Enter]** Win or **[return]** (Mac), then type the following as a single line of code:

   fishBtn.addEventListener(MouseEvent. CLICK, loadMovie1);

   This creates an event listener for a mouse event for the fishBtn and names a function, loadMovie1.

5. Press **[Enter]** Win or **[return]** (Mac) to add a new line, then type the following lines of code, as shown in Figure 19:

   function loadMovie1(event:MouseEvent)

   {

   myLoader.load(new URLRequest("fish. swf"));

   addChild(myLoader);

(continued)

Figure 19 *ActionScript to define the loadMovie1 function*

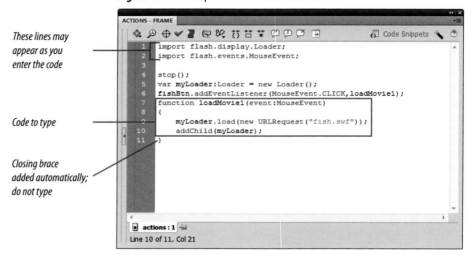

These lines may appear as you enter the code

Code to type

Closing brace added automatically; do not type

```
import flash.display.Loader;
import flash.events.MouseEvent;

stop();
var myLoader:Loader = new Loader();
fishBtn.addEventListener(MouseEvent.CLICK,loadMovie1);
function loadMovie1(event:MouseEvent)
{
    myLoader.load(new URLRequest("fish.swf"));
    addChild(myLoader);
}
```

Using ActionScript to Enhance User Experience

Figure 20 *ActionScript to add event listener for the frogBtn object*

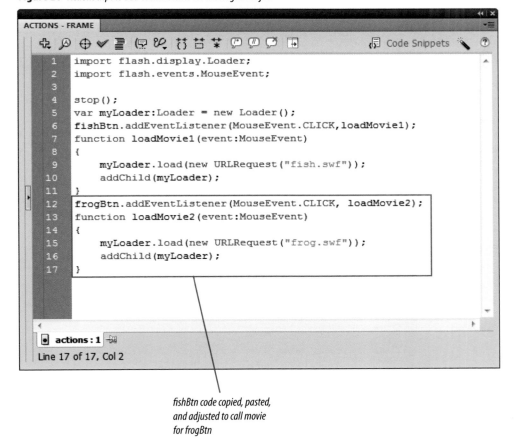

```
1    import flash.display.Loader;
2    import flash.events.MouseEvent;
3
4    stop();
5    var myLoader:Loader = new Loader();
6    fishBtn.addEventListener(MouseEvent.CLICK,loadMovie1);
7    function loadMovie1(event:MouseEvent)
8    {
9        myLoader.load(new URLRequest("fish.swf"));
10       addChild(myLoader);
11   }
12   frogBtn.addEventListener(MouseEvent.CLICK, loadMovie2);
13   function loadMovie2(event:MouseEvent)
14   {
15       myLoader.load(new URLRequest("frog.swf"));
16       addChild(myLoader);
17   }
```

Code Snippets

actions : 1

Line 17 of 17, Col 2

fishBtn code copied, pasted, and adjusted to call movie for frogBtn

This defines the function loadMovie1. The myLoader line uses the URLRequest class to specify the SWF file to load into the myLoader variable. The addChild line places the variable myLoader on the display list so that it is visible on the screen.

6. Test the movie, then click the **fish button**.

 The fish animation appears on top of the F.

7. Close the Flash Player window.

8. Copy and paste the code used for the fish button to add the event listener and function for the **frogBtn object**, then adjust the wording in the code, as shown in Figure 20, to correspond to the frogBtn. Change fishBtn to frogBtn, fish.swf to frog.swf and loadMovie1 to loadMovie2 (2 occurrences).

9. Click the **Check syntax button** ✔, then click the **Auto format button** ▤.

10. Test the movie, click the **frog button**, then click the **fish button**.

11. Close the Flash Player window.

12. Save your work.

You created the ActionScript to load external SWF files at runtime.

Unload movies

1. Add a new **blank line** below the last line of code, which is a closing brace, then type the following as a single line of code:

   unloadBtn.addEventListener(MouseEvent. CLICK, removeMovie);

   This creates an event listener for a mouse event that calls a function named removeMovie when the unloadBtn object on the Stage is clicked.

2. Press **[Enter]** Win or **[return]** (Mac) to add a new line, then type the following lines of code, as shown in Figure 21:

   function removeMovie(event:MouseEvent)

   {

   removeChild(myLoader);

   This defines the removeMovie function and uses the removeChild method to remove the myLoader variable from the display list so it is no longer visible on the screen.

3. Click the **Check syntax button** ✔, then click the **Auto format button** ▤.

4. Play the movie, click the **fish button**, then click the **unload button**.

5. Close the Flash Player window.

6. Save your work.

You used the removeChild method to remove a movie from the screen.

Figure 21 *ActionScript to define the removeMovie function*

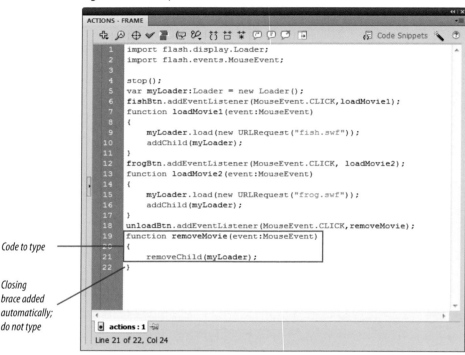

Code to type

Closing brace added automatically; do not type

Figure 22 *Changing the y coordinate value*

Code to set the placement of the SWF file

```
ACTIONS - FRAME

                                                    Code Snippets

1    import flash.display.Loader;
2    import flash.events.MouseEvent;
3
4    stop();
5    var myLoader:Loader = new Loader();
6    myLoader.x = 0;
7    myLoader.y = 50;
8    fishBtn.addEventListener(MouseEvent.CLICK,loadMovie1);
9    function loadMovie1(event:MouseEvent)
10   {
11       myLoader.load(new URLRequest("fish.swf"));
12       addChild(myLoader);
13   }
14   frogBtn.addEventListener(MouseEvent.CLICK, loadMovie2);
15   function loadMovie2(event:MouseEvent)
16   {
17       myLoader.load(new URLRequest("frog.swf"));
18       addChild(myLoader);
19   }
20   unloadBtn.addEventListener(MouseEvent.CLICK,removeMovie);
21   function removeMovie(event:MouseEvent)
22   {
23       removeChild(myLoader);
24   }

    actions : 1
Line 7 of 24, Col 16
```

NEW Set the Stage position when loading a movie

1. Insert a **new line** below the var myLoader:Loader=new Loader(); line, then type the following lines of code:

   myLoader.x = 0;

   myLoader.y = 0;

   This code sets the x and y coordinates for the myLoader variable, which determines where the movie will appear on the screen.

2. Test the movie, then click the **fish button**.

   The fish appears in the center of the screen.

3. Close the Flash Player window.

4. Change the myLoader.y value from 0 to **50**, as shown in Figure 22.

5. Test the movie, then click the **fish button**.

   The fish appears lower on the screen.

6. Close the Flash Player window.

7. Close the Actions panel.

8. Save your work, then close the document.

You set and then changed the Stage position when loading a movie.

Work With CONDITIONAL ACTIONS

What You'll Do

In this lesson, you will work with conditional actions and use ActionScript to duplicate movie clip symbols.

Using the Else and Else If Statements

In Chapter 9, you used the *if* statement to test for a condition. If the condition was true, the *if* statement ran a series of actions enclosed in curly braces. Otherwise, it skipped the actions in braces and ran the next set of actions in the Script pane.

ActionScript also includes an *else* statement you can use to create more sophisticated branching. An *else* statement lets you specify one set of actions to run if a condition is true, and an alternate set to run if the condition is false. If a condition has more than two possible states, you can use *else if* to set up a series of possible branches. For example, if you are creating an online test, there might be several possible answers a student could provide, and you might want to create a different branch for each answer. Figure 23 shows ActionScript that uses *else if* to create multiple branches.

Creating Conditional Loops

A **loop** is an action or set of actions that repeat as long as a condition exists. Creating a loop can be as simple as taking a variable, assigning a value to it, executing a statement, and if the statement is false, adding one to the variable and trying again. You can often just use an *if* action to create a loop, which is what you did when you created the preloader in an earlier chapter.

ActionScript includes other actions you can use to create more sophisticated conditional loops. The *for*, *while*, and *do while* loops all let you set up conditions for a loop and actions to run repeatedly. The *for* loop uses a series of arguments to set up a condition, a series of actions to take if the condition is true, and a counter that keeps track of the number of loops. This counter is often used in conjunction with the condition, for instance, to run the loop a user-specified number of times. The *while* and *do while* loops let you enter a series of actions to run while a condition is true. The difference is that *do while* runs the actions at least one time, then evaluates if the condition is true, whereas *while* evaluates the condition and then runs the actions if the conditions are met. Figure 24 shows an example of using the while statement to create a loop.

Using the Password Line Type in an Input Field

You may not want passwords to be visible onscreen as users enter them. For security, you can set an input text field to display asterisks rather than the actual keystrokes being typed by a user. To do this, click the Text tool, be sure the text type is set to Input Text, display the Properties panel for the Input Text field, click the Line type list arrow for the Behavior option in the PARAGRAPH area, and then click Password.

NEW Using the Math.random Function

There are times in a Flash movie that you may need to generate numbers at random. For example, you may be developing a game and want a character to appear on the screen in a different position each time the user clicks a button. The x and y Stage coordinate values for the character could be generated using the Math.random function.

This function returns a random number that is equal to or greater than 0 and less than 1 (that is 0 to .999 ...). This random number can be used to obtain a value that is in a desired range. For instance, if you want to calculate a number that is equal to or above 100 and less than 200, you would take the number generated by the random function and multiply it by 100, then you would add 100. If the random number that is generated is 0, the calculated number would be 100 ((0*100) + 100). If the random number that is generated is .999, the calculated number would be 199.9 ((.999*100)+100).

Figure 23 *ActionScript using else if statements to create multiple branches*

```
5
6
7    {
8        if (answer == "A")
9        {
10           gotoAndStop(2);
11       }
12       else
13       {
14           if (answer == "B")
15           {
16               gotoAndStop(3);
17           }
18           else
19           {
20               if (answer == "C")
21               {
22                   gotoAndStop(4);
23               }
24           }
25       }
26   }
27
```

actions : 1
Line 27 of 27, Col 1

Figure 24 *ActionScript to create a loop using the while statement*

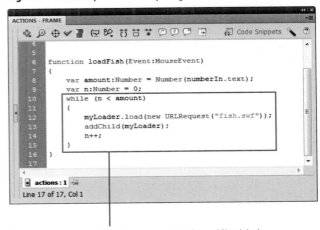

This code creates a loop that continues to load the fish.swf file while the variable n is less than the value in the variable named amount

Create conditional branching using if and else statements

1. Open fl10_3.fla, then save it as **branching.fla**.

2. Drag the **playhead** to view the three screens.

   This movie has three screens. The first screen requires a user to type a password and click a login button, the second screen displays Access Granted, and the third screen displays Access Denied.

3. Use the Selection tool ![pointer] to click the **white input text box** in frame 1 on the Stage, display the Properties panel, then type **pwEntered** for the instance name.

4. Click the **login button** on the Stage to select it, then give it an instance name of **loginBtn**.

5. Click **frame 1** on the actions layer, open the Actions panel, then click below the stop(); line.

6. Press **[Enter]** (Win) or **[return]** (Mac), then type the following as a single line of code:

   loginBtn.addEventListener(MouseEvent. CLICK, checkPW);

   This creates an event listener for the loginBtn object and names the function, checkPW, that will be called when the loginBtn object is clicked.

7. Press **[Enter]** (Win) or **[return]** (Mac), then type the following lines of code, as shown in Figure 25:

   function checkPW(Event:MouseEvent)

   {

   if (pwEntered.text == "letmein")

   The first line identifies the function (checkPW). The if line checks to see if the text typed by the user in the password input text box is letmein.

   (continued)

Figure 25 *The function that includes an if statement*

This line may appear as you enter the code

Code to type

Closing brace added automatically; do not type

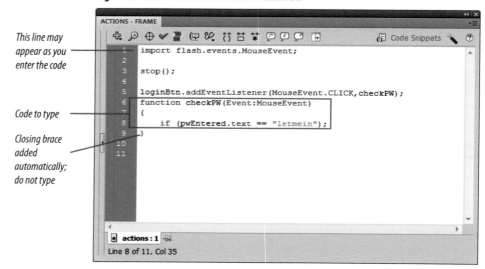

Using ActionScript to Enhance User Experience

Figure 26 *The completed code to test user input*

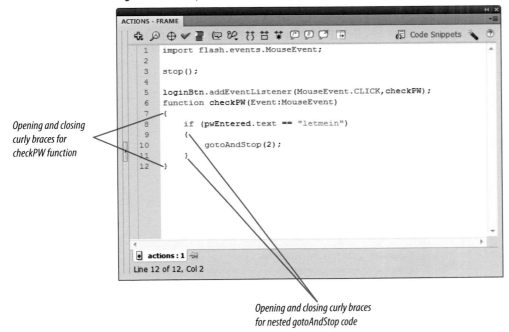

Opening and closing
curly braces for
checkPW function

```
ACTIONS - FRAME
                                                    Code Snippets
1    import flash.events.MouseEvent;
2
3    stop();
4
5    loginBtn.addEventListener(MouseEvent.CLICK,checkPW);
6    function checkPW(Event:MouseEvent)
7    {
8        if (pwEntered.text == "letmein")
9        {
10           gotoAndStop(2);
11       }
12   }

actions : 1
Line 12 of 12, Col 2
```

Opening and closing curly braces
for nested gotoAndStop code

8. Press **[Enter]** (Win) or **[return]** Mac to add a new blank line, then type the following lines of code as shown in Figure 26:

   {

   gotoAndStop(2);

   This code tells the program what to do if the If statement is true, that is, if the user typed letmein in the password input text box.

   Notice the two sets of curly braces. The gotoAndPlay code is nested inside the checkPW function code. Each set of codes (the checkPW function code and the gotoAndStop code) must have its own set of curly braces.

9. Click the **Check Syntax button** .

10. Click the **Auto format button** .

11. Test the movie, type **notsure**, then click the **login button**.

    Nothing happens using the text string notsure.

12. Change **notsure** to **letmein**, then click the **login button**.

    The second screen appears.

13. Close the Flash Player window.

14. Close the Actions panel.

15. Save your work.

You used an if statement to create a conditional branch based on user behavior (input of password).

Provide user feedback

1. Insert a **new layer** above the password input box layer, then name it **tries output box**.
2. Click the **Text tool** on the Tools panel, change the Text type to **Dynamic text**, then be sure Show border around text button 🔲 is not selected.
3. Draw the **text box** shown in Figure 27, then give it an instance name of **tries**.
4. Click **frame 1** on the actions layer, display the Actions panel, then click below the stop(); line.
5. Type **var n:Number = 0;** to create a numeric variable named n.
6. Click after the **right brace (})** below the gotoAndStop line to set the insertion line as shown in Figure 28.
7. Press **[Enter]** (Win) or **[return]** (Mac) to add a blank line, then type the following lines of code:

   else

   {

   This starts the else statement. The else statement will be executed if the user does not type in the correct password, letmein.
8. Press **[Enter]** (Win) or **[return]** (Mac), then type the following lines of code:

   n++;

   tries.text = "Sorry, "+(3-n)+" tries left";

   pwEntered.text = "";

   The first line increments the variable n by 1. The second line subtracts the value of n from 3, concatenates it with Sorry ... tries left, and places the text string in the tries dynamic text box. The third line clears the password that the user typed in the pwEntered input text box.

   (continued)

Figure 27 *Drawing the dynamic text box*

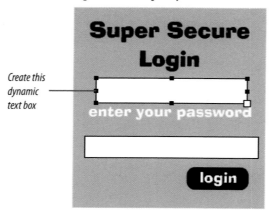

Create this dynamic text box

Figure 28 *Setting the insertion line*

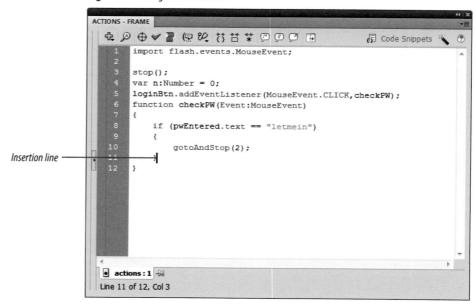

Insertion line

Figure 29 *Completed code to create a conditional branch based on user input*

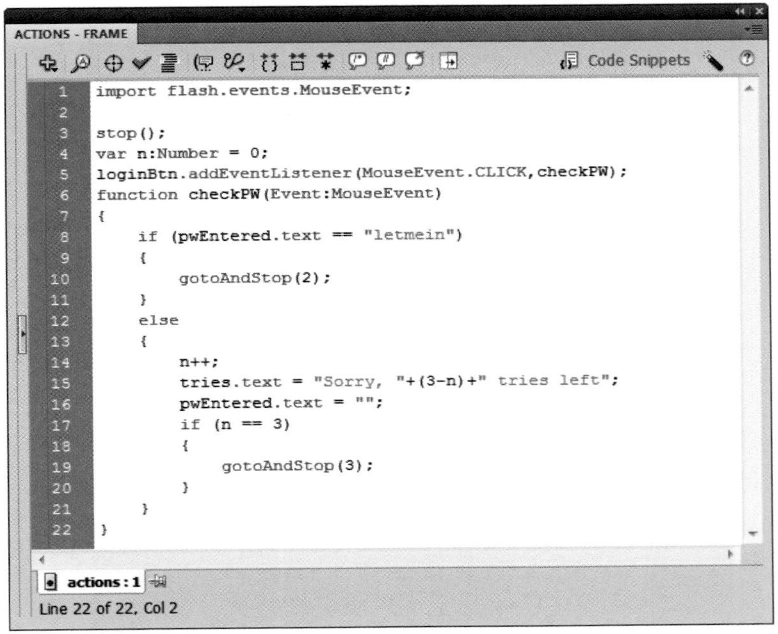

```
ACTIONS - FRAME

1   import flash.events.MouseEvent;
2
3   stop();
4   var n:Number = 0;
5   loginBtn.addEventListener(MouseEvent.CLICK,checkPW);
6   function checkPW(Event:MouseEvent)
7   {
8       if (pwEntered.text == "letmein")
9       {
10          gotoAndStop(2);
11      }
12      else
13      {
14          n++;
15          tries.text = "Sorry, "+(3-n)+" tries left";
16          pwEntered.text = "";
17          if (n == 3)
18          {
19              gotoAndStop(3);
20          }
21      }
22  }
```

actions : 1

Line 22 of 22, Col 2

9. Press **[Enter]** (Win) or **[return]** (Mac), then type the following lines of code:

    if (n == 3)

    {

    gotoAndStop(3);

    The first line checks to see if n is equal to 3. If so, the code within the braces is executed which jumps the playhead to screen 3. Screen 3 displays the words Access Denied.

10. Click the **Check Syntax button** , click the **Auto format button** , then compare your screen to Figure 29.

11. Test the movie, type **notsure** for the password, then click the **login button**.

12. Type **notsure** and click the login button two more times.

    The Access Denied screen appears and the number of tries left is displayed.

13. Close the Flash Player window.

14. Test the movie, type **letmein** for the password, then click the **login button**.

15. Close the Flash Player window, then close the Actions panel.

16. Click the **password input box** on the Stage to select it, click the **Behavior list arrow** in the PARAGRAPH area of the Properties panel, then click **Password**.

17. Test the movie, type **letmein**.

    Notice asterisks are displayed in place of the letters as you type.

    (continued)

18. Click the **login button**.

The Access Granted screen appears.

19. Close the Flash Player window, save you work, then close the movie.

You used if and else statements to provide feedback to the user.

Create a while loop to duplicate movie clip symbols

1. Open fl10_4.fla, then save it as **duplicator.fla**.

This movie has one screen that allows the user to determine how many times to duplicate the head on the screen. The user enters a number and clicks the duplicator button, which causes that number of heads to appear in random locations on the screen.

2. Insert a **new layer** above the duplicate button layer, then name it **number input box**.

3. Click the **Text tool** T on the Tools panel, change the text type to **Input**, click the Show border around text button 🔲 to make it active, change the Behavior to **Single line**, then draw the **text box** shown in Figure 30.

4. Enter **numberIn** for the instance name.

5. Click **frame 1** on the actions layer, open the Actions panel, then type the following as a single line of code below the stop(); line:

**duplicateBtn.
addEventListener(MouseEvent.CLICK,
runDuplicate);**

This creates an event listener for duplicateBtn (the instance name of the button) and names a function, runDuplicate, that is called when the duplicateBtn object is clicked.

(continued)

Figure 30 *Drawing the input text box*

Figure 31 *Setting the condition for the while loop*

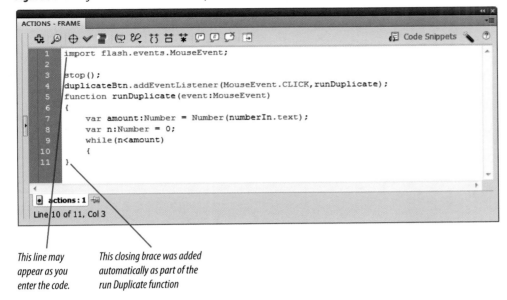

```
import flash.events.MouseEvent;

stop();
duplicateBtn.addEventListener(MouseEvent.CLICK, runDuplicate);
function runDuplicate(event:MouseEvent)
{
    var amount:Number = Number(numberIn.text);
    var n:Number = 0;
    while(n<amount)
    {
}
```

Line 10 of 11, Col 3

This line may appear as you enter the code.

This closing brace was added automatically as part of the run Duplicate function

6. Press **[Enter]** (Win) or **[return]** (Mac) to add a blank line, then type the following lines of code:

   function runDuplicate(event:MouseEvent)

   {

   The first line identifies the function (runDuplicate). The left brace ({) signifies the start of the code that defines the function.

7. Press **[Enter]** (Win) or **[return]** (Mac) to add a blank line, then type the following lines of code:

   var amount:Number = Number (numberIn.text);

   var n:Number = 0;

   The first line creates a numeric variable named amount and assigns it the number entered by the user in the numberIn input box. The second line creates a numeric variable named n and gives it a value of 0.

8. Press **[Enter]** (Win) or **[return]** (Mac) to add a blank line, then type the following lines of code, as shown in Figure 31:

   while (n < amount)

   {

   The first line sets the condition for the while loop. That is, the loop will continue as long as the value in the amount variable is less than the value in the n variable. The { brace signifies the start of the code contained in the loop.

   (continued)

9. Press **[Enter]** (Win) or **[return]** (Mac) to add a blank line, then type the following:

   var faceInstance:faceMC = new faceMC();

   This line creates a variable named faceInstance and creates an instance of the faceMC movie clip.

10. Press **[Enter]** (Win) or **[return]** (Mac) to add a blank line, then type the **addChild** code, as shown in Figure 32, and that follows:

    addChild(faceInstance).x = (Math. random()*150)+50, (faceInstance).y = (Math.random()*200)+50;

    This line adds the faceInstance object at a random location on the screen and keeps the object within the boundaries of the Stage.

    (continued)

Figure 32 *The addChild line*

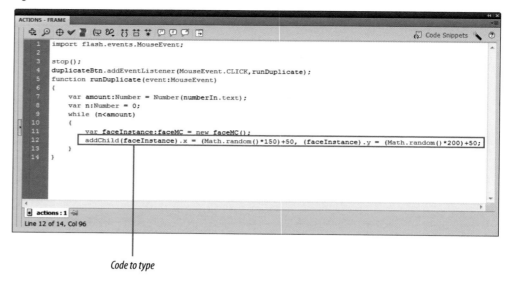

Code to type

Using ActionScript to Enhance User Experience

Figure 33 *Completed code to create a loop based on user input*

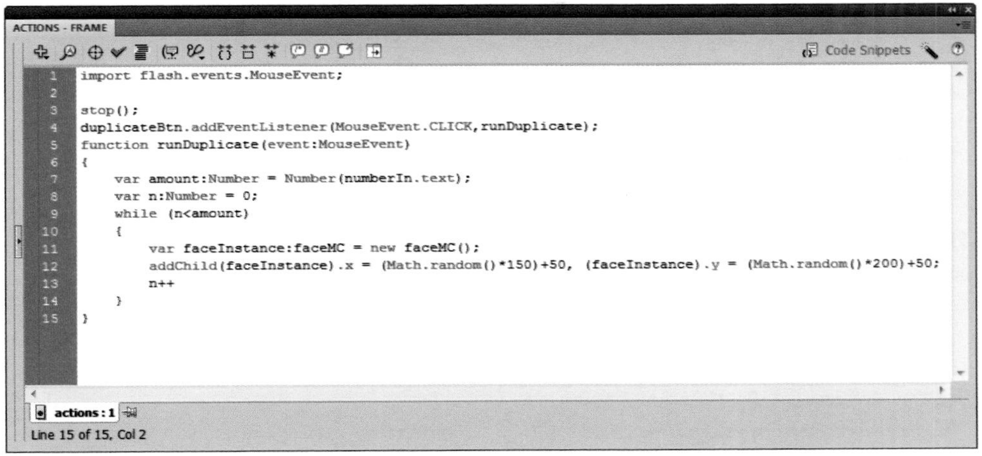

```
ACTIONS - FRAME

Code Snippets

1    import flash.events.MouseEvent;
2
3    stop();
4    duplicateBtn.addEventListener(MouseEvent.CLICK,runDuplicate);
5    function runDuplicate(event:MouseEvent)
6    {
7        var amount:Number = Number(numberIn.text);
8        var n:Number = 0;
9        while (n<amount)
10       {
11           var faceInstance:faceMC = new faceMC();
12           addChild(faceInstance).x = (Math.random()*150)+50, (faceInstance).y = (Math.random()*200)+50;
13           n++
14       }
15   }

actions : 1
Line 15 of 15, Col 2
```

11. Press **[Enter]** (Win) or **[return]** (Mac) to add a blank line, then type the following:

    n++;

    This line increments n by 1.

12. Click the **Check Syntax button** ✔, click the **Auto format button** ☰, then compare your Script pane with Figure 33.

13. Test the movie, type **5** in the enter number box, then click the **duplicate button**.

TIP Compare your Actions panel to Figure 33. If you encounter any errors, be sure the type is set to input text box and, if you see asterisks when you type, change the Behavior setting to Single line.

14. Close the Flash Player window, save your work, then close the document.

You used a while statement to create a loop that duplicates a movie clip symbol the number of times specified by the user.

Use ActionScript
TO CREATE EXTERNAL LINKS

What You'll Do

 In this lesson, you will create email and web page links.

Creating a Link to a Website

Many websites contain links to other sites. You might create links to lead the user to a related site or just to another site you want to share. The URLRequest class along with the navigateToURL function, shown in Figure 34, let you open another file or jump from a button or movie clip symbol to another website. The new site or file can appear in the same browser window as your site or in a new browser window. Table 1 displays the target options for a website and external file links.

When you use URLRequest to lead to another website, you must supply the URL for the file. Make sure to include the entire URL, including the protocol prefix, for example, *http://www.adobe.com*, which is known as an absolute path.

Figure 34 *ActionScript to display a website*

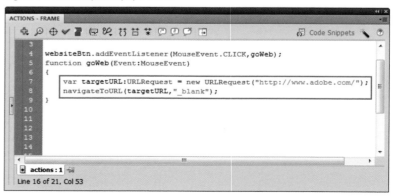

Using ActionScript to Enhance User Experience

Creating a Mailto: Link

You can also use URLRequest to create an email link from a button or movie clip symbol. When a user clicks an email link, a new email message window opens, with the TO: address field already filled in with an address you have specified, as shown in Figure 35. To create an email link, include mailto: and then the email address in the URL field of the URLRequest statement. If you want to create an email link from text, not a button or movie clip symbol, you can use the Properties panel.

TABLE 1: TARGET OPTIONS FOR WEBSITE LINKS	
Option	**Opens site or link in:**
_self	The current window
_blank	A new window
_parent	The parent of the current frame (a frame is a part of a web page)
_top	The top-level frame in the current window

Figure 35 *New message window for a maito:link*

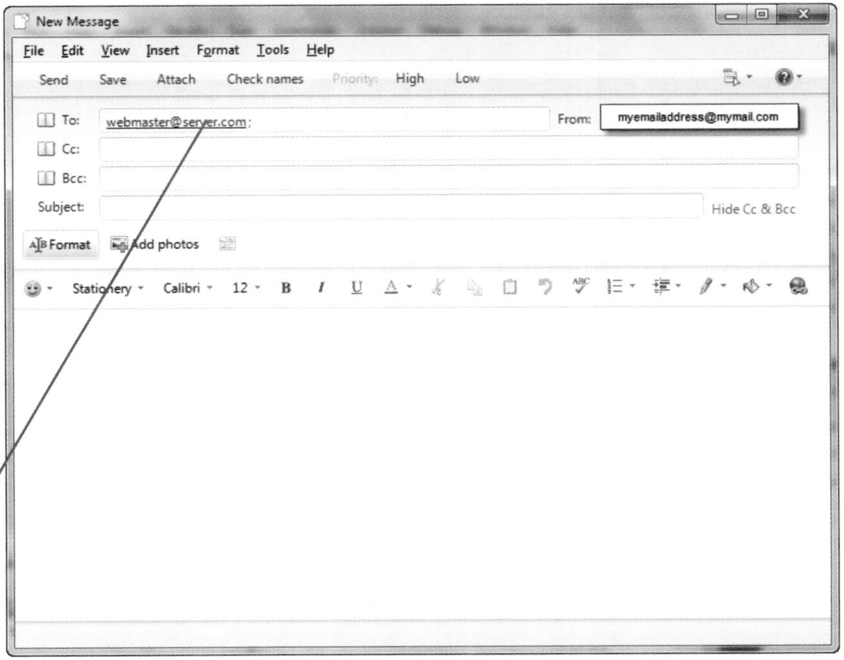

To: field filled in
with the address
you specified

NEW Create a website link

1. Open fl10_5.fla, then save it as **links.fla**.

2. Click **frame 1** on the actions layer, open the Actions panel, then type the following as a single line of code:

   websiteBtn.addEventListener(MouseEvent. CLICK, goWeb);

   This creates an event listener for a mouse event and names a function (goWeb) that is called when the websiteBtn object is clicked.

3. Press **[Enter]** (Win) or **[return]** (Mac) to add a blank line, then type:

   function goWeb(Event:MouseEvent)

   This starts the definition of the function goWeb.

4. Press **[Enter]** (Win) or **[return]** (Mac) to add a blank line, then type these three lines of code, as shown in Figure 36:

   {

   var targetURL:URLRequest = new URLRequest("http://www.adobe.com/");

   navigateToURL(targetURL,"_blank");

5. Compare your screen to Figure 36, test the movie, then click the Visit our Website button.

   The Adobe website opens in a browser window. If the browser does not open in a window, click the flashing or bouncing browser button on the taskbar to display the browser window.

   Note: If you are not connected to the Internet, you will not be able to view the site.

6. Close the browser, close the Flash Player window, then save your work.

You linked a button to a website.

Figure 36 *ActionScript code to create a website link*

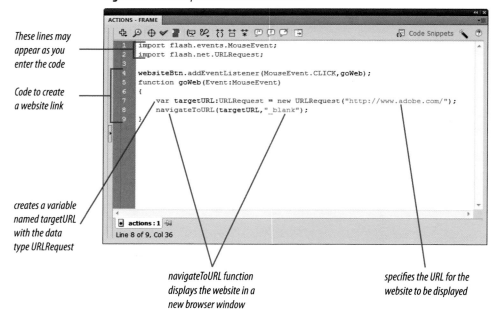

These lines may appear as you enter the code

Code to create a website link

creates a variable named targetURL with the data type URLRequest

navigateToURL function displays the website in a new browser window

specifies the URL for the website to be displayed

Figure 37 *ActionScript code to create an email link*

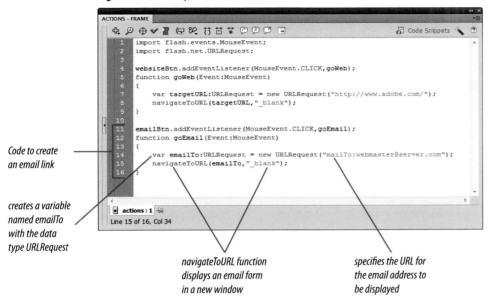

```
ACTIONS - FRAME
 1   import flash.events.MouseEvent;
 2   import flash.net.URLRequest;
 3
 4   websiteBtn.addEventListener(MouseEvent.CLICK,goWeb);
 5   function goWeb(Event:MouseEvent)
 6   {
 7       var targetURL:URLRequest = new URLRequest("http://www.adobe.com/");
 8       navigateToURL(targetURL,"_blank");
 9   }
10
11   emailBtn.addEventListener(MouseEvent.CLICK,goEmail);
12   function goEmail(Event:MouseEvent)
13   {
14       var emailTo:URLRequest = new URLRequest("mailTo:webmaster@server.com");
15       navigateToURL(emailTo,"_blank");
16   }
```

Code to create an email link

creates a variable named emailTo with the data type URLRequest

navigateToURL function displays an email form in a new window

specifies the URL for the email address to be displayed

actions : 1
Line 15 of 16, Col 34

Code Snippets

Create a link to an email address

1. Display the Actions panel, click after the **last curly brace** (}), Press **[Enter]** (Win) or **[return]** (Mac) twice to add two blank lines, then type:

   emailBtn.addEventListener(MouseEvent. CLICK, goEmail);

   This creates an event listener and names a function (goEmail) that is called when the emailBtn object is clicked.

2. Press **[Enter]** (Win) or **[return]** (Mac) to add a blank line, then type:

   function goEmail(Event:MouseEvent)

   This starts the definition of the function goEmail.

3. Press **[Enter]** (Win) or **[return]** (Mac) to add a blank line, then type the three lines of code, as shown in Figure 37:

   {

   var emailTo:URLRequest = new URLRequest ("mailTo:webmaster@server.com");

   navigateToURL(emailTo, "_blank");

4. Compare your screen to Figure 37, test the movie, then click the email button.

   A new email message window opens in your default email program, with the To: field already filled in.

   TIP If an email message window does not appear, your computer may not have access to an email program. If a security warning appears, click Allow.

5. Close the email form window without saving changes, then close the Flash Player window.

6. Save your work, close the document, then exit Flash.

You linked a button to an email address.

Create complex interactivity.

(*Note*: It is good practice to use the Check syntax button and the Auto format button each time you complete the code for an action. This allows you to troubleshoot the code as you go.)

1. Start Flash, open fl10_6.fla, then save it as **skillsDemo10.fla**.
2. Scrub the playhead to view the contents of the frames.

   This is a game in which the user tries to click a moving target, and then, when the user clicks the End button, he or she receives feedback that is based the number of hits. (*Note*: All of the buttons have been given intuitive instance names. For example, the button on the Stage with the text, Go, has an instance name of goBtn.)

3. Click frame 1 on the Timeline, click the white dynamic text box at the top of the Stage, then type **hitsBox** for the instance name.
4. Click frame 1 on the actions layer, open the Actions panel, then add a blank line below the stop(): line.

   You will hide the mouse cursor and enable a custom cursor named arrow. However, first you will create a variable named arrow with a data type of arrow_cursorMC, which is a movie clip in the Library that contains the custom cursor. (*Note*: The arrow_cursorMC movie clip has been given a linkage name, arrow_cursorMC, which means the Export for ActionScript is enabled.) Creating the variable will allow you to use the addChild method so that the cursor will appear on top of the other objects.

5. Type the following:
   var arrow:arrow_cursorMC = new arrow_cursorMC;
6. Move to the next line and type the mouse hide method, then move to the next line.
7. Add a stage mouse move event listener and specify **followMouse** for the function name, then move to the next line and type the code to associate the function with a mouse event.
8. Move to the next line and define the block of code for the followMouse function that will set arrow.x and arrow.y to follow the mouseX and mouseY, then move to the next line.
9. Type **addChild(arrow);** to add arrow to the display list. (*Note*: Be sure to enclose the lines that define what will be executed when the function is called within left and right braces ({}).)
10. Click after the right brace (}) that completes the function (*Note*: this right brace should have been added automatically while you were typing the function definition), then move to the next line.

Load movies at runtime.

1. Create a variable named **myLoader** with a data type of Loader and create a new instance of the Loader, then move to the next line. (*Note*: myLoader will be used to load an SWF file with animated text that will display on the first screen as the flash movie opens.)
2. Type the two lines that set the myLoader x and y properties to 0, then move to the next line.
3. Type the URLRequest statement so that myLoader loads "textAnimation.swf", then on the next line use the addChild method to add myLoader to the display list. (*Hint*: This is similar to the exercise you completed in Lesson 2.)

   This completes the code to load the SWF file into the movie. (*Note*: Be sure that the textAnimation.swf file is in the same folder as your skillsDemo10.fla file.)

4. Add a line to the bottom of the ActionScript code, then create a variable named **hits** with a Number data type and a value of 0.
5. Move to the next line and type an event listener that will call a function named **runIT** when the user clicks the goBtn object on the Stage.
6. Move to the next line and type the code to associate the function with a mouse event.

7. Move to the next line and define the block of code for the runIT function as follows. (*Note*: Be sure to enclose the lines of code that define what will be executed when the function is called within left and right braces ({}). After completing this Skills Review, you will have blocks of code that are nested within other blocks of code. It is important to be sure you always have an opening left brace and a closing right brace for each block of code.)

   ■ Create a variable named **heartInstance** with a targetMC data type and new targetMC instance. (*Note*: The movie clip named targetMC is in the Library and contains an animation of a heart moving around the screen.)

   ■ Use the addChild method to add an instance of the heartInstance object using an x coordinate of 260 and y coordinate of 220. *Hint*: This will keep the animation of the moving heart within the boundaries of the Stage. This one line of code is: addChild(heartInstance). x = **260**, (heartInstance). y = **220**;

   ■ Type an event listener that will call a function named **hitIT** when the user clicks the heartInstance object on the Stage.

   ■ Move to the next line and define the block of code for the hitIT function as follows: (*Note*: Be sure to enclose the lines of code that define what will be executed when the function is called within left and right braces ({}).)

   ● A line of code that increments the variable hits by 1.

   ● A line of code that takes the value in the hits variable and changes it to a string data type, then assigns it to the hitsBox text box. (*Note*: This will display the number of hits that are recorded as the user clicks on the heartInstance object.)

■ Move to the line after the closing brace and create an event listener that will call a function named **goto2** when the endBtn object is clicked.

■ Move to the next line and type the code to associate the function with a mouse event.

■ Move to the next line and define the block of code for the goto2 function as follows: (*Note*: Be sure to enclose the lines of code that define what will be executed when the function is called within left and right braces ({}).)

   ● A line of code that uses the removeChild method to remove myLoader from the display list so the animated text will not be visible on the next screen.

   ● A line of code that uses the removeChild method to remove heartInstance from the display list so the heart will not be visible on the next screen.

   ● A line of code that causes the playhead to go to and play frame 2.

8. Verify a right brace (}) ends the function.

9. Check the syntax and auto format the code.

10. Collapse the Actions panel, then click frame 2 on the Timeline.

11. Click the dynamic text box just below score, then give it an instance name of **scoreBox**.

12. Click the dynamic text box just above the Start Over button, then give it an instance name of **messageBox**.

13. Click frame 2 on the actions layer, open the Actions panel, then add a blank line below the stop(); line.

14. Type the statement that takes the value in the hits variable and changes it to a string data type and then assigns it to the scoreBox text box. (*Note*: This will display the number of hits the user had when trying to click on the heartInstance object. To increase the difficulty of the game, increase the frame rate. This causes the targetMC movie clip (the hearts) to change position more quickly.)

Work with conditional actions.

1. On the next line type the if-else code that will check the number of hits. If the number is greater than 4 have **Super!** appear in the messageBox text box. If not, have the message **Nice Try!** appear in the text box.
2. On the line after the closing brace create an event listener that calls a function named **goHome** when the user clicks the startoverBtn object.
3. Move to the next line and type the code to associate the function with a mouse event.
4. On the next line define the block of code for the goHome function to include:
   - A remove child method that removes arrow. (*Note*: This will remove the custom cursor because it will be added at frame 1.)
   - A gotoandPlay action that jumps the playhead to frame 1.

Use ActionScript to create an external link.

1. After the closing right brace for the goHome function, create an event listener that calls a function named goEmail when the user clicks the commentsBtn object.
2. Move to the next line and type the code to associate the function with a mouse event.
3. On the next line define the block of code for the goEmail function to include a URLRequest and navigateToURL method that will display an email form with the To line filled in.
4. Check the syntax and auto format the code.
5. Test the movie, compare your image to Figure 38, then save your work.

Figure 38 *Completed Skills Review*

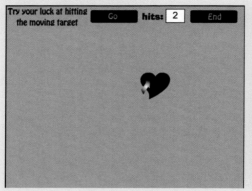

Ultimate Tours would like you to build a banner for its website which, when a button on the banner is clicked, will load a new movie containing its latest travel specials. By creating the banner in one SWF file and the specials in another, Ultimate Tours can update the specials at any time, just by replacing one file. As a way to encourage users to look at and interact with the banner, they would also like you to create a button, that links to the *www.weather.com* website.

1. Open fl10_7.fla, then rename the file **ultimateTours10**.

   This movie contains a heading, two buttons, and a red backdrop. The blank area on the left is where the new movie, named specials.swf, will be loaded.

2. Click the "see specials" button on the Stage, then give it an instance name of **specialsBtn**.

3. Click the "get weather" button on the Stage, then give it an instance name of **weatherBtn**.

4. Click frame 1 of the actions layer, then open the Actions panel.

5. Add a blank line beneath the stop(); line.

6. Type the code that creates a variable named **myLoader**, with a Loader data type, and creates an instance of the new Loader.

7. Type two lines of code to set the myLoader.x value to **20** and the myLoader.y value to **10**.

8. Type the code to create an event listener that calls a function when the user clicks on the specialsBtn object.

9. Type the block of code to define the function to use the URLRequest class to load specials.swf.

   Note: You will need to have the specials.swf file in the same folder as the ultimateTours10.fla file.

10. Use the addChild method to add the myLoader instance to the display list so that it becomes visible on the screen.

11. Add a blank line below the last line of code, then type the code to create an event listener that calls a function when the user clicks on the weatherBtn object.

12. Type the block of code to associate the function with a mouse event and to define the function to use the URLRequest class and the navigateToURL function to link to the http://www.weather.com website using a new window.

13. Check the syntax and auto format the code.

14. Test the movie, click the see specials button, then click the get weather button.

15. Close your browser, compare your image to Figure 39, then save your work.

Figure 39 *Sample completed Project Builder 1*

You have volunteered to use Flash to create an interactive, educational counting game that will get first-graders comfortable with computers. The game will display a random number of cookies spilled from a cookie jar, ask students to count the cookies, type the number, and then give feedback on whether or not the answer is correct.

1. Open fl10_8.fla, then save it as **counting_game10.fla**.
2. Click frame 1 on the Timeline, click the input box above the go button, then give it an instance name of **checkBox**.
3. Click frame 1 on the actions layer, then open the Actions panel.

   Notice that some code has already been included in the file. The code in Line 2 creates a numeric variable named numberOfCookies, which has been given the value of 0. This variable will be assigned a random number between 1 and 10 inclusive. The code in Line 3 is an event listener that calls a function named getCookies when the startBtn object is clicked. The code in Lines 4-8 defines the getCookies function. The code in Line 6 assigns a number between 1 and 10 inclusive to the numCookies variable. This is done using the Math.random and the Math.floor methods. The Math.random method returns a value between 0 and .999 that is multiplied by 10 and adds 1. So, the range for Math.random is 1 to 10.999. The Math. floor method takes the number that was calculated

using the Math.random method and changes it into a whole number that does not exceed the specified range (in this case 1 through 10). The code in Line 7 creates a numeric variable named n, which will be used in a counter.

4. Complete the getCookies function by typing code for the following before the closing right brace:
   - Add a line below the last line of code and before the closing right brace to create a while loop that loops while n is less than numberOfCookies.
   - Define the while loop as follows and place the code inside left and right braces.
     - Type a line that creates a variable named **cookieInstance** that has a **cookieMC** data type and then create a new instance of the cookieMC. *Note*: cookieMC is the movie clip that contains an image of the cookie.
     - Add another line of code that uses the addChild method to add cookieInstance to the display list and positions it in a random location. (*Hint*: See Figure 32 for the format. The x values should be 200 and 20, and the y values should be 150 and 220. This will ensure the cookies will overlap with the cookie jar.)
     - Add another line of code that increments n by 1.
   - Verify both the while loop block of code and the getCookies function block of code end with right braces (}).

5. After the closing right brace for the getCookies function, type an event listener that calls a function when the **goBtn** object is clicked. Name the function **checkNumberTyped**.
6. Define the function as an if-else statement. If the number entered by the user into the input box (checkBox.text) is equal to the number of cookies (numberOfCookies) generated by the random function, then have the playhead got to and play frame 2; else have the playhead go to and play frame 3.
7. Check the syntax and auto format the code.
8. Click frame 2 on the Timeline, click the dynamic text box just below the heading on the Stage and give it an instance name of **right**.
9. Click frame 2 on the actions layer, then display the Actions panel.

   The code in Line 2 adds an event listener that "listens" for an ENTER_FRAME event and names a function (**correct**). The enter frame event causes the function named correct to be executed when the playhead moves to frame 2.

10. Type the line of code between the left and right braces ({}) that takes the value in the numberOfCookies variable and changes it to a string data type, then assigns it to the dynamic text box named **right**. (*Hint*: The format to change a numeric var to a string is: Textboxname.text = String(var);)

11. Check the syntax and auto format the code.
12. Click frame 3 on the Timeline, click the dynamic text box on the Stage and give it an instance name of **wrong**.
13. Click frame 2 on the actions layer and copy the code for the event listener and the function called correct, then click frame 3 on the actions layer and paste the code on a new line following stop();.
14. Edit the code pasted into frame 3 on the actions layer so the function name is **incorrect** and the text box name is **wrong**.
15. Check the syntax and auto format the code.
16. Test the movie several times by entering both correct and incorrect numbers for the number of cookies displayed.
17. Compare your image to Figure 40, then save your work.

Figure 40 *Sample completed Project Builder 2*

Spill the Cookies

Click start to spill the cookies.

start

Type the number of cookies that have spilled from the jar in the box, then click go.

4

go

Figure 41 shows a page from a website created using Flash. Study the figure and complete the following. For each question, indicate how you determined your answer.

1. Connect to the Internet, then go to this URL: *http://v4.2a-archive.com/flashindex.htm*.

2. Open a document in a word processor or open a new Flash document, save the file as **dpc10**, then answer the following questions. (*Hint*: Use the Text tool in Flash.)
   - What is the purpose of this site? Does the design of the site contribute to its purpose?
   - Move the mouse pointer around the screen and note the different effects as you pass over links and buttons. How could these effects be achieved with ActionScript?
   - Click the links in the main navigation bar. What changes occur on the screen? Do you think the links are jumping to a different frame in this movie or loading a new movie? What specific actions could be used to achieve this effect?
   - List some of the advantages of loading a new movie for links, in the context of this site.
   - Click the Portfolio link, then click the VIEW button for the featured website. (*Note*: The VIEW button is under the slide show that is running for the featured website.) What happens? What specific actions might be associated with the View button to achieve this effect?

Figure 41 *Design Project*

You have decided to create a portfolio with five screens, each in a separate frame and on a separate layer. One screen contains examples of the Flash work you have done throughout this book, and one creates a password-protected, clients-only area. You will create the links to your Flash movies by loading new SWF files. You can use your favorites from the files you have developed throughout this book, or any other SWF files you have created on your own.

1. Open a new Flash document, then save it as **portfolio10.fla**.
2. Create a screen with a heading of **home** in frame 1 on a layer called Home Page. Add another layer named **Navigation-buttons** and create three buttons named **home**, **flash samples**, and **clients only**.
3. Create a screen in frame 2 on a layer called **Flash Samples**, using a format that fits in visually with the rest of your site. On this screen include a title and at least three buttons, each of which, when clicked, loads a new Flash movie. (*Hint*: New movies appear starting in the middle of the current movie. You may need to reduce the size of your SWF files or change the x and y coordinates of the loader to position the movies as desired. Be sure the SWF files are in the same folder as your movie.)
4. Create a screen in frame 3 on a layer called **Clients Only**. On this screen, create the text "Enter password" and an input text box with the instance name **enterPW**.
5. Create another screen that says: **Welcome to the client's area**.

6. Create another screen that says: **Sorry, that is not correct. Please contact me to receive or verify your password**. Then, add a button to the page which, when clicked, opens the user's default email program to a new mail message with your email address filled in.
7. On the Clients Only screen that prompts for a password, create a button with the text **Submit**. Set up a conditional action which, if the user types the word "password" in the input text box, jumps to the "welcome" screen,
or, if the user types anything else, jumps to the "sorry" screen.
8. Add events to the buttons on the home screen which, when clicked, jump to the appropriate screen: the home button goes to screen 1, the flash samples button goes to the flash samples screen, and the clients only button goes to the clients only screen.
9. Create a variable named myLoader with a Loader data type and add an instance of the loader. Specify the X and Y Stage location for the loader. (*Hint*: Place these three lines in frame 1 of your actions layer just below a stop(); statement.)
10. Add myLoader.unload(); event (assuming your loader variable is named myLoader) to the function called by the home, samples and clients only navigation buttons on the home screen. (*Note*: If you don't add this action, the movies you load on the Flash Samples screen will remain loaded, even when you navigate away from the samples screen. Add these statements above the goto statements in each function.)
11. Check the syntax and auto format the code.

12. Test the movie, then compare your movie to Figure 42.
13. Save your work.

Figure 42 *Sample completed Portfolio Project*

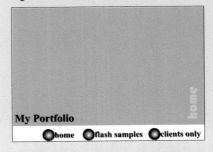

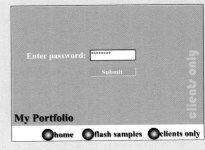

11
CHAPTER

ADDING SOUND
AND VIDEO

1. Work with sound

2. Specify synchronization options

3. Modify sounds

4. Use ActionScript with sound

5. Work with video

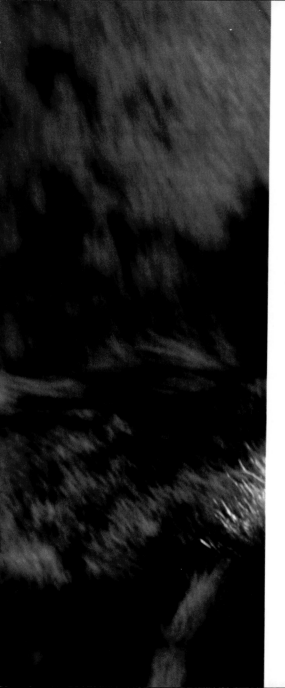

CHAPTER 11

ADDING SOUND
AND VIDEO

Introduction

Like animation and interactivity, sound and video are important tools you can use to express a message, engage users and make your site or application appealing to visitors. In an earlier chapter, you added sound to the Timeline and to a button and you added video to a Flash document. In this chapter, you will see that there is much more you can do with sound and video in Flash. For example, you can set a short sound clip to play continuously, creating a musical backdrop for your movie. Or, you can synchronize sound with an animation or movie clip, perhaps providing a voice-over that explains what's happening on the screen. You can use new video features, such

as adding cue points, which allow users to navigate to different parts of a video clip. You can add cue points to a video directly in Flash using the Properties panel.

Sound and video can add significantly to the size of published movies, so you should plan ahead and try to use them strategically. Apply sound and video only where it will have the most impact. Flash includes a number of compression options that can help you achieve a balance between quality and file size when using these elements in your movies. Effective and judicious use of sound and video are key ingredients in making a Flash site or application a truly multimedia experience.

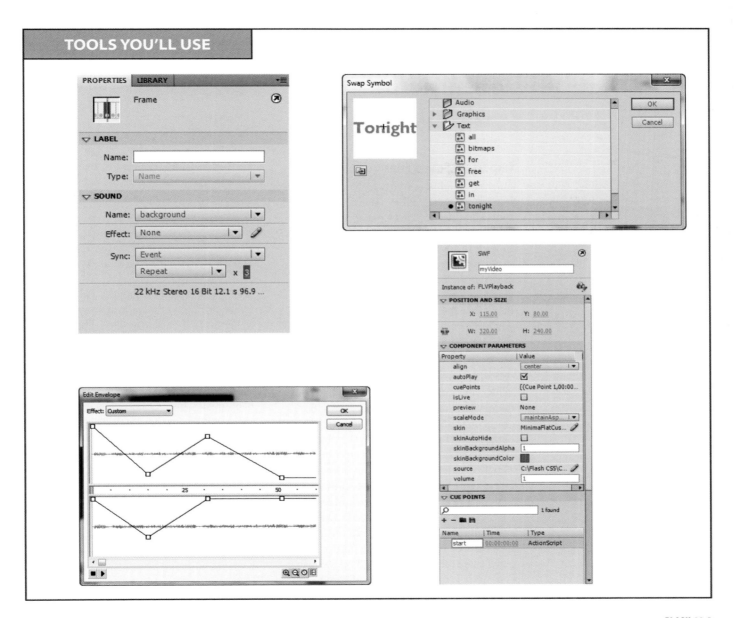

Work with
SOUND

What You'll Do

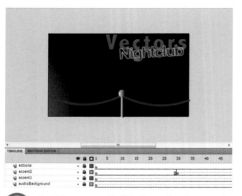

In this lesson, you will add background music to a movie
and work with layering and repeating sounds.

Importing Sound Files

One way to add sound to an object (such as a
button) or the Timeline in Flash, is to import
sound files to the Library panel. Table 1
shows the types of sound files you can
import. In addition to imported sound files,
Flash provides dozens of sound effects such
as sirens wailing, dogs barking, and lightning
cracking. These are found in the Common
Libraries panel on the Windows menu. Also,
you can use ActionScript to add a sound
during runtime.

Adding a Sound to the Timeline

When you want a sound to play in the
background, rather than tie it to a specific
object on the Stage, you can add an instance
of the sound to a frame on the Timeline.
You can select a keyframe on a layer on the
Timeline and then drag a sound from the
Library panel to the Stage to add the sound
to the selected keyframe, or you can select a
keyframe on a layer on the Timeline and then
add a sound to the selected keyframe through
the Properties panel. Using the Properties
panel is the recommended method because
you can select the sound file you want to use,
set the number of times you want the sound

file to repeat, and set effects related to the
sound file, such as fade in and fade out.

Sounds are represented on the Timeline by
either a straight or waveform line, as shown
in Figure 1. The approximate duration of the
sound is indicated by the number of frames
the line occupies. Although the line extends
no further than the last frame of the movie,
if the sound is longer in duration than the
length of the movie in seconds, the sound
may continue playing after the playhead has
reached the last frame of the movie.

You can play multiple sounds at once by
placing the sounds on different layers.
For example, you might have background
music that plays continuously, but then
play accent sounds at various points to
act as a supplement or counterpoint to
the background. Or you might have a
background sound on one layer and a voice-
over or narration on another layer. You can
stagger where each sound begins by creating a

keyframe at a later point on the Timeline, and then adding the sound to this keyframe.

Understanding Event Sounds

By default, sounds you add in Flash are considered **event sounds**. Like movie clip symbols, event sounds play independently of the Timeline. The sound starts in the keyframe to which you add it, but it can continue playing even after the last frame in the main Timeline is played. In addition, event sounds may play at a faster or slower rate than indicated by the frames on the Timeline, depending on the speed of the computer on which the movie is played.

Event sounds have an advantage in that you can use them as many times as you like in a movie, with no increase in the file size of your published movie. However, when a movie is played over the web, event sounds do not begin until the entire sound file is downloaded; this may cause a disconnect between sound and images for some users.

There is another type of sound in Flash, called **stream sound**. Stream sounds are similar to animated graphic symbols because they are closely tied to the main Timeline. Thus, even if a stream sound is longer than a movie, a stream sound stops at the end of the movie. When loading sound files externally, instead of from the Library panel, stream sounds can start playing as your computer begins to download them, which prevents users from waiting for the entire sound file to download before the movie starts. You will work with stream sounds in the next lesson. The same sound file can be designated as either an event sound or a stream sound, depending on the setting you choose.

Repeating Sounds

The Repeat feature lets you replay a sound a specified number of times. This is useful in certain situations, such as creating background music for a movie. If you want your audio to loop continuously, you can select the Loop option by clicking the Repeat list arrow in the SOUND area on the Properties panel, and then selecting Loop.

Figure 1 *A sound on the Timeline*

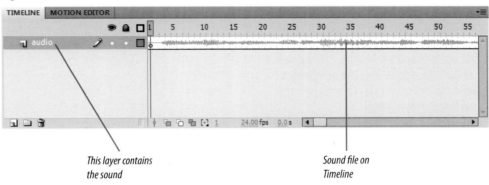

This layer contains the sound

Sound file on Timeline

TABLE 1: SOUND FILES THAT FLASH IMPORTS		
Sound type	**Windows**	**Mac**
Adobe Soundbooth (.asnd)	Yes	Yes
Waveform Audio File (.wav)	Yes	Yes, requires QuickTime
Audio Interchange File (.aiff), (.aif)	Yes, requires QuickTime	Yes
MPEG-1 Audio level 3 (.mp3)	Yes	Yes
Sound only QuickTime movies (.mov), (.qt)	Yes, requires QuickTime	Yes, requires QuickTime
System 7 sounds (.snd)	No	Yes, requires QuickTime
Sound Designer II (.sd2)	No	Yes, requires QuickTime
SunAU (.au)	Yes, requires QuickTime	Yes, requires QuickTime

Add sound to a Timeline

1. Open fl11_1.fla from the drive and folder where your Data Files are stored, then save it as **nightclub.fla**.

2. Display the Library panel, expand the Audio folder to display the list of audio files, click **accent1**, then click the **Play button** in the Item Preview area at the top of the Library panel to preview the sound.

3. Preview the **accent2** and **background** sounds.

4. Insert a **new layer** above the sign layer, then name it **audioBackground**.

5. Click **frame 1** on the audioBackground layer, display the Properties panel, click the **Name list arrow** in the SOUND area, click **background**, then verify that Event appears in the Sync sound list box, as shown in Figure 2.

    Flash adds the sound file to the layer, as indicated by the blue horizontal line through the frames on the audioBackground layer.

    TIP The Library panel already contains several sounds, so when you click the Name list arrow in the SOUND area, a list appears of all sound files that have been imported into the Library panel.

6. Test the movie.

    The background music sound clip plays, ending after about 12 seconds, which is how long it takes to play the sound file one time.

7. Close the Flash Player window.

You added a sound to the Timeline and verified it was an event sound.

Figure 2 *Selecting a sound file in the Properties panel*

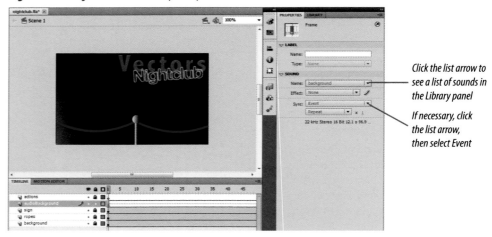

Click the list arrow to see a list of sounds in the Library panel

If necessary, click the list arrow, then select Event

Figure 3 *A Timeline with layered sounds*

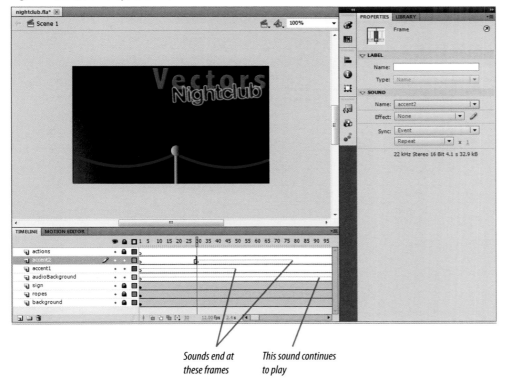

Sounds end at   This sound continues
these frames   to play

Layer sounds

1. Insert a **new layer** above the audioBackground layer, then name it **accent1**.

2. Click **frame 1** on the accent1 layer, click the **Name list arrow** in the SOUND area on the Properties panel, click **accent1**, then verify that Event appears in the Sync list box.

3. Insert a **new layer** above the accent1 layer, then name it **accent2**.

4. Insert a **keyframe** in frame 30 on the accent2 layer.

5. Click the **Frame view button** ▾≡ at the top right side of the Timeline, then click **Tiny** to display more frames.

6. Click the **Name list arrow** in the SOUND area on the Properties panel, click **accent2**, verify that Event appears in the Sync list box, then compare your screen to Figure 3.

7. Test the movie.

   All three sound files play simultaneously for a short time. However, since the sound clips are of different durations, they do not all play to the end of the movie.

   TIP When you look at the Timeline, sound lines are blue and layer border lines are black.

8. Close the Flash Player window.

You layered sounds of different durations.

Create a repeating sound

1. Click **frame 1** on the audioBackground layer, verify that Repeat is displayed in the SOUND area on the Properties panel, change the Number of times to repeat to **3**, then compare your screen to Figure 4.

   The sound line on the audioBackground layer now stretches to the end of the movie, frame 200.

2. Click **frame 1** on the accent1 layer, then use the Properties panel to change the Number of times to repeat to **5**.

3. Click **frame 30** on the accent2 layer, then use the Properties panel to change the Number of times to repeat to **4**.

   Since the accent2 sound starts in a later keyframe than the accent1 sound, you do not have to repeat it as many times to have it play until the end of the movie.

TIP You select Loop when you want a sound to play continuously. You select Repeat and select a number when you want a sound file to play a set number of times. The default setting is Repeat 1, which indicates the sound will play one time.

4. Lock the three audio layers.

(continued)

Figure 4 *Specifying the number of times a sound repeats*

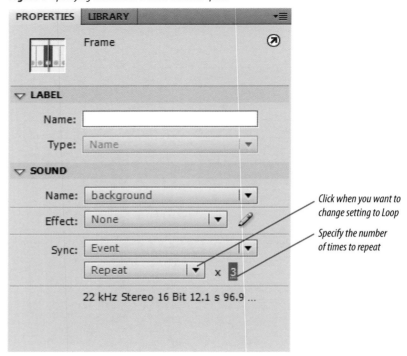

Click when you want to change setting to Loop

Specify the number of times to repeat

Figure 5 *Sounds in Timeline extend to end of movie*

5. Drag the **playhead** to frame 200 on the Timeline, as shown in Figure 5.

   All the sounds now extend to the same ending frame, frame 200, which is the frame where the animation of the sign ends.

6. Test the movie and let it play until all the sounds stop.

   The sound files play simultaneously during the animation of the sign. You can tell the animation has ended when the words "Vectors Nightclub" stop flashing. The blue lines on the Timeline representing the sound waves end at frame 200, the last frame of the movie. However, because the sounds are event sounds, they continue to play even after the playhead reaches frame 200, each stopping only when it reaches the end of the number of repetitions you specified.

7. Close the Flash Player window.

8. Click the **Frame view button**  at the top right of the Timeline, then click **Normal** to display fewer frames.

9. Drag the **scroll bar** at the bottom of the Timeline to the left to display frame 1.

10. Save your work.

You set three sounds to repeat, which causes them to play simultaneously to the same ending frame, frame 200.

Specify SYNCHRONIZATION OPTIONS

What You'll Do

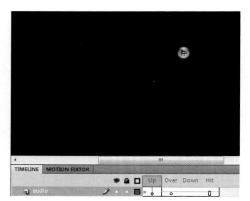

 In this lesson, you will synchronize a stream sound with an animation, and you will set a button to play a sound in the Over state and stop playing the sound in the Up state.

Understanding Synchronization Options

As you've seen, Event is the default synchronization sound option in the Properties panel. You can also choose from one of three other synchronization options: Start, Stop, and Stream, as shown in Figure 6.

Understanding Stream Sounds

Unlike event sounds, stream sounds are tied to the Timeline and the number of frames on the Timeline. When you add a sound and set it to stream, Flash breaks the sound into individual sound clips and then associates each clip with a specific frame on the Timeline. The frame rate of your movie determines the number of clips that Flash creates. If the sound is longer than the number of frames on the Timeline, the sound still stops at the end of the movie.

One important use of stream sounds is to synchronize animation and audio, since the sounds can be better coordinated with the Timeline during both development

and playback. If the computer playing a movie is slow, Flash will skip frames of an animation to maintain synchronization with a stream sound. To avoid a jumbled or jerky playback, you should try to keep your animation simple when using a stream sound.

QUICK TIP

Once you set a sound to a stream, you can preview the sound by playing the movie on the Stage.

Understanding the Start and Stop Synchronization Options

A Start sound is similar to an event sound, but it will not play again if an instance of that sound is already playing. The Start option is often used with sounds associated with buttons or with movies that loop back to the beginning, in order to avoid overlapping sounds.

The Stop option lets you end an event sound at a specific keyframe. For example, you can start an event sound in frame 1 and then stop it playing in frame 40, even if the sound file is of a much longer duration. You insert a keyframe in the frame where you want to apply a Stop option, then you specify the name of the sound you want to stop in the Properties panel. If you want to stop multiple event sounds, you must insert a separate Stop option in a keyframe on each sound layer. Flash indicates a Stop option with a small square in the keyframe, as shown in Figure 7.

QUICK TIP

You stop a stream sound at a specific frame by adding a keyframe with the stop(); command on the sound's layer. You stop an event sound by adding a Stop option to a keyframe and identifying via the Properties panel which sound to stop. Event sounds will continue to play through a keyframe, even one with a stop(); command, unless it includes a Stop option and the name of the sound to stop.

Figure 6 *The Sync sound options in the Properties panel*

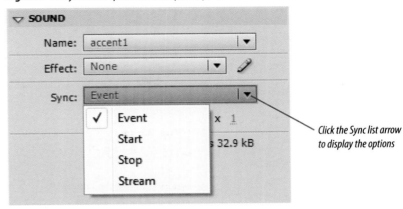

Click the Sync list arrow to display the options

Figure 7 *A Stop option on the Timeline and in the Properties panel*

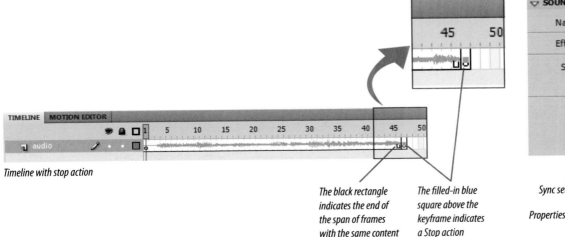

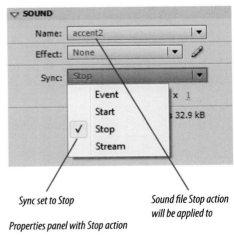

Timeline with stop action

The black rectangle indicates the end of the span of frames with the same content

The filled-in blue square above the keyframe indicates a Stop action

Sync set to Stop

Properties panel with Stop action

Sound file Stop action will be applied to

Set synchronization to the Stream option

1. Verify that the nightclub.fla movie is open, click **Insert** on the menu bar, then click **New Symbol**.

2. Type **wordAnimation** in the Name text box, select Movie Clip for the Type, then click **OK**.

   The edit window for the wordAnimation movie clip symbol opens.

3. Rename Layer 1 as **audio**.

4. Insert a **keyframe** in frame 50.

5. Display the Actions panel, then type **stop();** as shown in Figure 8.

   Inserting a keyframe creates a movie clip of sufficient length (frames 1–50) for the sound to play, and adding a stop action to the keyframe stops the movie clip Timeline from repeating.

6. Close the Actions panel, click **frame 1** on the audio layer, click the **Name list arrow** in the SOUND area on the Properties panel, then click **bitmaps_free_vo**.

7. Click the **Sync list arrow**, click **Stream**, then compare your screen to Figure 9.

8. Press **[Enter]** (Win) or **[return]** (Mac), then listen to the audio.

   The sound file plays, "Tonight all bitmaps get in for free."

You created a movie clip, specified a stop action, added a sound, and set the synchronization of a sound to stream.

Figure 8 *Adding a stop action*

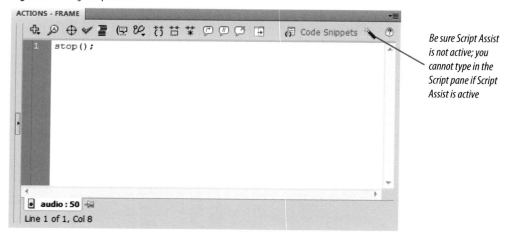

Be sure Script Assist is not active; you cannot type in the Script pane if Script Assist is active

Figure 9 *The streaming sound in the Timeline and Properties panel*

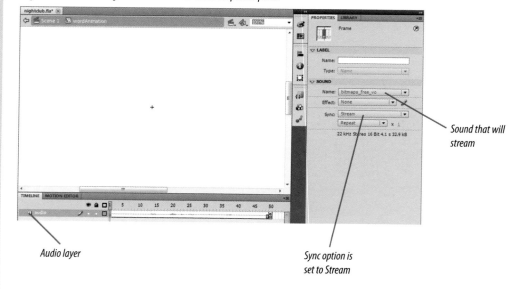

Sound that will stream

Audio layer

Sync option is set to Stream

Figure 10 *The Swap Symbol dialog box*

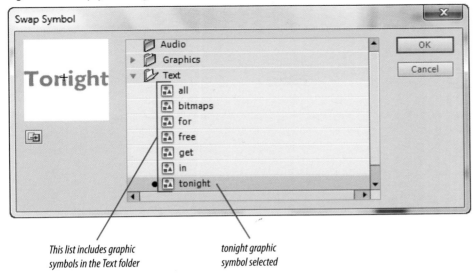

This list includes graphic symbols in the Text folder

tonight graphic symbol selected

Figure 11 *Selecting a symbol to swap*

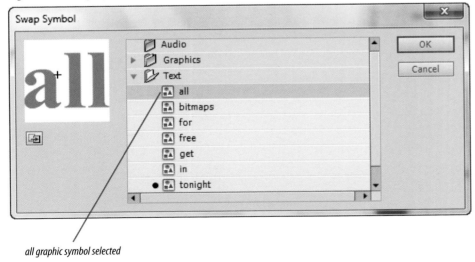

all graphic symbol selected

Synchronize a stream sound with an animation

1. Insert a new layer above the audio layer in the wordAnimation movie clip, then name it **text**.

   You will add text that synchronizes with a voice-over.

2. Insert a **keyframe** in frame 13 on the text layer, display the Library panel, expand the Text folder to view the text graphic symbols, then drag the **tonight graphic symbol** approximately to the middle of the Stage.

3. Change the view to **Fit in window**.

4. Display the Properties panel, change the X value to **−48.9**, change the Y value to **−8.5**, then press **[Enter]** (Win) or **[return]** (Mac).

   The word Tonight appears centered on the Stage.

5. Click the **Selection tool** ![selection tool] on the Tools panel, insert a **keyframe** in frame 19 on the text layer, click the word **Tonight** on the Stage to select it, click the **Swap button** in the Properties panel to open the Swap Symbol dialog box as shown in Figure 10.

TIP The Swap Symbol dialog box lets you replace an object on the Stage with a different object, keeping all other properties the same, including any actions you have assigned to the original object.

6. Click the **all graphic symbol** in the Swap Symbol dialog box as shown in Figure 11, then click **OK**.

   Flash replaces the instance of the tonight graphic symbol with an instance of the all graphic symbol.

(continued)

7. Insert a **keyframe** in frame 23 on the text layer, click the word **all** on the Stage to select it, click the **Swap button**, click the **bitmaps graphic symbol** in the Swap Symbol dialog box, then click **OK**.

8. Insert a **keyframe** in frame 31 on the text layer, click the word **Bitmaps** on the Stage to select it, click the **Swap button**, click the **get graphic symbol** in the Swap Symbol dialog box, then click **OK**.

9. Insert a **keyframe** in frame 32 on the text layer, click the word **Get** on the Stage to select it, click the **Swap button**, click the **in graphic symbol** in the Swap Symbol dialog box, then click **OK**.

10. Insert a **keyframe** in frame 35 on the text layer, click the word **in** on the Stage to select it, click the **Swap button**, click the **for graphic symbol** in the Swap Symbol dialog box, then click **OK**.

11. Insert a **keyframe** in frame 37 on the text layer, click the word **for** on the Stage to select it, click the **Swap button**, click the **free graphic symbol** in the Swap Symbol dialog box, click **OK**, then compare your Timeline to Figure 12.

12. Click **frame 1** on the Timeline, then press **[Enter]** (Win) or **[return]** (Mac), to view the words as they synchronize with sound.

13. Click **Scene 1** at the top left of the workspace to return to the main Timeline.

You created a text animation, then synchronized the appearance of each word in the animation with a voice-over saying the word.

Figure 12 *The wordAnimation movie clip symbol Timeline*

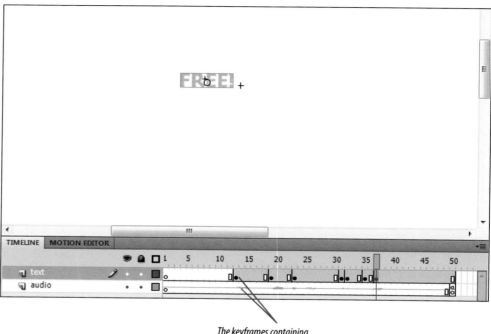

The keyframes containing graphic symbols on the text layer synchronize with the spoken words on the audio layer

Adding Sound and Video

Figure 13 *Movie clip symbol on the Stage*

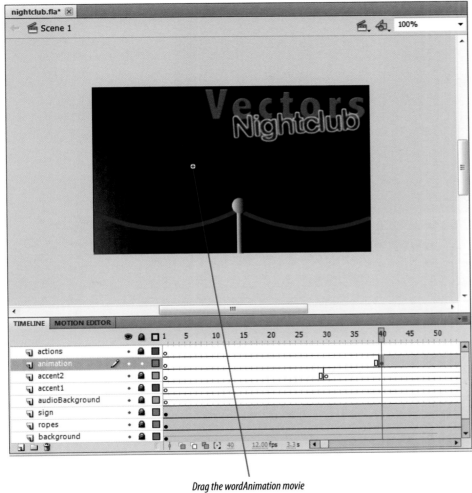

Drag the wordAnimation movie
clip symbol to this location

Add the synchronized animation to the Stage

1. Insert a **new layer** above the accent2 layer, then name it **animation**.

2. Insert a **keyframe** in frame 40 on the animation layer.

3. Display the Library panel, then drag the **wordAnimation movie clip symbol** from the Library panel to the left side of the Stage, as shown in Figure 13.

4. Test the movie.

   The words and stream sounds appear synchronized.

5. Close the Flash Player window.

6. Save your work.

7. Close the movie.

You added an animation synchronized with sound to the Stage.

Set synchronization to the Start option

1. Open fl11_2.fla, then save it as **superTips.fla**.

2. Display the Library panel, open the buttons folder, then double-click the **gel Right button** to display the edit window.

3. Drag the **playhead** through the Timeline.

   The gel Right button symbol currently has four layers, which create the visual effects of the button, such as the arrow changing color when the pointer rolls over it.

4. Insert a **new layer** above the button-arrow layer, name it **audio**, then insert a **keyframe** in the Over frame on the audio layer.

5. Display the Properties panel, click the **Name list arrow** in the SOUND area, then click **accent2**.

   Flash adds the sound file, as indicated by the straight line on the audio layer, which will start to play once you move the mouse pointer over the button, and it will continue to play even after you move off the button.

6. Click the **Sync list arrow**, click **Start**, then compare your screen to Figure 14.

7. Click **Scene 1** at the top left of the workspace to return to the main Timeline.

8. Test the movie, position the mouse pointer over a button, then move the mouse pointer off the button.

   The music starts playing when you hover over a button, and it continues even if you move the mouse pointer away from the button.

9. Close the Flash Player window.

You added sound to the Over state of a button.

Figure 14 *Inserting a Start option in the Over state of a button*

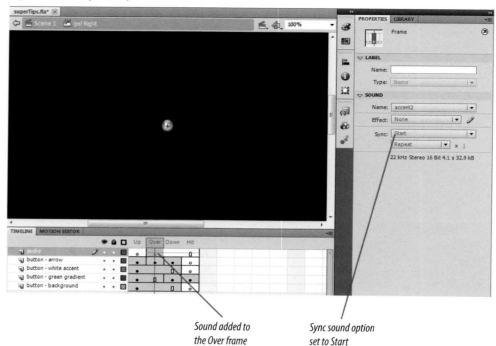

Sound added to
the Over frame

Sync sound option
set to Start

Adding Sound and Video

Figure 15 *Inserting a Stop option in the Up state of a button*

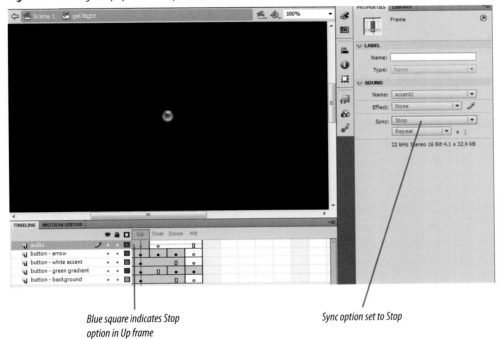

Blue square indicates Stop option in Up frame

Sync option set to Stop

Set synchronization to the Stop option

1. Display the Library panel, then double-click the **gel Right button** in the Library panel to open it in the edit window.

2. Click the **Up frame** on the audio layer.

3. Display the Properties panel, click the **Name list arrow** in the SOUND area, then click **accent2**.

4. Click the **Sync list arrow**, click **Stop**, then compare your screen to Figure 15.

5. Click **Scene 1** at the top left of the workspace to return to the main Timeline.

6. Test the movie.

7. Position the mouse pointer over a button, then move the mouse pointer off the button.

   Note: If you click a button, close the Flash Player window and repeat steps 6 and 7.

   The music stops playing when you move the mouse pointer away from the button.

8. Close the Flash Player window.

9. Save your work, then close the file.

You directed a sound to stop when a button is in the Up state.

Modify
SOUNDS

What You'll Do

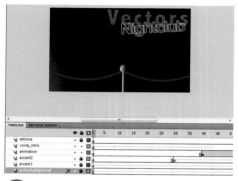

 In this lesson, you will edit when one sound begins and create a custom sound effect for another sound.

Editing Sounds for Length

In most cases, you will want to edit and enhance sounds in a sound-editing program before you import them into Flash. However, Flash does include some basic editing features you can use on sounds you have already imported.

You can trim the length of a sound file using the Edit Envelope dialog box, shown in Figure 16. By moving the Time In and Time Out controls, you can set where the sound will start and stop playing. Adjusting the controls lets you delete unwanted sounds and remove silent sections at the start and end of sounds, which reduces the file size of the published movie. You can preview the edits you make to a sound by clicking the Play button at the bottom-left corner of the Edit Envelope dialog box. Other buttons in this dialog box let you zoom the display of the sound in or out and set the units in the center of the dialog box to seconds or frames, which can help you determine the length of event sounds and make frame-by-frame adjustments to stream sounds.

Changing Sound Effects

Flash includes the following effects you can apply to sounds:

- Left Channel plays the sound only in the left channel or speaker.
- Right Channel plays the sound only in the right channel or speaker.
- Fade Left to Right gradually shifts the sound from the left channel to the right channel over the duration of the sound.
- Fade Right to Left gradually shifts the sound from the right channel to the left channel over the duration of the sound.
- Fade In increases the volume of the sound as it begins to play.
- Fade Out decreases the volume of the sound as it ends.

You can set these options either in the Properties panel of the frame to which you have added the sound, or in the Edit Envelope dialog box for the sound.

An additional option—Custom—lets you create your own volume variations over the duration of a sound. By clicking the channel

Adding Sound and Video

sound line and then moving the envelope handle toward the top (to make the sound louder) or bottom (to make the sound lower), you can specify up to eight locations where you want the sound to fade in, fade out, or play at less than 100% volume. For stereo sounds, you can set different custom envelopes for the two channels. Figure 17 shows a custom volume envelope.

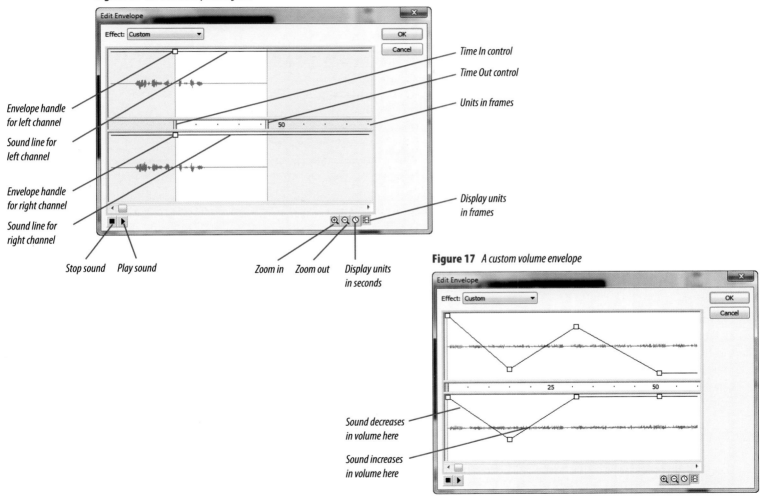

Figure 16 *The Edit Envelope dialog box*

Envelope handle for left channel

Sound line for left channel

Envelope handle for right channel

Sound line for right channel

Stop sound   Play sound

Time In control

Time Out control

Units in frames

Display units in frames

Zoom in   Zoom out   Display units in seconds

Figure 17 *A custom volume envelope*

Sound decreases in volume here

Sound increases in volume here

Edit a sound using the Time In control

1. Open nightclub.fla, then save it as **vectors.fla**.
2. Insert a new layer above the animation layer, then name it **voice_intro**.
3. Click **frame 1** on the voice_intro layer, click the **Name list arrow** in the SOUND area on the Properties panel, click **hello_vo**, click the **Sync list arrow**, then click **Stream**.
4. Test the movie, then close the Flash Player window.
5. Click the **Edit sound envelope button** in the Properties panel, click the **Effect list arrow**, then click **Custom**.

   You will edit the sound file so it plays only the words "Vectors Nightclub."
6. Click the **Frames button** in the Edit Envelope dialog box to select it, if it is not already selected.
7. Click the **Zoom out button** repeatedly until you can see the entire sound with the frames, as shown in Figure 18.
8. Click the **Play sound button** in the Edit Envelope dialog box.
9. Click and drag the **Time In control** to frame 30, then compare your image to Figure 19.
10. Click the **Play sound button** in the Edit Envelope dialog box.

    Only the last two words of the sound, "Vectors Nightclub," should play. If necessary, adjust the Time In control.
11. Click **OK** to close the Edit Envelope window, then test the movie.
12. Close the Flash Player window.

You changed the point at which a sound begins playing.

Figure 18 *Zooming the hello_vo sound in the Edit Envelope dialog box*

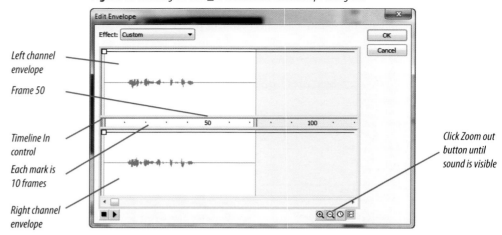

Left channel envelope

Frame 50

Timeline In control

Each mark is 10 frames

Right channel envelope

Click Zoom out button until sound is visible

Figure 19 *Trimming the length of a sound*

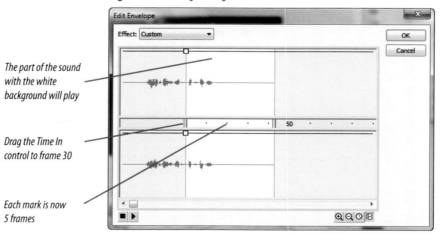

The part of the sound with the white background will play

Drag the Time In control to frame 30

Each mark is now 5 frames

Figure 20 *Decreasing the volume of both channels*

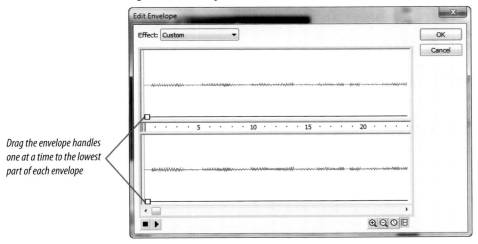

Drag the envelope handles
one at a time to the lowest
part of each envelope

Figure 21 *Increasing the volume of the left channel*

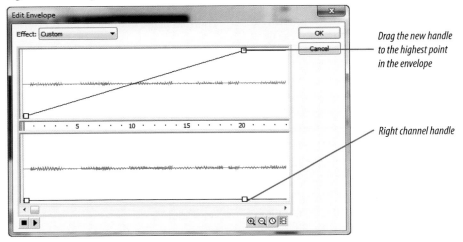

Drag the new handle
to the highest point
in the envelope

Right channel handle

Edit envelopes to create custom volume effects

1. Unlock the audioBackground layer, then click **frame 1** on the layer.

2. Click the **Effect list arrow** in the Properties panel, then click **Custom**.

   Note: You can also select Custom using the Effect list arrow in the Edit Envelope dialog box.

3. Click the **Zoom out button** 🔍 until the frames display 5, 10, 15, and 20, drag the **envelope handle** for the left channel and the **envelope handle** for the right channel down to the lowest point to decrease the sound in both channels, then compare your dialog box to Figure 20.

4. Click the **left channel sound line** on frame 20.

   New envelope handles appear on frame 20 for both the left and right channel envelope sound lines.

5. Drag the **new handle** on the left channel up to the highest point, as shown in Figure 21.

6. Drag the **new handle** on the right channel up to its highest point.

7. Click the **Play sound button** ▶ in the Edit Envelope dialog box.

   The music fades in gradually in both channels.

8. Click the **Stop sound button** ■ , then click **OK** in the Edit Envelope dialog box.

9. Lock the audioBackground layer, save your work, then close the movie.

You established a fade in effect for a sound file by dragging envelope handles to create a custom envelope.

Use ActionScript
WITH SOUND

What You'll Do

 In this lesson, you will use ActionScript to play and stop sounds.

Understanding ActionScript and Sound

ActionScript and sound are a powerful combination. You can use actions to set how and when sounds play in a movie, and to start or stop sounds in response to user interactions. You can also use events to trigger an action such as navigating to a frame or scene based on when a sound ends.

To reference a sound from the Library panel in ActionScript, you must enable the Export for ActionScript option in the Linkage area of the Sound Properties dialog box, as shown in Figure 22. In the dialog box, you make sure a sound in the Library panel that is referenced in ActionScript will be exported for use by the ActionScript, and you also assign a class name which is the name you will use to identify the sound in ActionScript. You can make the class name the same name as the sound name, or you can assign a new class name. By default, Flash assigns the sound name as the class name.

A **sound object** is a way for ActionScript to recognize and control a sound. Creating a sound object is similar to creating an instance of a sound on the Stage, except it happens entirely in ActionScript. First, you create a variable and then you give it a sound data type using the class name specified as the Linkage name in the Library panel. (*Note:* Flash knows that the class name represents the sound class because it was specified in the Sound Properties dialog box.) Then you assign an instance of the sound class to the variable, as shown in Figure 23. This links the sound file to the sound object.

Starting and Stopping Sounds with ActionScript

Once you have created a sound object and attached a sound to it, you can begin controlling the sound using ActionScript.

The Sound.play method starts a sound playing. When using this action, you substitute the variable name of a sound object for "Sound." For example, if you have a sound object named "BackgroundMusic," you would include the action BackgroundMusic.play to play the sound. Sound.play includes optional parameters that let you specify a sound offset (for example, if you want to start playing a sound that is 15 seconds long at the 10-second mark) and also the number of times to repeat the sound.

The stopAll method of the SoundMixer class stops all sounds currently playing, regardless of whether the sound is an event or stream sound. It's a good idea to include a stopAll statement at the end of a movie, especially if the movie uses event sounds.

To stop a single sound you can use the stop(); method of the SoundChannel class.

The ActionScript to assign a sound to a sound channel and to use the sound channel to control the playing of the sound follows.

`var channel1:SoundChannel;`

`channel1 = safariSnd.play()`

`channel1.stop();`

The first line of code creates a variable named channel1 with a SoundChannel data type. The second line of code plays a sound named safariSnd using the SoundChannel variable. The last line of code stops any sound assigned to the channel1 variable.

Figure 22 *The Sound Properties dialog box*

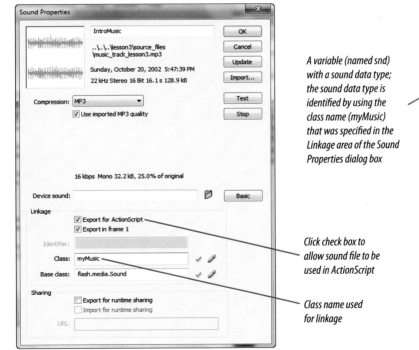

A variable (named snd) with a sound data type; the sound data type is identified by using the class name (myMusic) that was specified in the Linkage area of the Sound Properties dialog box

Click check box to allow sound file to be used in ActionScript

Class name used for linkage

Figure 23 *Example of ActionScript to create a sound object*

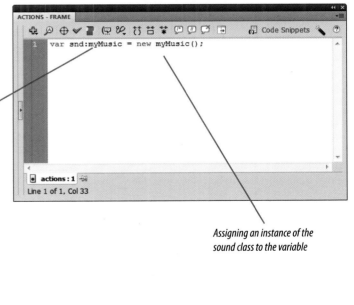

Assigning an instance of the sound class to the variable

Link a sound file with a movie

1. Open fl11_3.fla, then save it as **levels.fla**, then test the movie.

2. Click the **start button**, then click the **mute button**.

   The animation plays and stops, but there is no sound.

3. Close the Flash Player window.

4. Display the Library panel, right-click (Win) or [control]-click (Mac) the **song1 audio file**, then click **Properties** to open the Sound Properties dialog box.

5. Click the **Advanced button** to display the Linkage area if it is not already displayed, then click the **Export for ActionScript check box** to select it, as shown in Figure 24.

6. Click **OK**.

   A message appears indicating that Flash will automatically generate a definition for the class.

7. Click **OK**.

8. Display the Library panel, then notice that **song1** is displayed in the Linkage column.

You used the Sound Properties dialog box to create a linkage class and to ensure a sound will be exported for ActionScript.

NEW Start a sound using ActionScript

1. Click **frame 1** on the actions layer, then open the Actions panel.

   The current ActionScript code causes the playhead to go to and play the frame labeled startBars when the start button is clicked. The startBars frame is the first frame in the colorBars movie clip, and it is the frame where the animation starts. Remember a movie clip has its own Timeline.

   (continued)

Figure 24 *Using the Sound Properties dialog box to enable the Export for ActionScript option*

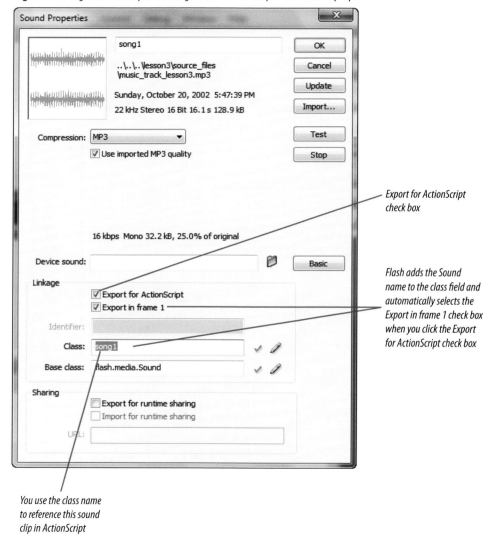

Export for ActionScript check box

Flash adds the Sound name to the class field and automatically selects the Export in frame 1 check box when you click the Export for ActionScript check box

You use the class name to reference this sound clip in ActionScript

Figure 25 *ActionScript to create a new sound object*

Creates a variable named snd and gives it a song1 data type (song1 is the new class you created), and creates an instance of the class

Figure 26 *ActionScript to stop all sounds when mute button is clicked*

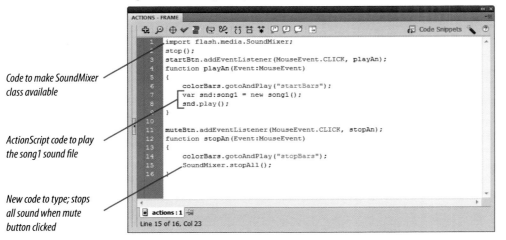

Code to make SoundMixer class available

ActionScript code to play the song1 sound file

New code to type; stops all sound when mute button clicked

2. Type the following line below the colorBars line in the playAn function, as shown in Figure 25:
   var snd:song1 = new song1();

3. Press **[Enter]** (Win) or **[return]** (Mac), then type the following line.
   snd.play();
   This line causes the snd variable containing the song1 instance to play.

4. Test the movie, click the **start button**, then click the **mute button**.
   The sound file plays when you click start; when you click mute, the color bars stop playing, but the sound file does not.

5. Close the Flash Player window.

You wrote the ActionScript for a button that creates a sound object, attaches a sound to the object, and plays the sound.

NEW Stop sounds using ActionScript

1. Display the Actions panel.

2. Type the following above the stop(); line:
   import flash.media.SoundMixer;
   This line makes the SoundMixer class available.

3. Type the following line below the colorBars line in the stopAn function, as shown in Figure 26:
   SoundMixer.stopAll();
   This line stops all sounds currently playing.

4. Close the Actions panel, then test the movie.

5. Click the **start button**, click the **mute button**, then click the **start button** again.
   The music plays when you click start, then stops when you click mute.

6. Close the Flash Player window.

7. Save your work, then close the document.

You added actions to stop sounds from playing.

Work with VIDEO

What You'll Do

In this lesson, you will import an external video, set cue points, and use ActionScript to allow users to navigate through the video.

[NEW] Understanding Loading an External Video

In a previous chapter, you learned how to convert a video clip to the flv file format. Then you embedded the video into a Flash movie. Embedded video becomes part of the SWF file similar to other objects, such as sound and graphics. Embedding video is best used with small video clips in order to keep the SWF file size small. Flash provides another process, progressive downloading, for including video in a Flash movie. Progressive downloading uses a video Component and ActionScript to load an external FLV file into an SWF file, allowing the video to play when the SWF file is played. The FLV file resides outside the SWF file and can begin playing soon after the first part of the file has been downloaded. This keeps the SWF file smaller than when the video is embedded. The video Component is a built-in object, with playback controls, that displays the video on the Stage.

The process for loading an external video follows:

- Start a Flash ActionScript 3.0 document and select the layer and frame where the video will be displayed.

- Import the video using the Import Video option from the Import command on the File menu.
- Use the Browse button in the Import Video dialog box to navigate to the folder where the video is located and choose the video. This will tell Flash where the video file is located. (*Note*: If the video file is not an .flv file you will need to use the Adobe Media Encoder to convert it.)
- Check the Load external video with playback component option, and click the Next button.
- The Skinning screen appears, as shown in Figure 27. The video's skin determines the appearance and position of the video controls. You use this screen to choose how the FLVPlayback Component will appear and what controls (play, pause, rewind, and so on) will be available. You can choose from a variety of predefined skins or you can choose not to have any skin or controls at all. You can obtain skins from third party developers and even create your own custom skins. When you are finished making your choices on this screen, you click the Next button.
- The Finish Video Import screen appears, indicating the file and its location as well as

Adding Sound and Video

information on the video Component and its skin. When you are finished reviewing the screen, you click the Finish button.

The FLVPlayback Component is displayed on the Stage. You can use the controls to play the video without having to publish the movie. This allows you to preview the video and to add features to the video, such as cue points.

NEW Introducing Cue Points

A new and extremely useful feature of Flash video is the ability to add cue points directly in Flash using the Properties panel. Cue points are indicators on the video timeline that you specify. For example, you may have a video that runs for 20 seconds and 12 seconds into the video there is a scene that you want the user to be able to jump to. You can specify a

cue point at the 12 second mark, give it a name, and use the name in ActionScript. This process is similar to creating frame labels on the Flash Timeline that are used in ActionScript to have the playhead jump to the frame when a button is clicked. To create a cue point, you scrub the seek bar to locate the desired position for the cue point, then use the CUE POINTS area of the Properties panel to add a cue point and give it a name, as shown in Figure 28.

NEW Using Cue Points in ActionScript

The FLVPlayback class allows you to load FLV video files. The findCuePoint method finds a cue point and the seek method seeks the time (in milliseconds) associated with the cue point. The code within a function called by a button click that displays the video at a cue point follows.

```
function goLion(Event:MouseEvent)
{
    var myvid:Object = MyVideo.
        findCuePoint("lion");

    MyVideo.seek(myvid.time);
}
```

The first highlighted line of code creates a variable named myvid with an object data type. MyVideo is the instance name of the video FLVPlayback Component and lion is the name of the cue point. Thus, the lion cue point is assigned to the myvid object.

The second highlighted line of code takes the time in the myvid object (that is the cue point time) and seeks (jumps to) it in the MyVideo instance (the video on the Stage).

Figure 27 *The Skinning screen in the Import Video dialog box*

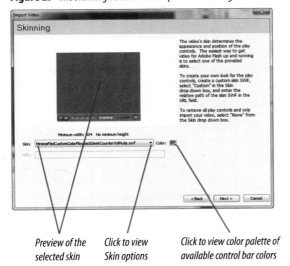

Preview of the selected skin *Click to view Skin options* *Click to view color palette of available control bar colors*

Figure 28 *Setting a cue point*

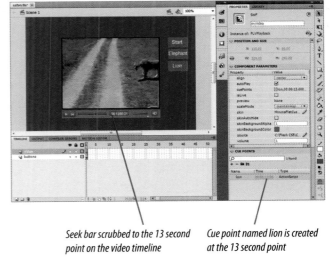

Seek bar scrubbed to the 13 second point on the video timeline *Cue point named lion is created at the 13 second point*

NEW Load an external video

1. Open fl11_4.fla, then save it as **safari.fla**.

2. Insert a **new layer**, name it **video**, then click **frame 1** of the video layer.

3. Click **File** on the menu bar, point to **Import**, then click **Import Video**.

   The Import Video dialog box opens with the Select Video screen active.

4. Click the **Browse** button, navigate to the folder where your data files are stored, click **safari.flv**, then click **Open**.

5. Verify Load external video with playback component is selected, as shown in Figure 29, then click the **Next** (Win) or **Continue** (Mac) button.

6. Read the information on the Skinning screen, then click the **Next** (Win) or **Continue** (Mac) **button**.

7. Read the information on the Finishing screen, then click the **Finish button**.

   The FLVPlayback Component appears, see Figure 30, centered on the Stage with the video loaded.

8. Click the center of the FLVPlayback Component on the Stage to select it, click the **play button** ▶ on the playback Component.

   The video plays in the FLVPlayback Component. Notice the video has three parts: the title, the elephant, and the lion.

9. Click the center of the FLVPlayback Component on the Stage to select it.

10. Display the Properties panel, then type **myVideo** for the instance name.

11. Save your work.

You imported a video that is loaded into an FLVPlayback Component, then you played the video on the Stage and in the Flash Player window.

Figure 29 *Completed Select Video screen*

Your file path may differ

Load external video option checked

Figure 30 *FLVPlayback Component on the Stage with video loaded*

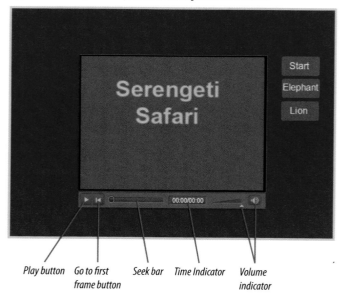

Play button   Go to first   Seek bar   Time Indicator   Volume
               frame button   indicator

Figure 31 *COMPONENT PARAMETERS area of the Properties panel*

Instance name of the FLVPlayback Component on the Stage

Properties of the FLVPlayback Component

Area to create and list cue points

Figure 32 *Adding a cue point named start*

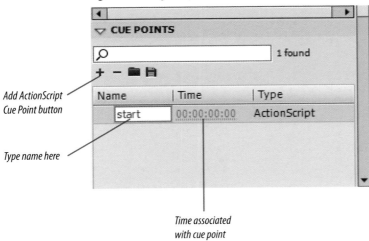

Add ActionScript Cue Point button

Type name here

Time associated with cue point

1. Click the **Go to first frame button** on the FLVPlayback component to set the time indicator to 0.

2. Display the Library panel and notice the FLVPlayback Component is listed.

3. Display the Properties panel, expand the COMPONENT PARAMETERS, then view the properties for the FLVPlayback Component as shown in Figure 31.

   This area has information about the FLVPlayback Component, including the alignment on the Stage, the skin, and the source video file. The CUE POINTS area is used to add and display cue points. Currently, there are no cue points.

4. Click the **Add ActionScript Cue Point button** +

5. Click **Cue Point 1** in the Name column, then type **start**, as shown in Figure 32.

   This creates a cue point named start at the beginning of the video (00:00:00:00).

6. Drag the **seek bar** on the FLVPlayback Component until the elephant appears (approximately 1 second as indicated by the time listed on the FLVPlayback Component control bar.

7. Click the **Add ActionScript Cue Point button** + , click **Cue Point 2** in the Name column, then type **elephant**.

8. Drag the **seek bar** on the FLVPlayback Component until the road appears that the lion crosses (approximately 11 seconds).

9. Click the **Add ActionScript Cue Point button** + , click **Cue Point 3** in the Name column, type **lion**, then press **[Enter]** (Win) or **[return]** (Mac).

10. Save your work.

You created three cue points for the video.

NEW Use ActionScript with cue points

1. Insert a new layer, name it **actions**, click **frame 1** on the layer, open the Actions panel, then type the following as a single line of code:

   lionBtn.addEventListener(MouseEvent. CLICK, goLion);

2. Press **[Enter]** (Win) or **[return]** (Mac) to move down a line, then type the following:

   function goLion(Event:MouseEvent)

3. Press **[Enter]** (Win) or **[return]** (Mac) to move down a line, type **{**, then press **[Enter]** (Win) or **[return]** (Mac):

4. Type the following between the curly braces as a single line of code:

   var myvidLion:Object = myVideo. findCuePoint("lion");

5. Press **[Enter]** (Win) or **[return]** (Mac) to move down a line, then type the following:

   myVideo.seek(myvidLion.time);

   This line takes the time in the myvidLion variable (that is the cue point time) and seeks (jumps to) it in the myVideo instance on the Stage.

6. Test the movie, click the **Lion button**, then close the Flash Player window.

7. Display the Actions panel, then use Figure 33 to complete the ActionScript code for the other two buttons.

8. Test the movie, click all the buttons, then close the Flash Player window.

9. Save your work, then close the document.

You created a navigation process for the user by using cue points in ActionScript.

Figure 33 *The completed ActionScript for the cue points*

```
import flash.events.MouseEvent;

lionBtn.addEventListener(MouseEvent.CLICK, goLion);
function goLion(Event:MouseEvent)
{
    var myvidLion:Object = myVideo.findCuePoint("lion");
    myVideo.seek(myvidLion.time);
}
elephantBtn.addEventListener(MouseEvent.CLICK, goElephant);
function goElephant(Event:MouseEvent)
{
    var myvidElephant:Object = myVideo.findCuePoint("elephant");
    myVideo.seek(myvidElephant.time);
}
startBtn.addEventListener(MouseEvent.CLICK, goStart);
function goStart(Event:MouseEvent)
{
    var myvidStart:Object = myVideo.findCuePoint("start");
    myVideo.seek(myvidStart.time);
}
```

Creates an event listener that calls the goLion function when the lionBtn object is clicked

Creates a variable named myvidLion that has an object data type and assigns the lion cue point to the variable

Figure 34 *The completed ActionScript to play and stop a sound*

Creates a variable name safariSnd with a sound (safari) data type and creates an instance of the sound class

Creates a variable named channel1 with a SoundChannel data type

Plays the sound (safariSnd) using the SoundChannel channel1 variable

Code to stop a sound

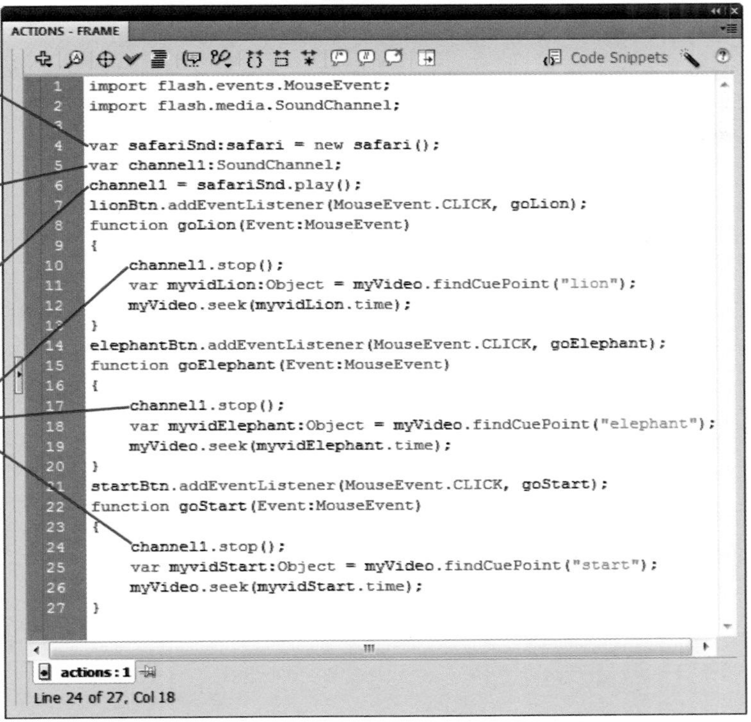

```
ACTIONS - FRAME

 1   import flash.events.MouseEvent;
 2   import flash.media.SoundChannel;
 3
 4   var safariSnd:safari = new safari();
 5   var channel1:SoundChannel;
 6   channel1 = safariSnd.play();
 7   lionBtn.addEventListener(MouseEvent.CLICK, goLion);
 8   function goLion(Event:MouseEvent)
 9   {
10       channel1.stop();
11       var myvidLion:Object = myVideo.findCuePoint("lion");
12       myVideo.seek(myvidLion.time);
13   }
14   elephantBtn.addEventListener(MouseEvent.CLICK, goElephant);
15   function goElephant(Event:MouseEvent)
16   {
17       channel1.stop();
18       var myvidElephant:Object = myVideo.findCuePoint("elephant");
19       myVideo.seek(myvidElephant.time);
20   }
21   startBtn.addEventListener(MouseEvent.CLICK, goStart);
22   function goStart(Event:MouseEvent)
23   {
24       channel1.stop();
25       var myvidStart:Object = myVideo.findCuePoint("start");
26       myVideo.seek(myvidStart.time);
27   }
```

actions : 1

Line 24 of 27, Col 18

Combine sound and video

1. **Double-click** the Elephant button on the Stage to open it in the edit window.

2. Click the **Down frame**, display the Properties panel, click the **Name list arrow** in the SOUND area, then click **elephant.wav**.

3. Verify Sync is set to Event, then click **Scene 1** to return to the main Timeline.

4. Repeat Steps 1-3 for the **Lion button** using the **lion.mp3** sound file.

5. Click **Scene 1** to return to the main Timeline, display the Library panel, then play the **safari. wav** sound.

6. Click **frame 1** on the actions layer, then open the Actions panel.

7. Type the following 3 lines of code above the lionBtn event listener line:

   var safariSnd:safari = new safari();

   var channel1:SoundChannel;

   channel1 = safariSnd.play();

8. Type the following within the function for each of the buttons as shown in Figure 34:

   channel1.stop();

   This stops the playing of the safariSnd sound file.

9. Test the movie, click each button, then close the Flash Player window.

10. Save your work, then close the document.

You added event sounds to buttons and used ActionScript to play and stop a sound.

Work with sound.

1. Start Flash, open fl11_5.fla, then save it as **skillsDemo11.fla**.
2. Move the playhead through the Timeline of the movie. Notice there are two screens that are partially completed. The callouts in Figure 35 indicate the types of changes you will make to the movie.
3. Insert a new layer above the buttons layer, then name it **ambient1**.
4. Click frame 1 on the ambient1 layer, then select the background_loop1 sound from the Name list in the SOUND area on the Properties panel, which adds it to frame 1 on the ambient1 layer.
5. Set the synchronization for the sound on the ambient1 layer to Event, then set the number of times to repeat to 10.
6. Insert a new layer above the ambient1 layer, then name it **ambient2**.
7. Click frame 1 on the ambient2 layer, then select the background_loop2 sound from the Name list in the SOUND area on the Properties panel, which adds it to frame 1 on the ambient2 layer.
8. Verify the synchronization for the sound on the ambient2 layer is set to Event, then set the number of times to repeat to 10.
9. Insert a new layer above the ambient2 layer, name it **song**, then add an instance of the song1 sound to frame 15 on the song layer. (*Hint*: Insert a keyframe in frame 15 before you add the sound.)
10. Verify the synchronization for the sound on the song layer is set to Event, then set the number of times to repeat to **10**.
11. Save your work.

Specify synchronization options.

1. Create a new movie clip symbol named **animated_text**.
2. Name Layer 1 of the animated_text movie clip symbol **audio**, click frame 1 on the audio layer, select the music_selector_audio sound from the Name list in the SOUND area on the Properties panel, which adds it to frame 1 on the new layer, then set the synchronization to Stream.
3. Insert a keyframe in frame 75 on the audio layer, then add a stop action to the keyframe. (*Hint*: Adding a keyframe lets you see the full stream sound. Adding the stop action keeps the movie clip from repeating.)
4. Insert a new layer above the audio layer, name it **text**, insert a keyframe in frame 13 on the layer, then drag the Welcome graphic symbol from the Text folder in the Library panel to the Stage.

5. Display the Properties panel, change the value in the X text box to **−58.5** and the value in the Y text box to **−16.7**, then press [Enter] (Win) or [return] (Mac).
6. Insert a keyframe in frame 17 on the text layer, select the word "Welcome" on the Stage, click the Swap button on the Properties panel, click the "to" graphic symbol, then click OK.
7. Insert a keyframe in frame 20 on the text layer, select the word "to" on the Stage, click the Swap button on the Properties panel, click the "the" graphic symbol, then click OK.
8. Insert a keyframe in frame 23 on the text layer, select the word "the" on the Stage, click the Swap button on the Properties panel, click the "music" graphic symbol, then click OK.

Figure 35 *Completed Skills Review*

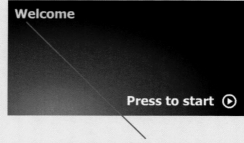

Voice-over and background music begin when screen is displayed; voice-over is synchronized with words

Click the mute button to stop all sounds

Click the start over button to stop currently playing sounds and restart song from the beginning

9. Insert a keyframe in frame 27 on the text layer, select the word "Music" on the Stage, click the Swap button on the Properties panel, click the "selector" graphic symbol, then click OK.
10. Insert a blank keyframe in frame 45 on the text layer.
11. Play the movie clip symbol.
   Note: The audio includes the words online, but no text appears on the Stage.
12. Return to the main Timeline.
13. Create a new layer above the song layer, name it **animation**, click frame 1 on the layer, then add an instance of the animated_text movie clip symbol from the Library panel to anywhere on the Stage.
14. Display the Properties panel for the movie clip symbol instance, change the value in the X text box to **120** and the value in the Y text box to **40**, then press [Enter] (Win) or [return] (Mac).
15. Click frame 1 on the buttons layer, double-click the right arrow button on the Stage to open it in the edit window, add a layer, then name it **sound**.
16. Insert a keyframe in the Down frame on the sound layer, then use the Properties panel to add an instance of the Plastic Click sound to the frame and set the synchronization to Start.
17. Click the Up frame on the sound layer, add an instance of the Plastic Click sound to the frame, then set the Sync sound to Stop.
18. Return to the main Timeline, test the movie, then save your work.

Modify sounds.

1. Open the animated_text movie clip in the edit window, then click frame 1 on the audio layer.
2. Display the Properties panel, then click the Edit sound envelope button on the Properties panel.
3. Show units in Frames, then zoom out the view in the Edit Envelope dialog box until you can see the waveform for the entire sound, as shown in Figure 36.
4. Play the sound.
5. Drag the Time Out control (located on the Timeline at the end of the waveform, about frame 70) left to approximately frame 31, then play the sound in the Edit Envelope dialog box to verify that the word "online" does not play.

6. Click OK, then return to the main Timeline.
7. Click frame 1 on the ambient1 layer, then click the Edit sound envelope button on the Properties panel.
8. Play the sound, then stop the sound.
9. Reduce the volume by dragging the envelope handles in both channels so the sound line is just above the bottom of the envelope, as shown in Figure 37 on the next page.
10. Play the sound. (*Hint*: If you do not hear the sound, drag the envelope handles up slightly. Adjust the sound lines as needed until you hear the sound playing softly.)
11. Click OK to accept changes and close the Edit Envelope dialog box.

Figure 36 *The Edit Envelope dialog box*

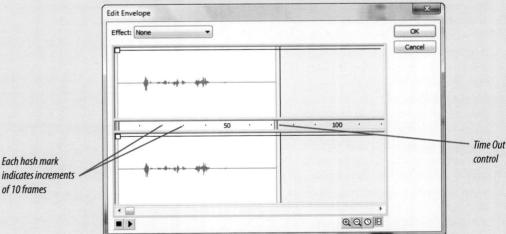

Each hash mark indicates increments of 10 frames

Time Out control

12. Click frame 1 on the ambient2 layer, then click the Edit sound envelope button on the Properties panel.
13. Play the sound, then stop the sound.
14. Drag the envelope handles in both channels to just above the bottom of the envelope, then play the sound. (*Note*: Continue to adjust the handles and play the sound until you are satisfied that the sound plays softly in the background.)
15. Click OK to accept changes and close the Edit Envelope dialog box.
16. Save your work.

Use ActionScript with sound.

1. Select the song1 sound in the Sounds folder in the Library panel, then display the Sound Properties dialog box for the song1 sound symbol. (*Hint*: Click the Panel options list arrow in the Library panel title bar, then click Properties.)
2. Select the Export for ActionScript check box in the Linkage area of the Sound Properties dialog box, then click OK twice.
3. Unlock the actions layer, click frame 14 on the actions layer, then open the Actions panel.
4. Add a SoundMixer.stopAll(); statement below the gotoAndPlay statement within the function that is called when the startBtn object is clicked.
5. Move down a line and create a variable with the name **snd** and a data type of song1 (the class name specified when you completed the Linkage area of the Sound Properties dialog box) and create an new instance of the sound object.
6. Move down a line and add a snd.play(); statement to play the sound object.

7. Use the Check syntax and Auto format buttons to check your code.
8. Click frame 30 on the actions layer, then display the Actions panel.
   There are two event listeners, one for the mute button and one for the start over button. Each function for the event listeners has a gotoAndPlay action that plays a section of the waveform (a movie clip) Timeline.
9. Add a SoundMixer.stopAll(); statement below the gotoAndPlay ("mute"); statement.

10. Add the following two lines of code below the gotoAndPlay ("start"); statement:

    var snd:song1 = new song1();
    snd.play();

11. Use the Check syntax and Auto format buttons to check your code, then lock the actions layer.
12. Test the movie, then save your work.
13. Close the file, then exit Flash.

Figure 37 *Volume adjusted by changing the placement of the sound line in each channel*

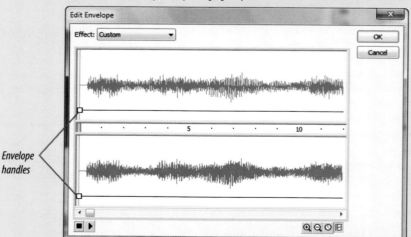

Work with video.

1. Create a new ActionScript 3.0 file, then save it as **skillsDemo11-video.fla**.
2. Rename Layer 1 as **buttons**.
3. Refer to Figure 38 as you set the Stage background color and create two buttons at the bottom right side of the Stage with labels Lake and Waterfall, then give them instance names of **lakeBtn** and **waterfallBtn**. (*Note*: You do not need to match the Figure exactly, use colors and shapes that appeal to you.)
4. Add a layer, name it **video**, then select frame 1.
5. Import wilderness.flv as an external video.
6. Give the FLVPlayback Component an instance name of **myVideo**.
7. Use the Properties panel to add cue points named **lake** and **waterfall** at the points they appear in the video.
8. Add a layer and name it **actions**.
9. Open the Actions panel, then complete the ActionScript to add an event listener for each button that calls a function (goLake and goWaterfall, respectively) to seek the location on the video corresponding to the respective cue points.
10. Test the movie, click each button, compare your screen to Figure 38, then close the Flash Player window.
11. Save your work.

Combining sound and video

1. Import the waterfall.wav file from the drive and folder where your Data Files are stored to the Library, change the properties to Export for ActionScript, then specify **waterfall** for the Class name.

2. Click frame 1 on the actions layer, then open the Actions panel.
3. Position the insertion point above the waterfallBtn event listener statement, then create a variable named **waterfallSnd** with a waterfall data type (waterfall is the sound class you created in Step 1), and create a new instance of the sound.
4. Move down a line and create a variable named **channel1** with a **SoundChannel** data type.
5. Add a statement within the goWaterfall function that uses the channel1 variable to play waterfallSnd.
6. Add a statement as the first line of code within the goLake function that stops the sound being played in the channel1 variable.
7. Test the movie, click the Waterfall button first, then click the Lake button.
8. Close the Flash Player window, save your work , then close the Flash document.
9. Exit Flash.

Figure 38 *Completed Skills Review - Video*

Ultimate Tours would like you to create a banner promoting its "Japan on a Budget" tours. The graphics for the banner are complete; now you need to add music and a voice-over. Ultimate Tours would like a musical background to play continuously while the banner is displayed, and they have also provided a voice-over they would like to be synchronized with text on the screen, as shown in Figure 39. Finally, Ultimate Tours would like an accent sound to play when a visitor clicks the navigation button on the banner.

1. Open fl11_6.fla, then save the file as **ultimateTours11.fla**.
2. Test the movie and notice the text banner that appears across the screen against a series of background images.
3. Insert a new layer above the text animation layer, name it **audio**, use the Properties panel to add the sound named ultimate_background to frame 1 on the layer, then set synchronization to Event.
4. Set repetition for the sound to **2** to ensure the music plays the entire time the banner is displayed.
5. Display the Library panel, open the movie clips folder, then open the words movie clip symbol in the edit window.
6. Insert a new layer above the text layer, name it **audio**, use the Properties panel to add the ultimate_voiceover sound to the layer, then set synchronization to Stream.

7. Move the keyframes that control when each word of text appears on the Stage to synchronize with when the word is spoken in the voice-over. (*Hint*: Use the playhead to hear the stream sound and use the wave pattern as a clue to when a sound is played. Drag the keyframes on the text layer to create the synchronization effect. *Note*: To move a keyframe, click the keyframe you want to move to select it. Press and hold (Win) or hold (Mac) the mouse pointer on the keyframe until the pointer changes to. Use the pointer to drag the keyframe to the new location, then release the mouse button.)

8. Return to the main Timeline, open the Library panel, open the buttons folder, then double-click the Circle with arrow button to open it in the edit window.
9. Edit the arrow button to play the Switch Small Plastic sound when a visitor clicks the button. (*Hint*: Be sure to specify an Event sound.)
10. Return to the main Timeline, test the movie, then close the Flash Player window.
11. Select frame 1 on the audio layer, then use the Edit Envelope dialog box to reduce the volume of the ultimate_background sound.
12. Test the movie, then close the Flash Player window.
13. Save your work.

Figure 39 *Sample completed Project Builder 1*

Voice-over is synchronized with appearance of words

Sound plays when visitor clicks button

You work for a software game company. Your newest game, "Match the Shapes," will be developed in Flash and marketed to preschoolers. You are working on a prototype of the game to show upper management. You have already completed the visual aspects of the prototype; now you must add sound.

1. Open interactive.fla, then save it as **game_prototype11.fla**. (*Note:* You created the interactive.fla file in Chapter 10.)
2. Test the movie to see how the matching game works, then close the Flash Player window.
3. Change the frame rate to 12 frames per second.
4. Import the following sound files to the Library click File on the menu bar, point to Import, then click Import to Library:
   ambient_audio.wav
   welcome_voiceover.wav
   crowd_yes.wav

5. Create a new folder in the Library panel named **sounds**, then drag the files to the sounds folder in the Library panel.
6. Add a new layer above the cursor layer and name it **ambient**.
7. Using the Properties panel, add the ambient_audio sound as an event sound to frame 1 only. Repeat the sound **2** times to ensure it plays the entire time the visitor is viewing the screen. Set the Effect in the Properties panel to Fade in. Remove frame 2 on the ambient layer.
8. Test the movie, then close the Flash Player window.

9. Create a movie clip named **welcome** with three layers, each extending 50 frames. The first layer should have the welcome_voiceover audio clip as a stream sound. The second layer should have text blocks with the words **"Welcome to Match the Shapes"** that are synchronized with the welcome_voiceover audio clip. Each word in the phrase appears one at a time and stays on the Stage as new words are added to the phrase. Use two lines for the text and keep the total width below 200 pixels. (*Hint:* You can display the Rulers to check the width.) The third layer should have a stop action at the end of the movie clip.

10. Display the first screen and delete the Welcome to Match the Shapes heading and the Instructions text block from the backdrop layer, but be sure the rest of the elements, such as the orange background, stay.

11. Add a new layer above the backdrop layer and name it **welcome**. Then add the welcome movie clip to frame 1 of the layer. Remove frame 2 of the layer.

12. Add a statement to the Start button function that stops all sounds before the playhead jumps to frame 2.

13. Have a sound play each time the user correctly drags an object from the start bin to the drop bin. (*Note*: Be sure you set the audio file to Export to ActionScript and give the file a linkage name, such as goodSnd.

Insert two lines of ActionScript in frame 2 on the actions layer that create a sound variable, then play an instance of the sound variable. Be sure to add these two lines of code above the reply.text = "Good Job!"; line for each shape.)

14. Test the movie, then close the Flash Player window.

15. Save your work and compare your screens to Figure 40.

Figure 40 *Sample completed Project Builder 2*

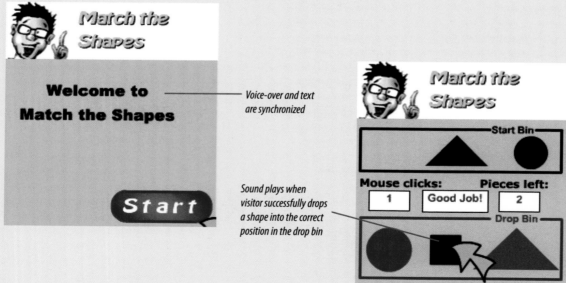

Voice-over and text are synchronized

Sound plays when visitor successfully drops a shape into the correct position in the drop bin

Figure 41 shows a page from a website that might have been created using Flash. Study the figure and complete the following. For each question, indicate how you determined your answer.

1. Connect to the Internet, then go to *http://www.americaslibrary.gov/jp/bball/jp_bball_early_2.html.*
2. Open a document in a word processor or open a new Flash document, save the file as **dpc11**, then answer the following questions. (*Hint:* Use the Text tool in Flash.)
   - Currently, this site does not have any sounds. How might sound be used to enhance this site?
   - If this site were created in Flash, how might you incorporate sounds?
   - What user controls might be appropriate when including sound in a Flash movie and why?

Figure 41 *Sample Design Project*

★ Home ★ About this site ★ Help ★ Search ★ The Library of Congress

America's Story from **America's Library**

Meet Amazing Americans   Jump Back in Time   Explore the States   **Join America at Play**   See, Hear and Sing

Join America at Play ▶ Play Ball!

Union prisoners at Salisbury, North Carolina play baseball in 1863

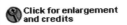
Click for enlargement and credits

How Baseball Began

When a group in New York City got together in 1845 to regulate the rules of baseball, they decided that to get a base runner out, an opposing player need only tag him with the ball instead of hitting him with it. From then on, baseball was played using a hard ball, and soon the game began to be played on a much larger scale. Baseball became an organized sport in the 1840s and 1850s. People even played it during the Civil War. In this print you can see Union soldiers playing a baseball game in a Confederate prisoner-of-war camp in North Carolina. Do you know where the first baseball teams were established?

◀ BACK   page 2 of 4   NEXT ▶

Library Of Congress | Legal Notices | Privacy | Site Map | Contact Us

In the previous chapter, you created a portfolio for your work samples and a password-protected, clients-only area. Now you will add sound to the Flash movie. If you have access to sound-recording software, you can record your own voice-overs that describe the samples being shown. You can import sound clips or use the sounds found in the Sounds area of the Common Libraries panel. Alternatively, use can use the sample files provided in this chapter as musical background sounds. Finally, you add a video to your portfolio.

Work with sound.

1. Open portfolio10.fla, then save it as **portfolio11.fla**.
2. Use sound files from the Common Libraries panel, or import to the Library panel sound files you have acquired or created, such as voice-overs describing your work, or import the following sound files from the drive and folder where your Data Files are stored:
   accent1.mp3
   accent2.mp3
   background.mp3
   portfolio_voiceover.wav
3. Add a new layer named **music**, then add a background sound that plays when the movie starts. Have the background sound stop when a user clicks any of the buttons.
4. Add a sound to each button on the home page that is heard when the button is clicked.
5. Use ActionScript to add a sound from the Library panel to the Games button on the flash samples page.

6. Add a sound when the user successfully enters the correct password and gains access to the clients area.
7. If you are using the musical backgrounds, experiment with adding effects to the sounds, such as fades or shifts between channels.
8. Test the movie.
9. Save your work, then compare your movie to Figure 42.

Work with video.

1. Save portfolio11.fla as **portfolio11-video.fla**.
2. Add a new layer to the Timeline, name it **video**, then insert a keyframe in frame 6 of the layer.
3. Add keyframes to frame 6 of the Navigations-buttons, Border, and actions layers.
4. Add a keyframe to frame 4 of the video layer, then add a button with a label **Video** to the Stage to the right of My Portfolio.
5. Name the instance of the button, **videoBtn**.
6. Click frame 4 on the actions layer and open the Actions panel.
7. Type the code to add an event listener to the videoBtn object so that a function named **goVideo** is called when the button is clicked.

Figure 42 *Sample completed Portfolio Project*

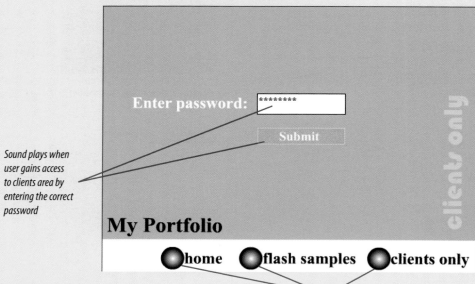

Sound plays when user gains access to clients area by entering the correct password

Background music stops and sound plays when buttons are clicked

Adding Sound and Video

8. Type the code to create the goVideo function that jumps the playhead to frame 6.
9. Click frame 6 on the video layer, then import the flv file named catFun.flv.
10. Play the video on the Stage, then create two cue points: one named **bag** that starts near the beginning of the video and the other named **string** that is near the middle of the video. Also create two buttons to the right of the FLVPlayer Component: one labeled bag and the other labeled string. Give the buttons instance names of **bagBtn** and **stringBtn** respectively.
11. Click frame 6 on the actions layer and open the Actions panel.
12. Type the code to add event listeners to the bagBtn and stringBtn objects that call functions when they are clicked.
13. Type the code for the function for each event listener that creates a variable as an object type and assigns an instance of the video with the findCuePoint method and cue point name. Then type the code to seek the time for each cue point of the video.
14. Test the movie, navigate to the clients area screen, enter the correct password (*Hint*: password), click submit, click the Video button, click the bag button, compare your screen to Figure 43, then click the string button.

15. Close the Flash Player window, then save your work.
16. Open the Library panel.
17. Open Sounds from the Common Libraries option of the Window menu.
18. Select Animal Mammal Carnivore Cat Domestic Cat Meow 02.mp3, then drag it to the Library panel.
19. Change the properties to Export for ActionScript with a class name of **cat**.
20. Display the Actions panel, then type the code at the top of the panel that creates a variable with a sound (cat) data type.

21. On the next line add a variable with a **SoundChannel** data type.
22. On the next line add the code to have the cat sound play.
23. Test the movie, navigate to the clients area screen, then click the Video button.
24. Close the Flash Player window, save your work, then close the document.
25. Exit Flash.

Figure 43 *Completed Portfolio - Video*

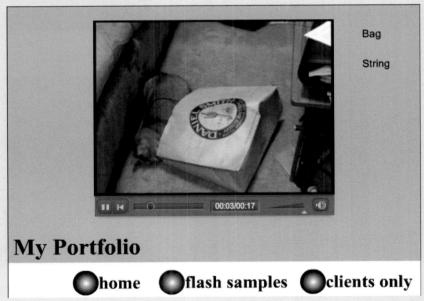

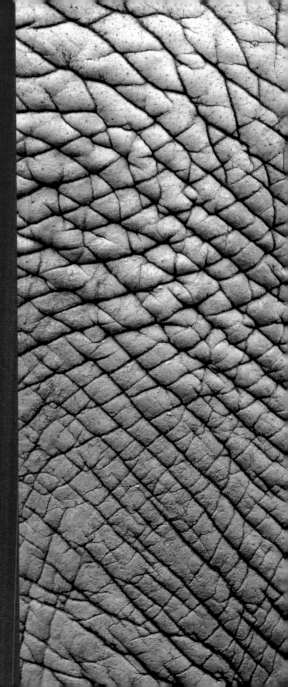

CHAPTER 12

WORKING WITH
COMPONENTS

1. Use Components in a Flash Movie

2. Work with Components and ActionScript

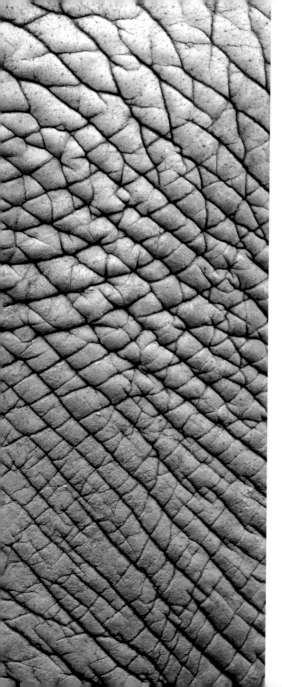

CHAPTER 12 **WORKING WITH**
COMPONENTS

Introduction

Completion of an effective Adobe Flash application depends on several factors, including the nature of the application (straightforward versus complex), the allotted development time, and the developer's expertise. Flash provides a feature, Components, that enables developers to speed up the development process and create effective applications without writing ActionScript code. Components are another time-saving feature of Flash. There are three categories of Components:

- **User Interface (UI)**—Components (such as buttons and menus) that are used to create the visual interface for a Flash application.
- **Video**—Components used to insert an flv video file into a Flash document and allow the user to control the playback of the video including start, stop, and mute controls. You used the video FLVPlayback Component in Chapter 11.

- **Flex**—Contains the FlexComponentBase class that is used to develop and deploy cross-platform applications.

Components are commonly used for creating check boxes, drop-down menus, and forms with boxes for entering user data, such as name and address. You can quickly add functionality to a movie by dragging and dropping Components (predeveloped movie clips) from the Components panel to the Stage.

You are not required to enter ActionScript code when using Components. However, you can use ActionScript to enhance the functionality of a Component. When you select a Component to use, it is placed in the Library panel for reuse in another part of the movie.

In addition to the Components provided in Flash, you can obtain other Components from third-party companies and individuals. Often these are mini-applications, such as calendars, photo galleries, and preloaders, that add functionality to a Flash movie.

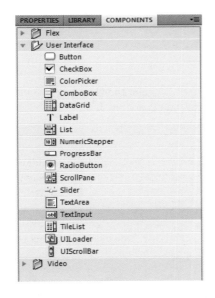

COMPONENTS panel

PROPERTIES LIBRARY COMPONENTS

- ▶ 🗋 Flex
- ▼ 🗋 User Interface
  - ☐ Button
  - ☑ CheckBox
  - ▓ ColorPicker
  - 🗗 ComboBox
  - 🎹 DataGrid
  - T Label
  - 🗐 List
  - 🔟 NumericStepper
  - ▭ ProgressBar
  - ◉ RadioButton
  - ▒ ScrollPane
  - ∿ Slider
  - ▤ TextArea
  - 🔲 TextInput
  - ▦ TileList
  - 🖼 UILoader
  - 🖁 UIScrollBar
- ▶ 🗋 Video

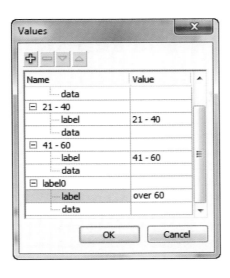

Values

Name	Value
⌐ data	
⊟ 21 - 40	
⌐ label	21 - 40
⌐ data	
⊟ 41 - 60	
⌐ label	41 - 60
⌐ data	
⊟ label0	
⌐ label	over 60
⌐ data	

OK   Cancel

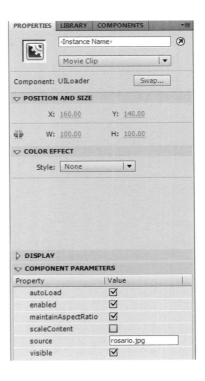

PROPERTIES LIBRARY COMPONENTS

‹Instance Name›

Movie Clip

Component: UILoader   Swap...

▽ **POSITION AND SIZE**

X: 160.00   Y: 140.00

W: 100.00   H: 100.00

▽ **COLOR EFFECT**

Style: None

▷ **DISPLAY**

▽ **COMPONENT PARAMETERS**

Property	Value
autoLoad	☑
enabled	☑
maintainAspectRatio	☑
scaleContent	☐
source	rosario.jpg
visible	☑

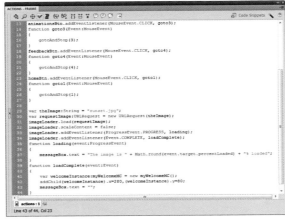

```
ACTIONS - FRAME
animationsBtn.addEventListener(MouseEvent.CLICK, goto3);
function goto3(Event:MouseEvent)
{
    gotoAndStop(3);
}
feedbackBtn.addEventListener(MouseEvent.CLICK, goto4);
function goto4(Event:MouseEvent)
{
    gotoAndStop(4);
}
homeBtn.addEventListener(MouseEvent.CLICK, goto1);
function goto1(Event:MouseEvent)
{
    gotoAndStop(1);
}
var theImage:String = "sunset.jpg";
var requestImage:URLRequest = new URLRequest(theImage);
imageLoader.load(requestImage);
imageLoader.scaleContent = false;
imageLoader.addEventListener(ProgressEvent.PROGRESS, loading);
imageLoader.addEventListener(Event.COMPLETE, loadComplete);
function loading(event:ProgressEvent)
{
    messageBox.text = "The image is " + Math.round(event.target.percentLoaded) + "% loaded";
}
function loadComplete(event:Event)
{
    var welcomeInstance:myWelcomeMC = new myWelcomeMC();
    addChild(welcomeInstance).x=280,(welcomeInstance).y=80;
    messageBox.text = "";
}
```

actions : 1
Line 43 of 44, Col 23

Use Components
IN A FLASH MOVIE

What You'll Do

 In this lesson, you will learn how to use Components to load external graphics and animations, and to create forms.

Using Components

Figure 1 shows the Components panel and the list of available User Interface Components displayed. Each Component name and icon provides a clue to its type, such as Button, CheckBox, and ScrollPane. Many of the User Interface Components are used as part of forms that can gather data from a user. Some, such as the UILoader Component, are used to display content. The UILoader Component can load external .jpg graphic files and .swf movie files. The files do not have to be in the Library panel or on the Stage in the original movie, instead, they can be loaded from a folder, using either a relative or an absolute path, when the movie is running. This can reduce the size of the movie and allow for easy updating of website content by simply changing the .jpg or .swf files on the external site. You learned to load external files using ActionScript in a previous chapter. You can also use the UILoader to accomplish this same task.

Figure 1 *Components panel showing the User Interface Components*

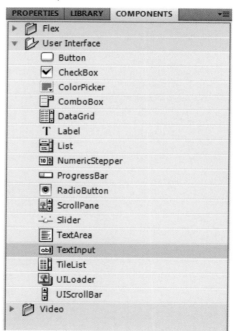

Working with Components

Depending on the type of Component used, you will need to specify one or more of the following parameters:

- source—This parameter is used to specify the location (server, directory, folder, and so on) for the content that is to be displayed using the Component. For example, when using the UILoader Component, if the jpg file is not located in the same folder as the movie file, a path to the jpg file needs to be specified.
- scaleContent—This parameter can be turned on and off. If it is turned on, the content will automatically resize (reduce or enlarge but not crop) to the size of the Component. For example, a UILoader Component has a default size of 100 px by 100 px. If an object with dimensions of 50 px by 50 px is loaded and the scaleContent parameter is active, the object will expand to the larger size of the UILoader Component. If it is not active, the UILoader Component will be scaled to the smaller size associated with the object. The opposite is true as well. That is, if an object with dimensions of 200 px by 200 px is loaded and the scaleContent parameter is active, the object will be scaled to fit the smaller size of the UILoader Component. If the scaleContent parameter is not active, the UILoader Component will expand to be the larger size associated the object.
- autoLoad—This parameter can be turned on and off. If it is turned on, the Component will automatically display the specified contents. If it is turned off, the contents will not be displayed until some other action you specify, such as a button click, occurs.
- label—This parameter allows you to type a text label. For example, you could type Contact Us as the text label for a button Component. The text label appears on the button graphic.

To use a Component, you first select the frame and layer where the Component will be placed, then drag the Component from the Components panel to the desired location on the Stage. To complete the process, you use the Properties panel to set the Component parameters. Figure 2 shows the Component parameters for a UILoader component that is used to display the rosario.jpg image.

Figure 2 *The completed Component parameters to load a .jpg image*

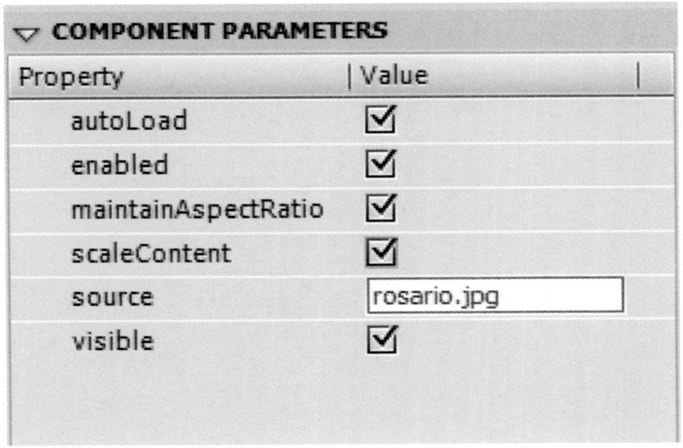

Property	Value
autoLoad	☑
enabled	☑
maintainAspectRatio	☑
scaleContent	☑
source	rosario.jpg
visible	☑

COMPONENT PARAMETERS

Set up the workspace

1. Open fl12_1.fla from the drive and folder where your Data Files are stored, then save it as **mySamples.fla**.

   The Stage size is set to width: 800 px and height 600 px.

2. Change the view to **Fit in Window**.

3. Click **Control** on the menu bar, point to **Test Movie**, then click **in Flash Professional**.

4. Click each of the **navigation text buttons** at the bottom of the screen.

   This is a basic website with simple screen headings. There is no content on the screens except for the Feedback form, which has several labels, but the Components associated with the labels have not been created yet.

5. Close the Flash Player window.

6. Click **Window** on the menu bar, then click **Components**.

7. Dock **the Components panel** with the Library panel and the Properties panel, as shown in Figure 3.

8. View the Timeline and notice there is a layer for each screen associated with a link, such as photos, animations, and feedback.

9. Drag the **playhead** to view each frame from frame 1 to 4 and notice how the objects on the Stage change.

You configured the workspace by displaying and arranging panels and setting the magnification. You then viewed each frame of the movie.

Figure 3 *Docking the Components panel*

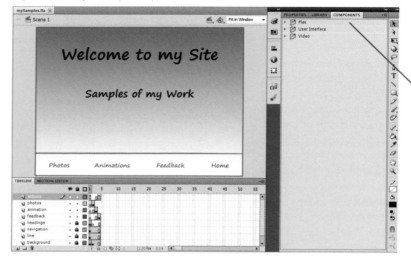

Components panel grouped with the Library and Properties panels

Note: The Components panel may be grouped with other panels. If so, drag the Components panel tab to on top of the tab of the Library panel and, when a blue rectangle appears, release the panel to dock it. Then, close the other panels.

Figure 4 *Positioning the UILoader Component*

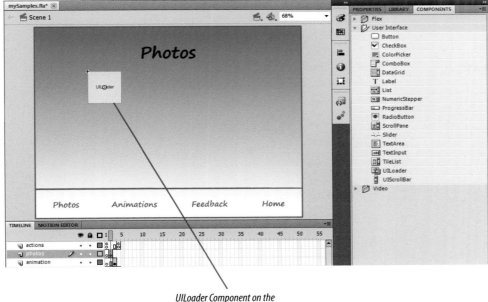

UILoader Component on the
Stage; UILoader Component
default size 100 px by 100 px

Use Components to load graphics

1. Click **frame 2** on the photos layer.

2. Display the Components panel, click the **User Interface expand icon** ▶ , drag the **UILoader Component** from the Components panel to the left side of the Stage, then release the mouse button.

   The UILoader Component appears on the Stage, as shown in Figure 4.

3. Verify the UILoader Component is selected on the Stage, click the **Properties panel**, then display the COMPONENT PARAMETERS area.

TIP Throughout this chapter, you will be using both the Components panel and the Properties panel. Click the tab to activate the panel you need.

4. Click the **source text box** in the Value column in the COMPONENT PARAMETERS area, type **rosario.jpg**, then press **[Enter]** (Win) or **[return]** (Mac).

   The rosario.jpg file should be in the same folder as the mySamples.fla file. If it is not, the complete path to the rosario.jpg file needs to be specified.

5. Verify that autoLoad and scaleContent have check marks to indicate they are turned on.

6. Test the movie, then click **Photos**.

   Notice the display size of the image, which is determined by the size of the UILoader Component. Because scaleContent is active, the image was resized to the size of the UILoader.

7. Close the Flash Player window.

   (continued)

8. **Uncheck** the scaleContent check box to turn it off, as shown in Figure 5.

9. Test the movie, then click **Photos**.

   Notice the displayed image is larger. This is because the UILoader has increased to the size of the image.

10. Close the Flash Player window.

    Note: Be careful when using the scaleContent parameter and resizing the UILoader. The dimensions of the image should be taken into account. If you have a small image that is enlarged to fit the UILoader dimension, the image may lose clarity as the pixels increase.

You placed the UILoader Component on the Stage and specified the graphic to be loaded. You also changed the parameters to have the Component scale to the size of the graphic.

Use Components to load text

1. Display the Components panel, then drag the **TextArea Component** to the Stage and position it to the right of the UILoader and under the ending "s" in Photos.

2. Display the Properties panel, be sure the Lock Icon is broken, then set the TextArea Component width to **300** and the height to **60**.

3. Uncheck the **editable** parameter, then verify the wordWrap parameter is turned on in the COMPONENT PARAMETERS area of the Properties panel.

4. Use your file management program to navigate to the drive and folder where your Data Files are stored, then double-click **rosario.txt** to open the file in a text editor, as shown in Figure 6.

TIP If the text appears on one long line in Notepad, click Format on the menu bar, then click Word Wrap.

(continued)

Figure 5 *Unchecking the scaleContent option*

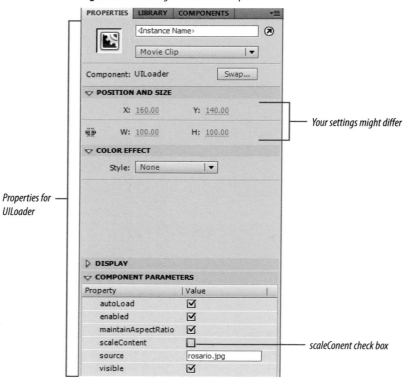

Your settings might differ

Properties for UILoader

scaleConent check box

Figure 6 *The rosario.txt file in a text editor*

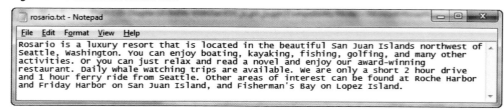

Figure 7 *The rosario text pasted into the text text box*

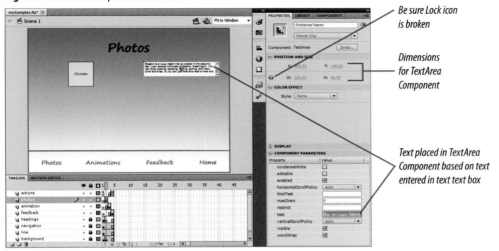

Be sure Lock icon is broken

Dimensions for TextArea Component

Text placed in TextArea Component based on text entered in text text box

Figure 8 *Setting animation.swf as the source file*

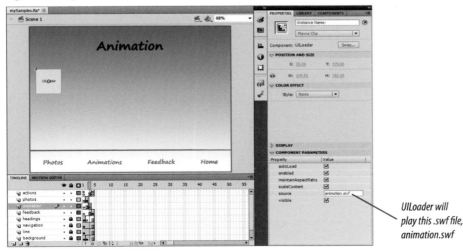

UILoader will play this .swf file, animation.swf

Lesson 1   Use Components in a Flash Movie

5. Use the text editor menu commands (usually available via the Edit menu) to **select all** the text, repeat to **copy** all the text, then close the text editor window.

6. Return to the Flash document, click in the **text text box** in the COMPONENT PARAMETERS area of the Properties panel, press and hold **[Ctrl]**, press **[V]** (Win) or **[command]+V** (Mac), then press **[Enter]** (Win) or **[return]** (Mac) to paste the text into the text box, as shown in Figure 7.

7. Test the movie.

8. Click **Photos**, then scroll to read all the text in the text box.

Note: If the text box overlaps the photo, you can adjust the position of either object when you return to the Flash workspace.

9. Close the Flash Player window, then save your work.

You used the TextArea Component to display text by copying the text to the text text box in the Properties panel.

Use Components to load an animation (.swf file)

1. Click **frame 3** on the animation layer.

2. Display the Components panel, then drag the **UILoader Component** from the Components panel to the Stage and position it on the Stage below and to the left of the heading Animation.

3. Display the Properties panel, then verify autoLoad and scaleContent have check marks.

4. Click in the **source text box**, type **animation.swf** as shown in Figure 8, then press **[Enter]** (Win) or **[return]** (Mac).

(continued)

The animation.swf file should be in the same folder as the mySamples.fla file. If it is not, the complete path to the animation.swf file needs to be specified.

5. Test the movie, then click **Animations**.

   Notice the size of the stick figure. Because the scaleContent parameter is active, the size of the animation is determined by the size of the UILoader. See the top of Figure 9.

6. Close the Flash Player window, then **uncheck** the scaleContent check box.

7. Test the movie, then click **Animations**.

   The UILoader is resized to the size of the animation.swf movie clip. See the bottom of Figure 9.

8. Close the Flash Player window.

9. Save your work.

You used a UILoader Component to display a .swf file by specifying the contentPath and scaleContent parameters.

Figure 9 *Effect of scaleContent on display*

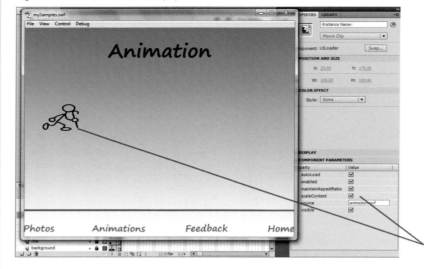

scaleContent checked so animation in animation.swf resized to size of UILoader

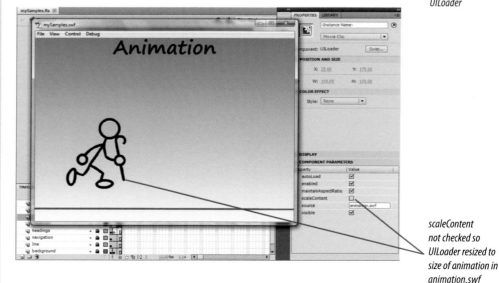

scaleContent not checked so UILoader resized to size of animation in animation.swf

Figure 10 *The completed form with the position of the Components*

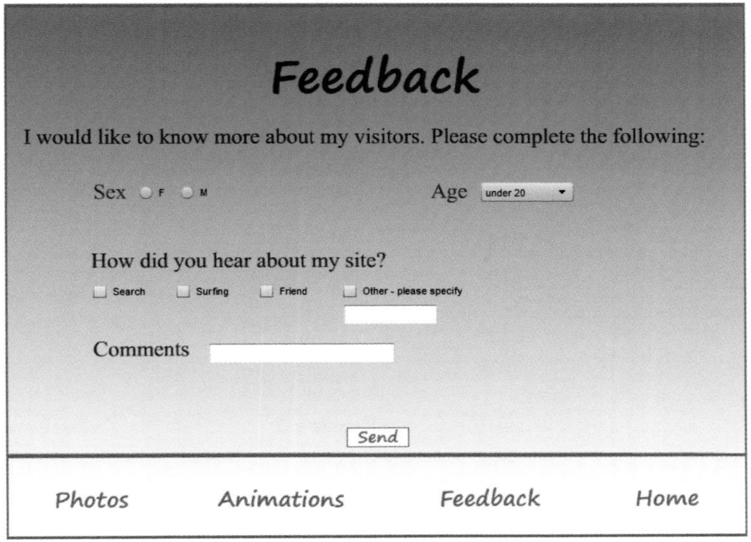

Use Components to create a form

1. Click **frame 4** on the feedback layer, then click a blank area of the Stage to deselect the objects.

   Figure 10 shows the form with the position of the Components.

2. Display the Components panel, then drag the **RadioButton Component** to the Stage and position it next to Sex. (*Hint*: Use the arrow keys on the keyboard to adjust the position of the Component.)
3. Change the label in the label text box in the COMPONENT PARAMETERS of the Properties panel to **F**.
4. Repeat Steps 2 and 3 to add a second RadioButton with the label set to **M**.
5. Drag the **ComboBox Component** from the Components panel and position it next to Age.

   A ComboBox allows you to enter values that appear when the user clicks the list button. Then the user can select a value.

6. In the Properties panel, click [] next to **dataProvider** in the Value column.

   The Values dialog box opens.

(continued)

7. Click the **Add value button** ⊕ , click **label0** in the Value column, then type **under 20**.

8. Click the **Add value button** ⊕ , click **label0** in the Value column, then type **21 – 40**.

9. Click the **Add value button** ⊕ , click **label0** in the Value column, then type **41 – 60**.

10. Click the **Add value button** ⊕ , click **label0**, then type **over 60**.

    Your Values dialog box should resemble Figure 11.

11. Click **OK**.

12. Drag the **CheckBox Component** from the Components panel and position it below "How did you hear about my site?"

13. Change the label in the label text box in the COMPONENT PARAMETERS area of the Properties panel to **Search**.

14. Repeat Steps 12 and 13 to add three more check boxes for **Surfing**, **Friend**, and **Other – please specify**.

15. Click **Other – please specify**, then use the Properties panel to change the width to 150.

(continued)

Figure 11 *The completed Values dialog box*

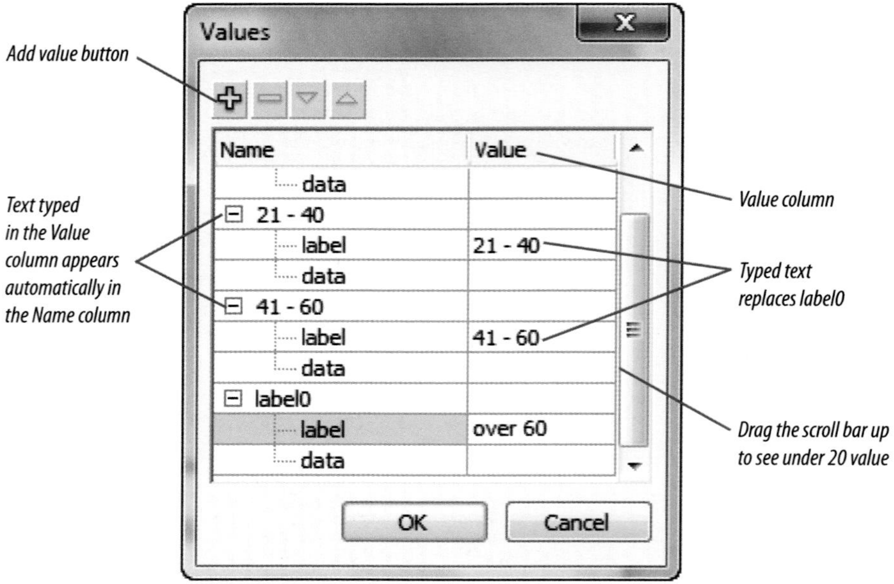

Add value button

Text typed in the Value column appears automatically in the Name column

Value column

Typed text replaces label0

Drag the scroll bar up to see under 20 value

Figure 12 *Changing the width of the TextInput Component*

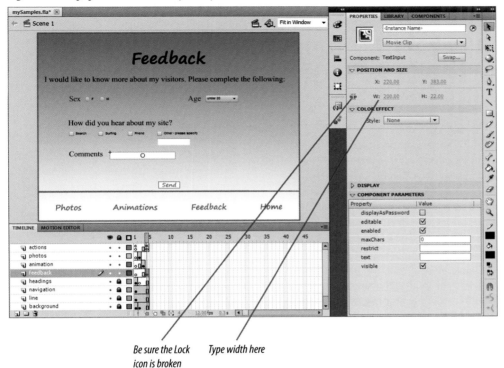

Be sure the Lock icon is broken   Type width here

16. Drag the **TextInput Component** from the Components panel and position it below the Other – please specify check box.

17. Verify editable is active in the Properties panel.

18. Type **20** for the maxChars.

19. Drag the **TextInput Component** from the Components panel and position it next to Comments.

20. Verify the TextInput Component next to Comments is selected on the Stage, display the Properties panel, then change the width to **200**, as shown in Figure 12.

21. Use the arrow keys to adjust the placement of the Component as needed, then click the **Pasteboard** to deselect the Component.

22. Test the movie, click **Feedback**, then fill in the form.

    Notice that you can only select one radio button, and you can only select one option from the list in the combo box. You can select as many check boxes as you want, and you can type freely in the Comments text input box. As you type in the Comments input box, the text scrolls horizontally to allow additional text. You are limited to 20 characters in the Other – please specify input box. *Note*: The Send button is not active.

23. Close the Flash Player window, then save your work.

You used Components to create a form.

Work with Components
AND ACTIONSCRIPT

What You'll Do

In this lesson, you will learn how to add ActionScript to Components to enhance the user experience.

Adding ActionScript to Components

While it is comparatively easy to use Components to create parts of websites and applications, ActionScript can be used to enhance the user experience. In fact, in some cases it is necessary to use ActionScript along with Components. For example, the form you developed in the previous lesson has a send button that is designed to send the user data to a server to be processed, which is accomplished using ActionScript. Another example of using ActionScript to enhance the use of Components would be to add feedback, similar to the preloader you created in an earlier chapter, that lets the user know the progress of an image as it is being loaded and that determines when the image has been loaded. This feedback is especially useful for large images that may take a few moments to appear because it lets the user know that something is happening and how long the wait may be before the loading process is done. In addition, it allows developers to add code, such as to play an animation, that is triggered after an image has been loaded. Figure 13 shows a message that is displayed

as an image is being loaded. The message includes text ("Image is... loaded") and a percent that changes as the image is loaded. When the image has loaded, the message is removed and an animation plays, as shown in Figure 14.

The URLRequest class is used to provide the data (name and location of the image file if it is not in the same folder as the movie) to the load method that will allow an image to be displayed in a UILoader Component on the Stage. Once the image is associated with the UILoader, parameters such as scaleContent can be specified using ActionScript rather than using the Properties panel. In addition, event listeners can be created to "listen" for events such as PROGRESS (the status of the loading) and COMPLETE (when the image is finished loading). Then functions can be created that are called when these events occur. The process for using ActionScript for loading an image into a Component; checking the loading progress, displaying a message about the loading, checking for when the loading is complete; and playing an animation after the image loads follows.

- Create an input text box on the Stage and give it an instance name, such as messageBox. This text box will display a message showing the percentage of the image that is loaded.
- Place an instance of the UILoader on the Stage and give it an instance name, such as imageLoader.
- Create a string variable (theImage) that holds the image to be loaded. This allows you to use the variable name (theImage) in your ActionScript code.

```
var theImage:String = "myImage.jpg";
```

- Create a URLRequest variable (requestImage) that specifies the object (theImage) to pass to the loader.

```
var requestImage:URLRequest = new
URLRequest(theImage);
```

- Use the instance name of the UILoader (imageLoader) to do three things:
  - Load the image.

```
imageLoader.load(requestImage);
```

  - Determine the progress of the loading of the image.

```
imageLoader.addEventListener
    (ProgressEvent.PROGRESS, loading);
```

  - Determine when the image has been completely loaded.

```
imageLoader.addEventListener(Event.
    COMPLETE, loadComplete);
```

- Create the function (loading) that displays a message in a text box indicating the percentage of the image loaded. *Note*: event.target specifies where the percentLoaded method will get the percentage. That is, target refers to the object being loaded).

```
function loading(event:ProgressEvent)

{

messageBox.text = "The image is " +
    (event.target.percentLoaded) + "% loaded"

}
```

- Create a function (loadComplete) that plays an animation (myWelcomeMC) when the image has been loaded.

```
function loadComplete(event:Event)

{

var welcomeInstance:myWelcomeMC =
    new myWelcomeMC();

addChild(welcomeInstance);

}
```

Additional code could be added to set parameters for the UILoader using ActionScript code rather than the Properties panel, such as to set the scaleContent, to round the percentage number to a whole number, and to set the x and y Stage position for the animation.

This example works well for images that have a large file size. If you are loading an image with a small file size or one that is located on your computer or a local network you may not experience any measurable wait time during the loading process. To test this example, you could go to a website that has a large jpg image (over 300 kb) you can load, and depending on the file size, you may be able to see to see how the above code works.

Figure 13 *A message displayed while an image is loading*

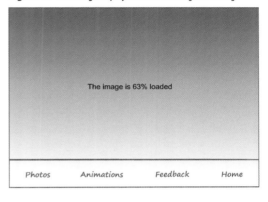

The image is 63% loaded

Photos   Animations   Feedback   Home

Figure 14 *An animation that plays after an image has been loaded*

Photos   Animations   Feedback   Home

Welcome text is animated

Set the objects on the Stage

1. Save the mySamples.fla file as **mySamplesAS3.fla**.

2. Click **frame 1** on the Timeline, delete the **headings layer** to remove the Welcome . . . and Samples . . . headings from the Stage.

3. Insert a **new layer** above the photos layer, name it **message box**, then click **frame 1** on the message box layer.

4. Click the **Text tool** T on the Tools panel, then specify the following: Text type: **Dynamic Text**, Character: **Arial**, Style: **Bold**, Size: **24**; Color: **Blue**, **No border around text**, Format: **Align left**, Behavior: **Single line**.

5. Click the **Embed button**, check **Uppercase**, **Lowercase**, **Numerals**, and **Punctuation** for the Arial Bold font, click the **Add new font button** ➕, then click **OK**.

6. Draw a **text box** at the top of the Stage, then use the Properties panel to specify the following: x value: **100**; y value: **10**; Width: **300**; Height: **40**.

7. With the text box selected use the Properties panel to give it an instance name of **messageBox**.

8. Insert a **blank keyframe** in frame 2 on the message box layer.

9. Insert a **new layer** above the message box layer, then name it **loader**.

10. Click **frame 1** on the loader layer, open the Components panel, drag the **UILoader Component** to the Stage, then use the Properties panel to set the x value to 100 and y value to 50, as shown in Figure 15.

11. Give the UILoader an instance name of **imageLoader**.

(continued)

Figure 15 *Positioning the UILoader Component on the Stage*

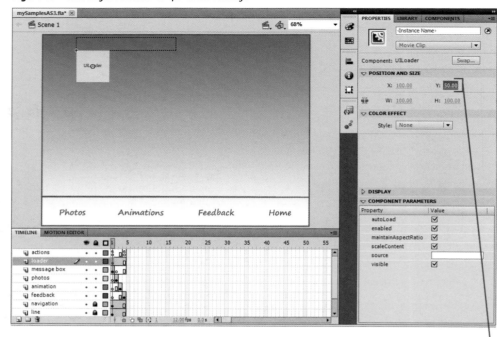

Type x and y values here

Figure 16 *The partially completed code*

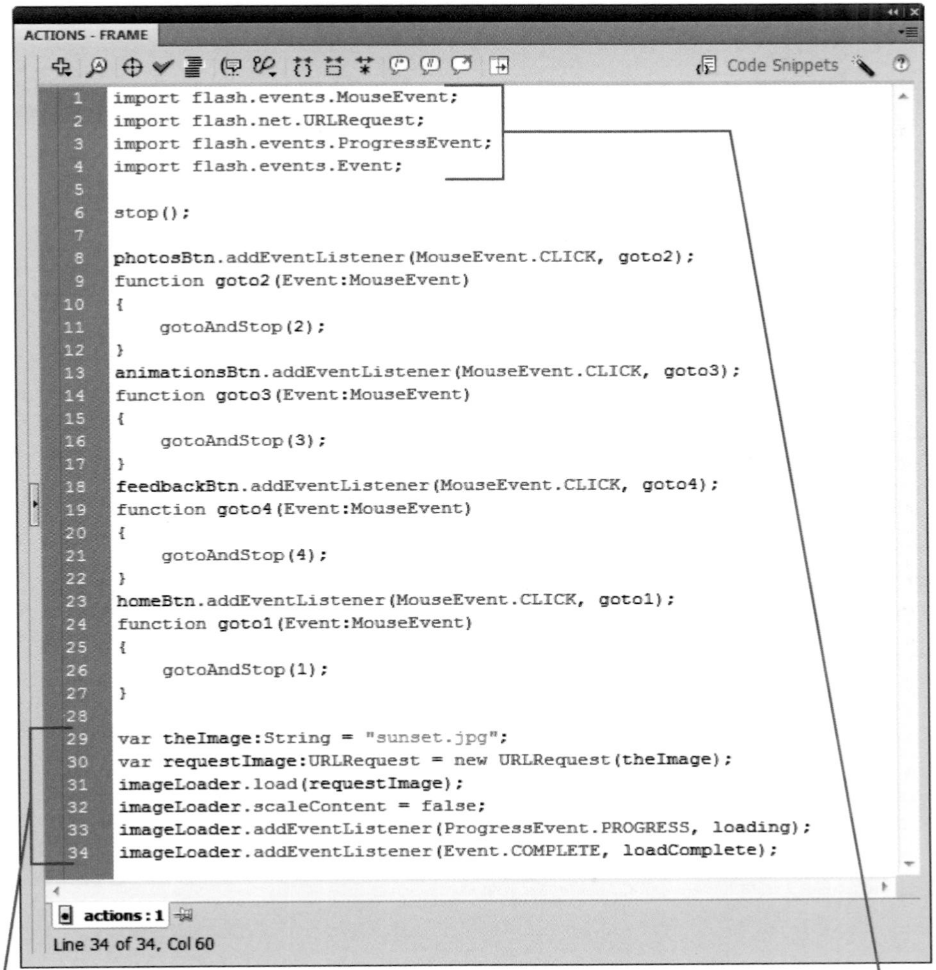

```
ACTIONS - FRAME

                                                    Code Snippets

 1    import flash.events.MouseEvent;
 2    import flash.net.URLRequest;
 3    import flash.events.ProgressEvent;
 4    import flash.events.Event;
 5
 6    stop();
 7
 8    photosBtn.addEventListener(MouseEvent.CLICK, goto2);
 9    function goto2(Event:MouseEvent)
10    {
11        gotoAndStop(2);
12    }
13    animationsBtn.addEventListener(MouseEvent.CLICK, goto3);
14    function goto3(Event:MouseEvent)
15    {
16        gotoAndStop(3);
17    }
18    feedbackBtn.addEventListener(MouseEvent.CLICK, goto4);
19    function goto4(Event:MouseEvent)
20    {
21        gotoAndStop(4);
22    }
23    homeBtn.addEventListener(MouseEvent.CLICK, goto1);
24    function goto1(Event:MouseEvent)
25    {
26        gotoAndStop(1);
27    }
28
29    var theImage:String = "sunset.jpg";
30    var requestImage:URLRequest = new URLRequest(theImage);
31    imageLoader.load(requestImage);
32    imageLoader.scaleContent = false;
33    imageLoader.addEventListener(ProgressEvent.PROGRESS, loading);
34    imageLoader.addEventListener(Event.COMPLETE, loadComplete);

  actions : 1
Line 34 of 34, Col 60
```

New code; your line numbers might differ, depending on if import code is added at top of panel

Your Actions panel might not display all these lines of code

12. Insert a **blank keyframe** in frame 2 on the loader layer.

You added a dynamic text box and the UILoader Component to the Stage and gave them instance names.

Use ActionScript with a Component

1. Click **frame 1** on the actions layer, then open the Actions panel.

2. Refer to Figure 16 as you type the code that follows:

var theImage:String = "sunset.jpg";

This code creates a variable named theImage that uses a String data type and that has sunset.jpg assigned to it.

3. Move to the next line, then on one line type:

var requestImage:URLRequest = new URLRequest(theImage);

This code creates a variable named requestImage that has a data type of URLRequest and specifies theImage as the object to pass to the loader.

4. Move to the next line, then type:

imageLoader.load(requestImage);

This line of code starts the load process.

5. Move to the next line, then type:

imageLoader.scaleContent = false;

This code sets the scaleContent parameter of the UILoader (imageLoader is the instance name of the UILoader) to "false". False is the code that will turn off the scaleContent parameter. This means that the image will retain its original size; it will not scale to the size of the UILoader.

(continued)

6. Move to the next line, then type the following as one line of code:

**imageLoader.
addEventListener(ProgressEvent.
PROGRESS, loading);**

This line of code creates an event listener for a progress event that calls a function named loading when the image begins loading.

7. Move to the next line, then type the following as one line of code:

**imageLoader.addEventListener(Event.
COMPLETE, loadComplete);**

This code creates an event listener for an event that calls a function named loadComplete when the image has finished loading.

8. Click the **Check Syntax button** ✔ and the **Auto format button** ▤, then compare your screen to Figure 16 on the previous page.

9. Move to the next line, then type the code that follow:

**function loading(event:ProgressEvent)
{**

The first line code identifies the loading function as a progressEvent. The second line of code creates the left brace that will enclose the action to be executed when the function named loading is called.

10. Press **[Enter]** (Win) or **[return]**(Mac), then type the following as 1 line of code between the curly braces, as shown in Figure 17.

**messageBox.text = "The image is " + Math.round(event.target.
percentLoaded) + "% loaded";**

(continued)

Figure 17 *The code to display a message while image is being loaded*

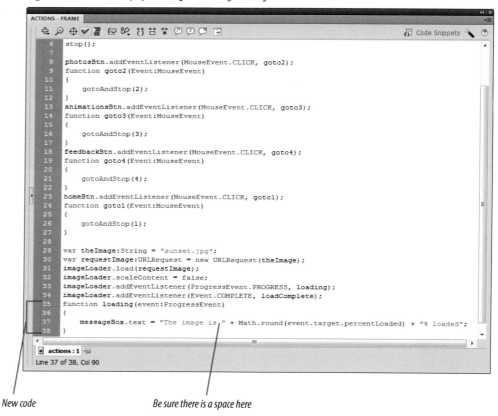

New code

Be sure there is a space here

Working with Components

Figure 18 *The completed code*

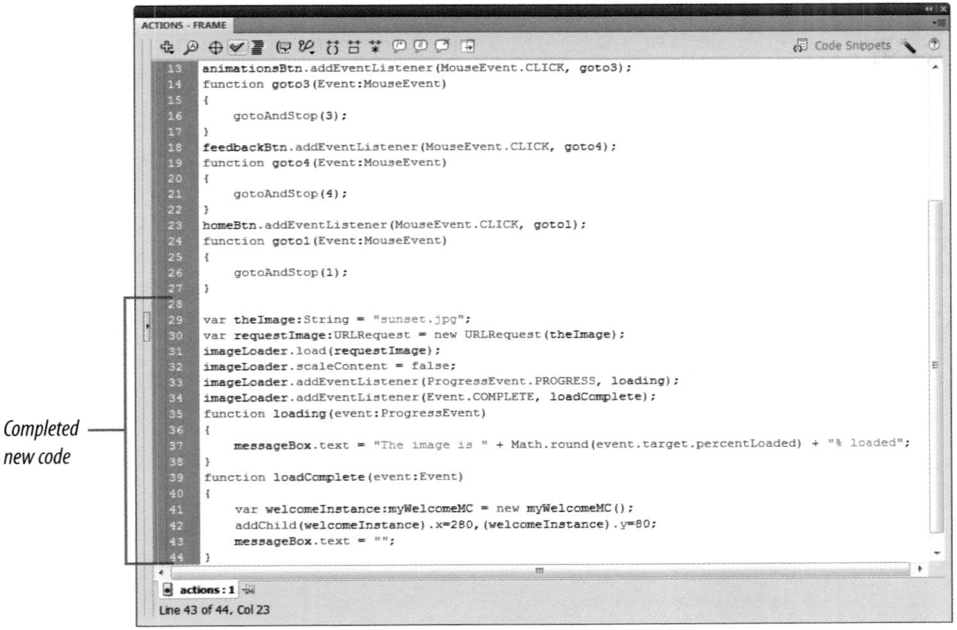

Completed new code

```
13  animationsBtn.addEventListener(MouseEvent.CLICK, goto3);
14  function goto3(Event:MouseEvent)
15  {
16      gotoAndStop(3);
17  }
18  feedbackBtn.addEventListener(MouseEvent.CLICK, goto4);
19  function goto4(Event:MouseEvent)
20  {
21      gotoAndStop(4);
22  }
23  homeBtn.addEventListener(MouseEvent.CLICK, goto1);
24  function goto1(Event:MouseEvent)
25  {
26      gotoAndStop(1);
27  }
28
29  var theImage:String = "sunset.jpg";
30  var requestImage:URLRequest = new URLRequest(theImage);
31  imageLoader.load(requestImage);
32  imageLoader.scaleContent = false;
33  imageLoader.addEventListener(ProgressEvent.PROGRESS, loading);
34  imageLoader.addEventListener(Event.COMPLETE, loadComplete);
35  function loading(event:ProgressEvent)
36  {
37      messageBox.text = "The image is " + Math.round(event.target.percentLoaded) + "% loaded";
38  }
39  function loadComplete(event:Event)
40  {
41      var welcomeInstance:myWelcomeMC = new myWelcomeMC();
42      addChild(welcomeInstance).x=280, (welcomeInstance).y=80;
43      messageBox.text = "";
44  }
```

actions : 1

Line 43 of 44, Col 23

This code creates the message "The image is ... % loaded" and displays it in the messageBox text box on the screen. The percentLoaded property returns a number between 0 and 100 indicating what percentage of the event.target (imageLoader) is loaded. The Math.round method rounds the value up or down to the nearest integer.

11. Move to below the right brace (}), then type the two lines of code that follow:

    function loadComplete(event:Event)

    {

    The first line identifies the loadComplete function as a loadComplete event. The second line of code creates the left brace that will enclose the action to be executed when the function named loadComplete is called.

12. Press **[Enter]** (Win) or **[return]** (Mac), then type the following three line between the curly braces:

    var welcomeInstance:myWelcomeMC = new myWelcomeMC();

    addChild(welcomeInstance) .x=280, (welcomeInstance) .y=80;

    messageBox.text = "";

    The first line creates a variable named welcomeInstance with a myWelcomeMC (movie clip) data type and creates an instance of the movie clip. The second line adds the welcomeInstance object to the display list so that it will be visible on the screen, and sets the location on the screen. The third line places a blank in the messageBox.text text box so that the loading message disappears.

13. Click the **Check Syntax button** and the **Auto format button** , then compare your screen to Figure 18.

(continued)

14. Test the movie.

The sunset.jpg image appears and the animation plays. *Note*: The loading percentage message may not appear because the image is located on your computer or a network computer that requires minimal loading time.

15. Close the Flash Player window.

16. Save your work.

You used ActionScript with a Component to check the loading of an image, display a message on the status of the loading, and play an animation when the loading is done.

Test loading an image from a website

1. Save the file as **mySamplesAS3_altImage.fla**, then open your web browser, go to a search engine site such as Google or Bing, then select the images option that allows you to search for photo images on the web.

2. Search a category (such as mountains), then select a photo image with a large (over 300 kb) file size and dimensions of less than 800 px wide and 600 pixels high. *Note*: You may choose to copy the URL in Figure 19.

3. Right-click (Win) or [control]-click (Mac) the **image**, then choose **Properties**. *Note*: Depending on your browser, the process for copying an image URL may vary.

4. Select the URL address in the Properties dialog box, as shown in Figure 19, press **[Ctrl][C]** to copy the address.

Note: Make sure that the address starts with http:// and ends with .jpg or .jpeg.

(continued)

Figure 19 *Copying the URL address*

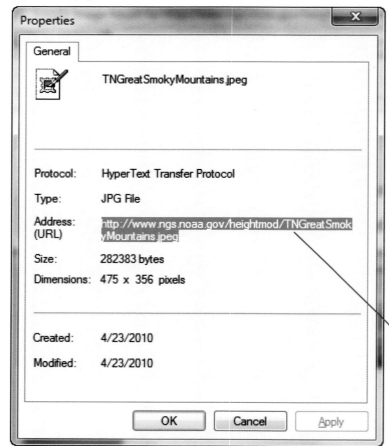

Highlighting the URL in order to copy it Note: If the complete URL is not visible, use the arrow keys to move to the beginning or end of the URL, then drag the pointer to select the complete URL.

Figure 20 *Replacing the sunset.jpg text*

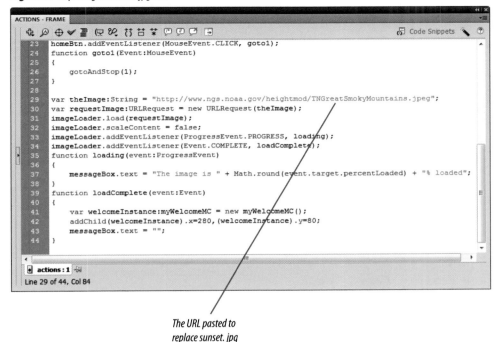

```
ACTIONS - FRAME

                                                              Code Snippets

23    homeBtn.addEventListener(MouseEvent.CLICK, goto1);
24    function goto1(Event:MouseEvent)
25    {
26        gotoAndStop(1);
27    }
28
29    var theImage:String = "http://www.ngs.noaa.gov/heightmod/TNGreatSmokyMountains.jpeg";
30    var requestImage:URLRequest = new URLRequest(theImage);
31    imageLoader.load(requestImage);
32    imageLoader.scaleContent = false;
33    imageLoader.addEventListener(ProgressEvent.PROGRESS, loading);
34    imageLoader.addEventListener(Event.COMPLETE, loadComplete);
35    function loading(event:ProgressEvent)
36    {
37        messageBox.text = "The image is " + Math.round(event.target.percentLoaded) + "% loaded";
38    }
39    function loadComplete(event:Event)
40    {
41        var welcomeInstance:myWelcomeMC = new myWelcomeMC();
42        addChild(welcomeInstance).x=280,(welcomeInstance).y=80;
43        messageBox.text = "";
44    }

  actions : 1
Line 29 of 44, Col 84
```

The URL pasted to
replace sunset. jpg

5. Return to the Flash document, then display the Actions panel.

6. Select sunset.jpg in the line of code that reads var theImage:String = "sunset.jpg";, then press **[Ctrl][V]** to paste the URL address in place of sunset.jpg text, as shown in Figure 20.

7. Test the movie, then maximize the player window if it is not already maximized.

8. Close the Flash Player window.

   Note: If the image does not appear on the screen the way you want it to, try repositioning the UILoader or try unchecking the scaleContent check box, and test the movie again.

9. Save your work, close the document, then Exit Flash.

You tested the load progress and load complete ActionScript features using an image from the web.

Set up the workspace.

1. Start Flash, open fl12_2.fla, then save it as **skillsDemo12.fla**.
2. Test the movie and click the buttons.
3. Close the Flash Player window.
4. Open the Components panel if it is not already open, then dock the Component panel with the Library and Properties panels if they are not already grouped.

Use Components to load graphics.

1. Select frame 2 on the loading graphics and text layer.
2. Drag the UILoader Component to the left side of the Stage.
3. Set the width to **200** and the height to **200** in the POSITION AND SIZE area of the Properties panel.
4. Click the source text box in the COMPONENT PARAMETERS area of the Properties panel, type **kayaking.jpg**, then press [Enter] (Win) or [return] (Mac).
5. Verify that autoLoad and scaleContent are active.
6. Verify that the kayaking.jpg file is in the same folder as the skillsDemo12.fla file.
7. Save your work.

Use Components to load text.

1. Drag the TextArea Component to the Stage and position it to the right of the UILoader.
2. Verify editable and wordWrap are active.
3. Change the width to **250** and the height to **100**.
4. Use your file management program to navigate to the drive and folder where your Data Files are stored, then open the file kayaking.txt in a text editor.

5. Select and copy the text in the kayaking.txt file, close the text editor, then paste the text into the text text box in the COMPONENT PARAMETERS area in Properties panel and press [Enter] (Win) or [return] (Mac).
6. Test the movie, then click the arrow button for Loading graphics and text.
7. Use the scroll bar to read the text, as needed.
8. When done, close the Flash Player window, then save your work.

Use Components to load an animation.

1. Select frame 3 on the loading animations layer.
2. Drag the UILoader Component to the left edge of the Stage beneath the heading.
3. Use the Properties panel to verify autoLoad is active, then uncheck the scaleContent check box to make scaleContent not active.
4. Type **kayaker.swf** for the source, then press [Enter] (Win) or [return] (Mac).
5. Test the movie and click the Loading animations arrow button to view the animation.
6. When done, close the Flash Player window.
7. Save your work.

Use Components to create a form.

1. Select frame 4 on the "a form" layer.
2. Drag two RadioButton Components to the right of the financial aid question and label them **yes** and **no**.
3. Drag four CheckBox Components to the right of the Areas of Interest question and label them: **Arts/ Hum**; **Business**; **Science**; and **Soc Science**.
4. Drag the CheckBox Component to below the Arts/Hum check box and label it: **Other (specify)**.

5. Change the width of the check box to **110**.
6. Drag the TextInput Component to the right of the Other (specify) check box and set the maximum characters to **30**.
7. Drag the ComboBox to the right of Highest degree earned.
8. Click the brackets for the dataProvider Property in the COMPONENT PARAMETERS area of the Properties panel.
9. Use the Values dialog box to add the following labels: **none**; **High School**; **2-Year**; **4-Year**; **Masters**; **Doctorate**.
10. Drag Text Input Components to the right of First Name and Last Name.
11. Test the movie, click the A Form arrow button, compare your screens to Figure 21 on the next page, then test each Component. *Note*: The Submit button is not active.
12. Close the Flash Player window, then save your work.

Work with Components and ActionScript.

1. Save skillsDemo12.fla as **skillsDemo12_AS3.fla**. (*Note*: You will load a photo from the web and add an animated title to the photo.)
2. Add a new layer above the loading photos layer, then name it **message box**.
3. Insert a keyframe in frame 5 of the message box layer.
4. Select the Text tool, then use the Properties panel to specify the following: Text type: **Dynamic**; Character: **Arial**, Style: **Regular**; Size: **24**; Color: **Black**, **No border around text**; Format: **Align center**, Behavior: **Single line**.

Figure 21 *Completed Skills Review - Adding components*

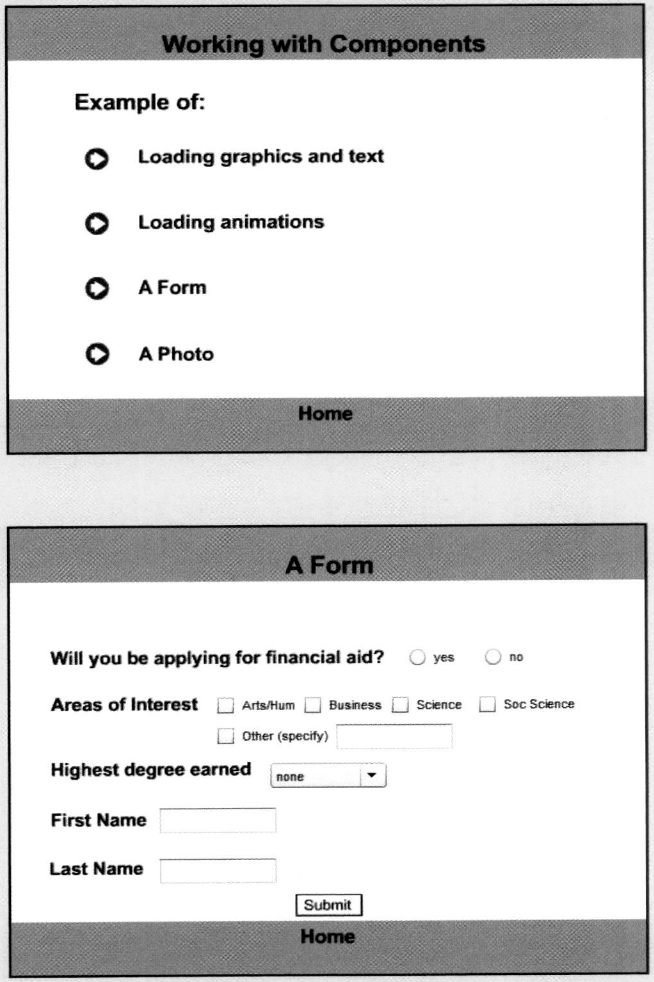

5. Click the Embed button, check Uppercase, Lowercase, Numerals and Punctuation for the Arial Regular font, click the Add new font button, then click OK.
6. Draw a dynamic text box on the center of the Stage, then change the width to **300** and the height to **40**.
7. Change the X coordinate value to **125** and the Y value to **180**.
8. Give the text box an instance name of **loadMessage**.
9. Insert a new layer above the message box layer, then name it **loader**.
10. Insert a keyframe in frame 5 of the loader layer.
11. Drag the UILoader Component to the Stage, then make the following changes in the Properties panel: X coordinate: **0**; Y coordinate: **50**; Width: **550**; Height: **300**.
12. Give the UILoader Component an instance name of **photoLoader**.
13. Create a new movie clip symbol that has an animation and name the movie clip **animationMC**. For example, you might create a title for the photo you are loading from the web then animate the title, perhaps to fade in or to follow a path across the screen.
14. Display the Library panel, right-click (Win) or [control]-click (Mac) animationMC, click Properties, then use the Symbol Properties dialog box to enable Export for ActionScript using animationMC as the class name.

15. Click frame 5 on the actions layer, open the Actions panel, then add code below the stop(); line for the following:
    - A variable named **thePhoto** with a String data type that is assigned a web URL for a .jpg image. (*Note*: Find an image on the web available for download and that has no copyright restrictions, such as an image available at a government website. Also be sure the photo is a minimum of 300 kb.)
    - A variable named **requestPhoto** with a URLRequest data type and a new URLRequest that specifies thePhoto as the object to be passed to the loader.
    - A statement that sets the scaleContent property of the photoLoader to **true**.
    - A statement that begins the load process for the photoLoader.
    - A ProgressEvent event listener that calls a function named **loadingPhoto** as the photo is being loaded.
    - An Event.COMPLETE event listener that calls a function named **loadingComplete** when the photo has been loaded.
    - The loadingPhoto function that displays a message with the percentage of loading compete in the loadMessage text box.
    - The loadingComplete function with the following:
      • The addChild method that adds the instance of the animation to the display list and specifies the location for the object. (*Note*: This is the animationInstance referred to in Step 16 below. The x and y coordinates are 280 and 120, respectively.)
      • A statement to assign a blank to the loadMessage text box.
16. Click frame 1 on the actions layer, then add the following single line of code below the stop(); line:

- A variable named **animationInstance** that is a movie clip data type, named **animationMC**, and the code to create an instance of the movie clip.
- The following four lines of code placed above the goto statement for the function called by the home button so the animation does not play when the Home button is clicked.

```
if (animationInstance.parent != null)
{
animationInstance.parent.removeChild
(animationInstance);
}
```

(*Note*: animationInstance is the instance name for the animation that is played after the photo is loaded in frame 5. The animationInstance object was added to the Display List using the addChild method so that it would be visible at runtime. The removeChild method is used to remove the animationInstance from the Display List. However, you must use parent in the code to target the instance on the Stage. The if statement checks to make sure there is an object on the stage before executing the removeChild statement.

17. Click the Check Syntax button, then click the Auto format button.
18. Test the movie, click the A Photo button, then view the animation. (*Note*: You may not see the loading message if the file size of the photo you referenced is small and loads quickly.)
19. Compare your screen to Figure 22, close the Flash Player window, then save your work.
20. Exit Flash.

Figure 22 *Completed Skills Review - Enhancing components with AS3*

The Ultimate Tours travel company wants to promote a special destination that changes periodically. They have asked you to design a page that will be called "Destination Revealed." The page is to contain an animated heading, photo of the site, and short description. The page is to link to the home page. You decide to create the page using Components so that the company can easily update the photo, description, and sound. Figure 23 shows the link on the home page, the destination page UILoader Components for the animated heading and photo, and a TextArea Component for the description.

1. Open fl12_3.fla, then save it as **ultimateTours12.fla**. (*Hint*: If the font used in this file is not available on your computer, you can choose to use a default font or substitute another font.)
2. Insert a new layer above the Destination_btn layer, name it **Destination page**, then add a keyframe to frame 2 on the layer.
3. Click frame 1 on the Timeline, select the button with the question mark (?), give it an instance name of **questionBtn**, then use the Actions panel to add an event listener that will call a function to cause the playhead to jump to frame 2 when the button is clicked.
4. Create the function that is called in Step 3.

5. Add the UILoader Component to the top of the destination page and change the width to **550** pixels and the height to **50** pixels.
6. Set the X coordinate value to **0** and the Y value to **30**.
7. Have the UILoader Component load the **destination.swf** file as the source file. (*Note*: Be sure this file is stored in the same folder as your ultimateTours12 movie.)
8. Add the UILoader Component to the middle of the destination page and change the height and width to **200** pixels.
9. Set the X coordinate value to **175** and the Y value to **100**.
10. Have the UILoader Component load the **kapalua.jpg** file as the source file. (*Note*: Be sure this file is stored in the same folder as your ultimateTours12 movie.)

11. Add the TextArea Component below the graphic UILoader Component and change the width to **200** pixels and height to **60** pixels.
12. Set the X coordinate value to **175** and the Y value to **320**.
13. Use your file management program to open kapalua.txt in a text editor, then copy the text to the text text box in the COMPONENTS PARAMETER area of the Properties panel.
14. Click frame 2 on the actions layer, insert a keyframe, then use the Actions panel to add a **stop()**; action.
15. Test the movie, click the question mark (?) button, then compare it to the sample images shown in Figure 23.
16. Close the Flash Player window, then save your work.

Figure 23 *Sample completed Project Builder 1*

The International Student Association (ISA) is interested in obtaining information that could be used to determine the effectiveness of its website and improve the site contents. Management would like to add a page with a survey form to its website and has asked you to develop two sample forms. After reviewing the forms, management will select one to be linked to the ISA home page. The intent is to keep the survey short so that site visitors are encouraged to complete and submit it. Figure 24 shows a sample form. Using Figure 24 as a guide, create this introductory survey form, then create one additional similar survey form.

1. Create a new Flash document, then save it as **isa_survey12_1**.
2. Add a background color.
3. Place the following on separate layers:
   - a border
   - the ISA heading
   - the text for the form
   - radio buttons for the ratings with appropriate labels
   - comboBox for the times visited with appropriate choices
   - check boxes for the sections visited with appropriate labels
   - TextInput box for the comments
   - button Component

   Make sure the parameters of the Components have the appropriate settings, such as editable for the TextInput Component.

4. Test the movie, then close the Flash Player window.
5. Publish the movie and display it in a browser.
6. Close your browser, then save your work.
7. Create one more form with similar content for ISA, then test the form.
8. Save your work.

Figure 24 *Samle completed Project Builder 2*

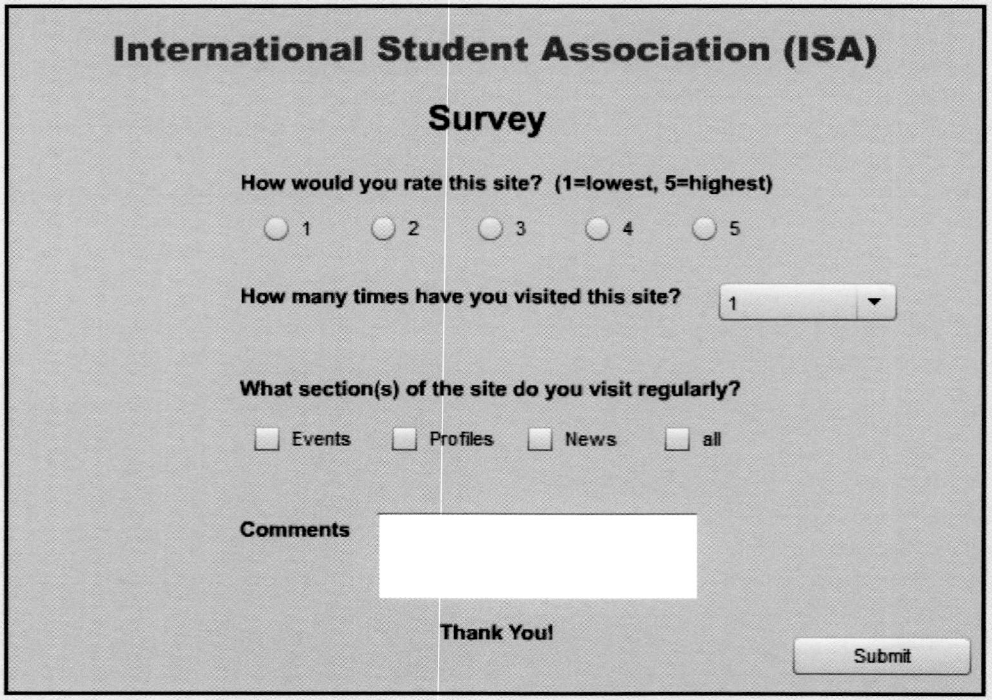

Figure 25 shows part of a form displayed on a website. After connecting to the website, scroll the page to view the entire form and complete the following questions. For each question, indicate how you determined your answer.

1. Connect to the Internet, then go to *http://www.nleb.org/SL_tissue_request.cfm.*
2. Open a document in a word processor or create a new document in Flash, save the file as **dpc12**, then answer the following questions.
   - Whose website is this?
   - What is the goal of the site? (*Note*: Click on the SightLife logo in the upper left of the screen to display the home page to answer this question.)
   - Who is the target audience?
   - How might Components be used in this site? (*Note*: Return to the Tissue Request Form page or refer to Figure 25 to answer this question.)
   - What other types of forms might the site developers create?

Figure 25 *Design Project*

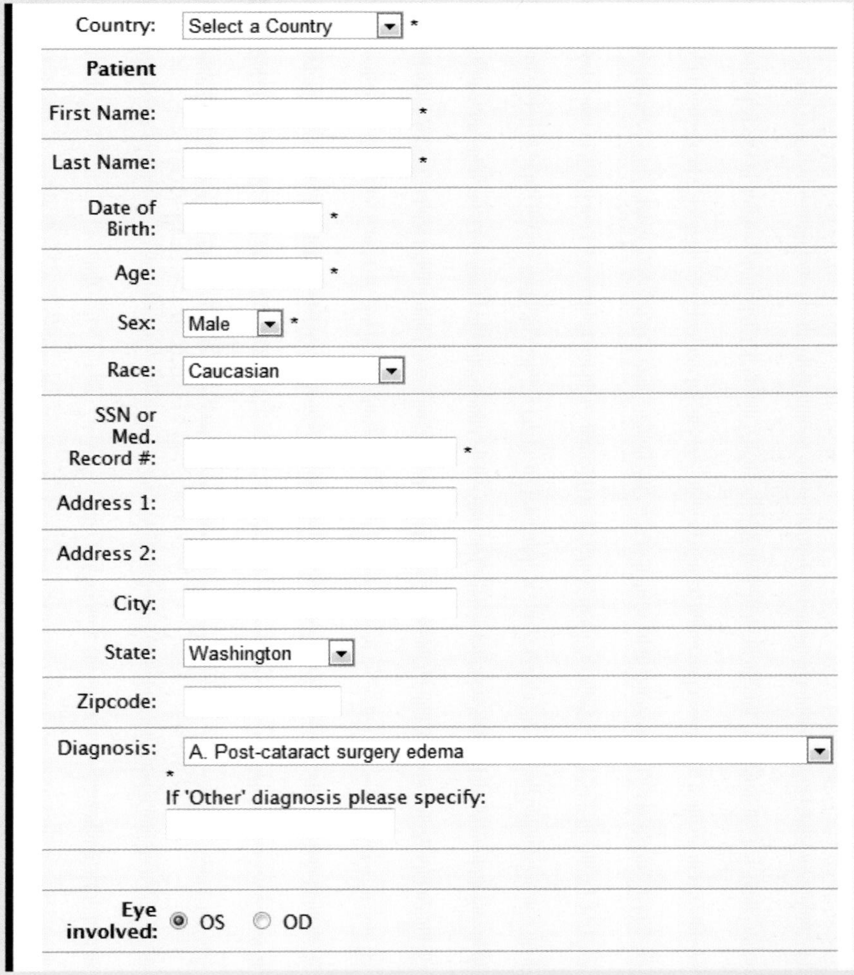
Country: Select a Country *
Patient
First Name: *
Last Name: *
Date of Birth: *
Age: *
Sex: Male *
Race: Caucasian
SSN or Med. Record #: *
Address 1:
Address 2:
City:
State: Washington
Zipcode:
Diagnosis: A. Post-cataract surgery edema
*
If 'Other' diagnosis please specify:
Eye involved: OS OD

You have been asked by a local artist to help design the gallery page for her website. The page will include samples of her artwork and will be linked to her home page. The gallery page could be used to showcase her work as an online portfolio. Figure 26 shows the home page and a sample gallery page.

1. Open fl12_4.fla, then save it as **gallery.fla**.
2. Select the Gallery button, give it an instance name of galleryBtn, select frame 1 of the actions layer, then use the Actions panel to enter the ActionScript code that adds an event listener with a function to display frame 2 when the button is clicked.
3. Use the following steps to create the Gallery page. Use frame 2 for the Gallery page. Add layers as indicated and name them appropriately.
   - Extend the background, border, and copyright layers to frame 2.
   - Insert a new layer, name it **gallery heading**, add a keyframe in frame 2, then type the **Gallery** heading.
   - Insert a new layer above the gallery heading layer, name it **paintings**, add a keyframe in frame 2, then use UILoader Components to have the six paintings appear on the Gallery page. Set the scaleContent parameter so that the UILoader scales to the size of the .jpg file. (*Note*: Use the captions on the images in Figure 26, as well as the filenames, to know which .jpg image to associate with which UILoader.)
   - Insert a new layer above the paintings layer, name it **captions**, add a keyframe to frame 2, then use TextArea Components to have the six painting captions appear on the Gallery page, as shown in Figure 26. Set the width of each TextArea Component to **150** and the height to **24**.
   - Insert a new layer above the captions layer, name it **home button**, insert a keyframe in frame 2, then create a Home button with an instance name of **homeBtn**.
   - Insert a keyframe in frame 2 of the actions layer, then use the Actions panel to add stop(); action and the ActionScript that adds an event listener with a function to display frame 1 when the Home text button is clicked.
4. Verify that all of the .jpg files are in the same folder as the gallery.fla file.
5. Test the movie and test the Gallery and Home buttons.
6. Close the Flash Player window.
7. Publish the movie and display it in a browser.
8. Close the browser window, then save your work.

Figure 26 *Sample completed Portfolio Project*

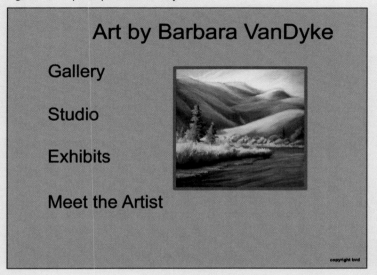

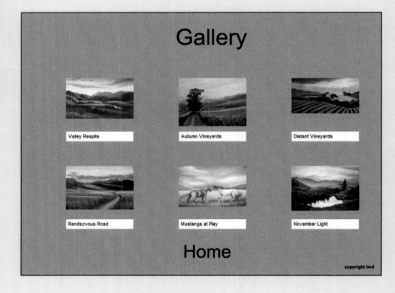

Some of the ACE exam objectives are covered in material posted on the Online Companion for this book. To access the Online Companion, take the following steps:

1. Open your web browser and go to: **http://www.cengagebrain.com/**.
2. Type the author, title or ISBN of this book in the Search window.
3. Locate and click on the book title.
4. When the book's main page is displayed, click the Access Now button.
5. Click the **Student Resources link** in the left navigation pane to access the resources.

ADOBE CERTIFIED EXPERT EXAM OBJECTIVES		
Topic	**Objective**	**Chapter (s)**
1.0 Planning and designing Flash applications	1.1 Given a requirement based on your audience, determine the appropriate Flash features and options used to meet the needs of your audience and target platform. (Audience requirements include: publishing to AIR, accessibility, player version)	1 (p. 1-40-43) 6 (p. 6-26-27)
	1.2 Given a scenario, explain how Flash can be used in an application. (Scenarios, include: Creating a banner, full Web application, mobile application, desktop AIR application, or visual element)	1 (p. 1-40) 6 (p. 6-26-27)
	1.3 Given an asset type, explain the benefit of that asset type for a given application. (Asset types include: raster, vector, FXG, XFL)	1 (p. 1-2) 7 (p. 7-4-7, 7-12, 7-16)
	1.4 Understand the benefits and uses of FLA source files versus XFL packages.	Online Companion

ADOBE CERTIFIED EXPERT EXAM OBJECTIVES		
Topic	**Objective**	**Chapter (s)**
2.0　Creating and managing assets	2.1　Given an option in the Library panel, explain the purpose of and how to use that option.	3 (p. 3-10-15)
	2.2　Given a tool, work with an existing asset by using that tool. (Tools include: Transform, 3D Rotation, Bone)	2 (p. 2-22, 24, 25, 27, 28) 5 (p. 5-26-39)
	2.3　Import external assets into Flash. (External assets include: XFG, XFL, Photoshop files, Illustrator files, and images)	7 (p. 7-2, 7-4-10)
	2.4　Create and manage text fields by using the Text tool including using the Text Layout Framework.	2 (p. 2-32-41)
	2.5　Embed and manage fonts. (Methods include: using the Font Embedding dialog box, Library)	9 (p. 9-31, 9-33-34)
	2.6　Given an asset, convert that asset to a symbol and explain the capabilities of that symbol.	3 (p. 3-4-9)
	2.7　Given a component, explain the purpose of or how to use that component.	12 (p. 12-2,12-4-11)
	2.8　Edit the skin of a component.	11 (p. 11-26-28)
	2.9　Manage performance by utilizing bitmap techniques.	7 (p. 7-4-7, 7-10-18)

ADOBE CERTIFIED EXPERT EXAM OBJECTIVES

Topic	Objective	Chapter (s)
3.0 Creating Flash interactive and visual output	3.1 Given a tool, create a shape by using that tool. (Tools include: Deco, Spray Brush, Rectangle Primitive)	2 (p. 2-2, 2-4-13) 5 (p. 5-40-45)
	3.2 Given an asset, modify individual properties to achieve specific design requirements. (Design requirements include: advanced text controls including anti-aliasing, stroke control and styling)	2 (p. 2-32-41)
	3.3 Create animations by using the Timeline.	4 (p. 4-2, 4-4-35)
	3.4 Edit animations by using the Motion Editor.	8 (p. 8-28-31)
	3.5 Create and use Motion Presets.	1 (p. 1-21, 1-28-29)
	3.6 Incorporate and manage audio and video in your movie.	5 (p. 5-8-17) 11 (all)
	3.7 Apply filters and effects to Movie Clips and text.	2 (p. 2-35)
	3.8 Add queue points to the FLV playback component on the stage for synchronized content.	11 (p. 11-27-31)
	3.9 Add basic interactivity by using code snippets.	9 (p. 9-24-29)

ADOBE CERTIFIED EXPERT EXAM OBJECTIVES		
Topic	**Objective**	**Chapter (s)**
4.0 Programming with ActionScript 3.0	4.1 Given an ActionScript class, create an instance from and work with the properties of that class.	9 (p. 9-4-14)
	4.2 Given an object-oriented concept, explain the definition of or purpose associated with that concept. (Object-oriented concepts include: Classes, Interfaces, Inheritance, Polymorphism, and Packages)	Online Companion
	4.3 Create custom classes. (Options include: Extending, Subclassing)	Online Companion
	4.4 Explain how to use the Document class.	Online Companion
	4.5 Load and use content and data from external sources. (Sources include: XML, SWF, and remote objects)	10 (p. 10-18-23), 11 (p. 11-26-28), 12 (p. 12-4-5, 12-7-11, 12-4-21)
	4.6 Create code snippets.	Online Companion
	4.7 List and describe the benefits and limitations of code hinting.	Online Companion
	4.8 Understand the use of the ExternalInterface class for execution with JavaScript.	Online Companion

ADOBE CERTIFIED EXPERT EXAM OBJECTIVES		
Topic	**Objective**	**Chapter (s)**
5.0 Testing Flash applications	5.1 Recognize effective optimization considerations when testing and debugging Flash applications.	6 (p. 6-10-15)
	5.2 Test an application by using Device Central, AIR Debug Launcher, or within Flash Pro.	1 (p. 1-13, 1-16) 6 (p. 6-26-31)
	5.3 Given a Debug panel, explain how to use that panel. (Panels include: Debug Console, variables, output)	Online Companion

ADOBE CERTIFIED EXPERT EXAM OBJECTIVES

Topic	Objective		Chapter (s)
6.0 Publishing and deploying Flash applications	6.1 Given a scenario, select the appropriate Publish settings to deploy a Flash movie. (Scenarios include: Web delivery, AIR, mobile)		1 (p. 1-36-38) 6 (p. 6-26)
	6.2 Understand the publish settings. (Publish settings include: HTML container page, script settings, SWF settings)		6 (p. 6-4-9, 6-22-25)
	6.3 Understand the implications of and how to implement cross-domain security for SWF, data, and visual assets.		Online Companion
	6.4 Understand how to enable and explain the limitations of functionality related to fullscreen.		Online Companion

ADOBE RICH MEDIA COMMUNICATIONS: ADOBE CERTIFIED ASSOCIATE EXAM OBJECTIVES

Topic	Objective	Chapter(s)
Domain 1.0 Setting Project Requirements	1.1 Identify the purpose, audience, and audience needs for rich media content.	1 (p. 1-40, 1-41)
	1.2 Identify rich media content that is relevant to the purpose of the media in which it will be used (websites, mobile devices, and so on).	1 (p. 1-40, 1-41)
	1.3 Understand options for producing accessible rich media content.	1 (p. 1-40, 1-41)
	1.4 Demonstrate knowledge of standard copyright rules (related terms, obtaining permission, and citing copyrighted material).	7 (p. 7-7)
	1.5 Understand project management tasks and responsibilities.	1 (p. 1-43-44)
	1.6 Communicate with others (such as peers and clients) about design and content plans.	1 (p. 1-43-44)

ADOBE RICH MEDIA COMMUNICATIONS: ADOBE CERTIFIED ASSOCIATE EXAM OBJECTIVES

Topic		Objective		Chapter(s)
Domain 2.0	Identifying Rich Media Design Elements	2.1 Identify general and Flash-specific best practices for designing rich media content for a website.		1 (p. 1-40-44)
		2.2 Demonstrate knowledge of design elements and principles.		1 (p. 1-40-44)
		2.3 Identify general and Flash-specific techniques to create rich media elements that are accessible and readable.		1 (p. 1-41)
		2.4 Use a storyboard to produce rich media elements.		1 (p. 1-42)
		2.5 Organize a Flash document.		1 (p. 1-4, 1-8)

ADOBE RICH MEDIA COMMUNICATIONS: ADOBE CERTIFIED ASSOCIATE EXAM OBJECTIVES

Topic	Objective	Chapter(s)
Domain 3.0 Understanding Adobe Flash CS5 Interface	3.1 Identify elements of the Flash interface.	1 (p. 1-2-11)
	3.2 Use the Property inspector.	1 (p. 1-5, 1-6, 1-25)
	3.3 Use the Timeline.	1 (p. 1-5, 1-11, 1-30-35)
	3.4 Adjust document properties.	1 (p. 1-17)
	3.5 Use Flash guides and rulers.	2 (p. 2-7, 2-14-15, 2-50-51)
	3.6 Use the Motion Editor.	8 (p. 8-28-31)
	3.7 Understand Flash file types.	1 (p. 1-12, 1-36-37)
	3.8 Identify best practices for managing the file size of a published Flash document.	6 (p. 6-10)

ADOBE RICH MEDIA COMMUNICATIONS: ADOBE CERTIFIED ASSOCIATE EXAM OBJECTIVES			
Topic	**Objective**		**Chapter(s)**
Domain 4.0 Building Rich Media Elements by Using Flash CS5	4.1	Make rich media content development decisions based on your analysis and interpretation of design specifications.	1 (p. 1-40-44)
	4.2	Use tools on the Tools panel to select, create, and manipulate graphics and text.	2 (p. 2-4-7, 2-9-13)
	4.3	Import and modify graphics.	3 (p. 3-30-35) 7 (p. 7-4-11)
	4.4	Create text.	2 (p. 2-32-34)
	4.5	Adjust text properties.	2 (p. 2-34-41)
	4.6	Create objects and convert them to symbols, including graphics, movie clips, and buttons.	1 (p. 1-22) 2 (p. 2-2-23) 3 (p. 3-2-6, 3-16-21) 4 (p. 4-36-41)
	4.7	Understand symbols and the library.	3 (p. 3-2-15)
	4.8	Edit symbols and instances.	3 (p. 3-7-9)
	4.9	Create masks.	5 (p. 5-4-7)
	4.10	Create animations (changes in shape, position, size, color, and transparency).	1 (p. 1-19-29) 4 (p. 4-2-35)

ADOBE RICH MEDIA COMMUNICATIONS: ADOBE CERTIFIED ASSOCIATE EXAM OBJECTIVES		
Topic	**Objective**	**Chapter(s)**
	4.11 Add simple controls through ActionScript 3.0.	9 (p. 9-2, 9-8-9, 9-20-21)
	4.12 Import and use sound.	5 (p. 5-8-11) 11 (p. 11-4-25)
	4.13 Add and export video.	5 (p. 5-12-17) 11 (p. 11-26-31)
	4.14 Publish Flash documents.	1 (p. 1-36-39) 6 (p. 6-2-15, 6-22-25)
	4.15 Make a document accessible.	1 (p. 1-41)
Domain 5.0 Evaluating Rich Media Elements by Using Flash CS5	5.1 Conduct basic technical tests.	3 (p. 3-20-21) 6 (p. 6-10-14)
	5.2 Identify techniques for basic usability tests.	6 (p. 6-10-15)

DATA FILES LIST

Read the following information carefully!

Find out from your instructor the location where you will store your files.

- To complete many of the chapters in this book, you need to use the Data Files provided on the CD at the back of the book.
- Your instructor will tell you whether you will be working from the CD or copying the files to a drive on your computer or on a server. Your instructor will also tell you where you will store the files you create and modify.

Copy and organize your Data Files.

- Use the Data Files List to organize your files to a USB storage device, network folder, hard drive, or other storage device if you won't be working from the CD.
- Create a subfolder for each chapter in the location where you are storing your files, and name it according to the chapter title (e.g., chapter_1).
- For each chapter you are assigned, copy the files listed in the **Data File Supplied** column into that chapter's folder. Note that you can also copy each folder and its contents to the storage location rather than creating the folders yourself.
- If you are working from the CD, you should still store the files you modify or create in each chapter in the chapter folder.

Find and keep track of your Data Files and completed files.

- Use the **Data File Supplied** column to make sure you have the files you need before starting the chapter or exercise indicated in the **Chapter** column.
- Use the **Student Creates File** column to find out the filename you use when saving your new file for the exercise.
- The **Used in** column tells you the lesson or end of chapter exercise where you will use the file.

Files Used in this Book

ADOBE FLASH CS5			
Chapter	**Data File Supplied**	**Student Creates New File**	**Used In**
1		workspace.fla	Lesson 1
	fl1_1.fla		Lesson 2
		tween.fla	Lesson 3
	*tween.fla	layers.fla	Lesson 4
	*layers.fla		Lesson 5
			Lesson 6
	fl1_2.fla		Skills Review
		demonstration.fla	Project Builder 1
	fl1_3.fla		Project Builder 2
		dpc1.fla	Design Project
			Portfolio Project

*Created in a previous Lesson or Skills Review in current chapter

ADOBE FLASH CS5			
Chapter	**Data File Supplied**	**Student Creates New File**	**Used In**
2	fl2_1.fla		Lesson 1
	fl2_2.fla		
	fl2_3.fla		
	fl2_4.fla		Lesson 4
	fl2_5.fla		Lesson 5
	fl2_6.fla		Skills Review
		ultimateTours2.fla	Project Builder 1
		theJazzClub2.fla	Project Builder 2
		dpc2.fla	Design Project
		portfolio2.fla	Portfolio Project

ADOBE FLASH CS5			
Chapter	Data File Supplied	Student Creates New File	Used In
3	fl3_1.fla		Lesson 1
	fl3_2.fla		Lessons 2-4
	islandview.jpg	sailing.fla	Lesson 5
	sailboat.ai		
	fl3_3.fla		Skills Review
	BeachScene.jpg		
	**ultimatetours2.fla		Project Builder 1
	UTLogo.jpg		
		isa3.fla	Project Builder 2
		dpc3.fla	Design Project
	**portfolio2.fla		Portfolio Project

**Created in a previous chapter

ADOBE FLASH CS5			
Chapter	**Data File Supplied**	**Student Creates New File**	**Used In**
4	fl4_1.fla		Lesson 1
	fl4_2.fla		
	fl4_3.fla		Lesson 2
	fl4_4.fla		Lesson 3
	fl4_5.fla		
	fl4_6.fla		Lesson 4
	fl4_7.fla		
	fl4_8.fla		
	fl4_9.fla		Lesson 5
	fl4_10.fla		Lesson 6
	fl4_11.fla		Skills Review
	**ultimatetours3.fla		Project Builder 1
	ship.gif		
		jumper4.fla	Project Builder 2
		dpc4.fla	Design Project
	**portfolio3.fla		Portfolio Project

**Created in a previous chapter

ADOBE FLASH CS5			
Chapter	Data File Supplied	Student Creates New File	Used In
5	fl5_1.fla		Lesson 1
	fl5_2.fla		Lesson 2
	CarSnd.wav		
	beep.wav		
	fl5_3.fla		Lesson 3
	fireworks.mov		
	fl5_4.fla		Lesson 4
	fl5_5.fla		Lesson 5
	fl5_6.fla		
	fl5_7.fla		Lesson 6
	fl5_8.fla		Lesson 7
	fl5_9.fla		Skills Review

ADOBE FLASH CS5			
Chapter	**Data File Supplied**	**Student Creates New File**	**Used In**
5, continued	fl5_10.fla		
	fl5_11.fla		
	*decoLand.fla		
	tour-video.mov		
	fl5_12.fla		Project Builder 1
	**ultimatetours4.fla		
	fl5_13.fla		Project Builder 2
		dpc5.fla	Design Project
	**portfolio4.fla		Portfolio Project

*Created in a previous Lesson or Skills Review in current chapter
**Created in a previous chapter

ADOBE FLASH CS5			
Chapter	**Data File Supplied**	**Student Creates New File**	**Used In**
6	fl6_1.fla	planeLoop.gif	Lesson 1
		planeLoop.jpg	
	fl6_2.fla		Lesson 2
	fl6_3.fla		Lesson 3
	*planeFun.fla	planeFun-caption.html	Lesson 4
	palmTrees.jpg	palms.fla	Lesson 5
	fl6_4.fla	skillsdemo6.jpg	Skills Review
		skillsdemo6-caption.html	
	**ultimatetours5.fla	ultimatetours6.gif	Project Builder 1
		ultimatetours6.jpg	
		ultimatetours6-caption.html	
		publish6.gif	Project Builder 2
		publish6.jpg	
		publish6-caption.html	
		dpc6.fla	Design Project
	**portfolio5.fla	portfolio6.jpg	Portfolio Project
		portfolio6-caption.html	

*Created in a previous Lesson or Skills Review in current chapter
**Created in a previous chapter

ADOBE FLASH CS5			
Chapter	**Data File Supplied**	**Student Creates New File**	**Used In**
7	dragonfly.png	gsamples.fla	Lesson 1
	tree.ai, background.psd		
	meadow.jpg		Lesson 2
	moon.jpg		Lesson 3
	fl7_1.fla		Lesson 4
	rose.jpg		
	dayMoon.jpg	skillsDemo7.fla	Skills Review
	logo.png		
	nightsky.jpg		
	mountain.jpg		

ADOBE FLASH CS5			
Chapter	**Data File Supplied**	**Student Creates New File**	**Used In**
7, continued	gtravel1.jpg	ultimateTours7.fla	Project Builder 1
	gtravel2.jpg		
	gtravel3.jpg		
	gtravel4.jpg		
	gtravel5.jpg		
	gtravel6.jpg		
	gantho1.jpg	anthoArt7.fla	Project Builder 2
	gantho2.jpg		
	gantho3.jpg		
	gantho4.jpg		
		dpc7.fla	Design Project
	portfolioCase.jpg	portfolio7.fla	Portfolio Project

ADOBE FLASH CS5			
Chapter	Data File Supplied	Student Creates New File	Used In
8	fl8_1.fla		Lesson 1
	fl8_2.fla		Lesson 2
	fl8_3.fla		Lessons 3-4
	**dragonfly.fla		Lesson 5
	fl8_4.fla		Skills Review
		ultimatetours8.fla	Project Builder 1
		ocean_life8.fla	Project Builder 2
		dpc8.fla	Design Project
		portfolio8.fla	Portfolio Project

**Created in a previous chapter

ADOBE FLASH CS5			
Chapter	**Data File Supplied**	**Student Creates New File**	**Used In**
9	fl9_1.fla		Lesson 1
	fl9_2.fla		
	fl9_3.fla		Lesson 2
	fl9_4.fla		Lesson 3
	fl9_5.fla		Lesson 4
	fl9_6.fla	skillsDemo9-object.fla	Skills Review
	**ultimatetours8.fla		Project Builder 1
		dragToMatch.fla	Project Builder 2
		dpc9.fla	Design Project
	**portfolio8.fla		Portfolio Project

**Created in a previous chapter

ADOBE FLASH CS5			
Chapter	**Data File Supplied**	**Student Creates New File**	**Used In**
10	fl10_1.fla		Lesson 1
	fl10_2.fla		Lesson 2
	fl10_3.fla		Lesson 3
	fl10_4.fla		
	frog.swf		
	fish.swf		
	fl10_5.fla		Lesson 4
	fl10_6.fla		Skills Review
	textAnimation.swf		
	fl10_7.fla		Project Builder 1
	specials.swf		
	fl10_8.fla		Project Builder 2
		dpc10.fla	Design Project
	shirt.swf	portfolio10.fla	Portfolio Project
	shirt2.swf		
	math.swf		

ADOBE FLASH CS5			
Chapter	Data File Supplied	Student Creates New File	Used In
11	fl11_1.fla		Lessons 1-2
	accent1.mp3		
	accent2.mp3		
	background.mp3		
	fl11_2.fla		Lesson 2
	*nightclub.fla		Lesson 3
	fl11_3.fla		Lesson 4
	fl11_4.fla		Lesson 5
	safari.flv		
	fl11_5.fla		Skills Review
	waterfall.wav		

*Created in a previous Lesson or Skills Review in current chapter

ADOBE FLASH CS5			
Chapter	**Data File Supplied**	**Student Creates New File**	**Used In**
11, continued	wilderness.flv		
	fl11_6.fla		Project Builder 1
	**interactive.fla		Project Builder 2
		dpc11.fla	Design Project
	**portfolio9.fla		Portfolio Project
	accent1.mp3		
	accent2.mp3		
	background.mp3		
	catFun.flv		
	portfolio_voiceover.wav		

**Created in a previous chapter

ADOBE FLASH CS5			
Chapter	**Data File Supplied**	**Student Creates New File**	**Used In**
12	fl12_1.fla		Lesson 1
	rosario.jpg		Lesson 2
	rosario.txt		
	animation.swf		
	fl12_2.fla		Skills Review
	*mySamples.fla		
	kayaking.jpg		
	kayaking.txt		
	kayaker.swf		
	sunset.jpg		
	fl12_3.fla		Project Builder 1
	destination.swf		

*Created in a previous Lesson or Skills Review in current chapter

ADOBE FLASH CS5			
Chapter	**Data File Supplied**	**Student Creates New File**	**Used In**
12, continued	kapalua.jpg		
	kapalua.txt		
		isa_survey1.fla	Project Builder 2
		dpc12.fla	Design Project
	fl12_4.fla		Portfolio Project
	AutumnVineyrds.jpg		
	DistantVineyards.jpg		
	Mustangs.jpg		
	Novlight.jpg		
	Rendezvous.jpg		
	ValleyRespite.jpg		
	yakimariver.jpg		

3D Effects
A process in Flash that animates 2D objects through 3D space with 3D Transformation tools.

――――――― **A** ―――――――

Absolute path
A path containing an external link that references a link on a web page outside of the current website, and includes the protocol "http" and the URL, or address, of the web page.

Actions panel
The panel where you create and edit Action Script code for an object or a frame.

Actions Toolbox pane
The section of the Actions panel displaying the categories of actions that can be selected to build ActionsScript code.

ActionScript
The Adobe Flash scripting language used by developers to add interactivity to movies, control objects, exchange data, and create complex animations.

ActionScript 3.0 (AS3)
The version of Flash ActionScript that is based on Object Oriented Programming (OOP) standards that provides a way to organize code (a set of instructions).

Adobe Flash CS5
A development tool that allows you to create compelling interactive experiences, often by using animation.

Animated graphic symbol
An animation stored as a single, reusable symbol in the Library panel.

Animation
The perception of motion caused by the rapid display of a series of still images.

――――――― **B** ―――――――

Balance
In screen design, the distribution of optical weight in the layout. Optical weight is the ability of an object to attract the viewer's eye, as determined by the object's size, shape, color, and other factors.

Bandwidth Profiler
A feature used when testing a Flash movie that allows you to view a graphical representation of the size of each frame and the frame-by-frame download process.

Bitmap image
An image based on pixels, rather than mathematical formulas. Also referred to as a raster image.

Break apart
The process of breaking apart text to place each character in a separate text block. Also, the process of separating groups, instances, and bitmaps into ungrouped, editable elements.

Broadband
A type of data transmission, such as DSL and cable, in which a wide band of frequencies is available to transmit more information at the same time.

Button symbol
Object on the Stage that is used to provide interactivity, such as jumping to another frame on the Timeline.

――――――― **C** ―――――――

Class
ActionScript 3.0 code that defines the attributes and functionality of an object.

Code hints
Hints appearing in a pop-up window that give the syntax or possible parameters for an action.

Code Snippets
Predefined blocks of ActionScript 3.0 code which provide a quick way to insert AS3 code into the Script pane.

Components
Predeveloped movie clips that can quickly add functionality to a movie by dragging and dropping them from the Components panel to the Stage. Commonly used for creating forms with boxes for entering user data (name, address, and so on), check boxes, drop-down menus and video playback objects.

Conditional action
ActionScript that tests whether or not certain conditions have been met and, if so, can perform other actions.

Controller
A window that provides the playback controls for a movie.

Coordinate
The position on the Stage of a pixel as measured across (X coordinate) and down (Y coordinate) the Stage.

Copyright
A legal protection for the particular and tangible expression of an idea.

Cue Points
Indicators on the video timeline that can be used in ActionScript. For example, you could specify a cue point at a location in a video that you want the user to be able to jump to by clicking a button.

———————— **D** ————————

Deco Tool
Tool used to create drawing effects that can be used to quickly create environments, such as city landscapes, and to create various animations

Decrement action
An ActionScript operator, indicated by—(two minus signs), that subtracts 1 unit from a variable or expression.

Device Central
A program used to test Flash movies on various models of mobile devices.

Display list
A list used by Flash to make objects visible to the user when a movie is published. Objects are added to the display list using the **addChild()** method of ActionScript 3.0.

Dock
A collection of panels or buttons surrounded by a dark gray bar. The arrows in the dock are used to maximize and minimize the panels.

Document
A Flash file which, by default, is given the .fla file extension.

Drop Zone
A blue outline area that indicates where a panel can be moved.

DSL
A broadband Internet connection speed that is available through phone lines.

Dynamic text field
A text box created on the Stage with the Text tool that displays information derived from variables.

———————— **E** ————————

Embedded fonts
Fonts that are available to the users no matter what fonts they have on their computer and ensures the text maintains the desired appearance. A font file is created that accompanies the swf file when the Flash document is published.

Embedded video
A video file that has been imported into a Flash document and becomes part of the SWF file.

Event Listener
ActionScript 3.0 code that "listening" to "hear" when an event occurs. For example, a button object might listen for a mouse click.

Event sound
A sound that plays independently of the Timeline. The sound starts in the keyframe to which it is added, but it can continue playing even after a movie ends. An event sound must download completely before it begins playing.

Expressions
Formulas for manipulating or evaluating the information in variables.

External links
Links from a Flash file or movie to another website, another file, or an e-mail program.

———————— **F** ————————

File Transfer Protocol (FTP)
A standard method for transferring files from a development site to a web server.

Filters
Special effects, such as drop shadows, that can be applied to text using options on the Filters area in the Properties panel.

Flash Lite
A program specifically developed to optimize the playing of Flash movies using mobile devices.

Flash Player
A free program from Adobe that allows Flash movies (.swf and .exe formats) to be viewed on a computer.

Flowchart
A visual representation of how the contents in an application or a website are organized and how various screens are linked.

Frame-by-frame animation
An animation created by specifying the object that is to appear in each frame of a sequence of frames (also called a frame animation).

Frame label
A text name for a keyframe, which can be referenced within ActionScript code.

Frames
Individual cells that make up the Timeline in Flash.

Function
An ActionScript 3.0 statement that executes a block of code in response to the event. For example, a function might include a gotoAndPlay action in response to a mouse click on a button.

——————— G ———————

Gradient
A color fill that makes a gradual transition from one color to another causing the colors to blend into one another.

Graphic Symbols
Objects, such as drawings, that are converted to symbols and stored in the Library panel. A graphic symbol is the original object. An instance (copy) of a symbol can be made by dragging the symbol from the Library to the Stage.

Graphics Interchange Format (GIF)
A graphics file format that creates compressed bitmap images. GIF graphics are viewable on the web.

Guide layers
Layers used to align objects on the Stage.

——————— I ———————

Increment action
An ActionScript operator, indicated by ++ (two plus signs), that adds 1 unit to a variable or expression.

Input text field
A text field created on the Stage with the Text tool that takes information entered by a user and stores it as a variable.

Instances
Editable copies of symbols that are placed on the Stage.

Inverse Kinematics
A process using a bone structure that allows objects to be animated in natural ways, such as a character running, jumping or kicking.

——————— J ———————

Joint Photographic Experts Group (JPEG)
A graphics file format that is especially useful for photographic images. JPEG graphics are viewable on the web.

——————— K ———————

Keyframe
A frame that signifies a change in a movie, such as the end of an animation.

——————— L ———————

Layers
Rows on the Timeline that are used to organize objects and that allow the stacking of objects on the Stage.

Level
A hierarchical designation used when loading new movies into the current movie; similar to layers on the Timeline.

Library panel
The panel that contains the objects (graphics, buttons, sounds, movie clips, etc.) that are used in a Flash movie.

Linkage class name
The name used to identify a sound from the Library panel in an ActionScript statement. You specify a linkage identifier in the Sound Properties dialog box.

Loader Component
A Component that can load external jpg graphic files and swf movie files.

——————— M ———————

Main Timeline
The primary Timeline for a Flash movie that is displayed when you start a new Flash document.

Mask layer
A layer used to cover up the objects on another layer(s) and, at the same time, create a window through which you can view various objects on the other layer.

Menu bar
A bar across the top of the program window that is located under the program title bar and lists the names of the menus that contain commands. Also called the application bar.

Merge Drawing Model
A drawing mode that causes overlapping drawings (objects) to merge so that a change in the top object, such as moving it, may affect the object beneath it.

Method
In ActionScript 3.0, the functionality of an object, that is, what it can do. For example, a button can listen for a mouse click.

Morphing
The animation process of changing one object into another, sometimes unrelated, object. For example, animating a car to change into a bus.

Motion Editor
Used to edit motion tween animations by changing the property values such as the position, rotation, color effects, and ease value.

Motion guide
Feature that allows you to draw a path and attach motion-tweened animations to the path. A motion guide has its own layer.

Motion Tween Presets
Pre-built animations that can be applied to objects in Flash. For example, applying a bouncing effect to a ball.

Motion tweening
The process used in Flash to automatically fill in the frames between keyframes in an animation that changes the properties of an object such as the position, size, or color. Motion tweening works on symbols and groups.

Movement
In screen design, the way the viewer's eye moves through the objects on the screen.

Movie clip symbol
An animation stored as a single, reusable symbol in the Library panel. It has its own Timeline, independent of the main Timeline.

MP3 (MPEG-1 Audio Layer 3)
A sound compression option primarily used for music and longer streaming sounds, but which can also be applied to speech.

—————— N ——————

Nesting
Including another symbol within a symbol, such as nesting a graphic symbol, button, or another movie clip symbol within a movie clip symbol.

Number variable
In ActionScript, a variable type that contains a number with which you can use arithmetic operators, such as addition and subtraction. To create a number variable use the Number data type.

—————— O ——————

Object Drawing Model
A drawing mode that allows you to overlap objects, which are then kept separate, so that changes in one object do not affect another object. You must break apart these objects before being able to select their stroke and fills.

Objects
Items, such as drawings and text, that are placed on the Stage and can be edited and manipulated. In ActionScript 3.0, an instance of a class that inherits the attributes (properties) and functionality (methods) of a class.

Onion Skin
Feature that displays the outlines of an animated object so that the positions of the object in a series of frames can be viewed all at once.

—————— P ——————

Panels
Individual windows in Flash used to view, organize, and modify objects and features in a movie.

Parameters
Properties of Components, such as autoload, that can be changed using the Properties panel or the Component Inspector.

Parent-child relationship
A description of the hierarchical relationship that develops between nested symbols, especially nested movie clip symbols. When you insert a movie clip inside another movie clip, the inserted clip is considered the child and the original clip is the parent.

Pasteboard
The gray area surrounding the Flash Stage where objects can be placed and manipulated. Neither the pasteboard nor objects placed on it appear in the movie unless the objects move onto the Stage during the playing of the movie.

Persistence of vision
The phenomenon of the eye capturing and holding an image for one-tenth of a second before processing another image. This enables the rapid display of a series of still images to give the impression of motion and creates an animation.

Pixel
Each dot in a bitmap graphic. Pixels have an exact position on the screen and a precise color.

Playhead
An indicator specifying which frame is playing in the Timeline of a Flash movie.

Portable Network Graphics (PNG)
A graphics file format developed specifically for images that are to be used on the web.

Preloader
An animation and ActionScript code (which could be a movie clip) that is played at the beginning of a movie to provide feedback to the viewer on the progress of downloading the movie frames.

Progressive download
The process of delivering an external Flash FLV video file at runtime.

Projector
A standalone executable movie, such as a Windows .exe file.

Properties panel (also called Property inspector)
In Flash, the panel that displays the properties of the selected object, such as size and color, on the Stage or the selected frame. The Properties panel can be used to edit selected properties.

Property
An attribute of an object such as its size or color.

Property inspector
A panel that allows you to display and edit the properties of a selected object or frame. See Properties panel.

Publish
The process used to generate the files necessary for delivering Flash movies on the web, such as swf and HTML files.

----------- **Q** -----------

QuickTime
A file format used for movies and animations that requires a QuickTime Player.

----------- **R** -----------

Raster image
An image based on pixels, rather than mathematical formulas. Also referred to as a bitmap image.

Raw
A sound compression option that exports a sound with no compression. You can set stereo to mono conversion and a sampling rate.

Registration point
The point on an object that is used to position the object on the Stage using ActionScript code.

Relative path
A path to a file based on the current location of the Flash .swf file referencing the file.

Rulers
On screen markers that help you precisely measure and position an object. Rulers can be displayed using the View menu.

----------- **S** -----------

Scene
A Timeline designated for a specific part of the movie. Scenes are a way to organize long movies by dividing the movie into sections.

Script Assist
A feature found in the Actions panel which can be used to generate ActionScript without having to write programming code.

Script Navigator pane
The section of the Actions panel that provides a list of elements (objects, movie clips, frames) that contain scripts. It can be used to quickly locate an object, such as a button, or a frame and display the ActionScript code.

Script pane
The section of the Actions panel that displays the code and a toolbar for editing the code. Also, displays the Script Assist dialog box.

Shape hints
Indicators used to control the shape of a complex object as it changes appearance during an animation.

Shape tweening
The process of animating an object so that its shape changes. Shape tweening requires editable graphics.

Sound object
A built-in object that allows ActionScript to recognize and control a sound. To associate a specific sound with a sound object, use a variable with a sound class type.

Speech compression
A sound compression option best used for voice-overs and other speech. You can set a sampling rate when you choose this option.

Stage
The area of the Flash workspace that contains the objects that are part of the movie and that will be seen by the viewers.

Stage-level object
A vector object that you draw directly on the Stage, unlike a symbol, which you place on the Stage from the Library panel.

Start synchronization option
A synchronization option that can be applied to sounds and that acts just like event sounds, but that will not begin again if an instance of the sound is already playing.

Stop synchronization option
A synchronization option that can be applied to sounds and lets you end an event sound at a specific keyframe.

Storyboard
A sketch showing the layout of the various screens. It describes the contents and illustrates how text, graphics, animation, and other screen elements will be positioned. It also indicates the navigation process, such as menus and buttons.

Streaming sound
A sound that is tied to the Timeline. No matter its length, a streaming sound stops at the end of the movie. Streaming sounds can start playing as they download.

Streaming video
The process of delivering video content using a constant connection established with a Flash Communication Server.

String variable
In ActionScript, a sequence of characters including letters, numbers, and punctuation. To create a string variable, use the Sting data type and enclose the string in double quotation marks.

Symbols
The basic building blocks of a Flash application. There are three types: graphic, button, and movie clip.

——————— **T** ———————

T1
An extremely fast Internet connection that is widely used by businesses.

Target
A reference in an action to a movie clip symbol or other object that includes a path and name.

Text Layout Format (TLF)
A text tool option that provides advanced text features such as flowing text, character coloring and column creation.

Time In control, Time Out control
Controls in the Edit Envelope dialog box that let you trim the length of a sound file.

Timeline
The component of Flash used to organize and control the movie's contents over time by specifying when each object appears on the Stage.

Tools panel
The component of Flash that contains a set of tools used to draw, select, and edit graphics and text. It is divided into four sections.

Trace
The process of turning a bitmap image into vector paths for animation and other purposes.

Transformation point
The point used to orient an object as it is being animated. For example, a rotating object will rotate around the transformation point. Also, the point of an object that snaps to a motion guide.

Tweening
The process of filling the in-between frames in an animation.

——————— **U** ———————

Unity
Intra-screen unity refers to how the various screen objects relate in screen design. Inter-screen unity refers to the design that viewers encounter as they navigate from one screen to another.

——————— **V** ———————

Variable
A container that holds information and is used in ActionScript code.

Vector image
An image calculated and stored according to mathematical formulas rather than pixels, resulting in a smaller file size and the ability to resize the image without a loss in quality.

——————— **W** ———————

Web server
A computer dedicated to hosting web sites that is connected to the Internet and configured with software to handle requests from browsers.

Workspace
The area in the Flash program window where you work with documents, movies, tools, and panels. The Flash workspace can be customized.

FLASH ART CREDITS	
Chapter	**Art credit for opening pages**
Chapter 1	© Neal Cooper	Dreamstime.com © iStockphoto.com/ETIEN
Chapter 2	© Bruce Turner	Dreamstime.com © 123RF LIMITED/cbpix
Chapter 3	© Richard Carey	Dreamstime.com © iStockphoto.com/Alex Bramwell
Chapter 4	© Chris Lorenz	Dreamstime.com © Vladimir Sazonov	Shutterstock Images
Chapter 5	© Gkuna	Dreamstime.com © Tony Emmett	Shutterstock Images
Chapter 6	© iStockphoto.com/Nico Smit Photography © iStockphoto.com/Freder
Chapter 7	© Morten Elm	Dreamstime.com © Michael Zysman	Dreamstime.com
Chapter 8	© iStockphoto.com/Malsbury Enterprises Ltd © iStockphoto.com/charcoal design
Chapter 9	© Jemini Joseph	Dreamstime.com © Janice Mccafferty	Dreamstime.com

ART CREDITS

(CONTINUED)

FLASH ART CREDITS	
Chapter	**Art credit for opening pages**
Chapter 10	© Christian Bech | Dreamstime.com © iStockphoto.com/ThaiEagle
Chapter 11	© Jay Bo | Shutterstock Images © 123RF LIMITED | Kitch Bain
Chapter 12	© Kendrick Moholt Photography © Creativemarc | Dreamstime.com
ACE Grid/Data Files/Glossary/Index	© Davthy | Dreamstime.com © Michael Zysman | Dreamstime.com